HISTORY

OF THE

CHURCH OF JESUS CHRIST

OF

LATTER-DAY SAINTS

PERIOD II

FROM THE MANUSCRIPT HISTORY OF BRIGHAM
YOUNG AND OTHER ORIGINAL DOCUMENTS

VOLUME VII

AN INTRODUCTION AND NOTES

BY

B. H. ROBERTS

PUBLISHED BY THE CHURCH

DESERET BOOK COMPANY
SALT LAKE CITY, UTAH

1980

Lithographed by

DESERET PRESS

in the United States of America

MOUNT ENSIGN
(Cover Indent-gravure)

"All ye inhabitants of the world, and dwellers on the earth, see ye, when he lifteth up an Ensign on the mountains; and when he bloweth a trumpet, hear ye."—(Isa. xviii:3)

On the cover of each of the six preceding volumes of this series of the *History of the Church*, Period I, there has appeared in low relief an indent-gravure of some prominent place: the Hill Cumorah, the Kirtland Temple, the Liberty Prison, the Nauvoo Mansion, and the Carthage Jail; and for this Period II, volume VII, since it brings us in its action into Salt Lake valley, a Utah subject of first importance is selected, *viz.* "Mount Ensign". It is generally referred to as "Ensign Peak". Elder Woodruff, among those who first climbed the Mount, says in his Journal entry of that date—July 26, 1847:

"We went on the top of a high peak in the edge of the mountain, which we considered a good place to raise an Ensign. So we named it 'Ensign Peak', or 'Hill'."

Captain J. W. Gunnison, refers to it in his *The Mormons*, 1856, (pp. 33-4), as "Ensign Mound".

President Young refers to the Mount as "Ensign Hill", on the occasion of recording the incident of Addison Pratt receiving his endowments on its summit, in October, 1849. (See *Comprehensive History of the Church*, Century I, vol. iii, p. 386, footnote 10); so that while referred to generally in early days as "Ensign Peak", it was not exclusively known by that name; and as it was dedicated for such purpose and used as a "House of the Lord" for giving the sacred mysteries of the Temple ritual—a new sanctity attaches to it. It is a sacred "Mount", as much so as "Mount Lebanon", the "Mount of Transfiguration", "Mount Sinai", or "Mount Zion", where the Temple of Jerusalem stood. And since this western mountain in the edge of a group of mountains was used as a Temple of God, "Mount" is both more euphonious and implies sacredness rather than "Peak" does. Hence the name here used is suggested—"Mount Ensign".

The significance of "Ensign" in the literature of the Church of the New Dispensation—in connection with this "Mount"—is that it has reference to the intent of the church "in these last days", to raise an "Ensign" to the nations, known as the "Standard of Zion", which would be an "Ensign" made up of the flags of all nations, indicating that its message was to be to "every nation, kindred, tongue and people", symbolized in this flag, or "Ensign". The matter is referred to in some remarks of President Young made on the 29th of May, 1847, when he mentioned to his Camp of Pioneers the raising of such an "Ensign" in the place to which they were going. Elder Woodruff made note of it in his daily Journal of that date, and drew in the margin of his Journal the rough outline of such a flag. It was to this "Ensign" that the small group of Pioneers referred to when on the top of the "Mount" to which they had climbed, as being "a good place to raise an Ensign."

TABLE OF CONTENTS
Volume VII

PART I

CHURCH HISTORIANS' EXCERPT FROM FORD'S HISTORY OF ILLINOIS

CHAPTER I

CONDITIONS IN HANCOCK COUNTY REVIEWED BY GOVERNOR FORD—THE STATE ARMS OF THE LEGION SURRENDERED ON THE DEMAND OF THE GOVERNOR

CHAPTER II

SUBMISSION OF THE PROPHET TO THE REQUIREMENTS OF THE GOVERNOR— GATHERING OF THE ENEMY FORCES OF THE PROPHET—GOVERNOR FORD'S DEFENSIVE JUSTIFICATION FOR HIS PLACEMENT OF THE HOSTILE FORCES AT CARTHAGE AND THE DISMISSAL OF OTHERS

CHAPTER III

GOVERNOR FORD'S VISIT TO NAUVOO—FEARS ON THE WAY—INSULTING SPEECH
TO THE CITIZENS—RESENTED—HEARS OF THE ASSASSINATION OF
JOSEPH AND HYRUM SMITH

PART II

EXTENSION OF QUOTATIONS FROM FORD'S HISTORY OF ILLINOIS

CHAPTER IV

GOVERNOR FORD'S COMMENTS ON THE CHARACTER OF JOSEPH SMITH AND HIS
FOLLOWERS—HIS CONJECTURES ON THE FUTURE OF MORMONISM

CHAPTER V

POLITICAL CONSIDERATIONS OF THE PERIOD FOLLOWING THE DEATH OF THE
PROPHET—"TRIAL" OF THE MURDERERS—STATUS OF CIVIL GOVERNMENT
IN HANCOCK COUNTY

PART III

MEMOIRS OF THE LATE PRESIDENT JOHN TAYLOR RESPECTING AF-
FAIRS AT NAUVOO LEADING UP TO THE MARTYRDOM OF THE PROPHET
AND PATRIARCH: GOVERNOR FORD'S RESPONSIBILITY THEREIN

CHAPTER VI

THE MARTYRDOM OF JOSEPH SMITH: REVIEW OF CONDITIONS IN ILLINOIS
PRECEDING THAT EVENT

CHAPTER VII

JOHN TAYLOR AND DOCTOR BERNHISEL'S INTERVIEW WITH GOVERNOR FORD
PLEDGE OF GOVERNOR FORD FOR THE SECURITY OF JOSEPH SMITH IF HE WOULD
COME TO CARTHAGE

CHAPTER VIII

INTERVIEW BETWEEN JOSEPH SMITH AND GOVERNOR THOMAS FORD

CONTENTS

CHAPTER IX

THE ASSAULT UPON THE PRISON—THE MURDER OF JOSEPH AND HYRUM SMITH

CHAPTER X

WAS GOVERNOR FORD RESPONSIBLE FOR THE MURDER OF THE PROPHET AND PATRIARCH OF THE NEW DISPENSATION

PART IV

HISTORIANS' SECOND COMPILATION OF HISTORICAL ITEMS OF CHURCH HISTORY, FROM 22ND OF JUNE, 1844 TO 8TH OF AUGUST, 1844

CHAPTER XI

MISCELLANEOUS EVENTS APART FROM THE MAJOR FACTS OF THE MARTYRDOM OF THE PROPHET AND PATRIARCH FROM JUNE 22ND, 1844 TO JUNE 29TH, 1844

CHAPTER XII

MOVEMENTS IN HANCOCK COUNTY, CARTHAGE, NAUVOO, WARSAW AND QUINCY,
FOR THE MAINTENANCE OF PEACE FOLLOWING THE MARTYRDOM: LIST OF THE
NAMES OF THOSE WHO WERE IN THE MOB ASSEMBLED TO SLAY THE PROPHET

CHAPTER XIII

THE MARTYRDOM IN POETRY—EFFORTS FOR FOOD SUPPLIES AND PROTECTION FOR
THE PEOPLE OF NAUVOO—THE DANIELS AFFIDAVIT ON THE MARTYRDOM

CHAPTER XIV

A CHAPTER OF SUNDRY EVENTS AT VARIOUS PLACES AND DOCUMENTS FOLLOWING
THE MARTYRDOM: UNITED STATES PRESS COMMENTS ON THE MURDER

CHAPTER XV

CHAPTER OF MISCELLANEOUS DOCUMENTS, PRESS EXCERPTS AND MOVEMENTS
OF LEADING ELDERS OF THE CHURCH AT NAUVOO AND ELSEWHERE

CHAPTER XVI

THE MOVEMENTS OF THE APOSTLES AND OTHER LEADING BRETHREN IN THE
EAST AND AT NAUVOO—IMPORTANT COMMUNICATION FROM GOVERNOR FORD

CHAPTER XVII

GATHERING OF THE TWELVE AND OTHER LEADING ELDERS AT NAUVOO—DEATH
OF ELDER SAMUEL H. SMITH, BROTHER OF THE PROPHET, EARLY MISSIONARY
OF THE CHURCH AND ONE OF THE EIGHT WITNESSES OF THE BOOK OF MORMON

CHAPTER XVIII

THE GATHERING OF THE TWELVE APOSTLES FROM THE EAST TO NAUVOO:
PRELIMINARY MEETINGS LOOKING TO THE SETTLEMENT OF THE QUESTION OF
THE PRESIDENCY OF THE CHURCH

CHAPTER XIX

THE SETTLEMENT OF CHURCH LEADERSHIP—THE TWELVE APOSTLES ACCEPTED
AS THE PRESIDENCY OF THE CHURCH, BRIGHAM YOUNG AT THEIR HEAD

PART V

EXCERPTS FROM THE MANUSCRIPT HISTORY OF BRIGHAM YOUNG
FROM AUGUST 9, 1844, TO OCTOBER 8, 1848

CHAPTER XX

EVENTS IMMEDIATELY FOLLOWING THE SUSTAINING OF THE QUORUM OF THE
TWELVE AS THE PRESIDENCY OF THE CHURCH—RESUMPTION OF THE CHURCH
ACTIVITIES—PERPETUATION OF THE POLICY OF THE PROPHET

CHAPTER XXI

FORMAL TRIAL AND EXCOMMUNICATION OF PRESIDENT SIDNEY RIGDON—RESTLESS
MOVEMENTS OF JAMES EMMETT—MISSION ACTIVITIES OF THE CHURCH—
MOVEMENTS OF STATE OFFICIALS AND THE MOB OF HANCOCK COUNTY

CHAPTER XXII

EPISTLE OF THE TWELVE TO THE CHURCH—MORAL AND SPIRITUAL GUIDANCE

CHAPTER XXIII

MINUTES OF THE IMPORTANT CONFERENCE OF OCTOBER 6TH TO 8TH, 1844—
THE CHURCH SET IN ORDER—DUTIES OF THE PRIESTHOOD EXPOUNDED—
ECONOMICS CONSIDERED

CONTENTS

CHAPTER XXIV

THE PRELIMINARY STEPS TO THE FORTHCOMING PROSECUTION OF THE MURDERERS OF JOSEPH AND HYRUM SMITH—THE WORK IN THE SOCIETY ISLANDS—TEMPLE AFFAIRS—FINANCIAL EMBARRASSMENT

CHAPTER XXV

PROGRESS OF WORK ON THE TEMPLE—MISCELLANEOUS MOVEMENTS IN CHURCH AND STATE

CONTENTS

CHAPTER XXVI

THE GREAT CONFERENCE OF THE SEVENTIES AT NAUVOO—ORGANIZATION OF
NEW QUORUMS—DEDICATION OF THE SEVENTIES' HALL—NOTABLE DISCOURSES—
DOCTRINAL INSTRUCTIONS BY PRESIDENT BRIGHAM YOUNG ON PRIESTHOOD—THE
TWELVE—THE SEVENTY—AND THE BISHOPRIC

CHAPTER XXVII

CAMPAIGN AGAINST WICKEDNESS BOTH BY THE CHURCH AUTHORITIES AND THE
NAUVOO CITY COUNCIL—VILLAINY OF NAUVOO'S ENEMIES

CHAPTER XXVIII

THE STORY OF CONTINUED PROGRESS OF THE CHURCH IN NAUVOO, IN EUROPE
AND IN THE UNITED STATES—PLEA FOR THE RETURN OF JAMES EMMETT'S
COMPANY

CHAPTER XXIX

THE JAMES EMMETT COMPANY OFFICIALLY VISITED—APRIL CONFERENCE OF 1845—MUNICIPAL CORPORATIONS UNDER GENERAL STATE LAW—WESTERN MOVEMENT PROPOSED BY GOVERNOR FORD

CHAPTER XXX

AN APPEAL TO LYMAN WIGHT TO BE UNITED WITH THE TWELVE—LETTERS TO THE PRESIDENT OF THE UNITED STATES AND THE GOVERNORS OF THE RESPECTIVE STATES—LETTERS OF GOVERNOR FORD TO STATE MILITARY LEADERS—IMPORTANT DOCTRINAL LETTER OF THE TWELVE TO THE CHURCH

CHAPTER XXXI

SUNDRY EVENTS GROUPED TOGETHER LOOKING TO AN UNDERSTANDING WITH THE STATE GOVERNMENT AT NAUVOO—HARVEST FEAST AT NAUVOO

CHAPTER XXXII

PREPARATIONS FOR WESTWARD JOURNEY—THE FINAL WORD: THE CHURCH
MUST LEAVE ILLINOIS—DETAIL OF THE PLANS—AMERICAN GOVERNMENT FAILS
IN THE CASE OF THE LATTER-DAY SAINTS

CHAPTER XXXIII

LAST CONFERENCE AT NAUVOO—PLEA OF THE "MOTHER OF PROPHETS"—
PATHETIC

CHAPTER XXXIV

OFFICIAL MESSAGE TO THE SAINTS IN THE UNITED STATES—REMOVAL OF THE
CHURCH TO THE WEST—ORGANIZATION—OLIVER COWDERY'S TENDER OF SERVICES
—THE BIGELOW CASE—WARREN-YOUNG-TAYLOR OUTRAGE—THE POWER OF
PRAYER *vs.* MOBOCRACY—APPEAL TO GOVERNOR FORD

CHAPTER XXXV

IMPORTANT LETTERS, FRIENDLY AND OTHERWISE SUMMARY OF RECENT
PROCEDURE IN AND ABOUT NAUVOO WITH COMMENT OF AN
EDITORIAL FROM THE TIMES AND SEASONS

CHAPTER XXXVI

MURDERS BY MOBS CONTINUED—CONFESSION OF DR. ROBERT D. FOSTER—FAREWELL
OF ORSON PRATT TO EASTERN SAINTS—WESTWARD BY SHIPPING—
THE DURFEE MURDER CASE

CHAPTER XXXVII

DEDICATION OF PARTS OF THE TEMPLE—ENDOWMENTS GIVEN—ROMAN CATHOLIC
EFFORTS TO PURCHASE THE TEMPLE AND OTHER NAUVOO PROPERTY—THE CHURCH
IN ENGLAND—UNITED STATES FEDERAL CHARGES OF COUNTERFEITING AGAINST
CHURCH AUTHORITIES—CHURCH PUBLICATIONS FOR 1845

CHAPTER XXXVIII

LARGE NUMBER OF PERSONS ENDOWED IN THE TEMPLE—JANUARY AND FEBRUARY, 1846—CATHOLIC CHURCH EFFORTS TO PURCHASE L. D. S. PROPERTY—FRIENDLY ATTITUDE OF JUDGE JOSIAH LAMBORN—REPEATED HOSTILE EFFORTS OF STATE OFFICIALS—DEPARTURE OF THE TWELVE HASTENED BY FALSE REPORTS CIRCULATED BY GOVERNOR FORD.

CHAPTER XXXIX

DEPARTURE OF BRIGHAM YOUNG FROM NAUVOO—PROPOSITION OF "A. G. BENSON & CO."—PROPOSED CONTRACT—PUBLIC MEETING IN THE TEMPLE—MISSISSIPPI BRIDGED BY ICE—LIMITED NUMBER WHO CROSSED ON THE ICE WITH TEAMS AND FAMILIES—PETITION TO THE GOVERNOR OF IOWA—REFLECTIONS ON COMMENCEMENT OF EXODUS FROM NAUVOO

CHAPTER XL

DISCONTINUANCE OF DAILY QUOTATIONS FROM THE MANUSCRIPT HISTORY OF
BRIGHAM YOUNG—SUNDRY EVENTS IN THE MARCHING ENCAMPMENT
FROM THE CLOSE OF FEBRUARY TO MID-JUNE

CHAPTER XLI

THE RETURN TO WINTER QUARTERS—THE ORGANIZATION OF AND UNIVERSAL
ACCEPTANCE OF THE FIRST PRESIDENCY OF THE CHURCH, BRIGHAM YOUNG,
HEBER C. KIMBALL AND WILLARD RICHARDS—1847-8 PRESIDENT YOUNG'S LAST
JOURNEY OVER THE PLAINS

INTRODUCTION

Volume VII is divided into six parts:

I. *Church Historians' Excerpt from Ford's History of Illinois,* pp. 1 to 31.

II. *Later Church Historians' Extension of Quotations from Ford's History of Illinois,* pp. 33 to 51.

III. *Personal Account of the Martyrdom of Joseph and Hyrum Smith by the Late President John Taylor,* pp. 53 to 126.

IV. *Second Compilation of Historical Items of Period I of Church History, From 22nd of June, 1844, to 8th of August, 1844* (Compiled by Church Historians George A. Smith and Wilford Woodruff, from the Journals of Elders Willard Richards, Wilford Woodruff and others), pp. 127 to 243.

V. *Excerpts from the Manuscript History of Brigham Young from August 9, 1844, to October 8, 1848*—Apostolic Interregnum—Inauguration of, and Sustaining of the Second First Presidency of Three, pp. 245 to 630.

The Church Documentary History, Period I, (The History of Joseph Smith the Prophet by Himself—his daily Journal in fact), necessarily closed with Joseph's martyrdom to which was added a brief account of his obsequies, and of his various services to humanity. The Historians of the Church who brought to a close that Period, George A. Smith, cousin of the Prophet and one of the Twelve Apostles, and Wilford Woodruff, also one of the Twelve Apostles, immediately followed that close by publishing a long and unbroken excerpt from Governor Thomas Ford's *History of Illinois,* which was published in 1854, about six months after the governor's death. This posthumous work gave large space to the activities and adventures of the Prophet and his people in Illinois, from 1839 to 1846. This, in fact, constitutes about the only part of Ford's *History* that is of permanent value or importance.

George A. Smith and Wilford Woodruff's excerpt from Ford's *History of Illinois* extends from page 328 to page 354; which is about two-thirds of what the governor wrote on the Mormons. Their quotation ends in the middle of a sentence, this because they were unwilling, doubtless, to include the vicious assault upon the character of the Prophet with which the sentence ends. The saints may now, however, be indifferent to such assaults upon the character and life's work of their Prophet, since time has placed the true value upon his character and the success of his work, vindicating both; rendering the "pelting of his memory with vile epithets" as supremely vain. Besides Ford's treatise of the Mormons in Illinois has some valuable material for their history not to be had elsewhere. And the student will have the satisfaction of knowing that he has practically all that the governor-enemy of the saints has said against them, and that the Prophet's followers have not blanched from all that is written of him by this opponent. The governor closes his chapter xi with the account of the trial of the murderers of the Prophet and Patriarch with the concession that government in Illinois had failed so far as protecting the Latter-day Saints in their rights, and adds that "there can be no government in a free country where the people do not voluntarily obey the laws;" which, of course, closes his connection with the events that occurred during the lifetime of the Prophet.

For the rest of Ford's connection with the History of the Church of the Latter-day Saints, excerpts are given including official letters, etc., as the events are developed; and are chosen and used in this present edition, and constitute Part II of this volume.

Governor Ford's contributions to the history of that period are followed by a review and commentary upon them by the late President John Taylor, who was a contemporary with Governor Ford and a leading participant in those events. This constitutes Part III of this volume. It is a review and commentary of the period of highest value, a statesman-like paper, a document of highest historical value of the times; and one marvels at the high tone with which the document is planned, being dispassionate, and one might say, written unexpectedly in an impartial spirit. The balancing of the pros and cons as to the responsibility of Governor Ford for the murder of the martyred being surprisingly fair to the governor. In my study of historical documents in which judgment is rendered upon such questions, without exception I can say that I have examined nothing that is equal in spirit and justice to this review by President Taylor of Governor Ford's responsibility for the murder. The Church of Jesus Christ of Latter-day Saints can well be proud of this performance of their great Apostle and later President of the Church. It deserves to live forever.

Part IV treats the Apostolic succession to the Presidency of the Church, from the death of the Prophet to August 8, 1844, a compilation made by the Church Historians George A. Smith and Wilford Woodruff from the Journals of Elders Willard Richards and Wilford Woodruff and others. It considers, and settles the claims of guardianship to the church made by Sidney Rigdon; finally disposes of his case; and installs the Presidency of the Twelve Apostles which continued until the First Presidency of Three could be re-established.

This touches what may be regarded as an important factor in the matter of arranging the transition from one administration in the Presidency of the Church to another. On the 6th of April, 1830, it was declared that a record should be kept in the church and that in it Joseph Smith should be called a "seer, a translator, a prophet, an apostle of Jesus Christ, an elder of the church through the will of God the Father, and the grace of your Lord Jesus Christ, being inspired of the Holy Ghost to lay the foundation thereof and to build it up unto the Most Holy Faith."*

It will be recognized that there were thus provided, even on the day the church was organized, very great powers of Presidency and administrative functions for Joseph Smith in the leadership of the church.

Later the Lord referred to the matter again and that by way of warning to the Prophet: "And I have sent forth the fulness of my gospel by the hand of my servant Joseph; and in weakness have I blessed him; and I have given unto him the keys of the mystery of those things which have been sealed, even things which were from the foundation of the world, and the things which shall come from this time until the time of my coming, *if he abide in me*, and *if not, another will I plant in his stead*."†

In another revelation the Lord enlarged upon this theme as follows: "Hearken ye elders of my church, and give ear to the words which I shall speak unto you. For behold, verily, verily, I say unto you, that ye have received a commandment for a law unto my church, through him whom I have appointed unto you to receive commandments and revelation from my hand. And this ye shall know assuredly— that there is none other appointed unto you to receive commandments and revelations until he be taken *if he abide in me*. But verily, verily, I say unto you, that none else shall be appointed unto this gift except it be through him, for if it be taken from him he shall not have power except to *appoint another in his stead*."‡

This makes known the fact that though the Prophet should not even abide in the Lord he would still have power left to appoint another in his stead; and how much more would he be competent to appoint another in his stead if he continued to abide in the Lord!

This right to appoint another in his stead the Prophet Joseph exercised, occasioned by his own approaching martyrdom. At the October Conference—the 6th, 1844—the conference following the martyrdom of the Prophet—in the presence of thousands making up the congregation, President Young asked the question: "Did Joseph ordain any man to take his place? He did. Who was it? It was Hyrum [his brother], but Hyrum fell a martyr before Joseph did".§ Holding in mind that the Lord has said that the Prophet Joseph Smith should not have taken from him the splendid powers of Presidency given to him for the guidance of the church—if he would "abide in the Lord". ‖ And in the event of his *not* abiding in the Lord, then he should not have power—"except to appoint another in his stead." It is clear that the Prophet was acting within his rights to appoint another to succeed himself in the Presidency of the Church when he appointed

*Doctrine and Covenants, sec. xxi:1. 2
†Doctrine and Covenants, sec xxxv:17-18
‡Doctrine and Covenants, sec xliii. 1-4.
§Times and Seasons, October 15 1844 p 683
‖Doctrine and Covenants, sec xxxv 18

Hyrum to succeed him. For surely, if when *not* abiding in the Lord he would still have power to appoint another in the prophetic office, and to succeed him in the Presidency of the Church, much more would he have the right to make the appointment when continuing to abide in the Lord. And this power he exercised; according to President Young he even "ordained" Hyrum to succeed him; but Hyrum, according to Joseph's own statement, would not leave him.*

In like manner the Christ designated St. Peter to succeed him in the leadership of the church, by saying: "I will give unto thee the keys of the kingdom of heaven, and whatsoever thou shalt bind on earth shall be bound in heaven: and whatsoever thou shalt loose on earth shall be loosed in heaven."† Thus did the Christ before his crucifixion appoint his successor in the Presidency of the Church in that dispensation.

Thus the Prophet Joseph Smith in appointing Hyrum Smith to be his successor in the leadership of the New Dispensation Church, did but follow the example of his divine Lord. But with Hyrum Smith falling a martyr before the Prophet Joseph Smith himself did, there was, of course, an end to that appointment: it had no chance to be presented to the people for approval, which, of course, would have been necessary as in the case of all officers in the church, or before the sub-division of it over which it is proposed they should exercise presiding jurisdiction.‡ Also it amounts to certainty that had Hyrum Smith survived his brother, and his name had been presented to the church as its President, he would have been overwhelmingly sustained by the saints for the office. But Hyrum dead before the Prophet was killed, it left no one else designated for the place of President, and hence choice and reconstruction of the Presidency devolved upon the next quorum in authority—the Twelve Apostles, which also is not only the "next" quorum in authority, but also "equal" in authority to the First Presidency,§ and therefore capable of doing whatever the First Presidency could do. It was under this quorum and its authority that President Brigham Young and his fellow Apostles proceeded to their construction of the First Presidency.

Part V of volume VII constitutes the larger section of the volume and consists of transcriptions from the *Manuscript History of Brigham Young*, to the close of the year 1848, and is the most important quotation of original documents to be had covering that period of time, setting forth the administration of the Twelve Apostles under the leadership of President Young. The value of this collection from original sources is beyond instant realization. As in the quotations from the Journal of Joseph Smith in the preceding six volumes of this

---

*See *Comprehensive History of the Church*, Century I, vol. ii, p. 424, footnote.
†*Matt.* xvi:19.
‡*Doctrine and Covenants*, sec. xx:65; and elsewhere.
§*Doctrine and Covenants*, sec. cvii:24.

series, so this section in volume VII gives the day by day and incident by incident transactions of the Apostles, disclosing the very spirit and administrative effects of the procedure and policies of their period. It is a most profitable contribution to the annals of the Church of Jesus Christ of Latter-day Saints. In it are revealed the truly and highly spiritual and unselfish efforts of the Twelve in directing the affairs of the church to the advantage of the organization and to the welfare of the saints. Their solicitude, watchfulness and prayerful interest in all the departments of the work of God are marvelous. The missionary service of the church in all the world was universal and untiring: throughout the United States, the Pacific groups of islands, the work in England. Also the local interests: the building up of Nauvoo, the completion of the Temple, the unstinted pouring of the contributed wealth of the people into its structural completion and interior embellishment, notwithstanding that they knew they could hold possession of it but a few months, and then it must be abandoned. It was the heroic and unselfish adherence to a completion of a commandment of God.

Nor did their zeal and sacrifices go unrewarded; for from December 10th, 1845, when the first endowments were given, to the 7th of February, 1846—when the Temple was closed for ordinance work—5,669 ordinances had been performed. These mostly for full endowment ceremonies, as the church in the main knows those ordinances today. However, some baptisms for the dead merely may have been recorded in the enumeration; also there may be slight variations above or below the figures here given; as the daily numbers, from which this total is made up, are occassionally given in round numbers. But think of the work accomplished, 5,669 endowments given! After full allowance is made for all slight variations that may have occurred, the official report makes it certain that over 5,500 endowments had been given in the Nauvoo Temple! So many of the saints entrusted with the sacred mysteries of the House of the Lord!

Meantime both the officers and church membership were making every exertion to prepare the church for removal to the west in fulfillment of the predictions of the Prophet Joseph Smith sometime previous to his death. In addition to this was their contention with authorities in high station in the state, more menacing to their security than the murderous assaults of mobs. In all things there was manifested a union of spirit and effort of the Apostles that proclaimed them true disciples of the Lord. They were a perfect example of a group united in one, a well-nigh perfect unanimity of purpose and action seemed to prevail. The spirit of the Christian religion was manifested in their forebearance and long continued patience with men of restless ambition who sought to divide the people and lead away groups of them. Such men as James Emmett who led a company of people into the western wilderness; Lyman Wight one of the Quorum of the

Twelve, who led a company of people into Texas; Bishop George Miller, always restive under restraint, who broke away from the main group of the people, impatient with what he thought was the too slow action of President Young and his brethren; their patience with Wm. Smith; one of the Twelve, then, and later Patriarch to the church, and brother of the Prophet. Their action in his trying case was a model of brotherly forbearance. Their uniform kindness and care for the Mother of the Prophet exhibited a truly Christian spirit and disproves the charges against the Twelve, that are sometimes made by dissentients, of tyranny, self-aggrandizement, and inordinate, and self-seeking ambition.

In all things the Twelve manifested their faith in prayer. God was their only refuge, as manifested in their constant appeal, to him in their days of trial. No one can read the annals of this volume and be in doubt of that; in sickness, in danger; in missionary undertakings; against the violence of mobs; in coping with the cunningly devised plans of political leaders, corrupted courts and scheming adventurers —against all these forces they employed the power of faith and prayer. But read the annals of the trying years covered by this volume of the History of the Church of Jesus Christ of Latter-day Saints, and you have in hand the world's finest example of faith and trust in God through prayer. Was one sick, the others prayed; was some group wayward, and rebellious, a circle met in prayer; did influential men in high places meet to conspire against them, the brethren sought to thwart their plans by an appeal to God through prayer; was one or more unjustly haled into the courts before unjust judges, prayer softened their hearts or confused their judgments; did mobs assail, did hell rage—prayer was both sword and shield. That all this may appear I take a cross section in Nauvoo experiences for an illustration which is but characteristic of the whole period.

I select items from the record of the months of August and September, 1844—in free quotation—and set down the direct experiences which illustrate the procedure of these presiding brethren that will indicate the spirit of the work they undertook and carried through. Under date of August 10, 1844, the day following the settlement of the Twelve Apostles as the Presiding Authority of the Church—this:

"The city council subscribed about $80.00 for the aid of the police. In addition to this really inadequate compensation Brigham Young, Heber C. Kimball, George A. Smith and Hyrum Kimball relinquished their dues as councilors that the taxes might be lessened and the police be paid.* * * Daniel Spencer was elected to fill the remainder of the term of the late Mayor Joseph Smith. An ordinance was passed allowing $100.00 per year to the mayor, and $1.00 a day to the councilors and aldermen while in session. * * * Also an ordinance prohibiting brothels and for suppressing disorderly characters was passed.

Wednesday, August 14.—[Brigham Young recording the incidents throughout] I attended meeting of the Twelve, Temple Committee and Nauvoo House Committee and the stone cutters for the Temple. * * * Agreed to raise the wages of the windlass men to $1.50 per day. The meeting terminated in a feeling of renewed determination to prosecute the work on the Temple.

Thursday, August 15.—The Quorum of the Twelve Apostles met at my house. * * * The council resolved to bear off the kingdom of God in all the world in truth, virtue and holiness, and to continue to set their faces as a flint against every species of wickedness, vice and dishonesty in all its forms: I met in a prayer circle with the Twelve and a few others in the afternoon and prayed for the sick."

RECOGNIZING THE PROPHET JOSEPH'S PLACE IN THE NEW DISPENSATION

"Let no man presume for a moment that his place will be filled by another, for, remember, he stands in his own place, and always will; and the Twelve Apostles of this dispensation stand in their own place and always will both in time and eternity to minister, preside and, regulate the affairs of the whole church. * * * How vain are the imaginations of the children of men to presume for a moment that the slaughter of one, two, or a hundred of the leaders of this church could destroy an organization so perfect in itself and so harmoniously arranged that it will stand while one member of it is left upon the earth."

PROPHET'S COPY OF THE NEW TRANSLATION OF THE BIBLE

"*Monday, August* 19.—Elder Willard Richards called on Emma Smith, widow of the Prophet, for the new translation of the *Bible*. She said she did not feel disposed to give it up at present.

Wednesday, August 21.—Council of the Twelve Apostles at my house to meet Elder Lyman Wight. Elder John Taylor went after him with a carriage; found him sick and unable to attend. Sociable gathering of a number of the Twelve at Wilford Woodruff's. The brethren were accompanied with their wives. Elder Woodruff was blessed and set apart for his mission to England under the hands of the members of the quorum of the Twelve Apostles present."

BAPTISM FOR THE DEAD RESUMED

Several of the Twelve Apostles were baptized for their dead this same afternoon. This (August 24th) was the first renewal of baptisms for the dead since the death of the Prophet Joseph. The ordinance took place in the temporary baptismal font in the Temple.

"*Tuesday, August* 27.—Met with the officers of the Nauvoo Legion in council. Six of the Apostles were present. The council decided that they would carry out all the views of their martyred Prophet: The brethren felt very spirited on the subject.

Thursday, August 29.—This was fast day and I attended meeting at the stand and laid hands on several of the sick.

Wednesday, September 4.—Willard Richards sick. The Twelve

Apostles and a few others met at my house in the evening and prayed for the preservation of the church and ourselves and that the Lord might bind up the apostates and preserve the honest in heart.

Thursday, September 5.—Everyone attended public prayer meeting and exposed the false prophets.

Friday, September 6.—Elder Heber C. Kimball and I visited the sick until 2 p. m.

Saturday, September 7.—Accompanied by Elder Kimball I waited upon Elder John P. Greene and attended to ordinances for him: He was on his deathbed.

Monday, September 9.—I attended council with the Quorum of the Twelve at Elder Heber C. Kimball's. Thence I went in company with Elder Kimball through the city attending to business and visiting Elder John P. Greene and Parley P. Pratt who were sick.

Monday, September 9.—[The wayward labored with] Elder Heber C. Kimball and George A. Smith labored diligently with James Emmett that he might be persuaded to desist from his intended course of taking away a party of misguided saints into the wilderness.

Friday, September 13.—In company with Brother Heber C. Kimball and his wife, Vilate, I visited Mother Lucy Smith, Mother of the Prophet.

Same day.—Reports concerning the movement of the mob who are making preparations for what they call a 'wolf hunt' on the 26th and 27th of this month. * * * They design coming and attempting to drag some more authorities of the church out to Carthage to murder them.

Saturday, September 14.—In company with Elders Heber C. Kimball and George A. Smith I called on Sister Hyrum Smith.

Elder Amasa M. Lyman being very sick and reported to be dying, Brothers Kimball and George A. Smith and I retired to my upper room (prayer room) and prayed for him; he was healed from that very hour.

Evening, visited Brother Amasa M. Lyman (sick nigh unto death).

Monday, September 16.—Building of an arsenal in Nauvoo near the Temple for housing the arms of the people. I went to the ground secured for the Arsenal. We uncovered our heads and lifted our hands to heaven and I dedicated the ground by prayer to the God of the armies of Israel. I took the spade and broke the ground for the cellar.

Thursday, September 19.—At home, waiting upon my wife who is very sick. The saints called upon me for counsel and direction.

Friday, September 20.—Attending to ordinances in behalf of the saints and laying hands on the sick. The Lord is with me continually.

Sunday, September 22.—Governor's agent arrived in Nauvoo. Elder John Taylor made affidavits against T. C. Sharp and Levi Williams, two of the murderers of Joseph Smith.

Monday, September 23.—This evening Sheriff Deming came into Nauvoo for a Mormon *posse* to take Sharp and Williams. The Twelve decided that it was imprudent to take Mormons for that purpose and advised him accordingly.

Tuesday, September 24.—I attended council at Winsor P. Lyons. Six of the brethren of the Twelve were present, and Elder Joseph Young [senior President of the Seventy]. We selected seventy presidents to preside over the seventies—over the ten quorums of the seventies then in contemplation, and fifty high priests to preside over different sections of the country.

Thursday, September 26.—The Quincy militia [state troops] were escorted about town by the Nauvoo band—(act of courtesy on the part of the Nauvoo band).

Held a council at the Temple office and appointed four watchmen to watch the Temple tonight. Some of Wight's Company have come to town and they report that they have come to deface the capitals [placed upon the columns of the Temple] and burn the lumber around the Temple.

Friday, September 27.—This was the day set apart by the anti-Mormons for the great 'wolf hunt'.

Governor's troops came into Nauvoo to revert the purpose of it and the hunt failed. Several of the staff officers of the Nauvoo Legion appeared in uniform without arms, which the governor regarded as a hint to remind him of his disarming the Legion previous to the massacre of Joseph and Hyrum Smith.

Sunday, September 29.—I attended meeting. * * * Afternoon, I went to the Seventies' Hall *and ordained* the sixty-three members of the First Quorum of Seventy to be presidents over the quorums from the second to the tenth inclusive.

Monday, September 30.—I breakfasted at Elder Heber C. Kimball's. We laid hands on the sick and visited Mother Lucy Smith.

The Twelve used their influence to prevent the brethren and sisters from attending the ball given by William Marks. The same was to come off on Wednesday evening in the dining room of the Mansion, which was still stained with the blood which flowed from Joseph and Hyrum as their bodies lay in said room preparatory to burial.

Tuesday, October 1, 1844.—Evening, attended a meeting of the Quorum of the Twelve for prayer. A very interesting session.''

So throughout. These men, Apostles of the Lord Jesus Christ, were devoted to prayer and the power thereof, nor could aught shake them from that anchorage. It was *par excellence* the period of prayer in the church; and of works, too, for nothing could exceed their activity; faith and works were evenly balanced; none could be more thoroughly convinced than they that "faith without works is dead, being alone." And so faith and works went hand in hand in this period, and held a great and disinherited and expatriated people together; and transported them across the plains and over the mountains to where they found refuge from their temporary ills, and sanctuary; and place and means to lengthen their cords and strengthen their stakes—a period for development.

In no other way can men of this and future generations so well learn "the faith of their fathers", or their character, than by a study of this sector of the Church History recorded in the annals of volume VII.

I
CHURCH HISTORIANS' EXCERPTS FROM FORD'S HISTORY OF ILLINOIS

HISTORY

OF THE

CHURCH OF JESUS CHRIST

OF

LATTER-DAY SAINTS

PERIOD II

FROM THE MANUSCRIPT HISTORY OF BRIGHAM YOUNG AND OTHER ORIGINAL DOCUMENTS

CHAPTER I.

CONDITIONS IN HANCOCK COUNTY REVIEWED BY GOVERNOR FORD—THE STATE ARMS OF THE LEGION SURRENDERED ON THE DEMAND OF THE GOVERNOR

Explanation

THE following lengthy excerpt from the *History of Illinois* by Thomas Ford, Governor of that State from 1842-6 was made by the Historians of the Church of Jesus Christ of Latter-day Saints, George A. Smith and Wilford Woodruff—1862—and published in the *Millennial Star* of that year (Vol. xxiv, pp. 519-584 *passim*). It is taken from Ford's *History* in unbroken quotation from page 329 to page 354. In a brief paragraph preceding this quotation (p. 328) the governor had said in commenting upon the character of the Mormon people: "Upon the whole, if one-half of these reports had been true [i. e. reports derogatory of their character] the Mormon community must have been the most intolerable collection of rogues ever assembled; or, if one-half them were false, they were the most maligned and abused." The beginning of the Historians' excerpt:

REVIEW OF GOVERNOR FORD'S PERFORMANCES

"Governor Ford is certainly a man who performed mighty wonders. He not only compelled two inno-cent men, by virtue of his office as Governor of Illinois, to go before two different magistrates on the same charge, contrary to the Constitution and laws of the state; to surrender themselves into the custody of a mob magistrate (not the one who issued the writ); go to prison under a military guard on an illegal mit-timus, granted contrary to law, without any examina-tion; put in a criminal cell without having been examined for crime; brought them out of prison con-trary to law; thrust them back again under the most solemn and sacred pledges of his personal faith, and the faith of the state, for their protection; guarded them with men whom he knew to be treacherous, and to have resolved on the death of the prisoners, until they were murdered in cold blood, and then pro-fessed to be 'thunderstruck'!

It is our wish to do strict justice to the memory of this heroic governor, who, in addition to the above-named mighty achievements, on his deathbed be-queathed to the astounded world a volume of 447 pages, entitled, '*History of Illinois* from 1818 to 1847, containing a full account of the rise, progress, and fall of Mormonism', etc., from which we copy the follow-ing:—

GOVERNOR FORD'S STATEMENT

'But the great cause of popular fury was, that the Mormons at several preceding elections had cast their vote as a unit, thereby making the fact apparent that
Cause of Pop-
ular Fury.
no one could aspire to the honors or offices of the country, within the sphere of their influence, without their approbation and votes. It appears to be one of the principles by which they insist upon being governed as a community, to act as a unit in all matters of government and religion. They

express themselves to be fearful that if division should be encouraged in politics, it would soon extend to their religion, and rend their church with schism and into sects.

This seems to me to be an unfortunate view of the subject, and more unfortunate in practice, as I am well satisfied that it must be the fruitful source of excitement, violence, and mobocracy, whilst it is persisted in. It is indeed unfortunate for their peace that they do not divide in elections, according to their individual preferences or political principles, like other people.

This one principle and practice of theirs arrayed against them in deadly hostility all aspirants for office who were not sure of their support, all who have been unsuccessful in elections, and all who were too proud to court their influence, with all their friends and connections.

These also were the active men in blowing up the fury of the people, in hopes that a popular movement might be set on foot which would result in the expulsion or extermination of the Mormon voters. For this purpose, public meetings had been called, inflammatory speeches had been made, exaggerated reports had been extensively circulated, committees had been appointed, who rode night and day to spread the reports, and solicit the aid of neighboring counties. And at a public meeting at Warsaw, resolutions were passed to expel or exterminate the Mormon population.

Methods of Blowing up the Fury.

This was not, however, a movement which was unanimously concurred in. The county contained a goodly number of inhabitants in favor of peace, or who at least desired to be neutral in such a contest. These were stigmatized by the name of *Jack-Mormons,* and there were not a few of the more furious exciters of the people who openly expressed their intention to involve them in the common expulsion or extermination.

A system of excitement and agitation was artfully planned and executed with tact. It consisted in spreading reports and rumors of the most fearful character.

As examples: On the morning before my arrival at Carthage [June 21, 1844], I was awakened at an Illustrations of early hour by the frightful report, which False Reports. was asserted with confidence and apparent consternation, that the Mormons had already commenced the work of burning, destruction, and murder, and that every man capable of bearing arms was instantly wanted at Carthage for the protection of the country. We lost no time in starting; but when we arrived at Carthage we could hear no more concerning this story.

Again: during the few days that the militia were encamped at Carthage, frequent applications were made to me to send a force here and a force there, and a force all about the country, to prevent murders, robberies, and larcenies, which it was said were threatened by the Mormons. No such forces were sent, nor were any such offenses committed at that time, except the stealing of some provisions, and there was never the least proof that this was done by a Mormon.

Again: on my late visit to Hancock county, I was informed by some of their violent enemies that the larcenies of the Mormons had become unusually numerous and insufferable. They indeed admitted that but little had been done in this way in their immediate vicinity; but they insisted that sixteen horses had been stolen by the Mormons in one night, near Lima, in the county of Adams.

At the close of the expedition, I called at this same town of Lima, and upon inquiry was told that no horses had been stolen in that neighborhood, but that sixteen horses had been stolen in one night in Hancock county. This last informant being told of the Hancock story, again changed the venue to another distant settlement in the northern edge of Adams.

As my object in visiting Hancock [county] was expressly to assist in the execution of the laws, and not to violate them, or to witness or permit their violation, as I was convinced that the Mormon leaders had committed a crime in the destruction of the press, and had resisted the execution of process, I determined to exert the whole force of the state, if necessary, to bring them to justice.

Governor Ford's Zeal for the Law!

But seeing the great excitement in the public mind, and the manifest tendency of this excitement to run into mobocracy, I was of opinion that before I acted I ought to obtain a pledge from the officers and men to support me in strictly legal measures, and to protect the prisoners in case they surrendered; for I was determined, if possible, that the forms of law should not be made the catspaw of a mob, to seduce these people to a quiet surrender, as the convenient victims of popular fury.

I therefore called together the whole force then assembled at Carthage, and made an address, explaining to them what I could, and what I could not legally do, and also adducing to them various reasons why they, as well as the Mormons, should submit to the laws, and why, if they had resolved upon revolutionary proceedings, their purpose should be abandoned.

Illinois Militia Promise to Sustain Legal Procedure Only.

The assembled troops seemed much pleased with the address, and upon its conclusion the officers and men unanimously voted, with acclamation, to sustain me in a strictly legal course, and that the prisoners should be protected from violence.

Upon the arrival of additional forces from Warsaw, McDonough, and Schuyler, similar addresses were made, with the same result.

It seemed to me that these votes fully authorized me to promise the accused Mormons the protection of the law in case they surrendered.

They were accordingly duly informed that if they surrendered they would be protected, and if they did not, the whole force of the state would be called out, if necessary, to compel their submission. A force of ten men was despatched with the constable to make the arrests and to guard the prisoners to headquarters.

In the meantime, Joe Smith, as Lieutenant-General of the Nauvoo Legion, had declared martial law in Martial Law in the city. The Legion was assembled, and Nauvoo. ordered under arms. The members of it residing in the country were ordered into town. The Mormon settlements obeyed the summons of their leader, and marched to his assistance. Nauvoo was one great military camp, strictly guarded and watched, and no ingress or egress was allowed except upon the strictest examination.

In one instance, which came to my knowledge, a citizen of McDonough, who happened to be in the city, was denied the privilege of returning until he made oath that he did not belong to the party at Carthage, that he would return home without calling at Carthage, and that he would give no information of the movement of the Mormons.

However, upon the arrival of the constable and guard, the mayor, Joseph Smith, and common council at once signified their willingness to surrender, and stated their readiness to proceed to Carthage next morning at eight o'clock. Martial law had previously been abolished.

The hour of eight o'clock came, and the accused failed to make their appearance. The constable and his escort returned. The constable made no effort to arrest any of them, nor would he or the guard delay their departure one minute beyond the time, to see whether an arrest could be made.

Upon their return they reported that they had been informed that the accused had fled and could not be found.

I immediately proposed to a council of officers to march into Nauvoo with the small force then under my command, but the officers were of opinion that it was too small, and many of them insisted upon a further call of the militia.

Upon reflection I was of opinion that the officers were right in the estimate of our force, and the project for immediate action was abandoned.

I was soon informed, however, of the conduct of the constable and guard, and then I was perfectly satisfied that a most base fraud had been attempted; that, in fact, it was feared that the Mormons would submit, and thereby entitle themselves to the protection of the law.   A Base Fraud Attempted.

It was very apparent that many of the bustling, active spirits were afraid that there would be no occasion for calling out an overwhelming militia force, for marching it into Nauvoo, for probable mutiny when there, and for the extermination of the Mormon race. It appeared that the constable and the escort were fully in the secret, and acted well their part to promote the conspiracy.

Seeing this to be the state of the case, I delayed any further call of the militia, to give the accused another opportunity to surrender, for indeed I was most anxious to avoid a general call for the militia at that critical season of the year.

The whole spring season preceding had been unusually wet. No ploughing of corn had been done, and but very little planting. The season had just changed to be suitable for ploughing. The crops which had been planted were universally suffering, and the loss of two weeks, or even of one, at that time, was likely to produce a general famine all over the country.

The wheat harvest was also approaching; and if we got into a war, there was no foreseeing when it would end, or when the militia could safely be discharged.

In addition to these considerations, all the gristmills in all that section of the country had been swept away, or disabled, by the high waters, leaving the inhabitants almost without meal or flour, and making it impossible then to procure provisions by impressment or otherwise, for the sustenance of any considerable force.

This was the time of the high waters, of astonishing floods in all the rivers and creeks in the western Flood Conditions. country. The Mississippi river at St. Louis was several feet higher than it was ever known before; it was up into the second stories of the warehouses on Water Street. The steamboats ran up to these warehouses, and could scarcely receive their passengers from the second stories. The whole American [Missouri] bottom was overflowed from eight to twenty feet deep, and steamboats freely crossed the bottom along the road from St. Louis to the opposite bluffs in Illinois. Houses and fences and stock of all kinds were swept away, the fields near the river, after the water subsided, being covered with sand from a foot to three feet deep, which was generally thrown into ridges and washed into gullies, so as to spoil the land for cultivation.

Families had great difficulty in making their escape. Through the active exertions of Mr. Pratt, the mayor of St. Louis, steamboats were sent in every direction to their relief. The boats found many of the families on the tops of their houses, just ready to be floated away.

The inhabitants of the bottom lost nearly all their personal property. A large number of them were taken to St. Louis in a state of entire destitution, and their necessities were supplied by the contributions of the charitable of that city. A larger number were forced out on to the Illinois bluffs, where they encamped, and were supplied with provisions by the neighboring inhabitants.

This freshet nearly ruined the ancient village of Kaskaskia. The inhabitants were driven away and scattered, many of them never to return.

For many years before this flood there had been a

flourishing institution at Kaskaskia, under the direction of an order of nuns of the Catholic Church. They had erected an extensive building, which was surrounded and filled by the waters to the second story; but they were all safely taken away, pupils and all, by a steamboat which was sent to their relief, and which ran directly up to the building and received its inmates from the second story. This school was now transferred to St. Louis, where it yet remains.

All the rivers and streams in Illinois were as high, and did as much damage in proportion to their length and the extent of their bottoms, as the Mississippi.

This great flood destroyed the last hope of getting provisions at home, and I was totally without funds belonging to the state, with which to purchase at more distant markets, and there was a certainty that such purchases could not have been made on credit abroad. For these reasons I was desirous of avoiding a war, if it could be avoided.

In the meantime, I made a requisition upon the officers of the Nauvoo Legion for the state arms in their possession. It appears that there was no evidence in the quartermaster-general's office of the number and description of arms with which the Legion had been furnished. *State Arms Demanded.*

Dr. Bennett, after he had been appointed quartermaster-general, had joined the Mormons, and had disposed of the public arms as he pleased, without keeping or giving any account of them.

On this subject I applied to General Wilson Law for information. He had lately been the major-general of the Legion. He had seceded from the Mormon party; was one of the owners of the proscribed press, had left the city, as he said, in fear of his life; and was one of the party asking for justice against its constituted authorities. He was interested to exaggerate the number of arms rather than to place it at too low an estimate.

From his information I learned that the Legion had

received three pieces of cannon and about two hundred and fifty stand of small arms and their accoutrements. Of these, the three pieces of cannon and two hundred and twenty stand of small arms were surrendered. These arms were demanded because the Legion was illegally used in the destruction of the press and in enforcing martial law in the city, in open resistance to legal process and the *posse comitatus*.

I demanded the surrender also on account of the great prejudice and excitement which the possession of these arms by the Mormons had kindled in the minds of the people.

A large portion of the people, by pure misrepresentation, had been made to believe that the Legion had received of the state as many as thirty pieces of artillery and five or six thousand stand of small arms, which in all probability, would soon be wielded for the conquest of the country, and for their subjection to Mormon domination.

I was of opinion that the removal of these arms would tend much to allay this excitement and prejudice, and, in point of fact, although wearing a severe aspect, would be an act of real kindness to the Mormons themselves.' "

CHAPTER II.

SUBMISSION OF THE PROPHET TO THE REQUIREMENTS
OF THE GOVERNOR — GATHERING OF THE ENEMY
FORCES OF THE PROPHET — GOVERNOR FORD'S DE-
FENSIVE JUSTIFICATION FOR HIS PLACEMENT OF THE
HOSTILE FORCES AT CARTHAGE AND THE DISMISSAL
OF OTHERS

" 'ON the 23rd or 24th day of June, Joe Smith, the
mayor of Nauvoo, together with his brother Hyrum,
and all the members of the council, and all   *Surrender of
others demanded, came into Carthage and   Nauvoo's May-
or and City
surrendered themselves prisoners to the con-   Council.
stable on the charge of riot.

They all voluntarily entered into a recognizance
before the justice of the peace for their appearance at
court to answer the charge, and all of them were discharged from custody except Joe and Hyrum Smith,
against whom the magistrate had issued a new writ
on a complaint of treason. They were immediately
arrested by the constable on this charge, and retained
in his custody to answer it.

The overt act of treason charged against them consisted in the alleged levying of war against the state by
declaring martial law in Nauvoo, and in ordering out
the Legion to resist the *posse comitatus.* Their actual
guiltiness of the charge would depend upon circumstances.

If their opponents had been seeking to put the law
in force in good faith, and nothing more, then an
array of military force in open resistance to the *posse
comitatus* and the militia of the state most probably
would have amounted to treason.

But if those opponents merely intended to use the process of the law, the militia of the state, and the *posse comitatus*, as catspaws to compass the possessions of their persons for the purpose of murdering them afterwards, as the sequel demonstrated the fact to be, it might well be doubted whether they were guilty of treason.

Soon after the surrender of the Smiths, at their request I dispatched Captain Singleton with his com-
The Nauvoo Legion. pany from Brown county to Nauvoo, to guard the town, and I authorized him to take command of the Legion. He reported to me afterwards, that he called out the Legion for inspection, and that upon two hours' notice two thousand of them assembled, all of them armed, and this after the public arms had been taken away from them. So it appears that they had a sufficiency of private arms for any reasonable purpose.

After the Smiths had been arrested on the new charge of treason, the justice of the peace postponed the examination, because neither of the parties were prepared with their witnesses for trial. In the meantime, he committed them to the jail of the county for greater security.

In all this matter the justice of the peace and constable, though humble in office, were acting in a high and independent capacity, far beyond any legal power
Question of Jurisdiction. in me to control. I considered that the executive power could only be called in to assist, and not to dictate or control their action; that in the humble sphere of their duties they were as independent, and clothed with as high authority by the law, as the executive department, and that my province was simply to aid them with the force of the state.

It is true, that so far as I could prevail on them by advice, I endeavored to do so. The prisoners were not in military custody, or prisoners of war, and I could no more legally control these officers than I could the superior courts of justice.

Some persons have supposed that I ought to have had them sent to some distant and friendly part of the state for confinement and trial, and that I ought to have searched them for concealed arms; but these surmises and suppositions are readily disposed of by the fact, that they were not my prisoners, but were the prisoners of the constable and jailor, under the direction of the justice of the peace; and, also, by the fact that by law they could be tried in no other county than Hancock.

The jail in which they were confined is a considerable stone building, containing a residence for the jailor, cells for the close and secure confinement of the prisoners, and one larger room, not so strong, but more airy and comfortable than the cells. They were put into the cells by the jailor; but upon their remonstrance and request, and by my advice, they were transferred to the larger room, and there they remained until the final catastrophe. Neither they nor I seriously apprehended an attack on the jail through the guard stationed to protect it, nor did I apprehend the least danger on their part of an attempt to escape, for I was very sure that any such an attempt would have been the signal of their immediate death. Indeed, if they had escaped, it would have been fortunate for the purposes of those who were anxious for the expulsion of the Mormon population, for the great body of that people would most assuredly have followed their Prophet and principal leaders, as they did in their flight from Missouri.

I learned afterwards that the leaders of the anti-Mormons did much to stimulate their followers to the murder of the Smiths in jail, by alleging that the governor intended to favor their escape. If this had been true, and could have been well carried out, it would have been the best way of getting rid of the Mormons. These leaders of the Mormons would never have dared to return, and they would have been followed in their flight by all their church. *I had such plan in my mind*, but I had never breathed it to a living soul, and was thus thwarted in ridding the state of the Mormons two years before they actually left, by the insane frenzy of the anti-Mormons.

Joe Smith, when he escaped from Missouri, had no difficulty in again collecting his sect about him at Nauvoo; and so the Twelve Apostles, after they had been at the head of affairs long enough to establish their authority and influence as leaders, had no difficulty in getting nearly the whole body of Mormons to follow them into the wilderness two years after the death of their pretended Prophet.

The force assembled at Carthage amounted to about twelve or thirteen hundred men, and it was calculated that four or five hundred more were assembled at Warsaw. Nearly all that portion resident in Hancock were anxious to be marched into Nauvoo.

Forces at Carthage and Warsaw.

This measure was supposed to be necessary to search for counterfeit money and the apparatus to make it, and also to strike a salutary terror into the Mormon people by an exhibition of the force of the state, and thereby prevent future outrages, murders, robberies, burnings, and the like, apprehended as the effect of Mormon vengeance on those who had taken a part against them.

On my part, at one time, this arrangement was agreed to. The morning of the 27th day of June was appointed for the march, and Golden's Point, near the Mississippi river, and about equi-distant from Nauvoo and Warsaw, was selected as the place of rendezvous.

I had determined to prevail on the justice to bring out his prisoners, and take them along. A council of officers, however, determined that this would be highly inexpedient and dangerous, and offered such substantial reasons for their opinions as induced me to change my resolution.

Two or three days' preparation had been made for this expedition. I observed that some of the people became more and more excited and inflammatory the further the preparations were advanced. Occasional threats came to my ears of destroying the city and murdering or expelling the inhabitants.

I had no objection to ease the terrors of the people by such a display of force, and was most anxious also to search for the alleged apparatus for making counterfeit money; and, in fact, to inquire into all the charges against that people, if I could have been assured of my command against mutiny and insubordination. But I gradually learned, to my entire satis- Threats of Vi-faction, that there was a plan to get the olence Within the Governor's troops into Nauvoo, and there to begin the Forces. war, probably by some of our own party, or some of the seceding Mormons taking advantage of the night to fire on our own force, and then laying it on the Mormons.

I was satisfied that there were those amongst us fully capable of such an act, hoping that in the alarm, bustle and confusion of a militia camp, the truth could not be discovered, and that it might lead to the desired collision.

I had many objections to be made the dupe of any such or similar artifice. I was openly and boldly opposed to any attack on the city, unless it should become necessary, to arrest prisoners legally charged and demanded. Indeed, if anyone will reflect upon the number of women, inoffensive and young persons, and innocent children, which must be contained in such a city of twelve or fifteen thousand inhabitants, it would seem to me his heart would relent and rebel against such violent resolutions. Nothing but the most blinded and obdurate fury could incite a person, even if he had the power, to the willingness of driving such persons, bare and houseless, on to the prairies, to

starve, suffer, and even steal, as they must have done,
for subsistence. No one who has children of his own
would think of it for a moment.

Besides this, if we had been ever so much disposed
to commit such an act of wickedness, we evidently had
not the power to do it. I was well assured that the
Mormons, at a short notice, could muster as many as
two or three thousand well-armed men. We had not
more than seventeen hundred, with three pieces of
cannon, and about twelve hundred stand of small arms.
We had provisions for two days only, and would be
compelled to disband at the end of that time. To
think of beginning a war under such circumstances
was a plain absurdity.

If the Mormons had succeeded in repulsing our
attack, as most likely would have been the case, the
Pro et con of country must necessarily be given up to their
Militia-Mob ravages until a new force could be assembled,
Treachery. and provisions made for its subsistence. Or
if we should have succeeded in driving them from their
city, they would have scattered; and, being justly
incensed at our barbarity, and suffering with privation
and hunger, would have spread desolation all over the
country, without any possibility on our part, with the
force we then had, of preventing it. Again, they would
have had the advantage of being able to subsist their
force in the field by plundering their enemies.

All these considerations were duly urged by me
upon the attention of a council of officers, convened
on the morning of the 27th of June. I also urged
upon the council that such wanton and unprovoked
barbarity on their part would turn the sympathy of
the people in the surrounding counties in favor of the
Mormons, and therefore it would be impossible to raise
a volunteer militia force to protect such a people
against them. Many of the officers admitted that there
might be danger of collision. But such was the blind
fury prevailing at the time, though not showing itself
by much visible excitement, that a small majority of

the council adhered to the first resolution of marching into Nauvoo; most of the officers of the Schuyler and McDonough militia voting against it, and most of those of the county of Hancock voting in its favor.

A very responsible duty now devolved upon me, to determine whether I would, as commander-in-chief, be governed by the advice of this majority. I had no hesitation in deciding that I would not; but on the contrary, I ordered the troops to be disbanded, both at Carthage and Warsaw, with the exception of three companies, two of which were retained as a guard to the jail, and the other was retained to accompany me to Nauvoo.

The officers insisted much in council upon the necessity of marching to that place to search for apparatus to make counterfeit money, and more particularly to terrify the Mormons from attempting any open or secret measures of vengeance against the citizens of the county, who had taken a part against them or their leaders.

To ease their terrors on this head, I proposed to them that I would myself proceed to the city, accompanied by a small force, make the proposed search, and deliver an address to the Mormons, and tell them plainly what degree of excitement and hatred prevailed against them in the minds of the whole people, and that if any open or secret violence should be committed on the persons or property of those who had taken part against them, that no one would doubt but that it had been perpetrated by them, and that it would be sure and certain means of the destruction of their city and the extermination of their people.

I ordered two companies, under the command of Captain R. F. Smith, of the Carthage Greys, to guard the jail. In selecting these companies, and particularly the company of the Carthage Greys for this service, I have been subjected to some censure. It has been said that this company had already been guilty of mutiny, and had

Capt. R. F. Smith and the Carthage Greys left to Guard the Prisoners.

been ordered to be arrested whilst in the encampment at Carthage, and that they and their officers were the deadly enemies of the prisoners. Indeed, it would have been difficult to find friends of the prisoners under my command, unless I had called in the Mormons as a guard, and this I was satisfied would have led to the immediate war and the sure death of the prisoners.

It is true that this company had behaved badly towards the brigadier-general* in command on the occasion when the prisoners were shown along the line of the McDonough militia. This company had been ordered as a guard. They were under the belief that the prisoners, who were arrested for a capital offense, were shown to the troops in a kind of triumph, and that they had been called on as a triumphal escort to grace the procession. They also entertained a very bad feeling towards the brigadier-general who commanded their service on the occasion.

The truth is, however, that this company was never ordered to be arrested; that the Smiths were not shown to the McDonough troops as a mark of honor and triumph, but were shown to them at the urgent request of the troops themselves, to gratify their curiosity in beholding persons who had made themselves so notorious in the country.

When the Carthage Greys ascertained what was the true motive in showing the prisoners to the troops, they were perfectly satisfied. All due atonement was made on their part for their conduct to the brigadier-general, and they cheerfully returned to their duty.

Although I knew that this company were the enemies of the Smiths, yet I had confidence in their loyalty *The Governor's Defensive Explanations.* and integrity, because their captain was universally spoken of as a most respectable citizen and honorable man. The company itself was an old independent company, well armed,

*This was Brigadier-General M. R. Deming. see *Millennial Star* vol. xxiv. p. 423. B. H. R.

uniformed and drilled, and the members of it were the elite of the militia of the county.*

I relied upon this company especially because it was an independent company, for a long time instructed and practiced in military discipline and subordination. I also had their word and honor, officers and men, to do their duty according to law.

Besides all this, the officers and most of the men resided in Carthage, in the near vicinity of Nauvoo, and, as I thought, must know that they would make themselves and their property convenient and conspicuous marks of Mormon vengeance in case they were guilty of treachery.

I had at first intended to select a guard from the county of McDonough, but the militia of that county were very much dissatisfied to remain; their crops were suffering at home, they were in a perfect fever to be discharged, and I was destitute of provisions to supply them for more than a few days. They were far from

*The reader should be reminded that these statements of Governor Ford in justification of his placing the Carthage Greys on guard at the prison with Captain Robert F. Smith in command, is a labored defense written some years after the events, and for the purpose of justifying his course of procedure. A very lame and impotent defense it is. The governor should have remembered that in addition to the rebellious conduct of this company of Carthage Greys on the occasion of Joseph Smith and his brother Hyrum being introduced to the McDonough troops, there was the likewise boisterous reception of the Prophet and his company the night they arrived at Carthage, and under the very window of the hotel where the governor lodged, and within his hearing. On that occasion they exclaimed: "Where is the damned prophet?" "Stand away, you McDonough boys, and let us shoot the damned Mormons." "G—d— you, old Joe, we've got you now." "Clear the way and let us have a view of Joe Smith, the prophet of God. He has seen the last of Nauvoo. We'll use him up now, and kill all the damned Mormons." The rear platoon of the Carthage Greys repeatedly threw their guns over their heads in a curve so that the bayonets struck the ground with the breech of their guns upward, when they would run back and pick them up at the same time whooping, yelling, hooting and cursing like a pack of savages. Governor Ford was a witness of all this. For on hearing the above expressions, he put his head out of the window of the Hamilton Hotel at which he was stopping and very fawningly said, "I know your anxiety to see Mr. Smith, which is natural enough, but it is quite too late tonight for you to have the opportunity, but I assure you, gentlemen, you shall have that privilege tomorrow morning, as I will cause him to pass before the troops upon the square, and I now wish you, with this assurance quietly and peaceably to return to your quarters." When this declaration was made there was a faint "Hurrah for Tom Ford", and they instantly obeyed his wish. From all which it must appear that the governor could not fail but know the style of character of this company of militia, made up perhaps of the bitterest enemies of the Prophet and the Mormon people (See vol. vi. this *History*, Period I, pp. 559-60). B. H. R.

home, where they could not supply themselves, whilst
the Carthage company could board at their own houses,
and would be put to little inconvenience in comparison.

What gave me greater confidence in the selection of
this company as a prudent measure was, that the selection was first suggested and urged by the brigadier-
general in command, who was well known to be utterly
hostile to all mobocracy and violence towards the prisoners, and who was openly charged by the violent
party with being on the side of the Mormons.

At any rate, I knew that the jail would have to be
guarded as long as the prisoners were confined; that an
imprisonment for treason might last the whole summer
and the greater part of the autumn before a trial could
be had in the circuit court; that it would be utterly
impossible, in the circumstances of the country, to keep
a force there from a foreign county for so long a time;
and that a time must surely come when the duty of
guarding the jail would necessarily devolve on the
citizens of the county.

It is true, also, that at this time I had not believed
or suspected that any attack was to be made upon the
prisoners in jail. It is true that I was aware that a
great deal of hatred existed against them, and that there
were those who would do them an injury if they could.
I had heard of some threats being made, but none of
an attack upon the prisoners whilst in jail. These
threats seemed to be made by individuals not acting
in concert. They were no more than the bluster which
might have been expected, and furnished no indication
of numbers combining for this or any other purpose.

I must here be permitted to say, also, that frequent
appeals had been made to me to make a clean and
thorough work of the matter by exterminating the
Mormons or expelling them from the state. An opinion seemed generally to prevail that the sanction of
executive authority would legalize the act; and all persons of any influence, authority, or note, who conversed with me on the subject, frequently and repeated-

ly stated their total unwillingness to act without my direction, or in any mode except according to law.

This was a circumstance well calculated to conceal from me the secret machinations on foot. I had constantly contended against violent measures, and so had the brigadier-general in command; and I am convinced that unusual pains were taken to conceal from both of us the secret measures resolved upon. It has been said, however, that some person named 'Williams',* in a public speech at Carthage, called for volunteers to murder the Smiths, and that I ought to have had him arrested. Whether such a speech was really made or not is yet unknown to me.' "

*Yet so prominent was this "some person named 'Williams' " that he was the "Colonel Levi Williams" in charge of the mob forces from Warsaw (See *History of Hancock County*, Gregg. p. 324). B. H. R.

CHAPTER III.

GOVERNOR FORD'S VISIT TO NAUVOO—FEARS ON THE
WAY — INSULTING SPEECH TO THE CITIZENS —
RESENTED — HEARS OF THE ASSASSINATION OF
JOSEPH AND HYRUM SMITH

" 'HAVING ordered the guard, and left General Deming in command in Carthage, and discharged the residue of the militia, I immediately departed for Nauvoo,
eighteen miles distant, accompanied by Colonel Buck-
master, quartermaster-general, and Captain Dunn's
company of dragoons.

After we had proceeded four miles, Colonel Buck-
master intimated to me a suspicion that an attack
Uncertainty of the Reflections and Actions of Governor Ford. would be made upon the jail.   He stated the
matter as a mere suspicion, arising from hav-
ing seen two persons converse together at
Carthage with some air of mystery.   I myself entertained no suspicion of such an attack; *at any rate, none
before the next day in the afternoon,** because it was
notorious that we had departed from Carthage with
the declared intention of being absent at least two
days.†   I could not believe that any person would
attack the jail whilst we were in Nauvoo, and thereby
expose my life and the life of my companions to the
sudden vengeance of the Mormons upon hearing of
the death of their leaders.   Nevertheless, acting upon

*Italics are the Church Historians', George A Smith and Wilford Woodruff. B. H. R.

†The governor is most unfortunate here in his admissions that he did not
expect an attack "until the afternoon of the next day" following his departure for
Nauvoo; for since he had made provision for being absent in Nauvoo "two days" then
he did expect, from the language he here uses, that an attack would be made upon the
jail and the prisoners on the second day after his departure, and while he would
still be absent from Carthage. B. H. R.

the principle of providing against mere possibilities, I sent back one of the company with a special order to Captain Smith to guard the jail strictly, and at the peril of his life, until my return.

We proceeded on our journey four miles further. By this time I had convinced myself that no attack would be made on the jail that day or night. I supposed that a regard for my safety, and the safety of my companions, would prevent an attack until those to be engaged in it could be assured of our departure from Nauvoo. I still think that this ought to have appeared to me to be a reasonable supposition.

I therefore determined at this point to omit making the search for counterfeit money at Nauvoo, and defer an examination of all the other abominations charged on that people, in order to return to Carthage that same night, that I might be on the ground, in person, in time to prevent an attack upon the jail, if any had been meditated. To this end we called a halt; the baggage wagons were ordered to remain where they were until towards evening, and then return to Carthage.

Having made these arrangements, we proceeded on our march, and arrived at Nauvoo about four o'clock of the afternoon of the 27th day of June. Governor Ford in Nauvoo. As soon as notice could be given, a crowd of the citizens assembled to hear an address which I proposed to deliver to them. The number present has been variously estimated from one to five thousand.

In this address I stated to them how and in what their functionaries had violated the laws; also the many scandalous reports in circulation against them, and that these reports, whether true or false, were generally believed by the people. I distinctly stated to them the amount of hatred and prejudice which prevailed everywhere against them, and the causes of it, at length.

I also told them, plainly and emphatically, that if any vengeance should be attempted openly or secretly against the persons or property of the citizens who had taken part against their leaders, that the public hatred and excitement was such, that thousands would assemble for the total destruction of their city and the extermination of their people, and that no power in the state would be able to prevent it.

During this address some impatience and resentment were manifested by the Mormons at the recital of the various reports enumerated concerning them, which they strenuously and indignantly denied to be true. They claimed to be a law-abiding people, and insisted that as they looked to the law alone for their protection, so were they careful themselves to observe its provisions.

People of Nauvoo Resent Charges.

Upon the conclusion of this address I proposed to take a vote on the question, whether they would strictly observe the laws even in opposition to their Prophet and leaders. The vote was unanimous in favor of this proposition.

The anti-Mormons contended that such a vote from the Mormons signified nothing; and truly the subsequent history of that people showed clearly that they were loudest in their professions of attachment to the law whenever they were guilty of the greatest extravagancies; and, in fact, that they were so ignorant and stupid about matters of law that they had no means of judging of the legality of their conduct only as they were instructed by their spiritual leaders.*

A short time before sundown we departed on our return to Carthage. When we had proceeded two miles, we met two individuals, one of them a Mormon, who informed us that the Smiths had been assassinated in jail, about five or six o'clock of that day. The intelligence seemed to strike every one with a kind of dumbness. As to

Word of the Assassination of the Prophet Received.

---

*Governor Ford is not justified in making these observations based on anything in the "subsequent history" of the people. Examination of their conduct in "subsequent history" will reveal the fact that they had as an intelligent understanding of law as a community, far exceeding the average of American community in respect to things of the law. B. H R.

myself it was perfectly astounding, and I anticipated the very worst consequences from it.

The Mormons had been represented to me as a lawless, infatuated and fanatical people, not governed by the ordinary motives which influence the rest of mankind. If so, most likely an exterminating war would ensue, and the whole land would be covered with desolation.

Acting upon this supposition, it was my duty to provide as well as I could for the event. I therefore ordered the two messengers into custody, and to be returned with us to Carthage. This was done to get time to make such arrangements as could be made, and to prevent any sudden explosion of Mormon excitement before they could be written to by their friends at Carthage.

I also dispatched messengers to Warsaw, to advise the citizens of the event. But the people there knew all about the matter before my messengers arrived. They, like myself, anticipated a general attack all over the country. The women and children were removed across the river, and a committee was dispatched that night to Quincy for assistance.

The next morning, by daylight, the ringing of the bells in the city of Quincy announced a public meeting. The people assembled in great numbers at an early hour. The Warsaw committee stated to the meeting that a party of Mormons had attempted to rescue the Smiths out of jail; False Rumors at Quincy and Warsaw. that a party of Missourians and others had killed the prisoners to prevent their escape; that the governor and his party were at Nauvoo at the time when intelligence of the fact was brought there; that they had been attacked by the Nauvoo Legion, and had retreated to a house where they were then closely besieged; that the governor had sent out word that he could maintain his position for two days, and would be certain to be massacred if assistance did not arrive by the end of that time.

It is unnecessary to say that this entire story was a fabrication. It was of a piece with the other reports put into circulation by the anti-Mormon party, to influence the public mind and call the people to their assistance. The effect of it, however, was that by ten o'clock on the 28th of June, between two and three hundred men from Quincy, under the command of Major Flood, embarked on board of a steamboat for Nauvoo, to assist in raising the siege, as they honestly believed.

As for myself, I was well convinced that those, whoever they were, who assassinated the Smiths, meditated in turn my assassination by the Mormons. The very circumstances of the case fully corroborated the information which I afterwards received, that upon consultation of the assassins it was agreed amongst them that the murder must be committed whilst the governor was at Nauvoo; that the Mormons would naturally suppose that he had planned it; and that in the first outpouring of their indignation they would assassinate him by way of retaliation; and that thus they would get clear [rid] of the Smiths and the governor all at once. They also supposed, that if they could so contrive the matter as to have the governor of the state assassinated by the Mormons, the public excitement would be greatly increased against that people, and would result in their expulsion from the state at least.

Upon hearing of the assassination of the Smiths, I was sensible that my command was at an end, that The Governor's my destruction was meditated as well as that Plight.   of the Mormons, and that I could not reasonably confide longer in the one party or in the other.

The question then arose, what would be proper to be done. A war was expected by everybody. I was desirous of preserving the peace. I could not put myself at the head of the Mormon force with any kind of propriety, and without exciting greater odium against them than already existed. I could not put

myself at the head of the anti-Mormon party, because
they had justly forfeited my confidence, and my command over them was put an end to by mutiny and
treachery. I could not put myself at the head of either
of these forces, because both of them in turn had
violated the law, and, as I then believed, meditated
further aggression. It appeared to me that if a war
ensued, I ought to have a force in which I could confide, and that I ought to establish my headquarters
at a place where I could learn the truth as to what
was going on.

For these reasons I determined to proceed to Quincy,
a place favorably situated for receiving the earliest intelligence, for issuing orders to raise an army The Governor
if necessary, and for providing supplies for Establishes
its subsistence. But first, I determined to at Quincy.
return back to Carthage and make such arrangements
as could be made for the pacification and defense of
the country.

When I arrived there, about ten o'clock at night,
I found that great consternation prevailed. Many of
the citizens had departed with their families, and others
were preparing to go. As the country was utterly defenseless, this seemed to me to be a proper precaution.
One company of the guard stationed by me to guard
the jail had disbanded and gone home before the
jail was attacked, and many of the Carthage Greys
departed soon afterwards.

General Deming, who was absent in the country
during the murder, had returned. He volunteered to
remain in command of a few men, with orders to
guard the town, observe the progress of events, and to
retreat if menaced by a superior force.

Here, also, I found Dr. Richards and John Taylor,
two of the principal Mormon leaders, who had been
in the jail at the time of the attack, and who voluntarily addressed a most pacific exhortation to their
fellow citizens, which was the first intelligence of the
murder which was received at Nauvoo. I think it

very probable that the subsequent good conduct of the Mormons is attributable to the arrest of the messengers, and to the influence of this letter.

Having made these arrangements, I departed for Quincy. On my road thither, I heard of a body of militia marching from Schuyler, and another from Brown [counties]. It appears that orders had been sent out in my name, but without my knowledge, for the militia of Schuyler county. I immediately countermanded their march, and they returned to their homes.

When I arrived at Columbus, I found that Captain Jonas had raised a company of one hundred men, who were just ready to march. By my advice they postponed their march to await further orders.

I arrived at Quincy on the morning of the 29th of June, about eight o'clock, and immediately issued orders, provisionally, for raising an imposing force, when it should seem to be necessary.

I remained at Quincy for about one month, during which time a committee from Warsaw waited on me, with a written request that I would expel the Mormons from the state. It seemed that it never occurred to these gentlemen that I had no power to exile a citizen; but they insisted that if this were not done, their party would abandon the state. This requisition was refused, of course.

Demands Upon the Governor to Expel the Saints from Illinois.

During this time also, with the view of saving expense, keeping the peace, and having a force which would be removed from the prejudices in the country, I made application to the United States for five hundred men of the regular army, to be stationed for a time in Hancock county, which was subsequently refused.*

*The application here referred to by Governor Ford was unquestionably mere subterfuge. It is true he made application for a United States force of 500 men, but he made it in such form that it could not be otherwise than that he knew that the requisition would not be granted, for he made application for it at the wrong source; namely he wrote to Colonel S. W. Kearney (U. S. A.) Commander of the Third Military Department of the United States, at St. Louis, and made the appli-

During this time also, I had secret agents amongst all parties, observing their movements, and was accurately informed of everything that was meditated on both sides. It appeared that the anti-Mormon party had not relinquished their hostility to the Mormons, nor their determination to expel them, but had deferred further operations until the fall season, after they had finished their summer's work on their farms.

When I first went to Carthage, and during all this difficult business, no public officer ever acted from purer or more patriotic intentions than I did. I was perfectly conscious of the utmost integrity in all my actions, and felt *Perplexities of Governor Ford —Political Parties.* lifted up far above all mere party considerations. But I had scarcely arrived at the scene of action before the whig press commenced the most violent abuse, and attributed to me the basest motives.

It was alleged in the *Sangamon Journal,* and repeated in the other whig newspapers, that the governor had merely gone over to cement an alliance with the Mormons; that the leaders would not be brought to punishment, but that a full privilege would be accorded to them to commit crimes of every hue and grade, in return for their support of the democratic party. I mention this not by way of complaint, for it is only the privilege of the minority to complain, but for its influence upon the people.

I observed that I was narrowly watched in all my proceedings by my whig fellow citizens, and was suspected of an intention to favor the Mormons.

I felt that I did not possess the confidence of the

cation for the above mentioned force to him instead of making application to the President of the United States; and this fact General Kearney mentioned in his letter replying to Governor Ford, a copy of which reply Governor Ford included in his letter to the General Authorities of the Church at Nauvoo. Kearney's letter bears date of July 11, 1844, and in it he said to Governor Ford: "I have not the power of complying with your request, but will forward by tomorrow's mail a copy of your communication to be read before the authorities in Washington City." The letter of Governor Ford, explaining this matter, including also Kearney's letter will be found in *The Comprehensive History of the Church of Jesus Christ of Latter-day Saints,* Century I, vol. ii, pp. 302-7.   B. H. R.

men I commanded, and that they had been induced
to withhold it by the promulgation of the most abominable falsehoods.

I felt the necessity of possessing their confidence, in
order to give vigor to my action, and exerted myself
in every way to obtain it, so that I could control the
excited multitude who were under my command.   I
succeeded better for a time than could have been expected; but who can control the action of a mob without possessing their entire confidence?

It is true, also, that some unprincipled democrats all
the time appeared to be very busy on the side of the
Mormons, and this circumstance was well calculated
to increase suspicion of every one who had the name
of democrat.

It was many days after the assassination of the
Smiths before the circumstances of the murder fully
became known.   It then appeared that,
agreeably to previous orders, the *posse* at
Warsaw had marched on the morning of
the 27th of June in the direction of Golden's Point,
with a view to join the force from Carthage, the whole
body then to be marched into Nauvoo.

Movements of
the Mob from
Warsaw.

But by the time they had gone eight miles, they
were met by the order to disband; and learning at the
same time that the governor was absent at Nauvoo,
about two hundred of these men, many of them being
disguised by blacking their faces with powder and
mud, hastened immediately to Carthage.

There they encamped, at some distance from the
village, and soon learned that one of the companies
left as a guard had disbanded and returned to their
homes.   The other company, the Carthage Greys, was
stationed by the captain in the public square, a hundred and fifty yards from the jail, whilst eight men
were detailed by him, under the command of Sergeant
Franklin A. Worrell, to guard the prisoners.

A Communication was soon established between the conspirators and the company, and it was arranged that the guard should have their guns charged with blank cartridges, and fire at the assailants when they attempted to enter the jail. The Attack Upon the Prison.

General Deming, who was left in command, being deserted by some of his troops, and perceiving the arrangement with the others, and having no force upon which he could rely, for fear of his life retired from the village.

The conspirators came up, jumped the slight fence around the jail, were fired upon by the guard, which, according to arrangement, was overpowered immediately, and the assailants entered the prison, to the door of the room where the two prisoners were confined, with two of their friends, who voluntarily bore them company.

An attempt was made to break open the door, but Joe Smith being armed with a six-barrelled pistol, furnished by his friends, fired several times as the door was bursted open, and wounded three of the assailants. At the same time several shots were fired into the room, by some of which John Taylor received four wounds, and Hyrum Smith was instantly killed.

Joe Smith now attempted to escape by jumping out of the second story window, but the fall so stunned him that he was unable to rise; and being placed in a sitting posture by the conspirators below, they dispatched him with four balls shot through his body.

Thus fell Joe Smith, the most successful impostor in modern times*.' "   *   *   *   *   *

---

*Here ends the former Church Historians' (George A. Smith and Wilford Woodruff) quotation from Ford's *History of Illinois*.   B. H. R.

II
EXTENSION OF QUOTATIONS FROM
FORD'S *HISTORY OF ILLINOIS*

Explanation

THE former Historians of the Church, George A. Smith and Wilford Woodruff (see *Millennial Star*, Vol. xxiv, p. 584, 1862) end their quotation from Ford's *History of Illinois* at p. 354, and in the middle of an unfinished sentence. There are other matters however in the book that should be preserved to history, which deal with subsequent events of Mormon affairs in Hancock county, and as it is not likely that Ford's *History of Illinois* will ever be published again, and inasmuch also as his treatise upon Mormon affairs is the most important part of the book, we shall do a service both to the History of the Church and to the History of Illinois by publishing further excerpts. These quotations will make up chapters iv and v.

CHAPTER IV.

GOVERNOR FORD'S COMMENTS ON THE CHARACTER OF JOSEPH SMITH AND HIS FOLLOWERS—HIS CONJECTURES ON THE FUTURE OF MORMONISM

IT is necessary to repeat the part of the sentence with which the last chapter closed:

"Thus fell Joe Smith, the most successful impostor in modern times; a man who though ignorant and coarse, had some great natural parts, which fitted him for temporary success, but which were so obscured and counteracted by the inherent corruption and vices of his nature that he never could succeed in establishing a system of policy which looked to permanent success in the future.* His lusts, his love of money and power, always set him to studying present gratification and convenience, rather than the remote consequences of his plans. It seems that no power of intellect can save a corrupt man from this error. The strong cravings of the animal nature will never give fair play to a fine understanding, the judgment is never allowed

Governor Ford's Estimate of the Prophet's Character.

---

*In the light of the signal success which has attended upon the church which Joseph Smith under God founded, after one hundred years of existence, his followers may smile now at this pronouncement of his enemy, Governor Thomas Ford; as also they may quote without fear of creating disparagement for the Prophet the unfavorable estimate of his character. Joseph Smith belongs now to the ages; and nothing that Governor Ford said, or that any of his enemies have said could stay his triumphant march to an honorable place in the world's history, or prevent the church he founded from winning a permanent place in the world that is the astonishment of the thoughtful. "Traitors and tyrants now fight him in vain."

"The man who established a religion in this age of free debate, who was and is today accepted by hundreds of thousands [three quarters of a million now living, to say nothing of the hundreds of thousands of faithful disciples who have died in the faith within the first century of the existence of the church founded by him] as a direct emissary of the Most High—such a rare human being is not to be disposed of by pelting his memory with unsavory epithets" (*Figures of the Past*, "Joseph Smith at Nauvoo", Josiah Quincy, p. 376, Ed. 1901). B. H. R.

to choose that good which is far away, in preference
to enticing evil near at hand.   And this may be considered a wise ordinance of Providence, by which the
counsels of talented but corrupt men, are defeated in
the very act which promised success.

It must not be supposed that the pretended Prophet
practiced the tricks of a common impostor; that he was
Characteriza-
tion of Joseph
Smith. a dark and gloomy person, with a long
beard, a grave and severe aspect, and a re-
served and saintly carriage of his person; on
the contrary, he was full of levity, even to boyism
romping; dressed like a dandy, and at times drank like
a sailor and swore like a pirate.   He could, as occasion
required, be exceedingly meek in his deportment; and
then again rough and boisterous as a highway robber;
being always able to satisfy his followers of the propriety of his conduct. He always quailed before power,
and was arrogant to weakness.   At times he could put
on the air of a penitent, as if feeling the deepest humiliation for his sins, and suffering unutterable anguish, and indulging in the most gloomy forebodings
of eternal woe.   At such times he would call for the
prayers of the brethren in his behalf, with a wild and
fearful energy and earnestness.   He was full six feet
high, strongly built, and uncommonly well muscled.
No doubt he was as much indebted for his influence
over an ignorant people, to the superiority of his phys-
ical vigor, as to his greater cunning and intellect.

His followers were divided into the leaders and the
led; the first division embraced a numerous class of
broken-down, unprincipled men of talents, to be found
in every country, who, bankrupt in character and for-
tune, had nothing to lose by deserting the known
Character of
the Followers
of Joseph
Smith. religions, and carving out a new one of
their own.   They were mostly infidels, who
holding all religions in derision, believed
that they had as good a right as Christ or Mahomet,
or any of the founders of former systems, to create
one for themselves; and if they could impose it upon

mankind, to live upon the labor of their dupes. Those of the second division, were the credulous wondering part of men, whose easy belief and admiring natures, are always the victims of novelty, in whatever shape it may come, who have a capacity to believe any strange and wonderful matter, if it only be new, whilst the wonders of former ages command neither faith nor reverence; they were men of feeble purposes, readily subjected to the will of the strong, giving themselves up entirely to the direction of their leaders; and this accounts for the very great influence of those leaders in controlling them. In other respects some of the Mormons were abandoned rogues, who had taken shelter in Nauvoo, as a convenient place for the headquarters of their villainy; and others were good, honest, industrious people, who were the sincere victims of an artful delusion. Such as these were more the proper objects of pity than persecution. With them, their religious belief was a kind of insanity; and certainly no greater calamity can befall a human being, than to have a mind so constituted as to be made the sincere dupe of a religious impostor. * * *

* * * The world now indulged in various conjectures as to the further progress of the Mormon religion. By some persons it was believed that it would perish and die away with its founder. But upon the principle that 'the blood of the martyrs is the seed of the church', there was now really more cause than ever to predict its success. The murder of the Smiths, instead of putting an end to the delusion of the Mormons and dispersing them, as many believed it would, only bound them together closer than ever, gave them new confidence in their faith and an increased fanaticism.

World's Conjecture of the Mormon Religion.

The Mormon Church had been organized with a First Presidency, composed of Joe and Hyrum Smith and Sidney Rigdon, and Twelve Apostles of Jesus

Christ.   The Twelve Apostles were now absent, and until they could be called together the minds of the Settlement of the Question of Church Leadership. 'saints' were unsettled, as to the future government of the church.   Revelations were published that the Prophet, in imitation of the Savior, was to rise again from the dead.   Many were looking in gaping wonderment for the fulfilment of this revelation, and some reported that they had already seen him, attended by a celestial army coursing the air on a great white horse.*   Rigdon, as the only remaining member of the First Presidency, claimed the government of the church, as being successor to the Prophet.   When the Twelve Apostles returned from foreign parts, a fierce struggle for power ensued between them and Rigdon.   Rigdon fortified his pretensions by alleging the will of the Prophet in his favor, and pretending to have several new revelations from heaven, amongst which was one of a very impolitic nature.   This was to the effect, that all the wealthy Mormons were to break up their residence at Nauvoo, and follow him to Pittsburg.   This revelation put both the rich and the poor against him. The rich, because they did not want to leave their property; and the poor, because they would not be deserted by the wealthy.   This was fatal to the ambition of Rigdon; and the Mormons, tired of the despotism of a one-man government, were now willing to decide in favor of the Apostles.   Rigdon was expelled from the church as being a false prophet, and left the field with a few followers, to establish a little delusion of his own, near Pittsburg; leaving the government of the main church in the hands of the Apostles, with Brigham Young, a cunning but vulgar man, at their head, occupying the place of Peter in the Christian hierarchy.

Missionaries were dispatched to all parts to preach

---

*No such revelation is extant; and I know of no other writing where it is to be found.   B. H. R.

in the name of the 'martyred Joseph'; and the Mormon religion thrived more than ever.   For a while it was doubtful whether the reign of the military saints in Nauvoo would not in course of time supplant the meek and lowly system of Christ.   There were many things to favor their success. The different Christian sects had lost much of the fiery energy by which at first they were animated.   They had attained to a more subdued, sober, learned, and intellectual religion.   But there is at all times a large class of mankind who will never be satisfied with anything in devotion, short of a heated and wild fanaticism.   The Mormons were the greatest zealots, the most confident in their faith, and filled with a wilder, fiercer, and more enterprising enthusiasm, than any sect on the continent of America; their religion gave promise of more temporal and spiritual advantages for less labor, and with less personal sacrifice of passion, lust, prejudice, malice, hatred, and ill will, than any other perhaps in the whole world.   Their missionaries abroad, to the number of two or three thousand,* were most earnest and indefatigable in their efforts to make converts; compassing sea and land to make one proselyte.   When abroad, they first preached doctrines somewhat like those of the Campbellites; Sidney Rigdon, the inventor of the system, having once been a Campbellite preacher; and when they had made a favorable impression, they began in far-off allusions to open up their mysteries, and to reveal to their disciples that a perfect 'fulness of the gospel' must be expected. This 'fulness of the gospel' was looked for by the dreamy and wondering disciple, as an indefinite something not yet to be comprehended, but which was essential to complete happiness and salvation.   He was then told that God required him to remove to the place of gathering, where alone this sublime 'fulness of the gospel' could be fully revealed, and completely enjoyed.   When he arrived at the place of gathering.

*If this means at one time, it is a gross exaggeration.   B. H. R.

he was fortified in the new faith by being withdrawn from all other influences; and by seeing and hearing nothing but Mormons and Mormonism; and by association with those only who never doubted any of the Mormon dogmas. Now the 'fulness of the gospel' could be safely made known. If it required him to submit to the most intolerable despotism; if it tolerated and encouraged the lusts of the flesh and a plurality of wives; if it claimed all the world for the saints; universal dominion for the Mormon leaders; if it sanctioned murder, robbery, perjury, and larceny, at the command of their priests, no one could now doubt but that this was the 'fulness of the gospel', the liberty of the saints, with which Christ had made them free.

The Christian world, which has hitherto regarded Mormonism with silent contempt, unhappily may yet have cause to fear its rapid increase. Modern society is full of material for such a religion. At the death of the Prophet, fourteen years after the first Mormon Church was organized, the Mormons in all the world numbered about two hundred thousand souls (one-half million according to their statistics); *Possible Future of Mormonism.* a number equal, perhaps, to the number of Christians, when the Christian Church was of the same age.* It is to be feared that in course of a century, some gifted man like Paul, some splendid orator, who will be able by his eloquence to attract crowds of the thousands who are ever ready to hear, and be carried away by, the sounding brass and tinkling cymbal of sparkling oratory, may command a hearing, may succeed in breathing a new life into this modern Mahometanism, and make the name of the martyred Joseph ring as loud, and stir the souls of men as much, as the mighty name of Christ itself. Sharon, Palmyra, Manchester, Kirtland, Far West, Adamon Diahmon [Adam-ondi-Ahman], Ramus. Nauvoo, and the Carthage Jail, may become holy and

*Needless to say, these numbers are great exaggerations. B. H. R.

venerable names, places of classic interest, in another age; like Jerusalem, the Garden of Gethsemane, the Mount of Olives, and Mount Calvary to the Christian, and Mecca and Medina to the Turk. And in that event, the author of this *History* feels degraded by the reflection, that the humble governor of an obscure state, who would otherwise be forgotten in a few years, stands a fair chance, like Pilate and Herod, by their official connection with the true religion, of being dragged down to posterity with an immortal name, hitched on to the memory of a miserable impostor. There may be those whose ambition would lead them to desire an immortal name in history, even in those humbling terms. I am not one of that number.

About one year after the Apostles were installed into power, they abandoned for the present the project of converting the world to the new religion. All the missionaries and members abroad were ordered home; it was announced that the world had rejected the gospel by the murder of the Prophet and Patriarch, and was to be left to perish in its sins. In the meantime, both before and after this, the elders at Nauvoo quit preaching about religion. The Mormons came from every part, pouring into the city; the congregations were regularly called together for worship, but instead of expounding the new gospel, the zealous and infuriated preachers now indulged only in curses and strains of abuse of the Gentiles, and it seemed to be their design to fill their followers with the greatest amount of hatred to all mankind excepting the 'saints'. A sermon was no more than an inflammatory stump speech, relating to their quarrels with their enemies, and ornamented with an abundance of profanity. From my own personal knowledge of this people, I can say with truth, that I have never known much of any of their leaders who was not addicted to profane swearing. No other kind of discourses than these were heard in the city. Curses upon their enemies, upon the country, upon government, upon all public officers, were now the lessons taught by the elders, to inflame their people with the highest degree of spite and malice against all who were not of the Mormon Church, or its obsequious tools.   The reader can readily imagine how a city of fifteen thousand inhabitants could be wrought up and kept in a continual rage by the inflammatory harangues of its leaders.*

In the meantime, the anti-Mormons were not idle; they were more than ever determined to expel the Mormons; and being passionately inflamed against them, they made many applications for executive assistance.   On the other hand, the Mormons invoked the assistance of government to take vengeance upon the murderers of the Smiths. The anti-Mormons asked the governor to violate the Constitution, which he was sworn to support, by erecting himself into a military despot and exiling the Mormons.   The Mormons, on their part, in their newspapers, invited the governor to assume absolute power, by taking a summary vengeance upon their enemies, by shooting fifty or a hundred of them, without judge or jury.   Both parties were thoroughly disgusted with constitutional provisions restraining them from the summary attainment of their wishes for vengeance; each was ready to submit to arbitrary power, to the fiat of a dictator, to make me a king for the time being, or at least that I might exercise the power of a king, to abolish both the forms and spirit of free government, if the despotism to be erected upon its ruins could only be wielded for its benefit, and to take vengeance on its enemies.   It seems that, notwithstanding all our strong professions of attachment to liberty, there is all the time an unconquerable leaning to the principles of monarchy and despotism, whenever the forms, the delays, and the restraints of republican government fail to correct

Demand and Counter-Demand.

Reflections of Governor Ford.

---

*Reference to Part V of this volume where much of the preaching of the Apostles is given both in synopses of discourses and verbatim reports will prove how utterly untrue the above statements of Governor Ford are.   B. H. R.

great evils. When the forms of government in the United States were first invented, the public liberty was thought to be the great object of governmental protection. Our ancestors studied to prevent government from doing harm, by depriving it of power. They would not trust the power of exiling a citizen upon any terms; or of taking his life, without a fair and impartial trial in the courts, even to the people themselves, much less to their government. But so infatuated were these parties, so deep did they feel their grievances, that both of them were enraged in their turn, because the governor firmly adhered to his oath of office; refusing to be a party to their revolutionary proceedings; to set aside the government of the country, and execute summary vengeance upon one or the other of them."

CHAPTER V.

POLITICAL CONSIDERATIONS OF THE PERIOD FOLLOW-
ING THE DEATH OF THE PROPHET—"TRIAL" OF THE
MURDERERS — STATUS OF CIVIL GOVERNMENT IN
HANCOCK COUNTY

"ANOTHER election was to come off in August, 1844,
for members of congress, and for the legislature; and
an election was pending throughout the nation for a
president of the United States. The war of party
was never more fierce and terrible than during the
pendency of these elections. The parties in many
places met separately almost every night; not to argue
the questions in dispute, but to denounce, ridicule,
abuse, and belittle each other, with sarcasm, clamor,
noise, and songs, during which nothing could be heard
but hallooing, hurrahing, and yelling, and then to
disperse through town, with insulting taunts and yells
of defiance on either side.

In all this they were but little less fanatical and
frantic on the subject of politics, than were the Mormons about religion. Such a state of excitement could
not fail to operate unfavorably upon the
Mormon question, involved as it was in
the questions of party politics, by the former votes of the Mormons. As a means of allaying
excitement, and making the question more manageable,
I was most anxious that the Mormons should not
vote at this election, and strongly advised them against
doing so. But Colonel E. D. Taylor went to their city
a few days before the election, and the Mormons, being
ever disposed to follow the worst advice
they could get, were induced by him and
others to vote for all the democratic candidates. Colonel Taylor found them very hostile to the

*Political Fa-
naticism of the
anti-Mormon
Party.*

*Political
Course of Col.
E. D. Taylor—
Democrat.*

governor, and on that account much disposed not to vote at this election. The leading whig anti-Mormons, believing that I had an influence over the Mormons, for the purpose of destroying it had assured them that the governor had planned and been favorable to the murder of their Prophet and Patriarch. The Mormons pretended to suspect that the governor had given some countenance to the murder, or at least had neglected to take the proper precautions to prevent it. And yet it is strange that at this same election, they elected General Deming to be the sheriff of the county, when they knew that he had first called out the militia against them, had concurred with me in all the measures subsequently adopted, had been left in command at Carthage during my absence at Nauvoo, and had left his post when he saw that he had no power to prevent the murders. As to myself, I shared the fate of all men in high places, who favor moderation, who see that both parties in the frenzy of their excitement are wrong—espousing the cause of neither; which fate always is to be hated by both parties. But Colonel Taylor, like a skillful politician, denied nothing, but gave countenance to everything the Mormons said of the governor; and by admitting to them that the governor was a great rascal; by promising them the support of the democratic party, an assurance he was not authorized to make, but which they were foolish enough to believe, and by insisting that the governor was not the democratic party, he overcame their reluctance to vote. Nevertheless, for mere political effect, without a shadow of justice, the whig leaders and newspapers everywhere, and some enemies in the democratic ranks, immediately charged this vote of the Mormons to the governor's influence; and this charge being believed by many, made the anti-Mormon party more famous than ever in favor of the expulsion of the Mormons.

In the course of the fall of 1844, the anti-Mormon leaders sent printed invitations to all the militia cap-

tains in Hancock, and to the captains of militia in all
the neighboring counties in Illinois, Iowa, and Missouri, to be present with their companies at a great
A Proposed   wolf hunt in Hancock; and it was privately
"Wolf Hunt".   announced that the wolves to be hunted
were the Mormons and Jack-Mormons. Preparations
were made for assembling several thousand men, with
provisions for six days; and the anti-Mormon newspapers, in aid of the movement, commenced anew
the most awful accounts of thefts and robberies, and
meditated outrages by the Mormons. The whig press
in every part of the United States, came to their assistance. The democratic newspapers and leading democrats, who had received the benefit of the Mormon
votes to their party, quailed under the tempest, leaving
no organ for the correction of public opinion, either
at home or abroad, except the discredited Mormon
newspaper at Nauvoo. But very few of my prominent
democratic friends would dare to come up to the assistance of their governor, and but few of them dared
openly to vindicate his motives in endeavoring to keep
the peace. They were willing and anxious for Mormon
votes at elections, but they were unwilling to risk their
popularity with the people, by taking a part in their
favor, even when law and justice, and the Constitution, were all on their side. Such being the odious
character of the Mormons, the hatred of the common
people against them, and such being the pusillanimity
of leading men, in fearing to encounter it.

In this state of the case I applied to Brigadier-General J. J. Hardin, of the state militia, and to Colonels
Baker and Merriman, all whigs, but all of them men
of military ambition, and they, together with Colonel
William Weatherford, a democrat* with my own exertions, succeeded in raising about five hundred volunteers; and thus did these whigs, that which my own

*Of the officers who were out with me in this expedition, General Hardin.
Colonels Baker and Weatherford, and Major Warren, afterwards greatly distinguished
themselves in the Mexican War.   Ford.

political friends, with two or three exceptions, were slow to do, from a sense of duty and gratitude.

With this little force under the command of General Hardin, I arrived in Hancock county on the 25th of September. The malcontents abandoned their design, and all the leaders of it fled to Missouri. The Carthage Greys fled almost in a body, carrying their arms along with them. During our stay in the county the anti-Mormons thronged into the camp, and conversed freely with the men, who were fast infected with their prejudices, and it was impossible to get any of the officers to aid in expelling them. Colonels Baker, Merriman and Weatherford, volunteered their services if I would go with them, to cross with a force into Missouri, to capture three of the anti-Mormon leaders, for whose arrest writs had been issued for the murder of the Smiths. To this I assented, and procured a boat, which was sent down in the night, and secretly landed a mile above Warsaw. Our little force arrived at that place about noon; that night we were to cross to Missouri at Churchville, and seize the accused there encamped with a number of their friends; but that afternoon Colonel Baker visited the hostile encampment, and on his return refused to participate in the expedition, and advised all his friends against joining it. There was no authority for compelling the men to invade a neighboring state, and for this cause, much to the vexation of myself and several others, the matter fell through.

It seems that Colonel Baker had already partly arranged the terms for the accused to surrender. They were to be taken to Quincy for examination under a military guard; the attorney for the people was to be advised to admit them to bail, and they were to be entitled to a continuance of their trial at the next court at Carthage; upon this, two of the accused came over and surrendered themselves prisoners.

But at that time I was held responsible for this

Wolf Hunt Dispersed.

The Accused Murderers of the Prophet Dictate their Own Terms of Surrender.

compromise with the murderers. The truth is, that I had but little of the moral power to command in this expedition. Officers, men, and all under me, were so infected with the anti-Mormon prejudices that I was made to feel severely the want of moral power to control them. It would be thought very strange in any other government that the administration should have the power to direct, but no power to control. By the Constitution the governor can neither appoint nor remove a militia officer. He may arrest and order a court martial. But a court martial composed of military officers, elected in times of peace, in many cases upon the same principles upon which Colonel Pluck was elected in New York City, is not likely to pay much attention to executive wishes in opposition to popular excitement. So, too, in Illinois, the governor has no power to appoint, remove, or in anywise control sheriffs, justices of the peace, nor even a constable; and yet the active cooperation of such officers with the executive, is indispensable to the success of any effort the governor may take to suppress civil war. If anyone supposes that the greatest amount of talents will enable anyone to govern under such circumstances, he is mistaken. It may be thought that the governor ought to create a public sentiment in favor of his measures, to sway the minds of those under him to his own course, but if anyone supposes that even the greatest abilities could succeed in such an effort against popular feeling, and against the inherent love of numerous demagogues for popularity, he is again mistaken.

GOVERNOR FORD'S PLEDGE OF SAFETY TO THE PROPHET ADMITTED

I had determined from the first that some of the ringleaders in the foul murder of the Smiths should be brought to trial. If these men had been the incarnation of satan himself, as was believed by many, their murder was a foul and treacherous action, alike disgraceful to those who perpetrated the crime, to the state, and to the governor, whose word had been pledged for the protection of the prisoners in jail, and which had been so shamefully violated; and required that the most vigorous means should be used to bring the assassins to punishment. As much as anything else the expedition under General Hardin had been ordered with a view to arrest the murderers.

Determination of the Governor to Have the Ringleaders of the Murderers of the Prophet and Patriarch Tried.

Accordingly, I employed able lawyers to hunt up the testimony, procure indictments, and prosecute the offenders. A trial was had before Judge Young in the summer of 1845. The sheriff and panel of jurors, selected by the Mormon court, were set aside for prejudice, and elisors were appointed to select a new jury. One friend of the Mormons and one anti-Mormon were appointed for this purpose; but as more than a thousand men had assembled under arms at the court, to keep away the Mormons and their friends, the jury was made up of these military followers of the court, who all swore that they had never formed or expressed any opinion as to the guilt or innocence of the accused. The Mormons had one principal witness, who was with the troops at Warsaw, had marched with them until they were disbanded, heard their consultations, went before them to Carthage, and saw them murder the Smiths. But before the trial came on, they had induced him to become a Mormon; and being much more anxious for the glorification of the Prophet than to avenge his death, the leading Mormons made him publish a pamphlet giving an account of the murder; in which he professed to have seen a bright and shining light descend upon the head of Joe Smith, to strike some of the conspirators with blindness, and that he heard supernatural voices in the air confirming his mission as a Prophet! Having published this in a book, he was compelled to swear to it in court, which of course destroyed the credit of his evidence. This witness was afterwards expelled from the Mormons, but no doubt they will cling to his evidence in favor of the divine mission of the Prophet.*

THE "TRIAL"! THE STATE OF THE COURT

Many other witnesses were examined, who knew the facts, but under the influence of the demoralization of faction, denied all knowledge of them. It has been said, that faction may find men honest, but it scarcely ever leaves them so. This was verified to the letter in the history of the Mormon quarrel. The accused were all acquitted.

During the progress of these trials, the judge was compelled to permit the courthouse to be filled and surrounded by armed bands, who attended court to browbeat and overawe the administration of justice. The judge himself was in a duress, and informed me that he did not consider his life secure any part of the time. The consequence was, that the crowd had everything their own way; the lawyers for the defense defended their clients by a long and elaborate attack on the governor; the armed mob stamped with their feet and yelled their approbation at every sarcastic and smart thing that was said; and the judge was not only forced to hear it, but to lend it a kind of approval. Josiah Lamborn was attorney for the prosecution; and O. H. Browning, O. C. Skinner, Calvin A. Warren, and William A. Richardson, were for the defense.

At the next term, the leading Mormons were tried and acquitted for the destruction of the heretical press. It appears that, not being interested in objecting to

*The witness here referred to was one Wm M. Daniels, and he is doubtless worthy of all the scorn that Governor Ford here heaps upon him. But the "Mormons" do not "cling to his evidence in favor of the divine mission of the Prophet" since they concede the unreasonableness of his testimony as also the testimony of one Benjamin Brackenbury, as will be seen by the treatment of the testimony of these witnesses in *The Comprehensive History of the Church*, Century I, vol. ii, ch. lx pp. 324-6, notes 14-15. B. H. R.

the sheriff or the jury selected by a court elected by themselves, they in their turn got a favorable jury determined upon acquittal, and yet the Mormon jurors all swore that they had formed no opinion as to the guilt or innocence of their accused friends.

It appeared that the laws furnished the means of suiting each party with a jury. The Mormons could have a Mormon jury to be tried by, selected by themselves; and the anti-Mormons, by objecting to the sheriff and regular panel, could have one from the anti-Mormons. From henceforth no leading man on either side could be arrested without the aid of an army, as the men of one party could not safely surrender to the other for fear of being murdered; when arrested by a military force the Constitution prohibited a trial in any other county without the consent of the accused. No one would be convicted of any crime in Hancock; and this put an end to the administration of the criminal law in that distracted county. Government was at an end there, and the whole community were delivered up to the dominion of a frightful anarchy. If the whole state had been in the same condition, then indeed would have been verified to the letter what was said by a wit, when he expressed an opinion that the people were neither capable of governing themselves nor of being governed by others. And truly there can be no government in a free country where the people do not voluntarily obey the laws."*

*Ford's *History of Illinois*, pp. 354-369.

III

MEMOIRS OF THE LATE PRESIDENT JOHN TAYLOR RESPECTING AFFAIRS AT NAU-VOO LEADING UP TO THE MARTYRDOM OF THE PROPHET AND PATRIARCH: GOVERNOR FORD'S RESPONSIBILITY THEREIN

Explanation

FOLLOWING the preceding excerpts from Ford's *History of Illinois,* setting forth his views of Latter-day Saint affairs in the state of Illinois during his incumbency of the office of governor of that state, and also what really amounts to a defense of himself in relation to those events, I deem it important that a Latter-day Saint statement covering the same period of time and events, with comments thereon, should be made. Such a statement and comments I find in an historical document written by John Taylor, late President [the third] of the Church of Jesus Christ of Latter-day Saints, a close participant in these events; and second only in nearness to the Prophet Joseph Smith and his brother Hyrum in them; and who also was nearly made a complete martyr to the cause in which they suffered, being savagely wounded in Carthage Prison, and only narrowly escaping the death visited upon them. This statement and the comments upon this eventful period were made at a time far enough removed from the excitement of those days to enable the writer to speak temperately upon the events of that period, and at the same time in a judicial and statesmanlike spirit, that greatly enhances the value of the document.

As seen by the introductory paragraph, the paper was prepared at the request of George A. Smith and Wilford Woodruff, Church Historians, under the title of "The Martyrdom of Joseph Smith"; and was filed in the Historian's Office, Salt Lake City.

This document will make up chapters vi to x inclusive.

CHAPTER VI.

THE MARTYRDOM OF JOSEPH SMITH: REVIEW OF CONDITIONS IN ILLINOIS PRECEDING THAT EVENT

"BEING requested by Elders George A. Smith and Wilford Woodruff, Church Historians, to write an account of events that transpired before, and took place at, the time of the martyrdom of Joseph Smith, in Carthage Jail, in Hancock county, state of Illinois, I write the following, principally from memory, not having access at this time to any public documents relative thereto farther than a few desultory items contained in Ford's *History of Illinois*.   I must also acknowledge myself considerably indebted to George A. Smith, who was with me when   Introduction. I wrote it, and who, although not there at the time of the bloody transaction, yet, from conversing with several persons who were in the capacity of Church Historians, and aided by an excellent memory, has rendered me considerable service.

These and the few items contained in the note at the end of this account are all the aid I have had.   I would farther add that the items contained in the letter, in relation to dates especially, may be considered strictly correct.

After having written the whole, I read it over to the Hon. J. M. Bernhisel, who with one or two slight alterations, pronounced it strictly correct.   Brother Bernhisel was present most of the time.   I am afraid that, from the length of time that has transpired since the occurrence, and having to rely almost exclusively upon my memory, there may be some slight inaccuracies, but I believe that in general it is strictly correct. As I figured in those transactions from the commencement to the end, they left no slight impression on my mind.

In the year 1844, a very great excitement prevailed in some parts of Hancock, Brown and other neighboring counties of Illinois, in relation to the 'Mormons', and a spirit of vindictive hatred and persecution was exhibited among the people, which was manifested in the most bitter and acrimonious language, as well as by acts of hostility and violence, frequently threatening the destruction of the citizens of Nauvoo and vicinity, and utter annihilation of the 'Mormons' and 'Mormonism', and in some instances breaking out in the most violent acts of ruffianly barbarity. Persons were kidnapped, whipped, persecuted, and falsely accused of various crimes; their cattle and houses injured, destroyed, or stolen; vexatious prosecutions were instituted to harass, and annoy. In some remote neighborhoods they were expelled from their homes without redress, and in others violence was threatened to their persons and property, while in others every kind of insult and indignity were heaped upon them, to induce them to abandon their homes, the county, or the state.

Threatening Portents in Illinois, 1844.

These annoyances, prosecutions, and persecutions were instigated through different agencies and by various classes of men, actuated by different motives, but all uniting in the one object—prosecution, persecution, and extermination of the saints.

There were a number of wicked and corrupt men living in Nauvoo and its vicinity, who had belonged to the church, but whose conduct was incompatible with the gospel; they were accordingly dealt with by the church and severed from its communion. Some of these had been prominent members, and held official stations either in the city or church. Among these were John C. Bennett, formerly mayor; William Law, counselor to Joseph Smith; Wilson

Apostates at Nauvoo.

Law, his natural brother, and general in the Nauvoo Legion; Dr. R. D. Foster, a man of some property, but with a very bad reputation; Francis and Chauncey Higbee, the latter a young lawyer, and both sons of a respectable and honored man in the church, known as Judge Elias Higbee, who died about twelve months before.

Besides these, there were a great many apostates, both in the city and county, of less notoriety, who for their delinquencies, had been expelled from the church. John C. Bennett and Francis and Chauncey Higbee were cut off from the church; the former was also cashiered from his generalship for the most flagrant acts of seduction and adultery; and the developments in their cases were so scandalous that the high council, before whom they were tried, had to sit with closed doors.

William Law, although counselor to Joseph, was found to be his most bitter foe and maligner, and to hold intercourse [it was alleged], contrary to all law, in his own house, with a young lady resident with him; and it was afterwards proven that he had conspired with some Missourians to take Joseph Smith's life, and (the Prophet) was only saved by Josiah Arnold and Daniel Garn, who, being on guard at his house, prevented the assassins from seeing him. Yet, although having murder in his heart, his manners were generally courteous and mild, and he was well calculated to deceive.

General Wilson Law was cut off from the church for seduction, falsehood, and defamation; both the above were also court-martialed by the Nauvoo Legion, and expelled. Foster was also cut off I believe, for dishonesty, fraud, and falsehood. I know he was eminently guilty of the whole, but whether these were the specific charges or not, I don't know, but I do know that he was a notoriously wicked and corrupt man.

Besides the above characters and 'Mormonic' apos-

tates, there were other three parties. The first of these
Other anti-
Mormon Part-
ies. may be called religionists, the second politicians, and the third counterfeiters, black-
legs, horse thieves, and cutthroats.

The religious party were chagrined and maddened
because 'Mormonism' came in contact with their religion, and they could not oppose it from the scriptures. Thus like the ancient Jews, when enraged at
the exhibition of their follies and hypocrisies by Jesus
and his Apostles, so these were infuriated against the
'Mormons' because of their discomfiture by them; and
instead of owning the truth and rejoicing in it, they
were ready to gnash upon them with their teeth, and
to persecute the believers in principles which they
could not disprove.

The political party were those who were of opposite
politics to us. There were always two parties, the
Whigs and
Democrats. whigs and democrats, and we could not
vote for one without offending the other,
and it not unfrequently happened that candidates for
office would place the issue of their election upon opposition to the 'Mormons', in order to gain political
influence from religious prejudice, in which case the
'Mormons' were compelled, in self-defense, to vote
against them, which resulted almost invariably against
our opponents. This made them angry; and although
it was of their own making, and the 'Mormons' could
not be expected to do otherwise, yet they raged on
account of their discomfiture, and sought to wreak
their fury on the 'Mormons'. As an instance of the
above, when Joseph Duncan was candidate for the
office of governor of Illinois, he pledged himself to
his party that, if he could be elected, he would exterminate or drive the 'Mormons' from the state.* The
consequence was that Governor Ford was elected. The
whigs, seeing that they had been out-generaled by the
democrats in securing the 'Mormon' vote, became seri-

---

*See his remarks as contained in Ford's *History of Illinois*, p. 269.

ously alarmed, and sought to repair their disaster by raising a crusade against the people. The whig newspapers teemed with accounts of the wonders and enormities of Nauvoo, and of the awful wickedness of a party which could consent to receive the support of such miscreants. Governor Duncan, who was really a brave, honest man, and who had nothing to do with getting the 'Mormon' charters passed through the legislature, took the stump on this subject in good earnest, and expected to be elected governor almost on this question alone.

The third party, composed of counterfeiters, blacklegs, horse thieves, and cutthroats, were a pack of scoundrels that infested the whole of the western country at that time. In some districts their influence was so great as to control important state and county offices. On this subject Governor Ford has the following:

'Then, again, the northern part of the state was not destitute of its organized bands of rogues, engaged in murders, robberies, horse-stealing, and in making and passing counterfeit money. These rogues were scattered all over the north, but the most of them were located in the counties of Ogle, Winnebago, Lee and De Kalb.

Lawlessness in Northern Illinois.

'In the county of Ogle they were so numerous, strong, and well organized that they could not be convicted for their crimes. By getting some of their numbers on the juries, by producing a host of witnesses to sustain their defense, by perjured evidence, and by changing the venue of one county to another, by continuances from term to term, and by the inability of witnesses to attend from time to time at distant and foreign counties, they most generally managed to be acquitted.'*

There was a combination of horse thieves extending from Galena to Alton. There were counterfeiters engaged in merchandizing, trading, and storekeeping in most of the cities and villages, and in some districts, I have been credibly informed by men to whom they have disclosed their secrets; the judges, sheriffs, con-

*Ford's *History of Illinois*, p. 246.

stables, and jailors, as well as professional men, were
more or less associated with them. These had in their
employ the most reckless, abandoned wretches, who
stood ready to carry into effect the most desperate
enterprises, and were careless alike of human life and
property. Their object in persecuting the 'Mormons'
was in part to cover their own rascality, and in part
to prevent them from exposing and prosecuting them;
but the principal reason was plunder, believing that
if they [the 'Mormons'] could be removed or driven,
they would be made fat on 'Mormon' spoils, besides
having in the deserted city a good asylum for the
prosecution of their diabolical pursuits.

This conglomeration of apostate 'Mormons', religious bigots, political fanatics and blacklegs, all
united their forces against the 'Mormons', and organized themselves into a party, denominated 'anti-
Mormons'. Some of them, we have reason to believe,
joined the church in order to cover their nefarious
practices, and when they were expelled for their unrighteousness only raged with greater violence. They
circulated every kind of falsehood that they could collect or manufacture against the 'Mormons'. They
also had a paper to assist them in their infamous designs, called the *Warsaw Signal*, edited by a Mr.
Thomas Sharp, a violent and unprincipled man, who
shrunk not from any enormity. The anti-'Mormons'
had public meetings, which were very numerously attended, where they passed resolutions of the most
violent and inflammatory kind, threatening to drive,
expel and exterminate the 'Mormons' from the state,
at the same time accusing them of every evil in the
vocabulary of crime.

They appointed their meetings in various parts of
Hancock, McDonough, and other counties, which soon
resulted in the organization of armed mobs, under
the direction of officers who reported to their headquarters, and the reports of which were published in
the anti-'Mormon' paper, and circulated through the

adjoining counties. We also published in the *Times and Seasons* and the *Nauvoo Neighbor* (two papers published and edited by me at that time) an account, not only of their proceedings, but our own. But such was the hostile feeling, so well arranged their plans, and so desperate and lawless their measures, that it was with the greatest difficulty that we could get our papers circulated; they were destroyed by postmasters and others, and scarcely ever arrived at the place of their destination, so that a great many of the people, who would have been otherwise peaceable, were excited by their misrepresentations, and instigated to join their hostile or predatory bands.

Emboldened by the acts of those outside, the apostate 'Mormons', associated with others, commenced the publication of a libelous paper in Nauvoo, called the *Nauvoo Expositor*.

This paper not only reprinted from the others, but put in circulation the most libelous, false, and infamous reports concerning the citizens of Nauvoo, and especially the ladies. It was, however, no sooner put in circulation than the indignation of the whole community was aroused; so much so, that they threatened its annihilation; and I do not believe that in any other city in the United States, if the same charges had been made against the citizens, it would have been permitted to remain one day. As it was among us, under these circumstances, it was thought best to convene the city council to take into consideration the adoption of some measures for its removal, as it was deemed better that this should be done legally than illegally. Joseph Smith, therefore, who was mayor, convened the city council for that purpose; the paper was introduced and read, and the subject examined. All, or nearly all present, expressed their indignation at the course taken by the *Expositor*, which was owned by some of the aforesaid apostates, associated with one or two others. Wilson Law, Dr. Foster, Charles Ivins and the Higbees before referred to, some lawyers, storekeepers, and others in Nauvoo who were not 'Mormons', together with the anti-'Mormons' outside of the city, sustained it. The calculation was, by false statements, to unsettle the minds of many in the city, and to form combinations there similar to the anti-'Mormon' associations outside of the city. Various attempts had heretofore been made by the party to annoy and irritate the citizens of Nauvoo; false accusations had been made, vexatious lawsuits instituted, threats made, and various devices resorted to, to influence the public mind, and, if possible, to provoke us to the commission of some overt act that might make us amenable to the law. With a perfect knowledge therefore, of the designs of these infernal scoundrels who were in our midst, as well as those who surrounded us, the city council entered upon an investigation of the matter. They felt that they were in a critical position, and that any move made for the abating of that press would be looked upon, or at least represented, as a direct attack upon the liberty of speech, and that, so far from displeasing our enemies, it would be looked upon by them as one of the best circumstances that could transpire to assist them in their nefarious and bloody designs. Being a member of the city council, I well remember the feeling of responsibility that seemed to rest upon all present; nor shall I soon forget the bold, manly, independent expressions of Joseph Smith on that occasion in relation to this matter. He exhibited in glowing colors the meanness, corruption and ultimate designs of the anti-'Mormons'; their despicable characters and ungodly influences, especially of those who were in our midst. He told of the responsibility that rested upon us, as guardians of the public interest, to stand up in the defense of the injured and oppressed, to stem the current of corruption, and as men and saints, to put a stop to this flagrant outrage upon this people's rights.

He stated that no man was a stronger advocate for

the liberty of speech and of the press than himself; yet, when this noble gift is utterly pros- tituted and abused, as in the present in- stance, it loses all claim to our respect, and becomes as great an agent for evil as it can possibly be for good; and notwithstanding the apparent advantage we should give our enemies by this act, yet it behooved us, as men, to act independent of all secondary influ- ences, to perform the part of men of enlarged minds, and boldly and fearlessly to discharge the duties de- volving upon us by declaring as a nuisance, and re- moving this filthy, libelous, and seditious sheet from our midst.

Mental Atti-
tude of the
Prophet.

The subject was discussed in various forms, and after the remarks made by the mayor, every one seemed to be waiting for some one else to speak.

After a considerable pause, I arose and expressed my feelings frankly, as Joseph had done, and numbers of others followed in the same strain; and I think, but am not certain, that I made a motion for the re- moval of that press as a nuisance. This motion was finally put, and carried by all but one; and he conceded that the measure was just, but abstained through fear.

Several members of the city council were not in the church. The following is the bill referred to:

BILL FOR REMOVING OF THE PRESS OF THE NAUVOO EXPOSITOR*

'Resolved by the city council of the city of Nauvoo, that the printing office from whence issues the *Nauvoo Expositor* is a public nuisance; and also of said *Nauvoo Expositors* which may be or exist in said establishment; and the mayor is instructed to cause said estab- lishment and papers to be removed without delay, in such manner as he shall direct.

'Passed June 10th, 1844.   GEO. W. HARRIS, President *pro tem.*
'W. RICHARDS, Recorder.'

After the passage of the bill, the marshal, John P. Greene was ordered to abate or remove, which he forth- with proceeded to do by summoning a *posse* of men for

Deseret News, No. 29, September 23, 1857, p. 226.

that purpose. The press was removed or broken, I don't remember which, by the marshal, and the types scattered in the street.

This seemed to be one of those extreme cases that require extreme measures, as the press was still proceeding in its inflammatory course. It was feared that, as it was almost universally execrated, should it continue longer, an indignant people might commit some overt act which might lead to serious consequences, and that it was better to use legal than illegal means.

This, as was foreseen, was the very course our enemies wished us to pursue, as it afforded them an opportunity of circulating a very plausible story about the 'Mormons' being opposed to the liberty of the press and of free speech, which they were not slow to avail themselves of. Stories were fabricated, and facts perverted; false statements were made, and this act brought in as an example to sustain the whole of their fabrications; and, as if inspired by satan, they labored with an energy and zeal worthy of a better cause. They had runners to circulate their reports, not only through Hancock county, but in all the surrounding counties. These reports were communicated to their anti-'Mormon' societies, and these societies circulated them in their several districts. The anti-'Mormon' paper, the *Warsaw Signal,* was filled with inflammatory articles and misrepresentations in relation to us, and especially to this act of destroying the press. We were represented as a horde of lawless ruffians and brigands, anti-American and anti-republican, steeped in crime and iniquity, opposed to freedom of speech and of the press, and all the rights and immunities of a free and enlightened people; that neither person nor property was secure, that we had designs upon the citizens of Illinois and of the United States, and the people were called upon to rise *en masse,* and put us down, drive us away, or exterminate us as a pest to society, and alike dangerous to our neighbors, the state, and the commonwealth.

These statements were extensively copied and circulated throughout the United States. A true statement of the facts in question was published by us both in the *Times and Seasons* and the *Nauvoo Neighbor;* but it was found impossible to circulate them in the immediate counties, as they were destroyed at the post offices or otherwise by the agents of the anti-'Mormons', and, in order to get the mail to go abroad, I had to send the papers a distance of thirty or forty miles from Nauvoo, and sometimes to St. Louis (upward of two hundred miles), to insure their proceeding on their route, and then one-half or two-thirds of the papers never reached the place of destination, being intercepted or destroyed by our enemies.

Uncertainty of U. S. Mail.

These false reports stirred up the community around, of whom many, on account of religious prejudice, were easily instigated to join the anti-'Mormons' and embark in any crusade that might be undertaken against us; hence their ranks swelled in numbers, and new organizations were formed, meetings were held, resolutions passed, and men and means volunteered for the extirpation of the 'Mormons'.

On these points Governor Ford writes:

'These also were the active men in blowing up the fury of the people, in hopes that a popular movement might be set on foot, which would result in the expulsion or extermination of the 'Mormon voters. For this purpose public meetings had been called, inflammatory speeches had been made, exaggerated reports had been extensively circulated, committees had been appointed, who rode night and day to spread the reports and solicit the aid of neighboring counties, and at a public meeting at Warsaw resolutions were passed to expel or exterminate the 'Mormon' population. This was not, however, a movement which was unanimously concurred in. The county contained a goodly number of inhabitants in favor of peace, or who at least desired to be neutral in such a contest. These were stigmatized by the name of 'Jack-Mormons', and there were not a few of the more furious exciters of the people who openly expressed their intention to involve them in the common expulsion or extermination.

'A system of excitement and agitation was artfully planned and executed with tact. It consisted in spreading reports and rumors of the most fearful character. As examples: On the morning before my arrival at Carthage, I was awakened at an early hour by the frightful report, which was asserted with confidence and apparent consternation that the 'Mormons' had already commenced the work of burning, destruction, and murder, and that every man capable of bearing arms was instantly wanted at Carthage for the protection of the county.

Systematic anti-Mormon Agitation.

'We lost no time in starting; but when we arrived at Carthage we could hear no more concerning this story. Again, during the few days that the militia were encamped at Carthage, frequent applications were made to me to send a force here, and a force there, and a force all about the country, to prevent murders, robberies, and larcenies which, it was said, were threatened by the 'Mormons'. No such forces were sent, nor were any such offenses committed at that time, except the stealing of some provisions, and there was never the least proof that this was done by a 'Mormon'. Again, on my late visit to Hancock county, I was informed by some of their violent enemies that the larcenies of the 'Mormons' had become unusually numerous and insufferable.

'They admitted that but little had been done in this way in their immediate vicinity, but they insisted that sixteen horses had been stolen by the 'Mormons' in one night near Lima, and, upon inquiry, was told that no horses had been stolen in that neighborhood, but that sixteen horses had been stolen in one night in Hancock county. This last informant being told of the Hancock story, again changed the venue to another distant settlement in the northern edge of Adams.'*

In the meantime legal proceedings were instituted against the members of the city council of Nauvoo. A writ, here subjoined, was issued upon the affidavit of the Laws, Fosters, Higbees, and Ivins, by Mr. Morrison, a justice of the peace in Carthage, and the county seat of Hancock, and put into the hands of one David Bettisworth, a constable of the same place.

WRIT ISSUED UPON AFFIDAVIT BY THOMAS MORRISON, J. P., STATE OF ILLINOIS, HANCOCK COUNTY, ss

'The people of the state of Illinois, to all constables, sheriffs, and coroners of the said state, greeting:

'Whereas complaint hath been made before me, one of the justices of the peace in and for the county of Hancock aforesaid, upon the oath

*Ford's *History of Illinois*, pp. 330, 331.

of Francis M. Higbee, of the said county, that Joseph Smith, Samuel Bennett, John Taylor, William W. Phelps, Hyrum Smith, John P. Greene, Stephen Perry, Dimick B. Huntington, Jonathan Dunham, Stephen Markham, William Edwards, Jonathan Holmes, Jesse P. Harmon, John Lytle, Joseph W. Coolidge, Harvey D. Redfield, Porter Rockwell, and Levi Richards of said county, did on the 10th day of June instant, commit a riot at and within the county aforesaid, wherein they with force and violence broke into the printing office of the *Nauvoo Expositor*, and unlawfully and with force burned and destroyed the printing press, type and fixtures of the same, being the property of William Law, Wilson Law, Charles Ivins, Francis M. Higbee, Chauncey L. Higbee, Robert D. Foster, and Charles A. Foster.

'These are therefore to command you forthwith to apprehend the said Joseph Smith, Samuel Bennett, John Taylor, William W. Phelps, Hyrum Smith, John P. Greene, Stephen Perry, Dimick B. Huntington, Jonathan Dunham, Stephen Markham, William Edwards, Jonathan Holmes, Jesse P. Harmon, John Lytle, Joseph W. Coolidge, Harvey D. Redfield, Porter Rockwell, and Levi Richards, and bring them before me, or some other justice of the peace, to answer the premises, and farther to be dealt with according to law.

'Given under my hand and seal at Carthage, in the county aforesaid, this 11th day of June, A. D., 1844.

[Signed] THOMAS MORRISON, J. P.' (Seal)*

The council did not refuse to attend to the legal proceedings in the case, but as the law of Illinois made it the privilege of the persons accused to go 'or appear before the issuer of the writ, *or any other* justice *of peace'*, they requested to be taken before another magistrate, either in the city of Nauvoo or at any reasonable distance out of it.

Action of the City Council.

This the constable, who was a mobocrat, refused to do, and as this was our legal privilege, we refused to be dragged, contrary to law, a distance of eighteen miles, when at the same time we had reason to believe that an organized band of mobocrats were assembled for the purpose of extermination or murder, and among whom it would not be safe to go without a superior force of armed men. A writ of *habeas corpus* was called for, issued by the municipal court of Nauvoo, taking us out of the hands of Bettisworth, and placing us in the charge of the city marshal. We went

Deseret News, No. 30, Sept. 30, 1857, p. 233.

before the municipal court and were dismissed. Our refusal to obey this illegal proceeding was by them construed into a refusal to submit to law, and circulated as such, and the people either did believe, or professed to believe, that we were in open rebellion against the laws and the authorities of the state. Hence mobs began to assemble, among which all through the country inflammatory speeches were made, exciting them to mobocracy and violence. Soon they commenced their depredations in our outside settlements, kidnaping some, and whipping and otherwise abusing others.

The persons thus abused fled to Nauvoo as soon as practicable, and related their injuries to Joseph Smith, then mayor of the city, and lieutenant-general of the Nauvoo Legion. They also went before magistrates, and made affidavits of what they had suffered, seen, and heard. These affidavits, in connection with a copy of all our proceedings were forwarded by Joseph Smith to Mr. Ford, then governor of Illinois, with an expression of our desire to abide law, and a request that the governor would instruct him how to proceed in the case of arrival of an armed mob against the city. The governor sent back instructions to Joseph Smith that, as he was lieutenant-general of the Nauvoo Legion, it was his duty to protect the city and surrounding country, and issued orders to that effect. Upon the reception of these orders Joseph Smith assembled the people of the city, and laid before them the governor's instructions; he also convened the officers of the Nauvoo Legion for the purpose of conferring in relation to the best mode of defense. He also issued orders to the men to hold themselves in readiness in case of being called upon. On the following day General Joseph Smith, with his staff, the leading officers of the Legion, and some prominent strangers who were in our midst, made a survey of the outside boundaries of the city, which was very extensive, being about five miles up and down the river, and about two and a half back in the center, for the purpose of ascertaining the position of the ground, and the feasibility of defense, and to make all necessary arrangements in case of an attack.

It may be well here to remark that numbers of gentlemen, strangers to us, either came on purpose or were passing through Nauvoo, and upon learning the position of things, expressed their indignation against our enemies, and avowed their readiness to assist us by their counsel or otherwise. It was some of these who assisted us in reconnoitering the city, and finding out its adaptability for defense, and how to protect it best against an armed force. The Legion was called together and drilled, *Military Defensive Measures.* and every means made use for defense. At the call of the officers, old and young men came forward, both from the city and the country, and mustered to the number of about five thousand.

In the meantime our enemies were not idle in mustering their forces and committing depredations, nor had they been; it was, in fact, their gathering that called ours into existence; their forces continued to accumulate; they assumed a threatening attitude, and assembled in large bodies, armed and equipped for war, and threatened the destruction and extermination of the 'Mormons'.

An account of their outrages and assemblages was forwarded to Governor Ford almost daily; accompanied by affidavits furnished by eyewitnesses of their proceedings. Persons were also sent out to the counties around with pacific intentions, to give them an account of the true state of affairs, and to notify them of the feelings and dispositions of the people of Nauvoo, and thus, if possible, quell the excitement. In some of the more distant counties these men were very successful, and produced a salutary influence upon the minds of many intelligent and well-disposed men. In neighboring counties, however, where anti-'Mormon' influence prevailed, they produced little effect. At the same time guards were stationed around Nauvoo, and picket guards in the distance. At length opposing forces gathered so near that more active measures were taken; reconnoitering parties were sent out, and the city proclaimed under martial law. Things now assumed a belligerent attitude, and persons passing through the city were questioned as to what they knew of the enemy, while passes were in some instances given to avoid difficulty with the guards. Joseph Smith continued to send on messengers to the governor (Philip B. Lewis and other messengers were sent). Samuel James, then residing at La Harpe, carried a message and dispatches to him, and in a day or two after Bishop Edward Hunter and others went again with fresh dispatches, representations, affidavits, and instructions; but as the weather was excessively wet, the rivers swollen, and the bridges washed away in many places, it was with great difficulty that they proceeded on their journeys. As the mobocracy had at last attracted the governor's attention, he started in company with some others from Springfield to the scene of trouble, and missed, I believe, both Brothers James and Hunter on the road, and, of course, did not see their documents. He came to Carthage, and made that place, which was a regular mobocratic den, his headquarters; as it was the county seat, however, of Hancock county, that circumstance might, in a measure, justify his staying there.

To avoid the appearance of all hostility on our part, and to fulfill the law in every particular, at the suggestion of Judge Thomas, judge of that judicial district, who had come to Nauvoo at the time, and who stated that we had fulfilled the law, but, in order to satisfy all he would counsel us to go before Esquire Wells, who was not in our church, and have a hearing, we did so, and after a full hearing we were again dismissed.

The governor on the road collected forces, some

of whom were respectable, but on his arrival in the
neighborhood of the difficulties he received
as militia all the companies of the mob
forces who united with him.   After his
Governor
Ford's Arrival
at Carthage.
arrival at Carthage he sent two gentlemen from there
to Nauvoo as a committee to wait upon General Joseph
Smith, informing him of the arrival of his excellency,
with a request that General Smith would send out a
committee to wait upon the governor and represent to
him the state of affairs in relation to the difficulties
that then existed in the county. We met this committee while we were reconnoitering the city to find
out the best mode of defense as aforesaid. Dr. J. M.
Bernhisel and myself were appointed as a committee
by General Smith to wait upon the governor. Previous to going, however, we were furnished with affidavits and documents in relation both to our proceedings and those of the mob; in addition to the
general history of the transaction, we took with us a
duplicate of those documents which had been forwarded by Bishop Hunter, Brother James, and others.
We started from Nauvoo in company with the aforesaid gentlemen at about 7 o'clock on the evening of
the 21st of June, and arrived at Carthage about 11
p. m.

We put up at the same hotel with the governor,
kept by a Mr. Hamilton. On our arrival we found
the governor in bed, but not so with the other inhabitants. The town was filled with a perfect set of
rabble and rowdies, who, under the influence of
bacchus, seemed to be holding a grand saturnalia,
whooping, yelling and vociferating as if bedlam had
broken loose.

On our arrival at the hotel, and while supper was
preparing, a man came to me, dressed as a soldier, and
told me that a man named Daniel Garn had just been
taken prisoner, and was about to be committed to
jail, and wanted me to go bail for him. Believing
this to be a ruse to get me out alone, and that some

violence was intended, after consulting with Dr. Bernhisel, I told the man that I was well acquainted with
Mr. Garn, that I knew him to be a gentleman, and did
not believe that he had transgressed law, and, moreover, that I considered it a very singular time to be
holding courts and calling for security, particularly
as the town was full of rowdyism.

I informed him that Dr. Bernhisel and myself
would, if necessary, go bail for him in the morning,
but that we did not feel ourselves safe among such a
set at that late hour of the night.

After supper, on retiring to our room, we had to
pass through another, which was separated from ours
only by a board partition, the beds in each
room being placed side by side, with the
exception of this fragile partition. On the
bed that was in the room which we passed through I
discovered a man by the name of Jackson, a desperate
character, and a reputed, notorious cutthroat and
murderer. I hinted to the doctor that things looked
rather suspicious, and looked to see that my arms were
in order. The doctor and I occupied one bed. We
had scarcely laid down when a knock at the door,
accompanied by a voice announced the approach of
Chauncey Higbee, the young lawyer and apostate before referred to.

He addressed himself to the doctor, and stated that
the object of his visit was to obtain the release of
Daniel Garn; that Garn he believed to be an honest
man; that if he had done anything wrong, it was
through improper counsel, and that it was a pity that
he should be incarcerated, particularly when he could
be so easily released; he urged the doctor, as a friend,
not to leave so good a man in such an unpleasant situation; he finally prevailed upon the doctor to go and
give bail, assuring him that on his giving bail Garn
would be immediately dismissed.

During this conversation I did not say a word.

Higbee left the doctor to dress, with the intention of

John Taylor and Dr. Bernhisel at Carthage.

returning and taking him to the court. As soon as Higbee had left, I told the doctor that he had better not go; that I believed this affair was all a ruse to get us separated; that they knew we had documents with us from General Smith to show to the governor; that I believed their object was to get possession of those papers, and, perhaps, when they had separated us, to murder one or both. The doctor, who was actuated by the best of motives in yielding to the assumed solicitude of Higbee, coincided with my views; he then went to Higbee and told him that he had concluded not to go that night, but that he and I would both wait upon the justice and Mr. Garn in the morning.

That night I lay awake with my pistols under my pillow, waiting for any emergency. Nothing more occurred during the night. In the morning we arose early, and after breakfast sought an interview with the governor, and were told that we could have an audience, I think, at 10 o'clock. In the meantime we called upon Mr. Smith, a justice of the peace, who had Mr. Garn in charge. We represented that we had been called upon the night before by two different parties to go bail for a Mr. Daniel Garn, whom we were informed he had in custody, and that, believing Mr. Garn to be an honest man, we had now come for that purpose, and were prepared to enter into recognizance for his appearance, whereupon Mr. Smith, the magistrate, remarked that, under the present excited state of affairs, he did not think he would be justified in receiving bail from Nauvoo, as it was a matter of doubt whether property would not be rendered valueless there in a few days.

Knowing the party we had to deal with, we were not much surprised at this singular proceeding; we then remarked that both of us possessed property in farms out of Nauvoo in the country, and referred him to the county records. He then stated that such was the nature of the charge against Mr. Garn that he believed he would not be justified in receiving any bail. We were thus confirmed in our opinion that the night's proceedings before, in relation to their desire to have us give bail, was a mere ruse to separate us. We were not permitted to speak with Garn, the real charge against whom was that he was traveling in Carthage or its neighborhood; what the fictitious one was, if I knew, I have since forgotten, as things of this kind were of daily occurrence.''

CHAPTER VII.

JOHN TAYLOR AND DR. BERNHISEL'S INTERVIEW WITH
GOVERNOR FORD——PLEDGE OF GOVERNOR FORD FOR
THE SECURITY OF JOSEPH SMITH IF HE WOULD COME
TO CARTHAGE

"AFTER waiting the governor's pleasure for some time we had an audience; but such an audience!

He was surrounded by some of the vilest and most unprincipled men in creation; some of them had an appearance of respectability, and many of them lacked even that. Wilson, and, I believe, William Law, were there; Foster, Frank and Chauncey Higbee, Mr. Mar, a lawyer from Nauvoo, a mobocratic merchant from Warsaw, the aforesaid Jackson, a number of his associates, among whom was the governor's secretary; in all, some fifteen or twenty persons, most of whom were recreant to virtue, honor, integrity, and everything that is considered honorable among men.

I can well remember the feelings of disgust that I had in seeing the governor surrounded by such an infamous group, and on being introduced to men of so questionable a character; and had I been on private business, I should have turned to depart, and told the governor that if he thought proper to associate with such questionable characters, I should beg leave to be excused; but coming as we did on public business, we could not, of course, consult our private feelings.

The Character of Men Surrounding the Governor.

We then stated to the governor that, in accordance with his request, General Smith had, in response to his call, sent us to him as a committee of conference; that we were acquainted with most of the circumstances

that had transpired in and about Nauvoo lately, and
were prepared to give him all information; that, moreover, we had in our possession testimony and affidavits
confirmatory of what we should say, which had been
forwarded to him by General Joseph Smith; that communications had been forwarded to his excellency by
Messrs. Hunter, James, and others, some of which
had not reached their destination, but of which we
had duplicates with us. We then, in brief, related
an outline of the difficulties, and the course we had
pursued from the commencement of the troubles up
to the present, and handing him the documents, respectfully submitted the whole.

During our conversation and explanations with the
governor we were frequently rudely and impudently
contradicted by the fellows he had around him, and
of whom he seemed to take no notice.

He opened and read a number of the documents
himself, and as he proceeded he was frequently interrupted by 'That's a lie!' 'That's a G—— d——ned
lie!' 'That's an infernal falsehood!' 'That's a blasted
lie!' etc.

These men evidently winced at an exposure of their
acts, and thus vulgarly, impudently and falsely re-
pudiated them. One of their number, Mr. Mar, addressed himself several times to me while in conversation with the governor. I did not notice him until
after a frequent repetition of his insolence, when I
informed him that 'my business at that time was with
Governor Ford', whereupon I continued my conversation with his excellency. During the conversation,
the governor expressed a desire that Joseph Smith, and
all parties concerned in passing or executing the city
law in relation to the press, had better come to Carthage; that, however repugnant it might be to our
feelings, he thought it would have a tendency to allay
public excitement, and prove to the people what we
professed, that we wished to be governed by law. We
represented to him the course we had taken in relation
to this matter, and our willingness to go before another

magistrate other than the municipal court; the illegal refusal of our request by the constable; our dismissal by the municipal court, a legally constituted tribunal; our subsequent trial before Squire Wells at the instance of Judge Thomas, the circuit judge, and our dismissal by him; that we had fulfilled the law in every particular; that it was our enemies who were breaking the law, and, having murderous designs, were only making use of this as a pretext to get us into their power. The governor stated that the people viewed it differently, and that, notwithstanding our opinions, he would recommend that the people should be satisfied. We then remarked to him that, should Joseph Smith comply with his request, it would be extremely unsafe, in the present excited state of the country, to come without an armed force; that we had a sufficiency of men, and were competent to defend ourselves, but there might be danger of collision should our forces and those of our enemies be brought into such close proximity. He strenuously advised us not to bring our arms, and *pledged his faith as governor, and the faith of the state, that we should be protected, and that he would guarantee our perfect safety.*

Governor and State's Pledge of Security.

We had at that time about five thousand men under arms, one thousand of whom would have been amply sufficient for our protection.

At the termination of our interview, and previous to our withdrawal, after a long conversation and the perusal of the documents which we had brought, the governor informed us that he would prepare a written communication for General Joseph Smith, which he desired us to wait for. We were kept waiting for this instrument some five or six hours.

About five o'clock in the afternoon we took our departure with not the most pleasant feelings. The associations of the governor, the spirit he manifested to compromise with these scoundrels, the length of time that he had kept us waiting, and his general deportment, together with the infernal spirit that we saw exhibited by those whom he had admitted to his counsels, made the prospect anything but promising.

We returned on horseback, and arrived at Nauvoo, I think, at about eight or nine o'clock at night accompanied by Captain Yates in command of a company of mounted men, who came for the purpose of escorting Joseph Smith and the accused in case of their complying with the governor's request, and going to Carthage. We went directly to Brother Joseph's when Captain Yates delivered to him the governor's communication. A council was called, consisting of Joseph's brother, Hyrum, Dr. Richards, Dr. Bernhisel, myself, and one or two others.

We then gave a detail of our interview with the governor. Brother Joseph was very much dissatisfied with the governor's letter* and with his general deportment, and so were the council, and it became a serious question as to the course we should pursue. Various projects were discussed, but nothing definitely decided upon for some time.

In the interim two gentlemen arrived; one of them, if not both, sons of John C. Calhoun. They had come to Nauvoo, and were very anxious for an interview with Brother Joseph.

These gentlemen detained him for some time; and as our council was held in Dr. Bernhisel's room in the Mansion House, the doctor lay down; and as it was now between 2 and 3 o'clock in the morning, and I had had no rest on the previous night, I was fatigued, and thinking that Brother Joseph might not return, I left for home and rest.

Being very much fatigued, I slept soundly, and was somewhat surprised in the morning by Mrs.

The Prophet's Start for the West.

Thompson entering my room about 7 o'clock, and exclaiming in surprise, 'What, you here! the brethren have crossed the river some time since.'

*See Letter file in Church Historian's Office, "Ford", 1844. Contents of this letter sufficiently given in the conversation between Joseph Smith and Governor Ford in Carthage prison. (See chapter viii).

'What brethren?' I asked.

'Brother Joseph, and Hyrum, and Brother Richards', she answered.

I immediately arose upon learning that they had crossed the river, and did not intend to go to Carthage. I called together a number of persons in whom I had confidence, and had the type, stereotype plates, and most of the valuable things removed from the printing office, believing that should the governor and his force come to Nauvoo, the first thing they would do would be to burn the printing office, for I know that they would be exasperated if Brother Joseph went away. We had talked over these matters the night before, but nothing was decided upon. It was Brother Joseph's opinion that, should we leave for a time, public excitement, which was then so intense, would be allayed; that it would throw on the governor the responsibility of keeping the peace; that in the event of an outrage, the onus would rest upon the governor, who was amply prepared with troops, and could command all the forces of the state to preserve order; and that the act of his own men would be an overwhelming proof of their seditious designs, not only to the governor, but to the world. He moreover thought that, in the east, where he intended to go, public opinion would be set right in relation to these matters, and its expression would partially influence the west, and that, after the first ebullition, things would assume a shape that would justify his return.

I made arrangements for crossing the river, and Brother Elias Smith and Joseph Cain, who were both employed in the printing office with me, assisted all that lay in their power together with Brother Brower and several hands in the printing office. As we could not find out the exact whereabouts of Joseph and the brethren, I crossed the river in a boat furnished by Brother Cyrus H. Wheelock and Alfred Bell; and after the removal of the things out of the printing office, Joseph Cain brought the account books to me, that we might make arrangements for their adjust-

ment; and Brother Elias Smith, cousin to Brother
Joseph, went to obtain money for the journey, and
also to find out and report to me the location of the
brethren.

As Cyrus Wheelock was an active, enterprising man,
and in the event of not finding Brother Joseph I calculated to go to Upper Canada for the time being, and
should need a companion, I said to Brother Cyrus H.
Wheelock, 'Can you go with me ten or fifteen hundred miles?'

He answered, 'Yes'.

'Can you start in half an hour?'

'Yes.'

However, I told him that he had better see his family,
who lived over the river, and prepare a couple of horses
and the necessary equippage for the journey, and that,
if we did not find Brother Joseph before, we would
start at nightfall.

A laughable incident occurred on the eve of my
departure.   After making all the preparations I could,
previous to leaving Nauvoo, and having
bid adieu to my family, I went to a house
adjoining the river, owned by Brother Eddy.

Elder John
Taylor in Dis-
guise.

There I disguised myself so as not to be known, and
so effectually was the transformation that those who
had come after me with a boat did not know me.   I
went down to the boat and sat in it.   Brother Bell,
thinking it was a stranger, watched my moves for
some time very impatiently, and then said to Brother
Wheelock, 'I wish that old gentleman would go away;
he has been pottering around the boat for some time,
and I am afraid Elder Taylor will be coming.'   When
he discovered his mistake, he was not a little amused.

I was conducted by Brother Bell to a house that
was surrounded by timber on the opposite side of the
river.   There I spent several hours in a
chamber with Brother Joseph Cain, adjust-
ing my accounts; and I made arrangements
for the stereotype plates of the *Book of Mormon* and

The Prophet's
Return to Nau-
voo.

Doctrine and Covenants to be forwarded east, thinking to supply the company with subsistence money through the sale of these books in the east.

My horses were reported ready by Brother Wheelock, and funds on hand by Brother Elias Smith.   In about half an hour I should have started, when Brother Elias Smith came to me with word that he had found the brethren; that they had concluded to go to Carthage, and wished me to return to Nauvoo and accompany them.   I must confess that I felt a good deal disappointed at this news, but I immediately made preparations to go.   Escorted by Brother Elias Smith, I and my party went to the neighborhood of Montrose, where we met Brother Joseph, Hyrum, Brother Richards and others.   Dr. Bernhisel thinks that W. W. Phelps was not with Joseph and Hyrum in the morning, but that he met him, myself, Joseph and Hyrum, Willard Richards and Brother Cahoon, in the afternoon, near Montrose returning to Nauvoo.

On meeting the brethren I learned that it was not Brother Joseph's desire to return, but that he came back by request of some of the brethren, and that it coincided more with Brother Hyrum's feelings than those of Brother Joseph.   In fact, after his return, Brother Hyrum expressed himself as perfectly satisfied with the course taken, and said he felt much more at ease in his mind than he did before.   On our return the calculation was to throw ourselves under the immediate protection of the governor, and to trust to his word and faith for our preservation.

A message was, I believe, sent to the governor that night, stating that we should come to Carthage in the morning, the party that came along with us to escort us back, in case we returned to Carthage, having returned.

It would seem from the following remarks of Governor Ford, that there was a design on foot, which was, that if we refused to go to Carthage at the governor's request, there should be an increased force called for by the governor, and that we should be destroyed by them. In accordance with this project, Captain Yates returned with his *posse*, accompanied by the constable who held the writ.

The following is the governor's remark in relation to this affair:

'The constable and his escort returned. The constable made no effort to arrest any of them, nor would he or the guard delay their departure one minute beyond the time, to see whether an arrest could be made. Upon their return they reported that they had been informed that the accused had fled, and could not be found. I immediately proposed to a council of officers to march into Nauvoo with the small force then under my command, but the officers were of the opinion that it was too small, and many of them insisted upon a further call of the militia. Upon reflection I was of the opinion that the officers were right in the estimate of our force, and the project for immediate action was abandoned.

The Constable's Report to Governor Ford.

'I was soon informed, however, of the conduct of the constable and guard, and then I was perfectly satisfied that a most base fraud had been attempted; that, in fact, it was feared that the 'Mormons' would submit, and thereby entitle themselves to the protection of the law. It was very apparent that many of the bustling, active spirits were afraid that there would be no occasion for calling out an overwhelming militia force, for marching it into Nauvoo, for probable mutiny when there, and for the extermination of the 'Mormon' race. It appeared that the constable and the escort were fully in the secret, and acted well their part to promote the conspiracy.'*

In the morning Brother Joseph had an interview with the officers of the Legion, with the leading members of the city council, and with the principal men of the city. The officers were instructed to dismiss their men, but to have them in a state of readiness to be called upon in any emergency that might occur.

About half past six o'clock the members of the city council, the marshal, Brothers Joseph and Hyrum, and a number of others, started for Carthage, on horseback. We were instructed by Brother Joseph Smith not to take any arms, and we consequently left

*Ford's *History of Illinois*, p. 333.

them behind. We called at the house of Brother Fellows on our way out. Brother Fellows lives about four miles from Carthage.

While at Brother Fellows' house, Captain Dunn, accompanied by Mr. Coolie, one of the governor's aidde-camps, came up from Carthage en route for Nauvoo with a requisition from the governor for the state arms. We all returned to Nauvoo with them; the governor's request was complied with, and after taking some refreshments, we all returned to proceed to Carthage. We arrived there late in the night. A great deal of excitement prevailed on and after our arrival. The governor had received into his company all of the companies that had been in the mob; these fellows were riotous and disorderly, hallooing, yelling, and whooping about the streets like Indians, many of them intoxicated; the whole presented a scene of rowdyism and lowbred ruffianism only found among mobocrats and desperadoes, and entirely revolting to the best feelings of humanity. The governor made a speech to them to the effect that he would show Joseph and Hyrum Smith to them in the morning.

About here the companies with the governor were drawn up in line, and General Deming, I think, took Joseph by the arm and Hyrum (Arnold says that Joseph took the governor's arm), and as he passed through between the ranks, the governor leading in front, very politely introduced them as General Joseph Smith and General Hyrum Smith.*

---

*The Deseret News gives the following account of Joseph and Hyrum Smith's passing through the troops in Carthage:

'Carthage, June 25th, 1844.

'Quarter past 9. The governor came and invited Joseph to walk with him through the troops. Joseph solicited a few moment's private conversation with him, which the governor refused.

'While refusing, the governor looked down at his shoes, as though he was ashamed. They then walked through the crowd, with Brigadier-General Miner, R. Deming, and Dr. Richards, to General Deming's quarters. The people appeared quiet until a company of Carthage Greys flocked round the doors of General Deming in an uproarious manner, of which notice was sent to the governor. In the meantime the governor had ordered the McDonough troops to be drawn up in line, for Joseph

All were orderly and courteous except one company of mobocrats—the Carthage Greys—who seemed to find fault on account of too much honor being paid to the 'Mormons'. There was afterward a row between the companies, and they came pretty near having a fight; the more orderly not feeling disposed to endorse or submit to the rowdyism of the mobocrats. The result was that General Deming, who was very much of a gentleman, ordered the Carthage Greys, a company under the command of Captain [R. F.] Smith, a magistrate in Carthage, and a most violent mobocrat, under arrest. This matter, however, was shortly afterward adjusted, and the difficulty settled between them.

The mayor, aldermen, councilors, as well as the marshal of the city of Nauvoo, together with some persons who had assisted the marshal in removing the press in Nauvoo, appeared before Justice Smith, the

The City Council of Nauvoo Arraigned Before Justice Smith.

aforesaid captain and mobocrat, to again answer the charge of destroying the press; but as there was so much excitement, and as the man was an unprincipled villain before whom we were to have our hearing, we thought it most prudent to give bail, and consequently became security for each other in $500 bonds each, to appear

and Hyrum to pass in front of them, they having requested that they might have a clear view of the Generals Smith. *Joseph had a conversation with the governor for about ten minutes, when he again pledged the faith of the state that he and his friends should be protected from violence.*

'Robinson, the postmaster, said, on report of martial law being proclaimed in Nauvoo, he had stopped the mail, and notified the postmaster-general of the state of things in Hancock county.

'From the general's quarters Joseph and Hyrum went in front of the lines, in a hollow square of a company of Carthage Greys. At seven minutes before ten they arrived in front of the lines, and passed before the whole, Joseph being on the right of General Deming and Hyrum on his left, Elders Richards, Taylor and Phelps following. Joseph and Hyrum were introduced by Governor Ford about twenty times along the line as General Joseph Smith and General Hyrum Smith, the governor walking in front on the left. The Carthage Greys refused to receive them by that introduction, and some of the officers threw up their hats, drew their swords, and said they would introduce themselves to the damned 'Mormons' in a different style. The governor mildly entreated them not to act so rudely, but their excitement increased; the governor, however, succeeded in pacifying them by making a speech, and promising them that they should have 'full satisfaction'. General Smith and party returned to their lodgings at five minutes past ten ' (*Deseret News*, No. 35, Nov. 4, 1857, p. 274).

before the county court at its next session. We had engaged as counsel a lawyer by the name of Wood, of Burlington, Iowa; and Reed, I think, of Madison, Iowa. After some little discussion the bonds were signed, and we were all dismissed.

Almost immediately after our dismissal, two men—Augustine Spencer and Norton—two worthless fellows, whose words would not have been taken for five cents, and the first of whom had a short time previously been before the mayor in Nauvoo for maltreating a lame brother, made affidavits that Joseph and Hyrum Smith were guilty of treason, and a writ was accordingly issued for their arrest, and the Constable Bettisworth, a rough, unprincipled man, wished immediately to hurry them away to prison without any hearing. His rude, uncouth manner in the administration of what he considered the duties of his office made him exceedingly repulsive to us all. But, independent of these acts, the proceedings in this case were altogether illegal. Providing the court was sincere, which it was not, and providing these men's oaths were true, and that Joseph and Hyrum were guilty of treason, still the whole course was illegal.

The magistrate made out a mittimus, and committed them to prison without a hearing, which he had no right legally to do. The statute of Illinois expressly provides that 'all men shall have a hearing before a magistrate before they shall be committed to prison'; and Mr. Robert F. Smith, the magistrate, had made out a mittimus committing them to prison contrary to law without such hearing. As I was informed of this illegal proceeding, I went immediately to the governor and informed him of it. Whether he was apprised of it before or not, I do not know; but my opinion is that he was.

I represented to him the characters of the parties who had made oath, the outrageous nature of the charge, the indignity offered to men in the position which they occupied, and declared to him that he knew very well it was a vexatious proceeding, and that the accused were not guilty of any such crime. The governor replied, he was very sorry that the thing had occurred; that he did not believe the charges, but that he thought the best thing to be done was to let the law take its course. I then reminded him that we had come out there at his instance, not to satisfy the law, which we had done before, but the prejudices of the people, in relation to the affair of the press; that at his instance we had given bonds, which we could not by law be required to do to satisfy the people, and that it was asking too much to require gentlemen in their position in life to suffer the degradation of being immured in a jail at the instance of such worthless scoundrels as those who had made this affidavit. The governor replied that it was an unpleasant affair, and looked hard; but that it was a matter over which he had no control, as it belonged to the judiciary; that

Governor Ford's Reaction to the Representation of John Taylor.

he, as the executive, could not interfere with their proceedings, and that he had no doubt but that they would immediately be dismissed. I told him that we had looked to him for protection from such insults, and that I thought we had a right to do so from the solemn promises which he had made to me and to Dr. Bernhisel in relation to our coming without guard or arms; that we had relied upon his faith, and had a right to expect him to fulfill his engagements after we had placed ourselves implicitly under his care, and complied with all his requests, although extra-judicial.

He replied that he would detail a guard, if we required it, and see us protected, but that he could not interfere with the judiciary. I expressed my dissatisfaction at the course taken, and told him that, if we were to be subject to mob rule, and to be dragged, contrary to law, into prison at the instance of every infernal scoundrel whose oaths could be bought for a dram of whiskey, his protection availed very little, and we had miscalculated his promises.

Seeing there was no prospect of redress from the governor, I returned to the room, and found the Constable Bettisworth very urgent to hurry Brothers Joseph and Hyrum to prison, while the brethren were remonstrating with him. At the same time a great rabble was gathered in the streets and around the door, and from the rowdyism manifested I was afraid there was a design to murder the prisoners on the way to jail.

Without conferring with any person, my next feelings were to procure a guard, and, seeing a man habited as a soldier in the room, I went to him and said, 'I am afraid there is a design against the lives of the Messrs. Smith; will you go immediately and bring your captain; and, if not convenient any other captain of a company, and I will pay you well for your trouble?' He said he would, and departed forthwith, and soon returned with his captain, whose name I have forgotten, and introduced him to me. I told him of my fears, and requested him immediately to fetch his company.

He departed forthwith, and arrived at the door with them just at the time when the constable was hurrying the brethren downstairs. A number of the brethren went along, together with one or two strangers; and all of us safely lodged in prison, remained there during the night."

CHAPTER VIII.

INTERVIEW BETWEEN JOSEPH SMITH AND GOVERNOR THOMAS FORD

"At the request of Joseph Smith for an interview with the governor, he came the next morning, Thursday, June 26th, at half past 9 o'clock, accompanied by Colonel Thomas Geddes, when a lengthy conversation was entered into in relation to the existing difficulties; and after some preliminary remarks, at the governor's request, Brother Joseph gave him a general outline of the state of affairs in relation to our difficulties, the excited state of the country, the tumultuous mobocratic movements of our enemies, the precautionary measures used by himself (Joseph Smith), the acts of the city council, the destruction of the press, and the moves of the mob and ourselves up to that time.

The following report is, I believe, substantially correct:

Governor—'General Smith, I believe you have given me a general outline of the difficulties that have existed in the country in the documents forwarded to me by Dr. Bernhisel and Mr. Taylor; but, unfortunately, there seems to be a great discrepancy between your statements and those of your enemies. It is true that you are substantiated by evidence and affidavit, but for such an extraordinary excitement as that which is now in the country there must be some cause, and I attribute the last outbreak to the destruction of the *Expositor*, and to your refusal to comply with the writ issued by Esquire Morrison. The press in the United States is looked upon as the great bulwark of American freedom, and its destruction in Nauvoo was represented and looked upon as a high-handed measure, and manifests to the people a disposition on your part to suppress the liberty of speech and of the press. This, with your refusal to comply with the requisition of a writ, I conceive to be the principal cause of this difficulty; and you are moreover represented to me as turbulent, and defiant of the laws and institutions of your country.'

General Smith—'Governor Ford, you, sir, as governor of this state, are aware of the persecutions that I have endured. You know well that our course has been peaceable and law-abiding for I have furnished this state ever since our settlement here with sufficient evidence of my pacific intentions, and those of the people with whom I am associated, by the endurance of every conceivable indignity and lawless outrage perpetrated upon me and upon this people since our settlement here; and you yourself know that I have kept you well posted in relation to all matters associated with the late difficulties. If you have not got some of my communications, it has not been my fault.

'Agreeably to your orders, I assembled the Nauvoo Legion for the protection of Nauvoo and the surrounding country against an armed band of marauders; and ever since they have been mustered I have almost daily communicated with you in regard to all the leading events that have transpired; and whether in the capacity of mayor of the city, or lieutenant-general of the Nauvoo Legion, I have striven, according to the best of my judgment to preserve the peace, and to administer even-handed justice; but my motives are impugned, my acts are misconstrued, and I am grossly and wickedly misrepresented. I suppose I am indebted for my incarceration to the oath of a worthless man, who was arraigned before me and fined for abusing and maltreating his lame, helpless brother. That I should be charged by you, sir, who know better, of acting contrary to law, is to me a matter of surprise. Was it the 'Mormons' or our enemies who first com-

menced these difficulties?   You know well it was not
us; and when this turbulent, outrageous people commenced their insurrectionary movements I made you
acquainted with them officially, and asked your advice,
and have followed strictly your counsel in every particular. Who ordered out the Nauvoo Legion? I did, under
your direction.   For what purpose?   To suppress the
insurrectionary movements.   It was at your instance,
sir, that I issued a Proclamation calling upon the Nauvoo Legion to be in readiness at a moment's warning
to guard against the incursions of mobs, and gave an
order to Jonathan Dunham, acting major-general, to
that effect.

'Am I, then, to be charged with the acts of others?
and because lawlessness and mobocracy abound, am I,
when carrying out your instructions, to be charged
with not abiding law?   Why is it that I must be made
accountable for other men's acts?   If there is trouble
in the country, neither I nor my people made it; and
all that we have ever done, after much endurance on
our part, is to maintain and uphold the Constitution
and institutions of our country, and to protect an
injured, innocent, and persecuted people against misrule and mob violence.

'Concerning the destruction of the press to which
you refer, men may differ somewhat in their opinions
about it; but can it be supposed that after all the
indignities to which they have been subjected outside,
that people would suffer a set of worthless vagabonds
to come into their city, and, right under their own
eyes and protection, vilify and calumniate not only
themselves, but the character of their wives and daughters, as was impudently and unblushingly done in
that infamous and filthy sheet?

'There is not a city in the United States that would
have suffered such an indignity for twenty-four hours.
Our whole people were indignant, and loudly called
upon our city authorities for a redress of their grievances, which, if not attended to, they themselves would

have taken into their own hands, and have summarily
punished the audacious wretches as they deserved. The
principle of equal rights that has been instilled into
our bosoms from our cradles as American citizens
forbids us submitting to every foul indignity, and suc-
cumbing and pandering to wretches so infamous as
these. But, independent of this, the course that we
pursued we consider to be strictly legal; for, notwithstanding the result, we were anxious to be governed
strictly by law, and therefore we convened the city
council; and being desirous in our deliberations to
abide by law, we summoned legal counsel to be present
on the occasion. Upon investigating the matter, we
found that our city charter gave us power to remove
all nuisances. Furthermore, after consulting Blackstone upon what might be considered a nuisance, it
appeared that that distinguished lawyer, who is considered authority, I believe, in all courts, states among
other things that 'a libelous and filthy *press* may be
considered a nuisance, and abated as such.'* Here,
then, one of the most eminent English barristers, whose
works are considered standard with us, declares that
a libelous and filthy press may be considered a nuisance;
and our own charter, given us by the legislature of this
state, gives us the power to remove nuisances; and
by ordering that press to be abated as a nuisance, we
conceived that we were acting strictly in accordance
with law. We made that order in our corporate capacity, and the city marshal carried it out. It is possible there may have been some better way, but I must
confess that I could not see it.

'In relation to the writ served upon us, we were
willing to abide the consequences of our own acts, but

*The author referred to (Blackstone) says: "A fourth species of remedy by the
mere act of the party injured. is the abatement, or removal of nuisances." On this
the following commentary is made in note 6. "So it seems that a *libelous print*, or
paper [not the printing *press* on which they may have been printed] affecting a private
individual may be destroyed; or, which is the better course, taken and delivered to a
magistrate" (See Chitty's *Blackstone*, bk. ii, chs. i, iv, note 6). The destruction of
libelous "*prints and papers*" can scarcely be held to sustain the action of destroying a
"*printing press.*"

were unwilling, in answering a writ of that kind, to
submit to illegal exactions, sought to be imposed upon
us under the pretense of law, when we knew they were
in open violation of it.   When that document was
presented to me by Mr. Bettisworth, I offered, in the
presence of more than twenty persons, to go to any
other magistrate, either in our city, in Appanoose,
or any other place where we should be safe, but we
all refused to put ourselves into the power of a mob.
What right had that constable to refuse our request?
He had none according to law; for you know, Governor Ford, that the statute law in Illinois is, that the
parties served with the writ 'shall go before him who
issued it, *or some other justice of the peace.*'   Why,
then, should we be dragged to Carthage, where the
law does not compel us to go?   Does not this look
like many others of our persecutions with which you
are acquainted? and have we not a right to expect
foul play?   This very act was a breach of law on his
part, an assumption of power that did not belong to
him, and an attempt, at least, to deprive us of our
legal and constitutional rights and privileges.   What
could we do, under the circumstances, different from
what we did do?   We sued for, and obtained a writ
of *habeas corpus* from the municipal court, by which
we were delivered from the hands of Constable Bettisworth, and brought before and acquitted by the municipal court.   After our acquittal, in a conversation
with Judge Thomas, although he considered the acts
of the party illegal, he advised that, to satisfy the
people, we had better go before another magistrate
who was not in our church.   In accordance with his
advice, we went before Esquire Wells, with whom you
are well acquainted; both parties were present, witnesses were called on both sides, the case was fully
investigated, and we were again dismissed.   And what
is this pretended desire to enforce law, and wherefore
are these lying, base rumors put into circulation but
to seek, through mob influence, under pretense of law,

to make us submit to requisitions which are contrary to law and subversive of every principle of justice? And when you, sir, required us to come out here, we came, not because it was legal, but because you required it of us, and we were desirous of showing to you, and to all men, that we shrunk not from the most rigid investigation of our acts. We certainly did expect other treatment than to be immured in a jail at the instance of these men, and I think, from your plighted faith, we had a right so to expect, after disbanding our own forces, and putting ourselves entirely in your hands. And now, after having fulfilled my part, sir, as a man and an American citizen, I call upon you, Governor Ford, to deliver us from this place, and rescue us from this outrage that is sought to be practiced upon us by a set of infamous scoundrels.'

Governor Ford—'But you have placed men under arrest, detained men as prisoners, and given passes to others, some of which I have seen.'

John P. Greene, City Marshal—'Perhaps I can explain. Since these difficulties have commenced, you are aware that we have been placed under very peculiar circumstances; our city has been placed under a very rigid police guard; in addition to this, frequent guards have been placed outside the city to prevent any sudden surprise, and those guards have questioned suspected or suspicious persons as to their business. To strangers, in some instances, passes have been given to prevent difficulty in passing those guards; it is some of these passes that you have seen. No person, sir, has been imprisoned without a legal cause in our city.'

Governor—'Why did you not give a more speedy answer to the *posse* that I sent out?'

General Smith—'We had matters of importance to consult upon; your letter showed anything but an amiable spirit. We have suffered immensely in Missouri from mobs, in loss of property, imprisonment, and otherwise. It took some time for us to weigh duly these matters; we could not decide upon matters of such importance immediately, and your *posse* were too hasty in returning; we were consulting for a large people, and vast interests were at stake. We had been outrageously imposed upon, and knew not how far we could trust anyone, besides, a question necessarily arose, how shall we come? Your request was that we should come unarmed. It became a matter of serious importance to decide how far promises could be trusted, and how far we were safe from mob violence.'

Colonel Geddes—'It certainly did look from all I have heard, from the general spirit of violence and mobocracy that here prevails, that it was not safe for you to come unprotected.'*

Governor Ford—'I think that sufficient time was not allowed by the *posse* for you to consult and get ready. They were too hasty; but I suppose they found themselves bound by their orders. I think, too, there is a great deal of truth in what you say, and your reasoning is plausible, but I must beg leave to differ from you in relation to the acts of the city council. That council, in my opinion, had no right to act in a legislative capacity and in that of the judiciary. They should have passed a law in relation to the matter, and then the municipal court, upon complaint, could have removed it [i. e., the *Expositor* press]; but for the city council to take upon themselves the law-making and the execution of the law, is, in my opinion, wrong; besides, these men ought to have had a hearing before their property was destroyed; to destroy it without was an infringement on their rights; besides, it is so contrary to the feelings of American people to interfere with the press. And,

---

*Notwithstanding this sympathetic allusion by Colonel Geddes upon the situation, it is stated by Gregg that Geddes was really unfriendly to the Prophet and had no sympathy with him and the injustice which had been done him in his arrest and imprisonment, for after leaving the prison and carrying on a conversation with Governor Ford, he represents the governor as saying to him: "O, it's all nonsense; you will have to drive these Mormons out yet"! Then Geddes said to the governor: "If we undertake that governor, when the proper time comes, will you interfere?" "No, I will not", said the governor, after a pause adding, *"until you are through"* (Gregg's *History of Hancock County*, p. 372).

furthermore, I cannot but think that it would have been more judicious for you to have gone with Mr. Bettisworth to Carthage, notwithstanding the law did not require it. Concerning your being in jail, I am sorry for that; I wish it had been otherwise. I hope you will soon be released, but I can not interfere.'

Joseph Smith—'Governor Ford, allow me, sir, to bring one thing to your mind that you seem to have overlooked. You state that you think it would have been better for us to have submitted to the requisition of Constable Bettisworth, and to have gone to Carthage. Do you not know, sir, that that writ was served at the instance of an anti-'Mormon' mob, who had passed resolutions, and published them, to the effect that they would exterminate the 'Mormon' leaders? And are you not informed that Captain Anderson was not only threatened but had a gun fired at his boat by this said mob in Warsaw when coming up to Nauvoo, and that this very thing was made use of as a means to get us into their hands; and we could not, without taking an armed force with us, go there without, according to their published declarations, going into the jaws of death? To have taken a force with us would only have fanned the excitement, and they would have stated that we wanted to use intimidation; therefore, we thought it the most judicious to avail ourselves of the protection of law.'

Governor Ford—'I see, I see.'

Joseph Smith—'Furthermore, in relation to the press, you say that you differ from me in opinion. Be it so; the thing, after all, is only a legal difficulty, and the courts, I should judge, are competent to decide on that matter. If our act was illegal, we are willing to meet it and although I can not see the distinction that you draw about the acts of the city council, and what difference it could have made in point of fact, law, or justice between the city council's acting together or separate, or how much more legal it would have been for the municipal court, who were a part of the city council, to act separately instead of with the councilors, yet if it is deemed that we did a wrong in destroying that press, we refuse not to pay for it; we are desirous to fulfill the law in every particular, and are responsible for our acts. You say that the parties ought to have had a hearing. Had it been a civil suit, this, of course, would have been proper; but there was a flagrant violation of every principle of right—a nuisance; and it was abated on the same principle that any nuisance, stench, or putrefied carcass would have been removed. Our first step, therefore, was to stop the foul, noisome, filthy sheet, and then the next in our opinion would have been to have prosecuted the man for a breach of public decency. And, furthermore, again let me say, Governor Ford, I shall look to you for our protection. I believe you are talking of going to Nauvoo; if you go, sir, I wish to go along. I refuse not to answer any law, but I do not consider myself safe here.'

Governor—'I am in hopes that you will be acquitted, and if I go I will certainly take you along. I do not, however, apprehend danger. I think you are perfectly safe either here or anywhere else. I can not, however, interfere with the law. I am placed in peculiar circumstances, and seem to be blamed by all parties.'

Joseph Smith—'Governor Ford, I ask nothing but what is legal; I have a right to expect protection, at least from you; for, independent of law, you have pledged your faith and that of the state for my protection, and I wish to go to Nauvoo.'

Governor—'And you shall have protection, General Smith. I did not make this promise without consulting my officers, who all pledged their honor to its fulfillment. I do not know that I shall go tomorrow to Nauvoo, but if I do I will take you along.'

At a quarter past ten o'clock the governor left.''

CHAPTER IX

THE ASSAULT UPON THE PRISON—THE MURDER OF JOSEPH AND HYRUM SMITH

"AT about half past twelve o'clock, Mr. Reed, one of Joseph's counsel, came in, apparently much elated; he stated that, upon an examination of the law, he found that the magistrate had transcended his jurisdiction, and that, having committed them without an examination, his jurisdiction ended; that he had him upon a pinhook; *The Magistrate Exceeds His Jurisdiction.* that he ought to have examined them before he committed them, and that, having violated the law in this particular, he had no farther power over them; for, once committed, they were out of his jurisdiction, as the power of the magistrate extended no farther than their committal, and that now they could not be brought out except at the regular session of the circuit court, or by a writ of *habeas corpus;* but that if Justice Smith would consent to go to Nauvoo for trial, he would compromise matters with him, and overlook this matter.

Mr. Reed farther stated that the anti-'Mormons', or mob had concocted a scheme to get a writ from Missouri, with a demand upon Governor Ford for the arrest of Joseph Smith, and his conveyance to Missouri, and that a man by the name of Wilson had returned from Missouri the night before the burning of the press for this purpose.

At half past two o'clock Constable Bettisworth came to the jail with a man named Simpson, professing to have some order, but he would not send up his name, and the guard would not let him pass. Dr.

Bernhisel and Brother Wasson went to inform the governor and council of this. At about twenty minutes to three Dr. Bernhisel returned, and stated that he thought the governor was doing all he could. At about ten minutes to three Hiram Kimball appeared with news from Nauvoo.

Soon after Constable Bettisworth came with an order from Esquire Smith to convey the prisoners to
Prisoners Il-   the courthouse for trial. He was informed
legally Forced   that the process was illegal, that they had
into Court.   been placed there contrary to law, and that they refused to come unless by legal process. I was informed that Justice [Robert F.] Smith (who was also captain of the Carthage Greys) went to the governor and informed him of the matter, and that the governor replied, 'You have your forces, and of course can use them.' The constable certainly did return, accompanied by a guard of armed men, and by force, and under protest, hurried the prisoners to the court.

About four o'clock the case was called by Captain Robert F. Smith, J. P. The counsel for the prisoners called for subpoenas to bring witnesses. At twenty-five minutes past four he took a copy of the order to bring the prisoners from jail to trial, and afterwards he took names of witnesses.

Counsel present for the state; Higbee, Skinner, Sharp, Emmons, and Morrison. Twenty-five minutes to five the writ was returned as served, June 25th.

Many remarks were made at the court that I paid but little attention to, as I considered the whole thing illegal and a complete burlesque. Wood objected to the proceedings *in toto*, in consequence of its illegality, showing that the prisoners were not only illegally committed, but that, being once committed, the magistrate had no farther power over them; but as it was the same magistrate before whom he was pleading who imprisoned them contrary to law, and the same who, as captain, forced them from jail, his arguments availed but little. He then urged that the prisoners be remanded until witnesses could be had, and applied for a continuance for that purpose. Skinner suggested until twelve o'clock next day. Wood again demanded until witnesses could be obtained; that the court meet at a specified time, and that, if witnesses were not present, again adjourn, without calling the prisoners. After various remarks from Reed, Skinner, and others, the court stated that the writ was served yesterday, and that it will give until tomorrow at twelve m. to get witnesses.

We then returned to jail. Immediately after our return Dr. Bernhisel went to the governor, and obtained from him an order for us to occupy a large open room containing a bedstead. I rather think that the same room had been appropriated to the use of debtors; at any rate, there was free access to the jailor's house, and no bars or locks except such as might be on the outside door of the jail. The jailor, Mr. George W. Steghall, and his wife, manifested a disposition to make us as comfortable as they could; we ate at their table, which was well provided, and, of course, paid for it.

Some Concessions of Comfort to the Prisoners.

I do not remember the names of all who were with us that night and the next morning in jail, for several went and came; among those that we considered stationary were Stephen Markham, John S. Fullmer, Captain Dan Jones, Dr. Willard Richards, and myself. Dr. Bernhisel says that he was there from Wednesday in the afternoon until eleven o'clock next day. We were, however, visited by numerous friends, among whom were Uncle John Smith, Hiram Kimball, Cyrus H. Wheelock, besides lawyers, as counsel. There was also a great variety of conversation, which was rather desultory than otherwise, and referred to circumstances that had transpired, our former and present grievances, the spirit of the troops around us, and the disposition of the governor; the devising for legal and other plans for deliverance, the nature of testimony required; the gathering of proper witnesses, and a variety of other topics, including our religious hopes, etc.

During one of these conversations Dr. Richards remarked: 'Brother Joseph, if it is necessary that you die in this matter, and if they will take me in your stead, I will suffer for you.' At another time, when conversing about deliverance, I said, 'Brother Joseph, if you will permit it, and say the word, I will have you out of this prison in five hours, if the jail has to come down to do it.' My idea was to go to Nauvoo, and collect a force sufficient, as I considered the whole affair a legal farce, and a flagrant outrage upon our liberty and rights. Brother Joseph refused.

Elder Cyrus H. Wheelock came in to see us, and when he was about leaving drew a small pistol, a six-shooter, from his pocket, remarking at the same time,

Cyrus H. Wheelock's Visit to the Prison.
'Would any of you like to have this?' Brother Joseph immediately replied, 'Yes, give it to me,' whereupon he took the pistol, and put it in his pantaloons pocket. The pistol was a six-shooting revolver, of Allen's patent; it belonged to me, and was one that I furnished to Brother Wheelock when he talked of going with me to the east, previous to our coming to Carthage. I have it now in my possession. Brother Wheelock went out on some errand, and was not suffered to return. The report of the governor having gone to Nauvoo without taking the prisoners along with him caused very unpleasant feelings, as we were apprised that we were left to the tender mercies of the Carthage Greys, a company strictly mobocratic, and whom we knew to be our most deadly enemies; and their captain, Esquire [Robert F.] Smith, was a most unprincipled villain. Besides this, all the mob forces, comprising the governor's troops, were dismissed, with the exception of one or two companies, which the governor took with him to Nauvoo. The great part of the mob was liberated, the remainder was our guard.

We looked upon it not only as a breach of faith on

the part of the governor, but also as an indication of a desire to insult us, if nothing more, by leaving us in the proximity of such men. The prevention of Wheelock's return was among the first of their hostile movements.

Colonel Markham went out, and he was also prevented from returning. He was very angry at this, but the mob paid no attention to him; they drove him out of town at the point of the bayonet, and threatened to shoot him if he returned. He went, I am informed, to Nauvoo for the purpose of raising a company of men for our protection. Brother Fullmer went to Nauvoo after witnesses: it is my opinion that Brother Wheelock did also.

Harsh Treatment of Col. Markham.

Sometime after dinner we sent for some wine. It has been reported by some that this was taken as a sacrament. It was no such thing; our spirits were generally dull and heavy, and it was sent for to revive us. I think it was Captain Jones who went after it, but they would not suffer him to return. I believe we all drank of the wine, and gave some to one or two of the prison guards. We all of us felt unusually dull and languid, with a remarkable depression of spirits. In consonance with those feelings I sang a song, that had lately been introduced into Nauvoo, entitled, 'A Poor Wayfaring Man of Grief', etc.*

Wine Obtained.

The song is pathetic, and the tune quite plaintive, and was very much in accordance with our feelings at the time for our spirits were all depressed, dull and gloomy and surcharged with indefinite ominous forebodings. After a lapse of some time, Brother Hyrum requested me again to sing that song. I replied, 'Brother Hyrum, I do not feel like singing;' when he remarked, 'Oh, never mind; commence singing, and you will get the spirit of it.'

'A Poor Wayfaring Man of Grief.'

*The song is published in full this *History*. vol. vi, pp. 614-15. It was the composition of Montgomery. B. H. R.

At his request I did so.   Soon afterwards I was sitting
at one of the front windows of the jail, when I saw a
number of men, with painted faces, coming around
the corner of the jail, and aiming towards the stairs.
The Assault.   The other brethren had seen the same, for,
as I went to the door, I found Brother
Hyrum Smith and Dr. Richards already leaning against
it.   They both pressed against the door with their
shoulders to prevent its being opened, as the lock and
latch were comparatively useless.   While in this position, the mob, who had come upstairs, and tried
to open the door, probably thought it was locked,
and fired a ball through the keyhole; at this Dr. Richards and Brother Hyrum leaped back from the door,
with their faces towards it; almost instantly another
ball passed through the panel of the door, and struck
Brother Hyrum on the left side of the nose, entering
his face and head.   At the same instant, another ball
from the outside entered his back, passing through his
body and striking his watch.   The ball came from the
back, through the jail window, opposite the door,
and must, from its range, have been fired from the
Carthage Greys, who were placed there ostensibly for
our protection, as the balls from the firearms, shot
close by the jail, would have entered the ceiling, we
being in the second story, and there never was a time
after that when Hyrum could have received the latter
wound.   Immediately, when the ball struck him, he
fell flat on his back, crying as he fell, 'I am a dead man!'
He never moved afterwards.

I shall never forget the deep feeling of sympathy
and regard manifested in the countenance of Brother
Joseph as he drew nigh to Hyrum, and, leaning over
him, exclaimed, 'Oh! my poor, dear brother Hyrum!'
He, however, instantly arose, and with a firm, quick
step, and a determined expression of countenance, approached the door, and pulling the six-shooter left
by Brother Wheelock from his pocket, opened the door
slightly, and snapped the pistol six successive times;

only three of the barrels, however, were discharged. I afterwards understood that two or three were wounded by these discharges, two of whom, I am informed, died. I had in my hands a large, strong hickory stick, brought there by Brother Markham, and left by him, which I had seized as soon as I saw the mob approach; and while Brother Joseph was firing the pistol, I stood close behind him. As soon as he had discharged it he stepped back, and I immediately took his place next to the door, while he occupied the one I had done while he was shooting. Brother Richards, at this time, had a knotty walking-stick in his hands belonging to me, and stood next to Brother Joseph, a little farther from the door, in an oblique direction, apparently to avoid the rake of the fire from the door. The firing of Brother Joseph made our assailants pause for a moment; very soon after, however, they pushed the door some distance open, and protruded and discharged their guns into the room, when I parried them off with my stick, giving another direction to the balls.

It certainly was a terrible scene: streams of fire as thick as my arm passed by me as these men fired, and, unarmed as we were, it looked like certain death. I remember feeling as though my time had come, but I do not know when, in any critical position, I was more calm, unruffled, energetic, and acted with more promptness and decision. It certainly was far from pleasant to be so near the muzzles of those firearms as they belched forth their liquid flames and deadly balls. While I was engaged in parrying the guns, Brother Joseph said, 'That's right, Brother Taylor, parry them off as well as you can.' These were the last words I ever heard him speak on earth.

Every moment the crowd at the door became more dense, as they were unquestionably pressed on by those in the rear ascending the stairs, until the whole entrance at the door was literally crowded with muskets and rifles, which, with the swearing, shouting, and demoniacal expressions of those outside the door and on the stairs, and the firing of the guns, mingled with their horrid oaths and execrations, made it look like pandemonium let loose, and was, indeed, a fit representation of the horrid deed in which they were engaged.

After parrying the guns for some time, which now protruded thicker and farther into the room, and seeing no hope of escape or protection there, as we were now unarmed, it occurred to me that we might have some friends outside, and that there might be some chance of escape in that direction, but here there seemed to be none. As I expected them every moment to rush into the room—nothing but extreme cowardice having thus far kept them out—as the tumult and pressure increased, without any other hope, I made a spring for the window which was right in front of the jail door, where the mob was standing, and also exposed to the fire of the Carthage Greys, who were stationed some ten or twelve rods off. The weather was hot, we all of us had our coats off, and the window was raised to admit air. As I reached the window, and was on the point of leaping out, I was struck by a ball from the door about midway of my thigh, which struck the bone, and flattened out almost to the size of a quarter of a dollar, and then passed on through the fleshy part to within about half an inch of the outside. I think some prominent nerve must have been severed or injured for, as soon as the ball struck me, I fell like a bird when shot, or an ox when struck by a butcher, and lost entirely and instantaneously all power of action or locomotion. I fell upon the window-sill, and cried out, 'I am shot!' Not possessing any power to move, I felt myself falling outside of the window, but immediately I fell inside, from some, at that time, unknown cause. When I struck the floor my animation seemed restored, as I have seen it sometimes in squirrels and birds after being shot. As soon as I felt the power of motion I crawled under the bed, which was in a corner of the room, not far from the window where I

Taylor's Effort to Escape by the Window.

received my wound. While on my way and under the bed I was wounded in three other places; one ball entered a little below the left knee, and never was extracted; another entered the forepart of my left arm, a little above the wrist, and, passing down by the joint, lodged in the fleshy part of my hand, about midway, a little above the upper joint of my little finger; another struck me on the fleshy part of my left hip, and tore away the flesh as large as my hand, dashing the mangled fragments of flesh and blood against the wall.

My wounds were painful, and the sensation produced was as though a ball had passed through and down the whole length of my leg. I very well remember my reflections at the time. I had a very painful idea of becoming lame and decrepid, and being an object of pity, and I felt as though I would rather die than be placed in such circumstances.

It would seem that immediately after my attempt to leap out of the window, Joseph also did the same thing, of which circumstance I have no knowledge only from information. The first thing that I noticed was a cry that he had leaped out of the window. A cessation of firing followed, the mob rushed downstairs, and Dr. Richards went to the window. Immediately afterward I saw the doctor going towards the jail door, and as there was an iron door at the head of the stairs adjoining our door which led into the cells for criminals, it struck me that the doctor was going in there, and I said to him, 'Stop, Doctor, and take me along.' He proceeded to the door and opened it, and then returned and dragged me along to a small cell prepared for criminals.

Summary of Movements.

Brother Richards was very much troubled, and exclaimed, 'Oh! Brother Taylor, is it possible that they have killed both Brother Hyrum and Joseph? it cannot surely be, and yet I saw them shoot them;' and, elevating his hands two or three times, he exclaimed, 'Oh Lord, my God, spare Thy servants!' He then said, 'Brother Taylor, this is a terrible event;' and he dragged me farther into the cell, saying, 'I am sorry I can not do better for you;' and, taking an old, filthy mattress, he covered me with it, and said, 'That may hide you, and you may yet live to tell the tale, but I expect they will kill me in a few moments!' While lying in this position I suffered the most excruciating pain.

Soon afterwards Dr. Richards came to me, informed me that the mob had precipitately fled, and at the same time confirmed my worst fears that Joseph was assuredly dead. I felt a dull, lonely, sickening sensation at the news. When I reflected that our noble chieftain, the Prophet of the living God, had fallen, and that I had seen his brother in the cold embrace of death, it seemed as though there was a void or vacuum in the great field of human existence to me, and a dark gloomy chasm in the kingdom, and that we were left alone. Oh, how lonely was that feeling! How cold, barren and desolate! In the midst of difficulties he was always the first in motion; in critical positions his counsel was always sought. As our Prophet he approached our God, and obtained for us his will; but now our Prophet, our counselor, our general, our leader, was gone, and amid the fiery ordeal that we then had to pass through, we were left alone without his aid, and as our future guide for things spiritual or temporal, and for all things pertaining to this world, or the next, he had spoken for the last time on earth.

The Murder Accomplished —Reflections.

These reflections and a thousand others flashed upon my mind. I thought, why must the good perish, and the virtuous be destroyed? Why must God's nobility, the salt of the earth, the most exalted of the human family, and the most perfect types of all excellence, fall victims to the cruel, fiendish hate of incarnate devils?

The poignancy of my grief, I presume, however, was somewhat allayed by the extreme suffering that I endured from my wounds.

Soon afterwards I was taken to the head of the stairs and laid there, where I had a full view of our beloved and now murdered brother, Hyrum. There he lay as I had left him; he had not moved a limb; he lay placid and calm, a monument of greatness even in death; but his noble spirit had left its tenement, and was gone to dwell in regions more congenial to its exalted nature. Poor Hyrum! He was a great and good man, and my soul was cemented to his. If ever there was an exemplary, honest, and virtuous man, an embodiment of all that is noble in the human form, Hyrum Smith was its representative.

While I lay there a number of persons came around, among whom was a physician. The doctor, on seeing a ball lodged in my left hand, took a pen- Rough knife from his pocket and made an incision Surgery. in it for the purpose of extracting the ball therefrom, and having obtained a pair of carpenter's compasses, made use of them to draw or pry out the ball, alternately using the penknife and compasses. After sawing for some time with a dull penknife, and prying and pulling with the compasses, he ultimately succeeded in extracting the ball, which weighed about half an ounce. Some time afterwards he remarked to a friend of mine that I had 'nerves like the devil', to stand what I did in its extraction. I really thought I had need of nerves to stand such surgical butchery, and that, whatever my nerves may be, his practice was devilish.

This company wished to remove me to Mr. Hamilton's Hotel, the place where we had stayed previous to our incarceration in jail. I told them, however, that I did not wish to go: I did not consider it safe. They protested that it was, and that I was safe with them; that it was a perfect outrage for men to be used as we had been; that they were my friends; that it was for my good they were counseling me, and that I could be better taken care of there than here.

I replied, 'I don't know you. Whom am I among?

I am surrounded by assassins and murderers; witness your deeds. Don't talk to me of kindness or comfort; look at your murdered victims. Look at me! I want none of your counsel nor comfort. There may be some safety here; I can be assured of none anywhere,' etc.

They G— d— their souls to hell, made the most solemn asseverations, and swore by God and the devil, and everything else that they could think of, that they would stand by me to death and protect me. In half an hour every one of them fled from the town.

Soon after a coroner's jury were assembled in the room over the body of Hyrum. Among the jurors was Captain Smith of the 'Carthage Greys', who had assisted in the murder, and the same justice before whom we had been tried. I learned of Francis Higbee as being in the neighborhood. On hearing his name mentioned, I immediately arose and said, 'Captain Smith, you are a justice of the peace; I have heard his name mentioned; I want to swear my life against him.' I was informed that word was immediately sent to him to leave the place, which he did.

Brother Richards was busy during this time attending to the coroner's inquest, and to the re-moval of the bodies, and making arrangements for their removal from Carthage to Nauvoo.

<small>Activities of Willard Richards.</small>

When he had a little leisure, he again came to me, and at his suggestion I was removed to Hamilton's Tavern. I felt that he was the only friend, the only person, that I could rely upon in that town. It was with difficulty that sufficient persons could be found to carry me to the tavern; for immediately after the murder a great fear fell upon all the people, and men, women, and children fled with great precipi-tation, leaving nothing nor anybody in the town but two or three women and children and one or two sick persons.

<small>Flight of the People from Carthage.</small>

It was with great difficulty that Brother Richards

prevailed upon Mr. Hamilton, hotelkeeper, and his family, to stay; they would not until Brother Richards had given a solemn promise that he would see them protected, and hence I was looked upon as a hostage. Under these circumstances, notwithstanding, I believe they were hostile to the 'Mormons', and were glad that the murder had taken place, though they did not actually participate in it; and, feeling that I should be a protection to them they stayed.

The whole community knew that a dreadful outrage had been perpetrated by those villains, and fearing lest the citizens of Nauvoo, as they possessed the power, might have a disposition to visit them with a terrible vengeance, they fled in the wildest confusion. And, indeed, it was with very great difficulty that the citizens of Nauvoo could be restrained. A horrid, barbarous murder had been committed, the most solemn pledge violated, and that, too, while the victims were, contrary to the requirements of the law, putting themselves into the hands of the governor to pacify a popular excitement. This outrage was enhanced by the reflection that our people were able to protect themselves against not only all the mob, but against three times their number and that of the governor's troops put together. They were also exasperated by the speech of the governor in town.

The whole events were so faithless, so dastardly, so mean, cowardly, and contemptible, without one extenuating circumstance, that it would not have been surprising if the citizens of Nauvoo had arisen en masse. and blotted the wretches out of existence. The citizens of Carthage knew they would have done so under such circumstances, and, judging us by themselves, they were all panic-stricken, and fled. Colonel Markham, too, after his expulsion from Carthage, had gone home, related the circumstances of his ejectment, and was using his influence to get a company to go out. Fearing that when the people heard that their Prophet and Patriarch had been murdered under the above circumstances they might act rashly, and knowing that, if they once got roused, like a mighty avalanche they would lay the country waste before them and take a terrible vengeance—as none of the Twelve were in Nauvoo, and no one, perhaps, with sufficient influence to control the people, Dr. Richards, after consulting me, wrote the following note, fearing that my family might be seriously affected by the news. I told him to insert that I was slightly wounded.

WILLARD RICHARDS' NOTE FROM CARTHAGE JAIL TO NAUVOO*

'Carthage Jail, 8 o'clock 5 min. p. m., June 27th, 1844. 'Joseph and Hyrum are dead. Taylor wounded, not very badly. I am well. Our guard was forced, as we believe, by a band of Missourians from 100 to 200. The job was done in an instant, and the party fled towards Nauvoo instantly. This is as I believe it. The citizens here are afraid of the 'Mormons' attacking them; I promise them no.

[Signed] W. RICHARDS.

'N. B.—The citizens promise us protection; alarm guns have been fired.

[Signed] JOHN TAYLOR.

I remember signing my name as quickly as possible, lest the tremor of my hand should be noticed, and the fears of my family excited.

A messenger was dispatched immediately with the note, but he was intercepted by the governor, who, on hearing a cannon fired at Carthage, which was to be the signal for the murder, immediately fled with his company, and fearing that the citizens of Nauvoo, when apprised of the horrible outrage, would immediately rise and pursue, he turned back the messenger, who was George D. Grant. A second one was sent, who was treated similarly; and not until a third attempt could news be got to Nauvoo.

News of the Assassination Intercepted by Governor Ford.

Samuel H. Smith, brother to Joseph and Hyrum, was the first brother I saw after the outrage; I am not sure whether he took the news or not; he lived at the time in Plymouth, Hancock county, and was on his way to Carthage to see his brothers, when he was met by some of the troops, or rather mob, that had been dismissed by the governor, and who were on their way home.

Attempt on the Life of Samuel H. Smith, Brother of the Prophet.

On learning that he was Joseph Smith's brother they sought to kill him, but he escaped, and fled into the woods, where he was chased for a length of time by them; but, after severe fatigue, and much danger and excitement, he succeeded in escaping, and came to Carthage. He was on horseback when he arrived, and was not only very much tired with the fatigue and excitement of the chase, but was also very much distressed in feelings on account of the death of his brothers. These things produced a fever, which laid the foundation for his death, which took place on the 30th of July. Thus another of the brothers fell a victim, although not directly, but indirectly to this infernal mob.

I lay from about five o'clock until two next morning without having my wounds dressed, as there was scarcely any help of any kind in Carthage, and Brother Richards was busy with the dead bodies, preparing them for removal. My wife Leonora started early the next day, having had some little trouble in getting a company or a physician to come with her; after considerable difficulty she succeeded in getting an escort, and Dr. Samuel Bennett came along with her. Soon after my father and mother arrived from Oquakie, near which place they had a farm at that time, and hearing of the trouble, hastened along.

General Deming, brigadier-general of the Hancock county militia, was very much of a gentleman, and showed me every courtesy, and Colonel Jones also was very solicitous about my welfare.

I was called upon by several gentlemen of Quincy and other places, among whom was Judge Ralston, as well as by our own people, and a medical man extracted a ball from my left thigh that was giving me much pain; it lay about half an inch deep, and my thigh was considerably swollen. The doctor asked me if I would be tied during the operation; I told him no; that I could endure the cutting associated with the operation as well without, and I did so; indeed, so great was the pain I endured that the cutting was rather a relief than otherwise.

A very laughable incident occurred at the time; my wife, Leonora, went into an adjoining room to pray for me, that I might be sustained during the operation. While on her knees at prayer, a Mrs. Bedell, an old lady of the Methodist association, entered, and, patting Mrs. Taylor on her back with her hand, said, 'There's a good lady, pray for God to forgive your sins; pray that you may be converted, and the Lord may have mercy on your soul.'

The scene was so ludicrous that Mrs. Taylor knew not whether to laugh or be angry. Mrs. Taylor in-

The Hamiltons and the Murder.

formed me that Mr. Hamilton, the father of the Hamilton who kept the house, rejoiced at the murder, and said in company that 'it was done up in the best possible style, and showed good generalship,' and she farther believed that the other branches of the family sanctioned it. These were the associates of the old lady referred to, and yet she could talk of conversion and saving souls in the midst of blood and murder: such is man and such consistency!

The ball being extracted was the one that first struck me, which I before referred to; it entered on the outside of my left thigh, about five inches from my knee, and passing rather obliquely towards my body, had, it would seem, struck the bone, for it was flattened out nearly as thin and large as a quarter of a dollar.

The governor passed on, staying at Carthage only a few minutes, and he did not stop until he got fifty miles from Nauvoo.''

CHAPTER X.

WAS GOVERNOR FORD RESPONSIBLE FOR THE MURDER OF THE PROPHET AND PATRIARCH OF THE NEW DISPENSATION

"THERE had been various opinions about the complicity of the governor in the murder, some supposing that he knew all about it, and assisted or winked at its execution. It is somewhat difficult to form a correct opinion; from the facts presented it is very certain that things looked more than suspicious against him.

In the first place, he positively knew that we had broken no law.

Secondly. He knew that the mob had not only passed inflammatory resolutions, threatening extermination to the 'Mormons', but that they had actually assembled armed mobs and commenced hostilities against us.

Thirdly. He took those very mobs that had been arrayed against us, and enrolled them as his troops, thus legalizing their acts.

Fourthly. He disbanded the Nauvoo Legion, which had never violated law, and disarmed them, and had about his person in the shape of militia known mobocrats and violators of the law.

Fifthly. He requested us to come to Carthage without arms, promising protection, and then refused to interfere in delivering us from prison, although Joseph and Hyrum were put there contrary to law.

Sixthly. Although he refused to interfere in our behalf, yet, when Captain Smith went to him and informed him that the persons refused to come out, he told him that he had a command and knew what to do, thus sanctioning the use of force in the violation of law when opposed to us, whereas he would not for us interpose his executive authority to free us from being incarcerated contrary to law, although he was fully informed of all the facts of the case, as we kept him posted in the affairs all the time.

Seventhly. He left the prisoners in Carthage jail contrary to his plighted faith.

Eighthly. Before he went he dismissed all the troops that could be relied upon, as well as many of the mob, and left us in charge of the 'Carthage Greys', a company that he knew were mobocratic, our most bitter enemies, and who had passed resolutions to exterminate us, and who had been placed under guard by General Deming only the day before.

Ninthly. He was informed of the intended murder, both before he left and while on the road, by several different parties.

Tenthly. When the cannon was fired in Carthage, signifying that the deed was done, he immediately took up his line of march and fled. How did he know that this signal portended their death if he was not in the secret? It may be said some of the party told him. How could he believe what the party said about the gun signal if he could not believe the testimony of several individuals who told him in positive terms about the contemplated murder?

Incriminating Circumstances Against Governor Ford.

He has, I believe, stated that he left the 'Carthage Greys' there because he considered that, as their town was contiguous to ours, and as the responsibility of our safety rested solely upon them, they would not dare suffer any indignity to befall us. This very admission shows that he did really expect danger; and then he knew that these people had published to the world that they would exterminate us, and his leaving us in their hands and taking of their responsibilities was like leaving a lamb in charge of a wolf, and trusting to its humanity and honor for its safe-keeping.

It is said, again, that he would not have gone to Nauvoo, and thus placed himself in the hands of the 'Mormons', if he had anticipated any such event, as he would be exposed to their wrath. To this it may be answered that the 'Mormons' did not know their signals, while he did; and they were also known in Warsaw, as well as in other places; and as soon as the gun was fired, a merchant of Warsaw jumped upon his horse and rode directly to Quincy, and reported, 'Joseph and Hyrum killed, and those who were with them in jail.' He reported farther that 'they were attempting to break jail, and were all killed by the guard.' This was their story; it was anticipated to kill all, and the gun was to be the signal that the deed was accomplished. This was known in Warsaw. The governor also knew it and fled; and he could really be in no danger in Nauvoo, for the 'Mormons' did not know it, and he had plenty of time to escape, which he did.

It is said that he made all his officers promise solemnly that they would help him to protect the Smiths; this may or may not be. At any rate, some of these same officers helped to murder them.

The strongest argument in the governor's favor, and one that would bear more weight with us than all the rest put together, would be that he could not believe them capable of such atrocity; and, thinking that their talk and threatenings were a mere ebullition of feeling, a kind of braggadocio, and that there was enough of good moral feeling to control the more violent passions, he trusted to their faith. There is, indeed, a degree of plausibility about this, but when we put it in juxtaposition to the amount of evidence that he was in possession of it weighs very little. He had nothing to inspire confidence in them, and everything to make him mistrust them. Besides, why his broken faith? Why his disregard of what was told him by several parties? Again, if he knew not the plan how did he understand the signal? Why so oblivious to everything pertaining

Argument in Favor of Governor Ford.

to the 'Mormon' interest, and so alive and interested about the mobocrats? At any rate, be this as it may, he stands responsible for their blood, and it is dripping on his garments. If it had not been for his promise of protection, they would have protected themselves; it was plighted faith that led them to the slaughter; and, to make the best of it, it was a breach of that faith and a nonfulfillment of that promise, after repeated warning, that led to their death.

Having said so much, I must leave the governor with my readers and with his God. Justice, I conceive, demanded this much, and truth could not be told with less; as I have said before, my opinion is that the governor would not have planned this murder, but he had not sufficient energy to resist popular opinion, even if that opinion led to blood and death.

It was rumored that a strong political party, numbering in its ranks many of the prominent men of the nation, were engaged in a plot for the overthrow of Joseph Smith, and that the governor was of this party, and Sharp, Williams, Captain Smith, and others, were his accomplices, but whether this was the case or not I do not know. It is very certain that a strong political feeling existed against Joseph Smith, and I have reason to believe that his letters to Henry Clay were made use of by political parties opposed to Mr. Clay, and were the means of that statesman's defeat. Yet, if such a combination as the one referred to existed, I am not apprised of it.

Were National Characters Implicated in the Murder.

While I lay at Carthage, previous to Mrs. Taylor's arrival, a pretty good sort of a man, who was lame of a leg, waited upon me, and sat up at night with me; afterwards Mrs. Taylor, mother, and others waited upon me.

Many friends called upon me, among whom were Richard Ballantyne, Elizabeth Taylor, several of the Perkins family, and a number of the brethren from Macedonia and La Harpe. Besides these, many strangers from Quincy, some of whom expressed indignant feelings against the mob and sympathy for _{Visitors to} myself. Brother Alexander Williams called _{John Taylor.} upon me, who suspected that they had some designs in keeping me there, and stated that he had, at a given point in some woods, fifty men, and if I would say the word he would raise other fifty, and fetch me out of there. I thanked him, but told him I thought there was no need. However, it would seem that I was in some danger; for Colonel Jones, before referred to, when absent from me, left two loaded pistols on the table in case of an attack, and some time afterwards, when I had recovered and was publishing the affair, a lawyer, Mr. Backman, stated that he had prevented a man by the name of Jackson, before referred to, from ascending the stairs, who was coming with a design to murder me, and that now he was sorry he had not let him do the deed.

There were others also, of whom I heard, that said I ought to be killed, and they would do it, but that it was too damned cowardly to shoot a wounded man; and thus, by the chivalry of murderers, I was prevented from being a second time mutilated or killed. Many of the mob came around and treated me with apparent respect, and the officers and people generally looked upon me as a hostage, and feared that my removal would be the signal for the rising of the 'Mormons'.

I do not remember the time that I stayed at Carthage, but I think three or four days after the murder, when Brother Marks with a carriage, Brother James Allred with a wagon, Dr. Ells, and a number of others on horseback, came for the purpose of taking me to Nauvoo. I was very weak at the time, occasioned by the loss of blood and the great discharge of my wounds, so when my wife asked me if I could talk I could barely whisper no. Quite a discussion arose as to the propriety of my removal, the physicians and people of Carthage protesting that it would be my death, while my friends were anxious for my removal if possible.

I suppose the former were actuated by the above-named desire to keep me. Colonel Jones was, I believe, sincere; he had acted as a friend all the time, and he told Mrs. Taylor she ought to persuade me not to go, for he did not believe I had strength enough to reach Nauvoo. It was finally agreed, however, that I should go; but as it was thought that I could not stand riding in a wagon or carriage, they prepared a litter for me; I was carried downstairs and put upon it. A number of men assisted to carry me, some of whom had been engaged in the mob. As soon as I got downstairs, I felt much better and strengthened, so that I could talk; I suppose the effect of the fresh air.

Taylor's Painful Journey to Nauvoo.

When we had got near the outside of the town I remembered some woods that we had to go through, and telling a person near to call for Dr. Ells, who was riding a very good horse, I said, 'Doctor, I perceive that the people are getting fatigued with carrying me; a number of 'Mormons' live about two or three miles from here, near our route; will you ride to their settlement as quick as possible, and have them come and meet us?' He started off on a gallop immediately. My object in this was to obtain protection in case of an attack, rather than to obtain help to carry me.

Very soon after the men from Carthage made one excuse after another, until they had all left, and I felt glad to get rid of them. I found that the tramping of those carrying me produced violent pain, and a sleigh was produced and attached to the hind end of Brother James Allred's wagon, a bed placed upon it, and I propped up on the bed. Mrs. Taylor rode with me, applying ice water to my wounds. As the sleigh was dragged over the grass on the prairie, which was quite tall, it moved very easily and gave me very little pain.

When I got within five or six miles of Nauvoo the brethren commenced to meet me from the city, and they increased in number as we drew nearer, until there was a very large company of people of all ages and both sexes, principally, however, men.

For some time there had been almost incessant rain, so that in many low places on the prairie it was from one to three feet deep in water, and at such places the brethren whom we met took hold of the sleigh, lifted it, and carried it over the water; and when we arrived in the neighborhood of the city, where the roads were excessively muddy and bad, the brethren tore down the fences, and we passed through the fields.

Never shall I forget the differences of feeling that I experienced between the place that I had left and the one that I had now arrived at.   I had left a lot of reckless, bloodthirsty murderers, and had come to the City of the Saints, the people of the living God; friends of truth and righteousness, thousands of whom stood there with warm, true hearts to offer their friendship and services, and to welcome my return.   It is true it was a painful scene, and brought sorrowful remembrance to my mind, but to me it caused a thrill of joy to find myself once more in the bosom of my friends, and to meet with the cordial welcome of true, honest hearts.   What was very remarkable, I found myself very much better after my arrival at Nauvoo than I was when I started on my journey, although I had traveled eighteen miles.

The next day, as some change was wanting, I told Mrs. Taylor that if she could send to Dr. Richards, he had my purse and watch, and they would find money in my purse.

Previous to the doctor leaving Carthage, I told him that he had better take my purse and watch, for I was afraid the people would steal them.   The doctor had taken my pantaloon's pocket, and put the watch in it with the purse, cut off the pocket, and tied a string around the top; it was in this position when brought home.   My family, however, were not a little startled to find that my

Time Registrar of the Massacre.

watch had been struck with a ball. I sent for my vest, and, upon examination, it was found that there was a cut as if with a knife, in the vest pocket which had contained my watch. In the pocket the fragments of the glass were found literally ground to powder. It then occurred to me that a ball had struck me at the time I felt myself falling out of the window, and that it was this force that threw me inside. I had often remarked to Mrs. Taylor the singular fact of finding myself inside the room, when I felt a moment before after being shot, that I was falling out, and I never could account for it until then; but here the thing was fully elucidated, and was rendered plain to my mind. I was indeed falling out, when some villain aimed at my heart. The ball struck my watch, and forced me back; if I had fallen out I should assuredly have been killed, if not by the fall, by those around, and this ball, intended to dispatch me, was turned by an overruling Providence into a messenger of mercy, and saved my life. I shall never forget the feelings of gratitude that I then experienced towards my heavenly Father; the whole scene was vividly portrayed before me, and my heart melted before the Lord. I felt that the Lord had preserved me by a special act of mercy; that my time had not yet come, and that I had still a work to perform upon the earth.

[Signed]   JOHN TAYLOR.

JOHN TAYLOR'S NOTES

"In addition to the above I give the following:

Dr. Bernhisel informed me that Joseph, looking him full in the face, and as solemn as eternity, said, 'I am going as a lamb to the slaughter, but I am as calm as a summer's morning. I have a conscience void of offense toward God and man.' I heard him state, in reply to an interrogatory, made either by myself or some one in my hearing, in relation to the best course to pursue: 'I am not now acting according to my judgment; others must counsel, and not me, for the present,' or in words to the same effect.

COMMENT ON THE EXPOSITOR AFFAIR

The governor's remarks about the press may be partially correct, so far as the legal technicality was concerned, and the order of administering law. The proper way would perhaps have been for the city council to have passed a law in regard to the removal of nuisances, and then for the municipal court to have ordered it to be abated on complaint. Be this as it may, it was only a variation in form, not in fact, for the municipal court formed part of the city council, and all voted; and, furthermore, some time after the murder, Governor Ford told me that the press ought to have been removed, but that it was bad policy to remove it as we did; that if we had only let a mob do it, instead of using the law, we could have done it without difficulty, and no one would have been implicated. Thus the governor, who would have winked at the proceedings of a mob, lent his aid to, or winked at, the proceedings of mob violence in the assassination of Joseph and Hyrum Smith for removing a nuisance according to law, because of an alleged informality in the legal proceedings or a legal technicality.

I must here state that I do not believe Governor Ford would have planned the murder of Joseph and Hyrum Smith; but being a man that courted popular opinion, he had not the firmness to withstand the mob, even when that mob were seeking to imbrue their hands in the blood of innocence; he lent himself to their designs and thus became a partaker of their evil deeds.

I will illustrate this vexed question with the following official paper, which appeared in the *Deseret News*. No. 30.

'Two of the brethren arrived this evening (June 13th, 1844), from Carthage, and said that about 300 mobbers were assembled there, with the avowed intention of coming against Nauvoo. Also that Hamilton [the hotel proprietor] was paying a dollar per bushel for corn to feed their animals.'

The following was published in the *Warsaw Signal*
Office; I insert it as a specimen of the unparalleled corruption and diabolical falsehood of which the human
race has become capable in this generation:

'At a mass meeting of the citizens of Hancock county, convened at
Carthage on the 11th day of June, 1844, Mr. Knox was appointed
president, John Doty and Lewis F. Evans, vice presidents, and William
Y. Head, secretary.

'Henry Stephens, Esq. presented the following resolutions, passed
at a meeting of the citizens of Warsaw, and urged the adoption of
them as the sense of this meeting:

PREAMBLE AND RESOLUTIONS

'Whereas information has reached us, about which there can be no
question, that the authorities of Nauvoo did recently pass an ordinance
declaring a printing press and newspaper published by the opponents
of the Prophet a nuisance, and in pursuance thereof did direct the
marshal of the city and his adherents to enter by force the building
from whence the paper was issued, and violently (if necessary) to
take possession of the press and printing materials, and thereafter to
burn and destroy the same; and whereas, in pursuance of said ordinance,
the marshal and his adherents, together with a mob of Mormons, did,
after sunset on the evening of the 10th inst., violently enter said
building in a tumultuous manner, burn and destroy the press and
other materials found on the premises;

And whereas Hyrum Smith did, in the presence of the city council
and the citizens of Nauvoo, offer a reward for the destruction of the
printing press and materials of the *Warsaw Signal*, a newspaper also
opposed to his interest;

And whereas the liberty of the press is one of the cardinal principles
of our government, firmly guaranteed by the several Constitutions of
the states as well as the United States;

And whereas Hyrum Smith has within the last week publicly
threatened the life of one of our valued citizens, Thos. C. Sharp, the
editor of the *Signal*:

Therefore, be it solemnly *Resolved* by the citizens of Warsaw in
public meeting assembled,

That we view the recent ordinance of the city of Nauvoo, and the
proceedings thereunder, as an outrage of an alarming character, revolutionary and tyrannical in its tendency, and being under color of law,
as calculated to subvert and destroy in the minds of the community
all reliance on the law.

Resolved, That as a community we feel anxious, when possible,
to redress our grievances by legal remedies; but the time has now
arrived when the law has ceased to be a protection to our lives and

property; a mob at Nauvoo, under a city ordinance, has violated the highest privilege in our government, and to seek redress in the ordinary mode would be utterly ineffectual.

Resolved, That the public threat made in the council of the city not only to destroy our printing press, but to take the life of its editor, is sufficient, in connection with the recent outrage, to command the efforts and the services of every good citizen to put an immediate stop to the career of the mad Prophet and his demoniac coadjutors. We must not only defend ourselves from danger, but we must resolutely carry the war into the enemy's camp. We do therefore declare that we will sustain our press and the editor at all hazards. That we will take full vengeance—terrible vengeance, should the lives of any of our citizens be lost in the effort. That we hold ourselves at all times in readiness to cooperate with our fellow citizens in this state, Missouri, and Iowa, to *exterminate*—UTTERLY EXTER-MINATE, the wicked and abominable Mormon leaders, the authors of our troubles.

Resolved, That a committee of five be appointed forthwith to notify all persons in our township suspected of being the tools of the Prophet to leave immediately on pain of INSTANT VENGEANCE. And we do recommend the inhabitants of the adjacent townships to do the same, hereby pledging ourselves to render all the assistance they may require.

Resolved, That the time, in our opinion, has arrived when the adherents of Smith as a body, shall be driven from the surrounding settlements into Nauvoo; that the Prophet and his miscreant adherents should then be demanded at their hands, and if not surrendered, A WAR OF EXTERMINATION SHOULD BE WAGED, to the entire destruction, if necessary for our protection, of his adherents. And we do hereby recommend this resolution to the consideration of the several townships to the mass convention to be held at Carthage, hereby pledging ourselves to aid to the utmost the complete consummation of the object in view, that we may thereby be utterly relieved of the alarm, anxiety, and trouble to which we are now subjected.

Resolved, That every citizen arm himself, to be prepared to sustain the resolutions herein contained.

Mr. Roosevelt rose and made a brief but eloquent speech, and called upon the citizens throughout the country to render efficient aid in carrying out the spirit of the resolutions. Mr. Roosevelt then moved that a committee of seven be appointed by the chair to draft resolutions expressive of our action in future.

Mr. Catlin moved to amend the motion of Mr. Roosevelt so that the committee should consist of one from each precinct; which motion as amended, was adopted.

The chair then appointed the following as said committee: Colonel Levi Williams, Rocky Run precinct; Joel Catlin, Augusta; Samuel Williams, Carthage; Elisha Worrell, Chili; Captain Maddison, St.

Mary's; John M. Ferris, Fountain Green; James Rice, Pilot Grove; John Carns, Bear Creek; C. L. Higbee, Nauvoo; George Robinson, La Harpe, and George Rockwell, Warsaw.

On motion of Mr. Sympson, Walter Bagby, Esq. was requested to address the meeting during the absence of the committee. He spoke long and eloquently upon the cause of our grievances, and expressed his belief that the time was now at hand when we were individually and collectively called upon to repel the innovations upon our liberties, and suggested that points be designated as places of encampment at which to rendezvous our forces, that we may be ready, when called upon, for efficient action.

Dr. Barnes, one of the persons who went with the officers to Nauvoo for the purpose of arresting the rioters, having just arrived, came into the meeting, and reported the result of their proceedings, which was, that the persons charged in the writs were duly arrested, but taken from the officer's hands on a writ of *habeas corpus* from the municipal court and discharged, and the following potent words entered upon the records—HONORABLY DISCHARGED.

On motion of O. C. Skinner, Esq. a vote of thanks was tendered to Dr. Barnes for volunteering his services in executing said writs.

Francis M. Higbee was now loudly called for. He stated his personal knowledge of the Mormons from their earliest history, throughout their hellish career in Missouri and this state, which had been characterized by the darkest and most diabolical deeds which had ever disgraced humanity.

The committee appointed to draft resolutions brought in the following report, which after some considerable discussion, was unanimously adopted:

REPORT OF THE COMMITTEE

'Whereas the officer charged with the execution of a writ against Joseph Smith and others, for riot in the county of Hancock, which said writ said officer has served upon said Smith and others; and whereas said Smith and others refuse to obey the mandate of said writ; and whereas, in the opinion of this meeting, it is impossible for the said officer to raise a *posse* of sufficient strength to execute said writ; and whereas it is the opinion of this meeting that the riot still progressing, and that violence is meditated and determined on, it is the opinion of this meeting that the circumstances of the case require the interposition of executive power: Therefore,

'*Resolved*, That a deputation of two discreet men be sent to Springfield to solicit such interposition.

'2d. *Resolved*, That a said deputation be furnished with a certified copy of the resolution, and be authorized to obtain evidence by affidavit and otherwise in regard to the violence which has already been committed and is still farther meditated.'

Dr. Evans here rose and expressed his wish that the above resolutions would not retard our operations, but that we would each one arm and equip ourselves forthwith.

The resolutions passed at Warsaw were again read by Dr. Barnes, and passed by acclamation.

On motion of A. Sympson, Esq., the suggestion of Mr. Bagby appointing places of encampment, was adopted to wit: Warsaw, Carthage, Green Plains, Spilman's Landing, Chili, and La Harpe.

On motion, O. C. Skinner and Walter Bagby, Esqrs. were appointed a committee to bear the resolutions adopted by this meeting to his excellency the governor, requiring his executive interposition.

On motion of J. H. Sherman, a Central Corresponding Committee was appointed.

Ordered, That J. H. Sherman, H. T. Wilson, Chauncey Robinson, Wm. S. Freeman, Thomas Morrison, F. M. Higbee, Lyman Prentiss, and Stephen H. Tyler be said committee.

On motion of George Rockwell,

Resolved, That constables in the different precincts hold themselves in readiness to obey the officer in possession of the writs, whenever called upon, in summoning the posse.

On motion, the meeting adjourned.

JOHN KNOX, President.
JOHN DOTY
LEWIS F. EVANS
Vice Presidents.

W. Y. Head, Secretary.'

The following will conclude the 'Expositor Question' :

JOSEPH SMITH'S ACCOUNT OF THE EXPOSITOR AFFAIR

'Nauvoo, June 14th, 1844.

'Sir,—I write you this morning briefly to inform you of the facts relative to the removal of the press and fixtures of the *Nauvoo Expositor* as a nuisance.

'The 8th and 10th instant were spent by the city council of Nauvoo in receiving testimony concerning the character of the *Expositor*, and the character and designs of the proprietors.

'In the investigation it appeared evident to the council that the proprietors were a set of unprincipled, lawless debauches, counterfeiters, bogus-makers, gamblers, peace-disturbers, and that the grand object of said proprietors was to destroy our constitutional rights and chartered privileges; to overthrow all good and wholesome regulations in society; to strengthen themselves against the municipality; to fortify themselves against the church of which I am a member, and destroy all our religious rights and privileges by libels, slanders, falsehoods, perjury, etc. and sticking at no corruption to accomplish their hellish purposes; and that said paper of itself was libelous of the deepest dye.

and very injurious as a vehicle of defamation, tending to corrupt the morals, and disturb the peace, tranquility, and happiness of the whole community, and especially that of Nauvoo.

'After a long and patient investigation of the character of the *Expositor*, and the characters and designs of its proprietors, the Constitution, the Charter (see Addenda to Nauvoo Charter from the *Springfield Charter*, sec. 7), and all the best authorities on the subject (see *Blackstone*, iii, 5, and n, etc., etc.), the city council decided that it was necessary for the 'peace, benefit, good order, and regulations' of said city, 'and for the protection of the property', and for 'the happiness and prosperity of the citizens of Nauvoo', that said *Expositor* should be removed; and declaring said *Expositor* a nuisance, ordered the mayor to cause them to be removed without delay, which order was committed to the marshal by due process, and by him executed the same day, by removing the paper, press, and fixtures into the streets, and burning the same; all which was done without riot, noise, tumult, or confusion, as has already been proved before the municipality of the city; and the particulars of the whole transaction may be expected in our next *Nauvoo Neighbor*.

'I send you this hasty sketch that your excellency may be aware of the lying reports that are now being circulated by our enemies, that there has been a 'mob at Nauvoo', and 'blood and thunder', and 'swearing that two men were killed', etc. etc., as we hear from abroad, are false—false as satan himself could invent, and that nothing has been transacted here but what has been in perfect accordance with the strictest principles of law and good order on the part of the authorities of this city; and if your excellency is not satisfied, and shall not be satisfied, after reading the whole proceedings, which will be forthcoming soon, and shall demand an investigation of our municipality before Judge Pope, or any legal tribunal at the Capitol, you have only to write your wishes, and we will be forthcoming: we will not trouble you to file a writ, or send an officer for us.

'I remain, as ever, a friend to truth, good order, and your excellency's humble servant,

[Signed]   JOSEPH SMITH.

'His Excellency Thomas Ford.' "*

*See Tyler's *History of the Mormon Battalion*, Introduction, in which the Taylor document is published almost completely, also Captain Richard F. Burton's *City of the Saints*, 1862, Appendix III, pp. 517-547. The letter inserted by Burton at pp. 526-7. however, is not the letter to which Joseph Smith took exception (see p. 78 this volume) but is the letter received from Governor Ford written on his arrival at Carthage June 21, 1844, in which he asks for a committee to be sent to him giving the Latter-day Saint version of the proceedings which had taken place in Nauvoo up to that time. B. H. R.

IV

HISTORIANS' SECOND COMPILATION OF HISTORICAL ITEMS OF CHURCH HISTORY, FROM 22ND OF JUNE, 1844, TO 8TH OF AUGUST, 1844.

Explanation

PART IV is a second compilation following Period I of this *History,* made by the Church Historians George A. Smith and Wilford Woodruff from the Journals of Willard Richards, Wilford Woodruff and others and was published in the *Millennial Star,* 1862, Vol. xxiv, pp. 598-792; and 1863, Vol. xxv, pp. 6-280. See also *Deseret News,* Vol. vii, Dec. 9, 1857 to Jan. 20, 1858. This will comprise chapters xi to xix inclusive.

CHAPTER XI

MISCELLANEOUS EVENTS APART FROM THE MAJOR
FACTS OF THE MARTYRDOM OF THE PROPHET
AND PATRIARCH FROM JUNE 22, 1844,
TO JUNE 29, 1844.

"*Saturday, June 22, 1844.*—In the evening Major-
General Dunham issued orders to all the guards and
sentries on the road to La Harpe, to let persons pass
and repass, until further orders, except they discover
companies of men, when they must report the same to
headquarters immediately.

A conference was held at Eagle, Benton county,
Tennessee, Elder A. O. Smoot presiding,
during which a branch was organized of
seventeen members.   One elder, one priest
and one teacher were ordained.

Varied Incidents of Activity in the Church.

Sunday, 23.—At 5 a. m., [at Nauvoo] A. P. Rockwood and John Scott asked advice what to do with
the cannon, etc.

William Clayton got the public records together
and buried them.

5 p. m.—Captain Anderson, of the steamer *Osprey,*
conversed with Joseph, saying the mob at Warsaw
threatened firing into his vessel.

President Brigham Young attended meeting at
Lowell, Massachusetts.

Elder Heber C. Kimball preached at Wilmington,
Delaware, in the forenoon, to an attentive congrega-
tion: he had a chill after he got through.   Elder Lyman
Wight spoke in the afternoon.

A conference was held at Kirtland, and was addressed by Elder Lorenzo Snow and others.   Twelve
persons were baptized and confirmed, and eight ordained elders.

Monday, 24.—

AFFIDAVIT OF J. R. WAKEFIELD

'Territory of Iowa,⎰ sct.
Henry County. ⎱

Dr. J. R. Wakefield being duly sworn, deposeth and sayeth, that on the 10th of June he, in company with two others, went on the hill in the city of Nauvoo, and in the neighborhood of the printing press of the *Nauvoo Expositor*, when a company of men approached, headed by the marshal of the city, Mr. Greene, some armed, but not many. After marching in front of the printing office, the marshal demanded the keys of the office, in behalf of the mayor and municipal court of Nauvoo, to destroy the press, type and appurtenances of said press, and burn them in the street.

Calm Procedure in Destroying the Nauvoo Expositor Press.

Mr. Higbee replied, in behalf of the whole of the editors of said newspaper, that he would not give up the key—that he set the court and city at defiance, and should hold them and the marshal responsible for their acts in this affair.

Accordingly orders were given to an officer of the company to forcibly take from the building the press, and destroy it according to order. It was done without any noise, or confusion, shouting, or riotous proceedings, and further deponent saith not.

[Signed] J. R. WAKEFIELD.

Sworn to and subscribed before me this 24th day of June, 1844.

A. McKINNEY, J. P.'

Tuesday, 25.—Elder Cahoon returned from Carthage for some papers, which were sent out by A. P. Rockwood.

Orrin P. Rockwell met F. M. Higbee about 4 p. m. and accused him of seeking Joseph's life. Higbee made use of some very insulting language in reply, when a scuffle ensued, during which a letter dropped out of Higbee's hat, which stated that there were seventy of the mob ready in Iowa to come upon Nauvoo tonight.

F. M. Higbee's Designs Against the Prophet's Life.

It is currently reported that the mob intend to make a rush on the jail tonight.

A strong guard placed in and round the city.

About 9 p. m. it began to rain very heavily.

Wednesday, 26.— 8 a. m., Captain Singleton arrived, with about sixty mounted militia, to protect the city in case a mob should come against it. He was authorized to take command of the police, and to use such measures as he might consider necessary.

He read his orders from the governor, and wanted to know if our men would obey his orders, when the brethren responded 'yes', whereupon notification was sent to the police to meet at 6 p. m., in the Masonic Hall. He further reported that Dr. Foster had given him information at Carthage, where he would find three presses in Nauvoo, for making bogus money, and said that he wanted to get hold of them.

6 p. m.—The police assembled in the Seventies' Hall, and entered into a temporary organization to act under Captain Singleton. Many of the regular police being officers of the Legion, and on active service, their places were filled for the time.

At midnight Captain Singleton sent a notification to the major-general's quarters, that he wanted the Nauvoo Legion to be in readiness for parade at an hour's notice, when notifications were sent to the colonels of the several regiments accordingly.

Thursday, 27.—About 9 a. m., John P. Greene arrived in Nauvoo with subpœnas for witnesses for the expected trial on Saturday the 29th instant.

At 10 a. m., orders were received from Captain Singleton, to call out that portion of the Nauvoo Legion resident within the limits of the city, for review at noon. General Dunham immediately issued similar orders to the commandants.

At noon about two-thirds of the Legion turned out to parade, nearly all of whom were well armed, although all the state arms had been taken away, which caused Captain Singleton and his company to express their astonishment. The captain made a remark to the effect that it would not do to come against such a force as this. The Legion was soon dismissed, on account of a messenger from the governor reporting that all the troops were dismissed, except a small escort which was with him.

5 *p. m.*—Governor Ford, with about fifty men arrived at the Mansion, and gave notice that he would

The Arrival of Governor Ford in Nauvoo.

shortly address the citizens. In about half an hour he ascended the frame of a building opposite the Mansion, and addressed the people.

WHEREABOUTS OF THE TWELVE—THEIR DEPRESSION OF SPIRIT

We here insert the location of the Twelve Apostles on this memorable day:—

President Brigham Young and Elder Wilford Woodruff spent a portion of the day together in the city of Boston, and were sitting together in the railway depot at the time of the massacre of the Prophets; they felt very sorrowful, and depressed in spirits, without knowing the cause.

Elders Heber C. Kimball and Lyman Wight traveled from Philadelphia to New York by railway and steamboat. Elder Kimball felt very mournful as though he had lost some friend, and knew not the cause.

Elder Orson Hyde was in the hall occupied by the saints in Boston, examining maps, and designating or pointing out each man's district or field of labor, in company with Elders Brigham Young, Wilford Woodruff and others, a part of the day. He felt very heavy and sorrowful in spirit, and knew not the cause, but felt no heart to look on the maps. He retired to the further end of the hall alone, and walked the floor; tears ran down his face * * * . He never felt so before, and knew no reason why he should feel so then.

Elder Parley P. Pratt was on the canal boat between Utica and Buffalo, N. Y., on his return to Nauvoo, and was much depressed in spirit; his brother William Pratt came on board of the same boat, and Parley asked him if he had any books or pamphlets containing the gospel of Christ, or the words of life; if so, to put them under lock and key, for the people are not worthy of them for, said Parley, 'I feel that the spirit of murder is in the hearts of the people through the land.'

Elders Willard Richards and John Taylor were the only two of the Quorum of the Twelve who were not on missions, and the only two men who were with the martyrs when they fell and sealed their testimony with their blood.

Elder George A. Smith rode with Elder Crandall Dunn, from Napoleon, to Elder Noah Willis Bartholomew's, near Jacksonburg, Jackson county, Michigan, and felt unusually cast down and depressed in spirits. About five o'clock he repaired to an oak grove, and called upon the Lord, endeavoring to break the spell of horror which had dominion over his mind. He remained there a long time without finding any relief, and then went back to Brother Bartholomew's, and went to bed with Elder Crandall Dunn; he could not sleep, but spent the night in a series of miserable thoughts and reflections. Once it seemed to him that some fiend whispered in his ear, 'Joseph and Hyrum are dead; ain't you glad of it?'

Elder Amasa Lyman was in the city of Cincinnati, and felt that depression of spirit mentioned by his brethren.

Friday, 28.—News arrived in Nauvoo at daylight, that Joseph and Hyrum were murdered yesterday while in jail, committed upon an illegal mittimus by Robert F. Smith, justice of the peace and captain of the company stationed at the jail.

News of the Martyrdom of the Prophets Brought to Nauvoo.

General Deming issued the following proclamation:

PROCLAMATION OF GENERAL DEMING TO THE PEOPLE OF HANCOCK COUNTY

'Headquarters, June 28, 1844.
4 o'clock, a. m.

To the Citizens of Carthage and Hancock County:

In pursuance of an order from Governor Ford, instructing me to the exercise of such discretionary powers as I may deem necessary for the preservation of the public safety, and the lives and property of our citizens; I hereby invite all citizens to remain at their several homes in Hancock county and cooperate with me in establishing tranquility and safety throughout the county.

The most efficient means have been put in requisition for concentrating the military force of the neighboring counties at Carthage, and in twelve hours there will be a sufficient force for the protection of every citizen in the county.

I confidently believe there is no just apprehension of an attack upon any place by the Mormon citizens of our county. And I hereby strictly command all citizens of Hancock county to abstain from violence towards the Mormon population, under penalty of the severest inflictions of military law, and act in no case only on the defensive.

The corpses of the murdered men will be forthwith removed to Nauvoo, under an escort from headquarters.

Given under my hand this 28th June, 1844, 4 o'clock, a. m.

[Signed]   M. R. DEMING, Brigadier-General.
4th Brigade and 5th Division.

It is hoped and expected that the governor will be at headquarters in a few hours.'

At 7½ a. m., General Dunham issued orders for the whole of the Legion to meet on the parade ground, east of the Temple, at 10 a. m.   They met accordingly, when addresses were delivered, and exhortations given to the saints to keep quiet, and not to let their violently outraged feelings get the better of them.

The Nauvoo Legion Ordered Out—"Keep Quiet".

About noon a council of officers of the Legion was held, and from thence they went to meet the sad procession that accompanied the bodies of the murdered Prophet and Patriarch.

Arrival of the Bodies of the Martyrs at Nauvoo.

At 2½ p. m., the corpses arrived at Mulholland Street, on two wagons, guarded by a few men from Carthage, and nearly all the citizens collected together and followed the bodies to the Mansion, where the multitude were addressed by Dr. Richards, W. W. Phelps, and Messrs. Woods and Reid, who exhorted the people to be peaceable and calm and use no threats.

We here insert the names of Joseph's bodyguard:—

Alpheus Cutler, capt.	John Snyder,
Amos C. Hodge,	Christian Kreymer,
James Allred,	Lewis D. Wilson,
Thomas Grover,	William Marks,
Reynolds Cahoon,	James Emmet,
Shadrach Roundy,	John S. Butler,

Samuel H. Smith,

Edward Hunter, herald and armor bearer.

The following are the names of the martial band:—

NAMES OF THE NAUVOO LEGION BAND

E. P. Duzette, major,
L. W. Hancock, fife major,
Dimick B. Huntington, drum major,
Elisha Everett, leader,

William Carter,	——— Lyon,
Dominicus Carter,	Aroet Hale,
James W. Cummings,	Abram Day,
Joseph Richards,	L. W. Hardy,
Geo. W. Taggart,	Willard Smith,
Wm. D. Huntington,	Stephen Wilber,
Jesse Earl,	Lewis Hardy,
J. M. King,	James Leithead,
H. B. Jacobs,	J. M. Frink,
A. J. Clothier,	Eleazer King,
Sylvester Duzette,	——— Sprague.

In the afternoon Elders Heber C. Kimball, Lyman Wight, William Smith and wife, went by railway cars and steamboat to Boston.

Saturday, 29.—The Legion was out all last night, expecting a mob to come.

The following is from a letter addressed to President Joseph Smith, from Elders Lyman Wight and Heber C. Kimball:—

*LETTER FROM ELDERS LYMAN WIGHT AND HEBER C. KIMBALL TO
JOSEPH SMITH*

'Philadelphia, Pa., June 19, 1844.

To my well beloved brother and fellow prisoner, President Joseph
Smith—*

I take this opportunity of giving you an abridged history of my
transactions, together with Brother Heber C. Kimball, my fellow
traveler. We left Nauvoo the 21st day of May, amidst the acclama-
tions of three cheers from the shore, 'Joseph Smith, the next President
of the United States!'

We passed smoothly down the river; there were 165 passengers
on board the boat *Osprey*. I was called upon to deliver a political
address, and to show what right Joseph Smith had
to the presidential chair, which I did to the entire satisfaction of nearly all the passengers on board, not forgetting
at the same time to show that the other candidates had disqualified
themselves to all the right and title, by acts of meanness.

Lyman Wight's Political Address.

Whilst speaking of their mean acts I was frequently interrupted
with loud laughing and clapping of hands, by way of approbation.
A vote being taken on the presidential question, Joseph Smith received
a large majority over all the other candidates.

We reached St. Louis on the 22nd at 10 a. m. Here Brothers
Young and Kimball called the church together and instructed them
spiritually and politically. We learned that the church at St. Louis
numbered nearly 700 souls.

On the 23rd we left St. Louis on board the boat *Louis Phillippe*,
at half past 12 o'clock, with about 200 passengers on board; many
of the same that were on the *Osprey*, together with many new passengers.

There were at first some little prejudices existing, but
President Brigham Young, being called upon, delivered
a discourse upon the principles of our doctrine, which
entirely allayed the prejudices.

Brigham Young's Address on the Steamboat.

Next evening Brother William Smith was called upon to deliver
an address, which he did in the power and demonstration of the
spirit, and we were afterwards looked upon as their superiors.

On the 26th we reached Cincinnati, at 6 o'clock, p. m. Elders
Young and Kimball went to visit the church in that city, whilst I
changed our luggage on board the boat *Neptune* for Pittsburgh.
All the passengers on board the *Louis Phillippe* being bound for
Pittsburgh, came with us.

At 8 a. m. on the 27th, we held a conference with the elders in
Cincinnati. I addressed them on the subject of politics,
and perseverance in duty, and the great necessity of
reform in government. I was followed by Brothers
Kimball and Young on the same subjects.

Members of the Twelve in Conference at Cincinnati.

*This has reference to their imprisonment together in Liberty prison, Missouri,
winter of 1838. B. H. R.

We then instructed them to have 2,000 copies of your views on the Powers and Policy of the Government printed, and for the elders to scatter them with the velocity of lightning and the voice of thunder.

I had nearly forgotten to mention an important occurrence on board of the *Louis Phillippe*, with a Mr. David Guard, of Lawrenceburgh, Indiana: he is worth from $200,000 to $300,000; he emigrated to Cincinnati when there were but three log cabins in that place. He gave me his views on politics, which completely corresponded with yours. I then gave him two copies of your 'Views'. He was highly pleased with them, and pledged his word he would have them published in both the Lawrenceburgh papers, as they were both published under his roof, and if they did not comply with so reasonable a request, they (the editors) would have to seek shelter elsewhere.

A Pioneer Cincinnatian for Joseph Smith for President of the United States.

He also stated that Joseph Smith was the first man since the days of Washington and Jefferson, who had been frank and honest enough to give his views to the people before being elected; and said, that he would go his whole length for such a man, and that if you were not elected this time, you would be the next: let this be an ensample of numerous other cases, as you know it would be too irksome to write them all, or read them.

To return to the subject, at ten o'clock this morning (the 27th), we left for Pittsburgh with an addition of passengers. On this boat I was called upon to deliver an address showing the utility of the *Book of Mormon*, and the present situation of the world, which I did, and by this time we had a complete victory over both priests and people. On this boat a large majority of votes were given for yourself for president.

The Apostles en route for Pittsburgh.

We arrived at Pittsburgh on the 30th at 6 p. m. Here we left President Brigham Young. Brothers William Smith, Heber C. Kimball and myself left Pittsburgh on the 31st of May, at 10 o'clock, from thence by steamer, stage and railway, we passed over hills and dales, arriving at Washington city [D. C.] on the 2nd of June, preaching to, and thorning everybody with politics that came in our way.

Thus after a journey of thirteen days we arrived in the great metropolis of the United States; which, by-the-by, with the exception of the Pennsylvania Avenue, more resembles the *Methodist slough of despond* than anything like a decent city.

Lyman Wight in Washington, D. C.— Impressions.

At this time, being near the close of the session, [congress] it was filled up with demagogues, jackleg lawyers and blackleg gamblers, and *everything else but intelligence*. The senators and representatives generally rise at 8 o'clock in the morning, prepare themselves for business about 11 o'clock, commonly return at 3 and 4 in the afternoon. From 6 till 9 is the only time we could do any business whatever, hence we prepared and watched our opportunity, and did all the business we could betwixt those hours, for ten days, pleading the cause of the poor and oppressed.

We have got a petition signed, with our names attached, in behalf of the church, asking for a remuneration for our losses, and not for our rights, or redress, for they would not receive such a petition from

Petition to Congress for "Remuneration of Losses" of the Church in Missouri.

us. It was thought by Judge Semple, Judge Douglas, General [David R.] Atchison and Major Hughs, that our petition would carry if it was not too late in the season. Judge Semple handed it to the chairman of the Committee on Public Lands. He said he would do the best he could for us. General Atchison is of the opinion if we could sue the state of Missouri for redress of grievances, that there was virtue enough in the state to answer our demands, 'for', said he, 'they are ashamed of their conduct.' Douglas and Semple are of the same opinion.

Brother Kimball and myself spared no pains during our stay at Washington: we found six members of the church, and many attentive hearers. We purpose sending a steady, faithful elder, who we think can build up a large church. We found our time too limited to meet the conferences and transact our business, to tarry longer at present, but shall return, if we find it necessary, after the Baltimore Convention; for we will never leave them, nor forsake them, nor return home, while we think there is a stone unturned, or a conscience that is not harrowed up by our continued preaching.

On the 11th instant we left Washington, and arrived at Brother Saunders', Wilmington, Delaware, at 5 o'clock the same evening, distance 114 miles. We can assure you we found everything right in this place, and adjacent to it. We found about 100 members, and held two meetings with them, appointing a conference on the 22nd and 23rd inst.

On the 13th at 2 p. m., we left this place for Philadelphia, and arrived at Brother William Smith's at 5 p. m. Brother Kimball being exposed, had a slight attack of the chills and fever. Since that time we have preached alternately.

Members of the Twelve at Philadelphia— Righteousness and Union of Joseph and the Twelve Affirmed.

The church here numbers nearly 200, out of which number many have commenced sickening, and were growing faint at the many false reports in circulation, fearing that the Prophet had fallen and the Twelve were in transgression, but they have since learned that the Prophet is right, and that the Twelve are with him, and they are beginning to revive; they have stood six tremendous shocks, and I think if they stand the seventh, which is to come tomorrow evening they will survive.

We shall call on them to know whether they intend to gather with the living and sustain the cause of God by the mouth of his Prophets and Apostles, or die in Philadelphia. If they should choose the latter, we shall attend to the funeral ceremonies, and leave them to rest with the dead, and we will go on our way among the living.

If they should choose the former, we shall expect a glorious work in this place.

We shall leave here on the 21st for Wilmington, to attend conference, we shall then return to this place, and from here to New York and Boston, to meet the conferences in those cities, and so continue from place to place until we shall have accomplished the mission appointed unto us."*

*This letter represents Elder Lyman Wight at his best, and shows him to be an Apostle of the Lord Jesus of no inferior order. B. H. R.

CHAPTER XII

MOVEMENTS IN HANCOCK COUNTY, CARTHAGE,
NAUVOO, WARSAW AND QUINCY, FOR THE MAINTE-
NANCE OF PEACE FOLLOWING THE MARTYRDOM: LIST
OF THE NAMES OF THOSE WHO WERE IN THE MOB
ASSEMBLED TO SLAY THE PROPHET

"Saturday, June 29th, 1844.—About noon, General H. Swazey, of Iowa, called at Nauvoo and offered
assistance to the people.

The following article from Governor Ford, was
published in the *Times and Seasons:*—

GOVERNOR FORD TO THE PEOPLE OF THE STATE OF ILLINOIS

'I desire to make a brief, but true statement of the recent disgraceful
affair at Carthage, in regard to the Smiths, so far as circumstances
have come to my knowledge.

The Smiths, Joseph and Hyrum, have been assassinated in jail, by
whom it is not known, but will be ascertained. I pledged myself
for their safety, and upon the assurance of that pledge they surrendered
as prisoners. The Mormons surrendered the public arms in their
possession, and the Nauvoo Legion submitted to the command of
Captain Singleton, of Brown county, deputed for that purpose by me.

All these things were required to satisfy the old citizens of Hancock
that the Mormons were peaceably disposed, and to allay jealousy and
excitement in their minds.

It appears, however, that the compliance of the Mormons with
every requisition made upon them, failed of that purpose. The pledge
of security to the Smiths was not given upon my individual responsibility. Before I gave it, I obtained a pledge of honor by a unanimous
vote from the officers and men under my command, to sustain me in
performing it. If the assassination of the Smiths was committed by
any portion of these, they have added treachery to murder, and
have done all they could to disgrace the state, and sully the public
honor.

On the morning of the day the deed was committed, we had
proposed to march the army under my command into Nauvoo. I
had, however, discovered on the evening before, that nothing but

utter destruction of the city would satisfy a portion of the troops; and that if we marched into the city, pretexts would not be wanting for commencing hostilities. The Mormons had done everything required, or which ought to have been required of them. Offensive operations on our part would have been as unjust and disgraceful as they would have been impolitic in the present critical season of the year, the harvest and the crops. For these reasons I decided, in a council of officers to disband the army, except three companies, two of which were reserved as a guard for the jail.

With the other company I marched into Nauvoo, to address the inhabitants there, and tell them what they might expect in case they designedly or imprudently provoked a war. I performed this duty as I think plainly and emphatically, and then set out to return to Carthage.

When I had marched about three miles, a messenger informed me of the occurrences at Carthage. I hastened on to that place. The guard, it is said, did their duty, but were overpowered. Many of the inhabitants of Carthage had fled with their families. Others were preparing to go. I apprehended danger to the settlements from the sudden fury and passion of the Mormons, and sanctioned their movements in this respect.

General Deming volunteered to remain with a few troops to observe the progress of events, to defend property against small numbers, and with orders to retreat if menaced by a superior force. I decided to proceed immediately to Quincy, to prepare a force sufficient to suppress disorders, in case it should ensue from the foregoing transactions, or from any other cause. I have hopes that the Mormons will make no further difficulties. In this I may be mistaken. The other party may not be satisfied. They may recommence aggression.

I am determined to preserve the peace against all breakers of the same, at all hazards. I think present circumstances warrant the precaution of having a competent force at my disposal, in readiness to march at a moment's warning. My position at Quincy will enable me to get the earliest intelligence, and to communicate orders with great celerity.

I have decided to issue the following general orders:

GOVERNOR FORD'S GENERAL ORDERS TO THE MILITIA IN THE WESTERN COUNTIES OF ILLINOIS

'Headquarters, Quincy,
June 29, 1844.

It is ordered that the commandants of regiments in the counties of Adams, Marquette, Pike, Brown, Schuyler, Morgan, Scott, Cass, Fulton and McDonough, and the regiments composing General Stapp's brigade, will call their respective regiments and battalions together immediately upon the receipt of this order, and proceed by voluntary enlistment to enroll as many men as can be armed in their respective regiments. They will make arrangements for a campaign of twelve days, and will provide themselves with arms, ammunition and provisions accordingly, and hold themselves in readiness immediately to march upon the receipt of further orders.

The independent companies of riflemen, infantry, cavalry, and artillery in the above-named counties, and in the county of Sangamon will hold themselves in readiness in like manner.

[Signed] Thomas Ford,

Governor and Commander-in-Chief.'

Saturday, 29, 1 p. m.—Mayor Wood and ex-Mayor Conyers, from Quincy, arrived from the governor's

Movement of
Quincy Troops
to Warsaw.

headquarters, and said 244 troops from Quincy had arrived in Warsaw to protect the innocent, and they had come to ascertain the feelings of the people, and adopt measures to allay excitement.

We copy the following letter from Sheriff J. B. Backenstos:—

ROLL OF CARTHAGE GREYS AND OFFICERS JUNE 27th, A. D. 1844.

Robert F. Smith, Captain.

F. A. Worrell, ⎫
S. O. Williams, ⎬ Lieutenants.
M. Barnes, Jun., ⎭

Guard at the Jail, June 27, 1844.

F. A. Worrell, officer of the guard.

Franklin Rhodes.

William Baldwin.

Levi Street, lives near Mendon, Adams county, Illinois.

Joseph Hawley, lives in Carthage, Illinois.

Anthony Barkman, lives in Carthage, Illinois.

Clabourn Wilson, lives in Carthage, Illinois.

Balance of [Company of] *Greys.*

Edwin Baldwin, lives near Carthage, Ill.
James D. Barnes,   "   "
Frederick Loring,   in   "
Leyrand Doolittle,   "   "

Marvin Hamilton, lives in Carthage, Ill.
Ebenezer Rand,   "   "
John W. Maith,   "   "
Thomas Griffith,   "   "
Lewis C. Stevenson.   "   "
Noah M. Reckard,   "   "
Eli H. Williams,   "   "
H. T. Wilson,   "   "
Albert Thompson,   "   "
Walter Bagby, left the country, gone to Louisiana, and died.
George C. Waggoner, lives 2½ miles north of Carthage.
Crocket Wilson, lives 8 miles east of Carthage.
Thomas J. Dale,   5   "   "   "
Richard Dale,   5   "   "   "

The Carthage Greys never numbered more than about thirty, rank and file; during the June mob war, several joined for the time only, who reside at other places, and whose names are unknown to me. The Carthage Greys were nearly to a man parties in the June massacre.

Green Plains.

Captain Weir's company of about sixty men.

Warsaw.

Captain J. C. Davis' company of about sixty men.
Captain Wm. N. Grover's company of about sixty men.
Captain Mark Aldrich's company of about sixty men, comprising the entire settlement in and about Warsaw and Green Plains, with the exception of the Walkers, Gillhams, Paytons, Bledsors, Gallahers, Byrrs, Kimballs, Worthens, Summervilles, and Bedells, and the Mormon families who resided in that part of the county at that time.

Those active in the massacre at Carthage—supplied by Sheriff
J. B. Backenstos

The leaders of the Hancock mob, and those who took an active part in the massacre of Joseph and Hyrum Smith are—

Thomas C. Sharp, *Warsaw Signal*, Illinois, editor.
Colonel Levi Williams, Green Plains, Illinois, farmer.
William N. Grover, Warsaw, Illinois, lawyer.
Jacob C. Davis, Warsaw, Illinois, lawyer.
Mark Aldrich, Warsaw, Illinois, no business.
Henry Stephens, Warsaw, Illinois, lawyer.
George Rockwell, Warsaw, Illinois, druggist.

James H. Wood, Warsaw, Illinois, blacksmith.
Calvin Cole, Warsaw, Illinois, tavernkeeper.
William B. Chipley, Warsaw, Illinois, doctor.
———— Hays, Warsaw, Illinois, doctor.
J. D. Mellen, Warsaw, Illinois, merchant.
E. W. Gould, Warsaw, Illinois, merchant.
Samuel Fleming, Warsaw, Illinois, constable.
John Montague, Warsaw, Illinois, no business.
Jas. Gregg, Warsaw, Illinois, no business.
J. C. Elliot, Warsaw, Illinois, no business.
Lyman Prentiss, Warsaw, Illinois, no business.
D. W. Matthews, now St. Louis, Missouri, merchant.
J. B. Matthews, now St. Louis, Missouri, merchant.
Trueman Hosford, Warsaw, Illinois, farmer.
Four of the Chittendens, Warsaw, Illinois, different occupations.
J. W. Athey, Warsaw, Illinois, no business.
Onias C. Skinner, now of Quincy, Illinois, lawyer.
Calvin A. Warren, Quincy, Illinois, lawyer.
George W. Thatcher, Carthage, Illinois, county clerk.
James W. Brattle, Carthage, Illinois, land shark.
Alexander Sympson, Carthage, Illinois, land shark.
Jason H. Sherman, Carthage, Illinois, lawyer.
Michael Reckard, one-half mile west of Carthage, Illinois, farmer.
Thomas Morrison, Carthage, Illinois, lawyer.
E. S. Freeman, Carthage, Illinois, blacksmith.
Thomas L. Barnes, Carthage, Illinois, quack doctor.
John Wilson, Carthage, Illinois, tavernkeeper.
Edward Jones, 5 miles north of Carthage, farmer.
Captain James E. Dunn, Augusta, Illinois, tavernkeeper.
Joel Catlin, Augusta, Illinois, farmer, etc.
William D. Abernethy, Augusta, Illinois, farmer, etc.
Erastus Austin, constable, etc.
———— Austin, loafer.
Reuben Graves, St. Mary's, Illinois, farmer.
Henry Garnett, St. Mary's, Illinois, farmer.
F. J. Bartlett, St. Mary's, Illinois, miller.
Valentine Wilson, St. Mary's, Illinois, farmer.
Sylvester M. Bartlett, editor of the *Quincy Whig.*
Major W. B. Warren, a damned villain.
Colonel ———— Gettis, Fountain Green, Illinois, farmer.
Matthews McClaughny, Fountain Green, Illinois, farmer.
Nickerson Wright, Fountain Green, Illinois, farmer.
John McAuley, Camp Creek Precinct, Illinois, one of the worst men
in Hancock.
William H. Rollason, Pontusuc, Illinois.
John M. Finch, Pontusuc, Illinois.
Francis M. Higbee, Pontusuc, Illinois.

———————— Douglass, Pontusuc, Illinois, schoolmaster.

George Backman, one of the Durfee murderers.*

———————— Moss or Morse, one of the Durfee murderers.

Jacob Beck, one of the Durfee murderers.

Backman lives in Carthage, Moss or Morse, and Jacob Beck have left the country, but expect to return.

The foregoing is a pretty large list: there are others of the smaller fry which I deem unworthy of notice, inasmuch as they were led on through the influence of the leaders, and whiskey. I most cheerfully give you any information in my power in reference to this matter; the only thing that I regret about is, that these things I am fearful will be put off so long that I will not live to see or hear of the awful vengeance which will in the end overtake the Hancock assassins. I have long been of the opinion that forebearance is no longer a virtue, let the guilty be made to answer for their crimes. Let justice be done, and all will be well.

The bloodhounds are still determined on taking my life; I can hear from them every once in a while. I will have to be exceedingly careful this summer, or they will have my scalp. They still act upon the principle that had it not been for me in September last, Worrell and McBradney would not have been killed, and the city of Nauvoo burned to the ground. They want to hold me responsible for everything that was done to put them down in their mob doings last year.

In reference to my correspondence with the governor, I will say that I received but two letters from him during the difficulty, neither of which were received until after the arrival of General Hardin and the [state] government troops.

In my communications to Governor Ford, in relation to the riots in Hancock county, I made but one request of him, and that was, that no troops ought to be brought into Hancock county; that I had sufficient power within the limits of the county to suppress any further riots, and prevent any more burning.

I am certain that the letters which I received from the governor were either left in your hands, or in the hands of some one in your office at Nauvoo; at least I have not got them now. I recollect that you desired to get them for future use, and am sorry that I cannot forward them to you. You will find in my Proclamations† the historical part of the last mob war in Hancock.'

The following list is from the pen of Dr. Willard Richards:——

*The Durfee murder occurred at Green Plains in Hancock county, Illinois, during the renewal of mob violence in the latter part of 1845 (See Jenson's *Chronology,* November, 1845, also *Comprehensive History of the Church,* Century I, vol. ii, ch. lxvii). B. H. R.

†These Proclamations are five in number, and will be found *in extenso* in the *Comprehensive History of the Church,* Century I, vol. ii, pp. 490-503. B. H. R.

LIST OF THE MOB AT CARTHAGE ACCORDING TO WILLARD RICHARDS

'William Law,   Wm. A. Rollason,
Wilson Law,   Wm. H. J. Marr,
Robert D. Foster,   S. M. Marr,
Charles A. Foster,   Sylvester Emmons,
Francis M. Higbee,   Alexander Sympson,
Chauncey L. Higbee,   John Eagle,
Joseph H. Jackson,   Henry O. Norton,
John M. Finch,   Augustine Spencer.

The foregoing have been aided and abetted by—Charles Ivins and family, P. T. Rolfe, N. J. Higbee.

William Cook, and Sarah, his wife, formerly Sarah Crooks, of Manchester.'

Sunday, 30.—The governor wrote to General Deming, as follows:—

COMMUNICATION OF GOVERNOR FORD TO GENERAL DEMING

'Headquarters, Quincy, June 30, 1844.

Sir.—It is my present opinion that the Mormons will not commit any outbreak, and that no further alarm need be apprehended. I regret to learn that the party in Hancock, who are in favor of violent measures have circulated a thousand false rumors of danger, for the purpose of getting men together without my authority, hoping that when assembled, they may be ready to join in their violent councils. This is a fraud upon the country, and must not be endured.

I am afraid that the people of Hancock are fast depriving themselves of the sympathy of their fellow citizens, and of the world. I strictly order and enjoin on you that you permit no attack on Nauvoo or any of the people there without my authority. I think it would be best to disband your forces, unless it should be necessary to retain them to suppress violence on either side: of this you must be the judge at present.

I direct that you immediately order all persons from Missouri and Iowa to leave the camp and return to their respective homes without delay.

I direct, also, that you cause all mutinous persons, and all persons who advise tumultuous proceedings to be arrested; and that you take energetic measures to stop the practice of spreading false reports put in circulation to inflame the public mind.

[Signed] THOMAS FORD, Commander-in-Chief.

To Brigadier-General Deming, Carthage, Ill.'

A few of the brethren met in council, and agreed to send Brother George J. Adams to bear the news of the massacre to the Twelve.

Elder Willard Richards wrote the following, and sent it by George J. Adams:—

WILLARD RICHARDS TO BRIGHAM YOUNG—NAUVOO AFFAIRS, INCLUDING THE MARTYRDOM

'Nauvoo, Sunday, June 30, 1844,
6 p. m.

Beloved Brother Brigham Young,—For the first moment we have had the opportunity, by request of such brethren of the council as we could call, we write to inform you of the situation of affairs in Nauvoo and elsewhere.

On the 24*th inst.*, Joseph, Hyrum, and thirteen others went to Carthage, and gave themselves up to Robert F. Smith, a justice of the peace, on charge of riot, for destroying the *Nauvoo Expositor* press and apparatus.

25*th*. Were exhibited by Governor Ford to the troops assembled, like elephants,—gave bonds for appearance at court, were arrested on charge of treason, and committed to jail without examination.

26*th*. Brought out to the courthouse contrary to law, for examination,—returned to jail till witnesses could be procured.

27*th*. A little before 6 p. m. the jail was forced by an armed, disguised mob, of from 150 to 200; the guard was frustrated, Hyrum shot in the nose and throat and two other places, only saying, '*I am a dead man*'. Elder Taylor received four balls in left leg and left wrist and hand. Joseph received four bullets, one in right collar bone, one in right breast, and two others in his back, he leaped from the east window of the front room, and was dead in an instant. I remained unharmed. The bodies were removed to Nauvoo on the 28th, and buried on the 29th. Elder Taylor remains at Hamilton's Tavern yet; we heard today he is better.

Elder George J. Adams is deputed to convey this to you, together with today's *Extra Nauvoo Neighbor*, and other papers giving particulars which you may rely on.

The effect of this hellish butchery was like the bursting of a tornado on Carthage and Warsaw; those villages were without inhabitants, as in an instant they ran for their lives, lest the Mormons should burn and kill them suddenly—'the wicked flee when no man pursueth'.

The excitement has been great, but the indignation more terrible: a reaction is taking place, and men of influence are coming from abroad to learn the facts, and going away satisfied that the Mormons are not the aggressors.

You now know our situation, and the request of the council is, that the Twelve return to Nauvoo. The lives of twelve more are threatened with deadly threats. It has been suggested by the council, that if the Twelve approved, President Brigham Young, Heber C. Kimball, George A. Smith, Wilford Woodruff and Orson Pratt return immediately; and William Smith, whose life is threatened, with all the Smiths, John E. Page, Lyman Wight, Parley P. Pratt and Orson Hyde spend a little time in publishing the news in the eastern cities, and getting as many in the church as possible. This is for you to decide.

The saints have borne this trial with great fortitude and forbearance. They must keep cool at present. We have pledged our faith not to prosecute the murderers at present, but leave it to Governor Ford; if he fails, time enough for us by and by; vengeance is in the heavens. We have been in close quarters some time,—money and provisions are scarce. Will the eastern brethren contribute to our relief?

Governor Ford has taken away the state arms from the Legion. Your families are well, for aught I know. Sister Hyde has gone to Kirtland, I suppose. I have not been able to get any means for myself or anybody else.

The council consider it best for all the traveling elders to stop preaching politics—preach the gospel with double energy, and bring as many to the knowledge of the truth as possible.

The great event of 1844, so long anticipated, has arrived, without a parallel since the birth of Adam.

Jackson [W. H.] and his gang will try to waylay you coming up the river, if not before: look out for yourselves.

A little while since Parley wrote to Hyrum about Elder George J. Adams' proceedings and teachings in Boston. I heard Joseph tell Hyrum to let Adams alone, let Adams go back there and make all things right, that Parley had misapprehended some things, and acted in the matter rather injudiciously.

The saints have entered into covenants of peace with the governor and government officers, not to avenge the blood of the martyrs, but leave it with the executive, who had pledged the faith of the state for their safe-keeping. The elders cannot be too careful in all the world, to keep from saying anything to irritate and vex the governor, etc., for at present we must conciliate: it is *for our salvation*. The governor has *appeared* to act with honest intentions; we bring no charge against him—will wait patiently his proceedings in the matter. Let the elders keep cool, *vengeance rests in heaven.*—Yours as ever,

WILLARD RICHARDS'.

A council was held by the brethren, at which Messrs. Wood and Conyers from Quincy were present, also Colonel Richardson, lawyer, from Rushville. The council again expressed their de-

Peace Council at Nauvoo.

termination to preserve the peace in the city, and requested those gentlemen to use their influence to allay the excitement abroad, which they promised to do.

Colonel Richardson agreed to use all his influence to stay all illegal writs, and all writs for the present.

General Dunham requested a guard might be sent to Golden's Point, to protect the people there from the mob.

Father John Smith was present, and spoke of the destruction of crops by the McDonough troops.

We extract from Elder Woodruff's Journal:—

EXCERPTS FROM WILFORD WOODRUFF'S JOURNAL—THE TWELVE IN BOSTON

'The Boston branch of the Church of Jesus Christ of Latter-day Saints, and many elders from various parts, met in conference in Franklin Hall, Boston, on the 29th day of June, 1844.

Present: a majority of the Quorum of the Twelve, *viz.*, President Brigham Young, presiding; Elders Heber C. Kimball, Orson Hyde, Orson Pratt, William Smith, Wilford Woodruff, and Lyman Wight.

Conference opened by prayer.

Elder Orson Hyde occupied the forenoon in an interesting manner.

Elders Young, Kimball, and Wight severally addressed the meeting in the afternoon, much to the edification of the people.

Resolved that James H. Glines and Wm. Henderson be ordained elders: they were ordained under the hands of Elders Brigham Young and Heber C. Kimball.

Conference adjourned till Sunday morning.

The Twelve met in council in the evening.

30th. 10 *a. m.* Conference met pursuant to adjournment.

Elder Orson Pratt addressed the meeting, and ably removed the objections generally urged against new revelation.

In the afternoon, Elder Lyman Wight preached on the immortality of the body and the spirit, and also the principle of charity, connecting it with baptism for the dead.

In the evening, Elder Wilford Woodruff preached from the words of Jesus: 'Ye are my friends, if ye do whatsoever I command you.'

The house was full through the day and evening, and much instruction was given during the conference by those who spoke.'

Monday, July 1.—A. Jonas and Colonel Fellows arrived in Nauvoo, with a message from the governor to the city council. We copy their instructions:—

A. Jonas and Col. Fellows at Nauvoo— Their Instructions.

THE GOVERNOR'S INSTRUCTIONS

'Colonel Fellows and Captain Jonas are requested to proceed by the first boat to Nauvoo, and ascertain what is the feeling, disposition, and determination of the people there, in reference to the late disturbances; ascertain whether any of them propose in any manner to avenge themselves, whether any threats have been used, and what is proposed generally to be done by them.

They are also requested to return to Warsaw and make similar inquiries there; ascertain how far false rumors have been put afloat for the purpose of raising forces; what is the purpose of the militia assembled, whether any attack is intended on Nauvoo.

Ascertain also, whether any person from Missouri or Iowa intends to take part in the matter, and in my name forbid any such interference, without my request, on pain of being demanded for punishment.

                              [Signed] THOMAS FORD.

June 30th, 1844.'

They wrote as follows:—

COMMISSIONERS' NOTE TO THE NAUVOO CITY COUNCIL

                              'Nauvoo, July 1, 1844.

To the City Council of Nauvoo:

Gentlemen,—With this you will receive a copy of instructions from Governor Ford to us. You will understand from them what we desire from you in action on your part, as the only authorities of your city now known to the country, of such a character as will pacify the public mind and satisfy the governor of your determination to sustain the supremacy of the laws, which will, we are sure, be gratifying to him, and as much so to

                              Yours respectfully,
                              [Signed] HART FELLOWS,
                                   A. JONAS.'

We copy from the *Times and Seasons*:—

RESOLUTIONS OF THE CITY COUNCIL OF NAUVOO

'At a meeting of the city council, held in the council room, in the city of Nauvoo, on the first day of July, 1844, having received instructions from Governor Ford, through the agency of A. Jonas, Esq., and Colonel Fellows, it was unanimously

Resolved, For the purpose of insuring peace, and promoting the welfare of the county of Hancock and surrounding country, that we will rigidly sustain the laws and the governor of the state, so long as they, and he, sustain us in all our constitutional rights.

Resolved, secondly, That to carry the foregoing resolutions into complete effect, that inasmuch as the governor has taken from us the public arms, that we solicit of him to do the same with all the rest of the public arms of the state.

Resolved, thirdly, To further secure the peace, friendship and happiness of the people, and allay the excitement that now exists, we will reprobate private revenge on the assassinators of General Joseph Smith and General Hyrum Smith by any of the Latter-day Saints. That instead of 'an appeal to arms', we appeal to the majesty of the law, and will be content with whatever judgment it shall award and should the law fail, we leave the matter with God.

Resolved, unanimously, That this city council pledge themselves for the city of Nauvoo, that no aggressions by the citizens of said city shall be made on the citizens of the surrounding country, but we invite them, as friends and neighbors, to use the Savior's golden rule, and 'do unto others as they would have others do unto them', and we will do likewise.

Resolved, lastly, That we highly approve of the present public pacific course of the governor to allay excitement and restore peace among the citizens of the country; and while he does so, and will use his influence to stop all vexatious proceedings in law, until confidence is restored, so that the citizens of Nauvoo can go to Carthage, or any other place, for trial, without exposing themselves to the violence of assassins, we will uphold him, and the law, by all honorable means.

[Signed] GEORGE W. HARRIS, President *pro tem.*
Willard Richards, Recorder.'

'A Jonas, Esq., and Colonel Fellows:—

Messrs.,—In reply to your communication to the city council of the city of Nauvoo, on behalf of His Excellency Governor Ford, I have been instructed by the council to communicate the foregoing resolutions which I respectfully solicit for your consideration, and at the same time would inform you that a public meeting of our citizens will take place at the stand, east of the Temple, at 4 p. m., and solicit your attendance.

Most respectfully, your obedient servant,
[Signed] W. RICHARDS.'

ACTION OF THE CITY COUNCIL—EXPRESSIONS OF APPRECIATION

'At a meeting of a large portion of the citizens of Nauvoo, convened at the stand, in the afternoon of July 1, 1844, after hearing the above instructions and resolutions of the city council read, and being addressed by A. Jonas, Esq., and others, the meeting responded to the same with a hearty AMEN!

The citizens then passed a vote of thanks to the governor's agents for their kindly interference in favor of peace among the citizens of Hancock county and elsewhere around us.

They also passed a vote of thanks to Messrs. Woods and Reid, the counsel for the Generals Smith, for their great exertions to have even-handed justice meted to the Latter-day Saints, and they also passed a vote of thanks to Messrs. Chambers and Field, the former one of the editors of the *Missouri Republican*, and the latter, one of the editors of the *Reveille*, of St. Louis, for their honorable course of coming to Nauvoo for facts, instead of spreading rumors concerning the Latter-day Saints.

Mr. Chambers made a very appropriate speech, containing inuendos for the benefit of our citizens, that appeared as the wise man said, '*like apples of gold in pictures of silver*'.

They also passed a vote of thanks to Messrs. Wood and Conyers, mayor and ex-mayor of Quincy, for their friendly disposition in establishing peace in this region, and we are happy to say that all appears to be *peace at Nauvoo*.'

ADDRESS TO THE CHURCH OF JESUS CHRIST OF LATTER-DAY SAINTS
—A WORD OF CONSOLATION

'Deeply impressed for the welfare of all, while mourning the great loss of President Joseph Smith, our 'Prophet and Seer', and President Hyrum Smith, our 'Patriarch', we have considered the occasion demanded of us a word of consolation.

As has been the case in all ages, these saints have fallen martyrs for the truth's sake, and their escape from the persecution of a wicked world, in blood to bliss, only strengthens our faith, and confirms our religion as pure and holy.

We, therefore, as servants of the Most High God, having the *Bible, Book of Mormon*, and the *Book of Doctrine and Covenants*, together with thousands of witnesses, for Jesus Christ, would beseech the Latter-day Saints, in Nauvoo and elsewhere, to hold fast to the faith that has been delivered to them in the last days, abiding in the perfect law of the gospel.

Be peaceable, quiet citizens, doing the works of righteousness, and as soon as the Twelve and other authorities can assemble, or a majority of them, the onward course to the great gathering of Israel, and the final consummation of the dispensation of the fulness of times will be pointed out, so that the murder of Abel, the assassination of hundreds, the righteous blood of all the holy Prophets, from Abel to Joseph, sprinkled with the best blood of the Son of God, as the crimson sign of remission, only carries conviction to the bosoms of all intelligent beings, that the cause is just and will continue; and blessed are they that hold out faithful to the end, while apostates, consenting to the shedding of innocent blood, have no forgiveness in this world nor in the world to come.

Union is peace, brethren, and eternal life is the greatest gift of God. Rejoice, then, that you are found worthy to live and die for God. Men may kill the body, but they *cannot* hurt the soul, and wisdom shall be justified of her children. Amen.

[Signed] W. W. PHELPS,
WILLARD RICHARDS,
JOHN TAYLOR.

July 1, 1844'."

CHAPTER XIII

THE MARTYRDOM IN POETRY—EFFORTS FOR FOOD
SUPPLIES AND PROTECTION FOR THE PEOPLE OF
NAUVOO—THE DANIELS AFFIDAVIT ON THE
MARTYRDOM

"THE following appropriate and expressive poetry we
copy from the *Times and Seasons*:—

*THE ASSASSINATION OF GENERALS JOSEPH AND HYRUM
SMITH, FIRST PRESIDENT AND SECOND PATRIARCH
OF THE CHURCH OF LATTER-DAY SAINTS, WHO
WERE MASSACRED BY A MOB, IN CARTHAGE,
HANCOCK COUNTY, ILLINOIS, ON THE
27TH OF JUNE, 1844*

BY MISS ELIZA R. SNOW

'And when he had opened the fifth seal, I saw under the altar the
souls of them that were slain for the word of God, and for the testimony which they held.

And they cried with a loud voice, saying, how long, O Lord,
holy and true, dost thou not judge and avenge our blood on them
that dwell on the earth?

And white robes were given unto every one of them; * * * that
they should rest yet for a litle season, until their fellow servants also,
and their brethren, that should be killed as they were, should be
fulfilled' (*Rev.* vi:9, 10, 11).

'Ye heavens attend! Let all the earth give ear.
Let God and seraphs, men and angels hear—
The worlds on high—the universe shall know
What awful scenes are acted here below!
Had nature's self a heart, that heart would bleed
At the recital of that horrid deed;
For never, since the Son of Man was slain
Has blood so noble flowed from human vein
As that which now on God for vengeance calls
From freedom's ground—from Carthage prison walls.

Oh! Illinois! thy soil has drank the blood
Of Prophets martyr'd for the truth of God.
Once lov'd America, what can atone
For the pure blood of innocence thou'st sown?
Were all thy streams in teary torrents shed
How vain the tribute, for the noblest worth
That graced thy surface, O degraded earth!
Oh wretched murd'rers! fierce for human blood!
You've slain the Prophets of the living God,
Who've borne oppression from their early youth,
To plant on earth the principles of truth.

Shades of heroic fathers! Can it be
Beneath your blood-stained flag of liberty,
The firm supporters of our country's cause,
Are butchered while submissive to her laws?
Yes, blameless men, defam'd by hellish lies,
Have thus been offered as a sacrifice
T'appease the ragings of a brutish clan,
That has defied the laws of God and man!
'Twas not for crime or guilt of theirs they fell—
Against the laws they never did rebel;
True to their country, yet her plighted faith
Has proved an instrument of cruel death!
Where are thy far-famed laws—Columbia, where
Thy boasted freedom—thy protecting care?
Is this a land of rights? Stern facts shall say,
If legal justice here maintains its sway.
The official pow'rs of State are sheer pretense
When they're exerted in the Saints' defense.

Great men have fallen, and mighty men have died—
Nations have mourn'd their fav'rites and their pride;
But TWO so wise, so virtuous, great and good,
Before on earth, at once, have never stood
Since the creation—men whom God ordain'd
To publish truth where error long had reign'd,
Of whom the world itself unworthy prov'd,
It *knew them not;* but men with hatred mov'd,

And with infernal spirits have combin'd
Against the best, the noblest of mankind.
Oh persecution! shall thy purple hand
Spread utter desolation through the land?
Shall freedom's banner be no more unfurled?
Has peace indeed been taken from the world?

Thou God of Jacob, in this trying hour
Help us to trust in thy Almighty power;
Support thy Saints beneath this awful stroke,
Make bare thine arm to break oppression's yoke.
We mourn thy Prophet, from whose lips have flow'd
The words of life thy Spirit has bestow'd—
A depth of thought no human art could reach
From time to time, roll'd in sublimest speech
From the celestial fountain, through his mind,
To purify and elevate mankind;
The rich intelligence by him brought forth,
Is like the sunbeam spreading o'er the earth.

Now Zion mourns—she mourns an earthly head;
The Prophet and the Patriarch are dead!
The blackest deed that men or devils know,
Since Calv'ry's scene, has laid the brothers low!
One in their life, and one in death—they prov'd
How strong their friendship—how they truly lov'd;
True to their mission until death they stood,
Then seal'd their testimony with their blood.
All hearts with sorrow bleed, and every eye
Is bath'd in tears—each bosom heaves a sigh—
Heartbroken widows' agonizing groans
Are mingled with the helpless orphans' moans!
Ye Saints! be still, and know that God is just—
With steadfast purpose in his promise trust;
Girded with sackcloth, own his mighty hand,
And wait his judgment on this guilty land!
The noble martyrs now have gone to move
The cause of Zion in the courts above.

Nauvoo, July 1st, 1844.'

Tuesday, July 2, 1844.—We extract the following from Elders Kimball and Wight's letter:—

SECOND LETTER FROM ELDERS WIGHT AND KIMBALL—MOVEMENTS OF THE TWELVE*

'June 21st, 1844.

We again resume the pen to give you a few further particulars. We met the church in the city of Philadelphia last evening, pursuant to adjournment, the members being all present. The vote was taken to know whether they would sustain the First Presidency and the Twelve in their calling, and follow their counsel spiritually and temporally, lay aside all their prejudice and fears, and follow them through evil as well as through good report. There was not a dissenting vote. We think the church is in a good condition. There will be some added next Sabbath by baptism, and we trust more ere long. For our manner of preaching and instructing the church, we refer you to brothers Forgeus and Price.

We leave here today, at 4 o'clock, for the Wilmington conference; many of the brethren and sisters from this place are going with us. We have so many calls in this place, from those in the church and out of it, that we cannot stop a night in a place. We are at this time at Sister McMinn's, whose family treat us with all the kindness and attention that the servants of God could ask. They wish to be remembered to the Prophet and family, and so do all the saints in this place; and they are now determined to uphold you by their prayers in all things. I must confess this was not the case when we came here, with all. We learned that it is too much the case that the Twelve often find their way hedged up by the presiding elders endeavoring to exalt themselves and debase us, but you will find it different with your case in Philadelphia.

June 24th, 1844.

Just returned from Wilmington conference, accompanied by several of the brethren and sisters who went from this place. We can truly say that this was one of the most pleasant trips in our life. We went down on the steamer *Balloon*, and returned by railway.

Our conference commenced on Saturday, the 22nd. The brethren came in from the adjacent country, and after much instruction from Brothers Kimball and Wight, we took a vote to know whether they would go withersoever the Presidency, Patriarch and Twelve went, should it be to Oregon, Texas, or California, or any other place directed by the wisdom of Almighty God. The saints, numbering about 100, rose to their feet and exclaimed, Whithersoever they go, we go, without a dissenting voice. This was truly an interesting meeting. We have not the least idea that anyone will back out;

*For first letter see chapter xi this volume.

they are nearly all men of wealth, and have commenced this morning to offer all surplus property for sale, that whenever you say go, they are ready. We ordained ten as promising young elders as we ever laid hands upon. They pledged themselves to start this week and go through the state of Delaware from house to house, and proclaim that the kingdom of heaven is at hand.

On Sabbath, the 23rd, we preached alternately to a large and respectable congregation, and left the warmest of friends in that place, both in and out of the church. We have hundreds of pleasant sceneries in our journals, which are too numerous to mention at present.

Yours as ever,
[Signed] HEBER C. KIMBALL,
LYMAN WIGHT.'

Tuesday, 2—Elder John Taylor was brought home from Carthage to the joy of his friends.

ACTION OF CITY COUNCIL ON SUPPLYING FOOD FOR NAUVOO

'A special session of the city council was called to devise ways and means for supplying the city with provisions. Dr. Richards, Colonel Dunham, Marshal Greene, and others, stated to the council that many were destitute, and that unless active measures were taken, many must suffer with hunger, as some had already; wherefore it was

Resolved, by the city council of the city of Nauvoo ,that special committees be appointed to visit the different sections of the surrounding country, and solicit the benevolent for donations, or provisions and means for supplying the wants of the destitute of this city; and so far as donations fail, supply the deficiency by loans.

Resolved, That Charles Patten, W. H. Jordan, and L. S. Dalrymple be this committee for Iowa; that D. M. Repsher, A. Morrison, and Captain Ross go to Madison, Burlington, and the north country; that Benjamin Clapp, Samuel James, and Hiram Clark visit Ramus, La Harpe, and the eastern country, and that Isaac Morley assist the south to carry out the foregoing resolutions.

Resolved, That L. N. Scovil, Edwin D. Woolley, and William M. Gheen, be a standing committee to negotiate for all necessary supplies to those who are on duty by order of government.

Resolved, That each of said committees keep an accurate account of all donations and loans, and make returns of the same to the marshal of the city.

Passed July 2nd, 1844, 6 p. m.

[Signed] ORSON SPENCER, President *pro tem.*
W. Richards, Recorder.'

GEORGE J. ADAMS—MESSENGER TO BRIGHAM YOUNG—FAILURE OF

'To *whom it may concern*—
Elder George J. Adams has been deputed by council of the church

to bear despatches to Elder Young, president of the Quorum of the Twelve, relative to the death of the Prophet Joseph, and his brother Hyrum Smith, and the brethren are requested to see that no means are wanting to speed him on his important mission.

In behalf of the church,

[Signed] WILLARD RICHARDS,

Clerk of the Quorum of the Twelve.'

George J. Adams failed to perform this mission, although he had plenty of means, but Jedediah M. Grant went right through, and carried the word.

General Dunham wrote as follows:—

LETTER OF GENERAL DUNHAM TO GOVERNOR FORD—CALL FOR MORE MILITIA TROOPS TO CHECK MOB AT WARSAW AND GOLDEN'S POINT

'*His Excellency Governor Ford.*

I am sorry to inform you that the mob is still prowling between Warsaw and Golden's Point, waiting for an opportunity to come in and burn and destroy. The mob party are continually threatening us, and are driving our people away from their homes, and they are obliged to come here for protection.

I want you to send about one hundred or two hundred men whom you can depend upon as loyal, to quarter in the woods between here and Golden's Point, so that they can be between us and the mob, and protect us. Our troops are worn out, and I shall soon expect an order from you to discharge my men from the duty they are obliged to perform, to fulfil your order.

I am your Excellency's obedient servant,

[Signed] JONATHAN DUNHAM,

Major-General Commanding Nauvoo Legion.

July 2, 1844, 8 p. m.'

At a council of the Twelve and other elders, held in the Franklin Hall, Boston, there were ordained two elders, and arrangements made for dividing off into different parts of the vineyard. Each of the Twelve were appointed to attend several conferences. Council of the Twelve at Boston.

Elders Wilford Woodruff and Milton Holmes took steamer for Portland, Maine.

Colonel Lyman Wight delivered a political address at Bunker Hill, at 4 p. m.

Wednesday, 3.—We copy from the *Neighbor:*—

*THE ANSWER OF GOVERNOR FORD TO THE WARSAW COMMITTEE—
REVIEW OF MURDER OF THE GENERALS SMITH*

'Quincy, July 3, 1844.

To the Warsaw Committee:

Gentlemen,—I have received your communication on behalf of the citizens of Warsaw, stating their unalterable determination to compel the Mormons of your county to leave the state; or otherwise to abandon their own homes and evacuate the county, and asking my interference and influence to assist you in procuring the removal of the Mormons.

I have no reply whatever to make to that part of your letter which treats of the history, character, and offenses of the Mormons.   I deem this, however, a fit occasion to remark somewhat upon the character of the events which have just transpired.   These events present reasons for my determination which must be noticed.

When I came to your county I announced the policy by which I intended to be governed.   The law was to be my guide; and this you well understand.   I announced this determination in numerous public addresses, and uniformly in my private conversations.   I successively obtained a vote to sustain me in this course from every troop stationed at Carthage, or who was visiting there.

From the detachment of your town and vicinity, who visited Carthage the day before the surrender of the Smiths, I obtained a similar pledge.   I met them on the prairie, before they arrived in town, and as they must testify, stated to them at length, the reason which ought to influence them to keep the peace and abide the operation of the laws.   They gave every demonstration of satisfaction, and signified, with unanimous acclamation, that they would stand by me in taking a strictly legal course.

All the other portion of the Hancock forces under my command were repeatedly and deeply pledged to sustain me in the same course.   Under the firm and confident assurance of support thus obtained, I demanded the surrender of the Smiths, and promised them security.

In doing so, I now acknowledge that I erred, and erred grievously, in relying with too much confidence upon men with whom I was but little acquainted.   The idea that men could be treacherous under such circumstances was abhorrent to my nature, and rejected with indignation.

Whatever your hatred of the Smiths might be, I was too confident you would respect your honor—the honor of your country and state, and the rights of defenseless prisoners.   I could not believe that so much stupidity and baseness as was necessary for such an enterprise as the murder of defenseless prisoners in jail would be, could be mustered in Hancock county.

What aggravates the transaction, as a matter personal to myself,

is that you betrayed my honor as well as your own, and that of the
state; and you selected a time to commit the deed when you believed
I was in Nauvoo, in the power of the Mormons, and would most
probably be murdered by them by way of retaliation.

Upon the whole I cannot too strongly express my indignation
and abhorrence of the base and profligate act which has disgraced the
state and raised suspicions in the minds of many in regard to my
conduct in the matter of the most painful character to my feelings.

I am happy, however, to learn that these denunciations apply only
to a small portion of the people of Warsaw and Hancock county.
All the most responsible inhabitants ought to be acquitted of any
direct participation with the conspirators.

If they are culpable at all, it is for not using their influence against
the act, and for not communicating to me information which would
have enabled me to prevent it. The intention of the people must,
to some extent, have been whispered about and understood, and
ought to have been communicated to me as commander-in-chief.

Under these circumstances I am in but a poor situation to use
influence with the Mormons, to procure their removal. Your own
people have destroyed whatever influence I might otherwise have
possessed in that quarter to serve you.

Your own conduct has placed me in a painfully suspicious attitude;
and I have no hopes that I could now have a more persuasive influence
with the Mormons than I had with the perpetrators of the horrid
deed which I sought to prevent. Under the circumstances I cannot
ask the Mormons to confide in me.

It must appear to them that they have been betrayed by somebody,
and they do not know by whom.

If you mean to request me to exercise a forcible influence to expel
them from the state, I answer you now, as I have uniformly done,
that the law is my guide, and that I know of no law authorizing
their expulsion. From this determination I have not swerved for
an instant from the beginning until this time.

I see nothing now requiring any deviation, and besides, if I were
ever so much determined to drive them out, I believe such is the
abhorrence against the base deed which some of you have committed,
that I could not obtain voluntary aid from the people.

I suppose that you are aware that a call for volunteers is the only
mode in which a force can be raised, and the force when raised must
be provisioned by voluntary contribution.

You had better not make too loud a call upon your fellow citizens;
you may want their aid for defense; and may yet be glad to receive
aid for defense rather than aggression.

I know the apprehensions which you entertain of Mormon violence;
I will not now say whether your fears are well or ill founded; a little
time will develop what may be expected.

Taking the law for my guide, I can assure you that, although some of you have treated me badly, in thwarting my policy and violating my honor, and have acted basely towards defenseless prisoners, yet you are entitled to, and are assured of all the force of the state to prevent or avenge illegal violence towards any of you. An inquiry must be made concerning the murderers; they must for the honor and credit of the state be dealt with according to law.

You ask a small force to be stationed in your county as a protection against small parties. You have not probably duly considered how large a force would be necessary for this purpose. A small force could protect but a few points of attack, and must necessarily leave the residue of the county exposed.

A large force cannot be stationed there permanently. Your best protection is the assurance that upon the first aggression or well defined threats, an overpowering force is ready to march directly for the scene of action.

I am informed that a design is still entertained at Warsaw of attacking Nauvoo. In this you will not be sustained by myself or the people; it is a part of my policy that you remain quiet, and if you please, watchful, but strictly on the defensive; and I now announce to you that I will not be thwarted in this policy with impunity.

I am, most respectfully,

> Your obedient servant,
> [Signed] THOMAS FORD.'

Wednesday, 3.—Messrs. John B. Kimball, of Warsaw, and Elias Smith, of Nauvoo, reported that John Patrick Wells and W. Voorhees were wounded in the affray at Carthage.

The Members of the Mob Wounded at Carthage.

Elders Brigham Young and Heber C. Kimball spent the day together in the city of Boston, and in the evening visited the museum.

Thursday, 4.—Elder Samuel H. Smith received a letter from Richard Ballantyne, introducing Mr. William M. Daniels.

Mr. Daniels made the following affidavit:—

AFFIDAVIT OF WILLIAM M. DANIELS

'State of Illinois,   } ss.
Hancock county,

On the 4th day of July, 1844, came William M. Daniels before me, Aaron Johnson, a justice of the peace within and for said county, and after being duly sworn, deposeth and saith that on Saturday, the 22nd day of June, 1844, he came to the town of Warsaw, in said county of Hancock, and continued there until the Thursday following, the 27th day of June; that on that morning your affiant joined the rifle company commanded by Jacob Davis;

that the lieutenant and ———— Chittenden, Esq., said that as the governor would be absent from Carthage that day, that they would send ten men from each of the two companies to join the Carthage Greys, and kill the two Generals Smith, and if the governor opposed, to kill him too; that among those twenty men were Mr. Houck, a tailor, and Mr. Stephens, a cooper; the rest of the two companies marched towards Golden's Point to the railroad crossing, when they were met by the governor's order to disband all the troops, and Colonel Williams disbanded them.

That then the captains called them to order, saying they had no command over them, but wished them to form in line, which they did; that then Mr. Sharp, the editor of the *Warsaw Signal*, urged by a speech the necessity of *killing the two Smiths*, and a vote was then called who would go and do it.

Captain Davis and about twenty men went home, the residue, eighty-four men, went to Carthage, having six runners ahead to stop the twenty men who had before started for Carthage.

Soon after they started, one of the Carthage Greys met them with a letter, saying it was a most delightful time, the governor had gone, they could now kill Joseph and Hyrum Smith, and must do it quick before the governor returned; that they then turned to the left between the Warsaw and Nauvoo roads, and were not seen again by your affiant till they arrived at the jail in Carthage; that among the names of those who committed the murder at the jail in Carthage, Hancock county aforesaid, on the 27th day of June, 1844, at about 5 o'clock and 20 minutes, was Colonel Levi Williams, of Green Plains precinct, Captain Wires, ———— Chittenden, Esq., of Warsaw. ———— Houck, the tailor, Captain Grovenor, three brothers by the name of Stephens, coopers, ———— Allen, a cooper, all of Warsaw, and a man by the name of Mills, who was wounded in the right arm.

That your affiant would further state that this company before mentioned were painted black; that the guns of the guard at the jail were loaded with blank cartridges; that this was an arrangement entered into by the Carthage Greys, as said the messenger who came to meet said company in the morning.

That your said affiant saw Joseph Smith leap from the window of the jail, and that one of the company picked him up and placed him against the well curb, and several shot him, Colonel Williams exclaiming, 'Shoot him! Damn him! Shoot him!' and further your affiant saith not.*   [Signed]   WILLIAM M. DANIELS.'

*It is unfortunate that this affiant did not keep his subsequent statements at the trial within the limits of this affidavit as he would then have been a much more efficient witness at the subsequent trial of the murderers of the Prophet at which he was a witness and testified; but with the aid of a young typo in the *Times and Seasons* printing office at Nauvoo, he enlarged his affidavit to a sensational pamphlet detailing many miraculous occurrences in connection with the martyrdom which discredited him as a witness and did much towards making the murderers of the Prophet farcical.

The following anonymous letter was written:—

A PLEA FOR LIBERTY AND JUSTICE—ANONYMOUS

'For the *Lee County Democrat,*

Lee County, Iowa, July 4, 1844.

Mr. Editor:

Sir,—On this birthday of our common country, I am admonished

This pamphlet detailing the alleged miraculous incidents in the murder was brought out in the trial and Daniels confronted with it, swore to the statements. The counsel for the defendants asked the court to eliminate all consideration of such testimony from the record. The court granted the request in the following terms:

"That in making up their (the jury's) verdict they will exclude from their consideration all that was said by Daniels, Brackenbury, and Miss Graham (witnesses)."

It was supposed that the testimony of Brackenbury and Miss Graham would support the testimony of Daniels, but this support failed to appear. We quote what is alleged to be a reproduction of much of it, in a book published in Utah under the title of *The Martyrs*. The excerpt begins with the appearance of the Prophet in the window of the prison under the fire of the mob:—

"He sprang into the window; but just as he was preparing to descend, he saw such an array of bayonets below, that he caught by the window casing, where he hung by his hands and feet, with his head to the north, feet to the south, and his body swinging downwards. He hung in that position three or four minutes, during which time he exclaimed, two or three times, 'O, Lord, My God!!!' and fell to the ground. While he was hanging in that position, Colonel Williams hallooed, 'Shoot him! G—d d—n him! shoot the dam'd rascal!' However, none fired at him.

He seemed to fall easy. He struck partly on his right shoulder and back, his neck and head reaching the ground a little before his feet. He rolled instantly on his face. From this position he was taken by a young man, who sprang to him from the other side of the fence, who held a pewter fife in his hand, was barefoot and bareheaded, having no coat, with his pants rolled above his knees, and shirtsleeves above his elbows. He set President Smith against the south side of the well curb, that was situated a few feet from the jail. While doing this, the savage muttered aloud, 'This is Old Jo; I know him. I know you, Old Jo. Damn you; you are the man that had my daddy shot.' The object he had in talking in this way, I supposed to be this: He wished to have President Smith and the people in general, believe he was the son of Governor Boggs, which would lead to the opinion that it was the Missourians who had come over and committed the murder. This was the report that they soon caused to be circulated; but this was too palpable an absurdity to be credited.

* * * The ruffian, of whom I have spoken, who set him against the well curb, now secured a bowie knife for the purpose of severing his head from his body. He raised the knife and was in the attitude of striking, when a light, so sudden and powerful burst from the heavens upon the bloody scene, (passing its vivid chain between Joseph and his murderers), that they were struck with terrified awe and filled with consternation. This light, in its appearance and potency, baffles all powers of description. The arm of the ruffian, that held the knife, fell powerless; the muskets of the four, who fired, fell to the ground, and they all stood like marble statues, not having power to move a single limb of their bodies.

By this time most of the men had fled in great disorder. I never saw so frightened a set of men before. Colonel Williams saw the light and was also badly frightened; but he did not entirely lose the use of his limbs or speech. Seeing the condition of these men, he hallooed to some who had just commenced to retreat, for God's sake to come and carry off these men. They came back and carried them by main strength towards the baggage wagons. They seemed as helpless as if they were dead" (*The Martyrs*, pp. 79-81. For treatment somewhat in full see *Comprehensive History of the Church*, Century I, vol. ii, ch.lx, pp. 321-34; also *History of Hancock County*, Gregg, pp. 323-31). B. H. R.

by surrounding circumstances that something must be done by the friends of liberty, and that speedily too, or the star spangled banner of the American Eagle must soon cease to wave its golden pinions o'er the heads of freemen.

I was aroused to these reflections by the statements of Messrs, Reid and Woods in the *Nauvoo Neighbor Extra,* of Sunday, June 30th, 1844, 3 p. m., also of the *Neighbor* of yesterday. Mr. H. T. Reid is a gentleman of high legal attainments, of Madison, in our county, possessed of a character for truth and veracity not to be impeached. Mr. J. W. Woods is an attorney, of Burlington, in this territory, of the same character and standing. His word may be relied on; and as these gentlemen were in the midst of the circumstances which led to the horrid butchery of Generals Joseph and Hyrum Smith at Carthage, on the 27th ult., and as they, like myself, are no Mormons, and live in a neighboring territory, I hope the citizens of these United States will give their statements of this horrid affair, that confidence and calm deliberation which the case solemnly demands.

If the freeborn sons of American liberty can be incarcerated in prison for some supposed or real crime without the privilege of an investigation, and be murdered by a ruthless mob in that defenseless state, in open daylight, and in the presence of the authorities of the land too, where, I ask in the name of freemen, where is our freedom? Where is our security for all the blessings for which our fathers fought and bled? Who will ere long dare lay his head upon his pillow in his own habitation and say, I am safe? If the strong walls of a prison are not sufficient to guarantee safety to citizens of this republic, what may we soon expect who live in unwalled houses? I ask in the name of humanity, are not American liberties on the verge of a mighty precipice, just ready to plunge into the whirlpool of utter dissolution?

Perhaps it may be said the Mormons are to blame; and supposing they are, does this warrant death and destruction to be hurled at them without judge or jury? The riots at Philadelphia and other places have been sufficiently alarming, but the recent tragedy at Carthage mocks all parallel—history has no equal.

The page of time till June 27th, 1844, has been unstained by such a blot. I mourn for my country. How has the soil of an independent state been crimsoned with innocent blood? I say innocent, for the law holds every man innocent till he is proved guilty. Were the Smiths proved guilty? No! they had no trial. Where is the plighted faith of the state?

How is the honor of all this western country tarnished! How will the jealousies of the eastern states be excited by this unheard of butchery!

I am a native of New England. I know the prejudices of the eastern people concerning the west and south. They feel that a man cannot travel in safety in our region, in Illinois, in Iowa, and the surrounding states and territories, without a pistol and a bowie knife, and that we almost belong to another race of beings; and when our eastern friends shall read the true and frightful tale of Messrs. Reid and Woods, well may their fears be increased, their jealousies aroused, and they led to believe that all they had anticipated was true concerning us. But, Mr. Editor, I would undeceive them; and although not one palliating circumstance, to my knowledge, offers itself to the public mind in relation to the occurrence at Carthage, yet I would say to my friends in New England, and to all men, the citizens of the west do not approbate such proceedings.

More than nineteen-twentieths of the citizens of Iowa, and, I am confident, of Illinois, reprobate with unqualified abhorrence the atrocious deed.

The wise, the virtuous, the patriotic of all sects and denominations and parties, political or religious, hurl their anathemas at the barbarous deed which was transacted by a lawless mob, a few scores of desperadoes, if we can believe the most authentic intelligence from the scene of trouble.

The great, great mass of the people deprecate the event as much as would the inhabitants of Vermont, Massachusetts, or any other state, and why not? We are their sons, their brothers, their sisters, their daughters, nursed by the same mothers, cradled by the same firesides.

I repeat what is well known, I am no Mormon, and that they may be guilty of some things as a society. If they are, I do not know it. So far as I have seen their leaders, their teachings have been moral and upright, and their publications state if they have erred in anything, they have erred unintentionally, and they are ready to be set right by the powers above them.

Why then should not the law have its course? Why should any man be condemned without a hearing? If this thing is suffered to go any further, God knows where it will end; I fear a general civil war, and I do hope that every good man in the union will arise and stamp with infamy any such unlawful proceedings.

If the city of Nauvoo erred in declaring the printing press of the *Expositor* a nuisance, what then? I am no lawyer, but I suppose it could be no more than a trespass—they liable for damage only; and if they erred in judgment, it is not the first time a legislative body has erred. Congress might have done as much, and not be killed for it; then why kill them?

Mr. Editor, is the action of the government to bring the murderers of the Generals Smith to justice? I ask for information. Have the perpetrators been discovered? Have arrests been made? Have rewards been made? Have rewards been offered by the governor of Illinois? or has he been dilatory in his duties, as the respectable part of the community think him to be?

If he does his duty, I trust justice will be done to the assassins;

but it is not enough to deprecate alone, action, decided action should be had in the case, that our country may be saved from mobocracy and violence, and order and law bear rule again in our land.*

I am, sir,

[Signed] A FRIEND TO EQUAL RIGHTS.' "

---

*It is appreciated that this is an anonymous communication, and anonymous letters are not often woven into serious historical statements; but it must be remembered that this anonymous letter was written for and published in the *Lee County Democrat* of Iowa, and is such a truthful statement of the main facts connected with the martyrdom of Joseph and Hyrum Smith and discusses the points at issue in such a temperate and striking manner that it represents a fixed and important view of the whole case; and for these valuable elements in it, notwithstanding its defects of composition, is here presented for preservation. B. H. R.

CHAPTER XIV

A CHAPTER OF SUNDRY EVENTS AT VARIOUS PLACES
AND DOCUMENTS FOLLOWING THE MARTYRDOM:
UNITED STATES PRESS COMMENTS ON THE
MURDER

"*Thursday, July 4,* 1844.—Elders Brigham Young and Heber C. Kimball, with several other elders, visited the grand exhibition of fireworks on the Boston Common this evening. A great multitude were present.

Sundry Events and Activities.

Friday, 5.—Mr. Daniels started about 9 a. m. to go and see the governor, and tell him what he knew in relation to the massacre of the Generals Smith.

A raft of pine lumber arrived from the upper country.

Elders Young and Kimball took cars from Boston, and proceeded to Linn.

Saturday, 6.—General Deming and Mr. Robertson arrived in the city at 2 p. m. They expressed themselves abundantly satisfied with Dr. Richards' proceedings and agreement at Carthage, and said they believed the governor would do all in his power to quell further outrages, and preserve the peace.

William Clayton took charge of the raft of lumber which arrived yesterday, as agent for the trustee.

William Clayton saw the governor's reply to the letter from the Warsaw Committee of Safety, and recorded in his journal thus:—'The governor seems disposed to make the best of his situation, and try to restore the credit of the state by bringing the assassins to justice.'

A conference was held in Genessee, New York. Four branches were represented, containing 95 members, including 23 elders. Elder C. W. Wandell presided.

Sunday, 7.—Meeting at the stand.

Judge W. W. Phelps read Governor Ford's letter in reply to the Warsaw Committee.

President Marks addressed the meeting.

Dr. Willard Richards advised some of the people to go out and harvest, and others who stay to go on with the Temple, and make work in the city.

R. D. Foster arrived in the city. His presence produced some excitement in consequence of the saints believing he was accessory to the murder of the Prophets.

The following was sent to General Deming:—

LETTER TO GENERAL DEMING

'Nauvoo, Sunday, July 7, 1844.

General Deming, Acting-Commander of the Forces of Hancock County.

Sir,—We are informed that Dr. R. D. Foster is in this city, and that he has an order from Governor Ford to call out Captain Dunn's company of militia to guard him while here transacting business.

You must be aware, sir, at sight of such communication, the situation in which such an order of things must place this people, and of the difficulties which might grow out of such a course, and we earnestly desire your immediate action as agent of the governor for this county, to prevent any such occurrence.

We request General Deming to interfere in this matter. We request that no troops be quartered among us, for any such purpose, lest excitement arise between them and the citizens.

We desire that Dr. Foster's business be transacted by agency, or some way, so that there may be no cause of contention or excitement in our midst. Nothing shall be wanted on our part to keep the peace; but without the cooperation of government, it would seem impossible to accomplish it.

We are, sir, most respectfully, your servants and the friends of peace,

WILLARD RICHARDS,
W. W. PHELPS,
JOHN P. GREENE.

P. S.—General Deming knows the threats which have been made by Dr. Foster, and the cause we have to fear his presence, as well as troops in such a case.'

Elder Kimball's journal records a conference held this day at Salem. He preached in the fore-noon, Elder Lyman Wight in the afternoon, and Elder Orson Pratt in the evening.

Apostles at Salem. Mass.

The conference went off well, the brethren realizing they had a good time.

A conference was held in the Presbyterian meeting-house in Scarborough, Maine, which continued through the 6th and 7th. Elder Wilford Woodruff presided.

The conference was addressed, and business attended to by Elders Wilford Woodruff, M. Holmes, E. Tufts, and Samuel Parker.

A large mob assembled in Philadelphia on the 6th, and gathered in front of St. Philip's Church, with the intention of burning it, because of some difficulty existing between the Protestants and the Irish Catholics. The mob continued two days. The governor of the state called out 3,000 of the militia. There were 14 killed and 50 wounded during the riot.

Religious Riot at Philadelphia.

Monday, 8.—About this time a letter was received from D. S. Hollister, reporting progress for the Baltimore convention to nominate candidates for the presidency.

Elders Brigham Young, Heber C. Kimball, Orson Pratt, Lyman Wight, Erastus Snow, Daniel Spencer and J. L. Heywood, held three meetings in the concert hall, Salem. The house was full and the brethren felt well.

The following is extracted from the *New York Tribune*:—

THE TROUBLES AT NAUVOO

'We begin almost to fear that the terrible scenes of cruelty, devastation of peaceful homes, and indiscriminate hunting down of men, women and children, which disgraced Missouri a few years since, during the expulsion of the Mormons from that state, are to be reenacted in Illinois.

The history of these deeds has never been, and probably never will be written; but enough of their atrocities has been heard from casual recitals of eye and ear witnesses to make the soul sicken with horror at their contemplation.

We are not the apologists of Joe Smith, or of the mummeries of Mormonism; we are ready to admit that the existence of that sect in the shape which it would seem Smith is bent on imparting to it, is fraught with danger, and should be looked to by the proper power; but in the name of common humanity, we stand up for the lives and security of helpless women and innocent children.

The executives of Illinois and Missouri have had loud and fair warning by the meetings in Carthage, Warsaw and St. Louis, of the dreadful scheme of arson and assassination that is going on to exterminate the Mormons; and if they permit the monstrous crime of the sacking of a city, the murder of men in cold blood, and the sacrifice of women and children to the demoniac fury of an inflamed mob, they will not, they cannot be held guiltless.

There are other means by which the course of the Mormons, if unlawful or destructive of the rights of others, can be restrained and punished; but, even if there be no immediate legal redress, are murder, rapine, desolation, the brand of civil war hurled among those who should be friends and neighbors—are these a suitable substitute for a little time and patience?

Let the citizens of Illinois *look to their votes* when next they approach the ballot box, and examine well for whom and for what principles they are cast, and they can restore the government of their state to hands that will remove their grievances and reassure them in their rights much more speedily than they can rebuild one log hut sacrificed to brutal war, or atone for the blood of a single human victim.'

Tuesday, 9.—Elders Willard Richards and John Taylor wrote as follows:—

*LETTER OF INSTRUCTION AND INFORMATION TO THE PRESI-
DENT OF THE BRITISH MISSION*

'Nauvoo, Illinois, U. S.,
July 9th, 1844.

*Elder Reuben Hedlock, Presiding Elder of the Church of Jesus Christ
in England, and the Saints in the British Empire.*

Beloved Brethren,—As Elder James Parsons is about to leave for England, we embrace this, as the first opportunity, to communicate to you one of the most signal events which has ever transpired in the history of the church.

It has been declared by all the former Prophets and Apostles, that God had reserved unto himself a peculiar people for the last days, who would not only be zealous in good works, but who should be purified as gold in the furnace seven times, and who would have to endure through faith and patience in all long-suffering, in meekness, forbearance, love, and every God-like virtue unto the end as good soldiers, and meet all the scorn, scoff, and derision and chiding, buffeting and persecution a wicked world could heap upon them, and even death itself, not counting their lives dear unto themselves, that they might obtain their inheritance in that kingdom of their heavenly Father, which Jesus, their elder brother, had gone to prepare for them.

It is in this period of time that we are permitted to live. It is at the dawning of that day of days in which our heavenly Father is about to usher in that glorious period when times and seasons shall be changed and earth renewed, when after rumors and commotions, turmoils, strife, confusion, blood and slaughter, the sword shall be beaten into ploughshares, and peace and truth triumphantly prevail o'er all the footstool of Jehovah. The day of these events has dawned, although to human view a cloud has o'erspread the horizon.

You are acquainted with the general history of the church to which we belong. From our lips and pens you have learned its rise and progress; you have heard of the persecution of the saints in Missouri, and their expulsion from thence, together with their kind reception by the citizens of Illinois, where we have been located for the last four years.

For some months past we have been troubled with the wicked proceedings of certain apostates in our midst, who have striven to overthrow the church and produce trouble and anguish in the mind of every virtuous being, but their designs having been frustrated by the wise and judicious management on the part of the Prophet and the saints.

These apostates, reckless of all consequences, made a deadly thrust at our overthrow, leaving the city suddenly, and, afterwards, by themselves or agents, fired their own buildings, doubtless thinking they would charge it upon the saints, and by that means excite a mob in the surrounding country, who would fall upon and burn the city, but in this they were disappointed, our vigilant police discovered and extinguished the flames.

Their next course was to arrest the Prophet, the Patriarch, and others, by legal process and false pretense, and take them to Carthage, the county seat, for investigation; but they gave themselves up to the requisition of the law, on the pledge of Governor Ford that they should be protected from all personal violence, and went voluntarily to Carthage, without even the attendance of the officer.

Considerable excitement prevailed in the neighborhood, to allay which they voluntarily gave bonds for their appearance at the next session of the circuit court. Their voluntary and noble conduct should have satisfied every mind, but certain individuals of the basest sort swore out a writ for treason against the Prophet Joseph and the Patriarch Hyrum Smith, and they were thrust into jail *without trial, without examination, without any legal course or procedure*, on the 25th of June, where they remained till the next day, when they were brought before the magistrate, that a day might be set for their examination.

They were immediately remanded to prison, where they remained until the 27th, when but few of their friends were permitted to see them.

Between five and six o'clock p. m., of that day, a company of 150 or 200 armed, disguised and painted men rushed upon the guard who were set to watch the prison door, overpowered them, rushed upstairs into the entry adjoining the room where Joseph Smith and Hyrum Smith were, and John Taylor and Willard Richards sitting with them to keep them company.

As soon as the mob arrived at the head of the stairs, they fired through the door and shot Hyrum in the face. He fell instantly, exclaiming, 'I am a dead man'.

The mob instantly forced open the door with the points of the bayonets, and recommenced an indiscriminate discharge of firearms upon all in the room.

Mr. Taylor, in attempting to leap from the window, was shot and fell back in the chamber. Joseph, in attempting to leap from the same window, was shot, and fell on the outside, about 20 feet descent, when the mob gathered instantly round him and again shot him.

Joseph and Hyrum received each four balls, and were killed instantly. Elder Taylor received four balls in his left wrist and left leg—is doing well and is likely to recover.

Dr. Richards was marked on his left ear and cheek, otherwise remained unharmed. The whole scene occupied only two minutes, when the mob fled rapidly towards Warsaw.

The bodies of the murdered men were removed to Nauvoo on the 28th, and were buried on the 29th. This event has caused the deepest mourning among the saints, but they have not attempted to avenge the outrage.

The governor has promised that the whole treacherous proceedings shall be investigated according to law, and the saints have agreed to leave it with him, and with God to avenge their wrongs in this matter. There has been considerable excitement in the surrounding country, which is now in a great measure allayed. The action of the saints has been of the most pacific kind, remembering that God has said, 'Vengeance is mine, I will repay'.

For further particulars we refer you to the statements of Messrs. Reid and Woods, and other statements in the *Nauvoo Neighbor,* which we send you with this; and now, beloved brethren, we say to you all, as we say to the saints here, be still and know that God reigns. This is one of those fiery trials that is to try the saints in the last days.

These servants of God have gone to heaven by fire—the fire of an ungodly mob. Like the Prophets of ancient days they lived as long as the world would receive them; and this is one furnace in which the saints were to be tried, to have their leaders cut off from their midst, and not be permitted to avenge their blood.

God has said, 'Vengeance is mine; I have not called mine elders to fight their battles; I will fight their battles for them;' and we know, assuredly, that he will do it in his own due time, and we have only to wait in patience and pray for the fulfilment of the promise.

This event is one of the most foul and damnable that ever disgraced the earth, having no parallel in time. Innocent men imprisoned without law, without justice, and murdered in cold blood in the enlightened nineteenth century, in an enlightened country in open daylight.

It will call down the wrath and indignation of all nations upon the perpetrators of the horrid deed, and will prove the truth of the saying, 'The blood of the martyrs is the seed of the church.' They died for the word of God and the testimony of Jesus Christ.

God has not left his church without witnesses; as in former days, so shall it be in the latter days, when one falls another will arise to occupy a similar station. Our heavenly Father always has had a leader to his people, always will have, and the gates of hell can never prevail against the chosen of heaven.

The murder of Joseph will not stop the work; it will not stop the Temple; it will not stop the gathering; it will not stop the honest-in-heart from believing the truth and obeying it; but it is a proof of the revelations we have received from heaven through him. He has sealed his testimony with his blood. He was willing to die, and desired only to live for the sake of the brethren.

Two better men than Joseph and Hyrum Smith never lived. Two better men God never made. The memorial of their godly lives is embalmed, printed with indelible ink in the memory of every honest heart who knew their upright walk and conversation; but they are taken away by the hands of assassins, and of the foolish things of the earth God will raise up others to comfort and lead his people, and not one item of his word can fail.

Jerusalem must be rebuilt and Zion must be redeemed, the earth be cleansed from blood by fire, Jesus return to his own, and all who shall continue faithful unto the end shall rest in everlasting peace and blessedness.

We alone, of the Quorum of the Twelve Apostles, are here at this time to write to you, the remaining ten are in the eastern states preaching the gospel, and we expect them soon to return; and as soon as God will, we will write you again.

Proceed onward with all your labors as though nothing had happened, only, preach Joseph martyred for his religion, instead of living, and God will pour out his Spirit upon you, and hasten his work from this time.

Believe not every spirit, but try the spirits; believe not every report, for every false rumor that men and demons can invent is set afloat to gull the world. What we have told you by letter and papers is true, but time will not permit to tell you every particular now.

Be humble, prayerful, watchful, and let not the adversary get any advantage of one of you, and may the choicest blessings of Israel's God rest upon you and abide with you, that you may endure faithful in all tribulation and affliction, and be prepared to be gathered unto Mount Zion, and enter into celestial glory, is the earnest prayer of your brethren in the new and everlasting covenant. Amen.

[Signed] WILLARD RICHARDS,
JOHN TAYLOR.

P. S.—We would have said that while Joseph was on his way to Carthage, and on the prairie, he said to his friends around him, 'I am going like a lamb to the slaughter, but my mind is calm as the summer's morning, I have a conscience void of offense towards God and towards all men.' Joseph also said to his friends, 'I am going voluntarily to give myself up, and it shall be said of me that I *was murdered in cold blood.'*

Elders Brigham Young and Orson Pratt were at Boston when they first heard the rumors of the massacre of the Prophets, but did not believe the accounts were correct.

Members of the Twelve in Boston.

Elders Kimball and Wight were in Salem this morning, [July 9th] and heard of the death of the Prophets. Elder Kimball recorded he was unwilling to believe it, though it struck him to the heart. They took cars for Boston in the morning, where they stayed during the day. In the evening they proceeded to New York.

Elder Wilford Woodruff was in Portland, Maine, and ready to step on board of a steamer for Fox Islands, when he received the *Boston Times* newspaper, containing an account of the death of the Prophets. He immediately took cars and returned to Boston, stopping over night at Scarborough.

Wednesday, 10.—Elder Willard Richards, Patriarch John Smith, Elders Samuel H. Smith and W. W. Phelps, met in council in the council chamber.

Elder Willard Richards wrote as follows:—

LETTER TO A. JONAS—'ALL PEACE AT NAUVOO'

'Nauvoo, July 10, 1844.

A. Jonas, Esq.

Dear Sir,—Yours of the 6th, per Mr. Meetze, is received, and I have only time to thank you for the information it contained, and all your endeavors for the promotion of truth and justice, and can still give you the fullest assurance that all is perfect peace at Nauvoo,

calmly waiting the fulfilment of Governor Ford's pledge to redeem the
land from blood by legal process.   You can do much to allay the
excitement of the country in your travels, and the friends of peace
will appreciate your labors.

Most respectfully,
WILLARD RICHARDS.'

Elder Parley P. Pratt arrived at Nauvoo.

A committee of nine ladies, among whom were Mrs.
Hyrum Smith, Mrs. John Taylor, Mrs. Arthur Mil-
liken and Mrs. W. W. Phelps, waited upon
Mr. R. D. Foster, and told him they would
not bear his taunts and insults any longer.
They ordered him to leave the city forthwith, or he
would be visited by a stronger force tomorrow.   These
ladies having good reason to believe that Foster was
accessory to the murder of their relatives, the Prophets,
took the liberty of pursuing this course towards him.

Appeal of
Nauvoo Ladies
to Governor
Ford.

Mr. Hiram Kimball obligated himself that Foster
should leave before morning, accordingly he got his
team ready and took him out of the city that evening.
We copy from the *Neighbor*:—

ELDER JOHN TAYLOR AND ITEMS OF THE MARTYR-TRAGEDY

'Elder Taylor is recovering as fast as can be expected.   His wounds
are doing well.

The senior editor of this paper, Mr. Taylor, at the horrible assassination of Joseph and Hyrum Smith in Carthage jail, on the
afternoon of the 27th day of June, received three wounds in his left
thigh and knee, and one in his left wrist; besides which a *fifth ball*
spent its force against his *watch* in his *left* vest pocket.   This ball,
but for the *timely* interference of this valuable watch, must have
caused instant death, as it would have passed directly into his lungs.
This watch, though dreadfully shattered, is a friend that points to the
very moment when he stood between *life* and *death*, the hands pointing to 5 o'clock, 10 minutes and 26 seconds.

While upon this subject, Mr. Taylor and his friends wish, through
this channel, to tender their thanks to Mr. Hamilton and family, and
to all who assisted him in any manner during his stay at Carthage,
while unable to be removed to his own home.   Kindness, assistance,
and the tender offices of humanity in such times of deep distress,
give the noble mind a chance to appreciate *help when it is needed*, and

to remember such friends in future.   Nor should the assistance rendered to lay out the bodies of the Messrs. Smith, preparatory to their removal to Nauvoo, be forgotten.   Though the people of Carthage, under the excitement of the moment, generally fled, yet those who did stay did all they could to forward the bodies, as well as to make Mr. Taylor as comfortable as the circumstances of the case would permit.

One thing further: In this awful tragedy, Dr. Willard Richards, equally exposed to the shower of bullets which were fired into the room at the door and windows, *escaped unhurt,* and while he would render thanksgiving and praise to his God for this signal preservation of his life, he would also return his grateful acknowledgments to the Messrs. Hamilton and others, who rendered all the assistance in their power in this awful hour of murder and woe at Carthage.'

Elders Brigham Young and Orson Pratt went from Boston to Lowell.

Elders Kimball, Wight and William Smith, proceeded by railway from New York to Philadelphia.

Movments of Some of the Twelve— Boston, Philadelphia.

The *Neighbor* has the following notice:—

'THE PROPHET'—A NEW L. D. S. PUBLICATION

'A well disposed newspaper called *The Prophet,* was started in New York, in the month of May last.   The *ruptures* of our neighbors, and the murder of our best friends, have prevented us from giving our readers *timely* notice.   It is published by a society for the promotion of truth, and we must say that in a city so large as New York, if the people have virtue, holiness, and the kindred spirits which have ever won the affections of humanity, they will sustain the *Prophet* liberally.   Nor should the country be less magnanimous: by comparing opinions, and proving contrarieties, *truth* manifests itself.'

PUBLIC OPINION ON THE MURDER OF JOSEPH AND HYRUM SMITH FROM VARIOUS NEWSPAPERS

We copy from the *St. Louis Evening Gazette:*—

'Public opinion of the press on the assassination of Joseph and Hyrum Smith by a mob in the jail at Carthage, while under the sacred pledge of the state for the protection of their lives.

'With reference to the recent bloody affair at Carthage, the *O. S. Democrat* says:—

'From all the facts now before us, we regard these homicides as nothing else than murder in cold blood—murder against the plighted faith of the chief magistrate of Illinois—murder of a character so atrocious and so unjustifiable as to leave the blackest stain on all its perpetrators, their aiders, abettors, and defenders.'

The *Republican* pronounces the deed 'unprovoked murder'.

The *Reporter* says:—'The conduct of the mob at Carthage cannot be justified'.

The *Reveille* says:—'Joe Smith has been '*Lynched*' while under the protection of the '*Laws*'.'

The *New Era* says:—'It was cruel and cowardly to murder the unarmed prisoners when they had surrendered themselves, and were in custody of the laws.'

In fact, the press of St. Louis denounces this bloody deed without a dissenting voice*.'

From the *Lee County (Iowa) Democrat:*

'We also endorse the whole of the sentiments of the St. Louis press, and say it was a *premeditated murder,* and that the offenders ought to be ferreted out and dealt with according to the strict sense of the law.'

From the *Illinois State Register:*—

JOSEPH SMITH, THE MORMON PROPHET, AND HIS BROTHER, HYRUM, MURDERED IN PRISON

'The following particulars of the most disgraceful and cold-blooded murder ever committed in a Christian land, is copied from an extra from the office of the *Quincy Herald.* Rumors of the bloody deed reached this city several days ago, but were not believed until Tuesday evening, when there was no further room left for doubt. Next week we will have all the particulars. Every effort will be made to bring the assassins to punishment.'

FROM THE QUINCY HERALD EXTRA OF SATURDAY

'Governor Ford arrived in this city this morning, much worn down by travel and fatigue, having left Carthage yesterday. It is now certain that only Joe and Hyrum Smith are killed, and they were murdered in cold blood.

*This denunciation by the St. Louis press "without a dissenting voice" is all the more worthy of note because it was in western Missouri—in which state St. Louis is situated—that the same kind of lawless assault upon the Church of the Latter-day Saints was made and the murder of many of its membership occurred but a few years before; and the like proceedings in Illinois might have been held up as a justification of the action of mobs in western Missouri against the saints. B. H. R.

It seems that while Governor Ford was absent from Carthage to Nauvoo, for the purpose of ascertaining satisfactorily the strength of the Mormon force, an excited mob assembled near Carthage, disfigured themselves by painting their faces, and made a rush upon the jail where Joe and his fellow prisoners were confined.

The guard placed by the governor to protect the jail were overpowered by superior numbers, the doors of the jail forced, and Joe and Hyrum both shot.

Hyrum was instantly killed by a ball, which passed through his head. Joe was in the act of raising the window, when he was shot both from without and within, and fell out of the window to the ground.

Richards, whom we supposed yesterday was dead, escaped unhurt. Mr. Taylor, the editor of the *Nauvoo Neighbor*, was in the room with the Smiths, and received three balls in his leg, and one in his arm. He is not considered dangerous. Three of the assailants were slightly wounded.

It will probably never be known who shot Joseph and Hyrum Smith, but their murder was a *cold-blooded, cowardly act*, which will consign the perpetrators, if discovered, to *merited infamy and disgrace*. They have broken their pledges to the governor, disgraced themselves and the state to which they belong. *They have crimsoned their perfidy with blood*.

The dead bodies of the Smiths were conveyed to Nauvoo, by order of the governor yesterday. It was supposed by many, that the Mormons on seeing them would break away from all restraints and commence a war of extermination.

But nothing of the kind occurred. They received their murdered friends in sorrow—laid down their arms and remained quiet. Colonel Singleton and his company of 60 men are still in Nauvoo, and the Mormons submitted to their authority.

The 300 that left our city yesterday on the *Boreas* are at present in Warsaw. A man was knocked down with a musket in Warsaw yesterday, for *presuming* to express disapprobation at the murder of the Smiths.'

From the *Sangamon Journal*:—

THE MORMON DIFFICULTIES

'Notwithstanding all the rumors which are afloat, we are unable to state anything very definite in relation to affairs at Nauvoo, or in the region round about that city.

It is certain that the governor has called out some of the neighboring militia; that bodies of armed men had collected without waiting a call from the governor; that the governor had accepted the services of militia at St. Louis under certain contingencies; that he had demanded of Smith the state arms at Nauvoo; that it had been reported that they were given up; that Smith and his council had given themselves up to be tried by our laws for alleged offenses.

Thus far our news seems to be certain. Rumor says further, that on Thursday of last week Joe Smith, Hyrum Smith and Dr. Richards were shot by a mob at Carthage.

We are incredulous in regard to the truth of this rumor. We cannot think, under the circumstances of the case, the excitement against these men among the anti-Mormons, Governor Ford would have received them as prisoners, to be tried under our laws, had pledged himself for their protection, and then placed them in a situation where they would be murdered. The rumor is too preposterous for belief. We wait with much anxiety to hear the truth on this subject; and this feeling is general in this community.'

From the *Missouri Republican*:—

'*The Murders at Carthage.*—A letter from the editor, one from G. T. M. Davis, Esq., and a proclamation from Governor Ford, give all the information which we have been able to collect from the seat of civil commotion and murder in Illinois.

They were issued in an extra form yesterday morning, and are transferred to our columns today for the benefit of our numerous readers abroad.

All our information tends to fix upon the people concerned in the death of the *Smiths*, the odium of perfidious, blackhearted, cowardly *murder*—so wanton as to be without any justification—so inhuman and treacherous as to find no parallel in savage life under any circumstances.

Governor Ford declares his intention to seek out the murderers; and he owes it to his own honor and to that of the state, whose faith was most grossly violated, never to cease his exertions for this purpose.

The Mormons, it will be seen, were quiet, and not disposed to commit any acts of aggression; their enemies, on the other hand, were evidently disposed to push them to extremities, and to force them from the state.

This feeling may be checked by the alacrity with which Governor Ford's orders were being executed, but it will be some time before peace and order can be restored—the disgrace of past acts cannot be wiped out.'

The following extract of a letter from a highly respectable gentleman to his friend in Nauvoo, we copy from the *Nauvoo Neighbor*:—

'Fair Haven, Ct. July 10, 1844.
I have, by the papers, within a day or two, been informed of the

murder of Joseph and Hyrum Smith. This is an event which will be deeply lamented by all Mormons, and will appear, probably, to those who are not Mormons, as the final overthrow of their religious tenets.

I will, however, make the prediction that this diabolical butchery makes more Mormons than the *friendship* of half the inhabitants in Illinois could have done by their most devoted exertions.

The blood of saints is the seed of the church. It will be considered by an extensive portion of the world that the Smiths have suffered martyrdom for their religion, and their profoundest sympathies will be aroused in favor of those believing the same creed.

The inflammatory appeals to the bloodthirsty passions of the anti-Mormon populace will be universally condemned by the reflecting and moral part of every community, and thousands will now examine your tenets, who never thought of such a thing before.

Carthage and Warsaw will be denounced by the honorable, and the indelible disgrace with which they now stand covered, will cause them to be avoided by every person who has any regard to his personal safety.

It is now known here that the lazy speculators of Warsaw, and the still lazier office drones at Carthage, cared nothing for Joe Smith personally, or for his tenets either; but the prosperity of Nauvoo increasing as it did, beyond any former parallel, even in the western world, excited in their bosoms envy, hatred and all ungodliness.

This is the true secret of all their barbarous movements against Mormonism; and they supposed by destroying the Smiths they should extinguish their religion, disperse the Mormons, depopulating and desolating Nauvoo. Their folly and wickedness will produce a result exactly the reverse; Mormons will increase an hundredfold; they will, if possible, be more devoutly attached to their religion; will concentrate more closely together, for self-preservation, and their united industry will produce such a city at Nauvoo as does not exist west of the mountains.

From all accounts which have been published here, it does not appear that the slightest resistance was made to the execution of the law, and the inquiry is now made, what was all this clamor, excitement and military parade for?

The editor of the *Warsaw Signal* can answer the question; and if he had his deserts, it is probable no more unprincipled and inflammatory addresses to an infuriated mob would ever emanate from his pen. Not that I would wish any violence to him, but he should be tried by the laws of the state, and see how far his course renders him accountable for the murders which have been committed.

Nothing has ever given me greater gratification than the calm, dignified submission to the laws shown at Nauvoo since the death of the Smiths. This forbearance on your part is beyond all praise; let it continue. Give not the shadow of a pretext for another appeal to popular fury.   The demons are foiled, and let them gnash their teeth in silence over their disappointment.

The increase of population at Nauvoo can no more be prevented than the Mississippi can be stopped in its course.   Its triumph is inevitable, because the engine by which it is to be accomplished is irresistible.

What earthly power has ever yet stood before the overpowering energies of a religious creed?   But when religion is protected by law, as your religion ought to be, and will soon be, in Illinois, then such advances will be made by the Mormons as have never been dreamed of by the greatest enthusiast.'

The editor of the *Neighbor* adds:—

'Upon this letter, let it be remembered that the writer is not a Mormon or a western man, but a citizen of Connecticut, loving law, liberty and life.'

From the *Tompkins* (N. Y.) *Democrat*, we extract the following:—

'The report that a battle had been fought between the Mormons and anti-Mormons, in which some five hundred were slain, is all a hoax.   Such vile statements only serve to give strength to the Prophet's views.   Indeed, we do not know which has the worst effect on the community, the doctrines of Smith or the ten thousand false rumors constantly put in circulation against him.   One thing is certain, his name will survive when those who grossly misrepresent him have become blanks on the page of the future.' "

CHAPTER XV

CHAPTER OF MISCELLANEOUS DOCUMENTS, PRESS
EXCERPTS, AND MOVEMENTS OF LEADING ELDERS OF
THE CHURCH AT NAUVOO AND ELSEWHERE

Tuesday, July 11, 1844.—Elder Willard Richards called upon Elder Parley P. Pratt, likewise Brothers Samuel Russell, Hiram Kimball and Stephen Markham; also upon Brother Elijah Fordham, to inquire about the lumber for the Temple. *Movements of the Twelve et al.*

Elders Brigham Young and Orson Pratt traveled to Peterboro, for the purpose of attending conference.

Elders Kimball, Wight and others went to Wilmington, and preached in the evening: several saints from Chester county were present.

Elder Wilford Woodruff preached in Boston this evening, and endeavored to console the saints who were mourning the loss of the martyred Prophet and Patriarch.

Friday, 12.—President Marks consulted with William Clayton about calling a meeting of the presidents of various quorums to appoint a trustee-in-trust in behalf of the Church of Jesus Christ of Latter-day Saints. *At Nauvoo Question of Trustee-in Trust.*

A council was held at 3 p. m.; but as Dr. Willard Richards and Bishop Whitney considered it premature, the council was adjourned till Sunday evening, the 14th.

Messrs. Bedell and Backenstos arrived in Nauvoo, and reported that the governor had demanded the public arms at Warsaw, and was refused. *Governor's Order Disregarded at Warsaw.*

President Brigham Young spent the day with the brethren in Peterboro .

We learn from Elder Kimball's journal, that in company with Elder Lyman Wight and delegates to the convention from Pennsylvania, Delaware and Maryland, he proceeded to Baltimore.

Premonitory Anxieties.

He and Brother Wight, hearing so many contradictory reports concerning the death of the Prophets, felt very anxious to obtain some correct information. They went into their closets and prayed to the Lord to open the way whereby they might know the truth concerning it. Immediately Elder Kimball went to the post office, and got letters up to the 24th of June from his wife, informing him that Presidents Joseph and Hyrum Smith had delivered themselves up into the hands of their enemies to be tried, upon reading which they were immediately satisfied that the Prophets were massacred.

Elder Wilford Woodruff wrote a letter of exhortation to the saints, which was published in *The Prophet*.

Elder John E. Page wrote a long letter on Mormonism, which appeared in the *People's Organ*, of Pittsburgh.

Saturday, 13.—Dr. Willard Richards proposed the organization of a fishing company to help to supply the city of Nauvoo with food.

Elders Kimball and Wight returned to Wilmington, and from thence to Philadelphia, where they read letters giving a particular account of the martyrdom of their brethren.

Sunday, 14.—Meeting at the stand: Elder Parley P. Pratt preached.

Dr. Willard Richards proposed that the church postpone electing a trustee until the Twelve returned, and called a special conference.

6 p. m. Several councilors came to the council chamber to investigate the subject of choosing trustees, but decided to wait until the Twelve arrived.

We extract the following from President Brigham Young's Journal:—

'*Friday*, 12.—We held a meeting in Peterboro in the evening, preparatory to the conference tomorrow.

Saturday, 13.—Had a good time at conference all day. The brethren were very glad to see us, and the Lord gave us many good things to say to them. I preached to the saints and showed the organization and establishment of the kingdom of God upon the earth: that the death of one or a dozen could not destroy the priesthood, nor hinder the work of the Lord from spreading throughout all nations.

Sunday, 14.—Held three meetings, ordained 28 elders. We enjoyed ourselves well, and had an excellent conference.'

Elders Kimball and Wight went to meeting in Philadelphia, and read the account of the massacre to the saints, who all felt very sorrowful, and agreed to dress in mourning in token of their love and respect for the martyred Prophets.

Elder Kimball recorded, 'O Lord, how can we part with our dear brethren—O Lord, save thy servants the Twelve.'

The saints in Boston met in the Franklin Hall; the house was crowded to overflowing, and many could not get into the room. Numbers who had not been in the habit of attending the meetings, came to see what course the saints would pursue now their leaders were slain. Elder Wilford Woodruff, being the only one of the Twelve in the city, addressed the saints during the day, and also in the evening. He preached in the forenoon from *Rev.*, ch. vi, 9, 10 and 11th verses; in the afternoon from *Rev.*, ch. xiv, 6, 7 and 8th verses, and in the evening on the parable of the fig tree, as recorded by *St. Luke* in ch. xxi; and, in connection, read some of the revelations given through the martyred Prophet of our day. The Spirit of the Lord rested powerfully upon the speaker and the saints, and their hearts were comforted. *Elder Woodruff Preaches in Boston.*

Monday, 15.—Elders Parley P. Pratt, Willard Richards, W. W. Phelps and the bishops, with many brethren, assembled to organize a *Movements at Nauvoo.*

company of fishermen to supply the city with fish; twenty-eight volunteered, with eight boats and skiffs.

Isaac Higbee was appointed president, John S. Higbee and Peter Shirts counselors.

The *Times and Season* has the following editorial:—

REVIEW OF THE MURDER AT CARTHAGE

'*General Joseph Smith*, who was murdered in cool blood, in Carthage jail, on Thursday, the 27th day of June, was one of the best men that ever lived on the earth.

The work he has thus far performed, towards establishing pure religion and preparing the way for the great gathering of Israel, in the short space of twenty years, since the time when the angel of the Lord made known his mission and gave him power to move the cause of Zion, exceeds anything of the kind on record.

Without learning, without means, and without experience, he has met a learned world, a rich century, a hard-hearted, wicked and adulterous generation, with truth that could not be resisted, facts that could not be disproved, revelations whose spirit had so much God in them that the servants of the Lord could not be gainsaid or resisted, but, like the rays of light from the sun, they have tinged everything they lit upon with a lustre and livery which has animated, quickened and adorned.

The pages of General Smith's history, though his enemies never ceased to persecute him and hunt for offenses against him, are as unsullied as virgin snow; on about fifty prosecutions for supposed criminal offenses, he came out of the *legal fire*, heated like Nebuchadnezzar's furnace, seven times hotter than it was wont to be, *without the smell of fire*, or a thread of his garments scorched.

His foes of the world and enemies of his own household, who have sought occasions against him, in order secretly to deprive him of his life, because his goodness, greatness and glory exceeded theirs, have a poor excuse to offer the world for shedding his innocent blood, and no apology to make to the Judge of all the earth at the day of judgment. They have murdered him because they feared his righteousness.

His easy, goodnatured way, allowing everyone was honest, drew around him hypocrites, wicked and mean men, with the virtuous, and in the hour of trouble or trial, when the wheat was cleansed by water, the light kernels and smut rose upon the top of the water and had to be poured off, that the residue might be clean; or, to be still plainer, when they went through the machine for cleansing the grain, the chaff, light grain and smut, were blown off among the rubbish.

False brethren, or to call them by their right name, 'apostates', have retarded the work more, and combined more influence to rob him of life, than all Christendom; for they, having mingled in his greatness, knew where and when to take advantage of his weakness.

Their triumph, however, is one that disgraces their state and nation, ruins them in time and in eternity.

They cannot outgrow it, they cannot outlive it, and they cannot outdie it, from him that winked at it to him that shot the fatal ball, wherever there is moral honesty, humanity, love of life, liberty and the pursuit of happiness, there the breath of indignation, the whisper of 'those murders', the story of mobocracy and the vengeance of God will haunt the whole gang and their offspring and abettors with a fury like Milton's gates of hell,

'*   *   *   grating harsh thunder.'

In thus descanting upon the glory of General Joseph Smith and the cowardly disgrace of his assassins, let his noble-minded brother Hyrum have no less honor shown him. He lived so far beyond the ordinary walk of man, that even the tongue of the vilest slanderer could not touch his reputation.

He lived godly and he died godly, and his murderers will yet have to confess that it would have been better for them to have a mill-stone tied to them, and they cast into the depths of the sea, and remain there while eternity goes and eternity comes, than to have robbed that noble man of heaven of his life.

If there be such a thing as the greatest and least crimes among the archives of the better world, the wilful murder of Joseph and Hyrum Smith will be first and worst, without forgiveness in this world or the world to come, 'for no murderer hath eternal life abiding in him.'

The Savior said, woe unto the world because of offenses, but offenses must needs come; but woe unto him by whom they come!

Prophets have been sent, according to the sacred history, which all enlightened nations use as a guide of morality here, or for a rule to obtain heaven hereafter, to instruct and lead the people according to the pure purposes of God, and yet from Cain down to two or three hundred Americans, Illinoians, Missourians, Christians, even freemen, the lives of mostly all these good men, the servants of God, not omitting his own Son, have been taken from them by those who professed to be the most wise, enlightened, intelligent and religious, (that is nationally) that were on the earth when the hellish deeds were done.

But what has the next generation said? Ah! time thou art older and abler to tell the story than they that did the solemn act. No wonder the heathen nations will be God's in the day of his power; they have not killed the Prophets.

When General Smith went to Carthage, just as the cavalry met him for the purpose of obtaining the state arms, he said to a friend, *I am going like a lamb to the slaughter; but I am calm as a summer's morning*: *I have a conscience void of offense toward God, and toward all men*: *I shall die innocent.'*

Now ye great men who boast of great wisdom, what think ye of the Prophet's last prediction? How glorious! How mild! How God-like! No wonder the sympathies of all honest men are kindled in his behalf; the goodness of his deeds merit them.

The want of a perfect knowledge of the servants of God, of the Son of God, in all ages, down to this last, horrid, heart-sickening butchery of those two unoffending American freemen, must have been the great first cause of taking life contrary to the law of God or man.

Leaving religion out of the case, where is the lover of his country, and his posterity, that does not condemn such an outrageous murder, and will not lend all his powers, energies and influence to bring the offenders to justice and judgment?

Every good man will do it when he remembers that these two innocent men were confined in jail for a supposed crime, deprived of any weapons to defend themselves, had the pledged faith of the state of Illinois, by Governor Ford, for their protection, and were then shot to death, while with uplifted hands they gave such signs of distress as would have commanded the interposition and benevolence of savages or pagans.

They were both Masons in good standing.

Ye brethren of 'the mystic tie', what think ye! Where are our good Masters Joseph and Hyrum? Is there a pagan, heathen or savage nation on the globe that would not be moved on this great occasion, as the trees of the forest are moved by a mighty wind? Joseph's last exclamation was, 'O Lord, my God'.

If one of these murderers, their abettors or accessories before or after the fact, are suffered to cumber the earth without being dealt with according to law, what is life worth, and what is the benefit of laws? and more than all, what is the use of institutions which savages would honor, where civilized beings murder without cause or provocation?

Will the Americans look over the vast concerns that must, sooner or later, touch their welfare at home and abroad, and exalt or disgrace them among the kingdoms of the great family of man, and learn whether anarchy, mobbery and butchery are not swiftly hurrying the constituted authorities of our country into irretrievable ruin, while the inhabitants of the land must sink into wretchedness, bloodshed, revenge and woe?

Elder John Taylor and Dr. Willard Richards, who were in the jail at the time, innocently, as friends of these men, have only to thank God that their lives were spared.

Elder Taylor was wounded with four bullets, and a fifth ball, which, had it not been for his watch in his left vest pocket, would have passed into his vitals and destroyed his life instantly.

This memorable and very valuable watch saved his life, and will remain with its hands permanently pointing to '5 o'clock, 16 minutes and 26 seconds', as the moment when so small a machine interposed between time and eternity.

Dr. Richards was not wounded by a single ball, though one passed so near his ear as to leave a mark.

If such scenes do not awaken the best feelings of freemen for personal safety, what will? We pause! solemnly pause for the opinion of millions, because all are interested; life is the last boon, all is blank without it, death blots the rest, and where is man?

To conclude, if the good people of our common country, and our common world, do not arise with a union of feeling and energy to help to wash off the blood of these two innocent men from Hancock county, from the plighted faith of Illinois, from the boasted and widespreading fame of the United States, and from the dignity of our globe, then let all but the righteous be smitten with a curse; but, methinks I see a 'union of all honest men', aside from religion, stand forth to magnify the law, who will never rest till justice and judgment have made the offenders, abettors and accessories, whether apostates, officers or mere *men, atone for the innocent blood of Joseph and Hyrum Smith.'*

The following was written by the undersigned members of the council [i. e. of the Twelve]:—

LETTER TO THE SAINTS ABROAD

'*Dear Brethren,*—On hearing of the martyrdom of our beloved Prophet and Patriarch, you will doubtless need a word of advice and comfort, and look for it from our hands.

We would say, therefore, first of all, be still and know that the Lord is God, and that he will fulfil all things in his own due time, and not one jot or tittle of all his purposes and promises shall fail.

Remember, REMEMBER that the priesthood and the keys of power are held in eternity as well as in time, and, therefore, the servants of God who pass the veil of death are prepared to enter upon a greater and more effectual work, in the speedy accomplishment of the restoration of all things spoken of by his holy prophets.

Remember that all the prophets and saints who have existed since the world began, are engaged in this holy work, and are yet in the vineyard, as well as the laborers of the eleventh hour, and are all pledged to establish the kingdom of God on the earth, and to give judgment unto the saints: therefore, none can hinder the rolling on of the eternal purposes of the great Jehovah.

And we have now every reason to believe that the fulfilment of his great purposes are much nearer than we had supposed, and that not many years hence we shall see the kingdom of God coming with power and great glory to our deliverance.

As to our country and nation, we have more reason to weep for them than for those they have murdered, for they are destroying themselves and their institutions, and there is no remedy; and as to feelings of revenge, let them not have place for one moment in our bosoms, for God's vengeance will speedily consume to that degree that we would fain be hid away and not endure the sight.

Let us then humble ourselves under the mighty hand of God, and endeavor to put away all our sins and imperfections as a people and as individuals, and to call upon the Lord with the spirit of grace and supplication, and wait patiently on him until he shall direct our way.

Let no vain and foolish plans or imaginations scatter us abroad and divide us asunder as a people, to seek to save our lives at the expense of truth and principle, but rather let us live or die together and in the enjoyment of society and union.

Therefore, we say, let us haste to fulfil the commandments which God has already given us. Yea, let us haste to build the Temple of our God, and to gather together thereunto, our silver and our gold with us, unto the name of the Lord, and then we may expect that he will teach us of his ways, and we will walk in his paths.

We would further say, that in consequence of the great rains which have deluged the western country, and, also, in consequence of persecution and excitement, there has been but little done here, either in farming or building, this season; therefore, there is but little employment and but little means of subsistence at the command of the saints in this region; therefore, let the saints abroad and others who feel for our calamities and wish to sustain us, come on with their money and means without delay, and purchase lots and farms, and build buildings and employ hands, as well as to pay their tithings into the Temple and their donations to the poor.

We wish it distinctly understood abroad that we greatly need the assistance of every lover of humanity, whether members of the church or otherwise, both in influence and in contributions for our aid, succor and support.

Therefore, if they feel for us, now is the time to show their liberality and patriotism towards a poor and persecuted, but honest and industrious people.

Let the elders who remain abroad continue to preach the gospel in its purity and fulness, and to bear testimony of the truth of these things which have been revealed for the salvation of this generation.

[Signed] PARLEY P. PRATT,
WILLARD RICHARDS,
JOHN TAYLOR,
W. W. PHELPS.

Nauvoo, July 15, 1844.'

Elder Jedediah M. Grant returned to Philadelphia. Two weeks since he left Nauvoo, and reported that all was quiet and peace in the city since the burial of the martyrs.

LAMENTATION

Of a Jew Among the Afflicted and Mourning Sons and Daughters of Zion, at the Assassination of the Two Chieftains in Israel, Joseph and Hyrum Smith.

'Blessed the people knowing the shout of Jehovah,
In the light of his countenance they will walk.
How can we, a people in sackcloth,
Open our lips before thee?
They have rejected and slain our leaders,
Thine anointed ones.
Our eyes are dim, our hearts heavy;
No place of refuge being left.
Redeem the people that in thee only trusts:
There is none to stand between and inquire;
Thou art our helper,
The refuge of Israel in time of trouble.
O look in righteousness upon thy faithful servants,
Who have laid bare their lives unto death,
Not withholding their bodies;
Being betrayed by false brethren, and their lives cut off,
Forbidding their will before thine;
Having sanctified thy great name,
Never polluting it;
Ready for a sacrifice;—standing in the breach,
Tried, proved and found perfect.
To save the blood of the fathers;
Their children, brothers, and sisters;
Adding theirs unto those who are gone before them;
Sanctifying thy holy and great name upon the earth;
Cover and conceal not their blood.
Give ear unto their cries until thou lookest
And shewest down from heaven-taking vengeance
And avenging their blood—avenging thy people and
        thy law,

According to thy promises made
Unto our forefathers, Abraham, Isaac and Jacob.
Hasten the acceptable and redeeming year;
Shadday: remember unto us thy covenants:
All this heaviness has reached us;
Can any one be formed to declare
What has befallen us?
All this we bear, and the name of our God
We will not forget, nor deny,
The 'Hebrews' God' he is called,
Thou art clothed with righteousness,
But we are vile.
Come not in judgment with us.
Before thee nothing living is justified by their works.
But be with us as thou wast with our fathers.
Help thou, O Father; unto thee
We will lift our souls,
Our hearts in our hands;
We look to heaven,
Lifting our eyes unto the mountains,
From whence cometh our help.
Turn away thine anger,
That we be not spoiled.
O return and leave a blessing behind thee.'*

Tuesday, 16.—William Clayton finished measuring the last raft of lumber for the Temple, from the pineries, amounting to 87,732 feet.

The following was received by Dr. Willard Richards:—

LETTER REPORTING THREATENING PORTENTS AGAINST NAUVOO

'De Kalb, Hancock Co., Ill.,
July 1, 1844.
[In confidence]

Dr. Richards.

Dear Sir,—I hope the subject upon which this communication

---

*Times and Seasons, vol. v, p. 591. The author of this poem is Alexander Neibaur who is also the author of the hymn "Come Thou Glorious Day of Promise", see *L. D. S. Hymn Books*, current. The strong Hebraic character of the above poem will appear to the reader.

is written will be a sufficient apology for the privilege I have taken in addressing you, with whom I have not had the pleasure of an acquaintance.

I wish to apprise you that reports are in circulation, which no doubt are true, that the Warsaw and Green Plains mobocrats are making strong exertions to raise forces sufficient to mob and drive the people of your city from their present residences.

I think you should keep a steady lookout, for it seems that the cold-hearted murder of Generals Joseph and Hyrum Smith in Carthage jail has not satisfied the bloodthirsty dispositions of those demons, but they desire to prosecute their wretched purposes still further.

I, as one of General Deming's staff, have used my influence against calling out a large force to be stationed at Carthage, fearing that some might be influenced by those mobocrats to join them in their wretched purpose, for I have no idea they can get forces enough to leave their homes, neither in Illinois nor Missouri, for that purpose, to overcome you.

If we could have four or five hundred troops stationed at Carthage, of the right sort, that could be depended on, to suppress mobs, I should like it, but, fearing the influence of those desperadoes might cause them to disobey all orders and join the mob against you, I think it best not to risk it.

The murder of Generals Joseph and Hyrum Smith is deprecated by the community, almost at large, that is, those who are not lost to the principles of humanity; and there seems to be a general feeling of sympathy resting on the public mind.

I was pleased to hear of the prudent course that your people resolved to pursue, in acting only on the defensive and abiding the law, which is on your side.

> In haste, yours, etc.,
>
> THOS. H. OWEN.'

To which Dr. Willard Richards replied as follows:—

DECLARED INTENTION OF THE CHURCH TO TAKE NO PART IN THE TRIAL OF THE MURDERERS OF THE PROPHETS

'Nauvoo, July 16, 1844.

Sir,—I am sorry that there has been delay which caused your letter to arrive so late to hand, and I feel thankful for the very kind and sympathetic manner in which you express yourself towards us as a people, and shall be very thankful if you will continue your favors to me whenever anything may occur, and you may depend upon my doing the same to yourself.

In regard to the assassination of the Generals Smith, we do not intend to take any action in the case whatever, but leave ourselves entirely in the hands of the governor and the majesty of the law, to mete out just and retributive justice in the matter.

You may rest perfectly assured that we never did act on the offensive, or against the law, but shall continue the same course, which appears to have given you so much satisfaction, and act entirely on the defensive, and abide the law.

In haste, sir, I remain yours, etc.,
WILLARD RICHARDS.

Thos. H. Owen, Esq.'

Elder Wilford Woodruff wrote the following:—

WOODRUFF'S LETTER TO BRIGHAM YOUNG—REPORTING THE PROPHETS' DEATH

'Boston, July 16, 1844.

Elders Brigham Young and Orson Pratt.

Dear Brethren.—I hasten to inform you that I returned to this city on hearing the report of the death of Joseph and Hyrum, expecting to see you. I have waited a number of days in deep suspense, to obtain word I could rely on.

This morning two letters were put into my hands by Sister Phelps, one from Erastus Snow and one from John E. Page of Pittsburgh, both confirming the report of the death of Joseph and Hyrum—they were murdered in Carthage jail.

It is not for me to counsel you, but I would ask if it would not be well for you to come direct to Boston, and hold a council with the Twelve and decide what course to pursue. Things are still very critical in the west; we don't know where it will end.

I spent the Sabbath here, spoke three times, comforted the saints all I could and had a good time. The saints bear the shock well. I am well and in good spirits. I do not know where I can address my letters to reach you. I shall write to Lowell, Peterboro and Bradford, hoping they may reach you in one of those places.

I shall go immediately to Farmington, New Haven, Ct., and New York; if you wish to write to me, direct to Farmington, Ct.

Yours in the kingdom of God,
WILFORD WOODRUFF.'

President Young having received Elder Woodruff's letter at Peterboro, started for Boston, but on arriving at Lowell remained all night.

Wednesday, 17.—Mrs. Emma Smith, in company
Movement
Respecting the
Prophet's
Estate.
with Messrs. Woods and Wasson, went to Carthage for letters of administration on the estate of her deceased husband, Joseph Smith.

The following is from Elder Woodruff's Journal:—

EXCERPT

'Elder Brigham Young arrived in Boston this morning. I walked with him to 57 Temple Street, and called upon Sister Vose. Brother Young took the bed and gave vent to his feelings in tears. I took the big chair, and veiled my face, and for the first time gave vent to my grief and mourning for the Prophet and Patriarch of the church, Joseph and Hyrum Smith, who were murdered by a Gentile mob. After being bathed in a flood of tears I felt composed. Elder Young left the city. I spent the night at Brother Phelps.'

The following is extracted from the *St. Louis Transcript*, taken from the report of the editor of the *Republican*:—

REPORTS OF MOVEMENTS IN ILLINOIS OBSERVED FROM WARSAW

'On our return we stopped at Warsaw, where the state commissioners were joined by Colonel Wood, the mayor of Quincy, and Mr. Conyers. These gentlemen had returned from Nauvoo through Carthage, and had been laboring to establish peace between the parties.

The people of Hancock county, however, appear to be averse to any compromise short of the removal of the Mormons from the county. They assert that it is now absolutely necessary to peace and quietness that either the Mormons or citizens quit the county, and that sooner or later one must go, even if force be necessary to accomplish it.

Mr. Jonas, one of the commissioners, addressed the citizens of Warsaw, and called upon them to say whether they would support the governor in enforcing the law and upholding the Constitution, and they unanimously refused to give the pledge.

The same evening a Mr. Skinner of Carthage, who professed to speak in the name of the citizens of Hancock, uttered the same sentiment. He deprecated, as impossible, the idea of settlement if the Mormons were to remain.

A committee of the citizens waited upon Governor Ford, informing him of their fixed conviction that it was necessary one of the parties should leave the county, and desiring him to decide.

The governor replied that it was not for him to decide such a question, or to order any body of citizens, whether Mormons or anti-Mormons, out of the county or state.

From the feeling evinced by the most active in the anti-Mormon ranks, we came to the conclusion that nothing but a dread of consequences would prevent further outbreaks. The flame has been smothered for a time, but the fire has not been quenched, and slight causes may make it burst forth more fiercely than before.

Governor Ford has a most arduous duty to perform. Of his ability to discharge it we will not now speak. At our latest dates he was still at Quincy, and avowed the intention of maintaining the ascendancy of the law at all hazards. He has dismissed all the troops, and they have returned to their homes.' "

CHAPTER XVI

THE MOVEMENTS OF THE APOSTLES AND OTHER LEADING BRETHREN IN THE EAST AND AT NAUVOO— IMPORTANT COMMUNICATION FROM GOVERNOR FORD

"*Thursday, July* 18*th* 1844.—No rain since the night of the 29th ult., of any moment: excessively warm. Thermometer 92½ ° F. After sunset the clouds gathered dense and black, accompanied by lightning, which became so constant, and the flashes so near each other, as to be almost one continued flash, lighter than noonday; the rain descended in torrents, the wind tremendous, prostrating many trees and some houses.

Storm—Status of Weather.

The following is from Elder Woodruff's Journal:—

EXCERPTS

'President Brigham Young arrived in the city of Boston, also Elders Orson Hyde, Heber C. Kimball and Orson Pratt. We met together in council, and agreed to counsel the elders and brethren having families at Nauvoo, to return immediately to them. Elder Hyde advertised that he would preach on the subject of the massacre of Joseph and Hyrum Smith, the Prophet and Patriarch of the church.

Movements of the Twelve in the East.

According to appointment the saints and friends met in a hall in Washington Street. Elder Hyde preached from words in chapter xxiv of *St. Matthew*, 9th to 14th verse, and concluded with the following remarks:—

DISCOURSE OF ELDER ORSON HYDE AT WASHINGTON, D. C.

'In consequence of the death of the Prophets, the editors seem to get the spirit of prophecy, and say the work is done, and will stop and die; but, as I am in the midst of the prophetic editors, like Saul

I catch some of the spirit of prophecy, and so I will prophesy that instead of the work dying, it will be like the mustard stock that was ripe, that a man undertook to throw out of his garden, and scattered seed all over it, and next year it was nothing but mustard. It will be so by shedding the blood of the Prophets—it will make ten saints where there is one now.

Some said that he would be president [i. e. of the U. S.], but is now dead; now, what will he do? The Revelator says, 'He that overcometh will I give power over the nations, and he shall rule them with a rod of iron'; I don't know but he may hold the keys of the plagues that are to be poured out in the last days upon this and other nations.

Angels appeared anciently to John, who were his fellow servants, the Prophets. Joseph may appear in this day to his brethren.

This gospel of the kingdom must be preached in all the world for a testimony, then shall the end come; though they should be persecuted, if they endured to the end, they should be saved.

This generation speak much about the clouds and weather; they discern the face of the sky, but why can they not discern the signs of the times? The fig trees are leafing, and all things indicate the second advent of Christ.'

REMARKS OF BRIGHAM YOUNG

Elder Brigham Young arose, and said he felt disposed to add his testimony; be of good cheer. The testimony is not in force while the testator liveth; when he died it was in force; so it is with Joseph.

On the Day of Pentecost there were but 120 of the saints, but at that time there were added 3,000 souls. When God sends a man to do a work, all the devils in hell cannot kill him until he gets through his work; so with Joseph, he prepared all things, gave the keys to men on the earth, and said, 'I may soon be taken from you'.'

The following Epistle of the Twelve was published in the *Prophet*:—

AN EPISTLE OF THE APOSTLES TO THE SAINTS

'Boston, July 18, 1844.

To the Elders and Saints Scattered Abroad, Greeting.

Dear Brethren,—We take this method to notify you that the advice and counsel of the Twelve is, that all the brethren who have families in the west should return to them as soon as convenient, and that all the churches should remain humble and watch unto prayer, and follow the teachings that have been given them by the servants of God, and leave all things in the hands of God: all will be right; the name of the Lord will be glorified and his work will prosper. And we would warn the saints in all the world against receiving the teachings of any man or set of men who come professing to be elders of the Church of Jesus Christ of Latter-day Saints, who preach any doctrine contrary to the plain and holy principles of the gospel of Jesus Christ which have been delivered unto them.

We wish to see all the authorities of the church residing at Nauvoo, who at this time may be absent, such as the presidents of the different quorums, high priests, high council, seventies and bishops, that we may meet them in council as soon as convenient, as we expect to return immediately to Nauvoo.

Dear brethren, we are sensible that the account of the death of the Prophet and Patriarch of the church will be painful to your hearts: it is to ours. We feel and mourn their loss, but they have sealed their testimony with their blood; they have not counted their lives as dear unto themselves as the lives of the church; they have died in the Lord and their works will follow them.

The eyes of the Lord are upon those who have shed the blood of the Lord's anointed, and he will judge them with a righteous judgment. Let the saints cultivate a meek and quiet spirit, and all things shall in the end work together for your good.

By order of the Quorum of the Twelve,

[Signed] BRIGHAM YOUNG, *President,*
WILFORD WOODRUFF, *Clerk.'*

We copy from the *Prophet*:—

WARNING AGAINST FALSE DOCTRINES

'*Mr. Editor,*—I am requested to say to the saints, through the *Prophet*, by the counsel of the Twelve, that whereas certain strange doctrines have been taught and practiced in Boston and elsewhere, by men claiming higher authority than the Twelve,—

This is, therefore, to warn you, in the name of our Lord Jesus Christ, that you give no heed to men making these high pretensions, when they teach you things that are not in accordance with principles which you know to be correct.

And we would seriously caution all men to beware how they offer strange fire upon the altars of pure and innocent hearts, lest that flame consume them, root and branch, in an unexpected hour; for the authorities of God's house are not to be rode over by any man, and he escape without the rod.

A ship that carries more sail than her ballast will admit of, will surely capsize when the storm strikes her. This is a figure, and let it be remembered.

Yours truly,
ORSON HYDE.'

Friday, 19.—Elders Parley P. Pratt, Willard Richards, John Taylor and W. W. Phelps spent the afternoon in council.

Elders at Nauvoo.

Elder Kimball went to Salem, and preached to the saints in the evening.

Movements of Elders in the East.

Saturday, 20.—Elders Brigham Young and Heber C. Kimball spent the day together in the city of Boston. Elders Orson Hyde and Orson Pratt left for New York, and Elder Wilford Woodruff for Connecticut.

Sunday, 21.—Meeting at the stand. Elder Parley P. Pratt preached from the *Book of Mormon,* quoting from Moroni, 'Widows mourning for their husbands'.

Meetings at Nauvoo.

Afternoon.—The sacrament was administered. Elders Pratt, Cahoon and Richards spoke.

Elders Young and Kimball preached to the saints in Boston during the day and evening; congregations very attentive.

Monday, 22.—The following is from Governor Thomas Ford:—

LETTER OF GOVERNOR FORD TO WILLARD RICHARDS AND W. W. PHELPS

'Quincy, July 17, 1844.
[Confidential]

Gentlemen,—I have just returned from St. Louis. I should have gone on directly to Nauvoo, but I was aware that a visit to your place at this time would certainly be misrepresented by the public. I want very much to see some of you solely on the business of the late outrages at Carthage.

The mode of proceeding to be adopted is a matter for careful consideration. I wish to see some of you to consult on that one subject alone. Can one of you come down? If so, come immediately, or let me know.

I am, most respectfully,

Your obedient servant,
[Signed] THOMAS FORD.

Dr. Willard Richards,
W. W. Phelps, Esq.'

To which the annexed was sent in reply:—

REPLY OF RICHARDS AND PHELPS

'Nauvoo, July 22, 1844.

[Confidential]

His Excellency Governor Ford.

Sir,—We have, at this late hour, received your letter of the 17th inst., and would be gratified with an interview, agreeably to your Excellency's request; but the murder of our best men makes our time precious, and compels us to forego the interview.

We have delegated our friend, Mr. Orson Spencer, one of the aldermen of our city, to meet your Excellency on the arrival of the morning boat, answer any queries, and attend to all necessary business, having the fullest confidence in his ability and integrity to discharge the mission to your Excellency's satisfaction and the best interest of our bleeding and long-loved country.

We are, sir, most respectfully,

Your obedient servants,

[Signed] WILLARD RICHARDS,

W. W. PHELPS.'

Sister Leonora Taylor wrote as follows:—

LEONORA TAYLOR'S WOMANLY LETTER TO GOVERNOR FORD

'Nauvoo, July 22, 1844.

To His Excellency Thomas Ford.

Sir,—The peculiarity of my situation will, I hope, plead my excuse for troubling your Excellency on the present occasion.

Mr. Taylor, who was severely wounded in the jail at Carthage, is still ill, and obliged to be lifted in and out of bed; his wounds are slowly healing, and we hope he will finally get well, if suffered to do so. But, sir, I am sorry to say the murderers and mobbers are still at large in our neighborhood; as there has been no steps taken to bring them to justice, they have taken fresh courage and held meetings to carry out their work of destruction. I have been told they have sent messengers to Missouri to collect all the force they can, to come and exterminate the Mormons after harvest.

I have enclosed your Excellency a communication sent Mr. Taylor yesterday, which is a sample of many that are daily coming in. He does not know of my writing this letter. Nothing but the urgency of the case could have induced me to remind your Excellency of your promise to bring the *murderers* to *justice*. If a step of that kind is not taken soon, I much fear that it cannot benefit us as a people.

We are without arms, in a great measure, having delivered them up at your Excellency's request, and we are forbid to stand even in our own defense. In this peculiar position, without resources, we can only look to your Excellency for defense, to you, sir, for protection; and if it is not granted, we must be murdered in cold blood.

My feelings as a wife, and mother of helpless children, together with the afflictions of an injured people, all constrain me to beseech of you to exert the power and authority which the people and God has given you, in the cause of the oppressed. You shall have our prayers, that wisdom may be given you from on high to act in this case to the glory of God, your own honor and that of the state we live in.

Your Excellency was warned of our brethren's danger, who were murdered, but could not believe that men were so base and degraded. The same men are now plotting our destruction.

As an individual who feels herself injured, and also in behalf of an oppressed, injured and persecuted people, I again beg your official interference. Your Excellency cannot now be mistaken in the men nor their design; I beseech you then, for the honor of our bleeding country, for the sake of suffering innocence and the cause of humanity, by the wounds of my husband and the blood of those murdered victims, to use prompt measures for our protection and the bringing to justice of those murderers.

Sincerely praying that you, sir, may become a terror to evildoers and the praise of those that do well, with great respect

I have the honor to be

Your Excellency's humble servant,

LEONORA TAYLOR.'

Elder Wilford Woodruff went to Farmington, Ct., and spent the night at his father's house. He ordained his father a high priest.

Movements of Prominent Elders.

Tuesday, 23.—10 a. m. Elder Orson Spencer went down on the *Osprey* to Quincy, to wait upon the governor.

Elders Brigham Young and Heber C. Kimball spent the day in Boston. They attended meeting in the evening and ordained thirty-two elders.

Elder Woodruff parted with his father and mother at Farmington, and proceeded to New York.

Wednesday, 24.—Elders Parley P. Pratt, Willard Richards, W. W. Phelps, George Miller and L. Woodworth met in council. They anointed and administered to Elder Samuel H. Smith, who was very sick.

Elder Phelps received the following communication from the governor:—

IMPORTANT AND CONFIDENTIAL LETTER OF GOVERNOR FORD
TO ELDER W. W. PHELPS

'Quincy, July 22, 1844.

Sir,—On Thursday last I wrote to Dr. Richards and yourself,
requesting you to come or send some person to me at this place, to
confer with me in relation to the time and mode of proceeding
against the murderers of the Messrs. Smith; and I therein stated that
I would have come to Nauvoo for that purpose were it not for
the certainty that my motives and objects for so doing would be
misinterpreted. As none of you have come, and have probably not
received my letter, I have concluded to write you again and send this
letter by special messenger.

In this letter I will say to you what I intended to say in a personal
conference. In the beginning, then, you must allow me to say that
my position forbids that I should be a partisan on either side of your
unhappy controversy.

I may, for aught I know, have stern duties to perform in
relation to both parties. This, however, will depend on which side
may be the aggressor. Thus far, since the death of the Smiths, your
people have behaved well; much better than could have been expected
under the circumstances, and much better than the opposite party.
I anxiously hope that they may have the grace to continue in the
same line of conduct.

An unresisting, passive, peaceable, but defensive course on your
parts, will do much to disarm prejudices in the surrounding country.
That such prejudices do exist in the minds of the people you know
as well as I, though you may not be fully aware of their extent, or the
ferocity which they engender.

If I speak of those prejudices and the causes of them, I do not wish
you to misunderstand me, as some of you did on a former occasion,
and suppose that I am speaking my own opinions and feelings.

I say now, once for all, that I have nothing to do with those
prejudices further than as a practical man; they obtrude themselves
on my consideration, as presenting obstacles to me in the discharge
of my official duty. The more prejudice and bad feeling which is
gotten up against your people, whether by their own imprudence or
the malice of their enemies, the more difficult it is for me to do
anything effectually to protect either party according to law.

There are, I am informed, some few inflammatory and hot-blooded
individuals amongst you, who, by their imprudence and rashness, continue to give cause for those prejudices, and, of course, by so doing,
continue to involve you all in a common danger; I speak of the danger
of a mob.

I am also informed that most of you entertain the opinion that there
has been a great and universal reaction in the public mind since the
death of the Smiths.

On this subject I desire to tell you the naked truth. I am aware that you scarcely ever hear the truth, as to public sentiment abroad, from those who visit you in your city. The complaisance of such persons, and their desire to please, will induce them to omit the statement of disagreeable truths, and to say such things only as are pleasing and complimentary. You are bound, as men of sense, to receive all such statements with a great deal of allowance.

On my part, without desiring to please any of you, or to conciliate your favor, but certainly without any design to insult your misfortunes, and in a pure spirit of friendly concern for the peace and safety of all who repose under the shade of our political fig tree, I desire to state to you frankly, candidly and thoroughly, what I do know on this subject.

The naked truth then is, that most well-informed persons condemn in the most unqualified manner the mode in which the Smiths were put to death, but nine out of every ten of such accompany the expression of their disapprobation by a manifestation of their pleasure that they are dead.

The disapproval is most unusually cold and without feeling. It is a disapproval which appears to be called for, on their part, by decency, by a respect for the laws and a horror of mobs, but does not flow warm from the heart.

The unfortunate victims of this assassination were generally and thoroughly hated throughout the country, and it is not reasonable to suppose that their death has produced any reaction in the public mind resulting in active sympathy; if you think so, you are mistaken.

Most that is said on the subject is merely from the teeth out; and your people may depend on the fact, that public feeling is now, at this time, as thoroughly against them as it has ever been.

I mention this, not for the purpose of insulting your feelings, but to show you clearly how careful your people ought to be in future to avoid all causes of quarrel and excitement, and what little reliance could be placed on any militia force which I could send in your favor.

I ought, perhaps, to qualify what I have said, by remarking that but few persons from the surrounding counties could now be procured to join a mob force against you, without further cause of excitement to be ministered by some misguided imprudence of your people. But what I mean to say, and to say truly, is, that in the present temper of the public mind I am positively certain that I cannot raise a militia force in the state who would be willing to fight on your side, or to hazard their lives to protect you from an attack of your enemies.

The same state of things exists in relation to any force which might be ordered to arrest the murderers. If troops should be ordered for that purpose, I would expect that they would behave as the militia did in the late Philadelphia riots. The militia in that case sympathized with the native party and against their opponents. It was an unpopular service, and rather than fight they suffered themselves to be defeated and driven from the field.

It is true that I might call upon the Mormons themselves, and then I would have a reliable force. This, however, would be a dangerous experiment, and would, in my mind, inevitably lead to civil war, the result of which no man can foresee.

I think I may safely say, that if the Nauvoo Legion should be called out against the old citizens, the crimes which are sought to be punished would be instantly forgotten in the general and burning indignation which would be kindled.

Men would rally to their assistance who would otherwise be neutral. Your Legion has ever been regarded with a jealous eye; the arming and drilling of your people, with such exceeding industry, in a season of peace, (not wrong in itself,) has been looked upon by the great body of the people with suspicion, and as intended in due time for the subversion of the public liberty: in the beginning you would have been much better without it. If your people had never made any military pretensions, no military feeling would ever have been aroused against you.

This much I hope you will consider has been said from a friendly motive, and for the further purpose of showing you what a dangerous experiment it would be, and how well calculated to excite a civil war, in which your city might be utterly destroyed, if I should attempt to call out the hated Legion against the old citizens.

You may be disposed to ask, What use is there for law and government if these things be so? I answer you, that cases like the present do not seem to be fully provided for by our Constitutions; they were not anticipated to occur.

Upon the first institution of our governments, it was a season of internal peace and union among our people. The population was homogeneous, and all agreed together as brothers. It was supposed that the great body of the people would be always willingly submissive to the laws which they themselves had made. It was not foreseen that great and hostile parties would soon spring up and combine in large numbers to set the law at defiance.

A voluntary submission and obedience was supposed as the basis of government, for this reason no adequate provision was made in our state constitutions for coercing this submission, when the laws were to be trampled upon by the concerted action of large numbers.

The states are prohibited from maintaining standing armies; the only military force at their command, without aid from the general government, is the militia; and, as I have already shown you, this force can only be relied on to do effectual service where that service is popular and jumps with their inclinations.

For this same reason, I must beg leave to say that a party, as in your case, which is the object of popular odium, cannot be too circumspect in their behavior, so as to give no color to the hatred of your enemies. 'Truth is great and will prevail'.

From this you may be assured that if the conduct of your people shall be uniformly peaceably honest and submissive to the laws, even if they have to bear persecution for a season, such conduct must result in dissipating the unhappy prejudices which exist against you.

Truth and candor, however, compel me to say that the Mormons have not always acted in such a manner as if they intended to avoid the creation of prejudices.

The pretensions of your municipal court, the unheard of description of ordinances passed by your city council, the assault on Mr. Bagby, the attempt to kidnap persons from Missouri, the formal destruction of a printing office and the general tone of arrogance and defiance of some of your leaders, were well calculated to inflame the public mind against you.

I think that I have considered this difficult subject in every possible point of view. I am afraid to rely on the militia in the present temper of the public mind. To call on the Nauvoo Legion would be suicidal to any effort as pacification of existing troubles, and for that reason would fail to bring about an enforcement of the laws.

If the laws are to be enforced at all in your county, out of the ordinary way by courts alone, it must be done by a force which is indifferent as to both parties.

To call in one party to put down and subdue the other, would lead to the most disastrous consequences; all the pride of conquest and victory; all the shame of defeat by, and submission to an adversary; all the fury of unconquerable hate and exasperated feeling would necessarily be mingled with the contest, and render it bloody and bitter beyond anything we know of in this country.

For these reasons I have called upon the officers now in command, in the absence of General Gains, of the 3rd Military Department of the United States, for five hundred men of the regular army to be stationed in Hancock county, with whose aid I hope to be able to preserve order and proceed against all criminals whomsoever they may be. The following is a copy of the answer to the application:—

'Headquarters, 3rd Mil. Dept.,
St. Louis, Mo., July 11, 1844.

'*Sir*,—I have the honor to acknowledge the receipt of your Excellency's communication of this date, relating to the difficulties which have occurred between the Mormons and the people of Hancock county, Illinois, and the further difficulties apprehended by you, and requesting of me a force of some five hundred men from the regular army of the United States to be stationed for a time in Hancock county, and to act in conjunction with such forces as may be ordered on the part of the state of Illinois.

'I have not the power of complying with your request, but will forward by tomorrow's mail a copy of your communication to be laid before the authorities in Washington city, and will advise your Excellency of the result as soon as ascertained.

With great respect,

Your most obedient servant,

[Signed] S. W. KEARNEY,

Col. 1st Drags.

His Excellency Thomas Ford,

Governor of Illinois, St. Louis, Mo.'

By the above letter you will perceive that I cannot yet be enabled to say with certainty whether the application will be successful: we will know in two weeks, I think, at most.

The anti-Mormon party intend to renew the war this fall, and if it were known with certainty that the troops of the regular army would be obtained to prevent their operations, they would, most likely, hasten their plans and do all the mischief in their power before the force arrives. They are not afraid of the state militia, and would give themselves but little concern in fear of such opposition.

I therefore caution you not to let it be known beyond your most trusted men that a regular force is expected. I have myself not informed anyone who would make the matter public, and yet, most unaccountably, the fact has got into the newspapers.

Another caution I would give you, your people cannot pay too much attention to it. It is very natural and probable to suppose that with the prospect of such a force, and the increased security it may give, some of your people may be prompted to such audacity and imprudence as will tend to prolong angry feelings. They may thus be induced to do and say foolish and wicked things, uselessly vexatious and mortifying to the opposing party.

There are no doubt wicked people in Nauvoo, ready for the commission of crime, as well as in every other city of the same number of inhabitants. The well-disposed amongst you must restrain those persons, and, if need be, bring them to punishment. The public at large will not distinguish among you, but will involve you all in a common obloquy.

I have dwelt more, perhaps, than may be agreeable to you on this point; but I have done so in my anxiety that the Mormons may demonstrate to the world that they are no more deserving than their enemies.

Three or four of your people are reported to me as having already been threatening life, and publicly following men about the city with clubs, and that no effort was made to restrain them. An effectual stop must be put to all such vaporings, if you expect it to stop on the other side. You are interested in bringing all such men to immediate justice, if you can. If pacification is what you ask, you must restrain your own hostility.

It may be thought that there has already been too much delay in proceeding against the murderers, that a further delay will give an opportunity for many of the guilty to escape, and that the apparent impunity for the present will greatly encourage further outrages against you.

This last consideration is one of considerable force, and on that account I could wish to proceed without delay, if it could be done without exciting further troubles, or if I had a force at my command on which I could rely to suppress them.

I do not fear that any of the leaders will escape or flee from justice: they are determined to remain and brave it out to the end.

In my humble opinion there is no utility in proceeding against any but the leaders.

As to the misguided multitude who were the mere followers of others and the instruments of mischief, it has never been the practice of civilized states to proceed against them with rigor.

The punishment of some of the principal offenders has always been looked upon as sufficient to vindicate the majesty of the law and to deter others from the commission of like offenses, and this is the whole object of human punishment.

I do not apprehend that anything requiring my further stay here will happen immediately, and will return home tomorrow.

I am, most respectfully,

Your obedient servant,

[Signed] THOMAS FORD.

William W. Phelps, Esq., Nauvoo, Illinois.' "*

*This lengthy communication of Governor Ford to W. W. Phelps is quite characteristic of Thomas Ford in nearly all his relationships with the Latter-day Saints, both before and after the martyrdom of the Prophets; and bears witness of his weakness, and inclination to double-dealing with them. In nothing is this more apparent than in the letter enclosed in the above communication to Colonel S. W. Kearney of the First Dragoons, headquarters of the Third Military Department at St. Louis. Ford's appeal to this local commander of the First Dragoons can be no other than mere pretense at applying for U. S. military assistance to quell the riotous uprising of mobs and the rebellion of state military units inclined to mobocracy in western Illinois. The Constitution of the United States makes it possible by application of the legislature or of the executive of a state when the legislature can not be convened to appeal to the federal government for protection against invasion or against "domestic violence". But this application must be made to the federal government for the fulfillment of the guarantee against domestic violence and with his knowledge of the law governing the case, the inconsistency of the appeal of Governor Ford to Colonel Kearney could not be other than a mere pretense at securing aid against the domestic violence in western Illinois at that period. It was a mere "seeming" to invoke federal aid, well knowing that it could not be granted from that source, and in that manner; and evidently the governor sought to satisfy the leading elders at Nauvoo that he had vainly attempted to exercise this power lodged in him by the Constitution. His ignorance could not be pleaded in excuse of such artful dodging in the case. B. H. R.

CHAPTER XVII

GATHERING OF THE TWELVE AND OTHER LEADING
ELDERS AT NAUVOO—DEATH OF ELDER SAMUEL H.
SMITH, BROTHER OF THE PROPHET, EARLY MISSION-
ARY OF THE CHURCH AND ONE OF THE EIGHT
WITNESSES OF THE BOOK OF MORMON

"*Wednesday, July 24, 1844.*—The brethren of the
Twelve were delayed in Boston several days, waiting upon Elder Lyman Wight to accompany them to Nauvoo.

Elders Young, Kimball and Wight left Boston by railway in the morning for Nau- voo. On their arrival at Albany, in the evening, they were joined by Elders Orson Hyde, Orson Pratt, Wilford Woodruff and Sister Ruth Sayers, who had arrived from New York. They continued their journey by railway during the night. *(Preparations of the Twelve to Start for Nauvoo.)*

Thursday, 25.—Elder Orson Spencer returned from
Quincy.

Dr. Richards received the following from President
Brigham Young:—

LETTER OF ELDER BRIGHAM YOUNG TO WILLARD RICHARDS

'Salem, July 8, 1844.

Beloved Brother Willard Richards:

I sit down a few minutes to write you, as Brother Erastus Snow
is going to start for Nauvoo tomorrow. He has been laboring in
Vermont.

We cannot get one word from our families by letter of late. Sister
Ruth Sayers has received a letter from her husband, that, I understand,
gives some information which seems to be satisfactory.

According to what we hear in this country about the 'Mormons'
in the west, I should suppose that there is an election about to take
place, or the Prophet had offered himself for some office in the United States; for of all the howlings of devils and devil's whelps, this
season cannot be beat.

Sometimes the 'Mormons' are all killed; sometimes they are half killed; sometimes the blood is shoe-deep in Nauvoo; sometimes 'Old Joe', as they call him, is taken by the mob and carried to Missouri; sometimes he is gone to Washington; sometimes he has run away; then again he is given up to the authorities, etc., etc. One might suppose him to be a sectarian God, without body, parts or passions, his center everywhere and his circumference nowhere.

Since I left Nauvoo I have heard a great many expressions about the Prophet, but the prevailing opinion is, that he is the smartest man in the Union, and the people are afraid of his smartness. Some will vote for him for the novelty of the thing, and some to see what a Prophet will do at the head of government. We had a fine passage on the rivers; preached and lectured all the way round.

I lectured at Pittsburgh and in Kirtland. We held political meetings at Shalorsville and Hiram. I preached in the first house west of old Father Johnson's, where Brothers Joseph and Sidney were mobbed. I looked at the house a great many times.

I left Brothers Snow and Brooks in Ohio, doing well. The Twelve have been faithful in all things. Brother William Smith is a great man in his calling in this country. Brother Lyman Wight has never been with us before; he is a great, good, noble-hearted man. I love my brethren more and more.

I want to see you and the rest of the brethren in Nauvoo. Give my best love to Brothers Joseph and Hyrum. I cannot be there to see them, but I pray for them continually, and for you and all the brethren in our beloved city, and I pray my heavenly Father to preserve my brethren, my family and the whole city. I pray that we may finish the Temple and get our endowments.

We had a large congregation in Boston at our convention, though in the evening there were some who came in that made some disturbance. This proves that the voice of the people rules; that is, the voice of the rabble. One of the watch got some hurt, but all this did us good in Boston. Brother Heywood, from Quincy, is here with us and is doing much good. He is a faithful witness for Brother Joseph and the principles of righteousness.

We have baptized a good many since we left. The gospel is going ahead. All the stories that are going the rounds make no difference, the people will believe the gospel.

You might ask what we think about Brother Joseph's getting the election this year? You know all about it. We shall do all we can and leave the event with God—the God of heaven will do just as he pleases about it.

Brother Daniel Spencer and many others are here; they are awake to the subject. We are now in the concert hall in Salem. Brother Erastus Snow is now speaking.

We shall attend the conferences in this country, and then leave for the western states to attend the conferences, and get home as quickly as possible. If you are to have a little trouble there, we wish to have a hand in it with you.

I wish you would see my family and speak comfortably to them. Brother Tur, I hope all will go on well with him. If you get a chance to dispose of our property at a good rate, do so. If my wife can get anything to help her I should be pleased. Give my love to Sister Jennetta and all the household, and to all the saints.

Brothers Kimball and Wight will start for Baltimore tomorrow. The brethren in this country inquire after you and all the elders that they have seen; they are warm-hearted. I suppose you have received a letter from the Boston church, with Parley P. Pratt's name to it.

May the Lord bless you all,

BRIGHAM YOUNG.'

Elder Samuel H. Smith remains very sick.

Elder Erastus Snow, and many other elders, returned home today; all seemed weighed down with gloom.

Elders Young, Kimball, Hyde, Pratt, Woodruff and Wight arrived in Buffalo, and remained all night.

Friday, 26.—President Young and company took steamboat at Buffalo for Detroit.

Elder Orson Hyde took leave of his brethren at Fairport, to visit his family at Kirtland.

Saturday, 27.—We copy from the *Times and Seasons* the following from the pen of Miss E. R. Snow:—

TO ELDER JOHN TAYLOR

'Thou Chieftain of Zion! henceforward thy name
Will be classed with the martyrs and share in their fame;
Through ages eternal, of thee will be said,
'With the greatest of Prophets he suffered and bled'.
When the shafts of injustice were pointed at him—
When the cup of his suff'ring was filled to the brim—
When his innocent blood was inhumanly shed,
You shared his afflictions and with him you bled.
When around you, like hailstones, the rifle balls flew—
When the passage of death opened wide to your view—
When the Prophet's freed spirit, through martyrdom fled,
In your gore you lay welt'ring—with martyrs you bled.
All the scars from your wounds, like the trophies of yore,
Shall be ensigns of honor till you are no more;
And by all generations, of thee shall be said,
'With the best of the Prophets in prison he bled'.'

The brethren of the Twelve arrived at Detroit in the evening, and remained over night at the railroad hotel.

Sunday, 28.—Elders Parley P. Pratt, W. W. Phelps and others addressed the saints in Nauvoo.

On hearing of the death of the Prophet and Patriarch, Elders Charles C. Rich, David Fullmer, Graham

Elders Returning to Nauvoo. Coltrin, Samuel Bent, Ira Miles and George A. Smith were together in Michigan. Elder George A. Smith counselled the elders to return home. They accordingly started for Nauvoo. The roads were muddy, the waters high, and many of the bridges were gone. As they approached Nauvoo they found the people very hostile, however they preached at several places by the way.

Elder George A. Smith, and the brethren with him, arrived at Nauvoo near midnight.

The following is from Elder Wilford Woodruff's Journal:—

EXCERPT

'The brethren of the Twelve took the propeller *Hercules* for Chicago at 10 a. m. Fare in the cabin $7. We had comfortable staterooms. We spent the day in writing and in social conversation with each other concerning the death of Joseph and Hyrum and the welfare of the church and our families. A variety of subjects were called up, each one expressing his feelings freely. President Brigham Young said he wished me to keep an account of things as they were passing, as he should look to me for his journal at a future day. Elder Wight said that Joseph told him, while in Liberty jail, Missouri, in 1839, he would not live to see forty years, but he was not to reveal it till he was dead.'

Monday, 29.—Elder George A. Smith visited the Prophet's family.

Elders Willard Richards and George A. Smith visited Elder Samuel H. Smith and laid hands upon him. He expressed a strong desire to live: he was very low, being in the last stages of bilious fever.

Elders Richards and Smith met at Elder Richards',

and ordained two elders who were about leaving the
the city.   Brother Richards signed their licenses:—

'TWELVE APOSTLES,
President.

Willard Richards, Clerk.'

George Miller called on them and requested the
privilege of passing some resolutions against the murderers of Joseph and Hyrum.   The brethren   Bishop George
told him to be quiet and wait and see what   Miller's
Restiveness.
the governor and the state authorities would
do, that Dr. Richards had pledged himself that the
brethren would be quiet, and the Lord had said, 'Vengeance is mine, I will repay'.   Miller left the council,
saying, 'Fat men for patience'.

In the evening Elders Richards and Smith visited
Elder Taylor.

Tuesday, 30.—Elder Samuel H. Smith, brother of
the martyred Prophet and Patriarch, died.

DEATH OF SAMUEL H. SMITH

Elders W. Richards and George A. Smith met in
council with Elder Taylor at his house. Bishop George
Miller and Alexander Badlam wanted them   The Council
to call together the Council of Fifty and   of Fifty.
organize the church.   They were told that the Council
of Fifty was not a church organization, but was composed of members irrespective of their religious faith,
and organized for the purpose of consulting on the
best manner of obtaining redress of grievances from
our enemies, and to devise means to find and locate in
some place where we could live in peace; and that the
organization of the church belonged to the priesthood
alone.

The brethren of the Twelve arrived at Mackinaw.
The steamer stopped a short time, took in   Returning
some fish, and took some boats with Indians   Elders not of
the World.
in tow.   There was a feeling of prejudice
manifested by the passengers of the boat against the

brethren, because they did not mingle with them in their nonsense and folly, and this spirit is more or less manifest throughout the world.

Wednesday, 31.—Elder Amasa Lyman arrived in Nauvoo.

The following from the governor appeared in the *Neighbor*:—

GOVERNOR FORD TO THE PEOPLE OF WARSAW IN HANCOCK COUNTY

'I am continually informed of your preparations and threats to renew the war and exterminate the 'Mormons'. One would suppose that you ought to rest satisfied with what you have already done.

The 'Mormon' leaders, if they ever resisted the law, have submitted to its authority. They have surrendered the public arms, and appeared to be ready to do anything required to make atonement for whatever wrong may have been done.

Since the assassination of their two principal leaders, under circumstances well calculated to inflame their passions and drive them to excesses for the purposes of revenge, they have been entirely peaceful and submissive, and have patiently awaited the slow operation of the laws to redress the wrongs of which they complained. There has been no retaliation, no revenge, and, for anything I can ascertain, there will be none.

Those of your people who are charged with being the most hostile to them have lived, if they knew it, in perfect security from illegal violence.

I am anxious for a pacification of your difficulties. You cannot drive out or exterminate the 'Mormons'. Such an effort would be madness, and would not be permitted by the people of the state. You cannot be sustained in it either by force or law. You are binding yourselves to your weakness, and keeping up an agitation which must fail of the purpose intended and recoil with terrible energy upon your own heads.

I exhort you to reconsider your infatuated resolutions. Try your 'Mormon' neighbors again, and if you cannot dwell together in amity, you may at least refrain from injuring each other.

From the moderation of the 'Mormons', under what they conceive to be the deepest injury, you might well hope that if they ever entertained designs inconsistent with your liberty and happiness, that those designs have been abandoned. They are also interested in preserving the peace.

It is not natural to suppose that they, any more than yourselves, wish to live in continual alarm. They hope for quietness, and will be peaceful and submissive in order to enjoy it. But you are continually driving them to desperation by an insane course of threatening and hostility, and depriving yourselves of peace by the same means used to disquiet them.

If I have said anything severe in this address, I pray you attribute it to my deep conviction that your course is improper and unwarrantable. Such is the opinion of the people at large in the state and all over the country.

From being right in the first instance you have put yourselves in the wrong, and there are none who sustain you. As men of sense you are bound to see, if you will open your eyes, that you cannot effect your purposes. Nevertheless, you are still training and drilling, and keeping together, and threatening a renewal of the war.

I have said to you often that you cannot succeed; by this time you ought to see it yourselves. What can your small force do against two thousand armed men, entrenched in a city, and defending themselves, their wives and their children?

Besides, if you are the aggressors, I am determined that all the power of the state shall be used to prevent your success. I can never agree that a set of infatuated and infuriated men shall barbarously attack a peaceful people who have submitted to all the demands of the law, and when they had full power to do so, refrained from inflicting vengeance upon their enemies. You may count on my most determined opposition—upon the opposition of the law, and upon that of every peaceful, law-abiding citizen of the country.

This is not spoken in anger. God knows I would do no injury unless compelled to do so to sustain the laws. But mob violence must be put down. It is threatening the whole country with anarchy and ruin. It is menacing our fair form of government, and destroying the confidence of the patriot in the institutions of his country.

I have been informed that the 'Mormons' about Lima and Macedonia have been warned to leave the settlements. They have a right to remain and enjoy their property. As long as they are good citizens they shall not be molested, and the sooner those misguided persons withdraw their warning and retrace their steps, the better it will be for them.

[Signed] THOMAS FORD.

July 25, 1844.

Thursday, August 1.—The remains of the deceased Elder Samuel H. Smith were interred this morning at 10 a. m.

We extract the following from his obituary:—

BIOGRAPHICAL NOTE OF SAMUEL H. SMITH, BROTHER OF THE
PROPHET—IMPORTANT TESTIMONY TO THE BOOK OF MORMON

'Samuel Harrison Smith, the fourth son of Joseph and Lucy, was
born in the town of Tunbridge, Orange county, Vermont, on the 13th
day of March, 1808.

In his early life he assisted his father in farming. He possessed a
religious turn of mind, and at an early age joined the Presbyterian
Church, to which sect he belonged until he visited his brother Joseph
in May, 1829, when Joseph informed him that the Lord was about
to commence his latter-day work.

He also showed him that part of the *Book of Mormon* which he had
translated, and labored to persuade him concerning the gospel of Jesus
Christ which was about to be revealed in its fulness.

Samuel was not, however, very easily persuaded of these things;
but after much inquiry and explanation he retired and prayed that he
might obtain from the Lord wisdom to enable him to judge for himself; the result was that he obtained revelation for himself sufficient
to convince him of the truth of the testimony of his brother Joseph.

On the 15th day of May, 1829, having been commanded of the
Lord, Joseph Smith and Oliver Cowdery were baptized, and as they
were returning from the water to the house, they overheard Samuel
engaged in secret prayer. Joseph said that he considered that a sufficient testimony of his being a fit subject for baptism; and as they had
now received authority to baptize, they spoke to Samuel upon the
subject, and he went straightway to the water with them, and was
baptized by Oliver Cowdery, he being the third person baptized into
the Church of Jesus Christ in the last dispensation.

He was one of the eight witnesses of the *Book of Mormon*.

He was present at the organization of the church, April 6, 1830,
and was one of the six who at that time constituted the members of
the church. He was ordained to the priesthood on the 6th of April,
1830.

On the 30th of June following the organization of the church,
he took some *Books of Mormon* and started out on his mission, to
which he had been set apart by his brother Joseph, and on traveling
twenty-five miles, which was his first day's journey, he stopped at a
number of places in order to sell his books, but was turned out of
doors as soon as he declared his principles.

When evening came on he was faint and almost discouraged; but
coming to an inn, which was surrounded with every appearance of
plenty, he called to see if the landlord would buy one of his books.
On going in, Samuel inquired of him if he did not wish to purchase
a history of the origin of the Indians.

'I do not know', replied the host, 'how did you get hold of it?'

'It was translated', rejoined Samuel, 'by my brother, from some
gold plates that he found buried in the earth.'

'You damned liar', cried the landlord, 'get out of my house—you shan't stay one minute with your books.'

Samuel was sick at heart, for this was the fifth time he had been turned out of doors that day. He left the house and traveled a short distance, and washed his feet in a small brook as a testimony against the man.

He then proceeded five miles further on his journey, and seeing an apple tree a short distance from the road, he concluded to pass the night under it; and here he lay all night upon the cold, damp ground.

In the morning he arose from his comfortless bed, and observing a small cottage at no great distance, he drew near, hoping to get a little refreshment. The only inmate was a widow, who seemed very poor. He asked her for food, relating the story of his former treatment. She prepared him some victuals, and, after eating, he explained to her the history of the *Book of Mormon*. She listened attentively, and believed all that he told her; but, in consequence of her poverty, she was unable to purchase one of the books. He presented her with one, and proceeded to Bloomington, which was eight miles further.

Here he stopped at the house of one John P. Greene, who was a Methodist preacher and was at that time about starting on a preaching mission. He, like the others, did not wish to make a purchase of what he considered at that time to be a nonsensical fable; however, he said that he would take a subscription paper, and if he found any one on his route who was disposed to purchase, he would take his name, and in two weeks Samuel might call again, and he would let him know what the prospect was of selling. After making this arrangement, Samuel left one of his books with him and returned home.

At the time appointed, Samuel started again for the Rev. John P. Greene's, in order to learn the success which this gentleman had met with in finding sale for the *Book of Mormon*. This time his father and mother accompanied him, and it was their intention to have passed near the tavern where Samuel was so abusively treated a fortnight previous, but just before they came to the house a sign of smallpox intercepted them.

They turned aside, and meeting a citizen of the place they inquired of him to what extent this disease prevailed. He answered that the tavernkeeper and two of his family had died with it not long since, but he did not know that anyone else had caught the distemper, and that it was brought into the neighborhood by a traveler who stopped at the tavern over night.

Samuel performed several short missions with the books, and gave the following account of his third mission to Livonia:—

'When I arrived at Mr. Greene's, Mrs. Greene informed me that her husband was absent from home, that there was no prospect of selling my books, and even the one which I had left with them she expected I would have to take away, as Mr. Greene had no disposition to

purchase it, although she had read it herself and was much pleased
with it.

'I then talked with her a short time, and, binding my knapsack
upon my shoulders, rose to depart; but, as I bade her farewell, it was
impressed upon my mind to leave the book with her. I made her a
present of it, and told her that the Spirit forbade my taking it away.
She burst into tears, and requested me to pray with her. I did so,
and afterwards explained to her the most profitable manner of reading
the book* which I had left with her, which was, to ask God, when she
read it, for a testimony of the truth of what she had read, and she
would receive the Spirit of God which would enable her to discern
the things of God. I then left her and returned home.'

In December, 1830, Samuel was sent to preach in Kirtland, Ohio,
and the surrounding country. About that time Joseph, the Prophet,
went to Kirtland to preside, accompanied by Hyrum and many of the
saints, and soon after Joseph Smith, Sen's. family, and the saints who
were located in Waterloo, in Fayette township, also moved to Kirtland.

In June, 1831, he was called by revelation to go to Missouri on a
mission, in company with Reynolds Cahoon. They immediately
started, and while on their way called upon William E. McLellin,
and preached the gospel to him and a large assembly in a room which
he procured. William, being troubled about the things he heard, closed
up his business and proceeded after the brethren to Missouri, where
he was baptized before they arrived.

On their route to Missouri they [Elders Smith and Cahoon]
preached the gospel, traveling without purse or scrip, and enduring
much for the want of food and rest.

When they started for Missouri, about fifty brethren set out for the
same place, and when they all arrived, they met on the spot for the
Temple, in Jackson county, and dedicated the ground unto God.

Brothers Smith and Cahoon spent several days in Jackson county,
attended several conferences and were with Joseph when he received
several revelations. While in Missouri they were required to remain
together on their return mission until they reached home, which was
in September following.

Soon after their arrival in Kirtland they took a mission into the
southern townships and counties of Ohio. Brother Cahoon returned
after laboring about six weeks, but Samuel continued preaching through
the winter, strengthening the churches and comforting the saints.

---

*This *Book of Mormon* left at the home of the Greene's who were relatives
of the Young's finally fell into the hands of Brigham Young, and Heber C.
Kimball and was the means not only of bringing them directly to the knowledge
of the New Dispensation gospel, but was the means also of their conversion. This
copy of the *Book of Mormon* came into the hands of Phineas Young, the brother
of Brigham Young, and was by him given into the possession of Joseph F. Smith,
nephew of the Prophet Joseph and subsequently President of the Church. He in turn
presented it to his son Joseph Fielding Smith, who still (1932) has it in his possession.

In a revelation given January, 1832, Orson Hyde and Samuel H. Smith were called to go on a mission to the eastern country; accordingly they started in March, and traveled and preached the gospel through the states of Ohio, New York, Pennsylvania, Connecticut, Rhode Island, Massachusetts and Maine. They baptized several in Spafford, N. Y., in Boston and Linn, Mass., in Providence, R. I., and in Saco, Maine, preaching much from house to house, as well as in public congregations, and returning to Kirtland in November or December.

During the year 1833, Samuel preached among the churches as he had opportunity, and spent a good portion of his time laboring with his hands.

On the 17th of February, 1834, he was ordained and set apart as one of the high council in Kirtland, in which office he officiated until he went to Missouri in 1838.

August 13th, 1834, he married Mary Bailey, who was born in Bedford, Hillsborough county, New Hampshire, Dec. 20th, 1808.

September 16th, 1835, he was appointed, in company with David Whitmer, as a committee and general agent to act in the name of, and for the Literary firm. In the winter of 1835-6 he chopped cordwood for Lorenzo D. Young.

In 1838 he traveled, in company with his brother Joseph, from Kirtland to Missouri. He passed through the mobbing of that year in Far West and Adam-ondi-Ahman in Missouri, and his family suffered nigh unto death from exposure, as they were driven about by the mob.

He was in the Crooked River battle; and immediately after, by the counsel of President Brigham Young, with Brothers C. C. Rich, B. L. Clapp, L. D. Young and about twenty others, they fled for Illinois by the wilderness, through the north part of Missouri and the southern part of Iowa.

Messengers overtook them and informed them that General Clark had sent a company of fifty well armed men to follow them, with strict orders not to return until they had brought back the company either dead or alive.

When this word came a halt was called, and Samuel asked what they should do in case the enemy overtook them. After a few moments' consultation, the whole company covenanted with uplifted hands to Heaven, that if they were overtaken they would fight till they died, and not a man would fall into the hands of the enemy alive.

They then traveled on ten miles and camped on the edge of some timber on the north side of a four-mile prairie, and they afterwards learned that their enemies camped on the south edge of the same prairie, and would have overtaken them next day had not the Lord sent a heavy snowstorm during the night; and when the brethren arose in the morning, Phineas H. Young remarked that that snowstorm was their salvation. The air was so full of snow that they could hardly find their horses to saddle them, but they soon mounted their horses and continued their journey as fast as they could. The storm was from the north and in their faces; it filled their tracks in a few moments, so that Clark's men could not follow.

It was reported that this company of men, on their return, informed the general that they could not overtake the 'damned Mormons' for they were stopped by a 'damned snowstorm'.

After they had got some distance on their journey, the company divided into three parts, the three brethren named fell in company with Samuel; their provisions gave out, and, after spending several days without food, except eating linden buds and slippery elm bark, they camped upon a small stream, and the company, numbering eight, held a council and appointed Samuel president, that they might receive the word of the Lord in relation to the situation of Joseph the Prophet and those who were with him, also in relation to their families, and what they were to do to obtain food. They all knelt down in a circle, and each one prayed, then the Spirit of the Lord came upon Samuel, and, being filled with the Holy Ghost, he arose and said:—

'Thus saith the Lord—My servant Joseph is not injured, nor any of his brethren that are with him, but they will all be delivered out of the hands of their enemies. Your families are all well, but anxious about you. Let your hearts be comforted, for I, the Lord, will provide food for you on the morrow.'

They went to bed with glad hearts, and arose in the morning and prayed again, and went out two by two to hunt for food. Brother Clapp saw several squirrels and shot at them, but could not hit them. They were only to stay one hour. At the end of the time they all returned except C. C. Rich and Samuel.

Feeling very faint, one of the brethren proposed killing a horse. Brother Clapp said that when Brothers Rich and Samuel returned they would have food, as he never knew the Lord to give a false revelation to his servants; and, while conversing upon the matter, the brethren made their appearance with two silk handkerchiefs tied up full of bread and dried meat.

Samuel's mind was led in a certain direction, and following it they came to an Indian camp. They made known to the Indians by signs that they were hungry; upon this the squaw, with all possible speed, baked them some cakes, and gave each of them two, sending two to each of the six brethren in camp, giving them to understand that she would be glad to send more, but she had but little flour, and her papooses (children) would be hungry.

When they arrived in camp, all felt to rejoice. They formed a circle around the food and asked a blessing upon it. The bread was very good, being shortened with raccoon's oil. After eating they started upon their journey, and obtained food sufficient, so that none perished.

Samuel arrived in Quincy, and was there to assist his father and mother over the river on their arrival, and hired a house for them, into which he also assisted four other families of the saints; and, according to the word of the Lord unto him, his brothers, Joseph and Hyrum, were delivered, and they arrived in Quincy in April, 1839.

He moved, in company with Don Carlos, on to a farm which he rented near Macombe, McDonough county, where he spent the season farming.

Elders Wilford Woodruff and John Taylor called upon them as they went on their missions to England, and held a meeting with the saints in that place (Oct. 11th, 1839). Don Carlos preached, and was followed by Samuel, who enjoyed much of the Holy Spirit, and bore a strong testimony to the truth of the work of God. He assisted the brethren upon their journey.

In September, 1840, Samuel received the following blessing from under the hands of his father, Joseph Smith, Sen., upon his dying bed:—

'Samuel, you have been a faithful and obedient son. By your faithfulness you have brought many into the church. The Lord has seen your diligence, and you are blessed in that he has never chastised you, but has called you home to rest; and there is a crown laid up for you which shall grow brighter and brighter unto the perfect day.

'When the Lord called you he said, 'Samuel, I have seen thy sufferings, have heard thy cries and beheld thy faithfulnes; thy skirts are clear from the blood of this generation'. Because of these things, I seal upon your head all the blessings which I have heretofore pronounced upon you; and this, my dying blessing, I now seal upon you. Even so. Amen.'

His wife bore to him four children—*viz.*, Susannah B., Mary B., Samuel Harrison Bailey and Lucy B. His wife Mary died January 25th, 1841.

In April, 1841, he was sent on a mission to preach the gospel in Scott and adjoining counties, Illinois. May 3rd, he married Levira Clark, daughter of Gardner and Delecta, born in Livonia, Livingston county, New York, July 30th, 1815. He preached during the summer and fall, his wife remaining with his father-in-law.

In the month of November he returned to Nauvoo, taking his family with him, where he remained during the winter, and also the summer of 1842, during which time he worked mostly for Joseph and harvested in the country.

In the fall of 1842 he removed to his brother William's tavern at Plymouth. In the summer of 1843 he was often at Nauvoo. In the fall he chopped wood, and prepared his farm by making fences and clearing off the timber, preaching the gospel in the vicinity as he had opportunity.

In the spring of 1844 he cultivated his farm, and upon hearing of the imprisonment of his brothers in Carthage jail, he repaired thither on horseback to see them. While on the way he was pursued by the mobocrats; but in consequence of the fleetness of his horse, he was enabled to reach Carthage in safety, from whence he went to Nauvoo in company with the bodies of his martyred brothers, Joseph and Hyrum.

His wife, Levira, bore to him three daughters—*viz.*, Levira A. C., Louisa C. and Lucy J. C.

He was soon after taken sick of bilious fever, and died on the 30th of July, aged 36 years.'

The following extract is from his obituary notice, published in the *Times and Seasons*:—

'The exit of this worthy man, so soon after the *horrible butchery* of his brothers, Joseph and Hyrum, in Carthage jail, is a matter of deep solemnity to the family, as well as a remediless loss to all. If ever there lived a good man upon the earth, Samuel H. Smith was that person. His labors in the church from first to last, carrying glad tidings to the eastern cities, and finally his steadfastness as one of the [eight special] *witnesses* to the *Book of Mormon,* and many saintly traits of virtue, knowledge, temperance, patience, godliness, brotherly kindness and charity, shall be given of him hereafter as a man of God.' "

CHAPTER XVIII

THE GATHERING OF THE TWELVE APOSTLES FROM
THE EAST TO NAUVOO: PRELIMINARY MEETINGS
LOOKING TO THE SETTLEMENT OF THE QUESTION
OF THE PRESIDENCY OF THE CHURCH

"*Thursday, August* 1, 1844.—The brethren of the
Twelve arrived in Chicago in the evening, and tarried
over night at the Lake Street house.

Friday, 2.—A meeting of the citizens of
Hancock county was held at the grove, west
of the Temple. Great excitement prevailed
through the county. The mob party were determined
to elect officers who would screen the murderers of
Joseph and Hyrum Smith and exterminate the Mormons.

Political Election in Hancock Co., Illinois.

The meeting resolved to support candidates who
were in favor of preserving order and enforcing the
laws. The following candidates were agreed upon:—
Miner* R. Deming, sheriff; Daniel H. Wells, coroner;
George Coulson, commissioner; J. B. Backenstos and
A. W. Babbitt, representatives.

President Young and company took stage
at seven a. m., for Galena; passed over delightful country, but very bad roads; had
to walk over mudholes and bad places, and had to
carry poles or rails on their backs to pry out the stage
coach.

Movements of Brigham Young.

Saturday, 3.—Elder Sidney Rigdon arrived at Nauvoo from Pittsburgh.

Movements of Sidney Rigdon.

Elders Parley P. Pratt, Willard Richards
and George A. Smith invited President Rigdon to meet
in council at eight o'clock tomorrow morning, which
he agreed to.

*Sometimes spelled "Minor".

The Twelve continued their journey through the day and night by stage. While upon their journey

Brigham Young as Oxteamster— Anecdote.

they overtook a company of Norwegians who were traveling with oxteams, and heavily loaded wagons, one of which was stuck fast in the mud, blocking up the road, while several of them were whipping the oxen and bawling to them in the Norwegian language, which seemed to frighten the oxen, but they were unable to move the wagons on.

After sitting and looking at them a moment, President Young got out of the coach and stepped up, and took the whip out of the hands of one of the Norwegians, telling them all to stand out of the way.

He then talked to the oxen in a tongue which was not understood by Norwegians or English, and touching them lightly with the whip, they instantly pulled the wagon out of the mud and continued the journey, much to the astonishment of the Norwegians and the surprise and amusement of the passengers on the stage.

Sunday, 4.—Elders Parley P. Pratt, Willard Richards and George A. Smith met in council, and waited an hour for Elder Rigdon, who excused himself afterwards by saying he was engaged with a lawyer.

Sunday Service at Nauvoo—Sermon of Sidney Rigdon.

10 *a. m.* Meeting at the stand. Elder Rigdon preached fiom the words, 'For my thoughts are not as your thoughts, neither are your ways my ways, saith the Lord.'

He related a vision which he said the Lord had shown him concerning the situation of the church, and said there must be a guardian appointed to build the church up to Joseph, as he had begun it.

He said he was the identical man that the ancient prophets had sung about, wrote and rejoiced over, and that he was sent to do the identical work that had been the theme of all the prophets in every preceding generation. He said that the Lord's ways were not as our ways, for the Lord said he would 'hiss for the fly from the uttermost part of the rivers of Egypt, and for the bee that is in the land of Assyria,' and thereby destroy his enemies; that the time was near at hand when he would see one hundred tons of metal per second thrown at the enemies of God, and that the blood would be to the horses' bridles; and that he expected to walk into the palace of Queen Victoria and lead her out by the nose, when none would have power to say, 'why do ye so?' and if it were not for two or three things which he knew, this people would be utterly destroyed, and not a soul left to tell the tale.

Elder Parley P. Pratt, in referring to the remarks of Brother Rigdon, on a subsequent occasion, said, 'I am the identical man the prophets *never* sang nor wrote a word about.' <abbr>Parley P. Pratt's Comment on Rigdon's Sermon.</abbr>

Public service meeting continued; afternoon: Elders Murdock and Rich preached. Elder William Marks, president of the stake, gave public notice (at the request of Elder Rigdon), that there would be a special meeting of the church at the stand, on Thursday, the 8th inst., for the purpose of choosing a guardian, (President and Trustee). <abbr>Appointment Attempted to Choose a "Guardian" for the Church.</abbr>

Elder Thomas Grover proposed waiting to examine the revelation.

Elder Marks said President Rigdon wanted the meeting on Tuesday, but he put it off till Thursday; that Elder Rigdon was some distance from his family, and wanted to know if this people had anything for him to do; if not, he wanted to go on his way, for there was a people numbering thousands and tens of thousands who would receive him; that he wanted to visit other branches around, but he had come here first.

Elder Rich called upon William Clayton, and said he was dissatisfied with the hurried movement of Elder Rigdon. He considered, inasmuch as the Twelve had been sent for and were soon expected home, the notice for meeting was premature, and it seemed to him a plot laid to take advantage of the situation of the saints.

President Young and his associates arrived at Galena at eight o'clock this morning (August 4th), nearly exhausted with fatigue, having traveled 48 hours without stopping, except to take meals and change horses, distance about 160 miles.

From the *Millennial Star*:—

MARK OF RESPECT SHOWN BY THE LATTER-DAY SAINTS IN LIVERPOOL FOR THE MARTYRS

'On Sunday, August 4th, very numerous congregations attended at the Music Hall, the majority of the saints in deep mourning, whilst the platform or raised gallery, where the priesthood sat, was handsomely decorated with black drapery. We would suggest to the saints generally, as far as their means will allow them, to pay respect to the memory of our lamented brethren.'

Monday, 5.—Elders Parley P. Pratt, Willard Richards, John Taylor, George A. Smith, Amasa Lyman and Bishop Whitney, waited upon Elder Rigdon in the morning. He said he would meet them in council at Elder Taylor's after dinner.

They accordingly met in council, and when Elder Rigdon came in, he paced the room and said, 'Gentlemen, you're used up; gentlemen, you are all divided; the anti-Mormons have got you; the brethren are voting every way, some for James, some for Deming, some for Coulson, and some for Bedell; the anti-Mormons have got you, you cannot stay in the county, everything is in confusion, you can do nothing, you lack a great leader, you want a head, and unless you unite upon that head you are blown to the four winds, the anti-Mormons will carry the election—a guardian must be appointed.'

The Agitation of Sidney Rigdon.

Elder George A. Smith said, 'Brethren, Elder Rigdon is entirely mistaken, there is no division; the brethren are united; the election will be unanimous, and the friends of law and order will be elected by a thousand majority. There is no occasion to be alarmed. President Rigdon is inspiring fears there are no grounds for.

The result was that it was one of the most unanimous elections held in Nauvoo, as there were only five opposition votes polled in the city, and Result of the Election. in the county the majority for the law and order candidates was over one thousand, notwithstanding the anti-Mormons smuggled a great many votes from other counties.

Elder Rigdon said he did not expect the people to choose a guardian on Thursday, but to have a prayer meeting and interchange of thought and feeling, and warm up each other's hearts.

Jesse Price made the following affidavit:—

AFFIDAVIT OF JESSE PRICE BEFORE AARON JOHNSON—MURDEROUS INTENTIONS OF WILLIAM LAW

'State of Illinois, County of Hancock, ss.

On the 5th day of August, 1844, personally appeared before me, Aaron Johnson, justice of the peace in and for said county, Jesse Price; and after being duly sworn according to law, deposeth and saith, that on or about the 18th of April, 1844, in the city of Nauvoo, county aforesaid, William Law said, 'I put pistols in my pockets one night, and went to Joseph Smith's house, determined to blow his infernal brains out, but I could not get the opportunity to shoot him then, but I am determined I will shoot him the first opportunity, and you will see blood and thunder and devastation in this place, but I shall not be here;' and deponent saith not further.'

The following letter was sent to Dr. Richards:—

LETTER OF JOSEPH M. COLE—ELECTION RETURNS THREATENED

'La Harpe, August 5, 1844.

Brother Richards,—I hasten to inform you that intelligence has arrived in this place today, by several persons, that the mobocrats at Carthage have concocted a plan to intercept the returns of the election at Nauvoo, and destroy them before they arrive at Carthage. The information is of such a nature that I deemed it necessary that you should be informed of the same, that you may act accordingly.

Respectfully,
JOSEPH M. COLE.'

President Young and the Apostles with him went on board the steamer *St. Croix* at Galena, for Nauvoo. They started in the afternoon.

Elder Kimball recorded the following dream:—

'I dreamed of speaking before a large congregation on the policy of the nation and the policy of our religion. I said that Joseph the Prophet had laid the foundation, and we would have to carry out his measures. Joseph was present, and heard all I said and sanctioned it. All seemed perfectly natural.'

Tuesday, 6.—Elders Parley P. Pratt, Willard Richards, John Taylor, George A. Smith and Bishop Whitney met in council at Elder Taylor's.

From the death of Joseph until the arrival of President Brigham Young and the Twelve, Elder Willard
Richards was the principal counselor of the saints in Nauvoo, and had scarcely a moment's rest. He answered the calls and inquiries of hundreds of the brethren, and was engaged every day until a late hour, or until exhaustion compelled him to lie down.

The following is extracted from Elder Woodruff's Journal:—

EXCERPT

'We (the brethren of the Twelve returning to Nauvoo) stopped at various places while going down the Mississippi, among others, the town of Burlington, after which we prepared our minds to once more behold the city of Nauvoo and embrace our families and friends.

We were landed at the upper stone house at eight in the evening, and were welcomed with joy by all the citizens we met. We hired a coach, and I accompanied my brethren to their families, after which I was conveyed to my own, and truly felt to rejoice to once more meet with my wife, children and friends. Thus it is with me, I have spent but one summer either at home or with the body of the church for the last ten years, as my lot has been cast abroad in the vineyard most of the time.

When we landed in the city a deep gloom seemed to rest over the city of Nauvoo, which we never experienced before.'

Wednesday, 7.—Elders Brigham Young, Heber C. Kimball, Parley P. Pratt, Orson Pratt, Willard Richards, Wilford Woodruff, George A. Smith and Lyman
Wight met in council with Elder Taylor at his house. They found him recovering from his wounds received at the massacre of the Prophets.

The Twelve felt to rejoice at having the privilege of again meeting in council together, after having passed through such trying scenes, and to be welcomed by the saints who considered it very providential for the Twelve to arrive at this particular juncture, when their minds were agitated, their hearts sorrowful, and darkness seemed to cloud their path, feeling like sheep without a shepherd, their beloved Prophet having been taken away.

4 p. m.—Meeting of the Twelve Apostles, high council and high priests at the Seventies' Hall.

Meeting of Church Authorities at Nauvoo.

President William Marks prayed.

President Brigham Young called upon President Rigdon to make a statement to the church concerning his message to the saints, and the vision and revelation he had received.

President Rigdon said:—

'The object of my mission is to visit the saints and offer myself to them as a guardian. I had a vision at Pittsburgh, June 27th. This was presented to my mind not as an open vision, but rather a continuation of the vision mentioned in the *Book of Doctrine and Covenants.**

It was shown to me that this church must be built up to Joseph, and that all the blessings we receive must come through him. I have been ordained a spokesman to Joseph, and I must come to Nauvoo and see that the church is governed in a proper manner. Joseph sustains

The Proposition of Elder Rigdon to Become "Guardian" to the Church.

the same relationship to this church as he has always done. No man can be the successor of Joseph.

The kingdom is to be built up to Jesus Christ through Joseph; there must be revelation still. The martyred Prophet is still the head of this church; every quorum should stand as you stood in your washings and consecrations. I have been consecrated a spokesman to Joseph, and I was commanded to speak for him. The church is not disorganized though our head is gone.

We may have a diversity of feelings on this matter. I have been called to be a spokesman unto Joseph, and I want to build up the church unto him; and if the people want me to sustain this place, I

---

*Undoubtedly Elder Rigdon referred to the continuation of the "Vision" of The Three Glories, now published in section lxxvi of the current edition of the *Doctrine and Covenants*, though what the connection could be is difficult to see.

want it upon the principle that every individual shall acknowledge it
for himself.

I propose to be a guardian to the people; in this I have discharged
my duty and done what God has commanded me, and the people can
please themselves whether they accept me or not.'

President Brigham Young said:—

'I do not care who leads the church, even though it were Ann Lee;
but one thing I must know, and that is what God says about it.

Attitude of
Brigham
Young—The
Twelve Hold
the "Keys".

I have the keys and the means of obtaining the mind of
God on the subject.

I know there are those in our midst who will seek
the lives of the Twelve as they did the lives of Joseph
and Hyrum. We shall ordain others and give the fulness of the
priesthood, so that if we are killed the fulness of the priesthood may
remain.

Joseph conferred upon our heads all the keys and powers belonging
to the Apostleship which he himself held before he was taken away,
and no man or set of men can get between Joseph and the Twelve in
this world or in the world to come.

How often has Joseph said to the Twelve, 'I have laid the foundation and you must build thereon, for upon your shoulders the kingdom
rests.'

The Twelve, as a quorum, will not be permitted to tarry here long;
they will go abroad and bear off the kingdom to the nations of the
earth, and baptize the people faster than mobs can kill them off. I
would like, were it my privilege, to take my valise and travel and
preach till we had a people gathered who would be true.

My private feelings would be to let the affairs of men and women
alone, only go and preach and baptize them into the kingdom of
God; yet, whatever duty God places upon me, in his strength I intend
to fulfill it.

I want to see this people, with the various quorums of the priesthood, assembled together in special conference on Thursday* next at
10 a. m.'

Which was carried unanimously by vote."

*In the previous publication of this historical item (*Millennial Star*, vol. xxv, p.
216) the language is "I want to see this people with their various quorums of the
priesthood assembled together in special conference on *Tuesday* next." This would have
brought the meeting on Tuesday the 13th of August. Evidently the word "Tuesday"
was a misprint and should have been, as changed above in the text, "Thursday",
which was the day following the council meeting and as a matter of fact it was the
next day following, August 8th, that the general public meeting of the church with
the quorums assembled in their order to settle this matter of the presiding council in
the church that the meeting was held. B. H. R.

CHAPTER XIX

THE SETTLEMENT OF CHURCH LEADERSHIP—THE
TWELVE APOSTLES ACCEPTED AS THE PRESIDENCY OF
THE CHURCH, BRIGHAM YOUNG AT THEIR HEAD

"*Thursday, August 8th,* 1844.—At a special meeting of the Church of Jesus Christ of Latter-day Saints held in Nauvoo, at 10 a. m. on Thursday, August 8, 1844, by the request of President William Marks, (who was then presiding over that stake of Zion) to choose a guardian, or President and Trustee, Sidney Rigdon took his position in a wagon, about two rods in front of the stand, and harangued the saints for about one and a half hours, upon choosing a guardian for the church. The meeting was then dismissed, when President Brigham Young gave out an appointment for the brethren to assemble at 2 p. m.

Special Public Meeting of the Church.

At the appointed time the brethren came together. Present, of the Twelve, Brigham Young, Heber C. Kimball, Parley P. Pratt, Orson Pratt, Willard Richards, Wilford Woodruff, George A. Smith.* The several quorums were organized on and around the stand according to order.

THE REMARKS OF PRESIDENT YOUNG IN BEHALF OF THE CLAIM OF
THE TWELVE TO LEAD THE CHURCH IN THE ABSENCE
OF THE FIRST PRESIDENCY

The meeting being opened, President Brigham Young arose and said:—

---

*It will be observed that there were seven of the Apostles present, a majority of the quorum. Of the absent ones, John Taylor was confined to his home, not yet recovered from his wounds, Orson Hyde, John F. Page and Wm Smith had not yet arrived in Nauvoo; and Lyman Wight was still in the east.

'*Attention all!* This congregation makes me think of the days of King Benjamin, the multitude being so great that all could not hear. I request the brethren not to have any feelings for being convened this afternoon, for it is necessary; we want you all to be still and give attention, that all may hear. Let none complain because of the situation of the congregation, we will do the best we can.

For the first time in my life, for the first time in your lives, for the first time in the kingdom of God in the 19th century, without a Prophet at our head, do I step forth to act in my calling in connection with the Quorum of the Twelve, as Apostles of Jesus Christ unto this generation—Apostles whom God has called by revelation through the Prophet Joseph, who are ordained and anointed to bear off the keys of the kingdom of God in all the world.

This people have hitherto walked by sight and not by faith. You have had the Prophet in your midst. Do you all understand? You have walked by sight and without much pleading to the Lord to know whether things were right or not.

Heretofore you have had a Prophet as the mouth of the Lord to speak to you, but he has sealed his testimony with his blood, and now, for the first time, are you called to walk by faith, not by sight.

The first position I take in behalf of the Twelve and the people is, to ask a few questions. I ask the Latter-day Saints: do you, as individuals, at this time, want to choose a Prophet or a guardian? Inasmuch as our Prophet and Patriarch are taken from our midst, do you want some one to guard, to guide and lead you through this world into the kingdom of God, or not? All that want some person to be a guardian or a Prophet, a spokesman or something else, signify it by raising the right hand. (No votes).

When I came to this stand I had peculiar feelings and impressions. The faces of this people seem to say, we want a shepherd to guide and lead us through this world. *All that want to draw away a party from the church after them, let them do it if they can, but they will not prosper.*

If any man thinks he has influence among this people to lead away a party, let him try it, and he will find out that there is power with the Apostles which will carry them off victorious through all the world, and build up and defend the church and kingdom of God.

What do the people want? I feel as though I wanted the privilege to weep and mourn for thirty days at least, then rise up, shake myself, and tell the people what the Lord wants of them; although my heart is too full of mourning to launch forth into business transactions and the organization of the church, I feel compelled this day to step forth in the discharge of those duties God has placed upon me.

I now wish to speak of the organization of the Church of Jesus Christ of Latter-day Saints. If the church is organized, and you want to know how it is organized, I will tell you. I know your feelings— do you want me to tell your feelings?

Here is President Rigdon, who was counselor to Joseph. I ask, where are Joseph and Hyrum? They are gone beyond the veil; and if Elder Rigdon wants to act as his counselor, he must go beyond the veil where he is.

There has been much said about President Rigdon being President of the Church, and leading the people, being the head, etc. Brother Rigdon has come 1,600 miles to tell you what he wants to do for you. If the people want President Rigdon to lead them they may have him; but I say unto you that the Quorum of the Twelve have the keys of the kingdom of God in all the world.

The Twelve are appointed by the finger of God. Here is Brigham, have his knees ever faltered? Have his lips ever quivered? Here is Heber and the rest of the Twelve, an independent body who have the keys of the priesthood—the keys of the kingdom of God to deliver to all the world: this is true, so help me God. They stand next to Joseph, and are as the First Presidency of the Church.

I do not know whether my enemies will take my life or not, and I do not care, for I want to be with the man I love.

You cannot fill the office of a prophet, seer and revelator: God must do this. You are like children without a father and sheep without a shepherd. You must not appoint any man at our head; if you should, the Twelve must ordain him. You cannot appoint a man at our head; but if you do want any other man or men to lead you, take them and we will go our way to build up the kingdom in all the world.

I know who are Joseph's friends, and who are his enemies. I know where the keys of the kingdom are, and where they will eternally be. You cannot call a man to be a prophet; you cannot take Elder Rigdon and place him above the Twelve; if so, he must be ordained by them.

I tell you there is an overanxiety to hurry matters here. You cannot take any man and put him at the head; you would scatter the saints to the four winds, you would sever the priesthood. So long as we remain as we are, the heavenly Head is in constant cooperation with us; and if you go out of that course, God will have nothing to do with you.

Again, perhaps some think that our beloved Brother Rigdon would not be honored, would not be looked to as a friend; but if he does right and remains faithful he will not act against our counsel nor we against his, but act together, and we shall be as one.

I again repeat, no man can stand at our head, except God reveals it from the heavens.

I have spared no pains to learn my lesson of the kingdom in this world and in the eternal worlds; and if it were not so, I could go and live in peace; but for the gospel and your sakes I shall stand in my place. We are liable to be killed all the day long. You have never lived by faith.

Brother Joseph, the Prophet, has laid the foundation for a great work, and we will build upon it; you have never seen the quorums built one upon another. There is an almighty foundation laid, and we can build a kingdom such as there never was in the world; we can build a kingdom faster than satan can kill the saints off.

What do you want? Do you want a patriarch for the whole church? To this we are perfectly willing. If Brother Samuel H. Smith had been living, it would have been his right and privilege; but he is dead, he is gone to Joseph and Hyrum, he is out of the reach of bullets and spears, and he can waft himself with his brothers, his friends and the saints.

Do you want a patriarch? Here is brother William [Smith] left; here is Uncle John Smith, uncle to the Prophet Joseph left; it is their right. The right of patriarchal blessings belongs to Joseph's family.

Do you want a Trustee-in-Trust? Has there been a bishop who has stood in his lot yet? What is his business? To take charge of the temporal affairs, so that the Twelve and the elders may go on their business. Joseph condescended to do their business for them. Joseph condescended to offer himself for president of the United States, and it was a great condescension.

Do you want a spokesman? Here are Elder Rigdon, Brother Amasa Lyman [whom Joseph expected to take as a counselor] and myself. Do you want the church properly organized, or do you want a spokesman to be chief cook and bottle-washer? Elder Rigdon claims to be spokesman to the Prophet. Very well, he was; but can he now act in that office? If he wants now to be a spokesman to the Prophet, he must go to the other side of the veil, for the Prophet is there, but Elder Rigdon is here. Why will Elder Rigdon be a fool? Who knows anything of the priesthood, or of the organization of the kingdom of God.* I am plain.

*It is rather singular that in the remarks of President Young and by none of the leading elders who spoke on that eventful 8th of August, 1844, that no adequate unfolding of the relationship of the respective presiding councils of the church was given. In the above I follow the punctuation as it stands in the records of the church, that is, as will be seen, the sentence, "Who knows anything of the priesthood, or of the organization of the kingdom of God", ends with a period. I wonder if the speaker's intent was not to make of it a question (?) For so far as the speeches are concerned there really was no adequate relationship of presiding councils of the priesthood given. It is quite possible that they had not been studied by the elders from the viewpoint of the relationship of these respective councils. In section cvii of the *Doctrine and Covenants*, which is *par excellence* the revelation on priesthood of the church, it is pointed out that "of necessity there are presidents, or presiding officers growing out of, or appointed from among those who are ordained to the several offices in these two priesthoods [Melchizedek and Aaronic. I refer only to the Melchizedek].

(1). "Of the Melchizedek priesthood three Presiding High Priests chosen by

Does this church want it as God organized it?   Or do you want to clip the power of the priesthood, and let those who have the keys of the priesthood go and build up the kingdom in all the world, wherever the people will hear them?

If there is a spokesman, if he is a king and priest, let him go and build up a kingdom unto himself; that is his right and it is the right of many here, but the Twelve are at the head of it.

I want to live on the earth and spread truth through all the world. You saints of latter-days want things right.   If 10,000 men rise up and say they have the Prophet Joseph Smith's shoes, I know they are imposters.   In the priesthood you have a right to build up a kingdom, if you know how the church is organized.

Now, if you want Sidney Rigdon or William Law to lead you, or anybody else, you are welcome to them; but I tell you, in the name of the Lord that no man can put another between the Twelve and the Prophet Joseph.   Why?   Because Joseph was their file leader, and he has committed into their hands the keys of the kingdom in this last dispensation, for all the world; don't put a thread between the priesthood and God.

I will ask, who has stood next to Joseph and Hyrum?   I have, and I will stand next to him.   We have a head, and that head is the Apostleship, the spirit and power of Joseph, and we can now begin to see the necessity of that Apostleship.

Brother Rigdon was at his side—not above.   No man has a right to counsel the Twelve but Joseph Smith.   Think of these things. You cannot appoint a prophet; but if you let the Twelve remain and act in their place, the keys of the kingdom are with them and they can manage the affairs of the church and direct all things aright.

Now, all this does not lessen the character of President Rigdon: let him magnify his calling, and Joseph will want him beyond the veil—

the body, appointed and ordained to that office and upheld by the confidence, faith, and prayer of the church, form a quorum of the Presidency of the Church.

(2) "The Twelve traveling councilors are called to be the Twelve Apostles, or special witnesses of the name of Christ in all the world. * * * They form a quorum equal in authority and power to the Three Presidents previously mentioned.

(3) "The Seventy are also called to preach the gospel and to be especial witnesses unto the Gentiles and in all the world.   * * * And they form a quorum equal in authority to that of the Twelve special witnesses or Apostles just named" (Doctrine and Covenants, sec. cvii).

It is not necessary to quote further, but it stands to reason that if for any cause the First Presidency goes out of existence, the council which is next to the first and equal in authority and power to it—the second council upon which presiding responsibility rests—is the Council of the Twelve.   Hence the Council of the Twelve Apostles logically and according to the constitutional organization of the church, becomes the de facto presiding authority of the church.   But this was not at the time definitely pointed out.

let him be careful what he does, lest that thread which binds us together is cut asunder. May God bless you all.'*

(Much more was said by President Young, but not written).

SPEECH OF AMASA M. LYMAN†

Amasa Lyman said:—

'I do not rise to electioneer. I am gratified with the open, frank and plain exposition of President Young. He has seen the relation I bear to my deceased brother [i. e. Joseph Smith]. I never did conceive it gave me a precedence to go before the Twelve.

I do not make exceptions to anything he has said. I believe there is no power, or officer, or means wanted to carry on the work, but

---

*It was while delivering this speech that a transformation of President Brigham Young is said to have occurred, that is to say in voice, person and manner. He seemed to be the personification of Joseph Smith, on the testimony of many who were present. The late President George Q. Cannon of this event said:

"If Joseph had arisen from the dead and again spoken in their hearing, the effect could not have been more startling than it was to many present at that meeting; it was the voice of Joseph himself; and not only was it the voice of Joseph which was heard, but it seemed in the eyes of the people as if it were the very person of Joseph which stood before them. A more wonderful and miraculous event than was wrought that day in the presence of that congregation we never heard of. The Lord gave his people a testimony that left no room for doubt as to who was the man chosen to lead them" (Life of Brigham Young, Tullidge, 1877, p. 115).

In the Journal of Elder Wm. C. Staines of the date of August 8, 1844, the following statement is recorded: "Brigham Young said: 'I will tell you who your leaders or guardians will be—the Twelve—I at their head.' This was with the voice like the voice of the Prophet Joseph. I thought it was he, and so did thousands who heard it. This was very satisfactory to the people, and a vote was taken to sustain the Twelve in their office, which with a few dissenting voices, was passed."

Wilford Woodruff described the event as follows: "If I had not seen him with my own eyes, there is no one that could have convinced me that it was not Joseph Smith, and anyone can testify to this who was acquainted with these two men" (Deseret Evening News, March 12, 1892).

†Amasa M. Lyman here making this speech had been ordained an Apostle (August 20, 1842) during a brief suspension of Elder Orson Pratt from the Quorum of the Twelve owing to a misunderstanding between Elder Pratt and President Joseph Smith; but on the reconciliation of Elders Pratt and Smith and the former's reinstatement into the Quorum of the Twelve, Elder Lyman had been taken by President Smith into the First Presidency (History of the Church, Period I, vol. v, pp. 255-6). However he was never formally presented to the people in that capacity, but meantime he had continued to act with the leaders of the church—the Apostles—and a few days following this 8th of August meeting, namely on the 12th of August at a council of the Twelve Apostles, he was received by vote as a member of the Quorum of the Twelve (See History of Brigham Young, Ms., August 12, 1844, p. 3).

what is in the Twelve. I am satisfied that no man can carry on the work, but the power that is in the Twelve, as has been stated.

There is one thing to secure the salvation of this people, and that is not in union alone, it is for you to know the right and be united—it has been presented to you by President Young, and I will back him up. All I design to do is to redeem my pledge.

President Young has stood next to the Prophet Joseph, with the Twelve, and I have stood next to them, and I will stand next to them. I have been at the back of Joseph Smith, and will be at the back of the Twelve forever, and then we will be saved.

There is no need of a President, we have a head here. What is that head? The Quorum of the Twelve Apostles are the head. We now see the necessity of the Apostleship.

I might rise up as well as any other man to ask for the Presidency, but I could not do it without endangering my salvation. This is the power that turns the key to bestow salvation through all the land, in the way that Joseph commenced it, the first one called to do the same in all the world. If Joseph Smith had any power to bear off the kingdom of God, the Twelve have the same.

I could not advocate a choosing of a President, and myself a candidate; so then you know the place I occupy is, to stand to the Twelve the same as the Twelve did to Joseph, either on one side or the other. I do not want to go before them or to fall asleep. I want to see the kingdom roll forth by our united faith and efforts.'

President Rigdon called upon W. W. Phelps to speak in his behalf, as he could not speak.

SPEECH OF ELDER W. W. PHELPS—NO SUPPORT TO SIDNEY RIGDON

W. W. Phelps arose and said: —

'With the knowledge that I have I cannot suppose but that this congregation will act aright this day. I believe enough has been said to prepare the minds of the people to act.

I have known many of them for 14 years, and I have always known them to submit with deference to the authorities of the church. I have seen the elders of Israel and the people—take their lives in their hands and go without purse or scrip in winter and in summer. I have seen them prepare for war, and ready to pour out their hearts' blood, and that is an evidence that they will walk by counsel.

I am happy to see this little lake of faces, and to see the same spirit and disposition manifested here today, as it was the day after the bloody tragedy, when Joseph and Hyrum Smith were brought home dead to this city. Then you submitted to the law's slow delay, and handed the matter over to God; and I see the same thing today—

you are now determined as one man to sustain the authorities of the church, and I am happy that the men who were on Joseph's right and left hand submit themselves to the authority of the priesthood.

I have feelings about this, especially for President Rigdon, and I want to say that there is a quorum that the Twelve belong to, and that the people will receive an endowment. I brought President Rigdon into that quorum, and he received in part the blessings. I could not bear the thought of President Rigdon going into the world without his endowment. He did obtain part, and I hope he will submit.

I want Brother Amasa to stand on the side of the Twelve, and they are wanted there still—let them go on and sustain them in that high office. You cannot put in a guardian of the church.

We have hitherto walked by sight, and if a man wanted to know anything he had only to go to Brother Joseph. Joseph has gone, but he has not left us comfortless.

I want to say that Brother Joseph came and enlightened me two days after he was buried. He came the same as when he was alive, and in a moment appeared to me in his own house. He said, 'Tell the drivers to drive on.' I asked if the building was on wheels? He said, 'certainly'. I spoke, and away it went. We drove all round the hills and valleys. He then told the drivers to drive on over the river into Iowa. I told him Devil Creek was before us. He said, 'Drive over Devil Creek; I don't care for Devil Creek or any other creek;' and we did so. Then I awoke.

There is a combination of persons in this city who are in continual intercourse with William and Wilson Law, who are at the bottom of the matter to destroy all that stand for Joseph, and there are persons now in this city who are only wanting power to murder all the persons that still hold on to Joseph; but let us go ahead and build up the Temple, and then you will be endowed. When the Temple is completed all the honorable mothers in Israel will be endowed, as well as the elders.

If you want to do right, uphold the Twelve. If they die, I am willing to die with them; but do your duty and you will be endowed. I will sustain the Twelve as long as I have breath.

When Joseph was going away he said he was going to die, and I said I was willing to die with him; but as I am now alive, as a lawyer in Israel, I am determined to live.

I want you all to recollect that Joseph and Hyrum have only been removed from the earth, and they now counsel and converse with the Gods beyond the reach of powder and ball.'

REMARKS OF ELDER PARLEY P. PRATT

Parley P. Pratt said:—

'What has been said has been well said. If there are men here who are our enemies, I'll tell you when they will cease to be here: they will

be here while you will deal with them.   If I exchange property or
deal with men, I do it with those whom I know to be faithful.

If there are wicked men here, it is because we support them.   Stop
dealing with them, and they will go away.   Will I support them?
No, I would deal with all honest men whom I know to be such.

I am willing to do good to all men, especially to the household of
faith.   Our enemies will cease to dwell here when you cease to deal
with them.   Mobs and wicked men will cease when you cease to
support them.

I know we can all live and be happy too, when we deal with
honest men.   If a man wants a doctor or a lawyer, he will send
directly for the worst man he can find.

I would die a natural death sooner than I would have a wicked
doctor to help me off.   I would go without sueing all the days of
my life before I would go to a lawyer to sue.   I will not say anything
about the merchants, because you all know them.

PRESIDENT BRIGHAM YOUNG'S SECOND SPEECH

President Brigham Young again arose and said:—

'There is more business than can be done this afternoon, but we
can accomplish all we want to have done without calling this convention of the whole church.   I am going to present to you the
leading items.

I do not ask you to take my counsel or advice alone, but every one
of you act for yourselves; but if Brother Rigdon is the person you
want to lead you, vote for him, but not unless you intend to follow
him and support him as you did Joseph.   Do not say so without
you mean to take his counsel hereafter.

And I would say the same for the Twelve, don't make a covenant to
support them unless you intend to abide by their counsel; and if they
do not counsel you as you please, don't turn round and oppose them.

I want every man, before he enters into a covenant, to know what
he is going to do; but we want to know if this people will support
the priesthood in the name of Israel's God.   If you say you will, do so.

We want men appointed to take charge of the business that did lay
on the shoulders of Joseph.   Let me say to you that this kingdom
will spread more than ever.

The Twelve have the power now—the seventies, the elders and all
of you can have power to go and build up the kingdom in the name
of Israel's God.   Nauvoo will not hold all the people that will come
into the kingdom.

We want to build the Temple, so as to get our endowment; and if
we do our best, and satan will not let us build it, we will go into the
wilderness and we will receive the endowment, for we will receive an
endowment anyhow.

Will you abide our counsel? I again say, my soul for any man's, if they will abide our counsel, that they will go right into heaven. We have all the signs and tokens to give to the porter at the door, and he will let us in.

I will ask you as quorums, Do you want Brother Rigdon to stand forward as your leader, your guide, your spokesman. President Rigdon wants me to bring up the other question first, and that is, Does the church want, and is it their only desire to sustain the Twelve as the First Presidency of this people?

Here are the Apostles, the *Bible*, the *Book of Mormon*, the *Doctrine and Covenants*—they are written on the tablet of my heart. If the church want the Twelve to stand as the head, the First Presidency of the Church, and at the head of this kingdom in all the world, stand next to Joseph, walk up into their calling, and hold the keys of this kingdom, every man, every woman, every quorum is now put in order, and you are now the sole controllers of it.

All that are in favor of this, in all the congregation of the saints, manifest it by holding up the right hand. (There was a universal vote). If there are any of the contrary mind, every man and every woman who does not want the Twelve to preside, lift up your hands in like manner. (No hands up). This supersedes the other question, and trying it by quorums.

We feel as though we could take Brother Rigdon in our bosom along with us; we want such men as Brother Rigdon. He has been sent away by Brother Joseph to build up a kingdom; let him keep the instructions and calling; let him raise up a mighty kingdom in Pittsburgh, and we will lift up his hands to Almighty God. I think we may have a printing office and a gathering there. If the devil still tries to kill us he will have enough to do.

The next is President Marks. Our feelings are to let him stand as president of the stake, as heretofore. We can build the Temple, etc.

You did not know who you had amongst you. Joseph so loved this people that he gave his life for them; Hyrum loved his brother and this people unto death. Joseph and Hyrum have given their lives for the church. But very few knew Joseph's character; he loved you unto death—you did not know it until after his death: he has now sealed his testimony with his blood.

If the Twelve had been here we would not have seen him given up —he should not have been given up. He was in your midst, but you did not know him; he has been taken away, for the people are not worthy of him.

The world is wide. I can preach in England, Ireland, Scotland, France, Germany, etc. I can preach in all the world, and the devils cannot find us. I'll swear to you I will not be given up.

There is much to be done. You have men among you who sleep with one eye open. The foundation is laid by our Prophet, and we will build thereon; no other foundation can be laid but that which is laid, and we will have our endowment, if the Lord will.

As the authorities do not want us to do military duty, don't do it. If it is necessary, my neck is ready for the knife; as for myself, I am determined to build up the kingdom of God: and by and by there will be a gleaning of grapes, and it may be said, 'To your tents, O Israel'.

We can build on the foundation that was laid by the Prophet. Joseph has finished his work, and all the devils in hell and all the mobbers on earth could not take his life until he had accomplished his work. God said, I will put a veil over his eyes and lead him up to the slaughter like a sheep to be killed, for the people are not worthy of him, though God loves this people.

Let no man suppose that the kingdom is rent from you; that it is not organized. If all the quorums of the church were slain, except the high priests, they would rise up with the keys of the kingdom, and have the powers of the priesthood upon them, and build up the kingdom, and the devil cannot help himself.

You can go to a healthy country, buy the land, and don't let a cursed scoundrel get in your midst. Let there be good men, good women, and whenever a man comes with a wheelbarrow-full of goods don't sell him land, don't let him a house, nor buy of him.

Suppose we had ten thousand such places, and increasing in greatness, perfectly free from these poor devils, we should feel better than we do now. Let us all be humble and get our endowments—all be humble, industrious and prudent, what sort of a kingdom would it be? The foundation is laid for more than we can think or talk about today.

Is it the will of this congregation that they will be tithed until the Temple is finished, as they have hitherto been? If so, signify it by the uplifted hand. (The vote was unanimous).

The men will act that have never acted before, and they will have the power and authority to do it. Is it the mind of this congregation to loose the hands of the Twelve, and enable us to go and preach to all the world? We want to know the feelings of the people. Is it your will to support the Twelve in all the world in their missions? (The congregation sustained this question by a unanimous vote). Will you leave it to the Twelve to dictate about the finances of the church? and will it be the mind of this people that the Twelve teach what will be the duties of the bishops in handling the affairs of the church? I want this, because twelve men can do it just as well as calling this immense congregation together at any other time. (A unanimous vote).

We shall have a patriarch, and the right is in the family of Joseph Smith, his brothers, his sons, or some one of his relations. Here is Uncle John, he has been ordained a patriarch. Brother Samuel would have taken the office if he had been alive; it would have been his right;

the right is in Uncle John, or one of his brothers (read sec. iii, par. 17, *Doctrine and Covenants**). I know that it would have belonged to Samuel. But as it is, if you leave it to the Twelve, they will wait until they know who is the man. Will you leave it to the Twelve, and they dictate the matter. (A unanimous vote). I know it will be let alone for the present.

I feel to bring up Brother Rigdon; we are of one mind with him and he with us. Will this congregation uphold him in the place he occupies by the prayer of faith and let him be one with us and we with him. (Unanimous). The Twelve will dictate and see to other matters. There will be a committee for the Temple; and now let men stand to their posts and be faithful.'

Adjourned to Oct. 6, Conference.
Benediction by Elder Parley P. Pratt.

COMMENT OF THE CHURCH HISTORIANS WHO COMPILED THIS DATA
OF THE CHURCH HISTORY

Thus closes the History of Joseph Smith, the great Prophet, Seer and Revelator, whom God has chosen to lay the foundation for the establishment of his church and kingdom upon the earth in the last dispensation and fulness of times.

He performed as great and mighty a work as any man that ever tabernacled in the flesh, save Jesus only. His mission lasted nearly seventeen years; from the time he received the plates from the angel Moroni on the 22nd day of Sept., 1827, to the 27th of June, 1844, when he was martyred in Carthage Jail, under the pledged protection of the governor of Illinois, Thomas Ford.

The History of Joseph Smith is now before the world, and we are satisfied that a history more correct in its details than this was never published. To have it strictly correct, the greatest possible pains have been taken by the historians and clerks engaged in the work. They were eye and ear witnesses of nearly all the transactions recorded in this history, most of which were reported as they transpired, and, where they were

---

*This would be the Nauvoo edition of the *Doctrine and Covenants*. In the current edition the passage is found in sec. cvii:39.

not personally present, they have had access to those who were.

Moreover, since the death of the Prophet Joseph, the history has been carefully revised under the strict inspection of President Brigham Young, and approved of by him.

TESTIMONY OF THE CHURCH HISTORIANS

We, therefore, hereby bear our testimony to all the world, unto whom these words shall come, that the History of Joseph Smith is true, and is one of the most authentic histories ever written.

We were, much of the time, associated with him in his travels and ministry since he organized the Church of Christ upon the earth. He labored diligently for the salvation and benefit of the human family. He ever taught and practiced, in public and in private, virtue, holiness and truth.

His brother Hyrum was martyred at the same time with him. He, also, was a great and good man, a wise counselor to his brother Joseph and a Prophet and Patriarch in the church, and the spirit of his office was with him up to the time of his death.

They were slain for the word of God and the testimony of Jesus Christ, and the people and nation who have persecuted them unto death and shed their blood will assuredly find their words fulfilled upon their heads, even in speedy and certain destruction, as were the words of the Savior fulfilled upon the Jewish nation for stoning and killing the Prophets and shedding the blood of the Lord's Anointed.

GEORGE A. SMITH,
WILFORD WOODRUFF, } Historians."

V

EXCERPTS FROM THE MANUSCRIPT
HISTORY OF BRIGHAM YOUNG
FROM AUGUST 9, 1844 TO
OCTOBER 8, 1848

Explanation

PART V deals with the actual beginning of the authorized administration by the Twelve Apostles in their
Presidency of the Church; and gives the detail of their
administration from August 9, 1844 to December 5.
1847, when Brigham Young was nominated by the
Council of the Twelve Apostles near Winter Quarters; and by October 8, 1848, the nomination had been
presented and unanimously sustained by all the major
divisions of the church. The subject matter of the
period is taken almost exclusively from *The History of
Brigham Young,* (*Ms.*)

This period officially shows the administration of
the Quorum of the Twelve acting as the Presidency
of the Church, and vindicates that Presidency for harmony and effectiveness. It has never before been published and will be found a rich mine of original information that will be of high value to the church for all
time, in that it will constitute an appeal to ultimate
authority for events of this period, and a vindication of
the men who functioned in the Presidency of the
Church during that time.

The main features covered in the period are the
church life in Nauvoo; the completion of the Temple
with the administration of the sacred ordinances therein; the establishment of the quorums of the priesthood.
especially the high priests and the seventies. It may be
said that it is especially a period of instruction for the
ministry of the church and important in developing
the seventies' organization therein. The period also
deals with the exodus of the church from Nauvoo, the
journey to the Missouri frontiers, thence westward over
the plains and the mountains to the Salt Lake Valley;
the beginning of settlements there and the installation
of the second First Presidency of the Church—Brigham Young, Heber C. Kimball and Willard Richards.

CHAPTER XX

EVENTS IMMEDIATELY FOLLOWING THE SUSTAINING OF THE QUORUM OF THE TWELVE—AS THE PRESIDENCY OF THE CHURCH—RESUMPTION OF CHURCH ACTIVITIES—PERPETUATION OF THE POLICY OF THE PROPHET

"*Friday, August* 9, 1844.—I met in council with Elders Heber C. Kimball, Parley P. Pratt, Orson Pratt, Wilford Woodruff, Willard Richards, George A. Smith, Amasa M. Lyman and eleven others at my house.

On motion of Elder Heber C. Kimball, Bishop Newel K. Whitney and George Miller were appointed to settle the affairs of the late Trustee-in-Trust, Joseph Smith, and be prepared to enter upon their duties as Trustees of the Church of Jesus Christ of Latter-day Saints.

Administrative Acts Following the Appointment of the Apostles to the Presidency.

The Nauvoo House Committee were instructed to wind up their business and report.

Patriarch John Smith [local] had the privilege of appointing another president at Macedonia in his stead and locating in Nauvoo at his option.*

Conversation ensued relative to the affairs and liabilities of the church and the building of the Nauvoo House.

Saturday. 10.—The following is an extract from the Minutes of the Nauvoo City Council:

'City council met at 9 a. m. and subscribed about $80.00 for the

---

*This was Patriarch "Uncle" John Smith, from now on prominent in the history of the church, and who was made Presiding Patriarch to the whole church Dec 24, 1847. He was paternal uncle of the Prophet Joseph.

Heretofore in this volume the footnotes are from various writers. Those supplied by the present editor up to now have been signed with his initials. Hereafter, as he supplies all the footnotes, they will not be so signed.

aid of the police.   Councilors (city) Brigham Young, Heber C. Kim-
Action of the
City Council
for the Sup-
pression of
Vice.
ball, George A. Smith and Hyrum Kimball in addition
relinquished their dues as councilors that the taxes might
be lessened and the police be paid. * * * Captain Hosea
Stout said the police were willing to watch the city while
it was necessary and all they wanted was to live [i. e. have their living
provided for] while they did it.

Daniel Spencer was elected to fill the remainder of the term of the
late martyred Mayor Joseph Smith.

An ordinance was passed allowing $100.00 per year to the mayor,
and $1.00 a day to the councilors and aldermen while in session.

Also an ordinance prohibiting brothels and disorderly characters.'*

Sunday, 11.—Forenoon meeting.   At the stand
Elder Lyman Wight preached about leading a company
away into the wilderness.   Afternoon, Elder Wm.
Hyde preached.   At 3 p. m. a few of the authorities met
at my house to pray for deliverance from the mob.

At a conference held in Southfield Center, Oakland
county, Michigan on the 9th, 10th and 11th inst. there
were represented 14 branches, containing upwards of
200 members and 37 officers.   Elders W. Burton and
Mephiboseth Sirrine, presidents.

Monday, 12.—The Twelve Apostles met in council
and made the following appointments:

That Elder Amasa Lyman, who was ordained an
Apostle by the direction of President Joseph Smith
Definite
Assignments
to Labors.
August 20, 1842, stand as a member of the
Quorum of the Twelve;

That Elder John Taylor hire the printing office and
establishment of the *Nauvoo Neighbor* and the *Times
and Seasons* from the church;

---

*The ordinance was signed by George W. Harris, president *protem* and Willard
Richards, recorder.   The ordinance was quite drastic.   It declared such places
(brothels) public nuisances and that the owners or keepers of such houses be fined
in the sum of not less than $50.00, nor more than $2,500.00 and imprisonment
for six months for each offense of one day's continuance of such establishments, and
that any person frequenting such establishments (except on lawful business) is to
be fined in any sum of not less than $50.00 or more than $500.00 and six months
imprisonment for each offense and further for every act of adultery or fornication
which can be proved.   The party is to be imprisoned six months and fined in the
sum of not less than $50.00 and not more than $2,500.00, and that the individual's
own acknowledgment shall be considered evidence in the case.

That Elder Wilford Woodruff go on a mission to England and preside over the churches there and on the adjacent isles and continent, taking charge of the printing and take his family with him;

That the general superintendencies' direction and control of the emigration from England be in the name of Brigham Young, President of the Quorum of the Twelve;

That the continent of America be organized into districts and high priests appointed to preside over each district;

That Brigham Young, Heber C. Kimball, and Willard Richards direct the continent and appoint presidents to manage the general affairs of the church;

That Lyman Wight go to Texas as he chooses, with his company, also George Miller and Lucine Woodworth, if they desire to go;

That Willard Richards continue the history of the church and be supported;

Elder Hyde arrived at Nauvoo from his eastern mission.

Wednesday, 14.—I attended meeting of the Twelve, Temple and Nauvoo House Committees and the stonecutters for the Temple at the Seventies' Hall. Agreed to raise the wages of the windlass men to $1.50 per day. The meeting terminated in a feeling of renewed determination to prosecute the work upon the Temple.

Thursday, 15.—The Quorum of the Twelve Apostles met at my house. Many matters were talked over. The council resolved to bear off the kingdom of God in all the world, in truth, honesty, virtue and holiness, and to continue to set their faces as a flint against every species of wickedness, vice and dishonesty in all its forms. _{Righteous Resolutions of the Twelve.}

I met in a prayer circle with the Twelve and a few others in the afternoon and prayed for the sick.

The following is from the *Times and Seasons*:

AN EPISTLE OF THE TWELVE TO THE CHURCH OF JESUS CHRIST OF LATTER DAY SAINTS, IN NAUVOO AND ALL THE WORLD—GREETING:

'*Beloved Brethren:*——Forasmuch as the saints have been called to suffer deep affliction and persecution, and also to mourn the loss of our beloved Prophet and also our Patriarch who have suffered a cruel martyrdom for the testimony of Jesus, having voluntarily yielded themselves to cruel murderers who had sworn to take their lives, and thus like good shepherds have laid down their lives for the sheep, therefore it becomes necessary for us to address you at this time on several important subjects.

The Saints Bereft of Their Prophet. You are now without a prophet present with you in the flesh to guide you; but you are not without Apostles, who hold the keys of power to seal on earth that which shall be sealed in heaven, and to preside over all the affairs of the church in all the world: being still under the direction of the same God, and being dictated by the same spirit, having the same manifestations of the Holy Ghost to dictate all the affairs of the church in all the world, to build up the kingdom upon the foundation that the Prophet Joseph has laid, who still holds the keys of this last dispensation, and will hold them to all eternity, as a king and priest unto the Most High God, ministering in heaven, on earth, or among the spirits of the departed dead, as seemeth good to him who sent him.

Let no man presume for a moment that his place will be filled by another: for, *remember he stands in his own place,* and always will: and the Twelve Apostles of this dispensation stand in their own place and always will, both in time and in eternity, to minister, preside and regulate the affairs of the whole church.

The Prophet Still at the Head of His Dispensation.

How vain are the imaginations of the children of men, to presume for a moment that the slaughter of one, two or a hundred of the leaders of this church could destroy an organization, so perfect in itself and so harmoniously arranged that it will stand while one member of it is left alive upon the earth. Brethren be not alarmed, for if the Twelve should be taken away still there are powers and offices in existence which will bear the kingdom of God triumphantly victorious in all the world. This church may have prophets many, and apostles many, but they are all to stand in due time in their proper organization, under the direction of those who hold the keys.

On the subject of the gathering, let it be distinctly understood that the city of Nauvoo and the Temple of our Lord are to continue to be built up according to the pattern which has been commenced, and which has progressed with such rapidity thus far.

Nauvoo the Place for the Gathering for the Present.

The city must be built up and supported by the gathering of those who have capital, and are willing to lay it out for the erection of every branch of industry and manufacture, which is necessary for the employment and support of the poor, or of those who depend wholly on their labor; while farmers who have capital must come on and purchase farms in the adjoining country, and improve and cultivate the same.—In this way all may enjoy plenty, and our infant city may grow and flourish, and be strengthened an hundred fold; and unless this is done, it is impossible for the gathering to progress, because those who have no other dependence cannot live together without industry and employment.

Therefore, let capitalists hasten here; and they may be assured we have nerves, sinews, fingers, skill and ingenuity sufficient in our midst to carry on all the necessary branches of industry.

The Temple must be completed by a regular system of tithing, according to the commandments of the Lord, which he has given as a law unto this church, by the mouth of his servant Joseph.

Therefore, as soon as the Twelve have proceeded to a full and complete organization of the branches abroad, let every member proceed immediately to tithe himself or herself, a tenth of all their property and money, and pay it into the hands of the Twelve; or into the hands of such bishops as have been, or shall be appointed by them to receive the same, for the building of the Temple for the support of the priesthood according to the scriptures, and the revelations of God; and then let them continue to pay in a tenth of their income from that time forth, for this is a law unto this church as much binding on their conscience as any other law or ordinance. And let this law or ordinance be henceforth taught to all who present themselves for admission into this church, that they may know the sacrifice and tithing which the Lord requires, and perform it; or else not curse the church with a mock membership as many have done heretofore. This will furnish a steady public fund for all sacred purposes, and save the leaders from constant debt and embarrassment, and the members can then employ the remainder of their capital in every branch of enterprize, industry, and charity, as seemeth them good; only holding themselves in readiness to be advised in such manner as shall be for the good of themselves and the whole society; and thus all things can move in harmony, and for the general benefit and satisfaction of all concerned.

The Law of Tithing to be Enforced.

The United States and adjoining provinces will be immediately organized by the Twelve into proper districts, in a similar manner as they have already done in England and Scotland, and high priests will be appointed over each district, to preside over the same, and to call quarterly conferences for the regulation and representation of the branches included in the same, and for the furtherance of the

The U. S. to be Organized into Church Districts Administered by High Priests.

gospel; and also to take measures for a yearly representation in a general conference. This will save the trouble and confusion of the running to and fro of elders; detect false doctrine and false teachers, and make every elder abroad accountable to the conference in which he may happen to labor. Bishops will also be appointed in the larger branches, to attend to the management of the temporal funds, such as tithings and funds for the poor, according to the revelations of God and to be judges in Israel.

The gospel in its fulness and purity, must now roll forth through every neighborhood of this widespread country, and to all the world; and millions will awake to its truths and obey its precepts; and the kingdoms of this world will become the kingdoms of our Lord and of his Christ.

As rulers and people have taken counsel together against the Lord, and against his anointed, and have murdered him who would have reformed and saved the nation, it is not wisdom for the saints to have anything to do with politics, voting, or president-making, at present. None of the candidates who are now before the public for that high office, have manifested any disposition or intention to redress wrong or restore right, liberty or law; and therefore woe unto him who gives countenance to corruption, or partakes of murder, robbery, or other cruel deeds. Let us then stand aloof from all their corrupt men and measures, and wait, at least, till a man is found, who, if elected, will carry out the enlarged principles, universal freedom, and equal rights and protection, expressed in the views of our beloved Prophet and martyr, General Joseph Smith.

Suggestion as to Policies.

We do not, however, offer this political advice as binding on the consciences of others; we are perfectly willing that every member of this church should use his own freedom in all political matters; but we give it as our own rule of action, and for the benefit of those who may choose to profit by it.

Now, dear brethren, to conclude our present communication, we would exhort you in the name of the Lord Jesus Christ, to be humble and faithful before God, and before all the people, and give no occasion for any man to speak evil of you, but preach the gospel in its simplicity and purity, and practice righteousness, and seek to establish the influence of truth, peace and love among mankind, and in so doing the Lord will bless you, and make you a blessing to all people.

Closing Admonition.

You may expect to hear from us again.

[Signed] BRIGHAM YOUNG
President of the Twelve.

Nauvoo, August 15th, 1844.

August 15, (continued).—Elders Noah Rogers and Benjamin F. Grouard wrote from Tahiti of this date that they and Elder Addison Pratt had arrived at the Society Islands. Their vessel had stopped at Toboui to refit and obtain supplies, where, being favorably received by the natives Elder Pratt remained. Elders Rogers and Grouard proceeded to Tahiti and found the people in great confusion in consequence of an invasion by the French. *Report of Mission Movements in the Pacific Islands.* The English missionaries opposed the elders bitterly, but having become alarmed in consequence of the war between the French and the Islanders they had mostly left the island. The elders found great difficulty in engaging the attention of the people in consequence of the excitement of the war. Queen Pomare's force having been defeated, the natives retired to the interior. Elder Pratt had baptized several Americans who were residing at Toboui which is a small island about 300 miles from Tahiti.

Saturday, 17.—In company with Elders Kimball, Woodruff and others I went on to the Temple walls, viewed the country, encouraged the workmen and counseled Brother Woodruff in relation to his mission to England.

Afternoon, spent considerable time in the Tithing Office.

Elder John Brown wrote from Monroe county, Mississippi, of his preaching in Kentucky, and in Hickman, Williamson, and Sumner counties, Tennessee; also in Tuscaloosa county, Alabama; thence he proceeded to Perry *Mission Movements in the Southern States.* county, Alabama, where he found a branch of fifteen raised up by Elder James Brown, and where he and Brother Haden W. Church, baptized forty-five. They continued their labors during last winter in Alabama and Mississippi. A conference was held in Alabama, in April, at which several elders were ordained. From this conference, Brother Church went to Tennessee and Brother B. L. Clapp and John Brown to Mississippi. Brother Clapp soon returned to Nauvoo and Brother Brown held a conference in July when thirty-nine were reported as having been baptized since last conference.

Sunday, 18.—I preached to the saints in the morning. The following synopsis of my discourse and minutes of the meeting were reported by Elder Woodruff:

PRESIDENT BRIGHAM YOUNG'S DISCOURSE

'I have many things to speak of. It was my mind in the first place that we should have a suitable time to meditate upon all matters, and weigh them, even every subject wherein we felt interested. When the question was asked me if the elders should continue to baptize for the dead, I replied that I had no counsel to give upon that subject at present, but thought it best to attend to other matters in the meantime.

Restless Elements at Nauvoo.

I have learned some things I did not know when I came home. I discover a disposition in the sheep to scatter, now the shepherd is taken away. I do not say that it will never be right for this people to go from here or scatter abroad; but I do say wait until the time comes, or until you are counseled to do so. The report has gone forth through the city that the Twelve have a secret understanding with those men who are going away and taking companies with them, that they shall take away all they can; and although the Twelve will blow it up in public, yet privately they wish it to go on, but if they were the last words I had to say before going into the eternal worlds I would swear by the Holy Trinity that such a report is utterly false, and there is not a word of truth in it. There is no man who has any right to lead away one soul out of this city by the consent of the Twelve, except Lyman Wight and George Miller, they have had the privilege of taking the 'Pine Company'* where they pleased, but not another soul has the consent of the Twelve to go with them. There is no man who has any liberty to lead away people into the wilderness

---

*This has reference to a company of men under the leadership of Lyman Wight to go into the pine country in the north to get out timber for the Temple.

from this church, or to lead them anywhere else, by the consent of the Twelve or the church, except in the case above named—and I tell you in the name of Jesus Christ that if Lyman Wight and George Miller take a course contrary to our counsel and will not act in concert with us, they will be damned and go to destruction—and if men will not stop striving to be great and exalted, and lead away parties from us, thereby weakening our hands, they will fall and not rise again—and I will destroy their influence in this church with the help of God and my brethren. I wish you to distinctly understand that the counsel of the Twelve is for every family that does not belong to the Pine Company to *stay here in Nauvoo,* and build up the Temple and get your endowments; do not scatter; 'united we stand, divided we fall'. It has been whispered about that all who go into the wilderness with Wight and Miller will get their endowments, but they cannot give an endowment in the wilderness. If we do not carry out the plan Joseph has laid down and the pattern he has given for us to work by, we cannot get any further endowment —I want this to sink deep into your hearts that you may remember it. If you stir up the flame of dissension, will you get an endowment? No! You get a party to run here and another there, to divide our strength, and weaken our hands, and our enemies will flock around us and destroy us—in that case you will not get your endowments, but will sink and not rise;— go to hell and not to the bosom of Abraham. Do the people leave here because they are afraid? Are you cowards? Do you fear those who have power to kill the body only? If you leave this place for fear of the mob, before God tells you to go, you will have no place of rest, but you will flee from place to place and go like the Jews, until God raises up some other people to redeem you, for if the devil scares you from this place he will scare you from all other places. Let no man go from this place but the pine country brethren, but stay here and sow, plant, build, and put your plowshares into the prairies: one plowshare will do more to drive off the mob than two guns. Let us stay here where the bones of Joseph, Hyrum, Samuel, Don Carlos, and Father Smith are. While Joseph was alive he said 'If I am slain in battle or fall by the hands of my enemies I want my body brought to Nauvoo and laid in the tomb I have prepared.' I would rather have the dead body of the Prophet than some men who are alive and I would rather have the clothes of the Prophet stuffed with straw for president of the United States than any man whose name is now before the nation as a candidate, for the straw would not do any harm.

We want to build the Temple in this place, if we have to build it as the Jews built the walls of the Temple in Jerusalem, with a sword in one hand and the trowel in the other. How easily some men are scared! I have not been frightened yet, and I know of other men who have not.

The Church not to be Deprived of Revelations. Do you suppose the mouth of God is closed, to be opened no more unto us? If this were the case I would not give the ashes of a rye straw for the salvation of the church. If God has ceased to speak by the Holy Ghost, or to give revelation, there is no salvation; but this is not the case.

There seems to be a disposition by many to leave Nauvoo and go into the wilderness or somewhere else. Suppose we should all go into the wilderness and then ask God to give us an endowment, and he should ask if we were driven from Nauvoo, and who drove us? The devil drove us would be the answer; he might say, well, did you not know that I had power over the devil? Yes, but one said I would not give a jackknife for all Nauvoo, and another said, I would not give a pair of mules for the best farm in Hancock county and I was afraid; would the Lord give an endowment to a people who would be frightened away from their duty?

Concerning those who are wishing to lead away parties contrary to counsel, I would not wish them damned worse, than to have a company after their own liking go with them, for they will soon quarrel among themselves; and if we should go to the wilderness and ask the Lord to give us an endowment, he might ask us, saying, Did I not give you rock in Nauvoo to build the Temple with? Yes. Did I not through my providence furnish men to quarry and cut the stone and prepare it for the building? Yes. Did I not give you means to build the Temple there? Yes. Very well, had you died in Nauvoo, on the walls of the Temple, or in your fields, I would have taken you to myself and raised up men to officiate for you, and you would have enjoyed the highest glory. Did you make a sacrifice by tithing? No. Well I do not wonder you did not believe I had power over the devil.

Such may go away but I want to have the faithful stay here to build the Temple and settle the city. We shall require the tenth of all your property as a tithing for the building of the Temple and for the poor and for the priesthood. I want my support and living by the church hereafter, so that I can give my whole time to the business of the church. I have always supported myself heretofore in all my travels and labors, with the aid of my brethren.

The Law of Tithing to be Enforced.

Joseph has always been preserved from his enemies, until now, but he has sealed his testimony with his blood, and his testament is now in force. While the testator lived it was all in his hands, but now he is dead.

There is no remission of sins without the shedding of blood.* You will soon wake up and know things as they are—there has been a great debt paid; there will be no need of more blood of the saints being shed at present, by and by you will understand and see that all is right.

Woe! woe! woe! unto all who have shed the blood of the saints and the Lord's anointed. It must needs be that offenses come, but woe unto that man through whom they come.

Woe! to Those by Whom Offenses Come.

*Heb. ix:22.

To those who want to go away from this place, I would say wait until the time comes. I will give you the key. North and South America is Zion and as soon as the Temple is done and you get your endowments you can go and build up stakes, but do not be in haste, wait until the Lord says go. If you have the Spirit of God you can discover right from wrong— when all is right with the priesthood and a man rises up and speaks by the Spirit of God and just right, all will say, Amen, but when a man rises up and talks as smooth as oil, if he is not right, there will be many queries about it, it will not edify the body [i. e. the people]. I give this as a key. You may go all over The Whole of North and South America and build up America Zion. stakes when the time comes. The whole continent of America must be organized into districts and presiding elders appointed over each district: the time has come when all things must be set in order.

I wish the saints to let their bickerings cease, and a strict order of things be introduced: we shall not harbor blacklegs, counterfeiters and bogus-makers; we know all about them, they have been in our midst long enough. I advise all the saints to have no dealings with such men; let them alone. The time has come that they should be wiped out of our midst, let the ungodly dealers alone; and as to the doctors who are in our midst, who are our enemies, I say let them alone, for I have no doubt but that three to one who have died in this place had a doctor. I say woe unto you lawyers, for your whole study is to put down truth and put a lie in its stead. I want the lawyers to know that we have common sense. They want to make you believe that when you spell 'baker' it means cider or whiskey. Now let the lawyers and doctors alone and leave off bitterness and evil speaking, and you will build the Temple and get an endowment. All ye lawyers go away and let us alone and when we get full of the devil and want you, we will send for you, we may then have a more convenient season.

I want to say to all who profess to be saints, do not harbor blacklegs, counterfeiters and bogus-makers, wipe them away; it is time to carry out the design of our Prophet; do cease to employ doctors, lawyers, and merchants who will empty your purses and then mob you. Store your grain in Nauvoo for you will want it here to eat while you are building the Temple. I say to the hands on the Temple, be united; and to the Temple Committee, do not turn away any person because he is an Englishman, Scotchman, Irishman or of any other nation; but employ every man you can and build the Temple and your homes. I would rather pay out every cent I have to build up this place and get an endowment, if I were driven the next minute without anything to take with me. As to the doctors, let them go. I can prove that a doctor in this place doctored a woman that was in the family way, and did not know it until she was delivered, and both woman and child died, and if you will employ them, you will all die.

The Ungodly Not to be Tolerated.

There is a distinction between the law of the land and the law of the church. You have the privilege of keeping all shops that do not come in contact with the law of the state, county, or city; so I will evade the law of the land, says the dealer, and give away whiskey and sell a little tobacco or something else and charge enough for both; but the law of the church will reach such men and if they are members they should be cut off. I dreamed that I saw a fruit tree in which I went in search of fruit. I soon discovered that some of the main branches on the top were dead. It seemed to me necessary to cut off the dead branches in order to save the tree so I told some person to help me cut them off. The person stepped on to a large green limb and was afraid it would break so I put my shoulder under it and held it up till the dead branch was cut off, the green limb cracked but did not break. After all the

Evasions not to be Practiced in Administering the Law of the Church.

The Removal of Dead Branches.

dry limbs were cut off the wounds healed up and the tree grew finely.

Let us cut off the dead branches of the church that good fruit may grow and a voice will soon be heard, go and build up Zion and the Temple of the Lord.

The seventies will be organized and a presidency of seven men will be chosen out of the first quorum to preside over the first ten quorums.'*

August 18, (*continued*).—At a conference in Tazewell county, Virginia, Richard H. Kinnamon presiding, Elders Hamilton and Park were appointed to labor in Tazewell, Smith and Washington counties.   Elders King and Lambson were appointed to labor in Greenbrier and Monroe counties, Elders Carter and Biles in Giles and Roanoke counties, Elder Hyatt in Patrick county, Elder Pitts in Giles county, Elders R. H. Kinnamon and Stephen Litz in South Carolina and Elder J. T. Crow was sent on a mission south.

The Work of the Church in the South.

Several were called to the priesthood; during conference the sacrament was administered and one person baptized.   Elder Robert Hamilton preached.

Monday, 19.—Elder Willard Richards called on Emma Smith, widow of the Prophet, for the new translation of the *Bible*:   She said she did not feel disposed to give it up at present.

The Prophet's "Translation" of the Bible Sought.†

I met in council with Elders Heber C. Kimball, Parley P. Pratt, Orson Pratt, Willard Richards, Wilford Woodruff, George A. Smith, Amasa M. Lyman, Erastus Snow, William W. Phelps and Jonathan Dunham at my house, when it was voted that Dan Jones

*These groups constituting the councils for the first ten quorums however did not cease to be members of the first quorum, on the contrary they continued to be the First Quorum of the Seventy one of the three great councils (the third) of the priesthood.   The First Presidency and the Twelve being the other two.   (*Doctrine and Covenants,* sec. cvii).

†It will be observed that I place "translation" in the sideheading in quotation marks.   I do this because the work of the Prophet was not really a translation of the *Bible* from ancient languages, but was a revision of the *English Bible* (King James' version), under inspiration.   (See this *History,* vol. i, p. 324, especially footnote; and p. 341; vol. iv, p. 137).

receive an order on Elder Woodruff, Liverpool, for five hundred dollars to assist him on his mission to Wales, having confidence that the Lord would bless him in preaching the gospel to that nation; Brother Jones having relinquished a certain sum due him to be applied to the benefit of the Temple.

Elder Willard Richards read a letter he received from James Arlington Bennett, in which he relates his dreams relative to the murder of Joseph and Hyrum. Elder Richards was instructed to write Bennett in reply, which was done. Afternoon, with Elder Kimball and Richards I visited Mr. Davidson Hibbard on business.

James Arlington Bennett.

Wednesday, 21.—Council of the Twelve Apostles at my house to meet Elder Lyman Wight. Elder John Taylor went after him with a carriage; found him sick and unable to attend.

I spent the evening and partook of supper at Elder Woodruff's with Elders Heber C. Kimball, Willard Richards, John Taylor and their wives.

Friday, 23.—The brethren of the Twelve got ready to go and dine at Father Mikesell's; but were called to go and see Lyman Wight near the upper stone house: he and thirty others were sick in the same house.

Saturday, 24.—Council of the Twelve Apostles, the Temple and Nauvoo House Committees and other elders at my house, when it was voted that I should take such measures as should seem best to gather men and means to this place to complete the Temple. Elder Lyman Wight was counselled to go north instead of going south.

Council Meeting to Give Impetus to Build the Temple.

After transacting the business presented, Elder Woodruff was blessed and set apart to his mission to England under the hands of the members of the Quorum of the Twelve Apostles present: Several of the Twelve Apostles were baptized for their dead this afternoon.*

*Also see p. 264, where President Young extended the privilege for the saints generally to be baptized for the dead. It is to be presumed that this was the

DISCOURSE OF ELDER WILFORD WOODRUFF

Sunday. 25.—Meeting at the stand.   Elder Wilford
Woodruff preached, he said:

'There is a spirit in man and the inspiration of the
Almighty giveth it understanding.   It is through this
principle that this congregation is assembled together at
this place; you had understanding of the things of God

announcement of the resumption of attending to baptisms for the dead under the
administration of Brigham Young and the Twelve Apostles which baptisms may well
have been interrupted during the exciting period just previous to and following the
martyrdom of the Prophet.   While Elijah revealed the keys of the priesthood
pertaining to this ordinance in the Kirtland Temple in 1836—April 3—the Prophet
Joseph did not begin teaching baptism for the dead until in October, 1840 (See letter
of President Smith to the "Traveling High Council"—the Twelve Apostles, then in
England—this *History*, vol. iv, p. 231).

On the introduction of this doctrine to the church it made a very strong appeal
to the members thereof and there was generally an earnest desire to attend to this
ordinance for the dead.   Some irregularities ensued, such as improper representatives
being baptized for the departed dead, and in some few instances women being
baptized for men and *vice versa*.   These ordinances for some time were performed in
the Mississippi river.   This procedure however was finally cancelled and at the
October conference, 1841, the Prophet Joseph made the announcement that there
should be no more baptisms for the dead until the ordinance could be attended to in
the Temple then building.   "For thus saith the Lord", declared the Prophet (this
History, vol. iv, p. 426).

Also there had been some irregularities in the matter of neglecting to make proper
records of baptisms for the dead.   These irregularities were corrected by careful
instructions from the Prophet.   (See two epistles of his in *Doctrine and Covenants*,
sec. cxxvii and cxxviii, bearing date of Sept. 1, 1842 and Sept. 6, 1842.)   Meantime
a rather fine temporary baptismal font was erected in the basement of the Temple
and enclosed by a temporary frame building, built of split oak clapboards (See
this *History*, vol. vi, p. 46).   Baptisms in this font were very numerous, even
in the days of the Prophet.   And now such baptisms were resumed under the direction
of President Brigham Young and his brethren.

The mission of Elijah in the New Dispensation was foreshadowed even on the
occasion of Moroni's first visit to the Prophet Joseph Smith on September 21, 1823,
when Moroni, in quoting prophecies of the scriptures which were soon to be fulfilled,
made reference to this mission of Elijah, saying: that the Lord would reveal unto
the Prophet Joseph the priesthood by the hand of Elijah before the coming of the
great and dreadful day of the Lord; and that he would plant in the hearts of the
children the promises made to the fathers, etc. (See Writings of Joseph Smith,
Pearl of Great Price, p. 21, current edition).   In section xx of the *Doctrine and
Covenants*, vv. 25-27, it is said "that as many as would believe and be baptized in his
holy name [in the New Dispensation then coming forth] and endure in faith to
the end, should be saved.   Not only those who believed *after* he came in the Meridian
of time in the flesh, but all those *from the beginning*, even as many as were *before*
he came who believed in the words of the holy prophets, who spake as they were
inspired by the gift of the Holy Ghost, who truly testified of him in all things—
should have eternal life as well as those who should come *after*, who should believe
in the gifts and callings of God, by the Holy Ghost, which beareth record of the
Father and of the Son."   So that almost from the commencement of the New Dispensation the work for the dead may be said to be in contemplation.

by the Spirit of God, and I have now one important declaration to make unto you, and that is, that inasmuch as you will be united in heart, mind and action in supporting your counsellors, Exhortation to Unity. the authorities of the church, the priesthood of God, and follow the counsel given you, as you have endeavored to follow the counsel of the Prophet while he was living, you will be safe and blessed and will prosper; but if you are divided and reject the counsel of God you will fall: union and faithfulness is your salvation. You have been led by one of the best men that ever graced humanity or tabernacled in flesh; but he has gone; he has sealed his testimony with his blood; he loved this people unto death.

I call upon this people to be united in building upon the foundation which the Prophet Joseph has laid. You have been called to suffer much in the cause in which you are engaged, but if judgment begins at the House of God, Babylon will not escape; and if there is fire in a green tree, a dry tree will not escape, and there are none more prepared for the shock that is coming upon the earth than the Latter-day Saints. The object we have in view is to secure blessings beyond the veil in the first resurrection; this is what The Prophet Joseph Sealed his Testimony with his Blood. we are preparing for. Again, I would say let not the saints be troubled because they have lost their Prophet. I would ask, because the Prophet has sealed his testimony with his blood, if that destroys the gospel—takes away the power of God—annihilates truth—or buries the priesthood? I tell you, nay! it does not. His testament is now in force; therefore my counsel is to follow the example of those who have gone before and be faithful unto death. If you will be united and go too with your mights in building the Temple you will have power to accomplish it and get an endowment. I exhorted the saints to faithfulness—and requested their prayers, and asked their forgiveness for anything that I might have done wrong and bade them farewell.'

Baptism for
the Dead
Resumed.
I [Brigham Young] spoke a few words to the saints; told them they were at liberty to be baptized for their dead relatives.

Elders Orson Hyde and Parley P. Pratt bore testimony that Joseph the Prophet had ordained, anointed Testimonies
on Various
Things. and appointed the Twelve to lead the church, and had given them the keys of the kingdom for that purpose.

Elder John Taylor bore testimony against those that murdered Joseph and Hyrum Smith; he said they should be cursed and the congregation said, Amen.

Elder William W. Phelps and Reynolds Cahoon bore testimony that Joseph said unto the Twelve 'upon you must rest the responsibility of bearing off the kingdom of God in all the world, therefore round up your shoulders and bear it.'*

Monday, 26.—Attended council held at my house. Afternoon attended a court martial.

Tuesday, 27.—I met with the officers of the Nauvoo Legion in council; six of the Apostles were present. The council decided that they would carry out all the views of our martyred Prophet: the brethren felt very spirited on the subject.

Departure
of Elders
Woodruff and
Jones for
England.
Wednesday, 28.—Elders Wilford Woodruff, Dan Jones, and Hiram Clark with their families started this afternoon for England.

Thursday, 29.—The Quorum of the Twelve Apostles met at my house, having notified Elders Elders Rigdon
and Marks
Cited Before
the Twelve. Rigdon and Marks to attend. This was fast day and I attended meeting at the stand and laid hands on several of the sick.

Friday, 30.—In company with my brethren of the

---

*This is important as corroborating a statement made many years subsequently by William Smith, brother of the Prophet at a court in Independence. He testified in that court in what is known as the "Temple Lot Suit" to obtain title to the Kirtland Temple by the organization known as the Josephite Church, vs. the Hedrickite Church, when he said President Joseph Smith ordained "him [Wm. Smith, who was one of the original members of the Quorum of the Twelve Apostles at Kirtland] a prophet, seer, revelator, and translator, and then informed him that he had all the necessary ordinations to lead the church in his time" (See *Succession in the Presidency of the Church*, B. H. Roberts, second edition, p. 104).

Twelve, Father John Smith and many others I visited at Father Mikesell's, partook of dinner and *A Social Function Under Armed Guards.* an abundance of peaches from his orchard: the family were glad to see us and we spent a pleasant day. Many of the brethren in the city being apprehensive that we might fall into the hands of the mob, took their guns and went a 'hunting' around and below Mikesell's along the timbered bluffs on the Mississippi River.

Saturday, 31.—Visiting the sick. Afternoon attended general meeting of the officers of the Nauvoo Legion. I was unanimously elected lieutenant-general and Charles C. Rich, major-general of the Nauvoo Legion. Evening, attended a school meeting."

CHAPTER XXI.

FORMAL TRIAL AND EXCOMMUNICATION OF PRES-
IDENT SIDNEY RIGDON——RESTLESS MOVEMENTS
OF JAMES EMMETT —MISSION ACTIVITIES OF
THE CHURCH——MOVEMENTS OF STATE OF-
FICIALS AND THE MOB OF HANCOCK
COUNTY

"*Sunday, September* 1, 1844.——I [Brigham Young]
went to the stand* in the forenoon. Elder
Sidney Rigdon preached. His discourse was
complicated and somewhat confused; he said
he had all things shown to him from this time to the
winding-up scene, or the great battle of Gog and Magog; there were great things to take place, but he did
not tell what the saints should do to save themselves.

Rigdon's Vagaries— Gog and Magog.

I met with the high priests' quorum in the afternoon
and spoke at some length to the brethren. Elder Heber
C. Kimball addressed the meeting; afterwards, we proceeded to the Seventies' Hall and instructed the seventies
pertaining to the organization of their quorums.

A conference was held at Philadelphia, August 31st,
and September 1st, at which Elder William
Smith [Apostle and brother of the Proph-
et] presided. Elder Jedediah M. Grant represented
three hundred and thirty-four members, including officers and gave much good instruction pertaining to
the duties of the saints, in building a Temple and
strengthening the hands of the saints at Nauvoo. Elders
Wm. Smith and William I. Appleby preached.

Conference in Philadelphia.

Monday, 2.——Visited Elders Willard Richards and
John P. Greene who were very sick.

---

*"I went to the stand." This had reference to an outdoor place of meeting on
the Temple site and was the only place of meeting sufficient to accommodate the large
congregations that were wont to assemble in Nauvoo during the summer time.

I wrote the following which was published in the *Times and Seasons*:

CONCENTRATION AT NAUVOO

'The Twelve would invite the brethren abroad, in obedience to the commandments of the Lord, to gather to Nauvoo with their means to help build up the city, and complete the Temple, which is now going forward faster than it has at any time since it commenced. Beware of the speculations about the Prophet! Believe no tales on the subject: Time will tell who are the friends of Joseph Smith, who laid down his life for his brethren. We have no new commandments, but beseech the brethren to honor and obey the old ones, for, wheresoever the carcass is, there will the eagles be gathered together.'

Tuesday, 3.—I had an interview with Brother Sidney Rigdon. He said he had power and authority above the Twelve Apostles and did not consider himself amenable to their counsel. In the evening, the Twelve had an interview with Brother Rigdon, who was far from feeling an interest with the Twelve. His license was demanded, which he refused to give up, and said the church had not been lead by the Lord for a long time, and he should come out and expose the secrets of the church.

Rigdon's License Demanded.

Wednesday, 4.—Elder Willard Richards sick. The Twelve Apostles and a few others met at my house in the evening and prayed for the preservation of the church and ourselves; and that the Lord might bind up the apostates and preserve the honest in heart.

Thursday, 5.—Brother Wm. Marks came to see me in relation to President Rigdon and his revelations. Afternoon, attended public prayer meeting and exposed the false prophets. Evening, Elder Hyde preached in the Masonic Hall on Elder Rigdon's conduct since his return to Nauvoo.

Friday, 6.—Elder Heber C. Kimball and I visited the sick till two p. m.

Brother Alonzo W. Whitney informed us of the proceedings of Elder Rigdon and others.

Elder Orson Pratt preached in the Seventies' Hall.

Saturday, 7.—Accompanied by Elder Kimball I waited upon Elder John P. Greene, and attended to ordinances for him: he was on his deathbed.*

Leonard Soby was disfellowshipped by the high council for following Elder Rigdon.

Sunday, 8.—I insert the following synopsis of minutes of Elder Sidney Rigdon's trial:

THE FORMAL TRIAL OF ELDER SIDNEY RIGDON

'Minutes of a meeting of the Church of Jesus Christ of Latter-day Saints held on the meeting ground in the city of Nauvoo. Present, of the Quorum of the Twelve, President Brigham Young, Heber C. Kimball, Parley P. Pratt, Orson Pratt, Orson Hyde, George A. Smith, John Taylor and Amasa M. Lyman.

The high council was organized with Bishop Newel K. Whitney at their head.†

President Young briefly addressed the congregation and introduced the business of the day, which he said would be this: All those who are for Joseph and Hyrum, the *Book of Mormon, Book of Doctrine and Covenants*, the Temple and Joseph's measures, they being

Testimony of Elder Brigham Young.

one party, will be called upon to manifest their principles openly and boldly, the opposite party to enjoy the same liberty and be as decided and manifest their principles as boldly as they do in their secret meetings and private councils. If they are for Sidney Rigdon, and believe he is the man to be the first President and leader of this people, they are requested to manifest it as freely as they do in other places, because this will form another party: President Young alluded to the course of Elder Rigdon.

Elders Orson Hyde, Parley P. Pratt, Amasa M. Lyman, John

Other Witnesses.

Taylor, William W. Phelps, Heber C. Kimball and William Marks bore testimony in relation to the course of Elder Rigdon, which is published in full in the fifth volume of the *Times and Seasons*.

Elder W. W. Phelps [after the above hearing] moved that Elder Sidney Rigdon be cut off from the church, and delivered over to the buffetings of satan until he repent.

Bishop Newel K. Whitney then presented the motion to the high

The Judgment.

council [who was trying the case] and the vote was unanimous in the affirmative.

*These were doubtless the usual ordinances for the sick and dedicating him to the Lord.

†This was the special high council provided for in the church for the trial of a president in the Presidency of the High Priesthood of the Church, which is presided over by the bishop of the church, assisted by twelve high priests chosen for the occasion. (See *Doctrine and Covenants*, sec. cvii:82-84). In this case Bishop Newel K. Whitney was the presiding bishop of the special court and the Apostles—the Twelve—were the accusers.

Elder Phelps then offered the same motion to the church, upon which President Young arose and requested the congregation to place themselves so that all could be seen who voted. He then called upon the church to signify whether they were in favor of the motion: the vote was nearly unanimous.

Those who were for Sidney Rigdon were requested to make it manifest: there were ten who voted for him.

Elder Phelps then moved that all who have voted to follow Elder Rigdon be suspended until they can have a trial before the high council. An amendment was offered as follows: 'or shall hereafter be found advocating his principles.'

The vote was unanimous in the affirmative.

President Young arose and delivered Sidney Rigdon over to the buffetings of satan in the name of the Lord, and all the people said, Amen.'*

Monday, 9.—I attended council with the Quorum of the Twelve at Elder Heber C. Kimball's; thence I went in company with Elder Kimball through the city, attending to business and visiting Elders John P. Greene and Parley P. Pratt who were sick.

Elder Heber C. Kimball and George A. Smith labored diligently with James Emmett that he might be persuaded to desist from his in- ^{Labors with James Emmett.}

---

*This is a very brief statement of the trial and final dismissal of Elder Sidney Rigdon from the church. The minutes of the trial with objections and remarks and complaints were published in the *Times and Seasons* of Sept. 15, Oct. 2, and Oct. 15, 1844, running through three numbers, and in all making fifteen pages of closely printed matter. Very serious charges are made against Elder Rigdon for insubordination, for claiming to hold keys and authority above any man or set of men in the church, even superior authority and keys thereof than those held by the Twelve; and likewise he had ordained men to positions—places and offices not recognized as properly belonging to the church. Among other things he somewhere about this time predicted that the building of the Temple would cease and prophesied that there would not be another stone raised upon the walls of the Temple. At one of the meetings where this was said, a Brother Wm. W. Player determined that Elder Rigdon should not prove a true prophet, in this instance at least, and took with him Archibald and John Held, and set a stone upon the Temple wall, making this prediction a failure; and of course the Temple was subsequently completed and dedicated, and ordinance work performed therein. The statement of Wm. W. Player is signed and recorded in the *History of Brigham Young, Ms.,* for December, 1844, p. 67.

After this trial at Nauvoo Sidney Rigdon returned to Pittsburg in Pennsylvania where he had something of a following; and he undertook to organize a church, choosing twelve apostles, etc.; his efforts however amounted to but little. He sent missionaries to many branches of the church to represent his claims, but his organization was never strong either in membership of leading men, and it soon crumbled into decay. Sidney Rigdon himself sank out of sight and in 1876 he died in obscurity in Allegheny county, state of New York. (See *Succession in the Presidency of the Church,* by the present writer, second edition).

tended course of taking away a party of misguided saints into the wilderness.*

Tuesday, 10.—Elder John P. Greene died.

Elder Orson Hyde started for Kirtland.

I attended council with the Twelve and others when orders to the mob given by Colonel Levi Williams were read. General Deming [sheriff of Hancock county] said he did not consider that a mob large enough to do any mischief could be raised.

Afternoon, with Elder Kimball visiting the saints.

Evening, attended a meeting of officers of the Legion, when a resolution was passed to build an arsenal and gunsmith's shop: one hundred and thirty dollars was subscribed towards the erection of the building.

Wednesday, 11.—Elder John P. Greene buried. * *

I attended council at Elder Erastus Snow's; afterwards in company with several officers of the Legion looking out a location for the arsenal.

Friday, 13.—I went to the parade ground where the officers were drilling. Jonathan Dunham was elected brigadier-general of the second cohort of the Nauvoo Legion: I addressed the officers.

In company with Brother Heber C. Kimball and his wife, Vilate, I visited Mother [Lucy] Smith.

There are many reports concerning the movements of the mob; who are making preparations for what they call a 'wolf hunt' on the 26th and 27th of this month; but the general apprehension is that they design coming and attempting to drag some more authorities of the church out to Carthage to murder them.

The "Wolf Hunt" Preparation.

Saturday, 14.—In company with Elders Heber C. Kimball and George A. Smith I called on Sister Hyrum Smith.

*James Emmett, born on February 22, 1803, in Boone county, Kentucky. He was quite active in the affairs of the church in Missouri; but just a bit uncertain in his conduct. In May of 1837, fellowship was withdrawn from him by a meeting of the presidency and high council of the church at Far West "for unwise conduct, until he should make satisfaction". This he did, and was returned to fellowship; but he was always a restless, impatient man and ambitious of leadership which led him into great trouble and final separation from the church as we shall see.

Elder Amasa M. Lyman being very sick and reported to be dying, Brothers Kimball, George A. [Smith] and I retired to my upper room and prayed for him: he was healed from that very hour.

Attended city council, Jonathan C. Wright was elected marshal and W. W. Phelps recorder of deeds. George A. Smith was elected councilor.

At two p. m., the second cohort of the Nauvoo Legion inspected: Brother John Taylor and I attended.

Evening, visited Brother Amasa M. Lyman.

Sunday, 15.—Elder Parley P. Pratt preached in the forenoon and Elder Orson Pratt in the afternoon.

Monday, 16.—At six a. m., accompanied by Elder Heber C. Kimball, Generals C. C. Rich, Jonathan Dunham and other officers of the Legion, I went to the ground secured for the arsenal, near the Temple. We uncovered our heads and lifted our hands to heaven and I dedicated the ground, by prayer, to the God of the armies of Israel. I took the spade and broke the ground for the cellar.

The Dedication of the Nauvoo Arsenal.

Evening, I attended council; Jared Carter was present and made confession and promised to return to the church.

Tuesday, 17.—The Legion trained. Afterwards the officers met when George A. Smith was elected quartermaster-general of the Nauvoo Legion, with the rank of colonel.

The following is from Elder Addison Pratt, Tubuai [sometimes written Tooboui or Toboui], Society Islands, of date of July 26, 1844.

LETTER OF ELDER ADDISON PRATT FROM THE SOCIETY ISLANDS

'July 26th, I baptized nine persons, four Americans, one Scotchman and four natives, having previously baptized one. On the 29th, I organized the Tubuai branch of the Church of Jesus Christ of Latter-day Saints, numbering eleven members, all in good standing.

On the 5th of August, I administered the sacrament. For wine I substituted cocoanut milk,* that was a pure beverage, which never

*Doctrine and Covenants, sec. xxvii.

had come to the open air till we broke the nut for that purpose. On the 8th I baptized another person.

The inhabitants here have resolved to build me a house. This climate is fine, never so cold as to freeze, though in July and August it is as cold as it can be and not freeze. January and February are the warmest months, though the heat is never so scorching as some days we have at home. In summer, however, the mosquitoes are innumerable and in winter the fleas are equally plentiful, though we have means to guard against them.

Before I came here King Tommatooah buried his wife; on the 14th July I married him to Toupah his queen; he has been very friendly with me ever since I came here.

Sometimes when I get to thinking about home I feel that I could leave all and return as quickly as possible. A few evenings since I fell into a train of thoughts and told my brethren. I went to bed, fell asleep and dreamed I had deserted my post and got to Nauvoo; the people all knew I had left without counsel and treated me with coolness and neglect. This mortified my feelings so much that I never thought of my family; I saw Brother Young, he was busily employed in sending a company of elders to Europe; I felt an anxiety to go with them, but I had deserted one station, and they never intended to send me to another. I then thought I would go back to the one I had left, but I had no means to get back, or to help myself with: I thought my shame was greater than I could bear, and with these reflections I awoke.*

I have lived at Mattaoora since I came here till the 23rd of August. I then removed to this place called Mahoo, which is the place where I first landed.

The second sabbath after I came here, the church [i. e. the saints] came over to visit me, and I baptized seven more, all natives and heads of families. I administered the sacrament and we felt that we were greatly blessed.

It is now a year since I have heard a syllable from home, and three months since I have heard from the brethren at Tahiti, though I have sent word by eight vessels bound thither.

On learning that missionaries [i. e. of sectarian churches] had arrived from Tahiti I called to see them. I had heard so much of their iniquity and I wanted to see how they looked; to me they looked guilty indeed. One of them named Howe very sanctimoniously remarked, 'I understand you have come among the Islands in the capacity of a preacher.' I answered, 'yes.' 'And what do you preach?' 'The sacred truths of the *Bible*,' I replied. 'I suppose you are aware,' said he, 'that many years ago the London Missionary Society established a mission here at a very great expense;' the whole stress was on the great expense, the cost of translating the *Bible*, etc.

---

*This is a very common experience with missionaries of the Church of the Latter-day Saints, as thousands will testify who read these words.

'Well,' said I, 'and now you are opposed to having the *Bible* preached after you have accomplished the translation?' He said, no: he had no objections to my preaching the *Bible*, but he understood I had another book I preached from. I told him that was a mistake, and went on to tell him what it was; a long dialogue ensued in which they all questioned me on the fundamental principles of the gospel, but they had to drop several points they introduced for fear of trapping themselves; at length they told me they found no fault with me as far as the *Bible* was concerned, but the *Book of Mormon* they had read and it was a bad book. I told them to show me some specimens of bad doctrine in it: they turned to the place where it says, 'Adam fell that man might be,' at which they flounced considerably, but I soon succeeded in proving that it was not contrary to *Bible* doctrine; they said they could find a worse place than that and turned to the passage:

'Adam had to know misery before he knew happiness.' This they spouted upon me in a great rage. I referred them to the temptations of the Savior and his sufferings that he might be perfected.

I questioned them about their belief in the *Bible*, and the coming of the Son of God the second time; contrasted this with the dispensation of Noah, told them the world was now being warned, and the consequences that would ensue if men did not give heed. I then raised my right hand towards heaven and called on all the heavenly hosts to witness the testimony I bore; that I knew Brother Joseph Smith to be a good man and a Prophet of the Lord. * * * The Spirit of the Lord rested upon me; it threw them into confusion, they knew not what to say. They finally told me as long as I preached the truth they would pray that I might be upheld, but if I preached error they should pray that it might fall to the ground. Then, I said, our prayers will be united.'

Wednesday, 18.—I attended council with the Twelve Apostles and Bishops Whitney and Miller, at Elder Taylor's. Several communications from the elders abroad were read.

It was voted that the profits arising from the publication of the *Book of Mormon* and *Book of Doctrine and Covenants* be devoted to the priesthood for the building up of the kingdom of God.

Disposition of the Profits Arising from the Sale of the Church Works.

Thursday, 19.—At home waiting upon my wife who was very sick. The saints called upon me for counsel and direction.

Friday, 20.—Attending to ordinances in behalf of

the saints, and laying hands on the sick. The Lord is with me continually.

Saturday, 21.—I visited the saints accompanied by Elders Kimball and Lyman. Received a letter from

Opposition of Benjamin Winchester Reported. Elder Jedediah M. Grant relating the slanderous course pursued by Elder B. Winchester against the Twelve, and informing us that at the Philadelphia conference he refused to vote to sustain the Twelve asserting that they gagged him while on his trial at Nauvoo.

Sunday, 22.—I preached to the congregation of the saints on the priesthood: had a good time.

High priests' quorum met at the Masonic Hall Elder George A. Smith preached.

Evening, attended council.

Murray McConnel, Esq., governor's agent from Morgan

Affidavit Against the Murderers of the Prophet. county arrived in Nauvoo, and Elder John Taylor made affidavit against Thomas C. Sharp and Levi Williams, two of the murderers of Joseph and Hyrum Smith.

Monday, 23.—The first capital weighing about two tons was raised on to the walls of the Temple.

This evening, Sheriff Deming came into Nauvoo for a Mormon *posse* to take Sharp and Williams. The Twelve decided that it was imprudent to take [use] Mormons for that purpose and advised him accordingly.

Received some arms and ammunition from the brethren in St. Louis, by the hands of Thomas McKenzie.

Tuesday, 24.—I attended a council at Winsor P.

Selection of Presiding Seventies and High Priests. Lyons: six of the brethren of the Twelve were present, and Elder Joseph Young; we selected seventy presidents to preside over the seventies* and fifty high priests to preside over different sections of the country.

The Quincy Greys under Captain Morgan and a company of Germans under Captain Swinder arrived

*See ch. xxii.

from Quincy and encamped in the east part of the city. These captains expected a general officer to direct their movements and expressed their astonishment at his non-arrival.

Received a letter from David Clayton containing an account of the sayings and doings of Lyman Wight, his opposition to the Twelve and Clayton's reasons for leaving Wight's company.

Wednesday, 25.—Sheriff Deming asked for wagons to take the Quincy militia to Warsaw to arrest Sharp. The marshal furnished teams and wagons, when the militia said they had no orders from the governor to go.

Attempt to Arrest Murderers of the Prophet.

An attempt was made under the directions of the governor's agent to arrest Thomas C. Sharp, but failed; it was reported that Colonel Levi Williams ran away.

Received a letter from Elder William A. Moore pertaining to the malicious and wicked course of Ben Winchester.

Thursday, 26.—I attended a council held at my house. Benjamin Winchester and wife were cut off from the church.

The Quincy militia escorted about town by the Nauvoo Band.

Held a council at the Temple Office and appointed four watchmen to watch the Temple tonight, some of Wight's company have come to town and they report that they

Night Watchman Appointed for the Temple.

have come to deface the capitals, and burn the lumber round the Temple.

General Charles C. Rich wrote the following:

'To His Excellency, Thomas Ford, Governor of the State of Illinois and Commander-in-chief of the Militia.

Sir: I received your letter by the hand of Major Bills last evening after dark and hastened to lay before you such information as is in my possession in regard to the movements at Warsaw and Carthage. The deputy sheriff arrived here last evening and informed us that he was at Warsaw and apprehended Thomas C. Sharp who was rescued from his hands by the citizens of Warsaw who stated that they would not let him be taken, law or no law, governor or no governor.

Judge Lot who also arrived here last evening from Quincy, passed through the neighborhood of Warsaw, and informed us that the country was in commotion, and that they had dispatched runners in all directions to raise a force and have it in readiness to act in defiance of all law; from all we have learned there is not much force assembled as yet in Carthage or Warsaw.

Everything is perfectly quiet here; we were, however, a little surprised on the arrival of two companies of militia from Quincy, such things being altogether unsuspected by us, having received no information from you in regard to such movements.

I had a conference with General Miller since the receipt of your letter, who informs me that he has as yet received no letter from you, though he has been expecting an answer for several days, consequently we are left in the dark in regard to your instructions for our intended movements.

Permit me sir, to introduce to your acquaintance Major John Pack and Mr. Snow, gentlemen, in whom we repose the utmost confidence and to whom you can communicate anything you wish concerning us.'

I received the following:

'SPECIAL ORDER NO. 10

Camp Pulasky, Sept. 26, 1844.

To the Commander of the Nauvoo Legion:

General Hardin having been commanded by the governor and commander-in-chief to take command of the Nauvoo Legion in the event of their being called into service will review the Legion tomorrow the 27th at 1 o'clock, p. m. It is not intended as a muster of the Legion into service but as a parade for inspection and review.

By order of Brigadier-General,

[Signed]   J. J. HARDIN,

W. B. Warren, Brigade-Major.   Commanding Illinois Volunteers.

Friday, 27.—This was the day set apart by the anti-Mormons for the great 'wolf hunt'.

A little before noon the governor and two of his aids arrived in Nauvoo. After viewing the Temple they went down towards the Mansion. About two p. m. his troops marched into the city, about five hundred in number. They had three six-pounders with them, two of which were brass. The whole company, halted on the first vacant block on the flat and tarried there some time. Many of the men visited the font and the Temple; they appeared astonished, but were civil.

I received my commission as lieutenant-general, and Charles C. Rich his as major-general.

Governor Ford said he had come to execute the law and was ready to proceed against the murderers of Joseph and Hyrum Smith as fast as the people get out writs. He issued a Proclamation offering a reward of two hundred dollars each for the arrest of Sharp, Jackson and Williams, and announced his intention of taking all the arms from this part of the state. His troops numbered four hundred and seventy, all that would volunteer in nine counties to help maintain the supremacy of the laws in Hancock and bring murderers to justice.

Saturday, 28.—I sent the following:

PRESIDENT YOUNG'S LETTER TO GOVERNOR FORD

'Headquarters, Nauvoo Legion,
Sept. 28, 1844.

His Excellency, Thomas Ford, Governor and Commander-in-Chief:

Sir: The review of the Nauvoo Legion will take place this day at twelve m., at which time the commander-in-chief, with his staff, is respectfully solicited to accept an escort from the Legion and be present at the review.

[Signed]   BRIGHAM YOUNG,
Lieutenant-General, Nauvoo Legion.

By E. H. Derby, Secretary.'

I reviewed the Legion. The governor, General J. J. Hardin and staff were present. Appropriate salutes were fired on the occasion.

The Legion made a creditable and soldier-like appearance. Several of the staff officers of the Legion appeared in uniform without arms, which the governor regarded as a hint to remind him of his disarming the Legion previous to the massacre of Joseph and Hyrum Smith.

Four p. m., the governor marched his militia force about three miles down the river and camped in the woods.

The governor called upon General George Miller to furnish boats to convey his command in the night to
Warsaw, who after making the necessary arrangements, accompanied by Cyrus H. Wheelock, two other brethren and one of the governor's officers, started to inform his Excellency that the boats were ready.   On reaching the neighborhood of the camp the officer requested the brethren to wait until he would go in and speak to the governor; after waiting a few minutes the brethren attempted to go in and see the governor for themselves but were prevented by a sentinel who cocked his gun.   Soon after three rounds of musketry were discharged by a detachment of the governor's troops, the bullets whistled all around Brother Miller and party, one ball taking effect upon the sentinel who cried out very loudly, 'I am a dead man': the officers subsequently remarked that they had forgotten to call in their sentinel.   Brother Miller and party rendered the wounded sentinel all the assistance they could until his comrades from the camp came to his relief, when Brother Miller learned the boats were not wanted; whereupon, accompanied by his party he started back for Nauvoo, when they got a few rods off twenty or thirty guns were fired after them: some of the balls skimmed the road near their feet: but they were preserved by the hand of God.''

CHAPTER XXII.

EPISTLE OF THE TWELVE TO THE CHURCH—MORAL AND SPIRITUAL GUIDANCE

"*Sunday. September* 29, 1844.—I [Brigham Young] attended meeting. Elder Parley P. Pratt preached on the duties of saints and advised all the drunkards and thieves to either quit their wickedness or leave the city, and not claim the name of Mormons, he exhorted the saints in the spirit of meekness to cherish the fruits of the Spirit and walk uprightly before God, and deal justly with all men and to shew by their walk and conduct that they had not taken upon them the name of Christ in vain, giving their enemies no occasion to say or print anything against them that was evil.

I made a few remarks endorsing the sisters' penny subscription* for the purpose of procuring glass and nails for the Temple and requested the saints to prepare themselves to entertain the elders who may be in attendance at conference.

Afternoon, I went to the Seventies' Hall and ordained the sixty-three members of the First Quorum of the Seventy to be presidents over the quorums from the second to the tenth inclusive.

All the First Quorum of the Seventy Ordained Presidents.

The high priests' quorum met.

Considerable sickness reported throughout the city and many deaths.

Monday. 30.—I breakfasted at Elder Heber C. Kimball's. We laid hands on the sick and visited Mother Smith.

Evening, went to the military school held at the Masonic Hall. Afterwards attended council with the

*This sisters' "penny fund" system was instituted by Patriarch Hyrum Smith.

Twelve and concluded to use our influence to prevent the brethren and sisters from attending the ball which

Elder Marks'
Ball
Boycotted. William Marks, landlord of the Nauvoo Mansion was making arrangements for; the same to come off on Wednesday evening in the dining room of the Mansion, which was still stained with the blood which flowed from Joseph and Hyrum, as their bodies lay in said room preparatory to burial.

Tuesday, October 1.—Evening, attended a meeting of the quorum for prayer: a very interesting session.

AN EPISTLE OF THE TWELVE,

'*To the Church of Jesus Christ of Latter-day Saints—Greeting*:

Dear Brethren: Having promised in our former epistles to address you from time to time, we now proceed to give you further information

Subjects of the
Epistle. relative to the welfare of the church both temporally and spiritually; the building up of Nauvoo; the gathering of the saints; the building of the Temple; the establishment of manufacturing and various branches of industry; the support of the poor, and the preserving of peace, good order, union, love, and truth: to the suppression of vice, and every kind of disorder, evil, and immorality.

The Temple, as a great and glorious public work, immediately connected with the completion of our preparation, and ordinances, touching our salvation and exaltation, and that of our dead,

The
Temple. necessarily claims our first, and most strict attention. And we rejoice to say for the encouragement of all, that its walls are now ready to receive the capitals, and the arches of the upper story windows; and in fact, seven of the capitals are already reared. The timbers are also being framed, and reared on the inside. In short it is progressing with a rapidity which is truly astonishing.

The gathering, next claims our attention as a work of salvation, to be accomplished in wisdom and prudence. Your Prophets and Apostles, have often told you, that the saints cannot gather together in

The
Gathering. large numbers, and be able to enjoy the comforts and necessaries of life, without the necessary calculations and preparations for their employment and support. Not only must farms be cultivated, houses built, and mills to grind the corn, but there must be something produced by industry, to send off to market in exchange for cash, and for such other articles as we need. This must be produced, not by singing, or praying, or going to meeting, or visiting, or friendly greetings, or conversation, *But, by the united industry, skill, and economy of the whole people.* Men, women, and children must be well, and constantly employed. In order the more effectually to do this, we must turn our attention to the erection of workshops for the manufacture of every useful article; and wares thus manufactured must find a market, not in Nauvoo alone but in all the wide country, and in cities and towns abroad.

If the saints will commence and follow out this plan, and lay out their cash for the raw material, and employ their friends and themselves at home, instead of sending away all our cash for manufactured goods, we can soon produce millions of wealth, and the poor will have no cause of complaint; for among a temperate people thus employed there would soon be no poor except the widow, the orphan, or the infirm, and these could be abundantly provided for.

The fact is, we have a country abundantly supplied with natural resources, and calculated for the production of wool, flax, hemp, cotton, and many other articles; and we have water power to any amount; and after all our troubles, a Economic prospect of peace and protection; in short everything Advantages at Nauvoo. for the encouragement of capitalists and workmen. Come on then, all ye ends of the earth, take hold together, and with a long, strong, steady and united exertion, let us build up a stronghold of industry and wealth, which will stand firm and unshaken amid the wreck of empires and the crash of thrones.

In regard to principle and doctrine, we know that we are founded upon the plain and manifest truth as The Conscious- revealed from on high; and which is sufficiently manifest ness of and plain to convince all honest men who look into it, Sound Doctrine. and to confound all who oppose. The main object then which remains to be carried out is to practice accordingly, and to live according to our knowledge.

Let the saints now send in their young men who are strong to labor, together with money, provisions, clothing, tools, teams, and every necessary means, such as they know they will want when they arrive, for the purpose of forwarding this work.

Brethren, bring all your tithings into the storehouse and prove the Lord, and see if he will not pour out a blessing, that there will not be room enough to receive.

Yes, brethren, we verily know and bear testimony, that a cloud of blessing and of endowment, and of the keys of the fulness of the priesthood, and of things pertaining to eternal life, is hanging over us, and ready to burst upon us; or upon Awaiting as many as live worthy of it, so soon as there is a place Spiritual Blessings. found on earth to receive it. Therefore, let no cunningly devised fable, no false delusive spirit, or vision, no man or set of men who go out from us, but are not of us, have any influence on your minds for a moment, to draw your minds away from this all important work. But enter steadily and regularly upon a strict observance of the law of tithing, and of freewill offerings, till Jehovah shall say it is enough; your offerings are accepted: then come up to the House of the Lord, and be taught in his ways, and walk in his paths; yea, enter his sanctuary; and receive the oil of joy for mourning, and the garment of praise for the spirit of heaviness.

In order to do this we must not only be industrious and honest, in providing abundantly for our temporal wants, and for those for whom duty and charity bind us to act, but we must abstain from all intemperance, immorality and vice of whatever name or nature; we must set an example of virtue, modesty, temperance, continency, cleanliness, and charity. And be careful not to mingle in the vain amusements and sins of the world.

In nearly all cities or towns of an extensive population there are certain vices, or crimes, not exactly tolerated by law, but yet, borne with by the people as a kind of unavoidable or necessary Against Vice in All its Forms. evil; such, for instance, as gambling, drunkenness, vain and wicked amusements and allurements, directly calculated to corrupt the morals of the people and lead them from the paths of virtue and truth. Among the most conspicuous and fashionable of these we might mention, balls, dances, corrupt and immodest theatrical exhibitions, magical performances, etc., all of which are apt not only to have an evil tendency in themselves, but to mingle the virtuous and the vicious in each others society; not for the improvement of the vicious but rather to corrupt the virtuous.

Nauvoo is now becoming one of the largest towns of the west, and as it was founded, and is still in a great measure managed by the saints, we greatly desire the united influence of all wellwishers to our society, and to good order and morality, to cooperate with us in preserving the general peace and quiet, and in suppressing these and all other vices and evils.

Or, to be plain on the subject, we wish to suppress all grogshops, gambling houses, and all other disorderly houses or proceedings in our city, and to tolerate no intemperance or vice in our midst. And so far at least as the members of the church are concerned, we would advise that balls, dances, and other vain and useless amusements be neither countenanced nor patronized; they have been borne with, in some instances heretofore for the sake of peace and good will. But it is not now a time for dancing or frolics but a time of mourning, and of humiliation and prayer.

If the people were all righteous, it would do to dance, and to have music, feasting and merriment. But what fellowship has Christ with Belial? Or what fellowship has light with darkness? or what union have the sons and daughters of God with the children of this world, who fear not God nor regard man. All amusements in which saints and sinners are mingled tends to corruption, and has a baneful influence in religious society.

There are amusements which are at once both innocent, instructive, and entertaining; and which the saints can enjoy, in honor to themselves, and without mingling with the world. Such for instance, as musical concerts, philosophical and astronomical exhibitions, etc. These, together with our religious devotions, and the increase of light, knowledge and intelligence which flows like a flood of glory from the upper world, are quite sufficient to exercise all our powers of enjoyment.

As the business of the conference is now fast crowding upon our time, we must cut short this communication by informing you that an organization and arrangement is now in progress, by which high priests and presiding officers will be appointed over each district of country, throughout the union, who will have entire charge, under the direction of the Twelve of all spiritual matters, superintending the labors of the elders and the calling of conferences. Arrangements will also be made, for the proper payment and reception of tithing, so that it may be duly received by responsible agents and recorded. Of these particulars you will receive further communication from us soon.

Organization for Effective Administration.

Done in council at Nauvoo, this first day of October, A. D. 1844.

[Signed] BRIGHAM YOUNG, President.'

Wednesday, 2.—At ten a. m., a council of the Twelve met at Elder Kimball's.

Elder A. W. Babbitt read a letter from Oliver Cowdery.

Governor Ford disbanded his troops. Sharp and Williams have given themselves up and gone to Quincy under a contract with the governor.

Sharp and Williams, Alleged Murderers of the Prophet Surrender.

Friday, 4.—I went up to the Temple in the forenoon. Attended council with the Twelve, the bishops and the Temple Committee at Sister Emma Smith's and expressed our feelings and intentions to her.

Elder Woodruff preached through the eastern states while traveling on his mission to England. He had an interesting time among his relatives at his father's house in Farmington, Connecticut, and this evening ordained his Uncle, Ozem Woodruff, a high priest."

Labors of Elder Woodruff Among Relatives.

CHAPTER XXIII.

MINUTES OF THE IMPORTANT CONFERENCE OF OCTO-
BER 6TH TO 8TH, 1844—THE CHURCH SET IN ORDER
—DUTIES OF THE PRIESTHOOD EXPOUNDED—
ECONOMICS CONSIDERED

"*Sunday, October 6, 1844.*—From the *Times and Seasons* (p. 682).

OCTOBER CONFERENCE MINUTES

'City of Nauvoo, Oct. 6, 1844.
Thousands having arrived on the ground by ten
o'clock a. m. Elder Parley P. Pratt called the people
to order. Singing by the choir—prayer by Elder
Phelps. Some instructions were given by Elder Pratt,
when President Brigham Young having arrived, arose
to lay before the brethren the matters to be attended to
during the conference.

THE DISCOURSE OF PRESIDENT BRIGHAM YOUNG

'This day' [he said], 'will be devoted to preaching
and instruction, and we will attend to business tomorrow. If the Twelve could have had their desires when
they returned home, they would have set their houses
in order, and devoted themselves to fasting and prayer.

*The Reasons
Given for
Haste in Set-
tling the Ques-
tion of Leader-
ship Before
Convening the
Conference.*
It has not been the Twelve who desired to
have business which pertains to this conference transacted previous, it was others
who urged it on. Some elders who have
known the organization of the church from
the beginning, have faltered and become darkened. We
feel to give the necessary instruction pertaining to the
church, and how it has been led, etc. It is necessary
that the saints should also be instructed relative to

building the Temple, and spreading the principles of truth from sea to sea, and from land to land until it shall have been preached to all nations, and then according to the testimony of the ancients, the end will come. When the Lord commences to work upon the earth he always does it by revealing his will to some man on the earth, and he to others. The church is built up by revelation, given from day to day according to the requirements of the people. The Lord will not cease to give revelations to the people, unless, the people trample on his laws and forsake and reject him. I request that the Latter-day Saints may pray that we may have the outpouring of the Spirit that we may hear, and I wish them to pray for me that I may have strength, and that I may make every principle I speak upon so perfectly plain, that we may all understand as quick as when we talk together upon our daily matters.

'This church has been led by revelation, and unless we forsake the Lord entirely, so that the priesthood is taken from us, it will be led by revelation all the time. The question arises with some who has the right to revelation? I will not ascend any higher than a priest, and ask the priest what is your right? You have the right to receive the administration of angels. If an angel was to come to you and tell you what the Lord was going to do in this day, you would say you had a revelation. The president of the priests has a right to the Urim and Thummim, which gives revelation. He has the right of receiving visits from angels. Every priest then in the church has the right of receiving revelations. Every member has the right of receiving revelations for themselves, both male and female. It is the very life of the church of the living God, in all ages of the world. The Spirit of Truth is sent forth into all the world to reprove the world of sin and unrighteousness, and of a judgment to come. If we were here today and had never heard this gospel, and a man was to come bounding into our

The Church Led by Revelation.

midst, saying, he had come to preach the gospel, to tell us that God was about to restore the priesthood, and save the people, etc., it would be your privilege, and my privilege to ask God in the name of Jesus Christ, as individuals, concerning this thing, whether it was of God, and get a testimony from God that it was true, and this would be revelation.   Let us take some of these old fathers for an example, they have heard the gospel, they have been baptized, etc., had hands laid on them for the gift of the Holy Ghost—he has got a family of children, he has been led all his days by his own spirit, but now begins to come to understand he has the right to bow before the Lord and receive instruction from God, from day to day, how to manage his family, his farm, his merchandise, and to govern all the affairs of his house.   I will take some of my younger brethren who have received the gospel, they have been ordained an elder to hold the keys, etc.   What is your privilege? It is your privilege to go and preach the gospel to the world, and to go by the power of the Holy Ghost, and you have no right to go without it.   You have been ordained to go forth and build up the kingdom to a certain extent.   No man ever preached a gospel discourse, nor ever will, unless he does it by revelation. You will do it by the Holy Ghost, or when you tell the history of the gospel, the gospel will not be there.   It has got to be done by revelation or the gospel you have not got, and when you preach, the people will still be left without the gospel.   There never was a prophet on the earth that dictated to the people, but he dictated their temporal affairs as well as spiritual.   It is the right

Self-Guidance by Revelation. of an individual to get revelations to guide himself.   It is the right of the head of a family to get revelations to guide and govern his family. It is the right of an elder when he has built up a church to get revelations to guide and lead that people until he leads them and delivers them up to his superiors.   An elder will always be a little in advance of those whom he has raised up if he is faithful.'

He [President Young] next showed how the saints are delivered up in their progress from those who give them up to the high council, and from the high council to the prophet, and from the prophet to the son, the elder brother, and from the son to his father.   (Then continued)—

'Are the keys of the kingdom taken from Joseph? Oh no; well then he still lives.   He that believes in Jesus as Joseph did, they will never die.   The Keys of Leadership not Taken from Joseph. They may lay down their lives, but they still hold the keys.   You are not going to be led without revelation.   The Prophet has stepped behind the veil and you have the right to obtain revelations for your own salvation.   Who stood next to the Prophet when he was here.   You have all acknowledged that the Twelve were the Presidents of the whole church when Joseph was not; and now he has stepped behind the veil, he is not here, and the Twelve are the Presidents of the whole church.   When did Joseph become a Prophet? I can tell you, when he became an Apostle.* Years and years before he had the right of holding the keys of the Aaronic priesthood, he was a Prophet, even before he was baptized.   There has been a perfect flood of revelation poured from this stand all the time and you did not know it.   Every spirit that confesses that Joseph Smith is a Prophet, that he lived and died a Prophet and that the *Book of Mormon* is true, is of God, and every spirit that does not is of anti-Christ.

'It is the test of our fellowship to believe   The Test of Fellowship. and confess that Joseph lived and died a Prophet of God in good standing; and I don't want

---

*This remark is a bit confusing because as a matter of fact Joseph Smith did not receive the Apostleship before he was baptized, for he was baptized on the visit of John the Baptist who restored the keys of the Aaronic priesthood May 15, 1829; and the restoration of the Apostleship came to him and Oliver Cowdery somewhat later, most likely sometime in June, 1829.   But President Young had in mind the fact of Joseph Smith becoming a Prophet from the time when he received his First Vision of God the Father and of the Son, early in the spring of 1820 and this constituted him a witness for God and likewise a Prophet; but he did not become authoritatively a Prophet to the church until he had been made an Apostle; for as stated by St. Paul, the order of these officers in the church is—"God hath set some in the church first apostles, secondarily prophets " etc.   (I Cor. xii:28.)

anyone to fellowship the Twelve who says that Joseph is fallen. If you don't know whose right it is to give revelations, I will tell you, It is I. There never has a man stood between Joseph and the Twelve, and unless we apostatize there never will. If Hyrum had lived he would not have stood between Joseph and the Twelve, but he would have stood for Joseph.—Did Joseph ordain any man to take his place? He did. Who was it? It was Hyrum, but, Hyrum fell a martyr before Joseph did. If Hyrum had lived he would have acted for Joseph, and then when we had gone up, the Twelve would have sat down at Joseph's right hand, and Hyrum on the left hand. The *Bible* says God hath set in the church, first Apostles, then comes Prophets, afterwards, because the keys and power of the Apostleship are greater than that of the Prophets. Sidney Rigdon cannot hold the keys without Joseph, if he had held the keys with Joseph and been faithful he would have been with us. If the Twelve do not apostatize they carry the keys of this kingdom wherever they go.'

Hyrum Smith Ordained to Take the Prophet's Office.

He [President Young] concluded by requesting all the brethren to tarry with us until all the business is through.

The meeting adjourned by blessing from Elder Heber C. Kimball, until 2 o'clock.

ELDER JOHN TAYLOR'S DISCOURSE

Two o'clock p. m.—The meeting was opened as usual by singing; and prayer by Elder W. W. Phelps. After which Elder John Taylor arose and addressed the people. He said it was with peculiar feelings that he arose to address the congregation.

'This is the first general conference' [he said], 'that has been held, where your beloved Prophet and Patriarch are not present. When I look at the many difficulties and severe trials we have passed through it fills me with peculiar feelings. I feel happy to see that the people still

Adherence to Principles Given by Revelation.

seem determined to hold on to those principles which
have been given to us through revelation.   Nothing
shall separate us from those principles which we have
imbibed, neither life nor death.   By the voice of Jehovah we have been sustained and will be sustained so
long as we put our trust in him.   We have not followed
'cunningly devised fables', but those principles which
have come from God.   So long as we are sustained
and upheld by the arm of Jehovah, we shall stand:
mobs may rage, and the rulers may imagine vain things;
but God has said, touch not mine anointed and do my
people no harm; and if harm does befall them, woe
to that man by whom it comes.   If our Prophets have
been taken, they are gone to plead our cause before the
Father.   And if we are deprived of their persons,
presence and counsel, that is no reason why we should
be deprived of the counsel of God to direct us in all our
movements whilst pressing on our journey here below.
We are in possession of the same principles, the same
priesthood, the same medium of communication and
intelligence, and of those things which will not only
secure our happiness here, but hereafter.   When we
speak of these matters, we speak of things which we
know assuredly, and although our Prophet and Patriarch are taken, all things pertaining to our salvation
will roll on and progress with as great rapidity, and
can be as effectually secured and accomplished as if they
[Joseph and Hyrum] were here themselves.   God has
secured to us those things in relation to our salvation
which have been in his bosom since the world
began.   He has in his providence seen fit to
call our brethren to himself; but he has left
others to take their places, who can teach us principles
and lead us to those things whereby we may ultimately
be clothed with glory, honor, immortality, and eternal
life.   If we had built upon a false foundation we might
have made a mistake in relation to our gathering together to be instructed; but we had not; our present
revelations agree with the past.   The prophets said

Perpetuation of the Plan of Salvation.

that the people would gather together, 'those who had
made a covenant with God by sacrifice', and the word
and purpose of God must stand unchanged, they do not
rest upon any mere casualty.   Did the Prophet ever
tell us that if a certain man should happen to die we
should scatter abroad?   No! no such thing ever ema-
nated from the lips of God.   We assembled together
to fulfill the revelations of the Great Jehovah, to bring
about the dispensation of the fulness of times, to build
up a Zion to the Most High; that he might be glorified.
We assembled here to bring about great events, to
fulfill the things spoken of by the prophets and secure
to ourselves an inheritance in the everlasting kingdom
of God.   Shall we then be led about by the foolish
notions of any man?   No! we will not, but we will
accomplish those things which are commanded us.   We
will not be diverted from our course, though earth and
hell oppose.   Shall we fear the puny arm of man, or
the prating of a wretched mobocrat?   No!   What have
we to fear?   We have nothing but God to fear.

'It is true we have not much to live for, and if we
have no hope beyond the grave we should be of all men
most miserable.   We are oppressed, and
slandered and persecuted all the day long;
all that I care for is to do the will of God,
and secure to myself all those blessings which the gospel
will warrant me.   I have been brought to the gates of
death, but I don't fear it; I care nothing about it.   You
feel as I do in relation to these matters, for your conduct
has proven it during the late difficulties.   I know that
the majority of the people are endeavoring to serve
God with all their hearts, and are they not prepared to
die?   There is nothing in death we have to fear; it is
not half as much to die as it is to be persecuted all the
day long.   Our great object then is to accomplish the
thing that we set out for.   When we gathered together
we expected to meet tribulation; the elders that
preached to you told you this or else they did not do

their duty. We have been told there would Expectation of Tribulation. be earthquakes in divers places, and pestilence, and war, and persecution, and distress, and famine. Do these things move us? If the bud is so bitter I wonder what the fruit will be. Don't you expect to be worse off than you are now. John saw an innumerable company and wanted to know where they came from; it was told to him that they are they which came out of great tribulation. That is the path we have to tread. The scripture says: 'woe unto you when all men shall speak well of you'; but that curse has never come upon us, for there are some few here and there who will not speak well of us. But 'blessed are ye when men shall revile you, and persecute you, and say all manner of evil against you falsely for Christ's sake.' Do you think there is any more evil that they have not said? If there is, let it come. What is it that makes you to be evil spoken of? you used to have a good name and reputation where you resided; what is the reason you are now so much spoken against? You have dared to believe the gospel; you have dared to obey it; and that is the reason why the world hates you. I know there is not a better set of men than these by which I am surrounded; I know there is not a more virtuous set of people on the earth, High Standing of the Saints of the New Dispensation. and yet all manner of evil is spoken of you. Shall we cry and go mourning all day long? No, we will rejoice and be exceeding glad, for great is our reward in heaven. I feel to rejoice; we have cause to rejoice for all manner of evil is spoken against us falsely, and I will say hallelujah, for the Lord God Omnipotent reigneth. What did we know of God, of religion, of heaven or hell, until it was made known to us through this gospel? We knew nothing. Why are we taking so much pains to build that Temple? That we may fulfill certain ordinances, and receive certain endowments and secure to ourselves an inheritance in the eternal world. Every man, woman and child within the sound of my voice, are interested in the building of that Temple. We know very little as a people yet, we don't know so much as the former day saints. The Savior said to his disciples, 'whither I go ye know, and the way ye know'; but how many of you know the locality of the Savior and the way to go to him? I know there are some here who know how to save themselves and their families, and it is this which occupies their attention all the day long, and it was this which occupied the attention of our beloved Prophet. Abraham obtained promises through the gospel, from God, for himself and his posterity. There were some upon this continent who also obtained promises, in consequence of which the *Book of Mormon* came forth. The first thing we have got to do is to build the Temple, where we can receive those blessings which we so much desire.

To Build the Temple the First Duty.

Never mind mobocrats, but let us do what God has commanded us. You that are living at a distance, don't fear these cursed scoundrels; we are all in the hands of God; we are all the servants of God; and we are going forth to do the things of God.'

He [Elder Taylor] exhorted the saints to be virtuous, humble and faithful, and concluded by blessing the saints.

He said further, in relation to the baptisms for the dead, that it would be better for the saints to go on and build the Temple before we urge our baptisms too much. There are cases which require being attended to, and there are provisions made for them; but as a general thing he would advise them not to be in too great a hurry. He said one of the clerks had asked whether any should be baptized who had

Baptism for the Dead and Tithing.

not paid their tithing; it is our duty to pay our tithing, one-tenth of all we possess, and then one-tenth of our increase, and a man who has not paid his tithing is unfit to be baptized for his dead. It is as easy for a man who has ten thousand dollars to pay one thousand, as it is for a man who has but a little to pay one-tenth. It is our duty to pay our tithing. If a man has not faith enough to attend to these little things, he has not faith enough to save himself and his friends. It is a man's duty to attend to these things. The poor are not going to be deprived of these blessings because they are poor; no, God never reaps where he has not sown. This command is harder for the rich than the poor; a man who has one million dollars, if he should give one hundred thousand, he would think he was beggared forever. The Savior said, how hardly do they that have riches enter the kingdom of heaven.

BISHOP MILLER'S REMARKS

Bishop Miller arose to say that on yesterday the bishops had to go in debt to get some wood to save some poor from suffering; and they wanted to take up a collection to pay the amount; he was opposed to taking up a collection in the congregation, but necessity required it on this occasion.

After the collection was taken up the conference adjourned until tomorrow morning at 10 o'clock.

Monday, October 7th, 1844, 10 o'clock, a. m.— Conference met pursuant to adjournment, and opened by singing, and prayer by Elder Parley P. Pratt, after which President Young arose to exhort the saints to keep their minds on the business before them, and not to be in a hurry to get away.

SUSTAINING OF THE SEVERAL AUTHORITIES OF THE CHURCH

The first business that we shall attend to will be to present the several quorums before the conference, for the purpose of taking an expression of the brethren and sisters, whether they will sustain the officers according to their several appointments.

I shall therefore give way, and I am to hear motions and present them to the conference for their action: wherefore,

It was moved by Elder Heber C. Kimball, that we

as a church endeavor to carry out the principles and measures heretofore adopted and laid down by Joseph Smith as far as in us lies, praying Almighty God to help us to do it. This motion was put to the conference by President Young and carried unanimously.

Policies of Joseph and Hyrum Smith Sustained by Vote.

President Young said by way of explanation. that this is as much as to say that we receive and acknowledge Joseph Smith as a Prophet of God; being called of God and maintaining his integrity and acceptance until death.

Elder Heber C. Kimball then moved that we carry out all the measures of Hyrum Smith, a Prophet and Patriarch in the church, so far as in us lies [the power], by the help of God.

This motion was also carried unanimously.

President Young said, this is an acknowledgment that he lived approved of God and died a martyr for the truth.

Elder W. W. Phelps moved that we uphold Brigham Young the president of the Quorum of the Twelve, as one of the Twelve and the First Presidency of the Church.

This motion was duly seconded, and put to the church by Elder John Smith (Uncle of the Prophet) and carried unanimously.

Moved by President John Smith and seconded, that we receive Elder Heber C. Kimball as one of the Twelve, and that he be sustained as such by the church. Carried unanimously.

Moved and seconded, that we receive Elder Orson Hyde as one of the Twelve, and that he be sustained as such by the church. Carried unanimously.

Moved and seconded, that we receive Elder Parley P. Pratt as one of the Twelve, and that he be sustained as such by the church. Carried unanimously.

Moved and seconded, that we receive Elder William Smith as one of the Twelve, and that he be sustained as such by the church. Carried unanimously.

Moved and seconded, that we receive Elder Orson Pratt as one of the Twelve, and that he be sustained as such by the church. Carried unanimously.

Moved and seconded, that we receive Elder John E. Page as one of the Twelve, and that he be sustained as such by the church. Carried unanimously.

Moved and seconded, that we receive Elder Willard Richards as one of the Twelve, and that he be sustained as such by the church. Carried unanimously.

Moved and seconded, that we receive Elder Wilford Woodruff as one of the Twelve, and that he be sustained as such by the church. Carried unanimously.

Moved and seconded, that we receive Elder John Taylor as one of the Twelve, and that he be sustained as such by the church. Carried unanimously.

Moved and seconded that we receive Elder George A. Smith as one of the Twelve, and that he be sustained as such by the church. Carried unanimously.

Moved by Elder H. C. Kimball, that Elder Amasa Lyman *stand in his lot.** The motion was seconded.

President Young said by way of explanation that Elder Amasa Lyman is one of the Twelve, just in the same relationship as he sustained to the First Presidency. He is one in our midst and a counselor with us.

An Explanation by President Young.

The motion was then presented and carried unanimously.

Moved and seconded, and after some discussion, carried unanimously that Elder Lyman Wight be sustained in his office to fill the place of Elder David W. Patten [martyred at Crooked River Battle, Missouri], but not

---

*Lyman "to stand in his lot". It will be observed here that if Amasa M. Lyman had been accounted as one of the Quorum of the Twelve Apostles, the quorum would have had thirteen in it instead of twelve. Elder Lyman had been ordained as an Apostle, and filled a vacancy that had been made by dropping Orson Pratt from the quorum before the death of the Prophet, but when Orson Pratt had been reinstated in his quorum, and the Prophet had decided that the action of the Twelve was illegal because it was not a majority that acted in the case, President Smith took Elder Lyman into the Council of the First Presidency and he was the Prophet's counselor. and now he was made counselor to the Twelve. as he had been to the Prophet—hence "Lyman to stand in his lot". (c. f. This *History*, vol. v, ch. xiii).

to take his crown, for that, as the Lord has said, no man can take.*

Elder Snow moved that George Miller be received as president of the high priests' quorum. Carried unanimously.

President John Smith moved that William Marks be sustained in his calling as president of this [Nauvoo] stake.

Elder W. W. Phelps objected inasmuch as the high council had dropped him from their quorum.

Elder S. Bent explained and said the reason why the high council dropped Elder Marks, was because he did not acknowledge the authority of the Twelve, but the authority of Elder Rigdon.

Difference of Effect in Dropping Officers from Positions.

President Young said that a president of a stake could be dropped without taking his standing from him in the church. But not so with the First Presidency or the Twelve. A president of a stake is only called for the time being, if you drop him he will fall back into the high priests' quorum.

The motion was then put, but there were only two votes. The contrary vote was put and carried by an overwhelming majority.

Elder H. C. Kimball moved that Elder John Smith stand as the president of this stake. Carried unanimously.

President Young then said, the Macedonia church must select their own man for a president, as Elder John Smith is coming here.

President John Smith moved that Elder Charles C. Rich be one of his council. Carried unanimously.

Moved and seconded, that S. Bent, James Allred, Dunbar Wilson, George W. Harris, Wm. Huntington,

The High Council.

Sen., Newel Knight, Alpheus Cutler, Aaron Johnson, Henry G. Sherwood, Thomas Grover, Ezra T. Benson, and David Fullmer, be sustained as the high council. Carried unanimously.

*Doctrine and Covenants, sec. cxxiv:130.

Elder H. C. Kimball moved that Elder Joseph Young stand as First President over all the quorums of the seventies. Carried unanimously. The First Council of the Seventy.

Moved and seconded, that Levi W. Hancock be sustained as one of the Presidents of Seventies. Carried unanimously.

Moved and seconded, that Daniel S. Miles be sustained as one of the Presidents of Seventies. Carried unanimously.

Moved and seconded, that Zerah Pulsipher, be sustained as one of the Presidents of Seventies. Carried unanimously.

Moved and seconded, that Josiah Butterfield be cut off from the church. Carried unanimously.

President Young showed that it was because he had got a little money, and was lifted up.

Moved and seconded, that Henry Harriman be sustained as one of the Presidents of Seventies. Carried unanimously.

President Young said, that the Seventies [First Council] had dropped James Foster, and cut him off, and we need not take an action upon his case.

Moved and seconded, that Jedediah M. Grant take the place of J. Butterfield in the Quorum of Seventies. Carried unanimously.

Elder H. C. Kimball moved that N. K. Whitney stand as our first bishop in the Church of Jesus Christ of Later-day Saints. Carried unanimously. The Bishopric.

Moved and seconded, that George Miller stand as second bishop. Carried unanimously.

Moved and seconded, that Samuel Williams retain his office as president of [in] the elders' quorum. Carried unanimously. The Elders.

Moved and seconded, that Jesse Baker and Joshua Smith be sustained as his counselors. Carried unanimously.

Moved and seconded, that Stephen M. Farnsworth retain his office as president of the priests.   Carried unanimously.

Moved and seconded, that E. Averett retain his standing as president of the teachers.   Carried unanimously.

Moved and seconded, that Jonathan H. Hale, Isaac Higbee, John Murdock, David Evans, Hezekiah Peck, Daniel Garns, Jacob Foutz, Tarlton Lewis, and Israel Calkins, be sustained as bishops in their several wards. Carried unanimously.

ELDER PARLEY P. PRATT'S DISCOURSE

President Young being fatigued gave place for Elder Parley P. Pratt, who got up to preach his 'old sermon', [not said in derision] *viz*.: that we continue our united and ceaseless exertions to build this Temple.   He referred to the discoveries of Elders Rigdon and Samuel James.   They said nothing about building the Temple, the city, feeding the poor, etc.   We heard a great deal about the Mount of Olives—Brook Kedron—Queen Victoria—great battles, etc.   This brought to my mind a good text in Webster's spelling book, 'The Country Maid and the Milk Pail'.   He then went on to show the importance of building the Temple.   He bore testimony that the people had hearkened to the voice of the Lord and to his commandments, and that they were still hearkening, and consequently we should be sustained here until we shall complete the Temple and receive our endowments.   He showed the consequences if we did not build it, 'that we should be rejected as a people with our dead.'   When the elders go abroad to teach the people, let them teach what we have to do, and what is depending on us and not spend their time in quoting multitudes of scripture to prove one point. We want to build up Nauvoo, never mind Gog and Magog, the Brook Kedron, etc., never mind the old countries; God has something to do there by and by, but not just now.   He recommended the brethren to make improvements and enlarge themselves without fear, for we shall not be moved till God suffers it. We are the only people who do not fear death, we have no need to fear it. He next said he would give the people a little religious advice. He advised those who had means to go to getting sheep to consume the vegetation and raise wool, by which means our women would be well employed in manufacturing the wool. He said in a proper time we will have gold and silver, and food and clothing, and palaces in abundance, we will create it by our labor.

President Young advised the saints to come after intermission prepared to tarry till evening if necessary. They [the authorities] have much instruction to give and want an opportunity to give it. He advised the saints to call and get Orson Pratt's *Mormon Almanac* which is something new. After some few exhortations he closed the meeting till 2 o'clock by blessing.

Two o'clock p. m.—Meeting opened by singing, and prayer by Elder John Taylor, after which Elder Taylor presented a communication from Mr. Small declaring his full faith in Elder Rigdon's doctrine. Moved and seconded, that he be cut off from the church. Carried unanimously.

A Rigdonite Excommunicated.

ELDER HEBER C. KIMBALL'S DISCOURSE

Elder Heber C. Kimball addressed the congregation on the principles of salvation by the celestial law. He went on to show the order of the resurrection and that there are different orders or degrees, wherever death finds us the resurrection will take hold of us. 'We desire to obtain a fulness of celestial glory, but many will be disappointed. It is for this that we pray every day that the Lord will spare our lives that we may obtain it. President Joseph Smith never rested till he had endowed the Twelve with all the power of the priesthood, because he was about to pass within the veil. He designed that we should give it to you and

The Resurrection.

you cannot be saved without it. You cannot obtain
these things until that house [The Temple] is built. I
and my brethren are willing to do all that lays in our
power to finish that house for your benefit, that you
may go where Joseph is gone. We have got to carry out
Joseph's measures and you have got to assist us. When
Jesus was upon the earth his time was spent in endow-
ing the Twelve Apostles that they might do the things
he had left undone and carry out his measures, and
upon the same principle we carry out Joseph's measures.
We have no rest—don't sleep half as much as you do.
We need your prayers.

'It is necessary to put away all wickedness from our
midst, all grogshops and bad houses. Drunkenness
All Evil to be and such things will be our overthrow if we
put Away.   are ever overthrown. The best way to put
these things away is to never frequent such places. It
is necessary for us to put away all this frolicking and
dancing over the blood of the Prophet, where it was
drenched by the blood from the coffin.* When the
Prophet had a dance at his house he said everything
against it he could, and now men go and practice the
same things. Shall we put these things away? I say
yes. We have got an ungodly race here among us
who are leading our young people away. They will
open their doors and let men go in and say everything
against the Twelve and the church they are capable of.
I never frequent such places; I cast them far from me.
Are you not under the same obligations and responsibility, ye elders, high priests, teachers, deacons and
members?'

He then went on to show that the saints could not
obtain the blessings they want until the Temple is
finished. We want all to pay their tithing that they
may receive the blessings.

PRESIDENT YOUNG PRESENTS A PATRIARCH

President Young arose and said that it had been

*See page 280 this volume.

moved and seconded that Asael Smith* should be ordained to the office of patriarch. He went on to show
that the right to the office of Patriarch to the whole
church belonged to William Smith† as a legal right by
descent. Uncle Asael [however] ought to receive the
office of [a] patriarch in the church.

The motion was put and carried unanimously.

President Young wanted to say a few words on the
principle of tithing. 'There has been so much inquiry
it becomes irksome: the law is for a man to
pay one-tenth of all he possesses for the
erecting of the House of God, the spread of
the gospel, and the support of the priesthood. When
a man comes into the church he wants to know if he
must reckon his clothing, bad debts, lands, etc. It is
the law to give one-tenth of what he has got, and then
one-tenth of his increase or one-tenth of his time. A
man comes and says he was sick six months and what is
required of me? Why go and pay your tithing for the
time you are able to work. Some say they have been
preaching and want to know if that doesn't pay their
tithing? Well, it will if you want to have it so.' He
then went on to recommend the brethren not to sell
their grain but to bring it into the city and store it, and
not take it to Warsaw.

The Principle of Tithing Expounded.

He next referred to Lyman Wight's going away be-

---

*This was the son of Asael Smith, brother of the Prophet Joseph's father, who
was the first Presiding Patriarch to the church. Asael Smith, here proposed as a
patriarch in the church, was not made the Presiding Patriarch to the church, as that
position was filled at this time by William Smith, the brother of Hyrum Smith, the
martyr, who had succeeded his father Joseph Smith, known in our annals as
Joseph Smith, Sen.

†William Smith was subsequently ordained to be the Presiding Patriarch to the
whole church. On this subject President Young says in his *Ms. History* under date
of May 24, 1845: "The brethren present expressed their feelings towards Elder
William Smith to which he responded. The Twelve then laid their hands upon him
and ordained him to be Patriarch to the whole church. There was a warm
interchange of good feelings between William Smith and the Quorum" (*History of
Brigham Young, Ms.* 1845, p. 84) But before he was sustained in that position
by the church, which in the due order of events would have taken place at the
October conference, 1845, his iniquitous life came fully to light and he was rejected
by the conference both as a member of the Quorum of the Twelve, and as Presiding
Patriarch to the church. (See Minutes of the Conference for October 1845, *Times
and Seasons,* vol. vi, p. 1009). On the 12th of October, 1845 he was excommunicated from the church (*Ibid*).

cause he was a coward, but he will come back and his
company, and James Emmett and his company will come back. How easy would it be for the Lord if an army of mobs was to come within one mile of this place, to turn the northwest winds upon them and with snow, hail and rain, make them so that they would be glad to take care of themselves and leave us alone. He then referred to the Missourians when Joseph and others went to jail, snapping their guns at the brethren but they would not go off, etc. The Lord never let a prophet fall on the earth until he had accomplished his work: and the Lord did not take Joseph until he had finished his work, and it is the greatest blessing to Joseph and Hyrum God could bestow to take them away, for they had suffered enough. They are not the only martyrs that will have to die for the truth. There are men before me today who will be martyrs, and who will have to seal their testimony with their blood. I believe this people is the best people of their age that ever lived on the earth, the church of Enoch not excepted. We want you to come on with your tithes and offerings to build this Temple, and when it is finished we want you to spend a year in it and we will tell you things you never thought of.

Reference to Lyman Wight's and James Emmett's Going Away.

The Twelve then proceeded to ordain Asael Smith as follows:

THE ORDINATION OF A PATRIARCH—ASAEL SMITH

'Brother Asael Smith in the name of the Lord Jesus Christ of Nazareth, we lay our hands upon your head to ordain you to the office of Patriarch in this last Church of Jesus Christ, and we bestow upon you the keys and power, and the right and authority of blessing as *a patriarch in the Church of Jesus Christ*—and we say unto thee, thou shalt be a father to many. Thou shalt feel the Spirit of the Lord more than thou hast ever done before. Thy heart shall be enlarged, and it shall be thy delight to bless thy family, and thy posterity, and the fatherless and widow; and the Spirit of the Lord will rest upon you to predict upon the heads of those on whom you lay your hands, things that shall be hereafter even in the eternal world. We ask thee O Lord in the name of Jesus Christ that thou wouldst send thy Spirit upon this thy servant, that his heart may circumscribe the wisdom and knowledge of this world, and be enlarged so as to comprehend the things of eternity. We say unto thee, thou art blessed: thou art of the royal blood, and of thy lineage shall arise great and powerful men in the earth. We seal upon you the powers we have mentioned with the keys thereof upon your head in the name of Jesus Christ. Thou art the anointed of the Lord, one who shall stand in the latter days and be a pillar in the church of the living God, and one in whom the saints of God may trust to ask counsel. These blessings we seal upon you in the name of Jesus Christ: Amen.'

THE BUSINESS OF THE CONFERENCE FOR OCTOBER 8TH OUTLINED

President Young then said, we want the conference to continue tomorrow for business. We want the high priests' quorum together. President Miller will organize them on the right of the stand.

The Presidents of Seventies will organize all the seventies. We want to select a number of high priests to go through the states to preside over congressional districts. Then we want to have the elders' quorum organized that we can take out of the elders' quorum and fill up the seventies. We want all the seventies to be here and their presidents. We want them organized and begin to fill up the second quorum and then the third and the fourth to the tenth. The business of the day will be to ordain the Presidents of the Seventies and then fill the quorums of seventies from the elders' quorums, and select men from the quorum of high priests to go abroad and preside.

The conference then adjourned until tomorrow at nine o'clock, by blessing from President John Smith.

REMARKS OF ELDER JOHN TAYLOR ON ECONOMIC POLICY TO BE INAUGURATED AT NAUVOO

Tuesday Morning, October 8th, 1844.—Previous to opening the services of the day, Elder John Taylor made some remarks on our temporal economy. He proceeded to say that we have the means of wealth within ourselves.

'We have mechanics of every description from every country; men who are capable of carrying through any branch of manufacture. We want capital to commence with; but it is not necessary to wait for a very large amount, for it is safer to go to work with small means, than with an immense sum; for a rich man is very apt to overlook himself, and for want of proper calculation often scatters his means without accomplishing any benefit to the community. We can be made rich by our own enterprise and labor. Look at Great Britain; how have they obtained it? They have obtained it by encouraging their own manufacturers. It is true the poor are oppressed there; but it is not the manufacturers that oppress the people. We are not going to start anything on a large scale; our calculation is to have the saints manufacture everything we need in Nauvoo, and all kinds of useful articles to send abroad through the states and bring money here. Franklin says, 'time is money', and we want to spend our time in something that is useful and beneficial. Since we came here we have labored under every disadvantage. We have purchased Nauvoo, and much of the surrounding country, which has taken all our money. We have no need now to purchase more land; we now want to hit upon a plan to enable you to take your hands out of your pockets and build work shops and other places of industry. We have silk weavers, and cotton weavers, and every kind of mechanics that can be thought of. We want these to come together, and we want those who have money to lay it out and find them work. We have men here who can take the raw silk and from that carry it through every process and manufacture the shawls and dresses our women wear. We want to purchase raw cotton and manufacture it into wearing apparel, etc. If we can manufacture cotton, silk and woolen goods, we can keep our money at home; we will encourage home manufacture, as the Quakers do. We want all the cutlers to get together and manufacture our knives and forks, etc., etc. I know that we, as a community, can manufacture every thing we need. But I must now desist as the time to commence meeting has arrived.'

ORGANIZATION OF THE HIGH PRIESTS AND THE SEVENTY

Elder Heber C. Kimball now appeared and took charge of the meeting, which was opened by singing and prayer by Elder W. W. Phelps.

Elder George A. Smith moved that all in the elders' quorum under the age of thirty-five should be ordained into the seventies', if they are in good standing, and worthy, and will accept it. The motion was seconded and carried unanimously.

Elder Heber C. Kimball stated that President Joseph Young's wife was very sick and he wished to have her blessed, that brother Young might tarry and perform the duties of his office, and if the congregation would bless her let them say amen, and all the congregation said, amen.

He then recommended all those elders who are under the age of thirty-five, and also all the priests, teachers, deacons and members, who are recommended to be ordained, to withdraw and receive an ordination into the seventies, which was done.

SPECIAL MISSION APPOINTED TO THE HIGH PRIESTS

President Brigham Young then appeared and proceeded to select men from the high priests' quorum, to go abroad in all the congressional districts of the United States, to preside over the branches of the church, as follows:

David Evans	Joseph Holbrook
A. O. Smoot	John Lawson
Edson Whipple	Abel Lamb
Harvey Green	J. H. Hale
J. S. Fullmer	G. D. Watt
J. G. Divine	J. W. Johnson
J. H. Johnson	L. T. Coons
Lester Brooks	J. L. Robinson
J. B. Noble	Howard Coray
Rufus Fisher	M. Sirrine
D. B. Huntington	Pelatiah Brown

Jefferson Hunt

Lorenzo Snow

William Snow

Noah Packard

A. L. Tippets

J. C. Kingsbury

Jacob Foutz

Peter Haws

Thomas Gates

Simeon Carter

Albert Brown

Levi Gifford

Elijah Fordham

Edward Fisher

Franklin D. Richards

Isaac Clark

J. S. Holman

Wandell Mace

Charles Thompson

John Murdock

John Chase

A. L. Lamoreaux

E. T. Benson

Thomas Grover

C. L. Whitney

Addison Everett

Moses Clawson

William Parks

George Colson

H. W. Miller

Isaac Higbee

Daniel Garn

E. H. Groves

G. P. Dykes

Willard Snow

Wm. Felshaw

Winslow Farr

Shadrach Roundy

S. B. Stoddard

E. D. Woolley

Solomon Hancock

Abraham Palmer

James Brown

R. McBride

W. D. Pratt

Martin H. Peck

Morris Phelps

D. McArthur

Archibald Patten

L. H. Ferry

Charles Crismon

Lyman Stoddard

Arnold Stevens

David Fullmer

Joseph Allen

Andrew Perkins

Daniel Carter

Wm. G. Perkins

Graham Coltrin

D. H. Redfield

Titus Billings

Harvey Olumstead

Daniel Stanton

EXPLANATION OF THE MISSION

President Young explained the object for which
these high priests were being sent out, and informed
them that it was not the design to go and tarry six
months and then return, but to go and settle down,
where they can take their families and tarry until the

Temple is built, and then come and get their endowments, and return to their families and build up a stake as large as this.

President Young then selected from the elders' quorums some to be ordained high priests, whose names for the want of room are omitted for the present.

He also selected a number more to go into the seventies after which the remainder of the morning was spent in calling out the several quorums of seventies, and giving charges to the several presidents.

Brother Joseph L. Heywood was ordained under the hands of Elder Brigham Young, Heber C. Kimball and Parley P. Pratt, to be a bishop to the church in Quincy, Illinois.

Previous to adjournment the Presidents of the Seventies ordained upwards of 400 into the quorums of the seventies, and the presidents of the high priests' quorum ordained 40 into their quorum.

The meeting then adjourned until 2 o'clock p. m.

INSTRUCTIONS TO SEVENTIES AND ELDERS

Two o'clock p. m.—Conference resumed business. Those presidents of the seventies who were present and had not received an ordination to the presidency over the seventies, were called out and ordained, under the hands of President Joseph Young and others.

The remainder of the afternoon was spent in filling up the quorums of seventies, and at the close, eleven quorums were filled and properly organized, and about 40 elders organized as a part of the twelfth quorum.

President Brigham Young then said that the elders young men who are capable of preaching, will be ordained; 'but do not be anxious. You must now magnify your calling. Elders who go to borrowing horses or money, and running away with it, will be cut off from the church without any ceremony. They will not have as much lenity as heretofore. The seventies will have to be subject to their presidents and council. We do not want any man to go to preaching until he is sent. If an elder wants to go to preaching let him go into the seventies. *You are all apostles to the nations to carry the gospel;* and when we send you to build up the kingdom, we will give you the keys, and power and authority. If the people will let us alone we will convert the world, and if they persecute us we will do it the quicker. I would exhort all who go from this place to do right and be an honor to the cause. Inasmuch as you will go forth and do right you shall have more of the spirit than you have heretofore. We have had a good conference; we have had beautiful weather and no accidents; and if you will go and do honor to the Lord for this, say amen;' and all the people said amen.

On motion the conference adjourned until the 6th of April next, at 10 o'clock a. m.

Meeting dismissed by prayer from Elder Heber C. Kimball.

[Signed] BRIGHAM YOUNG, President.
Wm. Clayton, Clerk.'

At this conference there were about sixty brethren ordained high priests and four hundred and thirty ordained seventies.

Wednesday, 9.—A council of the Twelve was held at my house.

At a meeting of the trades called for the purpose of discussing the propriety of manufacturing instead of importing articles of common use in the city of Nauvoo, —John Taylor was appointed chairman and W. W. Phelps, secretary.

An Industrial Committee Appointed.
Elders John Taylor, Orson Spencer and Phineas Richards were appointed a general committee to devise plans, and confer with the special committees of the several trades."

CHAPTER XXIV

PRELIMINARY STEPS TO THE FORTHCOMING PROSECU-
TION OF THE MURDERERS OF JOSEPH AND HYRUM
SMITH—THE WORK IN THE SOCIETY ISLANDS—
TEMPLE AFFAIRS—FINANCIAL EMBARRASSMENT

"*Wednesday, October 9, 1844 (continued)* :—Governor Ford wrote the following:

*LETTER OF GOVERNOR FORD AUTHORIZING THE USE OF THE NAUVOO
LEGION FOR PROTECTION OF THE COURTS*

'State of Illinois, Executive Department,
Springfield, October 9th, 1844.

To Lieutenant-General Brigham Young of the Nauvoo Legion:

Sir: It may be probable that there may be further disturbances in
Hancock county by those opposed to the prosecutions against the
murderers of Joseph and Hyrum Smith. They may combine together
in arms to subvert justice and prevent those prosecutions from going on.
They may also attack or resist the civil authorities of the state in that
county and they may attack some of the settlements or people there
with violence.

The sheriff of the county may want a military force to guard
the court and protect it or its officers or the jurors thereof or the witnesses attending court from the violence of a mob.

In all these cases you are hereby ordered and directed to hold in
readiness a sufficient force under your command of the Nauvoo Legion
to act under the direction of the said sheriff for the purposes aforesaid;
and also to suppress mobs which may be collected in said county to
injure the persons or property of any of the citizens. In testimony
whereof I have hereunto set my hand and affixed the seal of state the
day and year first herein above written.

[Signed]   THOMAS FORD,
Governor and Commander-in-Chief.'

NOTE ACCOMPANYING THE GOVERNOR'S LETTER

'The enclosed order is one of great delicacy to execute. I have
conversed with Mr. Backenstos and others and my opinion is the same
as theirs that employing the Legion even legally may call down the
vengeance of the people against your city. It if should be the means
of getting up a civil war in Hancock I do not know how much force

I could bring to the aid of government. A force to be efficient would have to be called out as volunteers; a draft would bring friends and enemies alike. I called for twenty-five hundred before and by ordering out independent companies got four hundred and seventy-five. Three of those companies, the most efficient, have since been broken up and would refuse to go again. I should anticipate but a small force to be raised by volunteers. I would not undertake to march a drafted militia there. Two-thirds of them would join the enemy. The enclosed order is more intended as a permission to use the Legion in the manner indicated, if upon the whole matter it is thought advisable, than a compulsory command.

Your most wise and discreet councilors and county officers will have to act according to their best judgment.

[Signed]   THOMAS FORD.*

Thursday, 10.—Elder Heber C. Kimball and myself spent most of the day at Father Ezra Chase's.

Friday, 11.—Evening, I attended prayer meeting at Elder Kimball's.

Saturday, 12.—I met with the city council.

Sunday, 13.—Meeting at the stand; Elder Parley P. Pratt preached.

The seventies met at their hall; Elder Orson Pratt preached and instructed the seventies in relation to their duties.

Tuesday, 15.—Accompanied by Elder Heber C.
Kimball and my brother Lorenzo D. Young
President
Young's Visit
to the East.
I started for Ottoway. We traveled to Ramus and stayed with Brother Erastus Bingham, where Parley P. Pratt joined us.

A meeting of delegates from Trades Committees was held in the Masonic Hall, Nauvoo, John Taylor chairman; at which it was reported that enough had been made manifest to ensure the practicability of making Nauvoo a great manufacturing depot.

Wednesday, 16.—Accompanied by the brethren before named I traveled to Brother Justus Ames's near Galesburg, forty miles. Next day, we traveled to LaFayette and stayed with Brother Austin Grant, and on the following day traveled to Providence encountering a wet snowstorm from which I took cold and suffered from diarrhea: we stayed at a tavern.

Saturday, 19.—We drove forty-four miles and arrived at Ottoway.

Sunday, 20.—We held two meetings at Brother Busard's.

Elders Heber C. Kimball and Parley P. Pratt and I preached: we had a profitable time.

The seventies met in their hall at Nauvoo.

After ordaining presidents who had been selected to preside over the quorums, a call was made by request of the major-general for thirty wagons and teams to be in readiness at the hall by daylight tomorrow, with three days' provisions and horse feed sufficient for the journey. Large Party of Witnesses From Nauvoo go to Carthage.
This call was made to convey witnesses to Carthage in safety, and for protection during the trials at court: as two of our best men were murdered in Carthage in June and that too under the faith and pledge of the state and since caution is the parent of safety, it was deemed inadvisable to venture upon the pledges and promises of others.

Monday, 21.—About one hundred and fifty brethren went from Nauvoo to Carthage early this morning and encamped near Crooked Creek; although they exhibited no arms their appearance created much excitement. The company consisted of the city council, police and those concerned in abating the *Nauvoo Expositor* nuisance with the witnesses and others who had business in Carthage: by encamping they avoided the necessity of paying hotel bills to enemies and the risk of being murdered in their beds.

With the brethren accompanying me I dined at Brother Reuben Miller's, crossed Fox river and proceeded to Brother Dunavan's and remained all night.

Tuesday, 22.—We visited the Norwegian branch in La Salle county, and met with the saints in the evening.

Misconduct
of William
Smith *et al*
Reported.

I received a lengthy communication from Elder Wilford Woodruff relative to the injudicious course pursued by Elders William Smith, George J. Adams and Samuel Brannan.

A correspondent wrote from Carthage to the *Nauvoo Neighbor* as follows:

'Court is in session. The mob is here but not in great numbers. They are fierce and vindictive and disposed to do harm if they dare.

Mob
Movements
at Carthage

They had a violent warlike meeting in the courthouse last night, in which they tried to get up a story that there were two hundred Mormons and three hundred Indians encamped near this place in hostile array for the purpose of an attack on the town. They passed panic resolutions, advising the court to adjourn and threatened if that was not done that they would raise an armed force as they say to protect themselves, but as all know, for the purpose of awing the court and juries and driving off witnesses. Rosevelt, Sharp, Williams and company were the leaders in getting up the excitement. They hope to get it believed abroad that they are about to be attacked by the Mormons as an excuse for some outrage which they wish, but have not the courage to perpetrate.'

Wednesday, 23.—In company with Elder Heber C. Kimball, Parley P. Pratt and Lorenzo D. Young, I

A Norwegian
Branch
Organized

called the brethren together as a conference of the Norwegian branch. We taught the principles of the gospel to them and appointed George P. Dykes, high priest, to preside over the Norwegian branch and the saints in that vicinity of country, and ordained Reuben Miller a bishop.

We bought one hundred acres of land from Brothers Goodman and Anderson, and thereupon laid out a city. We selected the ground for a meetinghouse and drove the southeast corner stake. We called the city Norway and dedicated it to the Lord. Evening, we ordained Brother Phillip Hammond Busard a high priest and set him apart as a counselor to Brother Dykes.

Thursday, 24.—We left Ottoway and drove forty-three miles to Brother Parley P. Pratt's farm. We found his brother, Anson Pratt, and family well: they were glad to see us.

The brethren who went to Carthage returned home to Nauvoo. The members of the city council who were not indicted by the grand jury, were released from their bonds; eleven brethren were indicted for riot: the judge and attorney advised the brethren to return to Nauvoo to allay the excitement. The trials are continued until next spring term of court: the Nauvoo Legion is a terror.

Return of the Nauvoo Witnesses.

Brother Hyrum Smith prophesied that the governor would call upon the Nauvoo Legion to maintain the supremacy of the law, which has been fulfilled according to [by] the governor's late order.

Willard Richards was subpoenaed to appear before the grand jury, but being unable and unwilling to go to Carthage application was made to the court to get an attachment for his person, the attorney averring that it was necessary to have someone to prove that Joseph and Hyrum were dead, and he presumed that Richards was in possession of that knowledge; the court however refused the attachment as they considered that fact could be proved without bringing a sick man out of his bed. The Twelve all left Nauvoo during the court except Elder Willard Richards who was confined to his bed, and Elder George A. Smith who gave such counsel as the excitement of the times required.

Willard Richards Subpoenaed a Witness at the Carthage Trial.

WORK IN SOCIETY ISLANDS REPORTED

Elder Noah Rogers wrote from Huahine, Society Islands, of date as follows:

'I have left Tahiti and am now on the Island of Huahine, which is about ninety or one hundred miles distant. The work on Tahiti has got a good start. We baptized several whites, and several more said that they believed and would be baptized soon, and several natives told me when I left Tahiti that they meant to be baptized soon.

I left Brother Grouard there, who has got the language very well, and I have no doubt of his faithfulness, because he is a firm and faithful brother, and seeks the good of the kingdom of God.

I have been but one week on Huahine. I expect soon to obtain a house and preach as there is one or two that show some disposition to assist me in getting one. Almost every white man on this island keeps a grogshop and a gambling house, which is a very bad example for the natives. If you say anything to them about it, they will say that the whites learned [taught] us. They are full of licentiousness, which the sailors are very willing to encourage. When I see so much iniquity and abomination, it makes me sick to the very heart, and I wonder that the Lord has spared the world so long as he has. There is but one missionary [i. e. sectarian] here, who rules the island, as it were. All the people say that he is a very nice man, but I cannot say so much of him as he refuses to talk with me.'

President Young's Return to Nauvoo.

Monday, 28.—I returned to Nauvoo with my brethren, we found our families well. During our absence it was unknown to the people whither we had gone.

The Neighbor announced that true bills of indictment had been found against several persons of Hancock county, for the murder of Joseph and Hyrum Smith on the 27th of June last.

Indictment of the Prophet's Murderers.

Among the most conspicuous are, Colonel Levi Williams, Thomas C. Sharp, Mark Aldrich and Jacob C. Davis. The latter a senator in the legislature of Illinois.

I attended a council with my brethren of the Twelve, the Trustees, the Temple Committee and Brother William Weeks the architect at the Temple Office, settling the differences existing between the Temple Committee and Brother Weeks.

Thursday, 31.—Elder Heber C. Kimball and I visited the Temple. I called at Sister Snively's with Brother Parley P. Pratt.

Friday, November 1, 1844.—The seventies met at 10 a. m.; President Joseph Young took the lead of business. Brother Eleazur Miller was ordained a president and twenty brethren were ordained seventies. I addressed the meeting on the subject of Elections, and voting for party candidates. I told them I wish I could communicate my feelings to them without speaking; and gave some of my views in relation to political men, and their principles.

Seventies' Meeting.

Sunday, 3.—I went to the Seventies' Hall in the forenoon, attended the high priests' quorum in the afternoon, and met again with the seventies in the evening.

At a conference held in Livonia, Wayne county, Michigan, on the 1st, 2nd and 3d inst., fourteen branches were represented, five elders volunteered to go and preach the gospel, and a resolution was passed to sustain the Twelve and all the authorities in carrying out the commandments of God that have been given through Joseph Smith, our martyred Prophet. The sacrament was administered, and much instruction given on the first principles of the gospel.*

Thursday, 7.—With Elders John Taylor and George A. Smith, I visited the Trustees, afterwards visited at Brother Joseph Bates Noble's with Elder Amasa M. Lyman, Sister Olive Frost and others.

A conference was held in New Trenton, Franklin county, Indiana, on the 6th and 7th inst. A good feeling prevailed, the Spirit of God was made manifest. President David Pettegrew baptized nine persons, and many were believing.

Friday, 8.—I went out to Fisher's Brick Yard and laid hands on the sick.

Saturday, 9.—I met with the city council. They passed an ordinance to prohibit the vending of spirituous liquors in the city under a penalty of not less than $25.00.

Sunday, 10.—I preached about two hours to the saints at the meeting ground; many present; had a good time.

Evening, seventies met: after the ordinations and business were attended to, Elder George A. Smith addressed the meeting on the progress of the kingdom.

At a quarterly conference held at St. Louis, present of the Twelve—1, high priests—4, seventies—15,

---

*The minutes of the conference were signed by Lyman Stoddard, President, William Burton, Clerk.

elders—21, priests—13, teachers—2, deacons—5, members—172. The congregation was large, and notwithstanding the crowd strict attention was given to the interesting discourse of Elder Orson Hyde.

During conference seventeen persons joined the branch by letter, and one by baptism.

Monday, 11.—Attended council with the Twelve, bishops, high council, mayor and policemen, and transacted business for the welfare of the church.

Tuesday, 12.—I went to the Temple; called on Elders Kimball and Richards and found them recovering. I attended and addressed a meeting of the various trades of the city; a committee of three were appointed to see to the erection of a cotton factory, inasmuch as the machinery could be obtained. Elders John Taylor and Orson Spencer addressed the meeting.

William Clayton recorded the following:

'As I was walking along Front Street, St. Louis, I saw a man engaged cutting a stone monument. I was amazed to see these words already cut on the monument, *viz.* 'Highwater June 27th, 1844', that was the day when this generation rejected the Prophet of God, when he and his brother Hyrum, the Patriarch, were murdered at Carthage jail by a wicked mob, and this was the day when the waters overflowed the Missouri at the highest, when the Front Street of St. Louis was covered eight feet deep with the flood.'

Thursday, 14.—Elder B. L. Clapp wrote the following brief account of his mission:

'I left Nauvoo August 12th, 1843, on a special mission to the south, and returned June 7th, 1844, during which time I traveled 4,444 miles, held 176 meetings and baptized 118 souls in the states of Alabama and Mississippi.'

Friday, 15.—I met with the authorities and held a council in relation to building the arsenal and carrying on the public works.

Sunday, 17.—Ten a. m. seventies met, Joseph Young presiding; twelve brethren were ordained to be seventies; several were recommended to the high priests' quorum. I attended in the evening and addressed the meeting.

Tuesday, 19.—Elder Orson Hyde and I visited the sick. A trades meeting was held in the Masonic Hall addressed by Elders Taylor, Scovil, Hunter and others. Elder J. W. Crosby wrote the following:

MISSION IN CANADIAN PROVINCES

'In August, 1843, Elder B. Brown and myself (having been appointed to visit the British provinces) proceeded to western New York, where we spent the winter. We organized several branches of the church, baptized upward of 150 souls, and held two conferences. After tarrying eight months, we went to Montreal and Quebec, making a short stay in each of these Catholic cities, preached some and circulated some books, pamphlets, etc. We proceeded to New Brunswick, and amid much opposition, persecution and personal violence, baptized 47; organized them into two branches, both in the county of York, above Frederickston. We returned to Boston in October and have spent a few weeks in the regions round about.'

Saturday, 23.—Bishop N. K. Whitney met with the lesser priesthood at the house of Samuel Gulley, and filled up the different quorums. I attended and in company with Elder Kimball and Bishop Whitney, ordained Brother Edward Hunter bishop, and set him apart to the care of the fifth ward [Nauvoo].

Edward Hunter Ordained a Bishop.

Sunday, 24.—Ten a. m. meeting of seventies in their hall. The seven presidents of the thirteenth quorum were ordained. Twenty brethren were ordained seventies, President Joseph Young preached.

Monday, 25.—A remonstrance against the division of Hancock county, numerously signed was placed in the hands of A. W. Babbitt, Esq., for presentation to the legislature of Illinois.

Saturday, 30.—Received a letter from Elder Wilford Woodruff, giving a particular account of the eastern branches of the church, which he had visited on his way to New York.

Sunday, December 1, 1844.—Elder Parley P. Pratt was appointed to go to the city of New York, and take charge of the press, regulate and counsel the immigra-

tion that may come that way from Europe and take
the presidency of all the eastern branches of the church.

Eleven a. m., seventies met in their hall, Joseph
Young presiding; sixteen brethren were ordained seventies; Elder George A. Smith preached at length on the
subject of Apostasy.

Monday, 2.—I extract from the *Times and Seasons*
(p. 728) the following:—

A VOICE FROM THE TEMPLE

By the Temple Committee

'We would say to all those who wish to bring tithes for the building of the Temple in the city of Nauvoo, that we have deemed it wisdom to remove our office, for the better accommodation

Change
of Office
Location.
of business, and of all who visit us on business, to the
new and commodious brick store of Elder Parley P.

Pratt, situated one block north from the west end of the
Temple; at which place we will attend every day in the week (Sunday excepted) from morning till evening, to receive donations for the
Temple and also attend to all other matters of business pertaining to
the Trustees. We publish this notice that the brethren may not need
to inquire where they shall deposit their donations. We have only
one place of deposit in the city of Nauvoo and that is the above mentioned brick store.

We would also once more offer a word of caution to all the saints
for their benefit, inasmuch as there are those who are going round

A Word of
Caution
Against
Frauds.
amongst the branches of the church to collect funds for
the Temple without authority, and who are all the while
practicing impositions upon the brethren. They generally use the property for their own individual benefit,
and make no returns of it to us, and consequently when the donors
come to see the records their names are not there. Many have felt to
censure us on this account, but censure in such a case is unjust, for we
have published notices repeatedly, warning the saints not to credit any
man's testimony as to his being an agent unless he can show written
authority from us or the Quorum of the Twelve, and all those who
entrust their means in the hands of unauthorized agents, do it at their
own risk, and not ours.

The presiding elders in the branches have a right to call for, and to
see the authority of any and every man professing to be an agent for

The Right
to Demand
Identification
of Agents.
the church, and if he is an honest servant and a man of
authority he will always be ready to produce his testimonials to proper authority, but if he is an impostor he
will either make excuses, or he will probably scorn at the
idea of your questioning a man of God as to his authority. In some

instances men have considered themselves insulted when asked by the presiding elders for their authority, but this is only an evidence either of their own wickedness, or that they come on an errand on which they were never legally sent.   Beware of wolves in sheep's clothing!

We are more particular on this subject because there have been instances, not a few, wherein men who are not Latter-day Saints, but on the contrary our most bitter enemies, have gone round gulling the churches and professing to be 'Mormons' and agents to collect funds for the building of the 'Temple and Nauvoo House', etc.; and they have taken advantage of the liberality of the brethren by all kinds of fine speeches and persuasive inducements to get away with their money, until they have accomplished their objects, and then they become 'missing'.   It is not our wish to see the brethren cheated so barefacedly after all the persecutions we have suffered, and we once more repeat the caution, be wise and careful.

There are instances where the saints rarely see an authorized agent, in consequence of the distance from Nauvoo, or, in consequence of their residing some distance from a regularly organized branch.   In such cases, when they want to send up their donations, let them do it by some man with whom they are well acquainted, and who they are well satisfied will do right, and carry their donation safe to its destination. And it would be well in all cases, where the brethren abroad send donations by authorized agents, to send a letter by mail (post paid), to the Trustees-in-Trust, informing them of the facts, and by whom their donations were sent, etc., and a good man will not blame you for being thus careful, for the same law that guards your rights will guard his rights, and the rights of every man.

It is our intention for the future to publish the names of our agents in the *Nauvoo Neighbor* and the *Times and Seasons*, which we consider to be safer and better than written authority, inasmuch as the latter can be 'forged', but the former can not, and the agents can carry a copy of the paper, having their authority with them wherever they go.   List of Church Agents to be Published.

There is also another subject which we would touch upon in this notice.   There have been instances wherein men have gone amongst the branches of the church, collecting money and agreeing to pay the same amount in labor on the Temple, which they represent will answer as good a purpose as the money.   We have to say on this subject that all   Promised Change of Labor for Money. such transactions are regarded as fraud, and is only a more crafty way of cheating the brethren.   It would be folly for us to tell a man that ten days labor on the Temple would answer the law of tithing as well as ten dollars in money, when he was possessed of one hundred dollars in money.   We know better, and every faithful brother and sister in the church will know better when they understand the principles of salvation as well as old Abraham, Isaac and Jacob did.   For Jacob said of all thou givest me, one-tenth I will give unto thee, and whoever will read the history of the ancients with care will find that the law was, that they must pay one-tenth of all in its kind, whether cattle, horses, sheep, or fruits of the field. 'Tis true there were laws of redemption, whereby a man might redeem 'ought of his tithing' but it was so strict, that it is far easier to pay the tithing in kind rather than redeem it.

Jesus said, all who do the works of Abraham are the children of Abraham, and he (Abraham) paid tithes of all. The Savior also said to the Pharisees, 'ye pay tithes of mint and annis and cummin, but neglect the weightier matters of the law, judgment, mercy and faith, these ought ye to have done, and not have left the others undone.'

We make reference to these subjects that the brethren may take the hint, and think for themselves for just so sure as there are laws established from before the foundation of the world for the government of the Church of Christ just so sure will we fail of obtaining a fulness of salvation if we do not abide by those laws. No man can obtain a celestial glory if he will not abide a celestial law, and the law of tithing is a celestial law, and always was in force where the Melchizedek priesthood was inherited.

Why did the Savior say, 'how hardly shall they that have riches enter the kingdom of heaven?' Just converse with a rich man upon the subject of tithing, and you will soon see a reason why the rich can hardly enter the kingdom of heaven. When you converse with a man who has got ten thousand dollars in money in his hands, and tell him that his tithing will be one thousand dollars in money, you generally will see the force of the words of Jesus. That man would consider himself almost ruined if he should donate his one thousand dollars, whereas a man who has only ten dollars in money in the world, will come forward with cheerfulness and donate his tenth with joy. Remember the widow with her two mites.

Operation of the Law of Tithing.

No man or woman who really desires to secure a fulness of salvation will wish to be kept ignorant of those principles, and laws and ordinances on which his salvation depends, and consequently we are free to give a hint on the subject of tithing, not because we take it upon us to instruct the people, but because we realize in some measure the importance of it ourselves to set the saints to 'thinking for themselves' on the subject.

The Saints Will Desire to Know.

When the saints ask for instructions, the Twelve are the proper authorities to refer to, and they will deal it out as fast as the saints are willing to obey.

The Twelve Willing to Impart Instructions

We are happy to have to say that the Temple has progressed more rapidly than our most sanguine expectations could have imagined. All the capitals are on the walls, except one, which if the weather permit, will be up in a few days. The weather has been remarkably favorable and continues so to the

Progress on the Temple.

present. The feelings of the saints are good and their hearts are cheered while they look upon the House of God and reflect on the prospects of its speedy completion. Their toils and poverty and persecutions are all swallowed up in the cheering prospects of their reward, only a little ways ahead.

Peace smiles upon our beloved city. And the great God looks down upon this people with sympathy and compassion from day to day, dispensing his heavenly blessings upon all the families of his saints according to his infinite wisdom and their willingness to receive them. The hearts of the saints are united firmer than ever, notwithstanding the vigorous efforts made by satan and dissenters to sow amongst us discord, strife, and confusion, and every evil work, scattering not excepted. Many houses are in progress of erection, which on account of the lateness of the season will have to stand unfinished until next spring. Every effort is being made to establish and put in operation various branches of manufacture for the employment of the saints, and the prospects are good, but not unattended with difficulty, toil and anxiety. But diligence, economy, and steady perseverance in a good cause, never fails to bring its reward, and very often the sweetest roses are surrounded by the sharpest thorns, and the greatest treasures deposited in places the most difficult of access, where we have to dig, and dig long and deep in order to obtain them.

We might prolong these remarks, but perhaps we have said enough for once. We will leave the subject, praying the blessings of our heavenly Father to rest upon all good men, and especially upon the saints, that they may have peace and joy in the Holy Ghost, and attain to that knowledge which will obtain for them an inheritance in the eternal kingdom of our God.

We have the honor to be

Your most obedient servants, and brethren in the faith of Christ,

N. K. WHITNEY,
GEORGE MILLER,
Trustees-in-Trust.

By Wm. Clayton, Recorder.
Nauvoo, Dec. 2, 1844.'

Monday, December 2, (continued).—I attended a council at Elder Willard Richards: present—the brethren of the Twelve, the Trustees; the Temple Committee and architect. The duties of the Temple Committee and architect were explained.

Evening; the Presidents of Seventies met.

Tuesday, 3.—City police met. Captain Hosea Stout instructed them pertaining to their duties.

Thursday, 5.—I insert the following minutes:

COUNCIL MINUTES OF FINANCIAL AFFAIRS

'Afternoon, a council was held in the recorder's office, President Brigham Young and Heber C. Kimball of the Quorum of the Twelve were present, also N. K. Whitney and George Miller, Trustees and Alpheus Cutler and Reynolds Cahoon, the Temple Committee. The council was called for the purpose of devising means to raise the sum of $3,100, which is due from the Trustees to several individuals for church lands, and which will have to be paid within three months or the lands be forfeited, worth from ten to fifteen thousand dollars. About one thousand dollars of the aforesaid sum must be paid in a few days. After conversing some time on the prospects of raising funds, President Young said that his feelings were to draw the money lying in the possession of Sisters Mary Smith and Mercy R. Thompson and A. Cutler, which money has been donated by the sisters of the church, by paying one cent a week, for the purpose of purchasing the nails and glass for the Temple and which amounted to five or six hundred dollars already collected. It is considered wisdom to do this to save the church property from the hands of our enemies; and the straitened circumstances under which the Trustees labor in consequence of persecution and oppression—we consider sufficient to justify the course. It is also considered certain that the money will be ready by the time the nails and glass are needed for the Temple, and that the money will be saving so much interest, whereas at the present it is lying useless. The suggestion by President Young seemed to meet the feelings of all the brethren, and it was concluded to draw an order for the money on Mrs. Mary Smith, and Mercy R. Thompson, which was immediately done.'

Action on Finance.

LETTER OF PRESIDENT YOUNG TO RELIEF SOCIETY PRESIDENCY

'To Mrs. Mary Smith and Mercy R. Thompson,

Dear Sisters:

We are under the necessity of raising a considerable sum of money for the use of the church within a few days. We have counseled together on the subject, and have considered it wisdom to call upon you for the money in your hands, donated by the sisters as penny subscription. You will therefore please deliver the same to Bishop Whitney when he presents this order.

Done by order of the Quorum of the Twelve, for and in behalf of the Church of Jesus Christ of Latter-day Saints.

[Signed] BRIGHAM YOUNG,

President of the Quorum of the Twelve.

William Clayton, Clerk.

Dec. 5, 1844.

N. B. Elder W. Richards, the clerk of the Quorum of the Twelve is very sick and unable to attend to business, which is the reason of the above signature as clerk.' "

CHAPTER XXV

PROGRESS OF WORK ON THE TEMPLE— MISCELLANEOUS MOVEMENTS IN CHURCH AND STATE

"*Friday, December* 6, 1844.—I [Brigham Young] insert the following minutes:—

THE PLACING OF THE LAST CAPITAL ON THE TEMPLE

'The last of the capitals was placed on the walls of the Temple. The workmen commenced raising the stone at half after 10 o'clock, but when about half way up one of the block shives broke in two. This placed the matter in a dangerous position, it was impossible to raise the stone higher without a new shive, and to attempt to let it down would have cut off the rope instantly. After much labor the workmen secured the tackle so that it could not move and having this done, they fixed a new shive in the block and after about an hour and a half's delay, at half after one p. m. the stone was safely fixed in its place in the wall. This stone is the largest one among the capitals and is supposed to weigh over two tons. There are thirty capitals around the Temple, each one composed of five stones, *viz.* one base stone, one large stone representing the sun rising just above the clouds, the lower part obscured; the third stone represents two hands each holding a trumpet, and the last two stones form a cap over the trumpet stone, and these all form the capital, the average cost of which is about four hundred and fifty dollars each. These stones are very beautifully cut, especially the face and trumpet stones, and are an evidence of great skill in the architect and ingenuity on the part of the stonecutters. They present a very pleasing and noble appearance, and seem very appropriate in their places. The first capital was set on the 23d of September last, making but a little over ten weeks between the first and the last, and out of that time the workmen lost about three weeks through bad weather, and having to wait for stone.

There has not been the slightest accident attending the raising of these large stones, except the second one which was set, the workmen, undertook to move the stone a little nearer the building without having first fixed the guy ropes to the crane, and while in the attempt the crane fell over with a tremendous crash and fell within about a foot of Brother Thomas Jaap, one of the workmen, who ran as soon as he saw the crane falling but happened to run in the same direction in which it fell. Providentially no further damage was done than to the crane which was partially broken.

The weather has been very favorable most of the time, but on account of its being so late in the season, it was generally feared we would not succeed in getting them [the capitals] up before winter set in, but it seems as though the Lord held up the storms and the cold for our advantage, until this important piece of labor has been accomplished to our utmost satisfaction and delight.

There are yet twelve of the capitals without trumpet stones, and will have to remain so until spring; three of them however are finished and several others nearly so.

The weather changed this morning. It rained nearly all the time the men were at work; and about two hours after the last capital was set, it commenced snowing and continued until the ground was covered about four inches deep. Nine o'clock p. m., it now freezes very sharp and to all appearance stern winter has taken possession of the atmosphere in earnest.'

Elder Wilford Woodruff and family, in company with Elder H. Clark and Dan Jones and their families, and Elders Milton Holmes and Leonard W. Hardy sailed from New York in the packet ship, *John B. Skiddy,* for Liverpool.

Departure of Elder Woodruff for England.

Sunday, 8.—The seventies met in their hall. Eight brethren were ordained seventies. A letter was read from Elder B. F. Grouard from the Society Isles. Elder Henry Harriman, George A. Smith and Joseph Young instructed the elders.

Elder Willard Richards, city recorder, opened office in his new house, and appointed Thomas Bullock his deputy. Thomas [Bullock] commenced putting the city records in order, which had been neglected some four months in consequence of Brother Willard's inability through sickness.

Monday, 9.—A conference was held in Comstock, Kalamazoo county, Michigan on the 8th and 9th inst.

Conference in Michigan.

Crandall Dunn presiding; five branches were represented numbering 107 members, 1 high priest, 16 elders, 1 teacher, and one deacon. Resolutions were passed to sustain the Twelve and agreeing to tithe themselves to aid in building the Temple. During the conference much good instruction was given by Elder Crandall Dunn, C. M. Webb, and D. Savage; one priest was ordained, 3 children blessed, and one person baptized.

Wednesday, 11.—Elder Willard Richards recommenced to gather materials for the Church History, assisted by W. W. Phelps.

Thursday, 12.—The high priests of the 5th ward met in the Concert Hall.

Friday, 13.—The Aaronic priesthood met. Bishop N. K. Whitney presided. He spoke on the subject of furnishing employment for the poor, the manufacturing of straw and palm leaf hats, and willow baskets. Two were ordained.

Saturday, 14.—Received a lengthy communication from A. W. Babbitt, Esq., house of representatives, Springfield. Advising in relation to his communications with the governor, the anticipated movements of the legislature, and his intended course pertaining to the chartered rights of the city of Nauvoo; to which a reply was written by Orson Spencer showing the injustice and unconstitutionality of a repeal of the Nauvoo Charter. *Repeal of Nauvoo Charters Proposed.*

In company with Elder Heber C. Kimball, Orson Hyde, Orson Pratt, John Taylor, and George A. Smith, I attended city council. An ordinance was passed organizing the Seventies' Library and Institute Association. The council expressed their views in relation to the illegality of the legislature interfering with the chartered right of the city of Nauvoo; when those rights had never been exercised to the hurt or the prejudice of the innocent. *City Council Meeting.*

Sunday, 15.—Ten a. m. meeting of seventies. President Joseph Young, presiding. Twenty-nine persons were unanimously received by vote and ordained to be seventies.

The ordinance of the city council in relation to the Seventies' Library and Institute Association was read.

Elder George A. Smith advised the elders to get up

schools, that all the seventies who would, might be
School for Seventies. taught in the branches of education, and
prepare themselves that the least might be
fully competent, to correspond with the wise men of
the world.

Good and useful instruction relative to manners,
order and good behavior were given by the president
and some of his council.

Monday, 16.—I extract from the *Tithing Record
No. 2:—*

'A few days ago the Twelve and the Trustees counseled together
on the propriety of employing a suitable number of carpenters this
winter to prepare the timbers for the Temple, so as to have them all
ready when the stone work was finished.

They concluded to employ fifteen persons steadily as carpenters,
and that the architect be authorized to select such men as he has confidence in—men who are well qualified to do the work
Carpenters Selected to Work on the Temple. that is wanted. It was also concluded to fix up a shop
in the Temple for the carpenters to work in. Accord-
ingly the south side of the lower story was weather-
boarded around and a convenient shop made of it on Saturday, and
today, the men have gone to work.

The names of the carpenters selected as steady hands are as follows:
viz: Truman O. Angel, William Felshaw, William F. Cahoon, Joseph
S. Schofield, Samuel Rolfe, Zimri H. Baxter, Addison Everett, John
Stiles, Hugh Riding, Miles Romney, Jabez Durfee, Stephen Long-
stroth, Benjamin Rolfe, Nicholas T. Silcock, William Carmichael,
Hiram Mace, Daniel Avery, Gideon Gibbs, and Wandel Mace.

N. B.—Daniel Avery is employed to take care of the shop and the
fires, etc.

The three last named are engaged in the sawmill shop.'

Tuesday, 17.—I copy the following minutes on
file:—

PRESIDENCY APPOINTED FOR KIRTLAND

'The Quorum of the Twelve and others in council assembled at the
office of President Brigham Young, at the corner of Kimball and
Granger Streets.

Moved and seconded that Brother Reuben McBride take the presidency over all the affairs pertaining to the Church of Jesus Christ of
Latter-day Saints in Kirtland—both spiritually and temporally—which
was carried by a unanimous voice of said council.

A letter was then read before the council which President Young
received from Brothers Joseph Parsons and James McDowell, residing

in Pittsburgh, containing an acknowledgment that they had been deceived by Elder Rigdon's false pretensions to the Presidency, and after a calm and careful investigation of the *Book of Doctrine and Covenants* and *Book of Mormon*, they had renounced the pretensions of Sidney Rigdon as being false and felt satisfied that the Quorum of the Twelve held the keys of the kingdom.

Elder Rigdon Rejected by Elders in Pittsburgh.

Voted unanimously that their acknowledgment be received and they be received into full fellowship with the saints.'

I received a letter from Horace R. Hotchkiss proposing to dispose of lots in Nauvoo, to be compensated by improvements on adjoining lots; also on the subject of home manufactures and building up the city of Nauvoo; to which I replied informing him that property was not so high as it had been, and referred him to Elder Taylor for information on the trades operations.

Hotchkiss Interests in Nauvoo.

The brethren of the Twelve visited Elder Willard Richards who was sick.

Wednesday, 18.—Evening with Elder Heber C. Kimball and Bishop N. K. Whitney. I attended the practice of music at the Concert Hall.

Friday, 20.—In company with Elder Heber C. Kimball and George A. Smith I spent a portion of the day at the Tithing Office regulating matters pertaining to tithings; called on Brother Willard Richards, found him some better.

William Clayton records he 'had some conversation with Brother Cahoon respecting making a feast for the poor and proposed to do it on New Year's day. Daniel H. Wells, Esq., agreed to give ten dollars to aid the feast for the poor.'

Sunday, 22.—I met as usual with the Twelve Apostles and others for prayer.

Ten a. m., seventies met at their hall, Joseph Young presiding: five presidents and forty seventies were ordained; fourteenth quorum organized; two brethren were recommended to the high priests' quorum.

Monday, 23.—The Aaronic priesthood met: Bishop

N. K. Whitney presiding; four persons were ordained to the office of priest.

Tuesday, 24.—The stockholders of the Seventies' Library and Institute Association elected Elder George A. Smith, Amasa M. Lyman, Joseph Young, Levi W. Hancock, Albert Carrington, John D. Lee and James M. Monroe trustees.

Wednesday, 25.—I spent an agreeable time at Brother Coolidge's, in company with Elders Heber C.

Banquet and Party. Kimball, George A. Smith, A. M. Lyman, John Taylor and their ladies. The band was in attendance. We partook of a substantial dinner; after which I made a few remarks expressive of my good feelings and love to my brethren. I remarked that the Lord would never suffer us to overcome our enemies while we cherished feelings of revenge, when we prevailed over our enemies it must be from a sense of duty and not of revenge.

Friday, 27.—I went to the Trustee's Office.

Evening, there was a meeting in the Seventies' Hall of the city council, the high council and leading authorities of the church.

Governor Ford's Message to the Illinois Legislature. Governor Ford's special message to the legislature was read. It was a very meager attempt to excuse himself from participation in the assassination of Joseph and Hyrum Smith, being full of misrepresentations, exaggerations and contemptible falsehoods.

Brother A. W. Babbitt made a report of his proceedings in Springfield.

Sunday, 29.—I published the following:

'*Brother Taylor on Church Periodicals.*—The question is asked in *The New York Prophet*: Why is it that there is no more interest manifested among the elders in enlisting support or subscriptions for our periodicals? For one I will answer the question. While I have been preaching abroad from place to place, the question being asked of me so many times by the saints, 'Why do not my papers come? I subscribed and sent the money long ago and have received but two or three numbers.' My reply has been, 'it seems the post office department is very uncertain.'

Realizing the very few that have been received by our brethren abroad, in proportion to the many that have been mailed at our establishment, my heart has fainted, and I have not asked men to pay their money fearing they would never receive their papers.' "

CHAPTER XXVI

THE GREAT CONFERENCE OF THE SEVENTIES AT
NAUVOO—ORGANIZATION OF NEW QUORUMS—DEDI-
CATION OF THE SEVENTIES' HALL—NOTABLE DIS-
COURSES—DOCTRINAL INSTRUCTIONS BY PRESIDENT
BRIGHAM YOUNG ON PRIESTHOOD—THE TWELVE—
THE SEVENTY—AND THE BISHOPRIC

"*Monday, December* 30, 1844.—The following is
extracted from the *Times and Seasons,* Vol. vi, p.
794:—

DEDICATION OF THE SEVENTIES' HALL

(*Five Days, Dec.* 26-30, 1844. *A Memorable Conference*)

'*Thursday, December* 26, *A. D.* 1844.—The services commenced under the direction of President Joseph
Young [the Senior President of the First Quorum of
the Seventy], who organized the meeting in the following order:

The stand was occupied by the Seven Presiding
Presidents of the Seventy, and the Twelve or as many
of them as were present. The senior president of each quorum was seated on the
right, the choir of singers on the left, and
the brass band in front. The second and third quorums in order, with their families, occupied the other
seats for the day. Each day afforded a new congregation, that all the seventies, with their families, might
in turn, participate in the privilege of the dedication,
according to their respective quorums, there being
fifteen quorums whose claims were equal, two of which
convened in the hall each day, beginning with the
second and third [quorums].

Arrangement of the Meeting.

The excellent melody of the choir and band, mingling with the devout aspirations of a congregation of all saints, gave the commencement of their services an air of interest, felicity and glory, at once feeling, touching, pathetic, grand, sublime!

A hymn, composed by Elder W. W. Phelps, for the dedication, entitled 'A Voice from the Prophet: Come to Me', was sung:

A VOICE FROM THE PROPHET

'COME TO ME'

(By W. W. Phelps, to the Tune—'Indian Hunter')

'Come to me, will ye come to the saints that have died—
To the next better world, where the righteous reside;
Where the angels and spirits in harmony be.
In the joys of a vast Paradise?　Come to me.

Come to me where the truth and the virtues prevail;
Where the union is one, and the years never fail;
Where the heart can't conceive, nor the nat'ral eye see,
What the Lord has prepar'd for the just: Come to me.

Come to me where there is no destruction or war;
Neither tyrants, nor mobbers, or nations ajar;
Where the system is perfect, and happiness free,
And the life is eternal with God:　Come to me.

Come to me, will ye come to the mansions above
Where the bliss and the knowledge, the light, and the love,
And the glory of God, do eternally be?
Death, the wages of sin, is not here:　Come to me.

Come to me, here are Adam and Eve at the head
Of a multitude quicken'd and rais'd from the dead:
Here's the knowledge that was, or that is, or will be—
In the gen'ral assembly of worlds:　Come to me.

Come to me; here's the myst'ry that man hath not seen;
Here's our Father in heaven, and Mother, the Queen,
Here are worlds that have been, and the worlds yet to be,
Here's eternity,—endless; amen:　Come to me.

Come to me all ye faithful and blest of Nauvoo:
Come ye Twelve, and ye High Priests, and Seventies, too;
Come ye Elders, and all of the great company;—
When you've finish'd your work on the earth:　Come to me,

Come to me; here's the future, the present and past:
Here is Alpha, Omega, the first and the last;
Here's the fountain, the 'river of life', and the Tree;
Here's your Prophet and Seer, Joseph Smith: Come to me.'

The dedication prayer by President Brigham Young, was in substance as follows:

PRAYER: A SUPPLICATION TO THE THRONE OF GRACE

'Thou God who dwellest in the midst of thine own kingdoms, and doeth thy pleasure in the midst of the same. We realize that we are thy children, although we have long wandered from thee. Yet we feel that it is thy good pleasure to bless us, when we come unto thee with hearts of humility. Therefore we desire to present ourselves before thee as dutiful children to an earthly parent, knowing that we are thine and ask thee for those things we need. We feel, our Father, that we are in a world of darkness, and trouble, and death, where we cannot behold thy glory; yet we come unto thee in the name of Jesus Christ, thy Son, and ask thee to forgive our sins and past offenses. Fill us with thy Spirit, and accept our praise, while we dedicate ourselves unto thee, and as we have approximated to behold this beautiful morning, the day in which begins a new year, do thou, our heavenly Father, look down in compassion upon us, the creatures of thy care and protection, who dwell upon thy footstool. Increase our knowledge, wisdom, and understanding, that we, thy servants, may be enabled to administer salvation to thy people, even as thou hast committed a dispensation of the same unto us; and while we call on thy name we desire union in thy presence, our Father, to dedicate unto thee this hall, the ground upon which it stands, and all things that appertain unto it. We ask thee to let thy blessing rest upon thy servant Edward Hunter, our beloved brother, who has donated to us the ground upon which this sacred edifice has been erected. We pray thee to enrich him and his family, not only with the good things of this world, but with the riches of eternity also. We ask thee, our Father, to accept the dedication of our hearts this morning, and may we feel the prelude of that power and authority with which thy servants shall be clothed, when they shall go forth and open the door of salvation to the nations and kingdoms of the earth; even thy servants, the seventies, upon whom the burden of thy kingdom does rest, and to whom the keys of the same shall be committed from time to time. We now dedicate this hall unto thee, our Father, and ask thee in the name of thy Son Jesus Christ, to sanctify it and make it holy, and may no foul spirit be suffered to enter it, but may it be filled with thy Spirit that it may be called the gate of heaven, and may all who enter within its doors be made to feel thy love and power. We ask thee to pour out thy Spirit upon the Presidency of the Seventies; wilt thou endow them with knowledge and understanding that they may be enabled to instruct thy servants over whom they are called to preside; and do thou let the same blessings flow freely upon each quorum, that all thy servants may be filled with thy Spirit, and become mighty men before thee that they may go forth and gather the pure in heart, Zion redeemed and Jerusalem rebuilt.   Help us O Lord to separate ourselves from all iniquity, that evildoers may not exist in our midst, but may this people become a holy people, peculiar to thyself, to show forth thy praise in all the world.   Our Father in heaven, we humbly beseech thee to shield and protect us in this city; provide for and sustain us by thy power, that we may be enabled to accomplish the work which thou hast commanded us to do.   Assist us to build the Temple and Nauvoo House; that the truth and light of the everlasting gospel may shine forth from this place, to the honor, praise and glory of thy name.   Regard in mercy the Quorum of the Twelve, at whom the arrows of the destroyer are directed.   Preserve them O Lord, by thine own omnipotent power, that they may stand in holy places and be enabled to disseminate the knowledge of thy kingdom to the inhabitants of the earth; wilt thou sustain us, our Father, that we may perform and accomplish the mighty work whereunto we are called.

'We feel to lament and mourn the loss of our beloved brothers, Joseph and Hyrum, the Prophet and Patriarch, whom thou hast suffered to be martyred for the testimony of the truth; but we thank thee our Father, that although they have been taken from us for the present, yet that same spirit which animated their bosoms, the fruits of which is peace and charity, still remains amongst thy people.   We now commit ourselves into thy care, and ask thee to guide and control us by the council of heaven, through all the shifting and various scenes of mortality, that the numbers of our days may be filled up in usefulness, and we be prepared for that exalted station and rest that remains for the people of God, and the honor, praise, and glory of our salvation, we will ascribe unto thee; for thine is the kingdom, power and glory, worlds without end: Amen.'*

A hymn composed by Elder John Taylor for the dedication of the Seventies' Hall and dedicated to President Brigham Young, was sung by Elder John Kay, assisted by the band, entitled 'The Seer'.

THE SEER

'The Seer;—the Seer;—Joseph the Seer—
I'll sing of the Prophet ever dear,
His equal now cannot be found,—
By searching the wide world around.

*It is doubtful if Brigham Young ever did anything better in oral expression than this beautiful and timely prayer.

With Gods he soared in the realms of day;
And men he taught the heavenly way.
'Mid the foaming billows of angry strife—
He stood at the helm of the ship of life.
The earthly Seer; the heavenly Seer,
I love to dwell on his mem'ry dear;—
The chosen of God, and the friend of men,
He brought the priesthood back again,
He gazed on the past, on the present too;—
And ope'd the heavenly world to view.

Of noble seed—of heavenly birth,
He came to bless the sons of earth;
With keys by the Almighty given,
He opened the full rich stores of heaven,
O'er the world that was wrapt in sable night
Like the sun he spread his golden light.
He strove,—O, how he strove to stay,
The stream of crime in its reckless way—
He urged the wayward to reclaim;
With a mighty mind, and a noble aim.

The saints;—the saints; his only pride,
For them he lived, for them he died!
Their joys were his;—their sorrows too;—
He lov'd the saints;—he lov'd Nauvoo.
Unchanged in death, with a Savior's love
He pleads their cause, in the courts above.
The Seer;—the Seer—Joseph the Seer!
O, how I love his memory dear,
The just and wise, the pure and free,
A father he was, and is to me.
Let fiends now rage in their dark hour;
No matter, he is beyond their power.

He's free;—he's free;—the Prophet's free!
He is where he will ever be.
Beyond the reach of mobs and strife,
He rests unharm'd in endless life.
His home's in the sky;—he dwells with the Gods
Far from the furious rage of mobs.
He died; he died—for those he lov'd
He reigns;—he reigns in the realms above,

He waits with the just who have gone before,
To welcome the saints to Zion's shore;
Shout, shout ye saints—this boon is given,
We'll meet our martyr'd Seer in heaven.'*

REMARKS OF ELDER HEBER C. KIMBALL

Elder Heber C. Kimball addressed the congregation in plain though impressive language, and in his usual philanthropic manner, used a chain as a figure to illustrate the principle of gradation, while in pursuit of celestial enjoyment in worlds to come.

ELDER GEORGE A. SMITH'S DISCOURSE AND ADMONITION ON UNION

Elder George A. Smith offered some very appropriate remarks relative to union. He referred to the Zion Camp, and their expedition to Missouri, and after giving an interesting account on that subject, concluded with an exhortation to union, firmness, and perseverance. He said that if we were of one heart and mind, we might be as the angels are. Perfect union and harmony exist among them. Hence their concert of action, and consequently their influence and power with God; and upon the same principle [continued he] we could make a heaven wherever in the dispensation of Providence, we might be placed, possessing this principle, consonant with the honors, glory and immortality of angels.

At 12 o'clock, a recess of one hour was given each day. At 1 o'clock the house was called to order by President Joseph Young.

DISCOURSE OF ELDER ORSON HYDE ON UNION—AN ILLUSTRATION

Elder Orson Hyde took the stand, and continued the

*This hymn under the circumstances of its rendition would be very impressive in the congregation of the seventies and their families. John Kay had a rich, deep baritone voice and sang with excellent taste and the martyrdom of the Prophet being so recent, within six months, the saints would be greatly affected by the noble sentiments of Elder Taylor's hymn, accompanied with the musical rendition of it.

same subject, [unity of spirit and action], and introduced for a comparison the circumstance of
Illustration of
the Force in
Unity.
the Assyrian king, who gave his son a bundle
of arrows bound in a quiver, and commanded him to break them, which he in vain attempted
to do while they were firmly bound together; but when
they were unbound and separated, the object was easily
effected. This circumstance he likened to this people,
and said that if we were united we would be able to
stand against all the fiery darts that could be hurled
upon us by the adversary of our salvation. Some
having a knowledge of this fact, have used every effort
to divide this people, in order to accomplish their
wicked designs. Some few have been led to the north,
others to the west, and some to the east. Those who
have separated may be broken; but those who remain
together firmly united can never be broken.

After speaking of authorities in the church or kingdom of God, he observed that 'Apostles in the primitive
age of Christianity were first made witnesses
Apostles
Witnesses
for God.
to all the nations of the earth. They were
afterwards made judges of that same people.
Hence the saying of the Apostles, 'know ye not that
the saints shall judge the world?' that is, that generation or people to whom they were sent as witnesses.
(See I Cor. vi:2,3). Indeed they were competent to sit
in judgment upon them, having had an experimental
knowledge of their course of conduct and barbarous
treatment towards the servants of God that were sent
to establish peace among them. Many of whom they
did not only reject, but tortured and slew them in a
cruel manner. This was the fate of the Prophets and
Apostles who vainly attempted to restore them from
their wickedness, assuring them, to use the language
of the scripture: 'As you mete out to others, so shall
it be measured to you again.'

'The declaration of John while on the Isle of Patmos,
through the Spirit of God, declaring things which

would come to pass, says: Give her double
for all her sins. The reason is obvious. The
debt was of a long standing; she had exercised unceasing tyranny over the servants of God, and
refused them justice and mercy. Therefore as they
meted out, double measure shall be given them in return. I have no doubt,' said he, 'but the old scribes,
and pharisees, after scourging the saints in the most
horrid manner, and causing many to seal their testimony with their blood, would go into the Temple with
all the sanctity imaginable and ask God to forgive their
sins; when in reality he would have nothing to do
with the matter, until they had first obtained forgiveness from those whom they had injured, by making
ample satisfaction to them. For proof of this fact just
examine the declaration of Jesus to the Apostles:
Whose soever sins ye remit on earth, shall be remitted
in heaven. And if they were retained on earth they
were to be retained in heaven also.

Measure to Babylon Double.

'Neither can this generation get forgiveness from
God, for the great injuries that they have done us as a
people, without first rendering perfect satisfaction to us
whom they have injured. The elders of this church
have been swift witnesses to Missouri, and all the
world. Hence in vain may they plead to have their
sins remitted until the proper steps are taken.

'Our Prophet has been slain, and the burden of the
kingdom has fallen upon us (the Twelve) and our
lives are sought after; but while the angel
that administers to man is still in attendance,
his life is protected, for the guardian angel
is stronger than death; but when he is withdrawn
humanity is easily overcome. Hence it was with the
Son of God while upon the cross, that even he, the
Savior of the world, could but exclaim: My God, my
God, why hast thou forsaken me! Referring to the
protecting angel whom the Lord had called away,
leaving Jesus in the arms of death; that he might be
taken away from this world of misery and pain to the

Burden of the Kingdom Has Fallen Upon the Twelve.

mansions of God, where he should turn and rule the nations with a rod of iron [i. e. the law, or word of God]. For proof of my assertion I have only to call upon the same individual who exclaimed on the cross: My God why hast thou taken away my protecting angel.

'At the time of his arrest he commanded Peter to put up his sword and gave him to understand that if it were the will of God that he should not drink of the bitter cup (death) that he could call on his Father for ten legions of angels who would eagerly fly to his deliverance. But had he been delivered from the cross, how could the scriptures have been fulfilled? * * *

'Another word respecting the arrows, which by the Spirit of God was made manifest to me last summer.

Efforts to Break up the Unity of the Saints.

There were certain persons who endeavored to divide and draw away the saints from this place, by telling them in secret councils: I have the wink from the Twelve; their minds are to sanction our going to build up, etc. I have got my work laid out by revelation; but you must not say a word to them (the Twelve) about this matter, for if you do you will not get any satisfaction, they will disclaim in public any knowledge of such a move; but I understand them; all is right; and thus hold them in ignorance; also, bind them by solemn oath, not to disclose the matter to any human being, not even to their wives, under the penalty of death. Through hypocrisy and false statements, a few, and but a few, have been deceived and torn from the bundle of arrows by those who have led off from this place. This is an aspiring spirit and is from the devil, and every spirit that refuses to make manifest, is from Lucifer, the prince of darkness. Now let the saints, from this time forth be guarded against all such secrets, councils or confirmations.'

ELDER AMASA M. LYMAN'S DISCOURSE

Elder Amasa M. Lyman expressed his gratitude to

God for the favorable circumstances under which we were placed at present.   Said he, when we contemplate the exalted station and high calling of this august body of elders, we can but associate it with their future destiny.   They, as a people are only forming a character for heaven and immortal happiness.   This certainly should stimulate each man of you to action, and remove every drowsy, careless, idle feeling from their minds, while in each heart the most lively sensations of joy should spring up.   He advised them to embrace every opportunity afforded them to improve their minds and obtain useful knowledge.   Just take the saints out of the world, said he, and soon destruction would sweep the land, as was the fact with Sodom and Gomorrah.

Effects of This Notable Meeting of Elders.

In speaking of the Seventies' Library and Institute Association, he remarked that the seventies were designed to be messengers to every land and kingdom under heaven, and consequently they will have ample opportunities to gather many antiquities, with various books, charts, etc., to deposit in the library for the advancement of art and science, which, with just principles, will go heart and hand unto perfection, being built upon truth, the foundation of the Apostles and Prophets, Jesus Christ the Chief Corner Stone, which shall sound out from this voluminous institute, and with its benign influence organize and harmonize the vast extent of the world.

The Seventies' Library and Institute.

Friday, December 27.—Fourth and fifth quorums met.   Prayer by Elder George A. Smith.

The order of the meeting was explained by President Joseph Young.

HEBER C. KIMBALL'S ADDRESS

Elder Heber C. Kimball then delivered a short address upon the authorities of the kingdom of God, and in passing on, he set forth the order as to endowment, and informed the saints that every man and woman must stand in his proper place and station, being subject to the powers that be, in order to be exalted to glory, honor, and immortality in the eternal world. 'It is even so in the resurrection from the dead, as St.

Joseph Smith's Place in the Resurrection.

Paul informs us that Christ is the first fruits of the resurrection from the dead in the primitive age, and so will Joseph Smith be in this dispensation. Joseph will be the first man who will rise from the dead, and then all men according to their proper order.

'I will tell the seventies and everybody else, if you cannot and will not submit to the authorities that God

Submit to the Powers That Be.

has placed in his church over you, you had better back out now, and not attempt to proceed further; if you are ever saved it will be by obedience to the order of God's kingdom here on the earth, and this order is in subordination to that order which is in the heavens. According to the important station the seventies are called to fill in this last dispensation, they should be careful to walk uprightly and act justly, shunning every appearance of evil and never condescend to do anything mean.'

Adjourned one hour.

Met pursuant to adjournment.

ELDER JOHN TAYLOR'S DISCOURSE—RELATIONSHIP OF
THE CHURCH TO GOD

Elder John Taylor took the stand and proceeded to lay before us the pure principles of life and salvation, reminding us that we were the people that the Lord had chosen and set apart to accomplish the great and mighty work of the last days, which was spoken of by the prophets of old. 'No other people,' said he, 'can possibly do this work, for unto us the keys of this last dispensation with the power of the priesthood is given; consequently there is no people under the whole heaven that sustain the same relationship with God, as we do. What knowledge have the world of God's laws or his ways? They don't know enough in reality to save a mosquito.

'I do not mean to say that there is no learning in the world, for I am aware of the fact that there is far more of what the world calls wisdom in the midst of the inhabitants of the earth than can be found here; but a learned fool is no better than an illiterate one, if the Apostle Paul's judgment can be admitted as proof. He told the people of his day that the wisdom of this world was foolishness with God. When I ask what knowledge the world has of God or his government, I mean to be understood as speaking of that knowledge that comes from God, communicated to us through the channel of revelation, for without it we know nothing correctly, no more than the brute beasts who are led by the instinct of nature. Consequently, brethren, when you go to declare the plain truth of the kingdom of God, the gospel of Jesus Christ, you should never shrink from your calling, nor succumb to the learned because of the advantage they have over you by reason of literary attainments, for God is with you, and will give you a mouth and wisdom by which you shall be delivered from the strong arm of violence.

The Elders of the Church and the Learning of the World.

'Remember the race is not to the swift nor the battle to the strong; but to those who trust in the Lord. When the Twelve were called to bear the gospel of this kingdom to the inhabitants of Europe, there were not many wise among them, speaking after the manner of men; yet we believed him faithful who had chosen us, and as little children we trusted in him for wisdom and understanding to do his will; for his will was our pleasure, and in the short space of two years, about two thousand souls were given to us in the ministry. I speak of these things that you may know in whom to put your trust and confidence; for should you desire self-esteem, and take the honor to yourselves, you soon would sink to shame and disgrace. You are the heralds of salvation, and through your faithfulness, obedience and persever-

The Race Not to the Swift Nor the Battle to the Strong.

ance, you may be exalted to kings and priests unto God
in the eternal worlds.

'Some of you may be called to go to foreign lands to
administer salvation to nations that are to you unknown. The redemption of your deceased
relatives are also required at your hands.
Hence you discover your relationship with
God and the responsibility under which you are acting.
Be faithful in him who has called you, and he will
deliver you from every snare, pit, and temptation that
awaits you. I would rather trust in God for bread,
than to trust in the princes of this world. I speak of
these things for your interest; then let your hearts be
comforted. When we (the Twelve) left this place,
on our mission to England, a journey of near five
thousand miles to be accomplished without a penny in
our pockets, our only resource was to trust in the Dis-
poser of all events to supply our returning wants. And
our prayers were heard and answered according to the
desires of our hearts.

Admonitions to the Seventies.

'When you go forth, lift up your heads like kings and
trust in the name of Israel's God; for the very hairs
of your head are numbered and will not fall
to the ground without notice. Remembering at all times to uphold each other by the
prayer and power of faith, and God will bless you
and your labors.'

Lift Up Your Heads Like Kings.

The following prayer was made by President Joseph
Young on the fourth day of the dedication.

PRAYER OF PRESIDENT JOSEPH YOUNG—SECOND PRAYER OF DEDICATION

'O God, our heavenly Father, we humbly pray thee in the name
of Jesus Christ, thy Son, to bless us with the remission of all our sins
and vanities; for we are subject to follies and vanities. But we thank
thee, our Father, that thou hast prepared a way and provided means
whereby we may be enabled to overcome, and elude the grasp of the
destroyer. We ask thee, our Father, to guide us by the Spirit, that

we may feel thy love shed abroad in our hearts, and fully appreciate every blessing that flows from thy liberal hands. As thou hast seen fit to break the silence of heaven, and again communicated thy will to the sons of men that dwell upon the earth, we ask thee to indict our petitions as we present ourselves in thy presence to dedicate this hall, for we now dedicate it and ourselves unto thee, and ask thee to let a special blessing rest upon him who has bequeathed to us the ground upon which this hall now stands. We remember before thee, our Father, the Building Committee, who were appointed to build the Temple. Let their hands be strengthened to carry on the work, and grant that the house may be finished according to thy commandments unto thy people, that thy servants may receive their endowments and be clothed upon with power and authority, to carry thy word to the scattered remnants of thy people. Let the Council of the Twelve come in remembrance before thee. Bless them, O Lord, with all that pertains to them. Also the quorums of the seventies, who have built this hall, not particularly by thy commandment, but in honor of thy name. Bless them and their families when they shall go to the islands of the sea, to preach the acceptable year of the Lord, and declare the truth of heaven, the gospel of the Son of God. Let them become mighty men in pulling down the strongholds of satan, and bursting the prison doors of darkness, and spread the light of the everlasting gospel to earth's remotest bounds. Bless the poor who are destitute; open the hearts of the rich, so that the principle of sympathy and charity may predominate and reign in their bosoms, that they may impart of their substance to feed the poor. Finally our Father, we ask thee to guide the destinies of this meeting to thy praise, for thine is the kingdom, power and glory, worlds without end: Amen.'

REMARKS OF ELDER JOHN E. PAGE, ONE OF THE TWELVE

Elder John E. Page having arrived here a short time previous with his family from Pittsburgh, being present, was requested to render an account of his stewardship, which he cheerfully assented to.

He arose and proceeded in a concise manner and gave a very interesting narrative of the events connected with his mission during his absence from this city. He also made many pertinent remarks upon the principles of the kingdom of God, and the organization of the same. He then added that the seventies were in the hands of God as a lever, by

The Seventies a Lever in the Hands of God.

which he would turn the world upside down and establish his covenant with the inhabitants of every land; that light and truth should prevail where the powers of darkness, superstition and error had long swayed universal dominion; and finally concluded by assuring the saints that he was one with them, and gave his testimony to the present organization of the church in the most solemn manner, and gave place.

THE GREAT DISCOURSE OF ELDER ORSON PRATT

Monday, December 30.—Elder Orson Pratt took the stand and after many appropriate remarks upon the principle of union, he made a quotation from the *Book of Mormon*: 'Adam fell that man might be—men are that they might have joy', and reasoned upon the correctness of the saying. He said that 'if Adam had not partaken of the fruit of the tree of life, he never could have obeyed the commandment enjoined upon him and the woman, which was to multiply and replenish the earth; (as will appear in the sequel) neither could he have appreciated the blessings of paradise without an experience of the opposite.

Adam Fell That Man Might Be

'The Apostle Paul plainly declared that the man was not in the transgression, but the woman; hence we infer that Adam was acquainted of the penalty annexed to the law of God, and with his future destiny, before he partook of the fruit. It might be said that out of two evils the man upon reflection chose the least. The first was the seduction of the woman, by the tempter, which evil would terminate in the banishment of the woman from the garden of paradise, it being one of the penalties annexed to the law for the offense already committed. Adam knowing this fact chose to suffer the penalty of the law with the woman, rather than to be deprived of her society; consequently he followed her into the transgression, as St. Paul remarks. The creature (Adam) was made subject to sin, not willingly; but by reason of him who has subjected the same in hope. The hope

Man and Woman in the Fall.

spoken of here, by Paul, must allude to the redemption of the woman and her posterity from the fall to immortality and eternal life.

'From this last quotation of the Apostle, we have reason to believe that Adam was encouraged to follow the woman into the transgression, and to people the earth. Whether Adam understood the law of redemption prior to the fall or not, I shall not decide; but shall be contented to submit the circumstance to your consideration. A word to the wise is sufficient.'

It was designed at the commencement to have continued each discourse throughout the week; but as that would occupy entirely too much space, we will conclude with these brief sketches, already given. Truly this was a time and season of rejoicing with the saints. Peace and harmony, brotherly love, kindness, and charity prevails throughout.

Comment on the Conference.

The remembrance of this glorious jubilee will never be erased from the minds of those who were participants. Each family was provided with fruits, nuts and every desert that heart could wish. Well might it be said that the saints enjoyed a feast of fat things.

JOHN D. LEE, Clerk.'

CHURCH PUBLICATIONS

The following works were published during the year 1844:

Times and Seasons, semi-monthly, twenty-three numbers, octavo, containing three hundred and sixty-seven pages.

Nauvoo Neighbor, folio, weekly.

Both of these papers were published at Nauvoo, John Taylor, editor. *The Times and Seasons* devoted principally to the publication of the faith and history of the church. The *Nauvoo Neighbor* included the principal items of news, general intelligence and advertisements.

Latter-day Saints Millennial Star, octavo 16 pp. monthly, Liverpool, England; Thomas Ward editor."

CHAPTER XXVII

CAMPAIGN AGAINST WICKEDNESS BOTH BY THE
CHURCH AUTHORITIES AND THE NAUVOO
CITY COUNCIL—VILLAINY OF
NAUVOO'S ENEMIES

"*Wednesday, January* 1, 1845.—Accompanied by
Elder Heber C. Kimball I went to Bishop David Evans'
ward south of Nauvoo City, and solemnized a marriage.

The following was written in council:

A WORD TO THE CHURCHES ABROAD FROM THE TWELVE

(*First Greeting of* 1845)

'The Twelve, feeling a great anxiety for the unity and prosperity
of the whole church, and, more especially, for the benefit of the
branches of the church abroad in the world, would, after mature
deliberation, and as a matter of counsel, (approving of the course,
management, and matter of the *Times and Seasons* and *Nauvoo
Neighbor*), recommend that suitable pains and exertions be taken by
both elders and members, to obtain these papers from Nauvoo. A
unity of effort, to circulate these papers, not only among the saints,
but among the people at large, will greatly facilitate the labors of the
traveling elders, while it disseminates correct principles, sanctioned by
the highest authorities in the church, and at the same time, opens a
channel of communication, best calculated to win the good feelings of
the community, while the affections, and zeal of the brethren, are
harmonized, by the same doctrines, the same rules; and the same
laudable purposes.

The kingdoms of the world continue and extend by division,
but the saints can only expect to prevail by wisdom and counsel;
we therefore, in connection with the union which prevails among
the saints here, and for the prosperity of the branches abroad, and as
a reward of merit to the honorable standing of the *Times and
Seasons* and *Nauvoo Neighbor*, and for their unyielding energies in
the cause of truth 'through good and through evil report', bespeak
for them a liberal subscription and ready remittance. May light and
liberality be equal.

We have just entered upon the threshold of a new year, and may our Father in heaven, have so much respect to his saints and people, as to bless the pure in heart, pure in purpose, and coworkers for the redemption of man, until the light from Zion extends round the globe and 'all Israel shall be saved'; and then we can rejoice and say: it was good for us that we followed the counsel of the Lord.

Brethren, we greet you with peace, and may the Lord bless you with righteousness.

Done in council, this first day of January, 1845.

[Signed]   BRIGHAM YOUNG, President.'

Elder Orson Hyde wrote an article which was published in the *Times and Seasons* advising the saints in the east to beware of land speculators professing to be Latter-day Saints, who were trying to sell lands in Illinois for lands and other property in the east.

ELDER ORSON HYDE'S LETTER OF CAUTION: BEWARE OF DECEPTION!

'Tidings have just reached us here [in Nauvoo] that certain men in the eastern countries, Ohio and other places, professing to be Latter-day Saints, are very busy in selling Illinois lands, and exchanging them for real estate and other property in the east. I would inform all the saints everywhere, that this operation is a field for greater and more extensive fraud than any other with which I am acquainted.

You may give some irresponsible, worthless creature a clear title to your homes in the east, with the expectation of finding good land here in exchange with a good title, etc., etc. But when you come, you may find your land in a swamp, in the middle of an extensive prairie, ten or fifteen miles from any timber. I will venture to give it as my opinion that those miserable speculators are knaves and villains; professing to be saints, and trying to help the church and build up the cause, when they have no license from the authorities of the church here.

I say again, beware of those 'wolves in sheep's clothing'. Whenever any such operation is deemed beneficial to the saints by those who know and understand these things, some competent responsible person will be sent, duly authorized with documents from under the hands of the Twelve that reside in this city. Otherwise you may find to your sorrow that you will have to pay for your lands twice over before you get good titles. I therefore warn you, as a watchman of your interests, to hold on upon your homes until you know certainly what you are doing.

[Signed]   ORSON HYDE.'

In company with Elders Heber C. Kimball, Orson Pratt, George A. Smith, Willard Richards and Amasa

M. Lyman, I spent the afternoon and evening, with our wives, at Hiram Kimball's; had a pleasant time: the propriety of settling a new country was discussed.

Settling in a New Country Discussed.

Mr. Jacob B. Backenstos delivered a speech in the house of representatives, Springfield, against the senate bill for the unconditional repeal of the Nauvoo Charter, wherein he ably set forth the injuries and persecutions suffered by the citizens of Nauvoo.

Repeal of Nauvoo Charter Before Illinois Legislature.

Elder Parley P. Pratt, having been appointed to the presidency of the eastern churches, published a proclamation to the saints in his presidency explaining the duties of his calling and the several duties of the officers and members under his special charge.

Elder Parley P. Pratt's Proclamation.

Thursday, 2.—Elders Heber C. Kimball, Orson Pratt and myself held a council at the Tithing Office with Bishops Newel K. Whitney and George Miller, Trustees and Alpheus Cutler and Reynolds Cahoon, Temple Committee: the object of the council was to inspire the Temple Committee with confidence and satisfaction.

Evening, in company with Elders Heber C. Kimball, John Taylor, and others I took supper with Dr. Willard Richards: sixteen of the brethren and sisters who first embraced the work in Preston, England, were present.

First Preston Reunion of Elders and Saints.

Friday, 3.—Elder Wilford Woodruff and accompanying missionaries landed in Liverpool having been twenty-five days at sea.

Saturday, 4.—A conference was held in Hartford, Connecticut, at which thirty-six members were represented including six officers. Elder M. Sirrine presided.

Work in Connecticut Extended.

Evening, I met with the city police at the Seventies' Hall and gave them suitable instructions.

DISCOURSES OF ELDERS YOUNG AND KIMBALL AGAINST
WICKEDNESS

Sunday, 5.—I went to the stand and addressed the saints on the necessity of having more order and putting down iniquity, and exhorted the brethren to rise up *en masse,* and put down the thieving, swearing, gambling, bogus-making, retailing spirituous liquors, bad houses, and all abominations practiced in our midst by our enemies, who, after they could not live among us any longer would go out to the world and publish that these things were practiced by us. I severely rebuked the civil authorities of the city for their want of energy in the discharge of their duty, and censured parents and guardians for not keeping their children from prowling round the streets at night; and remarked that if we did not as a people uproot such things, they would uproot us, and we would have to leave before we had done the things the Lord had commanded us to do. Elder Kimball followed me, treating on the same subject: a large congregation—pleasant day.

Movement of the Saints to California Considered.

Tuesday, 7.—I met in council with my brethren of the Twelve. The subject of sending a company to California was further discussed; also the propriety of sending to the branches of the church abroad for teams to help the expedition.

Wednesday, 8.—I attended a meeting which was got up by my brother, Joseph Young, of all our relatives and connections. Elder Phineas Richards presided. Elder Phineas Richards, John Haven, myself, Joseph Young, Heber C. Kimball, John Taylor, John Smith and Lucy Smith, mother of the Prophet, severally addressed the meeting.

The Young Family Social Reunion.

Evening, I met with the Twelve, bishops, high council, and city officials in relation to the election of city officers: the members of the Quorum of the Twelve present declined accepting any nomination.

The police held a meeting this afternoon; the Twelve

and Father John Smith attended and partook of dinner with them: it was an agreeable and interesting time.

Friday, 10.——The Twelve, the Temple Committee, the surveyors (Sherwood and Ripley) and Bishop Whitney, Trustee, met with the Committee of the Nauvoo Manufacturing Association respecting erecting the contemplated dam in the Mississippi.

The lesser priesthood met at the Music Hall. Bishop N. K. Whitney presided. He stated the object of the meeting was to fill up the quorums in order that the saints might be visited by the lesser priesthood; he recommended that the bishops establish in their respective wards the manufacturing of palm leaf and straw hats, willow baskets and other business that children are capable of learning, that they may be raised to industrious habits; he further stated his determination to have a feast prepared for the poor that their hearts might be made to rejoice. Bishops Edward Hunter, Isaac Higbee and others made some very interesting remarks. Bishop Whitney gave the lesser priesthood a faithful charge in relation to ferreting out iniquity. Four priests and ten teachers were ordained.

Lesser Priesthood Quorums Set in Order.

Saturday, 11.——City council met and transacted much business. Passed an ordinance authorizing and licensing Brigham Young to run a ferry across the Mississippi at Nauvoo in place of Joseph Smith, martyred.

With Elders Taylor, Richards and Phelps, I spent the evening writing an epistle to the churches on the gathering.

Sunday, 12.——A general meeting of the seventies convened at their hall; I attended and informed them that the Twelve designed to select a number of experienced elders from among the quorums to take short missions through this state and Iowa, for the purpose of frustrating the designs of wicked and ungodly men, who are endeavoring to poison the minds of the people by misrepresenting us and circulating base and false reports about us

Mission Projected for the Seventies.

as a people. There were a great many people who knew nothing about the true character of this church. From false reports many are led to suppose that we are all a set of thieves, blacklegs and bogus-makers, but we will undeceive them, that is, the honest in heart, who will listen to the elders sent among them. One hundred brethren were ordained into the seventies. The fifteenth and sixteenth quorums were organized.

IMPORTANT DISCOURSES BY ELDERS HEBER C. KIMBALL AND ORSON PRATT

Elder Heber C. Kimball preached to the saints in the Concert Hall on the subject of increase and expansion. Elder Orson Pratt advanced an idea pertaining to the magnitude of the planetary system, illustrative of the enlargement of the saints.

Elder Kimball and I attended the high priests' quorum and selected fifty of the members to go on missions till April 1st in the surrounding counties.

Evening, attended prayer meeting.

Monday, 13.—The city council met in Brother W. Richards' office, and adopted the following Preamble and Resolutions:

THE VOICE OF NAUVOO

(Proceedings of the City Council)

PREAMBLE

'It is with feelings of deep and inexpressible regret that we learn that the inhabitants of various parts of this state are seeking to accumulate all the real and supposed crimes of the whole community [of Nauvoo] for the secret or ostensible purpose of raising a tide of influence against the Mormon community that shall sweep them into irrecoverable ruin. This course of conduct, originating with our mortal enemies and gathering in its wake, other men that would revolt at the idea of lending a hand to oppress a long abused people that are struggling against foes within and foes without; [which] is at the present almost insupportable to our feelings. We have scarcely laid by our mourning weeds for murdered men, whom we promptly surrendered up to the state of Illinois for an equitable trial—And now we see in embryo another campaign to spill yet more blood and effect an utter extermination and massacre. We sought to rid our city of counterfeiters and blacklegs; these together with our foes without and within, had established a printing press of unparalleled rancor and malignity. But our efforts to obtain freedom from such vicious monsters cost us much tribulation and precious blood.

The impunity thus far granted the murderers by the senate and other authorities of the state of Illinois, has emboldened them and their apologists to set on foot a series of other exciting causes that they hope will either destroy this community, or prevent their criminals from being brought to punishment. We have not so much fear that our enemies will succeed in their fiendish designs against us, as we have that the peace and good order of the people of this state will be disturbed, and fearful anarchy and bloody misrule will ensue among those who listen to and countenance the fell designs of those who are stealing from quiet citizens of the state and palming upon them a spurious and false currency, and charging to the Mormons their own crimes. If they shall succeed, the citizens will be involved in continual larcenies, and neighborhood broils, and crimes, the end of which cannot now be foreseen. We deprecate such evils and calamities because we desire the good of all mankind; as the gratuitous labors of the greater portion of our citizens in spreading truth throughout the world under much poverty and suffering, abundantly prove.

As for us, our course is fixed, and while we are peaceable and loyal to the Constitution and laws of our country, and are ever willing to join hands with the honest, virtuous, and patriotic in suppressing crime and punishing criminals, we will leave our enemies to judge, whether it would not be better to make Nauvoo one universal burying ground, before we suffer ourselves to be driven from our hard-earned and lawful homes, by such high-handed oppression, and it may yet become a question to be decided by the community, whether the Mormons will, after having witnessed their best men murdered without redress, quietly and patiently, suffer their enemies to wrench from them the last shreds of their Constitutional rights; and whether they will not make their city one great sepulchre, rather than be the humble devotees at the shrine of mobocracy. But for the satisfaction of all concerned, we reiterate in the following resolutions, sentiments that we have always expressed in all places as occasion demanded:

Resolved; That the greater part of the thefts which have been complained of, are not, in our opinion, true in fact, but have been trumped up by inimical persons, in order to cover their aggressive doings, with plausibility, and entice honest and unwary citizens to unite with them in the same uncompromising hostility against this people.

Resolved; That we defy the world to substantiate a single instance, where we have concealed criminals, or screened them from justice; but, on the contrary, always have been, and now are, extremely anxious that they should be ferreted out and brought to justice; and to this end would esteem it a favor, that if any person should lose property, or have good and sufficient reason to suspect any place of containing apparatus for making bogus or counterfeit money, that such person would follow up, trace out, and make diligent search, for all such property and apparatus, and if they can trace it into this city, we pledge ourselves to assist them legally, to the extent of our abilities in so laudable an undertaking.

Resolved; That it is our opinion that very many scoundrels, such as thieves, robbers, bogus-makers, counterfeiters asd murderers, have been induced from reports published in the *Warsaw Signal,* to flock into this county in order to carry on their evil practices, knowing that it would be immediately charged upon the Mormons, and thereby they escape—and although we think that the reports of thefts have been very much exaggerated, yet we know from dear bought experience that such things do exist, and further we doubt not there may be some such characters prowling in and about our city.

Resolved; That we are extremely anxious to ferret out and bring to justice, all such persons, if any, that are within the limits of our city, and for this purpose we have authorized our mayor to enlarge the police, to any number, not exceeding five hundred, and we also pledge ourselves to double our diligence, and call upon our citizens to assist in ridding our city and country of all such infamous characters.

Done, in council, this 13th day of January, 1845.

[Signed]   DANIEL SPENCER, Mayor.

W. Richards, Recorder.'

Tuesday, 14.—

MEETING OF THE CITIZENS

'At a large meeting of the citizens of Nauvoo, convened at the stand, on the 14th day of January, 1845, Daniel Spencer, mayor of the city, was called to the chair, and James Sloan appointed secretary; and Samuel Bent, Alpheus Cutler, Charles C. Rich, Phineas Richards, and David Fullmer, were appointed a committee, to draft a Preamble and Resolutions, expressive of the sense of this meeting on the proceedings of the city council, and for the action of this meeting. The committee retired and in a short time, returned the following, which were adopted unanimously:

PREAMBLE

'Whereas, the city council of the city of Nauvoo, have presented to this meeting, a Preamble and sundry Resolutions setting forth the fact, that enemies to the people of this city, and as we believe, enemies to the common welfare of the people of this state, are attempting to get up an extensive popular excitement, prejudicial to this people and the country at large; and *whereas,* said Resolutions set forth an unqualified reprobation of all unlawful and villainous conduct whether under the false color of Mormonism, or the real guise of mobbers, blacklegs, bogus-makers, thieves, 'wolf hunters', or murderers; *therefore*, we hereby express our perfect concurrence in the said Preamble and Resolutions.

And *whereas*, the *Warsaw Signal*, the *Alton Telegraph*, and the *Quincy Whig*, have been, as we believe, industriously engaged in circulating falsehood; disseminating discord, and the principles of mobocracy; and *whereas*, Mormon extermination, pillage, robbery, and murder, have received both countenance and apology in these scurrilous prints, as we believe; and *whereas*, the pen of murderers, as we believe, has occupied the columns of these papers in order to defend the cries of innocent blood that ascends to heaven for vengeance; and *whereas*, a large share of the thefts spoken of and blazed through the land, are wholly without existence when traced out, as appears not only from the instance recorded in the Governor's Message concerning horse stealing, but from other similar instances, too numerous to mention; and *whereas*, it has been zealously reported, that much stolen goods could be traced to Nauvoo, and that no citizen could enter our city to search for thieves, and stolen goods, because the thief and goods would be screened from detection by the Mormon fraternity, and the person in search, would be in jeopardy of his life; and *whereas*, thieves and counterfeiters have in some instances fled to our city, either under the mistaken apprehension that we would screen them, or from a malignant design to palm upon us their own crimes, and thereby draw us under the lash of persecution; and *whereas*, it can be proved that individuals, in order to swell the list of Mormon depredations, have reported property to be stolen, which at another time they have acknowledged, they sold the same property and received pay; and *whereas*, bee yards have been robbed, the hives left at Mormon doors, to palm the theft upon us, when the honey has been found in the houses of our enemies; and *whereas*, an innumerable number of such infamous tricks have been played upon us, by our enemies, as we believe, for the purpose of blackening our character in the eyes of honest men; and *whereas*, our city is nightly infested with a set of outlandish men, who we believe, visit us for no good purpose, who do not appear to have any lawful business, but rather, as we believe, are endeavoring to scatter amongst us, their bogus and counterfeits, prostitute the virtue of the place, deposit stolen goods, or steal from us, and by every means in their power, sow the seeds of discord, strife, confusion, mobocracy, and murder, that in the end, they may uproot our beautiful city; and *whereas*, that in some instances, when the ministers of justice have visited our city, at the dark hour of midnight, for the purpose of making legal arrests, as they say; we believe what is reported to us, that they have employed runners to steal the saddles and bridles from their own horses, while in our city, for the purpose of damning us in the eyes of the community.

And *whereas*, the chief magistrate of this state, after a second and protracted visit to this city, and much pains taken to investigate the charge of promiscuous stealing, reports to the legislature as follows:

'Justice, however, required me here to say, that I have investigated the charge of promiscuous stealing, and find it to be greatly exaggerated. I could not ascertain that there were a greater proportion of thieves in that community, than in any other of the same number of inhabitants; and perhaps if the city of Nauvoo, were compared with St. Louis, or any other western city, the proportion would not be so great.'

And *whereas*, the printing office of our open and avowed enemy Dr. Foster, was set on fire, in this city by himself, or by his instruction, as we believe, to fan the flame of mobocracy, which fire was only prevented by our vigilant police.

And *whereas*, we firmly believe, that our enemies in this city, have several times attempted to fire their own buildings and have only been prevented by the diligence of our officers—

Therefore, be it resolved, unanimously, that we will use all lawful means in our power to assist the public to prevent stealing and bogus-making, and bring the offenders to justice.

Resolved, that to prevent further depredations in our city, by lawless desperadoes from abroad, we approve the raising of 500 police by this city.

Resolved, unanimously, That we invite all honest men to watch closely their property, and arrest all thieves; and if they shall catch a thief in the act of stealing, challenge him to stand, and if he refuses so to do, and flees, so far as the Mormons are concerned, we will be satisfied if the owners of the property shall speedily send after him a writ of *habeas corpus* sealed with lead to arrest his progress, but after all, should the thief prove to be a mobocrat, alas! alas!! O what a pity!

Resolved, unanimously, That 50 delegates be sent to the surrounding country to inform the people of the designs of our enemies now concocting in their secret and public meetings, so that the honest part of the community, may unite with us, to prevent stealing and secure peace.

Resolved, That these proceedings be published in the papers at Nauvoo, with a request that other papers copy them.

[Signed] DANIEL SPENCER, Chairman.

James Sloan, Secretary.'*

AN EPISTLE OF THE TWELVE TO THE CHURCH OF JESUS CHRIST OF LATTER-DAY SAINTS IN ALL THE WORLD, GREETING

'*Beloved Brethren*:—

As the purposes of God roll forth and the work of the Lord hastens to its accomplishment, it is necessary that we, as watchmen upon the towers of Zion, communicate with you from time to time,

Times and Seasons, vol. vi, pp. 773-5.

and put you in possession of such information as may be deemed necessary for your welfare, for the furtherance of the cause of God, and for the fulfilling of these great purposes which our heavenly Father has designed in the rolling forth of the dispensation of the fulness of times, 'spoken of by all the prophets since the world was.'

The Temple has progressed very rapidly since the death of our beloved Prophet and Patriarch. The diligence of those employed, and the willingness of the saints to contribute, have brought it to a state of forwardness, which has far exceeded our most sanguine expectations. You have already been informed that the capitals of the columns were all on; we have now to announce to you that by the time the spring opens we expect that every stone will be cut to complete the Temple, and it will not take long to lay them, when they are all prepared.

Progress on the Temple Since the Prophet's Death.

Great numbers of carpenters, masons, and other workmen are daily engaged in this arduous undertaking, so that not only is stone being prepared, but the sash, flooring, seats, and other things are progressing rapidly; and it is our design, if possible, so to rush the work forward that the building will be enclosed, and certain portions of it in that state of forwardness, so that we shall be prepared to commence giving the saints their endowments next fall; that the elders of Israel may be prepared by the power and spirit of the great Jehovah, to fulfill with dignity and honor, the great work devolving upon them to perform.

We wish to inform you brethren that the work in which we are engaged is great and mighty, it is the work of God and we have to rush it forth against the combined powers of earth and hell, we feel it to be an arduous undertaking whilst you, many of you have been enjoying ease, prosperity, and peace at home. We have had to combat mobs and to wade through blood to fulfill the work devolving upon us, and you: we have been exerting our energies, expended our money; and employing our time, our labor, our influence, and means for the accomplishment of this purpose; and feeling confident dear brethren, that you would like to share with us the labor, as well as the glory, we make the following requests:

Difficulties Under Which the Work Had to be Carried on

We wish all the young, middle aged, and able bodied men who have it in their hearts to stretch forth this work with power, to come to Nauvoo, prepared to stay during the summer; and to bring with them means to sustain themselves with, and to enable us to forward this work; to bring with them teams, cattle, sheep, gold, silver, brass, iron, oil, paints and tools; and let those who are within market distance of Nauvoo bring with them provisions to sustain themselves and others during their stay. And let all the churches send all the money, cloth, and clothing, together with the raw material for manufacturing purposes; such as cotton,

A Call For Help.

cotton yarn, wool, steel, iron, brass, etc., etc., as we are preparing to go into extensive manufacturing operations, and all these things can be applied to the furtherance of the Temple.

There was a font erected in the basement story of the Temple, for the baptism of the dead, the healing of the sick and other purposes; this font was made of wood, and was only intended for the present use; but it is now removed, and as soon as the stone cutters get through with the cutting of the stone for the walls of the Temple, they will immediately proceed to cut the stone for and erect a font of hewn stone. This font will be of an oval form and twelve feet in length and eight wide, with stone steps and an iron railing; this font will stand upon twelve oxen, which will be cast of iron or brass, or perhaps hewn stone. If of brass, polished; if of iron, bronzed;—upon each side of the font there will be a suite of rooms fitted up for the washings. In the recesses, on each side of the arch, on the first story, there will be a suite of rooms or ante-chambers, lighted with the first row of circular windows. As soon as a suitable number of those rooms are completed we shall commence the endowment.

Temporary Font in the Temple.

Brethren, inasmuch as you have long desired blessings, come up to the help of the Lord, and help to forward the work that we are engaged in; for we trust that these rooms will be finished by the first of December next, so that you may enter therein and receive wisdom, knowledge, understanding, and the power of the priesthood, which you have so long desired; that you may be prepared to go forth to the nations of the earth and build up the kingdom in all parts of the world; gather up Israel, redeem Zion; rebuild Jerusalem; and fill the whole earth with the knowledge of God.

While upon this subject we would remind the brethren of their duty in tithing according to the laws, and commandments given through Joseph the Prophet, it is the duty of all saints to tithe themselves one-tenth of all they possess when they enter into the new and everlasting covenant; and then one-tenth of their interest, or income, yearly afterwards. If the brethren will attend to this strictly, and send up the sum by agents appointed by us, whose names you will see in this paper, then we shall hold ourselves responsible for all monies and properties delivered to those agents that the names of the several individuals who send their tithing by the legal agents may be entered upon the book of the *Law of the Lord;* if this is not attended to strictly by the branches of the church abroad, they may be disappointed when they find that they have sent their means by unauthorized agents, who have not made returns to the Trustees, and their names are not recorded as they would have been if they had hearkened to counsel. On the subject of regular appointed agencies we would refer you to an article written by the Trustees, Bishops Whitney and Miller, and published in the *Times and Seasons* of December, 1844.

The Law of Tithing.

We would further say to the brethren that if there should be any of the churches to whom these agents do not come, let them send their means by honest men whom they may select from among themselves, and in whom they can place confidence; but we cannot be responsible for the conduct of any agents that we do not send, and can only give credit for that we receive. And as the churches abroad have been much imposed upon by designing men, without authority, we would warn them against such persons, and advise them not to pay their funds to traveling elders and others without a written authority from us to which shall be attached the private seal of the Twelve and their names published as above stated. Those men that we shall select for agents will be men of honor, men of integrity and respectability, in whom we can confide, and who are responsible, and able, and willing to enter into bonds for the faithful performance of their duty. This course will prevent those many impositions which have heretofore been practiced by villains wearing the garb of saints, and place the churches in a situation that they can forward their tithings with safety.

There is now in the city eight of the Twelve all in good health and spirits; our city is progressing, and the work of the Lord is rolling forth with unprecedented rapidity.

Thus, dear brethren, we have given you, in part, some of the measures and calculations, which we mean to carry into effect for your salvation, and for the furtherance of the salvation of the world. We have commenced a new year, and, as the Lord says: 'All victory and glory is brought to pass unto you through diligence, faithfulness and prayers of faith,' so we cannot but hope, that you will renew your exertions, your prayers, and your tithings, for the benefit of Zion, that she may arise and shine for the good of all people.

We cannot say everything in one short epistle, therefore, from time to time, as the Lord puts into our hearts instructions, we shall give them unto you: solemnly praying that you will increase your faith, double your diligence, walk by light and obedience, and be instant in season, to do the will of our Father in heaven:—Beware of ungodly men, who creep among you unawares; they are clouds without water, driven about by winds, and will finally be blown into outer darkness.

Our counsel to the traveling elders abroad is for them to return to Nauvoo by the 6th of April, to conference or as soon as possible afterwards, and before they leave, it will be necessary for them to ordain good and wise men to preside over the branches during their absence.

May the grace of our Lord Jesus Christ, a veneration for the names of the first Martyrs, first Elders, and first Prophets of the nineteenth century, inspire your hearts, to hear counsel, to keep counsel, to practice holiness, live the life of saints, and 'die the death of the righteous, that your last end may be like his'.

Done in council, at Nauvoo, this 14th day of January, 1845.

[Signed]   BRIGHAM YOUNG, President.

Willard Richards, Clerk.'*

Wednesday, 15.—I went to the Temple, afterwards to the stone quarry; Brother Albert P. Rockwood reported sixty-two hands and six teams engaged today in the quarry.

Evening, went to the Seventies' Hall.   The brethren of the Twelve, the high council, Trustees-in-Trust, Assignment of
Missionaries. many high priests and seventies were present.   The elders appointed on missions were assigned to their respective districts.   Elder Kimball instructed the elders to be fathers and not masters, and to be wise in their requirements of tithing from the saints abroad.   I gave some general instructions, and counseled the elders to gather all to Nauvoo who could leave their families and especially the young men to help complete the Temple.   Heavy thunder, lightning and rain.

Thursday, 16.—I spent most of the day with Elder Kimball correcting his history.

Friday, 17.—Mr. Joseph A. Kelting, deputy sheriff of Hancock county published the following in the *Times and Seasons* (p. 775):

TO THE PUBLIC

'Nauvoo, Jan. 17, 1845.

As much has been said concerning stealing and secreting property in this city, for the purpose of giving an impression abroad that Nauvoo was a grand *depot* for concealing stolen property, and that the Mormon community was concerned in it,—I will state, that so far as my knowledge extends, concerning the matter, I have ascertained that stolen property has been brought by way of Nauvoo, from the country, and then crossed over the Mississippi river to Iowa, and back into the territory some ten or twelve miles; where the thieves have some friends to conceal stolen property.

There seems to be a connection of these friends thirty or forty miles back into the country on this side of the river, who, with five or six in this city, seem to have a line for running stolen property through Nauvoo to the territory of Iowa; and I have good reason to believe

*Times and Seasons, vol. vi. p. 779-780.

that those in the country on this side of the river, those in the city, and those in the territory, are one clan, but they are not Mormons; nor have the Mormons any fellowship with them.

I have taken pains to go with a person from the country, with a writ, and have searched every house suspected, till the person was satisfied, and till I was satisfied myself that no such property, as claimed, was in the city.

I have good reason to believe that scoundrels stay in Nauvoo, and when stolen property comes into the city, they are ready to pass it on to the territory, and screen themselves under the cloak of Mormonism, in order that the Mormons may bear the blame. If people will satisfy themselves as I have done, they may find a *depot* in the regions of Iowa, containing the greater part of the property charged to the Mormons.

I would state further, that the Mormons had no agency in the searches I made, but that I made them, at the instance of men from the country, and that I spent three days in the territory of Iowa, searching into the facts and matters, and my statements are made up from personal observation.

[Signed]　Joseph A. Kelting,
Deputy Sheriff of Hancock County.'

Evening of Friday, 17.—Elder H. C. Kimball, John Taylor and George A. Smith met with me in my upper room: we counseled and prayed."

CHAPTER XXVIII

THE STORY OF CONTINUED PROGRESS OF THE CHURCH
IN NAUVOO, IN EUROPE AND IN THE UNITED
STATES—PLEA FOR THE RETURN OF
JAMES EMMETT'S COMPANY

"*Saturday, January* 18, 1845.—I called at Elder Willard Richards' and left some correspondence: proceeded to the Temple.

Sunday, 19.—The seventies met at their hall. Presidents for the sixteenth and seventeenth quorums were set apart; fifty persons were ordained. Afternoon the high priests' quorum met; President George Miller preached on the subject of Intemperance. In the evening I met the police and instructed them in their duties.

Monday, 20.—I called on Elder Willard Richards and found him engaged on the History.

Tuesday, 21.—Forenoon, with Elders Kimball and Richards at the Historian's Office. Wrote a letter to my brother, Phineas H., with counsel for the saints in Kirtland to come to Nauvoo, that all who have faith in the latter-day work may be united with us in building the Temple.

Evening, I met in council with Elders Heber C. Kimball, Willard Richards, George A. Smith and Amasa M. Lyman; we wrote to Elder Jedediah M. Grant, Philadelphia, counseling him to forward all the young men and other available help he could to build the Temple.

Wednesday, 22.—Forenoon, Elder Orson Pratt wrote a letter, in behalf of the council, to Elder Parley P. Pratt. Afternoon, I went to the Historian's Office accompanied by Elders Kimball and Taylor. The letters to Elders Grant and Pratt were read and approved.   A copy of Elder Pratt's letter was sent to Wm. Smith.

Evening, accompanied by my wife I attended a party at Brother Woodruff's, Heber C. Kimball, John Taylor, George A. Smith, W. W. Phelps and their wives were present.

Elder Elias Smith received a letter from A. W. Babbitt, Springfield, Ill., with the information that he was before the Legislative House Committee on Banks and Corporations pertaining to the bill for the unconditional repeal of the Nauvoo Charter.   Jacob A. Davis made a strong anti-Mormon speech before said committee and presented them with a full file of the *Nauvoo Neighbor* containing the ordinances passed by the city council.   Mr. Backenstos was also before the committee and pleaded like an apostle for the rights of his constituents.   The committee inquired of Mr. Babbitt as to 'bogus-making'—spiritual wife doctrine—and whether he believed in [Joseph] Smith's revelations. He had made two speeches before the committee, but believed they would recommend the passage of the bill.*

Thursday, 23.—I wrote to Elder Ezra T. Benson: called at the Trustees' Office; went to the Temple; called at Elder Richards', Kimball's, Taylor's and Hyde's.   Found Brother John Scott at my house who said Brother Aaron Smith had just returned from Appanoose and said Wilson Law was there lecturing to the mob; counseling them to drive the 'Mormons' from Nauvoo before the Temple was done or they never could.

Friday, 24.—Elders Heber C. Kimball and N. K. Whitney were at my house.   Elder Orson Hyde returned from St. Louis, Mo.

The plasterers finished plastering the Concert Hall. This building is thirty feet by fifty and eleven feet high. The ceiling is arched and has sounding jars.   It has

*The speeches in the Illinois legislature will be found *in extenso* in the *Comprehensive History of the Church,* Century I, vol. ii, ch. lxvii.

been built amidst difficulty and discouragement in consequence of poverty, and has cost nearly one thousand dollars: much of the burden has laid on the Trustees, Stephen H. Goddard, Wm. F. Cahoon, and Wm. Clayton.

Saturday, 25.—I went to the Temple this morning, thence with Elder Kimball, my brother Joseph, and Marshal Jon. C. Wright, to Brother Richards' office.

Sunday, 26.—I attended the regular meeting of the high priests' quorum at the Masonic Hall. George Miller presiding, who introduced the subject of building a hall for the use of the quorums of high priests one hundred and twenty feet long by eighty wide, and about thirty-three feet high. I asked all that were in favor of having such a hall built, and were willing to do something towards building it, and not merely look on and see their brethren build it, to raise their hands; all hands were raised. I told them such a building as had been proposed would not cost less than fifteen thousand dollars. Two years ago or even one year ago we had not a public hall in this city. The room in Brother Joseph's store was the only one where a congregation could convene. A year ago last fall I said to the seventies that if I were as strong and numerous a body as they were, I would go to work and put up a building that I might have a place to worship in. They put up their building, but the plan being altered, at the suggestion of Brother Hyrum, they had to wait for timber and could not finish it that season. Should the high priests commence the erection of the building proposed, next fall will come and even winter and the quorum will still be without a place to meet in, and probably the next season would pass away before it could be finished. I proposed to the quorum to finish off the upper story of the Temple in which they could receive their washings and anointings and endowments instead of undertaking a building from the commencement: this proposition was received by unanimous vote.

Elder Heber C. Kimball preached in the Concert Hall.

The seventies met in their hall. President Joseph Young presiding, James M. Munroe expressed his willingness to teach the seventies English grammar. Elder George A. Smith spoke on the benefits arising from education; he said, the saints should improve and be diligent in acquiring knowledge, this people and their gathering together has been made a political question, and we are a bone for all the world to pick at; Lawyer Babbitt had written that the legislature had repealed the city charter of Nauvoo, and there was a great rejoicing among the priests at their victory.

News of Nauvoo's Charter Being Repealed.

President Joseph Young spoke of the importance of being able to speak correctly. He lectured the youth who joined the quorums as to obedience; said, if he knew of a man belonging to these quorums stealing he would be cut off the church and published in the *Neighbor*. The saints had always taught honesty, virtue and uprightness—the lives of thousands were jeopardized by rascals and hypocrites, who would call you brother and pilfer your property; such were neither fit to be called saints nor decent human beings, they would go to hell. The names of several suspected of stealing were mentioned. James Dunn was cut off, two members were called in question for drunkenness.

Admonition by President Joseph Young.

Evening, I attended prayer meeting.

Monday, 27.—Attended to sending off fifty missionaries and forwarding letters to Elders Parley P. Pratt, Wm. Smith and J. M. Grant. Elder Kimball preached the funeral sermon of Sister Perrygrine Sessions.

Evening, at Dr. Richards' office; I dictated a letter to Joshua Grant and heard several articles read.

I insert minutes of meeting of the Presidents of Seventies:

MINUTES OF SEVENTIES COUNCIL

'Meeting opened by singing and prayer. President Joseph Young spoke upon the lack of wisdom and economy of the members of this church. As an example he quoted the teaching of a certain elder, a president of one of the quorums, who told the people he considered the Twelve Apostles to be God to us. This sentiment expressed to many was not only dangerous to the community, but was calculated to jeopardize the lives of the Twelve. The same allusion was made to Joseph, and the reply of the mob was, well if Jo Smith is their God we will kill their God, and so they did, and it may be so with the Twelve. The brethren should speak and act in wisdom for their own sake as well as for the truth's sake. There are brethren in these quorums and even presidents who are connected with a body of those consecrating thieves, who pretend to say that they have a right to consecrate from the Gentiles, but such will steal from their brethren as well as others.

Several elders spoke on the subject, expressing their sense of the propriety of expelling said members from the church and publishing their names.

The clerk, Elder John D. Lee, said that some of the brethren were probably too hasty in their decision according to his view of the matter. He considered that if the elders acted with discretion they must not be excited nor influenced by passion and remarked that did the elders possess the power of Jehovah in their present weak condition in less than twenty-four hours the earth would be depopulated, especially should the elders be vested with that power in turns, for what would be spared by one would likely be destroyed by another.

President Brigham Young arose and said, 'When men have come into our midst who were as corrupt as the devil himself, many have

Forbearance With Sinners as Some May Repent. supposed it would have been better to have cut their throats with a feather and exposed their sink of corruption, and let them go to hell where they belonged, than to have borne with them as Brother Joseph Smith did; but this course would meet with a conflicting argument. To stop a man in his career would be taking away his agency. Cain was permitted to live, peradventure, he might repent of his wickedness, and redeem a portion of his time, and thereby obtain a glory and salvation, though not a full salvation; and this is the reason that Brother Joseph bore so long with Jackson* and others, that peradventure they might, notwithstanding they had been guilty of murder and robbery, come to the waters of baptism through repentance, and redeem a part of their allotted time. If they were cut off from the earth they might with propriety come up in the day of judgment and say we took away their agency, which if we had let alone, they would

*This was a desperate character who appeared in Hancock county about the time the "Mormon" troubles approached a climax in the life of the Prophet. Jackson was supposed to be implicated in the murder of the Prophet. (See this *History*, vol. vi, pp. 149, 521, 560).

have repented of their sins and redeemed a part of their time. The presidents of seventies should be men of wisdom and know how to save men instead of destroying them; for example let a hot-headed president stand at the head of a quorum and let some of the members of his quorum be overtaken in a fault, it would make no difference how small or great the offense might be, the first steps that would be taken (instead of going in a private manner, as a prudent reflecting president should and teach the guilty the law of redemption, bind up the breach and thereby save a soul from ruin) would be to have the offense made public—have the accused arraigned before the quorum in order to ferret out the crime, thus increasing the wound, especially if it should be an interruption between a man and his wife; the offense having become public, confidence is lost, not only in the accused, but the parties concerned lose confidence in each other, their reputation sinks, consequently despair rushes into the troubled soul, who is thus rashly treated and he or they suppose they have not a friend on earth, consequently imagine it is useless for them to try to redeem their former standing, and in fact instances have been known of individuals under like circumstances giving up to intoxication and finally become the most miserable dissipated and abandoned wretches on earth; whereas, had wisdom been used, the soul might have been reclaimed and saved by casting the mantle of charity around them and thereby covering up a multitude of sins. This is what is meant by the mantle of charity that Paul speaks of [covering a multitude of sins].

We should be charitable, liberal, patient and forbearing with each other and above all never blast each others' characters, rather hide each others faults with the mantle of charity; for when but few know your faults they seem but few, but expose them and they become multitudes.'

Tuesday, 28.—I met in council with Elders Heber C. Kimball, John Taylor, John E. Page, Bishops Whitney and Miller, Reynolds Cahoon and Elias Smith, when was read a letter from Wm. P. Richards, Esq., Macomb, McDon-ough county, Illinois, to Bishop George Miller suggesting the propriety of petitioning congress for a grant of land twenty-four miles square in the pineries or other uninhabited portions of public domain to be set apart as a reserve for the saints, with power to make our own local arrangements, and enact laws not repugnant to the Constitution of the United States. This he considers necessary in consequence of the irreconcilable feelings of the public in relation to us as a religious

U. S. Land Grant Sought in Michigan.

body: his communication with the correspondence thereon was published in the *Neighbor*.

Wednesday, 29.—I called at Elder Richards' office with Elder Kimball and Thomas Kingston and read a letter* from J. B. Backenstos informing us of the strong prejudice entertained by the members of the legislative assembly and the determined spirit evinced to repeal the Nauvoo City Charter; also informing us that John Dougherty, senator from Union county, openly justified the murder of Joseph and Hyrum Smith, and that the senate had discharged from arrest Jacob C. Davis, one of their number, who was indicted for murder. Mr. Backenstos had appealed to the sense of justice, equal rights, patriotism and humanity possessed by the members of the house of representatives in vain. His colleague Mr. Babbitt and himself had done their duty.

Backenstos Reports Prejudice in Illinois Legislature.

Afternoon, attended council.

Evening, I assisted Brother Kimball to prepare his Journal for the press, and blessed his child, Brigham Willard.

Thursday, 30.—Attended council with the authorities of the city, pertaining to the action of the legislature in repealing the City Charter. The council agreed to have the city election go on tomorrow, not knowing whether the governor would pass or veto the bill. A committee was appointed to confer with legal gentlemen in relation to the legitimacy of the legislature repealing a charter granted for the term of perpetual succession.

Legality of Repeal of Nauvoo Charters Questioned.

* * *

Friday, 31.—Elders Heber C. Kimball, John Taylor, Willard Richards and W. W. Phelps engaged in writing letters to eminent jurists, inquiring as to the constitutionality of the action of the Illinois legislature in repealing the City Charter of Nauvoo.

Received a letter from Elder Parley P. Pratt in rela-

*See letter file in Historian's Office, box 7.

tion to the prosperity of the church under his care, [i. e. N. Y.] and the great demand for *Books* of *Doctrine and Covenants* and *Hymn Books.*

A meeting was held in the Seventies' Hall, for the purpose of forming a Mercantile and Mechanical Association, Elder John Taylor, chairman. Twelve trustees were elected to control the association, *viz.* Daniel Garn, Samuel Bent, Shadrach Roundy, Charles C. Rich, John D. Lee, L. N. Scovil, Joseph Worthen, Joseph Horn, Hosea Stout, Edward Hunter, Gustavus Williams and Charles A. Davis.

Bishops Whitney and Miller, Trustees-in-Trust for the church published the following:

AGENTS APPOINTED FOR RECEIVING DONATIONS AND TITHING FOR BUILDING THE TEMPLE

'To Whom It May Concern: This certifies that the following named elders have been appointed by the proper authorities of the Church of Jesus Christ of Latter-day Saints, agents to collect donations and tithings for the Temple in Nauvoo and for other purposes; and have complied with all necessary requirements by entering into bonds to our entire satisfaction. We hope they will be received as such by all people wherever they may travel. [Then follow the names of 46 elders so appointed].

We hope also that the brethren will have confidence in them, inasmuch as we hold ourselves responsible to credit on the *Book of Law of the Lord,* for all donations put into their hands, to the names of the donors on their tithing.

Inasmuch as this is a very good opportunity, and inasmuch as we feel very anxious that all should double their exertions in order to finish the building of the Temple the next season, that the saints may receive their endowments; we hope the saints universally will embrace the opportunity, and donate liberally, that they may the more speedily receive their reward, for great things depend on our finishing the building of the Temple with speed.'

Saturday, February 1, 1845.—At ten a. m. I met with Elders John Taylor, Willard Richards, Orson Spencer, George Miller, W. W. Phelps and L. R. Foster in committee to complete the letters to eminent jurists [i. e. on legality of the repeal of the Nauvoo Charter].

Sunday, 2.—I preached in the Concert Hall, to a crowded assembly. Elder Orson Hyde preached in the

Masonic Hall. Elder Heber C. Kimball preached at Brother Gully's at candle light; Father John Smith and Bishop Miller made a few remarks.

The seventies met at their hall in the evening, Elders George A. Smith, Joseph Young and others preached; several were ordained into the quorums, and several presidents were set apart for the eighteenth quorum. I spent the evening at home with my family.

City Election at Nauvoo. *Monday, 3.*—The following officers were elected without a dissenting vote (about 900 votes polled):

Mayor: Orson Spencer.

Aldermen: Daniel Spencer, N. K. Whitney, George W. Harris and Charles C. Rich.

Councilors: David Fullmer, John Pack, George Miller, W. W. Phelps, Jonathan C. Wright, Samuel Bent, Phineas Richards, James Sloan and Edward Hunter.

I received the following communication from the attorney-general of the state of Illinois:

A FRIENDLY LETTER FROM JOSIAH LAMBORN, STATE OFFICIAL

'Springfield, 28th Jan., 1845.

Dear Sir:

You and I were slightly acquainted heretofore, though I presume you have forgotten me. During my sojourn here this winter, I have carefully watched the progress of events and particularly so in reference to your friends and fellow citizens of Nauvoo. Throughout all the persecutions and abuses which have been heaped upon you, though I have been far removed from any political or pecuniary influence which might bias my mind; yet I have always considered that your enemies have been prompted by religious and political prejudices and by a desire for plunder and blood, more than for the common good. By the repeal of your charter and by refusing all amendments and modifications our legislature has given a kind of sanction to the barbarous manner in which you have been treated.

Your two representatives exerted themselves to the extent of their abilities in your behalf, but the tide of popular passion and frenzy was too strong to be resisted. It is truly a melancholy spectacle to witness the lawmakers of a sovereign state condescending to pander to the vices, ignorance and malevolence of a class of people who are at all times ready for riot, murder and rebellion. You had many true friends here. Most of the intelligent gentlemen out of the legislature felt that you were an injured and an outraged people. The members living nearest to your city and having better means of information than those living remotely, sustained and defended you to the last. The opposition was made up of the body of the whig party, together with such demagogues of the other party as could be cajoled and bamboozled by the whigs.

There is now presented to the house a new charter for your city. It is referred to a select committee. What its fate may be no man can tell. Your senator, Jacob C. Davis, has done much to poison the minds of members against anything in your favor. He walks at large in defiance of law, an indicted murderer. If a Mormon was in his position the senate would afford no protection, but he would be dragged forth to the jail or to the gallows or to be shot down by a cowardly and brutal mob.

All you have to do is to be quiet, submissive to the laws and circumspect in your conduct. Heap coals of fire on their heads by humility and kindness, and my word for it, there will be a mighty reaction in the public sentiment, which will ultimately overthrow all your enemies. The sober second thought of the people will always be right, and heaven will protect you against all the assaults of a corrupt and bloodthirsty rabble.

Excuse me for attempting to give you advice. I do not wish to interfere with your affairs or to dictate in any way to your minds. My motives are those of friendship springing warm from my heart and the same which would control in relation to all mankind.

Yours, etc.

[Signed]   JOSIAH LAMBORN.'

Tuesday, 4.—I met in council with the authorities of the church. Afternoon, Elder Kimball visited Mother Smith.

Thursday, 6.—I preached in the Concert Hall to a large congregation on the occasion of the death of Alonzo W. N. Whitney.

Friday, 7.—A meeting was held of the Council of the Trades Association. Elders John Taylor, George A. Smith and Amasa M. Lyman attended.

Sunday, 9.—Elder Kimball and I preached at Brother Horner's Mill; had a good meeting with the brethren: many came to hear us.

Meeting at the stand: Elders John Taylor and George A. Smith preached on the necessity of the

Seventy's
Quorums to
be Purged
of Wickedness. people sustaining themselves by home productions and their industry; manufacturing
their own clothing and being united and
keeping such good order that the repeal of the city
charters would be no injury to the community.

Afternoon, high priests' quorum met.

Seventies met in their hall. President Joseph Young
said he meant by the assistance of the great God to cut
off all liars, swearers, bogus-makers and bogus-circu-
lators and endeavor to purify the bodies of the seventies
from filth and wickedness. Seven presidents were set
apart, and thirty members ordained for the nineteenth
quorum. Elder Amasa M. Lyman addressed the meeting on the subject of order.

The branch at Quincy, Illinois, held a conference.
There were represented one hundred members, including nine high priests, one seventy, twelve elders and
two priests, one teacher and one deacon.

Monday, 10.—Meeting of the Presidents of Seventies at early candle light. After the business before the
Revelation
Doctrine. meeting was attended to, I instructed the
elders on the subject of revelation; showing
how the Lord dealt with his children in revealing to
them here a little and there a little, as they were capaci-
tated to receive, comprehend and improve upon, named
baptism for the dead in which the Lord first revealed
the principle, then the order. Elders John E. Page and
George A. Smith bore testimony.

Tuesday, 11.—Elders Kimball, Page, Taylor,
Smith, Lyman and myself met with the Trades Committee.

Afternoon, attended meeting at Elder Taylor's with
a Committee of the Agricultural and Manufacturing
Society. It was proposed that the citizens be invited
to subscribe twelve thousand days work, which it was
estimated would put a sufficient dam in the Mississippi
to propel machinery.

Mr. John C. Elliott, one of the murderers of Joseph
and Hyrum Smith was arrested by John Kay.

With other items, I wrote Elder Woodruff the following:

PRESIDENT YOUNG'S LETTER TO ELDER WOODRUFF IN ENGLAND

'It will rejoice your heart to hear that we have a remarkable mild winter, clear and pleasant, no snow, and peace in the city, as it does ours to live here and enjoy it. Though the papers report a total repeal of the Nauvoo Charter by a large majority in both houses, we remain undisturbed, and city affairs go on as usual. We expect to appeal to the U. S. court.

The stone is nearly hewn for the Temple; a stone font is about to be erected, the woodwork is progressing rapidly under a temporary roof in the basement story, and we hope to commence the endowments next fall or early in the winter. We will not send many elders to England until after the endowment.

You will please call at Stationer's Hall, London, the first opportunity, and get or by some means procure a copy of the 'copyright of the *Book of Mormon*' and safely keep it until further notice. The saints are more engaged than ever to finish the Temple, and it is desirable that tithings be forwarded from all branches at the earliest safe conveyance. Copyrights.

The different quorums are becoming perfected in their several organizations, by which means the elders are learning their duty. Union, love and peace were never more universal among the saints at Nauvoo, than at the present time. Brother Willard is convalescent, collecting materials for history and much regrets the absence of Elder Woodruff's Journals.'

Wednesday, 12.—Mr. Elliott was examined before Justices Aaron Johnson, Daniel H. Wells, Isaac Higbee and committed to Carthage jail to await his trial at the next term of the circuit court.

Thursday, 13.—I met in council with the Twelve and others. With Elders Willard Richards, George A. Smith, and others, I spent the evening at Elder Kimball's: had a good time.

Friday, 14.—Father Morley arrived from Yelrome near Lima, Adams county, bringing word that five of the brethren there had been arrested charged with larceny; he says that property had been concealed on their premises and recovered by a search warrant, on the principle 'those that hide can find'. These proceedings were had to produce Brethren Arrested at Yelrome on False Pretenses.

excitement, and a warrant is said to be out for Father Morley. I met with the Twelve and others and prayed for the deliverance of these brethren. Father Morley was counseled to remove his family to Nauvoo and Solomon Hancock was appointed to preside over that branch. Dr. John M. Bernhisel was appointed a Traveling Bishop to visit the churches. Some conversation ensued on the subject of sending six brethren with Brother Lewis Dana to the west and especially to Texas.

Saturday, 15.—A conference was held in Lipsey, Tuscaloosa county, Alabama. Five branches were represented containing one hundred and forty-one members, including twenty-four officers, A. O. Smoot, presided.

Died—in Nauvoo, Asa Works, Sen., aged eighty-three years, after a sickness of six months.

He served his country as a soldier in the American Revolution; was in the battles of Bennington and A Soldier of Monmouth, in the latter of which he received the American Revolution a wound in his left arm between the shoulder Dies. and elbow,—underwent a great deal of hardship, privation and hunger in helping to gain American independence.

In the year 1838, he emigrated to Far West, Missouri, at which place he was called to witness the violation of that liberty he fought to obtain. He endured with the Latter-day Saints all the persecution and suffering inflicted upon them in 1838 and 9 in Missouri; and since that time has lived in exile in the state of Illinois. Brother Asa Works was the father of my first wife, Miriam.

Sunday, 16.—Elder Amasa M. Lyman preached in the Masonic Hall. The seventies from the first to the eighth quorums met in their hall. Elder Zerah Pulsipher preached. Elder George A. Smith preached to the high priests: three persons were ordained high priests. Evening, I attended prayer meeting at the Trustees' Office.

Monday, 17.—Meeting of the Presidents of Seventies. Measures were adopted to facilitate the building of President Joseph Young's house.

Tuesday, 18.—The Board of the Mercantile and Mechanical Association met at the Masonic Hall and proceeded to organize.

I attended a council at President John Smith's, and ordained Wm. Perkins bishop of Macedonia and Andrew H. Perkins his counselor.

Thursday, 20.—I called at Elder W. Richards' office with Elders Joseph Young, George A. Smith and Amasa M. Lyman. I heard a recital of the Haun's Mill Massacre by my brother Joseph: afterwards went to the Temple.

Friday, 21.—I preached at Brother Robert Pierce's on the occasion of the funeral of Brother Morris Whitesides.

Saturday, 22.—I attended meeting of the high council in the Seventies' Hall: a full quorum present.

Sunday, 23.—I preached at Hiram Kimball's, Elders Heber C. Kimball and George A. Smith administered the sacrament: had a good meeting.

Meeting of seventies in their hall. Elders P. B. Lewis made a few remarks. President Joseph Young spoke of the principle of receiving revelation from God.

Meeting at Bishop Hale's. Elder Dunham preached, followed by Mother Smith, who gave a recital of the persecutions endured by her family, in establishing the church, and exhorted the brethren and sisters to bring up their children in the way they should go; there were meetings held in the Concert and Masonic Halls.

Afternoon, high priests quorum met, Elder Kimball preached.

Evening, the Twelve Apostles and others met in council and for prayer.

Monday, 24.—In company with Elders Heber C. Kimball, Orson Pratt, Amasa M. Lyman, George Miller, William Clayton, George D. Grant, E. D. Woolley, John Kay and John L. Smith I went to Macedonia:

we were armed with forty-six rounds, loaded pistols.

After the company partook of refreshments, we met at Brother Benjamin F. Johnson's and enjoyed a pleasant evening; Brother Kay sang a number of songs.

Evening, the Presidents of Seventies met in their hall. The charges against James Carrol and Hiram Gates, were investigated and they were expelled from the church. The brethren agreed to trade with those merchants who sustained good order and honored the laws of the city.

Tuesday, 25.—I spent the day in Macedonia, settling the church business with Elder B. F. Johnson. The company from Nauvoo dined at Elder Wm. G. Perkins'.

Afternoon, visited the saints. Evening. Elders Orson Pratt, Amasa M. Lyman, George Miller and I preached. Chatted at Brother Johnson's till after midnight. I told the brethren that all was not right and that we would have some of the brethren from Nauvoo before daybreak; George D. Grant and John Kay agreed to watch during the night. A rumor having reached Nauvoo that Elder Kimball and I were in Carthage jail, Elders John E. Page, John Taylor, Willard Richards, George A. Smith, and Charles C. Rich, met in Nauvoo at Elder Taylor's and investigated the report, and though they did not believe it, they deemed it prudent to dispatch Brother Hosea Stout and seven of the old police to Macedonia, as a protection for us.

Premonitions of President Young.

President John Smith very sick, several of the Twelve administered to him.

Wednesday, 26.—Brother Hosea Stout and company arrived in front of Brother Johnson's house; we at first thought it was the mob, but when Wm. H. Kimball cried out 'Father don't you know me', we immediately recognized the brethren and had a joyful meeting; they brought us word of the rumor which had arisen in Nauvoo from two suspi-

Friends Arrive—Not the Mob.

cious persons who had been at Brother Turley's inquiring for Elder Kimball and me.

At ten a. m. we started for Nauvoo, twenty-three of the brethren from Macedonia accompanying us through the timber about seven miles when we halted and Howard Egan recited a negro sermon; I made a few remarks by way of counsel to the Macedonia brethren and blessed them in the name of the Lord; they returned home; we proceeded and arrived in Nauvoo about three p. m.

Thursday, 27.—This morning in company with Elders George A. Smith, John E. Page, Willard Richards and John Taylor I proceeded to the bank of the river, in the lower part of the city, the site of the contemplated dam and in presence of about one hundred individuals consecrated the ground by prayer; Elder John E. Page being mouth. I made a few remarks.

The Twelve Apostles, Trustees, mayor, aldermen and councilors met in council. Moses Smith represented the condition of the company led into the wilderness by James Emmett. After mature deliberation on the situation and condition of James Emmett's company, it was unanimously voted that Elder Amasa M. Lyman visit them, and that he choose a companion to accompany him. Voted that Elder Orson Pratt write a fatherly epistle in behalf of this council and Elder Orson Spencer assist him: Elder Lyman chose Elder Daniel Spencer to accompany him.

Delegation Appointed to Visit James Emmett's Company in the Wilderness

The following is a copy of the letter written:

THE COUNCIL'S LETTER WRITTEN TO JAMES EMMETT AND COMPANY

'Nauvoo, February 27, 1845.

To James Emmett & Company,

Dear Brethren: We, the Twelve and some other of the authorities of the church, being in council assembled, send unto you this epistle by the hand of our beloved, trustworthy and faithful brother Amasa M. Lyman, whom we have counseled to visit you, and give you instruction for your good and salvation.

Though our counsel has been lightly esteemed and disregarded by Brother Emmett, yet we verily believe there are those among you who have been honestly and sincerely deceived by his vain pretenses and mis-representations. We labored long and faithfully to persuade Brother Emmett to hearken to the counsel of his friends to whom were committed the power, authority and keys for the salvation of Zion and the redemption of her children together with the keys of endowment for the lifting up and exaltation of the heirs of promise—the remnant of Joseph—but our counsels, our persuasions, our entreaties, and all our labors with him were in vain. He still persisted in his course and has led you forth from our midst and separated you from the body and like a branch severed from a tree you must and will perish together with your posterity and your progenitors unless you are engrafted again thereon before you wither and die; and because we know your unfortunate condition, and because we feel for your safety as a kind father feels for his tender offspring we therefore stretch out our arms to you and would feign welcome you to the bosom of our counsels and rescue you from the vortex of ruin and destruction into which you will inevitably and irrecoverably plunge yourselves by continuing to hearken to the counsels of one who will not regard the advice and counsel of the proper authorities of the kingdom of God.

Do you wish, dear brethren, to see the house of our God built up, adorned, and prepared according to the commandment and pattern given? Do you wish to enter into its sacred courts and receive your washings and anointings, and the keys of knowledge and power? Do you desire the eternal seal of the priesthood placed upon your head by which your progenitors for ages past and your posterity for endless generations to come shall be secured to you in a covenant that is everlasting? Do you desire to take part with the servants of God in teaching, civilizing, saving and exalting the Lamanites? And, in fine, do you desire to stand forth with the servants of God and in the majesty and strength and greatness of the everlasting priesthood rescue the earth from violence, oppression and wickedness and seal all things unto the end of all things that the saints alone may have dominion.

All of you are ready to answer yes, and respond with a hearty affirmative. But remember that there is but one way by which you can realize or partake of these things; it is by hearkening to our counsel in all things; and for this reason we send unto you Brother Amasa [M. Lyman], who will counsel you in all things according to the mind and will of God, according to the circumstances in which you are placed.

If Brother Emmett will receive our advice and continue so to do, it shall yet be well with him, but if not we say in the name of the Lord that it shall be ill with him and all that follow him.'

Evening, called on Father John Smith, who was still sick; united with the brethren and prayed for him: he felt blessed.

Friday, 28.—I went to the Temple and visited the Trustees, and counseled with them pertaining to business: all things going on well.

Saturday, March 1, 1845.—I met with the 'General Council'* at the Seventies Hall. We decided to send nine brethren westward, to search out a location for the saints; many eloquent speeches were made on the present position of affairs: had a good meeting, which continued all day.

The high council met: no business.

The overflowing of rivers in the north of China submerged whole provinces with populations respectively larger than some of the second class kingdoms of Europe. When the waters receded thousands of corpses were left on the ground. Upwards of seventeen millions of human beings who have escaped from the inundations have spread over the adjacent provinces, beggared of all things and crying for bread.

Sunday, 2.—At home—unwell. Elders Heber C. Kimball and John E. Page preached in the Music Hall. The seventies and their families met in their hall. Elders Luman A. Shurtliff, Hiram Dayton, and Joseph Young preached.

Evening, visited Father John Smith and the mother of the Prophet.

Monday, 3.—I accompanied Elder Heber C. Kimball at his request on to the hill to transact some business: returned home quite sick and went to bed.

Evening, the Presidents of Seventies met, and investigated the characters of several of their members. The choir had a concert at the Music Hall; Elders Taylor and Kimball addressed the assembly spiritedly.

Tuesday, 4.—Continued sickly. General Council met at Seventies Hall; Elder Kimball presided; the subject of the western mission was discussed.

---

*"General Council is the Council of Fifty." This is the footnote in *President Young's Ms. History.* This Council of Fifty is the legislature of the kingdom of God which includes the church. (For treatise see Note at end of chapter.)

Thursday, 6.—Elders Kimball and Richards called on me this evening. I sat up a little and felt better.

Friday, 7.—I walked over to my brother Joseph's: felt considerably better. I had no doctor in my sickness, but the Lord, my wife, and the laying on of hands of the elders.

Saturday, 8.—I rode up to the Temple. High council met—no business—adjourned.

Sunday, 9.—I attended council with Elders Heber C. Kimball, John Taylor, George A. Smith, N. K. Whitney and George Miller, most of the day; afterwards met with the high priests' quorum and preached. Evening, attended seventies meeting and addressed the brethren.

Elder Wilford Woodruff attended conference at Preston, England. Five hundred and five members were represented.

Monday, 10.—Forenoon, with Elders Kimball and Richards. Afternoon, Elders George A. Smith assisted Elder Richards to get out historical items.

Tuesday, 11.—I attended the General Council. The subject of writing to Governor Ford; also the present movements of the mob were discussed. It was considered best for those who are hunted with writs to go on missions; as the policy of commencing a mob persecution has always been to get out vexatious writs in order to provoke resistance to the form of legal authority and thereby produce a collision between us and the state; so that we may, if possible, evade the blow until we can finish the Temple and the Nauvoo House. It was also decided that the workmen on the walls of the Temple commence work tomorrow.

Wednesday, 12.—The sheriff is here with writs for several of the brethren. He says that the mob have sent messengers to the governor to inform him that the Mormons have resisted the officers and requesting him to order a *posse comitatus* to come and take Brackenbury: Mr. Brackenbury was a witness against the murderers of Joseph and Hyrum Smith.

Wm. Marks left town suddenly.

A dreadful earthquake occurred in the city of Mexico at fifty-two minutes past three p. m., which caused a great amount of suffering and great destruction of property.

Thursday, 13.—Several brethren accompanied Mr. Brackenbury to Augusta.

Friday, 14.—I attended meeting in the Masonic Hall and proposed that deacons be appointed to take care of the poor, in every neighborhood, with bishops at their head: agreed to meet the bishops and their counselors at the Masonic Hall on Monday morning to organize.

Brother A. P. Rockwood recorded the following:

'For the three and a half years that I have been in charge of the Temple quarry, with from twenty to one hundred and fifty hands, Brother Moses Horn has been the first person that has met with an accident by blasting. During this time there has been burned, according to my judgment, about one hundred casks of powder. Brother Horn had retired to the usual distance while blasting; he was struck on the head by a stone weighing one and a half pounds which fractured his skull; we immediately conveyed him home, sent for Dr. Bernhisel and other physicians, who pronounced the wound mortal: he died in three hours.' "

NOTE

President Young in writing a letter (May 3, 1844) to Reuben Hedlock, president of the European Mission at the time, said to him: "The kingdom is organized; and although as yet no bigger than a grain of mustard seed, the little plant is in a flourishing condition and our prospects brighter than ever. Cousin Lemuel is very friendly [referring to the Indians] and cultivating the spirit of peace and union in his family very extensively." *

Again in a discourse under date of July 8, 1855,† President Young said: "As was observed by Brother Pratt [this morning] that kingdom [i. e. of God] is actually organized and the inhabitants of the earth do not know it. If this people know anything about it, all right; it is organized preparatory to taking effect in the due time of the Lord, and in the manner that shall please him. As observed by

Millennial Star, vol. xxiii, p. 422.

†*Deseret News,* August 1, 1855, vol. v, p. 162; see also *Journal of Discourses,* vol. ix, pp. 309-17.

one of the speakers this morning that kingdom grows out of the Church of Jesus Christ of Latter-day Saints, but it is not the church; for a man may be a legislator in that body which will issue laws to sustain the inhabitants of the earth in their individual rights and still not belong to the Church of Jesus Christ at all.   And further though a man may not even believe in any religion it would be perfectly right, when necessary, to give him the privilege of holding a seat among that body which will make laws to govern all the nations of the earth and control those who make no profession of religion at all; for that body would be governed, controlled and dictated to acknowledge others in those rights which they wish to enjoy themselves. Then the Latter-day Saints would be protected, if a kingdom of this kind was on the earth, the same as all other people."

The late President George Q. Cannon while editor of the *Juvenile Instructor** said:

"We are asked, Is the Church of God, and the Kingdom of God the same organization? and we are informed that some of the brethren hold that they are separate.

This is the correct view to take.   The Kingdom of God is a separate organization from the Church of God.   There may be men acting as officers in the Kingdom of God who will not be members of the Church of Jesus Christ of Latter-day Saints.   On this point the Prophet Joseph gave particular instructions before his death, and gave an example, which he asked the younger elders who were present to always remember.   It was to the effect that men might be chosen to officiate as members of the Kingdom of God who had no standing in the Church of Jesus Christ of Latter-day Saints.   The Kingdom of God when established will not be for the protection of the Church of Jesus Christ of Latter-day Saints alone, but for the protection of all men, whatever their religious views or opinions may be.   Under its rule, no one will be permitted to overstep the proper bounds or to interfere with the rights of others."

Undoubtedly all this has reference to the time spoken of by St. John in *Revelation* when he said: "And the seventh angel sounded; and there were great voices in heaven, saying, The kingdoms of this world are become the kingdoms of our Lord, and of his Christ; and he shall reign forever and ever."†

However it is proper to note that sometimes these terms "the Church of Christ", "the Kingdom of God" and "the Kingdom of Heaven" are used interchangeably in the scriptures and hence the confusion in these terms sometimes obtains.

*Vol. xxxi, p 140.
†*Rev.* xi:15.

CHAPTER XXIX

THE JAMES EMMETT COMPANY OFFICIALLY VISITED—
APRIL CONFERENCE OF 1845—MUNICIPAL CORPORA-
TIONS UNDER GENERAL STATE LAW — WESTERN
MOVEMENT PROPOSED BY GOVERNOR FORD

"*Saturday, March* 15, 1845.—Attended council at the Trustees' Office: present—a quorum of the Twelve Apostles, Presidency of the Seventies, Temple Committee, Trustees and Architect. We decided to put all our help on the Temple—build a drain for the font—a wall on the south side of the Temple block—keep three cranes going, and stop building the dam in the Mississippi till next winter.

Afternoon, I attended the high council in company with Elders Heber C. Kimball, Orson Pratt, John Taylor, George A. Smith, and John E. Page.

Elders Amasa M. Lyman and Daniel Spencer returned from their visit to Emmett's company.

At five p. m., the Twelve and Trustees repaired to the Mansion and heard Elder Lyman give an account of his late mission to Emmett's company. He found them on the Iowa river one hundred and fifty miles west of the settlements in a deplorable condition, caused chiefly by the rigid enforcement of Emmett's measures; he having limited their food to three gills of corn each per day. The company were much distressed and in all probability many would soon return to Nauvoo.

Lyman and Spencer's Report of Emmett's Company.

The Twelve and Trustees partook of supper provided by Brother John Pack at the Mansion; after which the band discoursed sweet music.

Mr. Brackenbury and company returned from

Augusta; he had not been brought to trial, the party
Brackenbury—
Plot Against. prosecuting alleging they were not ready;
Brackenbury offered to admit the charge, and
give bonds for his appearance at next court, which was
all the justice of the peace could require, if the trial had
proceeded and the charge had been sustained; but the
justice would not do it, so determined were the mob
to annoy Brackenbury and get an opportunity to do
him personal violence. Mr. Brackenbury was arrested
for perjury; but the real intention of the mob was to
get him into their hands to murder him, to prevent his
being a witness against the murderers of Joseph and
Hyrum Smith.

Sunday, 16.—Elder Amasa M. Lyman preached at
the stand. He spoke as follows:

'I have been in the woods and have seen those people
who have gone into the wilderness to get their endow-
Amasa M.
Lyman's
Further Report
on the Emmett
Company's
Conditions. ment. They have suffered much—have been
reduced in their rations to three gills of corn
per day, and latterly to two gills, hence you
will not be surprised when I tell you that
they have grown very poor. This is the way they live
in the wilderness, still they profess to abide the counsel
of the Twelve. Emmett is trustee-in-trust and Butler
is second in command. Their countenances brightened
up when they saw Brother Spencer and me, and found
they were not all entirely cut off. The majority of
them were under the impression that their movement
was directed by the orders of the Twelve.

Brother Emmett did not manifest any disposition to
follow the counsel of the Twelve, he said if the Twelve
would live among the Gentiles longer he had no objections, but that he had endured the driving from
Missouri with patience, and that he was clear from
the blood of the Gentiles. He seemed determined to
go ahead against the advice of God, man or the devil.
He got his company to consecrate wife, children, clothing and everything they had, and place all their prop-

erty under the control of the bishop; there is not one who can control a second suit of clothes. Brother Hilmer wanted to come away. Emmett said to him, 'Did not you covenant to stand by us? If you want to be a covenant-breaker you can go.' They have more arms than men. More than one-half of the party were for stopping. Orders were given for the arms to be brought in and piled. Those who declared their determination to go ahead took the arms and the others were commanded to stand and have their tents searched. The suffering they have endured is too bad to talk about. Once in a while their cattle die; they have not the trouble of killing them; they then go to work and eat them. I stayed one night, my heart was sick; I left and wrote to them.'

REMARKS OF BRIGHAM YOUNG ON EMMETT'S COMPANY AND SUNDRY TOPICS

I [Brigham Young] also addressed the meeting and said: 'I will give a few of my own ideas in short. Living poor, being in the wilderness, etc., is nothing to me when I am called to endure it, but people who run headlong into misery and bring upon themselves suffering, do not arrive at anything but darkness and despair. There is not one of Emmett's company that can claim the protection of heaven or any blessing of the everlasting gospel; their sufferings add nothing to their exaltation, but if the Lord had called them to pass through trials, they would have visions, revelations and faith (if necessity required) to cause him to feed them like the children of Israel. We told James Emmett, if he went, he would get into trouble: this congregation can be led by a thread. Religion is one thing and fanaticism is another.

Spring is here; we covenanted to labor on the Temple until it was finished and do all we could towards its completion; but we have not done it; if the brethren had continued, they might have worked on those walls four days a week. The stonecutters and joiners have been at work; the joiners have far exceeded our expectations this winter. The timber holds out, we keep using and there is enough left; there will be no lack of timber. If the brethren will go to work now, there will be no lack of provisions. We want the brethren to pay up their tithing. If you will haul wood, timber, etc., and help on the Temple you will find that it will be made up to you in your crops.

Since N. K. Whitney and George Miller have taken charge of the business, no man has needed anything but what has been supplied. I can call scores of men around me, who would sooner sacrifice every dollar they have, than the work on the Temple should stop. We can set four hundred men to work on the Temple. I do not want any man to go to preach till he is sent. If the world want to hear preaching let them come here, and if they really want the gospel, let them clean [up] Carthage jail.

I have proposed to the leading men of the Water Power Company, to put their work on the Temple. I will call the stockholders together, and give my reasons to them. We want to press forward the work on the Temple. I now proclaim to all saints who control means, to go to the Trustees and see if they want means to procure provisions, etc., for the hands; and I ask you to use all your influence to strengthen the hands of the Trustees.

I swear by the God of heaven that we will not spend money in feeing lawyers. All the lawsuits that have been got up against the saints, have been hatched up to fee lawyers, tavernkeepers, etc. I would rather have a six-shooter than all the lawyers in Illinois. I am sworn not to pay lawyers, but to pay our debts, and it will relieve us from an immense tax. Do not let there be a lot laying vacant in this town, join fences, for there is land enough in this city without going on to the prairie. I am going to drop the name Nauvoo and call this the 'City of Joseph'. Tomorrow evening we want the bishops at the Masonic Hall, and we will

organize them according to our notion of things. We
have no police; the legislature has repealed our charter,
and we mean to have the 'City of Joseph' organized.
The streets shall be kept clear; and the poor cared for.

Brother Wm. Marks has gone without being 'whit-
:led' out. He would hire a man for twenty-
five cents a day and would make a man work Departure of
Wm. Marks
from Nauvoo.
two days in the harvest field for one bushel
of wheat, which is one of the most low, dishonest, mean
things a person can do.'

Elder Heber C. Kimball preached at Brother Luce's
on the occasion of the death of Brother Moses Horn.

Monday, 17.—One hundred and five extra laborers
and about thirty teams commenced work at the Temple
this morning in obedience to the call of yesterday to
hasten its completion.

Tuesday, 18.—I met with General Council all day.

Wednesday, 19.—Colonel Hosea Stout, who was on
duty this evening at my house [i. e. as watchman]
called upon me and I had some conversation with him
in regard to the saints settling the country near the
headwaters of the Colorado of the west.

Thursday, 20.—Elder Heber C. Kimball and I called
on Elder Richards and found him and his clerks engaged
on the history: we proceeded to the Temple.

Evening, attended prayer meeting at Brother Joseph
B. Noble's.

Friday, 21.—In company with Elders Heber C.
Kimball, Willard Richards, John E. Page and A. W.
Babbitt, I went to the Trustees' Office and Movement
as to
Brackenbury.
consulted in relation to the best course for
Mr. Brackenbury to pursue. We agreed that
he should sue out a writ of *habeas corpus* returnable
before Judge Young at Quincy, and that Brother Babbitt should accompany him thither.

Evening, attended prayer meeting at Brother Joseph
B. Noble's.

Saturday, 22.—I attended the General Council. The

subject of the western mission was considered and occupied the most of the day: the Nauvoo House, Printing Office, Church History and organization of the city were also matters of consideration.

Sunday, 23.—Elder Heber C. Kimball preached in the Music Hall on the building of the Temple.

Elder Wilford Woodruff attended a conference in Edinburgh, Scotland; four hundred and nine members were represented.

Monday, 24.—In company with the Twelve Apostles I attended a meeting at the Concert Hall in the evening. We ordained bishops who were directed to set apart deacons in their wards to attend to all things needful and especially to watch; being without any city organization, we deemed it prudent to organize the priesthood more strictly that the peace and good order hitherto sustained by the city might still be preserved.

Tuesday, 25.—I attended council with the Twelve and prayer meeting in the evening.

Wednesday, 26.—Elder Amos Fielding with about fifty saints arrived this evening, being a portion of the

Arrival of English Saints.

company who left Liverpool, England, on the ship *Palmyra;* many of the company were unable to get further than St. Louis. At nine p. m., I rode to the upper landing and welcomed the saints, and directed the schoolhouse to be opened for the use of the company during the night.

Brother Perkins from Macedonia, brought word that the mob were making active preparations to make a

Mob Movements.

break upon us about court time, which is the third Monday in May: they were collecting artillery and organizing themselves for a general raid.

Thursday, 27.—I attended council with the Twelve, the Trustees, the Temple Committee and Brother Amos Fielding at Father Cutler's. Church matters and the plans of the mob were canvassed.

At three p. m., Brother Wm. W. Player finished setting the last trumpet stone on the capitals of the pilasters of the Temple. All the capitals and trumpet stones are now safe on the walls, which is a matter of rejoicing to all who love to witness the prosperity of the work. The weather has been sometimes very cold and at other times very windy, so that it has been impossible for the hands to continue on the walls, much of the time of late.

Friday, 28.—I attended a party at the Mansion; most of the Twelve and their families and about one hundred and forty others were present: the brass band performed some good pieces.

Saturday, 29.—Elder Kimball and I called on Elder Richards at the Historian's Office; thence we proceeded to the Temple.

Elder Orson Hyde preached at the stand on the occasion of a Masonic funeral.

Sunday, 30.—I preached to the saints. It was very windy. It rained in the afternoon.

Monday, 31.—Elder Wilford Woodruff attended a conference at Liverpool, England: twelve branches were represented containing six hundred and seventy-six members.

I wrote to Governor Ford asking his counsel in relation to the reorganization of the militia of the city of Nauvoo, as the Legion was dissolved by a repeal of the charter, and soliciting his views on the great western measure: and also whether it would be the best policy to organize Nauvoo under the act for organizing towns. *Advice Sought From Governor Ford.*

Tuesday, April 1, 1845.—I commenced revising the History of Joseph Smith at Brother Richards' office: Elder Heber C. Kimball and George A. Smith were with me. President Joseph Smith had corrected forty-two pages before his massacre. It afforded us great satisfaction to hear Brother Richards read the history of the infancy of the church. Adjourned at eleven p. m. having read one hundred and forty pages in Book 'A'.

Wednesday, 2.—Engaged at Elder Richards' office

with Elders Kimball and Smith revising Church History.

Brother Jesse D. Hunter returned from his mission having visited the branches in the state of Tennessee since January last, and received two hundred and thirty dollars on tithing and offerings for the Temple mostly in property.

Thursday, 3.—Accompanied by Elders Heber C. Kimball, Willard Richards and George A. Smith, I went to the Temple.

Evening, the brethren of the Twelve and others met at Elder Richards' office and prayed; we remembered our enemies and prayed that their designs against Zion might fail; we felt the power of God.

Friday, 4.—I visited Brother Moore, who had been accidentally shot. Dr. Bernhisel decided that the wound was mortal; but by the blessing of God he recovered.

Elder Benjamin L. Clapp reported that he left Nauvoo on the twenty-third day of October, 1844, on a special mission to collect tithing throughout the southern states. He returned about this date, having held many meetings, baptized fifteen persons and collected one thousand and forty-seven dollars which he delivered to the Trustee-in-Trust.

The mob left notice with Sheriff Backenstos of Carthage to leave by three p. m. today. The Jack-Mormons (the name attached to those friendly to Mormonism), say they will defend him and are gathering a company for that purpose. Backenstos says he will not be driven, but will stand his ground: report says the mob are divided among themselves.

<small>Backenstos Threatened.</small>

Brother William W. Major exhibited a painting of the assassination of Joseph and Hyrum Smith by the mob at Carthage.

Sunday, 6.—The following Conference Minutes are extracted from the *Times and Seasons:*

CONFERENCE MINUTES

'Special conference of the Church of Jesus Christ of Latter-day Saints at Nauvoo, April 6, 1845; it being the first day of the sixteenth year (i. e. of the organization of the church).

The choir sang 'Hark the Jubilee' at quarter past ten o'clock, while the assembly was collecting.

Present—President Brigham Young, Heber C. Kimball, Orson Hyde, Orson Pratt, George A. Smith, John Taylor, John E. Page, Willard Richards, and Amasa M. Lyman of the Quorum of the Twelve—Father John Smith, president of the stake—Bishops Whitney and Miller—the high council—and about twenty-two thousand persons (in attendance).

Elder Kimball called the meeting to order at half past ten a. m.; and the choir sang the thirty-first hymn; followed by prayer by Elder Kimball; the choir then sang 'Come All Ye Sons of Zion'.

The morning was spent in teaching, on the baptism for the dead, by President Young.

Conference adjourned until two o'clock.

Two o'clock p. m.—Conference met pursuant to adjournment; the forepart of which was taken up by the blessing of children, but owing to the immense number it was found impossible to complete the whole, when it was accordingly dispensed with, and the remainder of the afternoon was occupied in exhortation from the stand, by Elder Page and President Young and the conference adjourned until tomorrow at ten o'clock a. m.

Monday, April 7, 1845, ten o'clock a. m.—Conference met pursuant to adjournment; after the conference was seated, in consequence of the high wind, it was thought best to remove into the valley, a little south; and the whole of this immense congregation was removed, and comfortably seated in the short space of about forty minutes. The choir sang 'The Heavenly Vision', and was followd by prayer, by Elder John Taylor, after which the choir sang another hymn. Elder Kimball then arose and stated to the congregation some of the items of business which would be necessary to attend to during the day, *viz.*: the building of the Temple, and the Nauvoo House; also, to take into consideration all old obligations against the church, which are pouring in like a torrent, also to ascertain the feelings of the people, in regard to sustaining the authorities of the church under the present organization.

President Brigham Young then arose, and said he would now present the first item of business, which would be to present the authorities of the church for the approval or disapproval of the conference. He also said he wanted to know if the saints are satisfied that Joseph Smith lived and died as a Prophet, Seer, and Revelator to this church.

The Saints Satisfied with Joseph Smith as a Prophet.

Whereupon Elder Phelps moved that we accept the labors of Joseph

Smith as a Prophet, Seer, and Revelator to the nineteenth century; and that we are satisfied that he lived according to his profession, and died a martyr to the truth. Carried unanimously.

Elder Phelps moved that we accept the labors of Hyrum Smith, believing that he lived according to his profession, and died a martyr to the truth. Carried unanimously.

Elder Phelps moved that this conference accept the Twelve as the First Presidency and leaders of this church. Carried unanimously. [After which each of the Twelve was sustained separately by unanimous vote].

* * *

The chairman then observed, concerning the course of Lyman Wight, his feelings are, that we should let him remain for the present,

Lyman Wight.

probably hereafter there may be a time that he will hearken to counsel, and do much good which he is capable of—for he is a noble-minded man.

The chairman then stated that the next item of business would be, to present to the conference, the presidency of the stake; moved and seconded that Patriarch John Smith continue in his office, as president of this stake, and that he be sustained in his office. Carried unanimously.

Moved and seconded that Charles C. Rich be continued and sustained in his office of counselor to Father Smith. Carried unanimously.

Moved and seconded that George Miller be continued and sustained in his office, as president of the high priests' quorum. Carried unanimously.

Moved and seconded that William Snow and Noah Packard be continued and sustained in their office as counselors to President Miller. Carried unanimously.

Moved and seconded that Samuel Bent, be continued and sustained in his office as president of the high council. Carried unanimously.

Moved and seconded that George W. Harris, Alpheus Cutler, William Huntington Sen., James Allred, Henry G. Sherwood, Thomas Grover, Newel Knight, Lewis D. Wilson, David Fullmer, Ezra T. Benson, and Aaron Johnson be continued and sustained in their office as members of the high council. Carried unanimously.

Moved and seconded that Joseph Young be continued and sustained as President of the First Presidency of the Seventy. Carried unanimously.

Moved and seconded that Levi W. Hancock, Henry Harriman. Zerah Pulsipher, Jedediah M. Grant, and Daniel S. Miles be continued and sustained in their office, as Associate Presidents to President Joseph Young. Carried unanimously.

Moved and seconded that if Roger Orton will reform and become a good man, he be received and ordained as a member of this presidency. Carried unanimously.

Moved and seconded that Samuel Williams be continued and

sustained in his office as the president of the elders' quorum.   Carried unanimously.

Moved and seconded that Jesse Baker, and Joshua Smith be continued, and sustained as counselors to President Williams.   Carried unanimously.

Moved and seconded that Newel K. Whitney and George Miller be continued and sustained in their offices as Bishops and Trustees-in-Trust, to the Church of Jesus Christ of Latter-day Saints.   Carried unanimously.

Moved and seconded that Alpheus Cutler and Reynolds Cahoon be continued and sustained as Temple Committee.   Carried unanimously.

On the subject of the old church debts coming, it was moved and seconded that the debts of Kirtland, and Missouri, and the debts that are said to be accrued in consequence of purchasing the Galland tract in Iowa territory, be dropt, and come up no more, and the Trustees shall be dunned for them no more forever;—neither shall they be sold into the hands of the Gentiles.   Carried unanimously.

Conference then adjourned until 2 o'clock.

Two o'clock p. m.—Conference met pursuant to adjournment. The choir sang a hymn, which was followed by prayer from Elder Orson Pratt; after which the choir sang another hymn.   By request of President Young, Elder Orson Pratt read the revelation, given January 19th, 1841, concerning the building of the Temple, Nauvoo House, etc.   After which he read an extract from the *Law of the Lord*, page 240.

The chairman then stated that he wanted to lay before the conference, the subject of completing the Nauvoo House, whereupon—

Elder Phelps moved 'that we fulfill the revelation, by completing the Nauvoo House, as soon as possible.'   Carried unanimously.

The chairman called for a show of hands from all those who could, and would, take one share of stock in the Nauvoo House, there were so many hands uplifted that they could not possibly be counted.

He next called for a show of hands from those who could and would, take two shares; quite a large number of hands were shown.

He then called for a show of hands from all, both male and female, who, after they had done all they could to finish the Temple are willing to sacrifice their all, to finish the Nauvoo House, rather than not have it done.   Every hand was raised in the congregation.

The President then proclaimed to the conference, that on next Monday, the books for the Nauvoo House Association would be opened in the upper part of the brick store on Water Street.

The conference then adjourned until tomorrow at 10 o'clock a. m.

Tuesday, April 8, 1845.—Conference met pursuant to adjournment at 10 a. m. and was addressed by Elders Kimball and Young, upon the propriety of the saints staying in Hancock county, and in the afternoon Elders Young, Page, and Hyde addressed the assembly.

Perfect union and harmony prevailed throughout the conference and there was but one dissenting vote in the entire congregation.

Nauvoo be-
comes City
of Joseph.

It was moved by the President, [Brigham Young] that henceforth and forever, this city shall be called 'The City of Joseph'. [Carried unanimously.]

Great praise is due to ex-Marshal A. P. Rockwood, and his associates for their unwearied exertion, to arrange and seat the numberless assembly, for the most perfect order was maintained by them throughout the whole city and the conference—and to the saints universally for seconding their movements.

On motion conference adjourned until the 6th of October next.

[Signed]   BRIGHAM YOUNG, President.

William Clayton⎞
            ⎬ Clerks of Conference.'
Thomas Bullock ⎠

COMMENTS ON THE CONFERENCE

'Elder George D. Watt, whose valuable services to this church as Professor of Phonography, are highly appreciated; has taken down the speeches delivered on this occasion, and they will appear from time to time as circumstances will allow.

Never have we seen the time before when the people were more willing to receive and listen to counsel than now. The high council have only had one case in about seven weeks. Our magistrates have nothing to do. We have little or no use for charter or law. Every man is doing his best to cultivate the ground, and all are anxious to provide things honestly in the sight of all men—to honor our God, our country and its laws. Whenever a dispute or difficulty arises, a word from the proper source puts all to right, and no resort to law. May God ever save us from this snare of men, this drainer of the purse, and this fruitful source of contention and strife.'*

Monday, April 7, 1845.—The stockholders of the Nauvoo House Association met. Elders George A. Smith and Amasa M. Lyman were appointed trustees in the place of Lyman Wight and John Snider; L. R. Foster was appointed clerk.

Tuesday, 8.—I had a conversation with Dr. W. G. Goforth on the principles of the gospel and baptized him, and in company with Brothers Heber C. Kimball and George A. Smith confirmed him a member of the church and ordained him a high priest.

Brother Elijah Fordham returned from New York

*Times and Seasons, vol. vi, pp. 869-871

and brought twelve hundred and sixty-three dollars for the Temple.

Wednesday, 9.—I met in council with the Twelve and bishops at the Trustees' Office. We agreed to advise Peter Maughan and Jacob Peart to return from Rock river whither they had been to work a coal mine; Reuben McBride to put the Kirtland property in the best state possible, without paying out money and to come to Nauvoo bye and bye. The bishops were instructed to sell the steamboat *Maid of Iowa* for what they could get for it.

Elder Lorenzo Snow returned to Nauvoo and brought some money and property and a six-pounder cannon on tithing.

Thursday, 10.—I met in council with Elders Heber C. Kimball, Orson Hyde, John Taylor, George A. Smith, Willard Richards and Amasa M. Lyman. We decided to print our own works at Nauvoo; remove the printing office into the Masonic Hall, and print the *Book of Doctrine and Covenants, Hymn Book* and *History* as soon as possible.

<small>Nauvoo to Become the Public Center for the Church.</small>

A resolution was passed to disfellowship George J. Adams and Sam Brannan, and a letter was written to Elder Parley P. Pratt on the subject.

The trustees of the Nauvoo House Association met and examined their books.

Evening, the Twelve and bishops met at the Historian's Office and prayed for rain; an abundant harvest; deliverance from our enemies and blessings on the saints.

Friday, 11.—I met with the General Council at the Masonic Hall.

Saturday, 12.—The trustees of the Nauvoo House Association met.

The old police invited the Twelve and their families to a party at the Masonic Hall, when a comfortable repast was partaken of. The police performed a new piece entitled, 'Father Marks' Return to Mormonism'.

Evening, the U. S. deputy marshal for the district of Illinois arrived in town with writs for myself and others.

Sunday, 13.—Meeting at the stand. Elders Heber C. Kimball and John Taylor preached. Several officers attended meeting. Elder Taylor gave them to understand that if they made an attempt to serve writs on him it would cost them their lives, and said, if they wished to magnify the law and make it honorable they should bring to justice the murderers of Joseph and Hyrum, two of our best men, who were treacherously butchered while in the custody of officers pledged for their safety; and that he would not submit any more to such outrages on our lives and liberties, for under present circumstances the law is only powerful to hold men still while the lawless massacre them.

I attended the high priests' quorum meeting and gave much counsel.

The following letter from the governor was read:

LETTER OF GOVERNOR FORD ON THE ORGANIZATION OF TOWN GOVERNMENT WITHIN NAUVOO

'Springfield, April 8, 1845.

General Brigham Young:

I have received your letter of March the 31st and have attentively considered its contents until this time. It is a matter of much delicacy and importance to answer in the best manner the inquiries contained in it. A town corporation under the general law, will evidently be insufficient for such a place as Nauvoo. The general law does not extend your limits over a mile square. This however may be remedied in some degree by making a number of corporations to include the whole territory of the city. In this case however you will be liable to a want of united action; and so many governments though less efficient must be more expensive than a city government.

I make no doubt also that you stand in need of a local court which however you cannot have higher than that of a justice of the peace under the present law. I would advise that you incorporate as many towns, one mile square as will cover the city; and I make no doubt but that your peaceable and orderly conduct, if continued, will be duly appreciated by the next session of the legislature. By that time the storm of passion produced by recent events will have subsided and I make no doubt a new charter will be granted.

The powers under your town charters will be but limited it is true.

They are to make and execute ordinances not inconsistent with law and the Constitution; to prevent and remove nuisances; to restrain and prohibit gaming and disorderly conduct; to prevent the indecent exhibition of horses; to license public shows; to sink and repair public wells; to open and repair the streets and alleys and make pavements and sidewalks, and to provide means to protect the town from injuries by fires, and to levy a tax on real estate for town purposes. These powers are somewhat better than none; and will give you some protection and provide somewhat for the advancement and comfort of your city. And I would advise the people to avail themselves of them until they can do better at another session. As to a want of legal united action, on the part of so many corporations in any common design for the good of the city; that must be supplied at present by their voluntary concurrence, which can be brought about by the influence of your leading citizens. There is no other way to do it that I can think of. Whether you have that spirit of unity amongst you which will enable them to do so, you know better than I can know.

As to your military affairs I have already written to the Hon. A. W. Babbitt concerning that subject and I refer you to that letter for my opinions at length as to your military organization. Since I wrote that letter I have been advised of the movement at Carthage in relation to the Hon. J. B. Backenstos, and also of the proceedings of the Carthagenians in removing the cannon from McComb. As yet I am ignorant of their design in this latter movement. Whether they intend it as a mere bravado, to keep up agitation and excitement, until after the trials; or whether there is to be a general move and renewal of the designs of last summer and fall I am not aware. I have seen the *Warsaw Signal* which again preached expulsion but beyond this I have seen nothing and know nothing of their designs. I have on Saturday last dispatched a bold and trusty man to demand the arms and cannon at Carthage and Warsaw. These events may for aught I know point to a new war against you. If they do you cannot be organized as a part of the state militia too soon.

I am aware that under such an organization there must be many persons exempt from military duty; but in case of danger no doubt they will voluntarily enroll themselves; there is no law to forbid their service; their exemption is not a disqualification to serve, but a privilege not to serve if they choose.

In case a mob should be raised against you it will be your privilege and one of your highest duties to society and yourselves to resist it. But you know your condition as a people. You know the prejudices which exist; and the disposition of the public mind to believe evil of you. You will therefore have to be cautious. Do nothing which will allow your opponents to say that you have begun a war. Place them clearly in the wrong and keep them so.

As to the great western measure if congress would grant you the land, I think it would be good policy for your people to move to some far distant country. Your religion is new and it surprises the people as any great novelty in religion generally does. They cannot rise above the prejudices excited by such novelty. However truly and sincerely your own people may believe in it; the impression on the public mind everywhere is that your leading men are impostors and rogues and that the others are dupes and fools. This impression in the minds of the great mass is sufficient to warrant them in considering and treating you as enemies and outcasts; as men to be cherished and trusted in nothing, because in their estimation some of you are deluded, and others designing in matters of religion. If you can get off by yourselves you may enjoy peace; but surrounded by such neighbors I confess that I do not foresee the time when you will be permitted to enjoy quiet. I was informed by General Joseph Smith last summer that he contemplated a removal west; and from what I learned from him and others at that time I think if he had lived he would have begun to move in the matter before this time. I would be willing to exert all my feeble abilities and influence to further your views in this respect if it was the wish of your people.

WESTERN MOVEMENT OF THE SAINTS SUGGESTED

I would suggest a matter in confidence, California now offers a field for the prettiest enterprise that has been undertaken in modern time. It is but sparsely inhabited and by none but the Indian or imbecile Mexican Spaniard. I have not inquired enough to know how strong it is in men and means. But this we know that if conquered from Mexico that country is so physically weak and morally distracted that she could never send a force there to conquer it. Why would it not be a pretty operation for your people to go out there, take possession of and conquer a portion of the vacant country, and establish an independent government of your own subject only to the laws of nations. [?] You would remain there a long time before you would be disturbed by the proximity of other settlements. If you conclude to do this your design ought not to be known or otherwise it would become the duty of the United States to prevent your emigration. But if you once cross the line of the United States territories you would be in no danger of being interfered with.

I am very respectfully
Your obedient Servant,
[Signed]   THOMAS FORD.'*

Sunday 13, (*continued*).—At four p. m., I met with the Quorum of the Twelve.

Evening, in company with several brethren I visited the U. S. deputy marshal at the Mansion; he was very polite."

*A facsimile of this paragraph of Governor Ford's letter will be found in the *Comprehensive History of the Church*, Century I, vol. iii, p. 420.

CHAPTER XXX

AN APPEAL TO LYMAN WIGHT TO BE UNITED WITH
THE TWELVE—LETTERS TO THE PRESIDENT OF THE
UNITED STATES AND THE GOVERNORS OF THE RE-
SPECTIVE STATES—LETTERS OF GOVERNOR FORD TO
STATE MILITARY LEADERS—IMPORTANT DOCTRINAL
LETTER OF THE TWELVE TO THE CHURCH

"*Monday, April* 14, 1845.—The public hands
commenced the foundation of the wall around the
Temple block.

Elder Richards and I attended the deacons' meeting.
The deacons have become very efficient looking after
the welfare of the saints; every part of the city is
watched with the strictest care, and whatever time of
night the streets are traveled at the corner of every
block a deacon is found attending to his duty.

Tuesday, 15.—Brother Heber C. Kimball, George
A. Smith and myself went to visit Philo Dibble, who
was sick. We then went to Isaac Higbee's
office and attended a council in relation to the organization of a town under the general incorporation act. Afterwards visited the arsenal and Uncle John Smith who let Dr. Cannon have his house and lot in Macedonia to cancel an obligation for four hundred dollars held by Dr. Cannon's wife and her sister against myself and Brother Kimball.
Proceeded to Bishop Whitney's and administered to his
wife who was sick; thence to the Seventies' Hall and
attended General Council, where the letter from Governor Ford was read. If the advice of Governor Ford
relative to organizing city government under the state
law, were complied with to the letter, it would require

Towns Under General State Corporation Act Considered.

twelve incorporations, as limited by the state statutes to supply the place of the Nauvoo Charter and cover the limits of the city with this species of complicated, restricted town protection.

Wednesday, 16.—At sunset, Brother Heber C. Kimball and I laid hands on Brother W. Richards who was sick. A small portion of the city was incorporated as the town of Nauvoo and Alpheus Cutler, Orson Spencer, Charles C. Rich, Theodore Turley and David Fullmer were appointed trustees; they selected policemen, and appointed Hosea Stout captain, they also appointed assessors, collectors and other officers.

Thursday, 17.—I met in council with Elders Orson Pratt, George A. Smith, Amasa M. Lyman, C. C. Rich, and Samuel Bent, at Elder Richards'. We wrote as follows:

LETTER TO LYMAN WIGHT ET AL: A PLEA FOR UNION

'To Brother Lyman Wight and All the Brethren With Him—
     Greeting:
We the Council of the Twelve being assembled and having learned your present circumstances and situation and also your future calculations with regard to your journey west, cannot feel justified without giving you a word of counsel and advice together with some information relative to our present prospects. We are prospering in this city both temporally and spiritually. Immigration continues to this city. Several hundred have arrived this spring. Great peace and union prevail among all the saints. There were many thousands present at our conference this month. All of our business was performed with the utmost peace and union and not a dissenting voice. We are rushing the Temple ahead with a strong hand. Tithings come in for the Temple more liberally than they have ever done before, and with but few exceptions the saints are willing to give their all for the Temple if required. There is every prospect of getting on the roof and finishing some rooms by next autumn when we shall commence administering the ordinances of endowment according to the commandment. We intend commencing again on the Nauvoo House within a few days. All the saints feel spirited and determined to carry out the measures of our martyred Prophet. There is no prospect of any mob at present, and all things bid fair for peace and prosperity.

And now, dear brethren, if you will hearken to our counsel you will give up all idea of journeying west at present. If you go westward before you have received your endowments in the Temple you will not prosper. And when you meet with trouble and difficulty let no one say that the counsel of the Twelve brought them into it, for we now in the name of the Lord counsel and advise you not to go west at present. We desire, dear brethren, that you should take hold with us and help us to accomplish the building of the Lord's houses. Come brethren, be one with us, and let us be agreed in all of our exertions to roll on the great wheel of the kingdom. We forward this letter by Brother Bent. He will give you further instructions relative to our proceedings and future calculations and we hope you will receive his counsel and do accordingly and all shall be well.'

Elder Samuel Bent was instructed to read the foregoing letter aloud to all the company.

Brother Lyman Wight has one hundred and thirty souls numbering forty able bodied men with him.

Evening, the Twelve and presiding bishops met and prayed.

Friday, 18.—As the workmen on the Temple had raised a large stone about fifteen hundred pounds weight, the chain broke and it fell fifty feet, but without injury to the building or any person.

Sunday, 20.—Elders Orson Pratt, Phineas H. Young and I preached. Afternoon, in council with the Twelve at the Seventies' Hall when four elders were set apart for missions.

Monday, 21.—Elder Wm. W. Player put up the first star on the southeast corner of the Temple. Elders Heber C. Kimball and William Clayton were watching the progress of the stone towards its destination: the 'stars' will add much to the beauty of the Temple.

Tuesday, 22.—Attended General Council.

Wednesday, 23.—Brother George A. Smith spent the evening with me.

Thursday, 24.—Elders Phineas H. Young, Jonathan Dunham, Charles Shumway, Lewis Dana and S. Tindale, started west on a mission to the Lamanites. Evening, attended prayer meeting with the Twelve at Elder Richards.

Realizing fully the insecurity of our position surrounded as we are by mob violence, and the constitution and laws of Illinois being powerless for our protection we deemed it wisdom, in General Council, to write as follows to the President of the United States and to the governor of every state in the Union except Missouri [and Illinois]:

LETTER TO THE PRESIDENT OF THE UNITED STATES AND THE GOVERNORS OF THE RESPECTIVE STATES

'Nauvoo, Illinois, April 24, 1845.

His Excellency James K. Polk,
President of the United States.

Hon. Sir:

Suffer us, Sir, in behalf of a disfranchised and long afflicted people to prefer a few suggestions for your serious consideration in hope of a friendly and unequivocal response, at as early a period as may suit your convenience, and the extreme urgency of the case seem to demand.

It is not our present design to detail the multiplied and aggravated wrongs that we have received in the midst of a nation that gave us birth. Most of us have long been loyal citizens of some one of these United States over which you have the honor to preside, while a few only claim the privileges of peaceable and lawful emigrants designing to make the Union our permanent residence.

We say we are a disfranchised people. We are privately told by the highest authorities of this state that it is neither prudent nor safe for us to vote at the polls; still we have continued to maintain our right to vote, until the blood of our best men has been shed, both in Missouri and Illinois, with impunity.

You are doubtless somewhat familiar with the history of our extermination from the state of Missouri, wherein scores of our brethren were massacred; hundreds died through want and sickness occasioned by their unparalleled sufferings; some millions of our property were confiscated or destroyed, and some fifteen thousand souls fled for their lives to the then hospitable and peaceful shores of Illinois; and that the state of Illinois granted to us a liberal charter (for the term of perpetual succession) under whose provision private rights have become invested, and the largest city in the state has grown up, numbering about twenty thousand inhabitants.

But Sir, the startling attitude recently assumed by the state of Illinois forbids us to think that her designs are any less vindictive than those of Missouri. She has already used the military of the state with the executive at their head to coerce and surrender up our best men to unparalleled murder, and that too under the most sacred pledges of protection and safety. As a salvo for such unearthly perfidy and guilt she told us through her highest executive officer, that the laws should be magnified and the murderers brought to justice; but the blood of her innocent victims had not been wholly wiped from the floor of the awful arena, where the citizens of a sovereign state pounced upon two defenseless servants of God our Prophet and our Patriarch, before the senate of that state rescued one of the indicted actors in that mournful tragedy from the sheriff of Hancock county and gave him an honorable seat in her hall of legislation, and all who were indicted by the grand jury of Hancock county for the murder of Generals Joseph and Hyrum Smith are suffered to roam at large watching for further prey.

To crown the climax of those bloody deeds the state has repealed all those chartered rights, by which we might have lawfully defended ourselves against aggressors.   If we defend ourselves hereafter against violence whether it comes under the shadow of law or otherwise (for we have reason to expect it both ways) we shall then be charged with treason and suffer the penalty; and if we continue passive and non-resistant we must certainly expect to perish, for our enemies have sworn it.

And here, Sir, permit us to state that General Joseph Smith, during his short life, was arraigned at the bar of his country about fifty times charged with criminal offenses, but was acquitted every time by his country, his enemies, or rather his religious opponents, almost invariably being his judges.   And we further testify that as a people, we are law abiding, peaceable, and without crime and we challenge the world to prove the contrary; and while other less cities in Illinois have had special courts instituted to try their criminals, we have been stripped of every source of arraigning marauders and murderers who are prowling around to destroy us except the common magistracy.

With these facts before you, Sir, will you write to us without delay as a father and friend and advise us what to do.   We are members of the same great confederacy.   Our fathers, nay some of us, have fought and bled for our country, and we love her Constitution dearly.

In the name of Israel's God and by virtue of multiplied ties of country and kindred, we ask your friendly interposition in our favor. Will it be too much for us to ask you to convene a special session of congress and furnish us an asylum, where we can enjoy our rights of conscience and religion unmolested?   Or, will you in a special message to that body, when convened recommend a remonstrance against such unhallowed acts of oppression and expatriation as this people have continued to receive from the states of Missouri and Illinois?   Or, will you favor us by your personal influence and by your official rank?   Or will you express our views concerning what is called the 'Great Western Measure' of colonizing the Latter-day Saints in Oregon, the northwestern territory, or some location remote from the states, where the hand of oppression shall not crush every noble principle and extinguish every patriotic feeling?

And now, Honored Sir, having reached out our imploring hands to you, with deep solemnity, we would importune with you as a father, a friend, a patriot and the head of a mighty nation, by the Constitution of American Liberty, by the blood of our fathers who have fought for the independence of this Republic, by the blood of the martyrs which has been shed in our midst, by the wailings of the widows and orphans, by their murdered fathers and mothers, brothers and sisters, wives and children, by the dread of immediate destruction from secret combinations now forming for our overthrow, and by every endearing tie that binds man to man and renders life bearable, and that too, for aught we know for the last time, that you will lend your immediate aid to quell the violence of mobocracy, and exert your influence to establish us as a people in our civil and religious rights where we now are, or in some part of the United States, or at some place remote therefrom, where we may colonize in peace and safety as soon as circumstances will permit.

We sincerely hope that your future prompt measure towards us will be dictated by the best feelings that dwell in the bosom of humanity, and the blessings of a grateful people and of many ready to perish shall come upon you.

> We are Sir,
> > with great respect,
> > > Your Obt. Servts.
> > > > [Signed]   BRIGHAM YOUNG,
> > > > WILLARD RICHARDS,
> > > > ORSON SPENCER,
> > > > ORSON PRATT,
> > > > W. W. PHELPS,
> > > > A. W. BABBITT,
> > > > J. M. BERNHISEL,

Committee in behalf of the Church of Jesus Christ of Latter-day Saints at Nauvoo, Illinois.'

'P.S.   As many of our communications, postmarked at Nauvoo have failed of their destination and the mails around us have been intercepted by our enemies, we shall send this to some distant office by the hand of a special messenger.'

The letters to the governors were the same as the above with slight requisite alterations.

Saturday, 26.—In company with Brothers Heber C. Kimball, George A. Smith, Amasa M. Lyman, and others I attended Brother George D. Watt's phonographic class from nine a. m. till noon.

Sunday, 27.—Elders A. W. Babbitt and John Taylor preached at the stand.   I met with the brethren of the Twelve at Elder W. Richards': we revised the conference minutes.

Evening, the Twelve Apostles, Presidents John Smith and Joseph Young met for prayer.

Monday, 28.—In council with Brothers H. C. Kimball, John Taylor and N. K. Whitney; we read letters from Parley P. Pratt in relation to his movements in the east; he thinks that he has influence with President Polk and other leading men of the nation, who are determined secretly to control the officers of Illinois so as to induce them to do away with mobs and mobocracy.

Tuesday, 29.—Evening, I attended General Council: Elder Samuel Bent reported the result of his visit to Lyman Wight's camp.

Thursday, May 1, 1845.—Accompanied by Brothers Heber C. Kimball, Newel K. Whitney, Alpheus Cutler and Wm. Clayton I rode to the river and bought lumber to the amount of sixteen hundred dollars. Brother Kimball and I gathered teams to draw it to the Temple. Evening, attended prayer meeting.

Saturday, 3.—Brother Ellis M. Sanders let the Trustees of the Temple have one thousand dollars in cash.

At a conference held in Batavia, N. Y., four branches containing seventeen elders, one priest and forty-two members were represented: Elder Winslow Farr presided.

Sunday, 4.—I attended meeting. Elder Orson Spencer and I preached. I dined at Brother Willard Richards' in company with Elders Kimball, Smith, Taylor and our wives. I met with the Twelve and wrote letters to Elders Parley P. Pratt and E. T. Benson, notifying the latter of his release and of Willard Snow's appointment as his successor in Massachusetts.

William Smith and family arrived from the east.

Elder Wilford Woodruff attended a conference in Blackburn, near Preston, England, and dedicated a new hall to worship; full house and interesting time.

Monday, 5.—Attended council of the Twelve at my house, on the case of Samuel Brannan and matters in the east. William Smith was present and expressed his satisfaction with the organization of the church.

Tuesday, 6.—The following was published in the *Nauvoo Neighbor*:

A VOICE FROM NAUVOO

'*Whereas* it is currently reported in various parts of this county, and in the adjoining counties, as we are creditably informed, that it is our intention to throng Carthage during the ensuing session of the circuit court of this county, for the purpose of awing or overruling the court so as to procure a conviction of certain men of the crime of murdering Joseph and Hyrum Smith; and *whereas* such reports are calculated to awaken an unjust prejudice against an innocent people; and *whereas* our enemies have jumped upon this stratagem as a hobby to raise an excitement against us; and *whereas* many honest and law abiding men are liable to be misled and imposed upon by these false, malicious, and envious reports; and *whereas* the governor of our state has solemnly pledged himself to us that the laws should be executed in justice in the premises; and *whereas* we did at that time pledge ourselves as a people to patiently wait their execution, and the action of the government; and *whereas* it is reported that certain individuals are trying to raise an excitement on the editorials of the *Nauvoo Neighbor*.

We *therefore*, in behalf of the church we represent do hereby publish to all men, that as a people and a council, we have no knowledge of the *Neighbor* until we read it as do others, and therefore cannot be responsible for it, and all we ask is the same consideration in the public mind, as is exercised towards the editorials of other papers in our land. And we further declare to all men, that as a people we are still determined to abide our pledge, and await the action of the executive and judiciary, and tarry at home and attend to our own business as usual during the sitting of the court except such as have lawful business with the court and are required to be in attendance, and hope that all men will do the same, and we wish, decidedly wish, that those whose business it is to keep the peace during court, should do it, and let us as a people alone, for we do not wish to be brought in collision with our neighbors and we are determined to abide the law.

In behalf of a General Council of the authorities of the Church of Jesus Christ of Latter-day Saints at Nauvoo.

[Signed]   WILLARD RICHARDS, Committe.'

Evening, I attended General Council, when it was agreed that letters should be written to Governor Ford and J. B. Hoge, M. C., in relation to the threats of the mob; and to take measures for the brethren to hold themselves in readiness for defense in case of an attack, and to pursue a medium course avoiding extremes that might raise an excitement in the country.

The Twelve met with the old police at the Masonic Hall to make preparations to prevent our surprise by the mob.

Wednesday, 7.—Brother Orson Hyde reported that a mob of about two hundred men were collected at Appanoose who had prevented some of the brethren from going to work on the Island. The mob captain told the brethren that they had arranged matters so as to cut off all communication with the governor.

The officers of the Legion met at the Masonic Hall.

Evening, attended prayer meeting with the Twelve, N. K. Whitney, and Levi Richards.

Thursday, 8.—I called at Elder Richards' office at ten a. m., and remained till five p. m., when Elder Richards accompanied me to Elder Kimball's.

Evening, met and prayed with the Twelve.

The council wrote to Elder Woodruff as follows:

COUNCIL'S LETTER TO ELDER WILFORD WOODRUFF—ENGLAND

'It is a part of our religion to support any government, wherever we may be, that will protect us in common with other citizens; for, to this end governments are instituted; and as England has ever been true and faithful to us, as a people in common with others, the elders cannot be too particular to enjoin on all the saints to yield obedience to the laws, and respect every man in his office, letting politics wholly, entirely and absolutely alone, and preach the principles of the gospel of salvation; for to this end were they ordained and sent forth. We are for peace, we want no contention with any person or government, and should war commence between England and America, it will probably be wisdom for you and all the American elders to return immediately home, and leave all parties to fight their own battles. * *

The stones are in rapid progress for the new font [i. e. of the Temple]. The wall for the foundation of the pickets or railing around the Temple block, and the block west of the Temple (to be in one) is also commenced. The bricks are making for the Nauvoo House; one hundred and forty thousand feet of pine timber was received last Saturday for our public buildings; another raft is expected soon and we anticipate they will be enclosed early in the fall. Immigration has been greater than usual this season; perfect peace and union prevail. It is also a time of health.

We have thought it would be very agreeable to the feelings of the English saints to furnish a bell for the Temple, if this is their pleasure you can forward it the first conveyance, and we will have it hung as the building is going up. We are but little acquainted with the weight of bells; we have thought of two thousand pounds weight, but we leave this to your judgment; we want one that can be heard night or day.

We forward you with this in a package a letter of attorney constituting you an agent to transact all necessary business for the church in the United Kingdom of Great Britain, and on the continent of Europe.'

Friday, 9.—I met with the Twelve in council, also Elders N. K. Whitney and W. W. Phelps and J. B. Backenstos.

Saturday, 10.—Brother George A. Smith called upon me this morning and I accompanied him to the Historian's Office where we read and revised Church History.

Afternoon, met in General Council.

Sunday, 11.—Elders William and George A. Smith and I preached at the stand. Evening, attended prayer meeting.

Elder Woodruff attended a quarterly conference at Clitheroe, England, and ordained one elder and several to the lesser priesthood. He had an interesting and affectionate time with those churches built up by Elder Heber C. Kimball on his first mission to England.

Conference at Clitheroe England.

Monday, 12.—Evening, with Brothers Heber C. Kimball, W. Richards and George A. Smith at Brother Edward Hunter's revising history.

Tuesday, 13.—With Elders Heber C. Kimball, W. Richards and George A. Smith reading and revising Church History at Brother Edward Hunter's where we had retired to keep out of the way of writs reported to have been issued against us.

Governor Ford wrote the following letters:

LETTERS FROM GOVERNOR FORD TO GENERAL DEMING

'Executive Department,
Springfield, Ill, May 13, 1845.

M. R. Deming, *Brigadier-General, Illinois Militia.*

Sir: I have received information which I do not know whether to credit or not, that certain persons in Hancock county are preparing a force, with a view to prevent the witnesses on the part of the state in the murder cases, now pending, from attending court at the term to be held this month. If such should be the case, and if it should become necessary to protect the court, the jurors or the witnesses whose duty it may be to attend; or to secure the custody of prisoners, you are hereby fully authorized and empowered to call out and employ a sufficient force of militia from your brigade for that purpose. This order to include the militia of Nauvoo.

[Signed]   THOMAS FORD, Governor and Commander-in-Chief.'

'Springfield, Ill., May 13, 1845.

Brigadier-General M. R. Deming:

Sir: I herewith send you authority to call out the militia of your brigade if necessary. The defendants in the murder cases have written here for Logan to defend them; and it is understood here that they do not intend to create any disturbance. The signs are not yet sufficiently certain to authorize me now to send militia there. I have employed Lamborn to assist in the prosecution. You will advise with him. If the defendants should organize a force to prevent a fair trial and keep off the witnesses I think it would be best to get the cases continued and at another term it will be so manifest that a force will be necessary to protect the court that I will be justified in sending one. But if at present I send one I will be laughed at and it will be universally believed that no necessity existed for it and that I have put the state to expense for nothing. If however you see that force is to be used and should think it most advisable to meet the crisis at this time, I give you power to employ your whole brigade including the Mormons of course. Upon the whole I think that they are the most fit material to be called on as their fidelity in doing their duty during the pending trials may be more thoroughly relied on than any troops I could send there.

I am most respectfully your obedient servant,
[Signed]   THOMAS FORD.'

GOVERNOR FORD'S LETTER TO. A. W. BABBITT—VACILLATION

'Springfield, May 13, 1845.

Hon. A. W. Babbitt:

Dear Sir: I received your favor from Galena last evening. If I thought that I could have the least influence in preventing a disturbance in Hancock county I would cheerfully go over there. My opinion however is that my presence there, and that of Mr. Hoge would only aggravate matters. I have employed Mr. Lamborn to assist the prosecution and have sent a military order to General Deming giving him authority to call out his whole brigade, including the Mormons of course if necessary to protect the court, the witnesses, the jurors; or to secure the custody of prisoners. He will use this order with discretion. You can certainly raise a force in Hancock amply sufficient to overpower any mob forces which can be got together. The defendants have written here for counsel, and it is universally understood here, that they do not intend to resist. At any rate the signs are not so definite as to authorize me now to call the militia. If I were to do so, the people would be made to believe all over the state that there was no necessity for it, and that the public had been corruptly put to this expense to serve the Mormon vote. Besides I very much question whether I could raise a force now, when there is so little apparent necessity for it; and I also question whether any force which I could send could be relied on to act efficiently. You suggest in your letter that if there shall be a disturbance the distance to this place where I reside, would prevent a messenger from arriving until after the event had occurred. Nearly the same thing would happen if I were at Carthage. If I were to call on the militia (other than the Mormons) I would have to send back an order to this side of the Illinois river before I could begin to find any that I could rely on. It is evident to my mind that it would not do to call on any of the militia of the military tract. They would either stand idle or join the enemy. If a force shall really become necessary I can think of none which can be embodied so soon, or who would be likely to act with the requisite zeal and fidelity as the Mormons themselves. General Deming has my orders for this purpose; and as I do not pretend to be a military man I do not see why he cannot act as efficiently with this force in my absence as if I were present.

I would make another suggestion: Possibly, if a mob should be organized to keep away the witnesses it may be the best for the prosecution to move for a continuance of the indictments grounded on the absence of testimony setting forth all the circumstances calculated to prevent a fair trial. And if the case shall have to be continued on account of a mob, the necessity will then be apparent to all the world for a force at the next term. But until such a necessity is manifest it is the very worst policy to be making frequent calls of the militia. The very idea that the necessity for protecting the Mormons and putting the state to expense for that purpose continually exists, creates a prejudice against them and a strong desire everywhere of getting them out of the state. Besides the mob party have this advantage that if I send a force there capable of overpowering them they can and will swear that they never had the least intention of creating the least possible disturbance. And what is more they will make the whole people of the state believe it. They will believe in such a case that I have been humbugged; and humbugged by the Mormons. You may well conceive what a prejudice this impression will create. Upon the whole I am decidedly of opinion that the local militia under the command of General Deming ought to be relied on; that even this force ought not to be called out until it is manifestly apparent that it is needed for the protection of the law against actual violence and that in fact it might be better to suffer a continuance of the prosecutions if it will be the means of shewing to the world what the defendants and their friends will do if not prevented. I have made these same suggestions to Mr. Lamborn and General Deming.

I am most respectfully,

Your Obedient Servant,

[Signed]   THOMAS FORD.'

Wednesday, 14.—Continued at Brother Edward Hunter's as yesterday; my health, and that of Brother Richards poor; but we read and revised history all day.

Thursday, 15.—I was quite unwell, Brother George A. Smith called in the forenoon and read the *Neighbor* to me: Brothers W. Richards and Amasa M. Lyman sick.

Fast day: all works were stopped. Meetings were held in the several wards and donations made to the bishops for the poor; enough was contributed to supply the wants of the poor until harvest. Evening, met at Brother Richards' for prayer.

Friday, 16.—I spent the day at Brother Hunter's in company with Brothers Heber C. Kimball, Willard Richards, George A. Smith and N. K. Whitney revising history: Thomas Bullock read for us. I wrote a letter to the architect directing him to place a stone in the west end (front) of the Temple with the inscription 'Holiness to the Lord' thereon. Isaac Chase agreed to let the church have one thousand dollars. Elder Orson Pratt called and reported that four hundred men had gone up the opposite side of the river.

Saturday, 17.—Revising history as yesterday, with the addition of Brother John Taylor: Brother Hunter and family were very kind to us. We wrote an epistle to the saints in Nauvoo dated at Point Clear and directed the same to Brother Orson Pratt.

Sunday, 18.—Elder Orson Pratt preached to the saints; also read the following epistle:

GENERAL LETTER OF THE TWELVE TO THE CHURCH FROM THEIR RETIREMENT

'Point Clear, Steamboat under way,
one o'clock Saturday morning,
May 17, 1845.

To the Church of Jesus Christ of Latter-day Saints
in the City of Joseph—Greeting:

Beloved Brethren: Our whole souls bless you; and we are happy in the privilege of communicating to you a few thoughts. Much more would we rejoice were it our privilege to be in your midst the coming Sabbath and tell you all that is in our hearts; but we are pilgrims in a world of sorrow and woe. In our journeyings to proclaim the gospel and bring about salvation to the honest in heart, God is with us and we prosper; though weary, we are not cast down nor discouraged, for we know that victory is with the upright.

We are happy to hear of the great union and love manifested at your recent fast, which also the Spirit bore witness of to us, and of your liberality towards the poor, and may the abundance which you have so liberally contributed in your penury in dealing your bread to the hungry be the omen of an abundant harvest of the fruits of the earth into your granaries the present and all future seasons.

Since we commenced our journey we have discovered some letters from Brother Joseph Smith to Bishop Partridge from which we extract the following for your edification and instruction:

MESSAGE OF NEWLY DISCOVERED LETTERS OF THE PROPHET ON CONSECRATION

'I proceed to answer your questions concerning the consecration of property. First, it is not right to condescend to very great particulars in taking inventories. The fact is this, a man is bound by the law of the church, to consecrate to the bishop, before he can be considered a legal heir to the kingdom of Zion; and this too without constraint; and unless he does this, he cannot be acknowledged before the Lord, on the church book: therefore to condescend to particulars, I will tell you that every man must be his own judge how much he should receive, and how much he should suffer to remain in the hands of the bishop. I speak of those who consecrate more than they need for the support of themselves and their families.

'The matter of consecration must be done by the mutual consent of both parties; for to give the bishop power to say how much every man shall have, and he be obliged to comply with the bishop's judgment is giving to the bishop more power than a king has; and upon the other hand, to let every man say how much he needs and the bishop be obliged to comply with his judgment is to throw Zion into confusion and make a slave of the bishops. The fact is, there must be a balance or equilibrium of power, between the bishop and the people; and thus harmony and good-will will be preserved among you.'

THE PRINCIPLE OF FASTS DEFINED

Let this be an ensample to all saints, and there will never be any lack for bread: When the poor are starving, let those who have, fast one day and give what they otherwise would have eaten to the bishops for the poor, and every one will abound for a long time; and this is one great and important principle of fasts approved of the Lord. And so long as the saints will all live to this principle with glad hearts and cheerful countenances they will always have an abundance.

We will give you another extract from the same author in a letter to Elder Phelps when in Zion:

FATE OF THE SONS OF PERDITION NOT REVEALED

'Say to the brethren Hulets and to all others that the Lord never authorized them to say that the devil, or his angels, or the son of perdition should ever be restored; for their state of destiny was not revealed to man, is not revealed, nor ever shall be revealed save to those who are made partakers thereof; consequently those who teach this doctrine have not received it of the Spirit of the Lord. Truly Brother Oliver declared it to be the doctrine of devils. We, therefore, command that this doctrine be taught no more in Zion. We sanction the decision of the bishop and his council in relation to this doctrine being a bar of communion.'

Let this extract remind the elders and all saints that a wise head keeps a still tongue. And that it is far better many times for men, yes and women too to forget all they know, than to tell all they know. And better still to forget than to tell some great things which they do not know. Probably the elders in Zion know about as much about the devil's being redeemed, as the elders know about the great God of the Gods, of the God of this world, which some have spoken of, concerning which they know nothing. There are Lords many and Gods many. But who are they, and what their relation to us, or this earth? Who can answer? This is a subject not revealed, therefore let the elders be silent concerning it. And who knows anything about our suffering in this world for sins committed in a former state of existence? Let him who had the answer by revelation speak: and if no such revelation exists, let this subject also live where it belongs in eternal forgetfulness to the ignorant until they shall be instructed from the right source.

Wisdom is justified of her children, therefore beloved brethren be wise and live up to the holy religion which you profess—to mind your own business and let your neighbors alone. Plant your gardens and till your farms; acknowledge your heavenly Father in all things; continue to raise up his house; walk humbly before him; watch and pray without ceasing; for ye know not what hour the thief will come. But be ye sure of this the thief will never come while he sees the good man of the house watching for him.

If ye are one, says Jesus, then are ye mine, and whatsoever ye shall ask the Father in my name he will give it unto you. Then brethren continue to be one and ask unceasingly and God will deliver you from all your enemies, break the oppressor's power and continue peace in the beloved city. Brethren pray for us that we may be prospered on our journey, and be returned to the saints in peace and safety when we shall have completed our mission. We bless you and praying the God of our fathers, Abraham, Isaac and Jacob to bless you with every blessing even unto everlasting life and salvation in his presence in the name of Jesus Christ, Amen.'

Sunday, 18, (continued).—At five p. m., the Presidents of Seventies met. President Joseph Young spoke emphatically as to putting down wickedness and evil known to exist among members of the quorums.

Evening, attended council and prayer meeting with the Twelve at Brother Richards': adjourned at 2 a. m.

Elder Woodruff attended a conference at Carlisle, England, one hundred and sixty-five members were represented including thirty-seven officers.

A conference was held in Ilion, Herkimer county, New York, fifty-two members, nine elders and two priests were represented.

Monday, 19.—Associated with Brothers Heber C. Kimball, John Taylor, and George A. Smith, I spent the day at Brother Robert Pierce's; Brother Pierce had gone to Carthage as a juror, his family made us very comfortable. Brothers W. Richards and George A. Smith went to Brother Elijah Fordham's.

Many brethren went to Carthage to attend the trial of the murderers of Joseph and Hyrum Smith: George D. Watt attended court and reported the proceedings.

Tuesday, 20.—With the brethren named I remained at Brother Pierce's; Willard Richards and George A. Smith joined us. We read and revised fifty-seven pages of History of Joseph Smith from Book 'B': Brothers Amasa M. Lyman and others called to see us.

Wednesday, 21.—Brother Richards went to Brother Fordham's. Brother George A. [Smith] visited the families of the Twelve who were from home and spent the afternoon with Brother Richards. At nine p. m., Brothers H. C. Kimball, J. Taylor, G. A. Smith, W. H. Kimball, Bishop Garn and I called at Brother Richards' and remained till midnight.

The following letter was sent to Josiah Lamborn, attorney-general of Illinois [by George A. and John Smith]:

REVIEW OF DIFFICULTIES ATTENDANT UPON COLLECTION OF EVI-
DENCE FOR THE PROSPECTIVE TRIAL OF THOSE CHARGED WITH THE
MURDER OF THE PROPHET AND PATRIARCH JOSEPH AND HYRUM
SMITH

'Sir: We are this evening informed by Mr. Scott that it is your wish as prosecuting attorney *vs.* the murderers of the Generals Smith that the Mormons should hunt up the witnesses in the case, and that Mr. Murray McConnell had conveyed the idea that there was a committee in the county whose business it was to collect and arrange the testimony against the day of trial and that said committee are supposed to be Mormons, etc. etc.

Now, Sir, in behalf of the Church of Jesus Christ of Latter-day Saints; or, if you choose, the Mormon fraternity, we beg leave to state to you, what has been often reiterated by us, and which is a well known fact, both to our people and the state, *viz*: that the difficulty causing the pending trials is not between the Mormons and anti-Mormons; nor between the Mormons and the murderers; but it is between the state and the prisoners or offenders.

The facts are, the Messrs. Smiths were murdered while in the charge of the state, relying on the plighted faith of the state for protection, and not in the presence of Mormon witnesses, for the Mormons were not there, but doubtless in the presence of many who were not Mormons

To show our loyalty to the institutions of our country and preserve peace in the county, as a people, we pledged ourselves to abide the operations of the law as directed by the proper authorities of the commonwealth; and that we would abide the decisions of the court, not taking vengeance into our own hands, (as was then feared by some) or commencing prosecutions, to which we have strictly adhered, and intend still to adhere, that our pledge may be honorably redeemed in the sight of all men, although we have been strongly solicited to enter the field of prosecution, and that, too, by the state or her agents: for instance when Mr. McConnell was engaged in preparation for the prosecution he came to Nauvoo and strongly solicited the Mormons to come out as complainants and assist in procuring witnesses, etc.; but we replied that we had had nothing to do with the affair, and wanted nothing to do with it; and for us to enlist in attempting to bring the murderers to justice, no matter how legal in our movements it would be construed into a persecution, or a desire to pick a quarrel on our part, which we were and still are determined to avoid, even every appearance of evil, and cut off every occasion of our enemies, or of those who are ready to seize upon any pretext to make us trouble.

We are decidedly for peace, and we ever have been and as the murders were committed while the murdered were in immediate charge of the state, all we ask is, that the state will prosecute the case to final judgment, and redeem her pledge, as we have ours; or if she choose to abandon the prosecution we shall submit peaceably; although, for public good, we would prefer that justice should take place.

We are unacquainted with the statute which suffers indicted murderers to roam at large month after month without arrest; or, after delivery, or surrender, to run at pleasure before trial, and we know not what other similar laws we might come in contact with, and be liable to break to our own endangering or disadvantage, should we attempt to have anything to do with the case in question.

It is reported to us, true or false we know not, that the sheriff of Hancock county and his deputies have been forbidden by the court to act in pending trials, and that the jurors have been discharged without impaneling. If this be true we are unacquainted with the statutes in the case and have nothing to say.

When Mr. McConnell was here last fall, at his earnest solicitation, we collected all the information in our possession and presented the same to him, supposing he would prosecute the case to final judgment. He took minutes at the time and probably has them now, if he has not handed them over, of which you must be acquainted, better than we, and of which we did not preserve minutes: we know of no new information since that period.

We were happy to hear that the trials had been committed to your able charge, and anticipated that you would have made us a visit before the sitting of the court; and we still anticipate that after court you will make us a visit, that we may have the pleasure of a more general acquaintance among our citizens; and we feel confident that such a visit would be higly appreciated by our friend, General Young, with whom we understand you are acquainted.

We shall be ever ready to assist in favoring the ends of right so far as we can do it and not give any occasion of excitement which would be detrimental to public peace.

We are Sir,

Most Respectfully
Your Servts.
[Signed]   GEORGE A. SMITH,
JOHN SMITH.'

Thursday, 22.—Elder Kimball and I spent the day at Brother Parley P. Pratt's.

Caroline Grant, wife of Elder Wm. Smith, died, aged thirty years and four months.

Evening, I attended council and prayer meeting.

Friday, 23.—Forenoon, Elder Heber C. Kimball, Willard Richards, John Taylor, George A. Smith, John E. Page and myself at Brother Taylor's. Afternoon, Samuel Brannan arrived from New York and in company with Wm. Smith visited us.

Brother John Kay was engaged in drilling out a six-pounder cannon and preparing it for service.

Evening, in council with the Twelve and Bishop Whitney: the improper course of Wm. Smith was the subject of conversation.

Saturday, 24.—A large number of the saints assembled to witness the laying of the capstone on the southeast corner of the Temple. Of the Twelve there were present, besides myself, Heber C. Kimball, John Taylor, Willard Richards, Amasa M. Lyman, George A. Smith, John E. Page, Orson Hyde and Orson Pratt, also Newel K. Whitney and George Miller the Presiding Bishops and Trustees-in-Trust, Alpheus Cutler and Reynolds Cahoon, Temple Committee, William Clayton, Temple recorder, John Smith, patriarch and president of the stake and several members of the high council. The brass band arranged themselves and played the 'Nightingale'.

Laying the Capstone of the Temple.

At six o'clock and eight minutes a. m., Brother Wm. Player commenced spreading the mortar, perfect silence prevailing; the stone being lifted to its place. I stepped on the same and fitted it precisely to its position with the large beetle, at twenty-two minutes past six a. m., the capstone was pronounced set; the band played the 'Capstone March' composed for the occasion by Wm. Pitt. I said:

'The last stone is now laid upon the Temple and I pray the Almighty in the name of Jesus to defend us in this place and sustain us until the Temple is finished and we have all got our endowments.'

The whole congregation then shouted, 'Hosanna, Hosanna, Hosanna, to God and the Lamb, Amen, Amen, and Amen,' which was repeated a second and third time. I concluded by saying, 'So let it be, O Lord Almighty. This is the seventh day of the week or the Jewish Sabbath. It is the day on which the Almighty finished his work and rested from his labors; we have finished the walls of the Temple and we may rest today from our labors.'

I dismissed the workmen for the day and requested them to spend the day in giving thanks to God; and dismissed the congregation, and with the brethren of the Twelve retired to our places of retreat, out of the way of constables and officers who are prowling around the city from Carthage.

The morning was wet and cold, but those present were highly interested with the morning's services, and felt well in consideration that the walls of the Temple were completed, notwithstanding the prophecies of our enemies and apostates.

Elder Orson Pratt preached the funeral discourse of Caroline, the daughter of Joshua and Thalia Grant and wife of Elder Wm. Smith, to a large assembly at the stand; her remains were deposited in the tomb of Joseph: she has left two children to mourn her loss.

At three p. m., a council of the Twelve met at Elder Taylor's and took into consideration the case of Elder Samuel Brannan who had been disfellowshiped; an investigation was entered into and Elder Brannan introduced testimony to prove his innocence of the charges made against him: he was restored to fellowship.

The brethren present expressed their feelings towards Elder Wm. Smith to which he responded. The Twelve then laid their hands upon him and ordained him to be a Patriarch to the whole church: there was a warm interchange of good feeling between William Smith and the quorum.

Wm. Smith Made Patriarch to the Whole Church.

Sunday, 25.—Elder John E. Page preached at the stand. The Presidents of Seventies met and preached to each other. Evening, the Twelve and others met for prayer.

Monday, 26.—I met with several of the Twelve and others in the Phonographic School at Brother Richards'. The Twelve and Trustees met in council at Bishop Miller's and wrote a long communication to Elder Parley P. Pratt.

Tuesday, 27.—I received a respectful letter from Governor Drew in reply to our Memorial to him as governor of Arkansas; stating his inability to protect us in the state of Arkansas, and suggesting the propriety of our settling in Oregon, California, Nebraska or some other country where we will be out of the reach of our persecutors."*

---

*The letter of Governor Drew will be found *in extenso* in *The Comprehensive History of the Church*, Century I, vol. ii. p. 525-6.

CHAPTER XXXI

SUNDRY EVENTS GROUPED TOGETHER LOOKING TO
AN UNDERSTANDING WITH THE STATE GOVERNMENT
AT NAUVOO—HARVEST FEAST AT NAUVOO

"Wednesday, May 28, 1845.—This morning the workmen commenced to raise the attic story of the Temple.

Thursday, 29.—Evening, met at Brother Richards' for prayer in company with Brothers Heber C. Kimball, Orson Hyde, Orson Pratt, Willard Richards, John Taylor, Amasa M. Lyman, N. K. Whitney, George Miller, Joseph Young and Levi Richards. Prayed that the Lord would overrule the movements of Wm. Smith who is endeavoring to ride the Twelve down; also that the Lord would overrule the proceedings of the mob so that we may dwell in peace until the Temple is finished.

Prayer and its Objective.

The court at Carthage heard the lawyer's pleas on the defense in the case the state of Illinois *vs.* the murderers of Joseph and Hyrum Smith; the counsel for the defense exhibited a cruel and mendacious spirit. Calvin A. Warren of Quincy made the most inflammatory speech.

Friday, 30.—I attended council with the Twelve at Elder Taylor's.

The jury at Carthage brought in a verdict of acquittal in favor of Levi Williams, Thomas C. Sharp, Mark Aldrich, Jacob C. Davis and William N. Grover —as we had anticipated: the court, attorneys, jury and bystanders being all fully satisfied of their guilt.*

---

*John Hay, secretary of state in two presidential administrations—McKinley's and Roosevelt's, 1898-1905—who as a boy was reared in Hancock county, in the *Atlantic Monthly* for December, 1869, contributed an article on the "Mormon Prophet's Tragedy", in which he reviews this mass trial of the above named characters, where at one point he writes: "The case was closed, there was not a man on the jury, in the court, in the county, that did not know the defendants had done murder. But it was not proven, and the verdict of 'not guilty' was right in law." Rather a sad comment on justice in Illinois at that time (See *Comprehensive History of the Church*, Century I, vol. ii, p. 327).

Brother George D. Watt attended the trial and took lengthy minutes from which the following is extracted:

GEORGE D. WATT'S REPORT OF THE CARTHAGE TRIAL

'District Court of Illinois,
Carthage, Hancock County, State of Illinois,
May 19, 1845.

The Hon. Richard M. Young of Quincy on the bench. The forenoon was spent in organizing. Adjourned at twelve m.

Court met at two p. m.

Colonel Levi Williams, Thomas C. Sharp, editor of the *Warsaw Signal*, Jacob C. Davis, state senator, Mark Aldrich and William N. Grover were held to bail with each other for sureties, in the sum of one thousand dollars each, to make their appearance in court each day of the term; they were indicted for the murder of Joseph Smith at Carthage jail on the twenty-seventh day of June, 1844.

The court decided that their case would be tried on Wednesday morning, May 21st.

Accordingly the sheriff notified the witnesses for both parties to make their appearance on said morning at seven o'clock; the court then proceeded to other business.

Wednesday Morning, May 21st.

Court opened.

The names of the counsel for the defense are as follows: William A. Richardson, O. H. Browning, Calvin A. Warren.

Josiah Lamborn, Esq. for the people.

Colonel Wm. A. Richardson presented before the court two affidavits drawn out by the defendants to quash the array. The charge of prejudice, consanguinity and partiality was preferred by these affidavits against the county commissioners, the sheriff and his deputies in the arrangement of the present panel of jurors; that their design was to hurt and prejudice the present trial, and thus endanger the lives of the defendants. On these grounds the defendants pleaded for the quashing of the array. After referring to the statute to show the provision made for such a proceeding he submitted to the court.

The attorney for the people then arose and made the following observations, *viz*.: That the doctrine advanced by Colonel Richardson was a novelty to him, as the affidavits of the defendants predicated no charge against the present panel of jurors, either individually or collectively; he showed from the statute that the array could not be quashed upon the above principle, neither did he believe the officers of the county could be discharged upon a mere *exparte* affidavit, but the charges ought to be made and affidavits filed and a trial had before the court. He said it was the first time he had heard of such a proceeding to quash the array, at the same time nothing alleged against it individually or collectively.

He showed that the statute referred to by Colonel Richardson applied to civil and not criminal cases. He could not suffer the idea of having the panel quashed by the discharge of all the officers of the county upon a mere *exparte* affidavit, and that too made by five men indicted for murder. He asked for a precedent in all the experience of this state or any other in criminal cases; he defied them to produce a single case.

Mr. Browning, for the defense, said, that although there had not been a precedent in the United States for such a proceeding, the reason is there has never been a case like this in the United States. He contended that such a proceeding is fully warranted by the English statutes and the statutes of the United States, that in a case like this the county commissioners, the sheriff and his deputies can be discharged, and in their place can be appointed elisors for the purpose of choosing another jury.

The court ruled that the jury be discharged and elisors appointed. The court then adjourned.

Thursday, May 22nd.

The court appointed Thomas H. Owen and William D. Abernethy elisors and they selected a full panel of jurors.

Four panels of jurors were successively called and out of the ninety-six men twelve were selected as a jury satisfactory to the defense.

Mr. Lamborn prosecuted before this jury in a manner which showed clearly to every bystander the certainty of the guilt of the prisoners who were honorably acquitted. Mr. Frank Worrell, who had command of the guard at the jail at the time of the massacre, being summoned as a witness, and being asked by the prosecuting attorney if the guard had their guns loaded with blank cartridges at the time of the attack on the jail refused to answer, assigning as a reason that he could not without incriminating himself.'

The *Nauvoo Neighbor* has the following:

THE CARTHAGE ASSASSINS

'On Friday last the trial terminated, and the prisoners were acquitted in the case of Joseph Smith. This accords with the vote of the city council last July, that when the law failed to atone for the blood of our Prophet and Patriarch shed at Carthage on the 27th of June last by a mob, we would refer the case to God for a righteous judgment, and we have never varied from that intention. If those men had been found guilty it would have been a novel case and a violation of all the rules of the world in all martyr cases before.

The murderers of Joseph and Hyrum Smith can rest assured that their case, independent of all earthly tribunals, will be tried by the Supreme Judge of the Universe, who has said, vengeance is mine and I will repay.'

Saturday, 31.—Brother George D. Watt returned from Carthage. Threats were made that his minutes should never go to Nauvoo, but he succeeded in passing them out of the court room about every hour.

Calvin A. Warren [counsel for the defense] said that if the prisoners were guilty of murder he himself was guilty alleging that it was the public opinion that the Smiths ought to be killed, and public opinion made the laws consequently it was not murder to kill the Smiths. [!]

Elder Orson Spencer made the following report:

REPORTED INTERVIEW WITH GOVERNOR FORD AND EX-GOVERNOR REYNOLDS

'By the appointment of the Twelve I went to Springfield, Illinois about the middle of June [a note in the manuscript changes this to 'the last of May'] in company with Brother Samuel Brannan in order to see Governor Ford. Immediately on our arrival we found his Excellency who received us politely and introduced us to the secretary of state, Mr. Campbell, and to ex-Governor Reynolds. After dinner we all repaired to the governor's office in the state house except Mr. Campbell. There we held a familiar interview for several hours; during which both governors spoke freely of the unreasonable prejudice of the people through the state especially in the southern part of it. They were requested to use their influence officially and personally to allay prejudice and rebut slanders that might ultimately endanger the safety of this people unless counteracted. Governor Reynolds said that he had attempted to speak in extenuation of the supposed faults of the saints at public meetings, but the people rudely resisted his efforts and accused him of being a 'Smithite' and a 'Mormon'; and he was seriously afraid they would mob us by making an attack by the cooperation of steamboats upon our city. Both governors strenuously urged the necessity that the saints should cease to gather in one place and also opposed my suggestion to buy out the anti-Mormons in the county. They alleged that we might spread through other counties as we had done in Hancock, which would increase the alarm in other counties and in the state generally. They said that our political influence was that which exasperated the people.

Governor Ford said he durst not trust the best militia in the state to defend the Mormons. They would go over to the side of the mob in the event of a collision. He said that even General Hardin could not be trusted in our defense against the mob. He further said that the conduct of Governor Boggs of Missouri was unlawful and barbarous and pledged himself never to act like him in driving the saints and confirmed a former pledge that he would never demand the leaders of this church on criminal writs to expose them to assassination as the Smiths had been, and to use his utmost endeavors to suppress all mobs. He said however that his official influence was only nominal, there was really no force in the government.

Large masses of people that might assemble for violent and tumultuous purposes could not be restrained by any law or government.

He was then assured that it was our intention as soon as we could finish the Temple to send off many of our people to distant parts of the earth and in the course of eighteen months very many of our people would colonize distant parts; and we were ready from that time forth to sell our property as soon as practicable and commence removals, if the people round about would buy us out.'

Sunday, June 1, 1845.—I attended meeting at the stand. Elder Heber C. Kimball preached.

[In the remarks of Elder Kimball the following occurs].

DISCOURSE OF ELDER KIMBALL

'I will mention one thing that we united in prayer for and called upon the Father in the name of Jesus: that our enemies should not have power to come in here with vexatious writs, for his servants during this court, and they have not done it. Is not this a miracle? Yes; and we have asked for rain, and it has rained; and we have asked for God to heal the sick, and he has healed them, or they are mending in answer to our prayers. Are not these great blessings? Does not this prove that God is with this people? Yes, verily, his name is to be praised, if this people will feel the same interest for the building up of this kingdom, and for the erecting of those houses, his will will be done, and there is no power that can stay them, and when that is done, I am satisfied; I do not care if I go into the wilderness the next day.'*

Elder John Taylor followed [Elder Kimball] on the subject of our persecutions. I made a few remarks.

At four p. m. the Presidents of Seventies met and preached to each other, and ordained four presidents for the twenty-seventh quorum.

Evening, I met for council and prayer with Elders H. C. Kimball, Orson Pratt, Willard Richards, John E. Page, John Taylor, George A. Smith, Amasa M.

*Times and Seasons, p. 987, vol. vi.

Lyman, John Smith, N. K. Whitney, George Miller, Levi Richards, Joseph Young and Wm. Clayton. Voted that Brother Peter O. Hanson translate the *Doctrine and Covenants* and *Book of Mormon* into the Danish Norwegian language and that Elder Orson Pratt assist him. Voted that the Trustees give George D. Watt a quarter of a lot and build him a house and employ him as reporter for the church and let his labors go towards paying for his house and lot. We prayed that justice might overtake the murderers of Joseph and Hyrum and that George J. Adams be stopped in his mad career.

A conference was held in Merthyr-Tydvil, Wales, Elder William Henshaw presided; forty had been baptized since the April conference, and the brethren felt determined to spread the gospel.

At a special conference held in Cincinnati, thirty-two members were represented.

Monday, 2.—I met with the Twelve in council.

Thursday, 5.—I met for prayer with the Twelve and other brethren.

Elder Parley P. Pratt wrote to the Twelve of date, as follows:

ELDER PARLEY P. PRATT'S LETTER TO THE TWELVE IN NAUVOO—CONDITIONS IN NEW YORK CITY

'As it regards publishing in this city [New York], if all the political and religious influence and support we have combined will support a periodical, even allowing the editor to work for nothing and live on sawdust pudding, it will be more than we have yet done, or are likely to do at present. There is little prospect of a periodical being supported by church or state, even if we give our time *gratis*, and use the utmost economy; therefore to divide it and either of us succeed seems at present impracticable; and I doubt very much whether we can continue to publish. The churches are few in number, we decrease while you increase. The law of tithing, emigration, the strengthening and defense of the City of Joseph has occupied the attention and employed the energies of the saints so entirely, since we came from the west and laid before them their duty and the necessity of immediate action, that it seems almost vain to mention subscriptions for papers in this country. If they have a dollar to spare, it is handed in for tithing, or used for the purchase of arms, clothing and ammunition, or to help themselves to emigrate and settle in the west.

Our teachings and influence, aided by yours and by the Spirit of God, have tended to produce this state of things, and it pleases us so well that we do not like to counteract it in the least; but it rather embarrasses us as to immediate means to clothe or to furnish us money for necessary expenses and involves us in debt, besides devoting our entire time.

I have become convinced that I can do no good here. The public are entirely indifferent, and will neither come to meeting, hear, nor read the truth. The saints are few, about fifty of them attended a Sunday meeting in a large hall, and perhaps half a dozen strangers come in and out to gaze and gape and wonder and perish.

I have labored hard for six months without an idle moment, and have used economy in living, traveling and clothing. I feel as if I was now done with this city, and nearly so with the nation. My garments are clear, if they all perish. If I tarry a little longer in the east it will necessarily be in Boston and vicinity, where there is more interest manifested for the truth.'

Saturday, 7.—Elder W. Woodruff visited the saints in London and secured the copyright of the *Book of Doctrine and Covenants* at Stationer's Hall, having published three thousand copies at Liverpool: he presented a copy to the Library of the British Museum. The copyright was secured in forty-eight hours after the last sheets were obtained from the printers; which defeated a secret plan of some of our enemies who were taking measures to print the book and secure the copyright.

Sunday, 8.—At four p. m., I met with the Twelve and others for counsel and prayer: we decided that Elder Orson Hyde go to the east and buy canvas for a Tabernacle [tent], and type to print the History of Joseph Smith. General Conference of Seventies met and proceeded with the organization of the quorums.

A conference was held in Florence, St. Joseph county, Michigan, when one hundred and twenty-eight members, one high priest, sixteen elders and four of the lesser priesthood were represented; Elder Crandall Dunn, president and Elder E. M. Webb, clerk.

Tuesday, 10.—I met in council with the brethren of the Twelve, and discussed the title of the Church History.

Thursday, 12.—I spent the afternoon with several of the Twelve.

Sunday, 15.—Elder Orson Hyde preached at the stand; Elder George A. Smith advocated the building of the Nauvoo House, and was followed by Elders Amasa M. Lyman and George Miller on the same subject. The high priests' quorum met. Evening, I met with the Twelve. The seventies met; Elder Joseph Young and others preached.

Monday, 16.—Council met on the Temple walls.

Tuesday, 17.—The Council of the Twelve wrote the following:

LETTER OF THE TWELVE TO THE SAINTS ABROAD

'To the Saints Abroad, Greeting:

The walls of our Temple are completed and the roof is nearly on. Through the liberality of the brethren that building is in a rapid state of advancement; but it will only accommodate a small portion of our congregation when completed.

Pursuant to the counsel of Joseph Smith given previous to his martyrdom, we now intend to erect a Tabernacle for the congregation made of canvas. It will take about four thousand yards, which, with other fixtures, will cost between one and two thousand dollars.

We have appointed Elder Orson Hyde one of our own quorum, a faithful, trusty and competent man of God, to go forth and raise all the necessary funds for the above purpose, to procure the materials and return with them to this place as soon as possible. Elder Hyde is authorized to raise the necessary funds by loan, by contribution, or tithing or donation; *Elder Hyde's Mission to Secure a Tent Tabernacle.* if by loan, the church here will refund the same in lands at a low rate, or in cash as soon as we can command it; and any contract that he may make in relation to the above, the church will be responsible for.

It is hoped that no brother or sister who has funds that he or she can spare for a season will withhold them from Brother Hyde, for it is the aid that he seeks for us. Also we hope that the saints will be liberal in their donations, and every other person that wishes well to the Temple of God and to the Tabernacle of the congregation in Zion. May God bless all that feel interested in the matter.'

Bishop Whitney started for St. Louis with $1,549 to purchase materials for the Temple.

Wednesday, 18.—I met with Elders Heber C. Kimball, John Taylor and George A. Smith at Brother Taylor's; we revised a portion of the History of Joseph Smith.

Elders Phineas H. Young and Charles Shumway returned from their missions and reported favorably.

Thursday, 19.—I spent the day with Brothers H. C. Kimball and George A. Smith revising history. Evening, the Twelve met for council and prayer.

I received a lengthy letter from Mr. H. R. Hotchkiss in relation to the necessity of establishing manufactories in Nauvoo for the employment of our rapidly increasing population of mechanics.

Friday, 20.—Elders H. C. Kimball, Orson Pratt, George A. Smith, and myself engaged revising Church History.

Sunday, 22.—Meeting at the stand; Elder Orson Pratt preached, but as it rained heavily, the meeting was dismissed. Evening, I met with the Twelve and others for prayer; Sister Jennetta Richards being very sick was administered to.

Monday, 23.—The sheriff came in with writs for a number of brethren and succeeded in arresting O. P. Rockwell and J. P. Harmon, but Rockwell got away from him. A constable from Le Harpe came in with writs for Brother Taylor, myself and others, but we kept out of the way.

Jonathan Dunham who was on a mission to the Lamanites received a notification from Ranes, the Indian Agent of the Neosha sub-agency to leave the country immediately.

Tuesday, 24.—I examined Church History with the brethren. Evening, Hiram Kimball and D. H. Wells returned from Carthage and brought word that Sheriff Deming had shot Sam Marshall.

Wednesday, 25.—At three p. m., I met with the Quorum of the Twelve for prayer; and in council in relation to a difficulty between William Smith and Brother Elbridge Tufts.

After council the Twelve met with the police at the

Masonic Hall when Wm. Smith delivered a very pathetic speech, delineating in a sectarian tone, the wrongs that his brothers and himself had sustained; asserting that we were all dependent upon his family for the priesthood, and pronouncing the most fearful anathemas upon all those who should not sustain him in his course, justifying his assault upon Brother Tufts, and demanding of the Twelve to inform the police that it was their duty to take his counsel in relation to the manner they discharge their duty. I told him that as an officer Brother Tuft was subject to the magistrates, and had no right to discharge a prisoner only by the order of the proper officer; that he (Brother William Smith) had no more right to interfere with the police than I had; that when he beat Brother Tufts for refusing to discharge his prisoner, he was doing wrong, and meddling with that which was not his business and should make satisfaction; that we received the priesthood from God through Joseph Smith and not through William, and that he had no authority or power to curse the Twelve Apostles who received the priesthood from Joseph; that we were not influenced by his curses, and that his prayers and imprecations upon the heads of those who were seeking to fulfill the instructions of Joseph to the letter would rise no higher than the smoke from a dung hill.

Brother William appeared humbled and agreed to make ample satisfaction to Brother Tufts.

Received a letter from James Arlington Bennett of New York, in which he applies to be consecrated a general of the Nauvoo Legion, that he may 'fight Napoleon's battles over again, either in Nauvoo or elsewhere.' This wild spirit of ambition has repeatedly manifested itself to us by many communications received from various sources, suggesting schemes of blood and empire, as if the work of the Lord was intended for personal aggrandisement.

James Arlington Bennett.

Thursday, 26.—The Twelve met for council and

prayer: several children were blessed. The first stone for the new font was laid in the Temple.

Friday, 27.—Elders Heber C. Kimball, Orson Pratt, Amasa M. Lyman, George A. Smith, Willard Richards, John E. Page, George Miller, Joseph Young and John Taylor met for fasting, prayer and counsel.

I wrote the following letter to Elder Woodruff:

BRIGHAM YOUNG'S LETTER TO WILFORD WOODRUFF IN ENGLAND— PROGRESS AND UNITY IN NAUVOO

'Nauvoo, June 27th, 1845.

Dear Brother Woodruff.—We sit down to acknowledge the receipt of your letters, and it being one year this day since the massacre of our beloved brethren Joseph and Hyrum, we have concluded to spend the day in conversation, counsel and prayer, and also to write answers to your letters, well knowing that a little information from this place must be acceptable to you at all times, for we feel it as a source of comfort to us to hear of your prosperity. We have met from time to time to offer up our prayers and thanksgivings before the Lord for the salvation and peace of the saints, and that the Lord would enable us to finish the Temple and the Nauvoo House that the brethren might obtain their endowments, for this we have supplicated by night and by day, and hitherto we have been prospered in a manner beyond our most sanguine expectations. Another subject for which we have constantly supplicated is the welfare and success of our dear brethren in England, Brother Parley P. Pratt in New York, and the brethren on the Islands of the Pacific, these with our petitions for the sick in our midst, and that God will preserve us from internal broils, has been the theme of our prayers from time to time, and we are happy to say that God has heard and answered our prayers, and has done all things well. The most perfect union, peace and good feeling has invariably prevailed in our midst and still continues. It seems like a foretaste of celestial enjoyment and Millennial glory.

* * *

The capstone of the Temple was laid by the Twelve on Saturday morning the 24th of May, at six o'clock, in the presence of many saints. It would have pleased you to have heard the hosannas on that occasion, and to have witnessed the short but interesting ceremony. The frame work of the roof is on the building, and the next week the brethren expect to put on the shingles; the frame work around the foundation of the tower is all up, and the first timbers for the tower itself were raised this day. The new stone front is mostly cut, and the first stone was laid today at about four o'clock. We expect in about five or six weeks the attic story of the Temple and the font will be all finished and ready for dedication, and just as soon as they are ready we shall dedicate them. We have all the timbers for the Temple on the ground, and above one hundred thousand shingles for the roof. The lead for the eaves and the tin for the dome of the tower are also bought. We have paid near 4000 dollars this spring for lumber (pine, boards, etc.) and near 1000 dollars for lead and tin, and have as yet lacked nothing. There is the most perfect union prevailing among the saints, and every man seems determined to do all he can to roll on the work of the Temple as fast as possible. Elder Hyde started east, about ten days ago, to purchase the cloth for the Tabernacle; and Elder Egan is gone to St. Louis to buy about 125 dollars worth of hemp to make cords for it.

The brethren are clearing the ground round the Temple, and we expect to have the Tabernacle reared, so as to be ready to meet in this fall.

We are building a stone wall around the Temple block, eight feet high and about five feet thick at the base, the wall on the north side is nearly built, the most of the woodwork for the Temple is finished, all the windowframes and sashes are made, and the glaziers are ready to set the glass, which we expect here in a few days, the frame and ornamental work of the tower is all ready to be put up, and the whole is far on the way of completion. The Nauvoo House Committee have reorganized, and the saints have appointed Elders A. Lyman and George A. Smith on that committee, in the place of Lyman Wight and J. Snider. A large quantity of brick is already made for the Nauvoo House, and considerable means are on hand to prosecute the work. We calculate to have it covered in before winter. The arsenal is ready for the roof timbers and the timbers on the ground. There are many good buildings erecting in different parts of the city, there is not much sickness in the place, and there never was a more prosperous time, in general, amongst the saints, since the work commenced. Nauvoo, or, more properly, the 'City of Joseph', looks like a paradise. All the lots and land, which have heretofore been vacant and unoccupied, were enclosed in the spring, and planted with grain and vegetables, which makes it look more like a garden of gardens than a city; and the season has been so favorable, the prospect is, there will be enough raised within the limits of the corporation to supply the inhabitants with corn, potatoes, and other vegetables. Hundreds of acres of prairie land have also been enclosed, and are now under good cultivation, blooming with corn, wheat, potatoes, and other necessaries of life. Many strangers are pouring in to view the Temple and the city. They express their astonishment and surprise to see the rapid progress of the Temple, and the beauty and grandeur of Mormon looks. Many brethren are coming from abroad, who seem highly delighted with the place and all its appendages.

We now conclude with our best wishes and prayers for your health and prosperity with that of your family, and those associated with you. Please remember us to Brothers Clark, Hedlock and families, and those of all the brethren with you, and believe us to be as ever—yours in the bonds of truth and righteousness.

[Signed]   BRIGHAM YOUNG.

P.S. *Sunday, June 29.*—This day the twenty-eighth quorum of the seventies has been organized, and is nearly full.   There are twenty-seven quorums duly organized and all appear united in the same interest, and firm in the faith.   Brother Milton Holmes is remembered by us in his station, he has been appointed one of the presidents of a quorum of seventies.'*

The saints in England observed this, the anniversary of the martyrdom of Joseph and Hyrum, by fasting and prayer: Elder Woodruff addressed a large assembly of saints at Birmingham.

Saturday, 28.—A number of brethren met and removed the stand and benches to the ground west of the Temple.

I rode out to the prairie with several of the Twelve: we felt thankful to God to see the crops looking so well.

Some of our wealthy brethren went to Carthage and became sureties on the bond upon which General Dem-

Bonds for General Deming—a Contrast.

ing was set at liberty: the sum required was ten thousand dollars.   Each signer was required to swear to the lowest cash value of his property and that it did not lie in the City of Nauvoo and he was then taken for one-half the sworn amount, so that twenty thousand dollars in property at its lowest cash value was held in security for General Deming's appearance at court. This contrasts strangely with the clemency extended by the court to Sharp, Williams, Aldrich, Grover, and Davis who were admitted to bail at the last court for one thousand dollars each on their own security; Deming having killed Marshall in self-defense, while the others violated the solemn faith of the state, pledged by its executive, and murdered innocent, unoffending men while confined in helpless condition in a prison awaiting examination!

Thirteen hundred dwellings were burned in Quebec, Canada, and at least six thousand persons were rendered homeless.

Millennial Star, vol. vi, pp. 91-2.

Father John Smith and Brother George A. Smith called upon William Smith in relation to his mother's visions. William evinced a very bitter spirit and declared himself President of the Church, and said that he would have his rights: his uncle reasoned with him and endeavored to show him the falsity of his position.

Attempted Reconciliation with William Smith and the Twelve.

Sunday, 29.—Elder Ezra T. Benson and I preached in the forenoon and Elders John Taylor and Amasa M. Lyman in the afternoon, at the grove west of the Temple. Evening, I met with the Twelve and others for prayer.

Monday, 30.—Visited Mother Smith in company with the Twelve and Bishops Whitney and Miller. William Smith was invited but did not attend. Mother Smith expressed herself satisfied with the Twelve and the course they were pursuing.

* * *

Tuesday, July 8, 1845.—Brother Joseph Toronto handed to me $2,500 in gold and said he wanted to give himself and all he had to the upbuilding of the church and kingdom of God; he said he should henceforth look to me for protection and counsel. I laid the money at the feet of the bishops.

Wednesday, 9.—Sister Jennetta Richards, wife of Dr. Willard Richards, died at 10:15 a. m.

At 2 p. m. the Smith family attended a public dinner at the Mansion which was given by Bishops Whitney and Miller in behalf of the church; seven widows and about fifty of the family were present. Brothers H. C. Kimball, John Taylor, Bishops Whitney, Miller and myself, assisted in waiting on the table; the band and a few friends attended: Mother Smith addressed her kindred and the audience in a feeling and pathetic manner.

* * *

Saturday, August 2, 1845.—In council with several of the Twelve and bishops. Brother Emmett desired in

behalf of his company to be retained in the fellowship
James
Emmett's
Desire to be in
Fellowship. of the church. I informed him that if he
and his company would follow the counsel
of the Twelve we would fellowship them,
but not otherwise.

Afternoon, I rode out in the new church carriage
with Brother Kimball and the bishops to look at two
[city] blocks of Emma Smith's which she has agreed
Kindness to
Mother
Lucy Smith. to sell the Trustees for $550.00. We se-
lected blocks 96 and 97 and then went to
Mother Smith's and brought her in the
carriage to choose which of the two blocks she would
have deeded to herself and her daughters. She selected block 96, and desired to have the church build
her a house like Brother Kimball's. She asked for
the carriage we rode in, a horse and a double carriage
harness. We gave her the use of the carriage during
her lifetime.

Monday, 4.—Elders Daniel Spencer and Charles
Shumway were appointed to go on a mission west in
company with Brothers Herring and Otis.

Afternoon, in council with the Twelve, James Emmett and others. Emmett wished to be restored to the
priesthood. He confessed his fault in leading away his
company contrary to counsel and promised to make
all the restoration in his power, he said he would abide
counsel. Council decided he should be restored.

Wednesday, 6.—In council with Brothers H. C.
Kimball, W. Richards, G. A. Smith and Amasa M.
Lyman.

From the *New York Sun.*

TEMPLE AT NAUVOO

'The building of the Mormon Temple under all the troubles by
which those people have been surrounded, seems to be carried on with
a religious enthusiasm which reminds us of olden times, by the
energy which controls all the movements towards its completion. It
occupies the highest and most imposing position in Nauvoo and is
built of fine limestone. Has thirty pilasters—six at each end and nine
at each side—each surmounted by a capital on which is carved a human
face with rays around it and two hands holding trumpets. The
Temple is 88 feet by 128 feet; from floor to ceiling is 65 feet; and

from the ground to the top of the spire is 165 feet. The baptismal font is in the basement, to be supported by stone oxen. Three hundred and fifty men are zealously at work upon the building, which it is supposed will be finished in a year and a half, probably at a cost of half a million of dollars. The spiritual concerns of the Mormons are governed by a Council of Twelve, composed of the following persons

Brigham Young—*The Lion of the Lord.*

H. C. Kimball—*The Herald of Grace.*

Parley P. Pratt—*The Archer of Paradise.*

Orson Hyde—*The Olive Branch of Israel.*

Willard Richards—*The Keeper of the Rolls.*

John Taylor—*The Champion of Right.*

Wm. Smith—*The Patriarchal, Jacob's Staff.*

Wilford Woodruff—*The Banner of the Gospel.*

George A. Smith—*The Entablature of Truth.*

Orson Pratt—*The Gauge of Philosophy.*

John E. Page—*The Sundial.*

Lyman Wight—*The Wild Ram of the Mountains.*

It is supposed that the Mormon inhabitants of this city are fully 12,000 souls, and of the surrounding country, 5,000 more. The only property owned in common is the Temple. The Mormons are industrious, good farmers, raise wheat plentifully, and are about to engage in manufactures. The whole community may be considered in their peculiar traits singular and remarkable and in after ages their Temple, like the ruins of Palenque may strike the beholder with wonder and history may be unable to explain what race worshiped there.'*

Tuesday, 12.—9 a. m., the Twelve, presiding bishops and others met in council, and wrote letters for H. G. Sherwood and John S. Fullmer, with authority to lead, direct and instruct Emmett's company who are now encamped among the Sioux on the Missouri river about thirty miles above the mouth of Big Sioux river. We laid our hands upon the heads of Brothers Sherwood, Fullmer and Emmett and blessed them for the mission. Brother Emmett declared he would be subject to counsel.

Sunday, 17.—I dreamed this morning I saw Brother Joseph Smith, and as I was going about my business, he said, 'Brother Brigham, don't be in a hurry', which was repeated the second and third times with a degree of sharpness.

*The author of the *Sun* article is supposed to be William W. Phelps, writing from Nauvoo.

Monday, 18.—I met with the brethren of the Council, and Trustees of the Nauvoo House on the walls of the building. Elder Kimball dedicated it to the Lord, asking his blessing to attend the work and those engaged upon it. The workmen then commenced: Brother Alonzo H. Raleigh laid the first brick.

Wednesday, 20.—A severe thunderstorm this morning, Brother Ralph was killed by lightning on Parley Street. Others were knocked down.

Governor Ford ordered the state arms in the possession of the Carthage Greys to be delivered to Sheriff Backenstos.

Friday, 22.—Elders W. Richards and George A. Smith commenced writing the History of Zion's Camp. Brother George A. Smith supplying many incidents from memory.

Sunday, 24.—Meeting at the stand: My brother Joseph Young, preached a funeral sermon. I made a few remarks.

Evening, the quorums all met at the stand and I instructed them about building the houses the Lord had commanded, called upon the bricklayers to come forward and put up the Nauvoo House, fifty came forward.

Elder David Foote was buried. He was born, August 7, 1769, Harrington, Litchfield county,

An L. D. S. American Revolution Soldier Dies. Connecticut. His father enlisted in the army of the Revolution and died in the service. David was reared by his uncle, Jonathan Barker.

In 1791 he married Irene, the eldest daughter of Matham and Dorcas Lane. He joined the Methodists and served as a class leader several years, he subsequently became a believer in universal restoration.

In the winter of 1830 he obtained a copy of the *Book of Mormon* which was read by himself and family, he considered it a true record. He was baptized by Elder John Murdock in Genesee, in the fall of 1833, and ordained an elder in 1834, commenced preaching and raised up a branch in Greenwood, New York, where he resided, and was called to preside over the same in 1835. Several elders visited him during the summer, and members were added to the branch.

In 1837, he moved with his family to Chester, near Kirtland, and in May, 1838, started for Missouri and arrived in Caldwell county in August in time to share in the persecutions that followed, and was driven to Adams county, Illinois. He was ordained a high priest in November, 1844.

August 14, 1845 he was taken sick with the chills and fever, his sickness continued till the night of the 22nd, when he fell asleep and all attempts to awake him proved ineffectual, he slept till 11 p. m., when he passed behind the veil without a struggle or a groan. Dying as he lived, a faithful saint.

Wednesday, 27.—Elder Parley P. Pratt gave an account of his mission in the east where he had been about 9 months (and returned on August 26th), preaching to and counseling the saints, and collecting tithing. Council voted they were satisfied with the course of Elder Pratt.

Monday, September 1, 1845. — Elders Daniel Spencer and Charles Shumway, who left Nauvoo on a mission to the west, on the fourth of last month returned with news confirmatory of the death of Brother Jonathan Dunham, which took place on the 28th of July last, a little before daylight.

Thursday, 4.—2 p. m., met for counsel and prayer with the Twelve and others.

Messrs. Elam Meacham, Phineas Richards, Levi R. Chase, Francisco Durphy, Isaac Houston, John Wait, Gardner Clark and Thomas Corbitt the trustees and officers of the Big Field Asso- A Harvest Feast Near Nauvoo. ciation having invited us to attend a public dinner, Elders H. C. Kimball, W. Richards, John Taylor, George A. Smith, Amasa Lyman, Father John Smith, Bishops George Miller and N. K. Whitney went to the field about six miles southeast from the city and partook with them of an excellent dinner. 616 adults sat down to the table: They had an ample bowery prepared for the occasion. I preached encouragingly to the brethren and advised them to store their grain in the city. They have 30,000 bushels of corn in the field."

CHAPTER XXXII

PREPARATIONS FOR WESTWARD JOURNEY — T H E
FINAL WORD: THE CHURCH MUST LEAVE ILLINOIS
—DETAIL OF THE PLANS—AMERICAN GOVERNMENT
FAILS IN THE CASE OF THE LATTER-DAY SAINTS

"*Tuesday, September 9, 1845.*—Forenoon, unwell.
Two p. m. General Council |Council of Fifty| met.
Resolved that a company of 1500 men be
selected to go to Great Salt Lake valley and
that a committee of five be appointed to
gather information relative to emigration,
and report the same to the council.

Salt Lake Valley Considered as place of Settlement.

Wednesday, 10.—I dreamed last night that I was
chased by a mob to a place like a barn full of corn or
grain, one chased me so close that he got into the same
room with me and it was Thomas Ford, who appeared
only two and one-half feet high, I took his wrist between my fingers and stepped to the door and knocked
down one after another of the mob with him till I
discovered he was dead.

News arrived that the mob are burning the houses
of the brethren at Yelrome.

Thursday, 11.—I received a letter from Sheriff J.
B. Backenstos announcing the death of General Miner
R. Deming, who died at half past ten o'clock
yesterday of congestive fever; during his ill-
ness his life was repeatedly threatened by the
mob, he was prevented from sleeping at night by their
yells and hideous screams, as they kept up a continual
row in the streets of Carthage near the general's residence which greatly aggravated his fever, and doubtless
caused his death.

Death of Miner R. Deming.

I answered Sheriff Backenstos' letter assuring him
of our regret at the loss the cause of liberty, law, and

order had sustained in the unexpected death of General Deming, and informed him of the burning of the houses of the citizens of Morley Settlement by the mob yesterday, and requested him to take immediate steps to suppress the mob, advised him to inform the governor that he may take the necessary measures to protect the lives and property of the people in this country.

A messenger from Lima reports eight houses burned.

The Twelve met in council; it was agreed to dispatch a messenger to the Lima branch and counsel the brethren to propose to sell their property to the mob and bring their families and grain here, and to send a messenger to Michigan to advise the brethren to sell their farms for stock, sheep, etc., also to Ottawa and recommend the brethren there to gather all the hay they can.

Prayers were offered up that the Lord would give us wisdom to manage affairs with the mob so as to keep them off till we can accomplish what he requires at our hands in completing the Temple and Nauvoo House, also for wisdom to manage the affairs in regard to the western emigration.

A selection was made of members of the council to start westward next spring.

Friday, 12.—Nine a. m., council met at Historian's Office, wrote and dispatched the following letter by James H. Woodland:—

BRIGHAM YOUNG'S LETTER TO SOLOMON HANCOCK

'Nauvoo, Sept. 12, 1845.

President Solomon Hancock,

Dear Brother: We have received your communication of last eve and taken it into consideration in council, and decided that it is wisdom for you to remove the women and children from Yelrome as fast as you can with what teams you have got, and we will send you more as fast as we can, and not only remove the women and children but your grain and let all the brethren stay there and keep 'bachelor's hall' and watch movements of the mob.

The object of our enemies is to get opposition enough to raise popular excitement but we think it best to let them burn up our houses while we take care of our families and grain.

Let the sheriff of Hancock county attend to the mob, and let us see whether he and the Jack-Mormons, so-called, the friends of law and order, will calmly sit down and watch the funeral processions of Illinois liberty; if so, they will all fall under the same condemnation. At a future day our course will be plain.

Be calm and patient till all things are ready. What is a little property or a few lives, compared with the properties and lives of a great people, and the house and ordinances on which the salvation of that people depend?

You will employ the best scribe you have, or half a dozen of them, if necessary, to pen minutely all the movements of the enemy and friends, what houses are burned, by whom, at what hour, who were present, and who saw them do it, etc.: even every particular and forward us a daily copy, if opportunity permits.

[Signed] BRIGHAM YOUNG, President.
W. Richards, Clerk.'

SOLOMON HANCOCK'S ANSWER TO BRIGHAM YOUNG

By letter from Solomon Hancock, Yelrome, we learn that the mob have burned all the houses on the south side of the branch [brook], and left last evening for Lima, said they would return this morning as soon as light, and swear they will sweep through and burn everything to Nauvoo. Colonel Levi Williams is at the head of the mob.

The following notice was issued by the council:

'Nauvoo, Sept. 12, 1845.

To the Brethren in and About Nauvoo, Greeting:

The Council of the Church requests every man who has a team to go immediately to the Morley Settlement, and act in concert with President Solomon Hancock in removing the sick, the women, children, goods and grain to Nauvoo.

Aid Sent to Morley Settlement.

[Signed] BRIGHAM YOUNG, President.
W. Richards, Clerk.'

The brethren at Yelrome made the following proposition to the mob:—

'Yelrome, Sept. 12, 1845.

We the undersigned, a committee appointed by the Morley and Hancock Settlement (a branch of the Mormon Church); *Whereas* there seemingly exists some difficulty between said body and anti-Mormons, we, as representatives of said body, wish to make some propositions so as to make peace;

Conciliation Offered to the Mob.

we wish to sell our deeded lands as well as our improvements as low as it could be reasonably expected, reserving to ourselves the crops now on the premises; and will take in exchange, working cattle, beef cattle, cows, sheep, horses, wagons, harness, store goods, and any available property and give possession as soon as our crops can be taken care of and we receive pay for the same; the whole of which may be purchased from the undersigned acting as committee or from owners.

> [Signed] DANIEL TYLER,
> HORACE RAWSON,
> MARCELLUS McCOWN,
> SAMUEL ALGER.'

An extra *Nauvoo Neighbor* was issued giving an account of the burning; and appealing to the citizens to come forward and magnify the laws.

Saturday, 13.—Brother H. C. Kimball and Andrew Perkins visited me. Brother Perkins wanted to know

Journey West to be made on the Apostles' Plan—"All things in common."

something about our going west; I told him that those who went must expect to go on the Apostles' doctrines and no man say aught that he has is his own, but all things are the Lord's: and we his stewards, and every man receive his stewardship.

George W. Lang reported that he had been among the mob at Green Plains and Lima. Esquire Hill of Lima told him they did not design gathering in large bodies, but go on as they had done and finish burning Yelrome, then attack some other place and drive the Mormons all into Nauvoo, then they had further plans to move them from there by help from abroad.

Afternoon, I visited the sick and met the Committee on Emigration and others at Brother Daniel Spencer's. Father Bent was instructed to organize a company of 100 families.

George Miller said he went to Carthage with his wife and was transacting business at the county clerk's office,

Arrest of George Miller —Resistance.

when he was arrested by Michael Barnes, constable, and taken before Captain Robert F. Smith, justice of the peace; was charged with treason and as the state was not ready for trial, and the offense not bailable, Captain Smith ordered him to be committed to jail, upon which Miller told him there was not enough men in the little town to put him in jail. Said he had served the United States government in two wars—had made the roads into this country and had killed snakes, and it was an imposition for these slinks that followed his tracks to charge him with treason, but if they wished to have an examination, he would come and attend court, but would not go into that jail alive. Upon which Esquire Smith took his verbal recognizance for his appearance at Carthage the next Saturday.

Sunday, 14.—* * * I prophesied we would have a winter of peace in Nauvoo.

I said, in relation to the mob burning houses, I was willing they should do so, until the surrounding counties should be convinced that we were not the aggressors, peradventure they may conclude to maintain the supremacy of the law by putting down mob violence and bringing offenders to justice.

I counseled the brethren to bring their families and grain here, and called for volunteers with wagons and teams to aid in removing the saints to this place; one hundred and thirty-four teams were procured and started forthwith. The brethren agreed to continue until they had brought in all their families, effects and grain of the saints in the settlements attacked by the mob.

Resolution to Help the Saints from Yelrome to Nauvoo.

I received a letter from John Loveless and Westley Knight informing me that the Highland branch was embodied [organized] by order of the sheriff to protect their property.

SUBSTITUTION OF MILITARY MEASURES FOR CIVIC MUNICIPAL ORGANIZATION

As the repeal of our City Charter had deprived us of our military organization, the following was issued by the council:—

'To Charles C. Rich:

  President of all the Organized Quorums of the Church of Jesus Christ of Latter-day Saints in Hancock County.

  Greeting: You are hereby instructed to hold the same [i. e. quorums of the priesthood] in readiness for all duties that shall be necessary in all emergencies.

  Done at the 'City of Joseph' this 14th day of September, A. D. 1845.

[Signed]   BRIGHAM YOUNG, President.'

Monday, 15.—Seven a. m., the police met at my house and put me up a stable.

Sheriff Backenstos went to Warsaw and tried his best to summon a *posse* to stop the burning but could not raise one.

Forty-four buildings have been burned by the mob. Several houses have been burned in the Prairie branch, Green Plain precinct.

Michael Barnes a constable from Carthage, and his brother came into Nauvoo with writs for H. C. Kimball, Willard Richards, John E. Page, Daniel Garn, Wm. and George A. Smith, and myself, issued by Captain Smith of the Carthage Greys, on the complaint of _____ Backman. The charges were for aiding and abetting Joseph Smith in treasonable designs against the state, for being officers in the Nauvoo Legion, for building an arsenal, for keeping cannon in times of peace, for holding a private council in Nauvoo, and for holding correspondence with the Indians.

Arrest of Prominent Citizens of Nauvoo Attempted.

He called on General Miller and made known his business. Miller told him he would get the men together and they would meet him at the Masonic Hall at 4 o'clock p. m. The constable said he did not wish to see Wm. Smith, but was anxious for all the others; before the time appointed he concluded to leave the names of the parties with General Miller and requested them to meet the justice at A. G. Fellow's house on the Prairie four miles this side of Carthage.

I wrote Elder Samuel Brannan in regard to the continuation of the *New York Messenger* as follows:

'Do as you and Brother Pratt think best, only do not think to sustain it [the *Messenger*] from the tithing. You know your circumstances and whether the subscription list will warrant its continuation or not.

I wish you together with your press, paper, and ten thousand of the brethren, were now in California at the Bay of San Francisco, and if you can clear yourself and go there, do so.'

Publication of Eastern Papers Referred to the Brethren in the East.

I received a letter from J. B. Backenstos, dated, Carthage, September 15th, in which he stated his inability to raise law and order citizens to quell the mob and requested us to hold two thousand well armed men in readiness for immediate service at any hour that he may call for them and added: that if we will not defend our own lives and property that we cannot reasonably expect any considerable support from those citizens commonly called 'Jack-Mormons'. 'Colonel Levi Williams has ordered out his brigade of militia, I am certain the turnout will be slim, we must whip them.'

Steps Attempted at the Maintainance of "Law and Order".

In reply I advised him to wait a few days and see if there are any law and order citizens in the county that are not Mormons, and if it proved there were none else to stand up for the Constitution and laws of the state, it would then be time enough for us, as the old citizens had heretofore advised us to 'hold still'! 'Keep cool'! 'Be quiet'! etc., etc., we were determined to do so.

The first regiment, second cohort of the Nauvoo Legion met and organized, choosing the old officers, to place themselves in readiness to act at the sheriff's call.

'There is grain enough growing within ten miles of this city, raised by the saints, to feed the whole population for two years if they were to sit down and do nothing but gather it in and feast upon it, and worship God. We expect to bring it all into the city or near it and the people too. The mob seem determined to drive us to our duty in gathering, and then drive us to carry the fulness of the gospel from among them and carry it to Israel. We are all well.

[Signed]   [BRIGHAM YOUNG].'

* * *

Tuesday, 16.—Sheriff Backenstos arrived in great haste and somewhat excited, said that the mob had Sheriff Backenstos Expelled from Carthage. driven him from his house in Carthage yesterday, and he went to Warsaw and stayed over night. He soon ascertained that the people were so enraged at him for trying to stop the house-burning that there was little probability of getting away alive, but finally prevailed on an influential mobocrat to escort him out of Warsaw this morning, who came with him about three and a half miles and on leaving cautioned him that if he saw two men together to avoid them for there were deep plans laid to kill him. Soon after he was pursued by a party of the mob on horseback, three of whom took the lead, one of the three had a swifter horse and gained a hundred yards in advance of his party in a short time when his horse stumbled and threw his rider. Backenstos maintained his speed, driving as fast as his horse could go.

The mob took the nearest road to cross his track and on his arrival at the old railroad crossing, the mob were within about 200 yards, they being on horseback and he in a buggy, they had gained on him considerably.

Orrin P. Rockwell and John Redding were refreshing themselves near the crossing as they had been out to bring in some of the burnt-out families who were sick, and on looking up saw Backenstos coming down the hill at full speed, and asked what was the matter. Backenstos replied the mob were after and determined to kill him and commanded them in the name of the people of the state to protect him. Rockwell replied, fear not, we have 50 rounds (two fifteen-shooter rifles besides revolvers).

Sheriff Backenstos then turned to the mob and commanded them to stop, and as they continued to advance Killing of Frank Worrell. raising their guns, he ordered Rockwell to fire; he did so aiming at the clasp of the belt on one of the mob, which proved to be Frank Worrell, who fell from his horse and the rest turned back and soon brought up a wagon and put his body into it.

* * *

Tuesday, 30.—Met in General Council at the Seventies' Hall. * * *

Parley P. Pratt said he had made a calculation for an outfit that every family of five persons would require: one good wagon, three yoke of cattle, two cows, two beef cattle, three sheep, one thousand pounds of flour, twenty pounds of sugar, one rifle and ammunition, a tent and tent poles; and that the cost would be about $250.00 provided the family had nothing to begin with, only bedding and cooking utensils; and the weight would be about twenty-seven hundred including the family, and calculating them to walk considerably would reduce it to about nineteen hundred weight.

Outfit
Required for
the Westward
Journey for a
Family of
Five Persons.

It was decided that all the council [i. e. of the Twelve] were to go west with their families, friends and neighbors.

General C. C. Rich reported that General J. J. Hardin with his troops had arrived in the city and were on the square northeast of the temple, waiting an interview with the Twelve and authorities of the place. Also that Sheriff Jacob B. Backenstos and Judge Stephen A. Douglas were at Elder Taylor's and wished to see me as soon as possible. Council adjourned.

Interview
of Church
Authorities
with Command-
ing General
Hardin *et al.*

I went with the Twelve to Elder Taylor's and saw Judge Douglas and Sheriff Backenstos.

They said it was hard to make the people, the other side of the Illinois river, believe that it was not the Mormons that were burning houses in Hancock county.

They wished us to go and see General Hardin. In company with H. C. Kimball, W. Richards, John Taylor, George A. Smith and Amasa M. Lyman, I went on to the hill and met General Hardin and staff surrounded by his troops, four hundred in number. He read us his orders from the governor to come here and keep the peace if he had to keep the county under martial law: said he wished to search for the bodies of two dead men who were last seen in Nauvoo and it was supposed they had been murdered.

I told him he was welcome to search for dead bodies or anything else he pleased. He inquired if I knew anything about them or of crimes having been committed in Nauvoo. I replied I knew nothing of the kind, but that I had reliable information that some hundred houses had been burned in the south part of the county and probably if he would go there, he would find the persons who had done it.

I tendered him the hospitality of the city and a home at my house, to which he replied drily, 'I always stay in camp.'

General Hardin marched his troops to, and searched the Temple, Masonic Hall, Nauvoo House, and the stables of the Mansion.

There were deposited some forty barrels of wild grape wine in the Masonic Hall which attracted the attention of some of the searchers and caused some delay.

While searching the Mansion stables, they found where a horse had been bled and sent for the landlord and demanded an explanation; after being shown the horse, the General and Judge Douglas ran their swords into the manure, as though they expected to prick some dead bodies and make them squeal. Almon W. Babbitt told them they must think we were fools to bury dead men in a stable when it was so easy to throw them into the Mississippi river, which was only a few rods off. They then marched off and camped on the south side of the city.

Caleb Baldwin was arrested and taken into camp, and examined as a witness. Most of the questions asked were designed to find out where the bodies of Joseph and Hyrum Smith were buried.

* * *

Wednesday, October 1, 1845.—Met in council at Elder Taylor's. General John J. Hardin, Hon. Stephen A. Douglas and J. A. Mc-Dougal were present.

E. A. Bedell, Esqr., asked General Hardin for three or four men to go to Warsaw and make arrests, which request was granted.

I asked the gentlemen present as to their feelings as friends and neighbors, and in relation to our propositions for removal.

General Hardin said he would do all in his power by counsel, etc., to help us, and approved of our proposed location at Vancouver's Island. He thought it desirable for our sakes that we should remove, also for the peace of the county.

Judge Douglas said Vancouver's Island was claimed by the United States, and he felt sure there would be no objection to its settlement, or to the settlement of Oregon.

General Hardin proposed that we should appoint trustees-in-trust to sell our property.

I proposed a committee of the whole on both sides, and informed them that we were not sowing any winter wheat, and a greater testimony of our intentions to remove should not be asked.

Judge Douglas said, all competent men must admit that the propositions of the committee of citizens of Nauvoo were just and fair.

General Hardin said he was satisfied we intended to remove but had not the assurance we could go if our property could not be sold.

We received the following:

Plans of the Saints' Proposition to Remove from Illinois.

Propositions of the Saints Admitted to be "just and fair".

LETTER FROM THE QUINCY COMMITTEE

'Nauvoo, October 1, 1845.

To the First President and Council of the Church at Nauvoo:

Having had a free and full conversation with you this day in reference to your proposed removal from this county, together with members

Church Leaders Requested to Place Terms of Departure in Writing.

of your church, we have to request you to submit the facts and intentions stated to us in the said conversation to writing, in order that we may lay them before the governor and the people of the state. We hope that by so doing it will have a tendency to allay the excitement at present existing in the public mind.

We have the honor to subscribe ourselves.

Respectfully yours etc.

[Signed]   JOHN J. HARDIN,
W. B. WARREN,
S. A. DOUGLAS,
J. A. McDOUGAL.'

Thursday, 2.—The council received the following from Camp Mississippi:

'To the First President and High Council of the
Church of the Latter-day Saints:

Since our conference with you yesterday, we have arrived at this place and have held free conversation with the anti-Mormons of this and the surrounding counties. We have read to them your statement made to us on the 1st instant.

Acquiescence of the Citizens of Illinois to the Agreed Removal of the Saints.

We have informed them that you individually made similar statements to us, with the most solemn protestations of truth, and with every appearance of earnest determination to carry out your expressed intentions in good faith.

In the Resolutions which were adopted yesterday, in this place, by the delegates from nine counties, (the citizens of Hancock being excluded from the meeting), it was resolved (as we are informed, not having seen a copy of the Resolutions), to accept your proposition to remove in the spring.

Since we have made public the statement by you made to us, there seems to be a general acquiescence in it by citizens of other counties, and of this, so far as to agree to restrain and withhold all further violence, and that you be permitted to depart in peace next spring.

We are convinced that affairs have reached such a crisis, that it has become impossible for your church to remain in this country.

After what has been said and written by yourselves, it will be confidently expected by us and the whole community, that you will remove from the state with your whole church, in the manner you have agreed in your statement to us.

Should you not do so, we are satisfied, however much we may deprecate violence and bloodshed, that violent measures will be resorted to, to compel your removal, which will result in most disastrous consequences to yourselves and your opponents, and that the end will be your expulsion from the state.

We think that steps should be taken by you to make it apparent that you are actually preparing to remove in the spring.

By carrying out, in good faith, your proposition to remove as submitted to us, we think you should be, and will be permitted to depart peaceably next spring for your destination, west of the Rocky Mountains.

For the purpose of maintaining law and order in this county, the commanding general purposes to leave an armed force in this county which will be sufficient for that purpose and which will remain as long as the governor deems it necessary. And for the purpose of preventing the use of such force for vexatious or improper objects, we will recommend the governor of the state to send some competent legal officer to remain here, and have the power of deciding what process shall be executed by said military force.

We recommend to you to place every possible restraint in your power over the members of your church, to prevent them from committing acts of aggression or retaliation on any citizens of the state, as a contrary course may, and most probably will bring about a collision which will subvert all efforts to maintain the peace in this county; and we propose making a similar request of your opponents in this and the surrounding counties.

With many wishes that you may find peace and prosperity in the land of your destination, which you desire, we have the honor to subscribe ourselves,

[Signed]   JOHN J. HARDIN,
W. B. WARREN,
S. A. DOUGLAS,
J. A. McDOUGAL.'

Friday, 3.—The following Resolutions by the citizens of Quincy were published in the *Quincy Whig,* October 1st:—

RESOLUTIONS IN THE QUINCY WHIG

'First, *Resolved,* That we accept and recommend to the people of the surrounding counties to accept the proposition made by the Mormons to remove from the state next spring: but we accept it as an unconditional proposition to remove. We do not intend to bring ourselves under any obligations to purchase their property or to furnish purchasers for the same, but will expect them to dispose of their property and remove at the time appointed.

Secondly, That we do not endorse the enumeration of grievances made by the Mormons in their printed proposition to remove, or in any degree yield our assent thereto: that we do not believe them to be a persecuted people, but believe whatever grievances they may suffer to be the legitimate consequences of their own conduct.

Thirdly, *Resolved,* That it is now too late to attempt the settlement of the difficulties in Hancock county upon any other basis than that of the removal of the Mormons from the state.

Fourthly, *Resolved,* That whilst we shall endeavor by all means in our power to prevent the occurrence of anything which might operate against their removal, and afford the people of Nauvoo any ground of complaint, we shall equally expect good faith upon their part; and if they shall not comply with their own propositions, the consequences must rest upon those who violate faith. And we now solemnly pledge ourselves to be ready at the appointed time to act as the occasion may require, and that we will immediately adopt a preliminary military organization, for prompt future action if occasion should demand it.

Fifthly, *Resolved,* That we respectfully recommend to the people of the surrounding counties, to wait with patience the time appointed for removal, and that if in their opinion the Resolutions passed by this meeting are such as the occasion requires they adopt them and send copies to the church authorities at Nauvoo.

Sixthly, *Resolved,* That in our opinion the peace of Hancock county cannot be so far restored as to allow the desired progress to be made in preparing the way for the removal of the Mormons while J. B. Backenstos remains sheriff of said county and that he ought to resign said office.

Seventhly, *Resolved,* That we recommend to all parties in Hancock county that they suspend all legal prosecutions for alleged offenses during the present state of excitement; and that all should be permitted to return to their homes in peace.

Eighthly, *Resolved,* That in our opinion it will only be necessary for the people of Nauvoo to appoint commissioners on their part to whom applications for the purchase of real estate may be made, and that there is no necessity to appoint commissioners on the other side.

Ninthly, *Resolved,* That in order to manifest our sympathies with the unoffending poor, the widow and orphans of Nauvoo, a committee of twenty with a treasurer, be appointed by the chairman, whose duty it shall be to receive subscriptions from all those desirous of contributing pecuniary aid for such persons and that the amount collected be paid over to such persons as they shall appoint to receive it upon their being ready to start upon their journey of removal.

Tenthly, *Resolved,* That we expect as an indispensable condition to the pacification of the county that the old citizens of Hancock county be permitted to return to their homes unmolested by the present sheriff, and the Mormons for the offenses alleged against them, and that any attempt on their part to arrest or prosecute such citizens will inevitably lead to a renewal of the late disorders.

Eleventh, *Resolved,* That the judge of this judicial circuit be requested not to hold any court in Hancock county this fall, with a view to prevent unnecessary excitement and collision in said county, which might inflame the passions of its citizens and so endanger its peace, it being well known that the unpleasant difficulties already existing there have entirely prevented the due impartial administration of justice.

Twelfth, *Resolved*, That this meeting deem it proper to recommend that a small military force be stationed in Hancock county until next spring to prevent depredations upon private property and preserve the peace of said county and that it be respectfully yet earnestly recommended to the executive of this state to furnish the same for the purpose above named.'

ADDITIONAL RESOLUTIONS ADOPTED AT THE SAME MEETING

'*Resolved*, That a committee of five be appointed for the purpose of adopting and carrying into operation a volunteer military organization for Adams county, and said committee are hereby authorized to do all things lawful, necessary and proper for the purpose of preparing such a force, without delay, to be used to preserve the peace of this and the adjoining counties.

Resolved, That the committee appointed to visit Nauvoo deserve and receive our warmest thanks, for the prompt, able and efficient manner in which they discharged the duties confided to them.

Resolved, That the chairman of this meeting be and he is hereby vested with full power and authority to call an adjourned meeting at any time he may deem the public exigencies require it.

Resolved, That the proceedings of this meeting be published in the city papers and copies thereof transmitted to the governor of the state, and to the church authorities of Nauvoo by the chairman and secretary of this meeting.'

Saturday, 4.—Attended General Council at Seventies' Hall. While riding to the hall with Elders H. C. Kimball and W. Richards, Elder Richards prophesied that we should have means to move all the poor and want for nothing. Elder Kimball said, amen. ^{A Prophecy of Good.}

The correspondence from General Hardin and suite, the governor, and the Resolutions by the citizens of Quincy were read to the council.

I proposed that we cease publishing the *Nauvoo Neighbor* and save our paper inasmuch as our papers rarely get beyond the hands of our enemies. Any information we want to send abroad we will publish in circulars and extras. ^{Resolution to Cease Publishing the *Nauvoo Neighbor* and the *Times and Seasons*.}

Elder Richards moved that the next number of the *Times and Seasons* close that paper and that the minutes of the conference be published in the *Nauvoo Neighbor.*

I proposed that we appoint a committee of three to select and preserve the statements of the press of the United States concerning us, and proposed that Elders Parley P. Pratt, Orson Spencer and Wm. W. Phelps be a committee to write a pointed document relating to the treatment we have received from the United States.*

The committee who were appointed by the President to acquire and lay before the council all the necessary information in regard to the outfitting of families for emigration west of the mountains submit the following report obtained from calculation and from the best works on the subject:

REQUIREMENTS OF EACH FAMILY OF FIVE FOR THE JOURNEY
ACROSS THE PLAINS

'Each family consisting of five adults, will require 1 good strong wagon, well covered. 3 good yokes of oxen between the ages of four and ten. Two or more cows. One or more good beeves, some sheep if they have them.

One thousand pounds of flour or other bread stuff and good sacks to put it in.

One bushel of beans.

One hundred pounds of sugar.

One good musket or rifle to each man.

One pound of powder and three lbs. lead (or perhaps more).

Two lbs. tea, 5 lbs. coffee.

Twenty-five pounds of salt.

A few pounds of dried beef, or bacon, as they choose.

A good tent and furniture to each two families.

From ten to fifty pounds of seed to a family.

And from twenty-five to one hundred pounds of farming or other tools.

Clothing and bedding to each family of five persons not to exceed five hundred pounds.

One or more sets of saw and gristmill irons to each company of one hundred families.

---

*This was in harmony with the revelation which was given some five years earlier to the Prophet Joseph Smith in which a commandment was given for the gathering up of all the libelous and damaging falsehoods that had been stated against the church by their enemies (See *Doctrine and Covenants*, sec. cxxiii, March, 1839).

Cooking utensils to consist of a bake-kettle, frying-pan, coffee pot, tin cups, plates, and forks, spoons, pans, etc., etc., as few as will do.

A few goods to trade with the Indians.

A little iron and steel, a few pounds of nails.

Each wagon supposed to be loaded on the start with one ton without the persons or twenty-eight hundred including them.

If going to the coast it is not necessary to carry seed wheat, oats or grass. Nor are cattle and sheep absolutely necessary except to live on while upon the journey, as the country abounds in both cattle and sheep. A few horses will be necessary for each company. Also a few cannon and ammunition for the same. The journey to the coast will require some four or five months, being upwards of two thousand miles.

There was also added two sets of pulley blocks and rope for crossing rivers to each company.

Two ferry boats to each company.

One keg of alcohol of five gallons for each two families.

Ten pounds of dried apples for each family.

Five pounds of dried peaches.

Twenty pounds of dried pumpkin.

Two pounds of black pepper.

One pound of cayenne.

One-half pound mustard.

Twelve nutmegs. One fish seine for each company. Hooks and lines for each family.' "

CHAPTER XXXIII

LAST CONFERENCE AT NAUVOO—PLEA OF THE
"MOTHER OF PROPHETS"—PATHETIC

"Sunday, October 5, 1845.—

FIRST MEETING IN THE TEMPLE

Through the indefatigable exertions, unceasing industry, and heaven-blessed labors, in the midst of trials, tribulations, poverty, and worldly obstacles, solemnized in some instances, by death, about five thousand saints had the inexpressible joy and great gratification to meet for the first time in the House of the Lord in the City of Joseph. From mites and tithing millions had risen up to the glory of God, as a Temple, where the children of the last kingdom could come together and praise the Lord.

It certainly afforded a holy satisfaction to think that since the sixth of April, 1841, when the first stone was laid, amidst the most straitened circumstances, the Church of Jesus Christ of Latter-day Saints had witnessed their bread cast upon waters, or more properly, their obedience to the commandments of the Lord, appear in the tangible form of a Temple, entirely enclosed, windows in; with temporary floors, pulpits and seats to accommodate so many persons preparatory to a General Conference; no General Conference having been held for three years past, according to the declaration of our martyred Prophet:—

'There shall be no more baptisms for the dead, until the ordinance can be attended to in the font of the Lord's House; and the church shall not hold another General Conference, until they can meet in said house. *For thus saith the Lord.*'

I [Brigham Young] opened the services of the day by a dedicatory prayer, presenting the Temple, thus far completed, as a monument of the saints' liberality, fidelity, and faith, concluding: 'Lord, we dedicate this house and ourselves, to thee.'   The day was occupied most agreeably in hearing instructions and teachings, and offering up the gratitude of honest hearts, for so great a privilege, as worshiping God within instead of without an edifice, whose beauty and workmanship will compare with any house of worship in America, and whose motto is:

'HOLINESS TO THE LORD'.

Monday, 6.——

CONFERENCE MINUTES

'*Minutes of the first General Conference, which was ever held by the Church of Jesus Christ of Latter-day Saints, in the House of the Lord in the City of Joseph, commencing on Monday, October 6th, 1845, ten o'clock forenoon.*

Present——Elder Brigham Young, President of the Quorum of the Twelve Apostles; also Elders Heber C. Kimball, Parley P. Pratt, Willard Richards, John Taylor, George A. Smith and Amasa M. Lyman; Patriarchs John Smith and Isaac Morley; Presiding Bishops Newel K. Whitney and George Miller; also the authorities of the church generally.

The conference was opened with singing by the choir, and prayer by Elder Parley P. Pratt.   Elder Willard Richards then arose and read over some notices concerning lost property, concerts, etc.   He then stated, that the President had waited from half past nine to near eleven o'clock, for the people to get together; he exhorted the brethren to be more punctual, as so much time lost could not be recalled, and we have a great amount of business, which must necessarily be attended to during conference.   He next stated that General Hardin had requested us to make out a list of all the buildings belonging to our brethren which have been burned by our enemies, and also had requested that all those who have had their buildings or other property destroyed should make affidavit of the same before a justice of the peace, and have their affidavits ready to be forwarded to him at as early a season as possible.

FIRST BUSINESS—PRESENTATION OF AUTHORITIES FOR APPROVAL

President Brigham Young then rose and said: the first business that will come before this conference, will be to present the authorities of the church to ascertain whether they are in good standing.

Father John Smith, the president of the stake, then arose and presented the Twelve as the Presidents of the whole church; which was seconded and carried unanimously.

It was then moved that Brigham Young be continued and sustained as the President of the Quorum of the Twelve Apostles; seconded and carried unanimously.

It was next moved that Heber C. Kimball be continued and sustained as one of the Twelve Apostles: seconded and carried unanimously.

It was next moved that Orson Hyde be continued and sustained as one of the Twelve Apostles; seconded and carried unanimously.

It was next moved that Parley P. Pratt be continued and sustained as one of the Twelve Apostles; seconded and carried unanimously.

It was next moved that Orson Pratt be continued and sustained as one of the Twelve Apostles; seconded and carried unanimously.

Orson Pratt's Objection to Sustaining William Smith.
It was next moved, that William Smith be continued and sustained as one of the Twelve Apostles; seconded. Whereupon Elder Orson Pratt arose and said:

'I have an objection to Brother William continuing in that office. I feel, as an individual, that I cannot, conscientiously, uphold and sustain Brother William as one of the Twelve Apostles, until he thinks different from what he does now. I have many reasons for this, but I will merely mention one or two, which must suffice for the present. In the first place, I have proof positive that he is an aspiring man; that he aspires to uproot and undermine the legal Presidency of the Church, that he may occupy the place himself. This he has avowed openly in the east, which I can prove by good and substantial witnesses. In the second place, while Brother William was in the east, to my certain knowledge, his doctrine and conduct have not had a savory influence; but have produced death and destruction wherever he went. This also I am well prepared to prove. I have been waiting in all long suffering, for an alteration in Brother William's course, but up to the present time, I have been disappointed. For these two reasons, I would plead for one, that we no longer sustain him in his office, till a proper investigation can be had, and he make satisfaction. I do this individually; I leave others to do as they please.'

The motion being seconded, a vote was then taken to sustain him, but was *lost* unanimously.

It was next moved that John E. Page be continued and sustained as one of the Twelve Apostles; seconded and carried unanimously.

It was next moved that Willard Richards be continued and sustained as one of the Twelve Apostles; seconded and carried unanimously.

It was next moved, that Wilford Woodruff be continued and sustained as one of the Twelve Apostles; seconded and carried unanimously.

It was next moved that John Taylor be continued and sustained as one of the Twelve Apostles; seconded and carried unanimously.

It was next moved that George A. Smith be continued and sustained as one of the Twelve Apostles; seconded and carried unanimously.

It was next moved that Lyman Wight be continued and sustained as one of the Twelve Apostles; whereupon Elder A. W. Babbitt said:

'As Elder Orson Pratt remarked, concerning William Smith, that he could not conscientiously vote to sustain him, so I say in regard to Lyman Wight, I cannot conscientiously give my vote in his favor. My reason is this: If there is a council in this church that ought to be united, and act in unison as one man, it is the Council of the Twelve. If the head is sick, the whole body is afflicted. If I am rightly informed concerning Brother Wight's conduct, for the past year, he has not acted in unison with the Twelve, nor according to their counsel. The last year has been one

A. W. Babbitt's Objection to Lyman Wight.

of affliction, persecution and sorrow, when the adversary has continually sought to destroy and mutilate the church; and it has required all the faith, prayers and perseverance of the leaders, to save this people from the grasp of the destroyer.   If the counsel of Brother Wight had been followed, this Temple would not have been built, nor the baptismal font erected.   He has sought to draw away a part of the force, which we ought to have had to build this Temple.   His teachings have been contrary to the counsel of the church, and his conduct calculated to destroy it.   Under circumstances of this kind, I cannot conscientiously vote to continue him in his standing, until he retracts, and makes satisfaction.   Brother Wight's course has been calculated to divide the church, and prevent those things being accomplished, which were commanded of God by the Prophet Joseph.'

Elder Kimball arose and said:—

'It is well known, that Brother Wight's case was had before the conference last spring, and that he was dropt, and then again retained; that is, that we would let him be, and see what he would do, and what course he would take.   He has been away ever since; and is with a small company somewhere; we cannot tell what he is doing; he may in his own mind, be acting in concert with the rest, and he may be acting for the good of this people.   It would be my mind, to let his case lay over for the present, until we can learn something from him.'

Whereupon it was moved, that we let the case of Brother Lyman Wight lay over for the present until we hear from him.   Seconded and carried unanimously.

It was next moved that Amasa M. Lyman be continued and sustained as one of the Twelve Apostles; seconded and carried unanimously.

Wm. Smith Rejected as Patriarch.

Elder Isaac Morley arose and said; he would next present William Smith as the Patriarch of the Church; and moved that he be continued and sustained in that office; seconded and *lost* unanimously.

Willard Richards Sustained as Church Historian.

President Brigham Young stated, that about three years ago, Elder Willard Richards was appointed by President Joseph Smith, as Historian for the Church, and general Church Recorder.   We have previously acted on his appointment to office, as Recorder, but not as Historian. He would therefore move, that we receive the appointment of Brother Joseph, and that we continue and sustain Elder Richards as Historian for the Church, and General Church Recorder; seconded and carried unanimously.

It was next moved that Father John Smith be continued and sustained as president of this stake of Zion; and that Isaac Morley and Charles C. Rich be continued and sustained as his counselors; seconded and carried unanimously.

It was next moved that Samuel Bent be continued and sustained in his office as president of the high council; seconded and carried unanimously.

It was next moved, that George W. Harris, Alpheus Cutler, James Allred, Thomas Grover, Henry G. Sherwood, William Huntington, Sen., Lewis D. Wilson, Newel Knight, David Fullmer, Aaron Johnson, and Ezra T. Benson each be continued and sustained as members of the high council; seconded and carried unanimously.

It was next moved that George Miller be continued and sustained as president of the high priests' quorum, and that William Snow and Noah Packard be continued as his counselors; seconded and carried unanimously.

It was next moved that Joseph Young be continued and sustained in his office as the Senior President of the First Quorum of the Seventy; seconded and carried unanimously.

It was next moved that Levi W. Hancock, Henry Harriman, Zera Pulsipher, Daniel S. Miles, Jedediah M. Grant, each be continued and sustained as one of the Seven Presidents over all the Seventies; seconded and carried unanimously.

Elder George A. Smith remarked that Roger Orton was one of the 'Old Camp'* and was selected a year ago to be one of the seven Presidents of the Seventy; but he had never received his ordination, nor done anything to magnify his calling. It is not to be expected that we

Elder Roger Orton dropped from First Council of Seventy.

---

*"Old Camp" (i. e. Zion's Camp) which went to Missouri to redeem Zion in 1834, and from which the Twelve Apostles and the first two quorums of Seventy were chosen.

shall wait year after year for men to come forward and fill their offices. Brother Orton was one of the Old Camp, and we love him on that account; we always called him the 'Big Major', and a first rate man; but he has not come forward since his appointment to magnify his calling.

Elder Joseph Young said:

'Last spring I visited Roger Orton and apprised him of his appointment. He agreed to come as early as convenient, and receive his ordination; and I gave him to understand, if he did not come and act in his office, he would be dropt. Brother Orton has always sustained Brother Joseph and the church, but he has very little of the spirit; he has been in the church about twelve years, but never has been active since his discharge from the camp that went up to Missouri in 1834. It was by the counsel of the Twelve that he was appointed one of the Presidents of the Seventy. I have no particular desire to plead for him, but if his case can be laid over, I think he can be saved in that office, but I will be subject to counsel. I have considerable feeling for him; he lost all his property in Missouri, and has since addicted himself to drinking whiskey; that seems to have ruined him, but he may be reclaimed.'

President Brigham Young arose and said, he would preach one of Dow's short sermons:—

'If you won't when you can, when you will you shan't'. 'I say if men will not act and magnify their calling, let more honorable men be appointed. Roger Orton is keeping a public house at Augusta and has had sufficient time to come and prove himself a worthy man in his office, but has not done it; and I say let a more honorable man take the crown. If he won't work now, when will he?'

It was then moved that we drop him; seconded and carried unanimously.

Moved that Samuel Williams be continued and sustained as president of the elders' quorum, and Jesse Baker and Joshua Smith be continued and sustained as his counselors; seconded and carried unanimously.

Moved that Newel K. Whitney be continued and sustained as the first Bishop of the Church; and that George Miller be continued and sustained as his associate; seconded and carried unanimously.

Moved that Stephen M. Farnsworth be continued

and sustained as president of the priests' quorum; and that William Carmichael and _____ Betts be continued and sustained as his counselors; seconded and carried unanimously.

Moved that Elisha Averett be continued and sustained as president of the teachers' quorum; as also his former counselors; seconded and carried unanimously.

President Brigham Young moved, that there be a quorum of deacons selected, and a president over them, and that the Presiding Bishops see to it, as soon as possible, and make report to this conference before its close; seconded and carried unanimously. Council of Deacons in the Church Provided.

Conference then adjourned till two o'clock p. m. Benediction by Elder G. A. Smith.

Two p. m.—The house was called to order by Elder Taylor; the choir sang 'The Prodigal Son'. Elder Taylor read a list of the sick, and offered up prayer; after which the choir sang another hymn.

Whereupon Elder Parley P. Pratt addressed the conference on the subject of our present situation and prospects. He referred to the great amount of expense and labor we have been at to purchase lands, build houses, the Temple, etc.; we might ask, why is it that we have been at all this outlay and expense, and then are called to leave it? He would answer that the people of God always were required to make sacrifices, and if we Elder Parley P. Pratt on the Situation and Prospects of the Saints. have a sacrifice to make, he is in favor of its being something worthy of the people of God.

'We do not want to leave a desolate place, to be a reproach to us, but something that will be a monument to those who may visit the place of our industry, diligence and virtue. There is no sacrifice required at the hands of the people of God but shall be rewarded to them an hundred fold, in time or eternity.

'The Lord has another purpose to bring about and to fulfill. We know that the great work of God must all the while be on the increase and grow greater. The people must enlarge in numbers and extend their borders; they cannot always live in one city, nor in one county;

they cannot always wear the yoke; Israel must be the head and not the tail. The Lord designs to lead us to a wider field of action, where there will be more room for the saints to grow and increase, and where there will be no one to say we crowd them, and where we can enjoy the pure principles of liberty and equal rights.

'When we settle a country where the air, the water, soil and timber is equally free to every settler without money or without price, the climate healthy, and the people free from unjust and vexatious lawsuits, mobocracy, and oppression of every kind, we can become vastly more wealthy, have better possessions and improvements, and build a larger and better Temple in five years from this time than we now possess.

'It has cost us more for sickness, defense against mobs, vexatious prosecutions, and to purchase lands in this place, than as much improvement will cost in another.

'One small nursery may produce many thousands of fruit trees, while they are small. But as they expand towards maturity, they must needs be transplanted, in order to have room to grow and produce the natural fruits. It is so with us. We want a country where we have room to expand, and to put in requisition all our energies and the enterprise and talents of a numerous, intelligent and increasing people. In our natural state, ask yourselves if you could be brought to endure and enjoy a celestial law, without an experience of the kind we have passed through for the last fifteen years?

'In short, this people are fast approaching that point which ancient prophets have long since pointed out as the destiny of the saints of the last days.'

After many other spirited remarks touching similar points, he was succeeded by Elder George A. Smith, on the same subject. Elder Smith observed that a revelation was given in Missouri in regard to the saints consecrating their property which was not understood at the time; but they were soon brought to their understanding, for the Lord in his providence caused it all to be consecrated, for they were compelled to leave it.

George A. Smith.

He is glad of the prospect of leaving this county and seeking a place where we can enjoy the fruits of our labors and God himself be the sole proprietor of the elements.

Here is one principle in which he wants this whole people to unite. When we were to leave Missouri the saints entered into a covenant not to cease their exertions until every saint who wished to go was removed, which was done.

We are better off now than we were then, and he wants to see the same principle carried out now, that every man will give all to help to take the poor; and every honest industrious member who wants to go. He wants to see this influence extend from the west to the east sea.

After which President Brigham Young moved that we take all the saints with us, to the extent of our ability, that is, our influence and property; seconded by Elder Kimball, and carried unanimously. Elder Brigham Young continued:

'If you will be faithful to your covenant, I will now prophesy that the great God will shower down means upon this people, to accomplish it [the resolution] to the very letter. I thank God that the time has come so much sooner than I expected, that that scripture is being fulfilled, 'My people shall be willing in the day of my power'; and I almost feel to thank our friends abroad for hastening it on now.' President Young's Prophecy of the Deliverance of the Saints.

Elder Parley P. Pratt made some remarks relative to the brethren being all on a level when they left Missouri. He referred to the Whitmer family monopolizing timber; advised liberality with wood.

Elder H. C. Kimball moved that every man who owned a woodlot should on application, let the poor, the sick, and the needy who wanted wood, have it; and those who have teams should assist in hauling it to them; seconded and carried unanimously.

It was requested by President Young that no man go into another's woods without the consent of the owner; and then take it clean and be careful of the timber.

Benediction by W. W. Phelps and adjourned until tomorrow at ten a. m.

Tuesday, October 7, 1845.—Conference met pursuant to adjournment at ten a. m. Meeting called to

order by president of the stake. Choir sang a hymn.
Prayer by Elder Phelps. Choir then sang another
hymn.

Elder Heber C. Kimball then addressed the conference.

'This is a hard place for anyone to speak in, and there are many
things still necessary to lay before this conference. For my part I am
done preaching to this nation; at least for the present.

Elder
Kimball I have been forth through the United States and Europe,
in fact, I have spent my whole time at it, since I came
into the church. It is now all counsel for me—We have a great many
things to say today; and I suppose we shall always have plenty to do.
I presume many have got out of business; but we will now have work
enough, to get ready to go to some other country; to get there, and
to plough our fields when we get there. I have seen people crying
and weeping, and mourning, because they had nothing to do; but
when we leave this place, you will never have cause to weep for not
having anything to do, from this time forth, and forever more, if you
are faithful to your calling. I am glad the time of our exodus is come;
I have looked for it for years. It is necessary for us to be faithful
and humble, and if we listen to counsel we shall prosper. And
although we leave all our fine houses and farms here, how long do you
think it will be before we shall be better off than we are now? I
have no farm to leave; I never had that privilege. Many of the
brethren have farms; but there are many who have spent their whole
time in the service of the church, for fourteen or fifteen years, who
never had a farm. When we get to a new country, some of these old
veterans will be looked after first; and I rejoice in it. We are now
about coming to the Apostolic religion; i. e., you will sell all, and
come and lay it down at the Apostles' feet. But it has taken a good
scourging for fifteen years to bring us to this. There may be individuals who will look at their pretty houses and gardens and say, 'it
is hard to leave them'; but I tell you, when we start, you will put
on your knapsacks, and follow after us. Before I was baptized, I
believed we should come into an Apostolic religion. As for a Common
Stock Business Religion, such as many preach, I do not believe in it.
Every man will be a steward over his house and property; and if he
is an unfaithful steward, his stewardship will be given to another. I will
prophesy in the name of Heber C. Kimball, that in five years, we will
be as well again off as we are now. Those brethren who have gone
off and labored among the Gentiles, are not as well off as we are;
some have eighty dollars, some an hundred, and some fifty dollars due
them; and their 'friends' have driven them away penniless; and they
have had to flee for safety to Nauvoo. Those who remained here, are
better off. Since we have had an invitation from our 'friends' to leave

the county, many have asked, shall we go and labor for them? They may go, if they have a mind to; but I won't do it; I'll see them go the other way first.

'I positively know men, that have gone to labor for those, who with uplifted hands, swore they would take President Brigham Young's life and my own. If it is your feeling to tarry here, and labor for each other to get away, manifest it (clear vote). At the last conference, a vote was passed that the Gentiles were cut off; and now, why do you want to labor for them. Inasmuch as the Gentiles reject us, lo! we turn to the Jews.

'Again; there is a constant running to the Twelve, and saying 'Can't we go in your company?' We calculate you are all going in the first company, both old and young, rich and poor; for there will be but one company. Probably we will sometimes be the first, and then again the last, sometimes in one place, sometimes in another. Some say, 'ah! you are going ahead, and taking the band;' but we will be with all of you.

'We first made a selection of one hundred, and when we had done, we found we could not be satisfied without taking the whole; and so we finally concluded we would take you all with us, and have but one company. There is no use in making selections, for you are all good; but there is still a chance for us all to be a great deal better. We have no partiality; we have a common interest, for the welfare of this whole people, and we feel to advocate your cause like a father would advocate the cause of his children.

'When men come in here to divide you, and when the mob came, did we flee? No! No! the hireling fleeth, but we felt like a father, and if you had to die, we would die with you. We want to feed the sheep, to nourish them; they have a tremendous journey to take; and when we see one that is weak and feeble, we will take it up, put it into a wagon, and take you all with us. We have had sorrow and could not sleep on your accounts: if we had no anxiety for you, we should have fled into the wilderness and left you.

'We want to take you to a land, where a white man's foot never trod, nor a lion's whelps, nor the devil's; and there we can enjoy it, with no one to molest and make us afraid; and we will bid all the nations welcome, whether Pagans, Catholics, or Protestants. We are not accounted as white people, and we don't want to live among them. I had rather live with the buffalo in the wilderness; and I mean to go if the Lord will let me, and spare my life. Let us become passive as clay in the hands of the potter: if we don't we will be cut from the wheel and thrown back in the mill again, like the Fosters, Higbees, and others. They want to come into Nauvoo again; but we won't let them, until we have all the good clay out, and have made it into vessels of honor to our heavenly Father: then they may come and be ground.'

Elder Lyman next arose and remarked:

'President Young says, we did not calculate to be in a hurry.   It would be a matter of gratification, if I could express my feelings; but I have so many of them that I can't do it. Elder Lyman's Remarks.

'There has been in the progress of this church an ample manifestation of the various windings and dispositions of man.   A person cannot fail to perceive it, when he will observe and reflect, and doubtless those who have reflected may be satisfied, that the course of this people is unalterably fixed.   I am glad it is not controlled by any human being.   We have contended with opposition when it appeared impossible for us to overcome, and yet we have triumphed; and this people are becoming great and numerous.

'Perhaps in the congregation before me there is every variety of feeling, which can be found on the face of the earth: yet we find their feelings undergoing a change, and that this people are approximating to a *Oneness;* the people are becoming one, and their interests one. When they first heard the gospel, they hailed and cherished it with joy; and they have come up here to receive additional instruction: yet perhaps, they have made but a limited calculation of how far they would have to go, in obedience and sacrifices, and to how much persecution and suffering they would be subject that they might come up out of the fire as gold seven times tried.

'It has been said, that after a time, the Lord will accomplish a certain something: That after men had endeavored to build up kingdoms, and seen them crumble to the dust and disappear; he had said, he would build up a kingdom which would stand forever, and become a universal kingdom: and moreover the Prophet said, 'it should break in pieces every other kingdom'.   If any man had preached this, he would have been considered guilty of treason.   But those whom the Christian world consider as better men than we are, have said it; men, whom they say were better, and had knowledge, power, and virtue, more than they will now admit is lawful for us in this enlightened age to enjoy.

'It has been said, that we should leave this country next spring; if the Lord is willing and the people have no objections.   (And we don't care much whether they have or not; we calculate to go about next spring).   And we calculate to go the same people we are now; preserving the same principles which have caused us to grow and expand as we have done.   This people have grown until there is not room for them to grow, and now they need transplanting, where they can have more room: and however much the people may seem disposed to not go, the sails are set, the wind is fair, and we are bound to weather the point, whether we will or no; for we are not at the helm; and whine and complain as much as you please, you have got to weather the point.   Brother Kimball says, the whiners will have to go behind! So if you want to go in the company of the Twelve, you must not whine. Some persons suppose that when they had once lost their all, they had suffered enough: to hear them talk you would suppose that John the Revelator, when they tried to boil him in oil, or the three Hebrew children in the fiery furnace, seven times heated—never suffered half as much, nor felt half so uncomfortable as they. They have to get rich, and be made poor, about twenty times over, before they will come straight. I expect the rich will have to be made poor until the poor are made rich; and then there will be nobody poor. When the rich are rich; and the poor are rich; then there will be nobody rich and nobody poor; for all will be on a level.

'God did not say, that this man or that man should build up the kingdom, that was to break in pieces all other kingdoms; but he said he would do it himself; and whenever this people were unwilling to do as the Lord would have them he has taken his rod and scourged them, until they were forced to do it. The Lord once said he would make Kirtland a stronghold for a time; and he has done it. He said in Missouri he would sustain the saints for a time; and he did it. And when we came here, the Lord said, that if the people of the state of Illinois would maintain us in our rights they would be blessed; if not we might find it to our advantage to leave them.'

The names of Company No. 5 were then called over, with orders to meet after meeting at the old stand.

Elder Taylor made some remarks in behalf of the suffering poor in the north part of town; and called upon all to come forward to aid the bishops in supplying these poor families. *Appeal in Behalf of the Poor.*

Elder George A. Smith said there were many coming to get leaders of the companies appointed; and remarked you need not be in a hurry for the Twelve will take care to have proper captains appointed in due time; and all will move on like clockwork. But we must not hurry business.

The Patriarch, John Smith, appointed four bishops to stand at the door, to take a collection for the benefit of the poor.

The choir sang and the meeting was dismissed until 2 o'clock p. m.

Benediction by George A. Smith.

All the single men who want to come into the 1st

company or company of the Twelve, were notified to give in their names.

At 2 o'clock.—President Brigham Young came to the stand and dismissed the meeting until tomorrow at 10 o'clock a. m. This was done on account of a body of armed men having suddenly entered the city. Not knowing but this was a move by the mob, the President requested all the brethren to go home and prepare themselves for any emergency. He, however, soon ascertained that W. B. Warren, Esq. was at the head of the troops and that they had come in on business.

Early Adjournment of Conference —Report of Troops in the City.

The President then informed the people of this fact; and requested them to retire to their homes in peace; concluding his remarks with these words, 'Be ye also ready'.

Wednesday, October 8, 1845.—Conference opened at the usual hour with singing and prayer.

Mother Lucy Smith, the aged and honored parent of Joseph Smith, having expressed a wish to say a few words to the congregation, she was invited upon the stand. She spoke at considerable length and in an audible manner, so as to be heard by a large portion of the vast assembly.

Appearance of Mother Lucy Smith Before the Conference.

She commenced by saying that she was truly glad that the Lord had let her see so large a congregation. She had a great deal of advice to give, but Brother Brigham Young had done the errand, he had fixed it completely. There were comparatively few in the assembly who were acquainted with her family. She was the mother of eleven children, seven of whom were boys. She raised them in the fear and love of God, and never was there a more obedient family. She warned parents that they were accountable for their children's conduct; advised them to give them books and work to keep them from idleness; warned all to be full of love, goodness and kindness, and never to do in secret, what they would not do in the presence of

millions. She wished to know of the congregation
whether they considered her a mother in Israel (upon
which President Brigham Young said: all who consider Mother Smith as a mother in Israel, signify it by
saying yes!—One universal 'yes' rang throughout).
She remarked that it was just eighteen years since
Joseph Smith the Prophet had become acquainted with
the contents of the plates; and then in a concise manner
related over the most prominent points in the early
history of her family; their hardships, trials, privations,
persecutions, sufferings, etc.; some parts of which
melted those who heard her to tears, more especially
the part relating to a scene in Missouri, when her beloved son Joseph was condemned to be shot in fifteen
minutes, and she by prodigious efforts was enabled to
press through the crowd to where he was, and to give
him her hand; but could not see his face; he took her
hand and kissed it she said, let me hear your voice once
more my son; he said, 'God bless you my dear mother!'
She gave notice that she had written her history, and
wished it printed before we leave this place. She then
mentioned a discourse once delivered by Joseph after
his return from Washington, in which he said that he
had done all that could be done on earth to obtain
justice for their wrongs; but they were all, from the
president to the judge, determined not to grant justice.
But, said he, keep good courage, these cases are recorded
in heaven, and I am going to lay them before the highest
court in heaven. 'Little', said she, 'did I then think
he was so soon to leave us, to take the case up himself.
And don't you think this case is now being tried? I
feel as though God was vexing this nation a little,
here and there, and I feel that the Lord will let Brother
Brigham take the people away. Here, in this city, lay
my dead; my husband and children; and if so be the
rest of my children go with you, (and would to God
they may all go), they will not go without me; and if
I go, I want my bones brought back in case I die away,
and deposited with my husband and children.' (Mother

Smith said many more good things, but the rest being inaudible to the reporters, they are lost).

President Brigham Young then arose and said he wanted to relate to the congregation the last closing remarks of Mother Smith; inasmuch as she could not be heard by all.

'Mother Smith proposes a thing which rejoices my heart: she will go with us. I can answer for the authorities of the church; we want her and her children to go with us; and I pledge myself in behalf of the authorities of the church, that while we have anything, they shall share with us. We have extended the helping hand to Mother Smith. She has the best carriage in the city and while she lives, shall ride in it when and where she pleases.

Considerate Pledges Made to the Smith Family.

'When William came here we furnished him a span of horses and a carriage and a house and Brother Kimball became responsible for the rent of it. He has run away in a time of trouble; but I suppose will come back when it is peace, and we mean to have him with us yet.'

(Mother Smith here interrupted President Young, but inaudible to the reporters). President Young continued:

'Mother Smith has been relating over the circumstances of her pecuniary life of late; she is perfectly satisfied, and all is right. I could have wished that the bishops would visit her more frequently; but they have done pretty well—and I say in the name of the Latter-day Saints, we will supply her wants; and I want the people to take anything they have for her to her, and let her do with it as she pleases. I have never asked her to go for she had told me she would not; but now she has offered it. Mother Smith proposes that she will go with us, if we will promise to bring back her remains in case of her death and deposit them with her husband's. Also Joseph once said, with outstretched arms, 'If I fall in battle in Missouri, I want you to bring my bones back, and deposit them in that sepulchre—I command you to do it in the name of the Lord.' And I pledge myself if Mother Smith goes with us and I outlive her, I will do my best to bring her bones back again, and deposit them with her children, and I want to know if this people are willing to enter into a covenant to do the same.' (Unanimous vote).

Pledge of President Young to Return the Remains of Mother Smith to Her Family at Nauvoo.

President Brigham Young continued:

'We are determined also to use every means in our power to do all that Joseph told us. And we will petition Sister Emma in the name of Israel's God, to let us deposit the remains of Joseph according as he commanded us. And if she will not consent to it, our garments are clear. Then when he awakes in the morning of the resurrection, he shall talk with them, not with me; the sin shall be upon her head, not ours.'

Meeting was adjourned to two p. m.

Benediction by President Brigham Young.

2 p. m.—Conference met pursuant to adjournment.

Meeting called to order by Elder Joseph Young. Choir sang 'The Spirit of God Like a Fire is Burning'. Prayer by Elder Taylor. Choir sang again.

Elder Taylor then arose and said:

'There is one piece of business which devolves upon me to bring before this conference; and that is the printing. As we have done preaching, so we have done printing to the people; and now let them alone and mind our own business, and let them print what they have a mind to. It has been thought best to publish the conference minutes, and let that finish the subject; but I have thought it would perhaps be better to continue the *Times and Seasons* until the volume be completed. And if we do not circulate them abroad, we can at home, in the neighborhood. There are reasons for it. First, many are anxious about items of doctrine which the saints want; and many want to have the volume completed. As to the *Nauvoo Neighbor*, it is more connected with temporal matters, news, etc., and we don't care so much about that. The world doesn't wish any news from us, and we don't wish to urge it upon them. I have read papers until I have become tired; for they are all villainy, corruption, deceit and abomination; and I shall be glad when we get to a place where we can be at peace. In regard to discontinuing the papers, I will do as I am counseled. Some may consider that they will be injured by stopping the paper; but I will give four or five dollars worth of obligations for everyone they can present against me. No man can say that I have asked pay for a paper, though hundreds here are owing me for it. I will abide counsel, but am willing to publish the *Times and Seasons* until the end of the volume.'

Proposal to Withdraw Publication of the Printed Word.

Elder Kimball moved that we discontinue the *Nauvoo Neighbor* after one number; and that the *Times and Seasons* continue from time to time, till the volume is closed; seconded and carried.

The next item of business is to appoint committees to sell houses, farms, lots, etc., that they can be referred to for sales,

Appointment
of Utility
Committees.
Nauvoo. — Winslow Farr, E d w a r d Hunter, Rufus Beach, A. W. Babbit, Joseph L. Heywood, John Benbow, and Daniel Russell.

La Harpe.—Lyman Corey, John Clark and John L. Bartolph.

Macedonia.—Wm. G. Perkins, Isaac Clark and Andrew H. Perkins.

Camp Creek.—L. A. Bingham.

Bear Creek.—Nelson Higgins, Samuel Shepherd and Daniel Allen.

Knowlton's Settlement. — Sidney A. Knowlton, Eleazer Brown and James Rawlins.

Highland Branch.—James Duncan, Wm. A. Duncan, and John Loveless.

Montebello—Eleazer Miller and Jesse Spurgin.

Yelrome.—Solomon Hancock and Horace Rawson.

In Iowa, every man is appointed to act as a committee of the whole for the sale of lands.

Elder Kimball said; there is yet another piece of business of great importance to all who have families; that is, to have some school books printed for the education of our children, which will not be according to the Gentile order.

Elder W. W. Phelps said:

'As a people we are fast approaching a desired end, which may literally be called a beginning. Thus far, we cannot be reproached with being backward in instruction. By revelation, in 1831, I was appointed to 'do the work of printing, and of selecting and writing books for schools in this church, that little children might receive instruction;' and since then I have received a further sanction. We are preparing to go out from among the people, where we can serve God in righteousness; and the first thing is, to teach our children; for they are as the Israel of old. It is our children who will take the kingdom and bear it off to all the world. The first commandment with promise to Israel was, 'Honor thy father and thy mother, that thy days may be long in the land, which the Lord thy God giveth thee.' We will instruct our children in the paths of righteousness; and we want that instruction compiled in a book.'

Provision
made for the
Publication of
School Books
for Children.

Moved that W. W. Phelps write some school books for the use of children; seconded and carried.

Elder Kimball said; the next item of business is whether or not there shall be a general settlement with the Trustees-in-Trust, the Twelve, the Temple Committee, and all others, so that we may not go away indebted to the Lord, and I want to know if it is wisdom to take such a course or not. But if we go away in debt, let it be to each other.

President Brigham Young said:

'One object of this settlement with us is, some of the Latter-day Saints believe that the Twelve are supported out of the funds belonging to this house; and I am not disposed to go away under the idea that I am in debt to the Trustees, when I have put more into their hands than I have taken out. Perhaps it will be a matter of curiosity to some how I get my living. It is not by stealing!—but by good luck, and the providence of God and good men. Those men who have done the most, are the nearest square. I want the Twelve, and the committee, and all the people to settle with the Trustees, and not go away in debt to the Lord; and then we will have abundance to take away the poor.'

Proposals for the Settlement of All Accounts.

Elder Kimball moved, that the Twelve, the Temple Commitee, and all others settle with the Trustees-in-Trust; and that the Trustees-in-Trust settle with the Presidency of the Church; seconded and carried. Elder Kimball remarked, we shall now expect a settlement from all those who have the wherewith, or you need not expect an endowment in this house. President Joseph Smith said he would stand at the door with the books; you will not see him, but you will see his successors, who will carry out his designs.

Elder George A. Smith said the next item was of very great importance:

'There has been more powder and ball wasted within the last two weeks, than would supply all the people with meat for three months if they were in a game country. What is the use of this waste? You cannot wake up in the night, but you hear them cracking away. You can hardly walk the streets, but sometimes a bullet will whistle over your head. Men say they are afraid their guns won't go off, it is wet; then I am in favor of getting something to draw (the charge from) them; I hope there will be no more firing. If there was a mob in sight, you have time enough to load your guns and fire on them. I want the powder and lead saved, so that when you get to your journey's end, you can sustain yourselves with food. Save your powder, caps and lead. I move that this conference discountenance all firing in the city, by any man, by night or by day, in every possible manner.'

Seconded and carried.

Elder H. C. Kimball said:

'There are a good many complaints of late, and I am sorry to hear it, of some of the neighbors having had their cattle shot. Brother John Benbow has had fifteen wounded. I am ashamed of a man who will do such things. The man that will destroy his neighbor's property in that way, I will prophesy that the hand of God will be upon him until he makes restitution, and he will not prosper.'

Sundry Practical Considerations Adopted.
Moved, that all persons who have been guilty, or may be hereafter, of shooting cattle, shall be cut off from the church, unless they make restitution; seconded and carried.

Moved that all persons who will not take care of their unruly cattle, shall be cut off from the church; seconded and carried.

President Young said:

'I have a little corn, if it is destroyed it may all go before I will have revenge. I am for keeping orderly and obeying counsel. When we first (again) preached in the grove, I charged the brethren not to let their cattle get into the gardens of the widows and the sick; and if the widows shot them, I would stand between them and harm, and someone, on the Friday following shot my only cow. I would have given five half eagles to bring her back again. She was reared by my wife, while I was on my mission to England, and was so gentle that my children could sit under her and milk her and play between her horns without fear of being hurt. Take care of your cattle, and feed them with your corn stalks, cabbage, slops, etc.'

And he again charged the brethren not to touch any property which did not belong to them; even if it be only a rail. He said:

'In Quincy they have decided that we shall not have any more law suits. Judge Purple has agreed not to hold any more courts in this county: (though we hear that he will). They are going to collect funds, as they say, to assist the poor to move out of Nauvoo. If they have a mind to bestow anything, let them give it to the Trustees, to be dealt out by them. We don't know but they will yet do as they did in Missouri—take our own property, and sell or bestow it upon us again at an extortionate price, and call it a deed of charity. I will tell you what it will be—a stink offering.'

Brother William Clayton then read a letter from Major Warren, respecting the arrest of one Smith, for felony, yesterday.

Moved that this conference adjourn until the 6th of April next; seconded and carried.

WILLIAM CLAYTON,
THOMAS BULLOCK,
Clerks of Conference.' "*

*Times and Seasons, vol. vi, pp. 1008-1016.

CHAPTER XXXIV

OFFICIAL MESSAGE TO THE SAINTS IN THE UNITED
STATES—REMOVAL OF THE CHURCH TO THE WEST—
ORGANIZATION — OLIVER COWDERY'S TENDER OF
SERVICES — THE BIGELOW CASE — WARREN-YOUNG-
TAYLOR OUTBREAK — THE POWER OF PRAYER *vs.*
MOBOCRACY — APPEAL TO GOVERNOR FORD

"*Wednesday, October 8, 1845.*—

*EPISTLE TO THE BRETHREN OF THE CHURCH OF JESUS CHRIST OF
LATTER-DAY SAINTS, SCATTERED ABROAD THROUGH
THE UNITED STATES OF AMERICA*

'*The Following Circular is Hereby Sent, Greeting*:
Beloved Brethren:

You will perceive from the foregoing interesting Minutes of the
General Conference, just held in the Temple in this place [see Chapter
XXXIII] not only the unparalleled union of the great
body of the saints convened, but also that a crisis of extraordinary and thrilling interests has arrived. The exodus of the nation of
the only true Israel from these United States to a far distant region of
the west, where bigotry, intolerance and insatiable oppression lose their
power over them—forms a new epoch, not only in the history of the
church, but of this nation. And we hereby timely advise you to consider
well, as the spirit may give you understanding, the various and momentous bearings of this great movement, and hear what the spirit
saith unto you by this our epistle.

Jesus Christ was delivered up into the hands of the Jewish nation
to save or condemn them, to be well or maltreated by them according
to the determinate counsel and foreknowledge of God.   And regard
not that even in the light of a catastrophe wholly unlooked for.
The spirit of prophecy has long since portrayed in the *Book of
Mormon* what might be the conduct of this nation towards the Israel
of the last days.   The same spirit of prophecy that dwelt richly in the
bosom of Joseph has time and again notified the counselors of this
church of emergencies that might arise, of which this removal is one;
and one too in which all the Latter-day Saints throughout the length
and breadth of all the United States should have a thrilling and
deliberate interest.   The same evil that premeditated
against Mordecai awaited equally all the families of his
nation.   If the authorities of this church cannot abide
in peace within the pale of this nation, neither can those

Exodus Announced. (margin note)

The Interest of Removal of the Church to the West to be Universal. (margin note)

who implicitly hearken to their wholesome counsel.   A word to the
wise is sufficient.   You all know and have doubtless felt for years the
necessity of a removal provided the government [U. S.] should not
be sufficiently protective to allow us to worship God according to the
dictates of our own consciences, and of the omnipotent voice of eternal
truth.   Two cannot walk together except they be agreed.   Jacob
must be expatriated while Esau held dominion.   It was wisdom for
the child of promise to go far away from him that thirsted for blood.
Even the heir of universal kingdoms fled precipitately into a distant
country until they that sought to murder (him) were dead.   The
ranklings of violence and intolerance and religious and political strife
that have long been waking up in the bosom of this nation, together
with the occasional scintilations of settled vengeance, and blood guiltiness cannot long be suppressed.   And deplorable is the condition
of any people that is constrained to be the butt of such
discordant and revolutionary materials.   The direful   Threatening
eruption must take place.   It requires not the spirit of   National
prophecy to foresee it.   Every sensible man in the nation has felt
and perhaps expressed his melancholy fears of the dreadful vortex into
which partizan ambition, contempt of the poor, and trampling down
the just as things of nought were fast leading the nation.   We therefore write unto you beloved brethren, as wise men that will foresee
the evil and hide yourselves until the indignation be overpast.

Concerning those who have more immediately instigated our removal by shedding the blood of our Prophet and Patriarch and burning
the habitations of scores of families in the midst of the most desolating
sickness ever known in the western valley; and who   The Church
oblige us to watch for our lives night and day—we   has Come to
have nothing to say.   We have told such tales to our   Silence.
father the president, and to all the high-minded governors, until we
are weary of it.   We look far beyond those by whom offenses come,
and discover a merciful design in our heavenly Father towards all
such as patiently endure these afflictions until he advises them that
the day of their deliverance has come.   It is our design to remove all
the saints as early next spring as the first appearance of thrifty vegetation.   In the meantime the utmost diligence of all the brethren at
this place and abroad will be requisite for our removal,   Intent to
and to complete the unfinished part of the Lord's House,   Complete the
preparatory to dedication by the next General Conference.   Temple.
The font and other parts of the Temple will be in readiness in a few
days to commence the administration of holy ordinances of endowments,
for which the faithful have long diligently labored and fervently
prayed, desiring above all things to see the beauty of the Lord and
inquire in his holy Temple.   We therefore invite the saints abroad
generally so to arrange their affairs as to come with their families
in sufficient time to receive their endowments, and aid in giving the last

finish to the House of the Lord previous to the great emigration of the church in the spring. A little additional help in the heat of the day from those abroad, to those here, who have been often driven and robbed will sweeten the interchange of fellowship, and so far fulfill the law of Christ as to bear one another's burdens. The sacrifice of property that will probably accrue from a virtually coerced sale in a given short time together with the exhaustion of available means, that has arisen from an extensive improvement of farms, and the erection of costly public and private edifices together with persecutions and abundant labors of elders in preaching the gospel to the nations, and also in self-defense from traitors and foes, hypocrites and knaves, are things that will suggest themselves to all the thoughtful humane and philanthropic. And we are confident in our Lord Jesus Christ that the balm and cordial adequate to the present crisis of affairs, will come from the saints abroad to the utmost of their ability. And you cannot furnish it better, than to come up unitedly to the counsel of our epistle promptly, diligently and to the letter. Therefore dispose of your properties and inheritance, and interests for available means, such as money, wagons, oxen, cows, mules, and a few good horses adapted to journeying and scanty feed. Also for durable fabrics suitable for apparel and tents; and some other necessary articles of merchandise. Wake up, wake up, dear brethren, we exhort you, from the Mississippi to the Atlantic, and from Canada to Florida, to the present glorious emergency in which the God of heaven has placed you to prove your faith by your works, preparatory to a rich endowment in the Temple of the Lord, and the obtaining of promises and deliverances, and glories for yourselves and your children and your dead. And we are well persuaded you will do these things, though we thus stir up your pure minds to remembrance. In so doing, the blessings of many, ready to perish like silent dew upon the grass, and the approbation of generations to come, and the hallowed joys of eternal life will rest upon you. And we can not but assure you in conclusion of our most joyful confidence, touching your union and implicit obedience to the counsel of the Great God through the Presidency of the saints. With these assurances and hopes concerning you, we bless you and supplicate the wisdom and furtherance of the Great Head of the Church upon your designs and efforts.

Admonition to Preparation for Western Move.

[Signed]　BRIGHAM YOUNG, President.

Willard Richards, Clerk.

N. B. Let all wagons that are hereafter built be constructed to the track of five feet width from center to center. Families may properly travel to this place during winter in their wagons.

There are said to be many good locations for settlements on the Pacific, especially at Vancouver's Island near the mouth of the Columbia.'

A general meeting of the seventies at 8 _{Seventies'} a. m.; twenty-two members were ordained _{Affairs.} for the thirty-first quorum.

Thursday, 9.—The seventies met in general conference. President Joseph Young counseled the seventies to pay strict attention to the call of their presidents and strongly exhorted them to pray unto the Lord day and night, and trust in him for deliverance, for the fervent prayers and faith of the saints would accomplish more than the strength of their arms, for the Lord holds the destinies of all men in his hands and he will control them according to his will and he has power to deliver us.

General Hardin has pledged himself to the mob that he will come to Nauvoo with his troops _{General Hardin's Threat Against Nauvoo.} and either arrest Orrin P. Rockwell and some others of the brethren or he 'will unroof every house in Nauvoo'. Three hundred of our enemies have volunteered to come with him from Quincy and they expect to be joined by others on the way.

There seems to be no disposition abroad but to massacre the whole body of this people, and nothing but the power of God can save us from the cruel ravages of the bloodthirsty mob.

We concluded to plead with our heavenly _{Reliance Upon Prayer.} Father to preserve his people, and the lives of his servants that the saints may finish the Temple and receive their endowments.

Saturday, 11.—The council met at Elder Taylor's. We joined in prayer, and wrote a circular for the agents to take abroad with them.

Afternoon, I remained at home being worn down with fatigue.

7 p. m., met for counsel and prayer. After prayer we finished an extract from the conference minutes for the circular. Also appointed additional captains of hundreds, making twenty-five companies, as follows: 1st, The Twelve; 2nd, Samuel Bent; 3rd, _{Organized Companies.} Alpheus Cutler; 4th, Isaac Morley; 5th,

Shadrach Roundy; 6th, Reynolds Cahoon; 7th, Daniel Spencer; 8th, Peter Haws; 9th, Joseph Fielding; 10th, John D. Parker; 11th, David Fullmer; 12th, Charles Shumway; 13th, Charles C. Rich; 14th, Jedediah M. Grant; 15th, Erastus Snow; 16th, Benjamin F. Johnson; 17th, Andrew H. Perkins; 18th, George Coulson; 19th, David Evans; 20th, Daniel C. Davis; 21st, Jonathan H. Hale; 22nd, George P. Dykes, (Ottoway); 23rd, Mephiboseth Sirrine, (Michigan); 24th, Hosea Stout; 25th, Wm. Huntington.

Bishop Miller, Sheriff Backenstos, and those who went with them to Quincy, have all returned safely.

Various Movements of Friends and Foes. Backenstos is bound over to court in three thousand dollar bonds.

General Hardin has gone to Springfield.

Tuesday, 14.—Major Warren came into the city with a detachment of the troops.

We prayed that they might not be permitted to do any injury to any of the saints; nor to interrupt our peace; they stayed but a short time.

Friday, 17.—Elder Orson Hyde returned from the east, having purchased between four and five thousand yards of canvas for the Tabernacle.

Wrote to General James Arlington Bennett in answer to several letters from him, and some he had written which we have not received, as he sent them by mail. We invited him to come out and see us, and make arrangements and go to the mountains with us.

I received a letter from Oliver Cowdery dated, Tiffin, Ohio, October 7th, advising us to seek

Tender of Services from Oliver Cowdery. aid from the United States government and offered his services as agent to see President Polk on the subject of removal westward if the council desired it.

2 p. m., attended council at Elder Heber C. Kimball's.

Last Meeting of High Council in Nauvoo. The high council met for the last time in Nauvoo, at least, it is the last minutes in their book.

Sunday, 19.—The congregation met in the Temple. Elder Orson Hyde preached.

William Smith who has published a pamphlet against the Twelve was excommunicated from the church by unanimous vote.

Excommunication of William Smith.

4 p. m., I met with the first Emigrating Company and proceeded with the organization by appointing captains of fifties and tens.

Monday, 20.—Elder Orson Hyde made returns of money collected for the Tabernacle $1415.38½c; he paid for canvas $1050.56c and other expenses $105.80c.

The Tabernacle for the Wilderness.

Evening, the Twelve met in council at Elder Taylor's, General James Arlington Bennett met with us, he expressed himself opposed to our selling out to gratify the mob, and would rather see us fight and maintain our ground.

Views of James Arlington Bennett.

Tuesday, 21.—We visited the Temple. General Bennett was highly pleased with it.

Judge Purple is holding a court in Carthage.

I received the following:

LETTER FROM J. B. BACKENSTOS

'Carthage, Illinois,
October 21, 1845.

My Dear Friend:

As yet nothing has been done to do us any good, the array of grand and petit jurors has been set aside upon an affidavit of one of the mobbers, William D. Abernethy, a notorious man has been appointed as an elisor. Thomas C. Owen is also appointed for the other elisor so things are taking a strong and decided stand against us and justice. Our judge has so far decidedly shown himself in favor of the mob faction, and has so far disgusted very many of the respectable persons at court, I confess I am perfectly displeased with such judicial 'humbugs'.

Our coroner, Henry W. Miller, has also been set aside as well as myself, so you may understand where we are, and what we may expect

Yours, etc.,

[Signed]   J. B. BACKENSTOS.'

Wednesday, 22.—General J. A. Bennett and Mr.

Booth, editor of the *Quincy Herald,* called at Dr. Richards' and tarried till noon. The conversation turned upon the saints going west. General Bennett asked Mr. Booth 'why don't you go with them'? Mr. Booth replied, 'To tell you the truth, that is my business here and I am not alone, for a number of others in Quincy are thinking of the same thing.'

Mr. Booth offered to publish in his paper anything to help the saints in the sale of their property, and any other communication from us which would not conflict with public opinion so far as to drive away his subscribers.

Evening, I met with the Twelve at Elder Taylor's. A letter was read from Reuben McBride, Kirtland, Hostility in Kirtland. stating that the apostates were doing everything they could to injure the saints. S. B. Stoddard, Jacob Bump, Hiram Kellogg, Leonard Rich, and Jewel Raney are the leaders of the rioters; they have broken into the House of the Lord, and taken possession of it, and are trying to take possession of the church farm.

Jesse P. Harmon and John Lytle who were charged with destroying the *Expositor* press were tried before Judge Purple.

The court decided in his charge to the jury, that Prosecutions for the Expositor Affair. the defendants acting under the municipal authorities of Nauvoo, were acting without authority, and if it could be proven that they had taken any part in the destruction of the press they were to be found guilty.

Rollison was the principal witness for the prosecution and gave a minute detail of the manner in which the nuisance was abated and stated that Mr. Harmon took the lead of the police on the occasion. On being asked if it was Appleton M. Harmon or Jesse P. Harmon, he replied it was the policeman and on being informed they were both policemen, he became confused and said he could not tell which it was.

The witness was asked whether it was John Lytle or Andrew Lytle, he replied, it was the Policeman

Lytle, on being informed that they were A Muddled Witness.
both policemen, he answered it was the
Blacksmith Lytle and on being told they were both
blacksmiths, he declared that he could not identify the
persons. The jury brought in a verdict of 'not guilty'
and the defendants were acquitted accordingly.

Thus were the words of the Prophet Joseph fulfilled,
who told the police (when they reported to him that
they had abated the nuisance) that not one of them
should ever be harmed for what they had done, and
that if there were any expenses consequent he would
foot the bill.

Thursday, 23.—A detachment of the governor's
troops came in from Carthage to search for In Search for a Bogus Press.
a bogus press. They searched Lucien Wood-
worth's house in vain.

By letters from Jonathan H. Hale and Jacob B.
Backenstos we learn that Alpheus Cutler, John Lytle,
Jesse B. Harmon and _____ Holmes were acquitted,
as the prosecution failed to prove they were the men
who destroyed the *Expositor* press.

All the affidavits of the sufferers in the house-burning in Hancock county were called for to be presented
before the grand jury.

Friday, 24.—Evening, council met at Elder Taylor's. Some of the mob went to Nathan Bigelow's
near Camp Creek and ordered him to leave before
Thursday for they were coming to burn his house, he
sent his son to Nauvoo for counsel, and he was advised
to go to Carthage and make the facts known to Major
Warren.

He accordingly went and told Warren who replied,
that the troops were gone elsewhere and he had nobody
to send. But told the young man to tell his father to
defend his house, and call on his neighbors Tragedy of the Bigelow Home Attack.
to assist him. It appears that on Thursday
the young man did not get back to tell his
father that night. Soon after this, Warren sent five
of his men to Father Bigelow's to defend his house.

They missed their way and did not get there till 11 o'clock at night. On arriving they tied their horses; and their commander, Lieutenant Edwards from Quincy, went straight to the door and undertook to go in without knocking. Father Bigelow expected it was the mob coming and asked who was there, but the man did not answer but still attempted to open the door. Father Bigelow again asked who was there, and what he wanted, but could get no answer. He then told the man if he opened the door he should shoot him. The man finally opened the door and Father Bigelow discharged a pistol at him loaded with buckshot; he then snatched up a musket and shot that. The shot took effect on Edwards' hip and three balls entered his breast. He fell and called to the others to come and help him. They then told Father Bigelow they were the governor's troops and had come to protect him. Father Bigelow said if that was the case he was sorry, and went to work and made a fire and got the man in and took care of him. This morning they brought Father Bigelow to Carthage a prisoner, but his case was not disposed of when the brethren left. Warren justified the act.

Saturday, 25.—4 p. m., A. W. Babbitt arrived from Carthage and stated that when the brethren went in yesterday as witnesses of the house-burning the grand jury refused to hear their testimony, or to admit any of them into the jury room, which effectually shields the house-burners from justice and blockades the way for the sufferers to obtain redress.

Refused Hearing Before the Carthage Grand Jury.

The steamer *Sarah Ann* passed up the river, Doctor Foster and Lyman E. Johnson were on board. When the boat landed Jackson Redden was standing by and L. E. Johnson stepped up to him to counsel concerning his father and brother's case. Dr. R. D. Foster got a number of men from the boat and undertook to haul Redden on board and take him off with them. Redden

knocked the first man down that undertook   The Redden Affair.
to lay hands on him; a few of the brethren
who were not far off ran to Redden's assistance and
with sticks and stones soon drove the whole crew on
board; the captain started immediately, without unloading; the clerk left the bills of lading with a man
who handed them to Albert P. Rockwood, but appeared not to know what he did. After the boat started
Doctor Foster shot his pistol at the brethren but hurt
no one. One of the brethren was cut on the back of
the neck with a stone.

This morning Hosea Stout and John Scott stationed
themselves at the mound, seven miles east of Nauvoo,
and extended a few men for miles north   Nauvoo East-ern Outpost.
and south to ascertain and express any hos-
tile movements which might be made towards Nauvoo.

Major Warren, Judge Purple, J. B. Backenstos,
Judge Ralston and Mr. Brannan with a detachment of
troops came into town and Warren demanded an explanation in relation to seeing some fifteen or twenty
of our express men on the prairie.

I went to the Mansion and in plain but mild language stated the reason why our men were there. War-
ren in a great rage declared he would issue   Warren-Young-Taylor Outburst of Feeling.
his manifesto on Monday morning and put
the county under martial law. After this
Elder John Taylor made some very just and spirited
remarks in relation to the foul treachery or criminal
imbecility of the governor's protection, telling Mr.
Warren that we had placed our express men in a position to communicate the earliest intelligence should
any mob violence be attempted upon our brethren
while at Carthage and further said: 'We lack confidence
in the governor's troops under your command while
hundreds of murderers, robbers and house-burners
roam at large unwhipped of justice. We shall take
measures to protect ourselves. I, Sir, have been shot all
to pieces under the 'protection' of the governor's troops.
Our leading men have been murdered in Carthage and

we shall not trust ourselves unprotected again until the state gives some evidence more than it has done of its justice and humane intentions to enforce its laws.'

Judge Purple said: 'Mr. Taylor do not talk on such an exciting topic.'

Elder Taylor ordered wine for the company, Judge Purple and all except Warren drank.

Elder Hyde commenced to make an apology for Elder Taylor. Elder Taylor interrupted him, saying, 'Do not offer any apology for me'. Judge Purple said, 'We accept the wine for Mr. Taylor's apology.'

Evening, I met with the council at Elder Taylor's. We prayed that the Lord would overrule the matter

Resort to Prayer.

and remove from Warren's heart the disposition to declare martial law or otherwise let his hand be heavy upon him with judgment that he may not be able to bring trouble upon the saints.

James Arlington Bennett's Message.

Brother Hedlock called upon Dr. Richards with a message from General Bennett, saying that he had left Carthage and gone to Quincy that he would write Dr. Richards soon, and that he would cross the Rocky Mountains with us in the spring.

Enos Curtis made the following affidavit:

MORE HOUSE-BURNING

'State of Illinois ⎱ ss.
Hancock County ⎰

On the 25th day of October, A. D. 1845, personally appeared before me E. A. Bedell one of the justices of the peace in and for said county, Enos Curtis, who after being duly sworn according to law deposeth and saith:—that on or about the eighteenth day of October A. D. 1845, in the Morley Settlement in said county he saw two houses and three stables burning and also saw two mobbers armed with guns going away from the same. And the deponent further saith that on Monday the twenty-first inst. he saw another house burning, said to belong to the widow Boss containing her potatoes and other vegetables. And further the deponent saith not.

[Signed]   ENOS CURTIS.

Subscribed and sworn to before me this 25th day of October, A. D. 1845.

[Signed]   E. A. BEDELL, J. P.'

Sunday, 26.—This morning Bishop Miller waited upon Judges Purple and Ralston and showed them the Temple.

Eight a. m., the seventies met in the Temple and proceeded with the organization of the thirty-first quorum.

P. M., council met at Elder Taylor's. Elder Orson Spencer in behalf of the council wrote the following:

AN APPEAL TO GOVERNOR FORD

'City of Nauvoo, Oct. 26, 1845.

To his Excellency Thomas Ford.

Sir: Fresh occasion from an occurrence of last evening appears to have arisen for this council to address you by the bearers E. A. Bedell, Esq. and Mr. George Miller. Having learned two or three days since that a number of houses and outbuildings were burned in the south part of the county and the utter impotency or negligence of the state forces to stop the work of burning, and having also learned that the mob intended next to burn houses in the north part of the county, at Camp Creek, and application having been made to Major Warren without obtaining sufficient aid to protect the citizens a number of our men in small companies not exceeding four in a company were ranging on the prairies in order to make a prompt report of any fresh depredations that might be made upon our property or persons.

At this time last evening Judge Purple, Major Warren and a portion of the bar, after adjourning the court were crossing the prairie to this place, when Major Warren discovered a portion of our men, say fifteen or twenty in their detached order. An inquiry into their business was made, and the answers not being sufficiently definite and satisfactory owing to weariness of watching and sense of their wrongs, the major took considerable umbrage and immediately upon his arrival demanded a satisfactory explanation. It was promptly given by President Young in a conciliatory spirit.

The major peremptorily avowed that he would issue his manifesto tomorrow and put the whole county under martial law, after which Elder Taylor made some spirited but not unjust remarks on his own responsibility.

If the major should impose martial law upon the county it would be a matter greatly to be deplored.

It would tend to obstruct the ends of peace and prevent that arrangement of affairs so necessary to our peaceful departure with our poor and helpless in the spring. It has been our continued effort and prayer to God that we might be unmolested until we can depart in the spring. For this purpose we still desire of you as our honored chief magistrate and the friend of the oppressed that the state troops may be speedily withdrawn. From this no danger will arise, even to our worst enemies, as our past forbearance and long suffering will abundantly prove. We would respectfully apprise you that the work of burning still goes on in the southern part of the county, as affidavits forwarded showing a number of buildings burned in the last two weeks will prove.

Our people are continually harrassed with threats of burning, and assassination up to last evening: and as astonishing as it may seem to you some of the house-burners are actually in the *posse* of state troops and are prowling round in Nauvoo every few days. Judge then of our feelings and situation and show us that favor that will merit the blessings of thousands upon your honored head.

Concerning what has been written and other matters of importance to us, we refer your honor to the bearers, who will give you the necessary information.

With sentiments of high consideration I have the honor to remain in behalf of the council your obedient servant,

W. RICHARDS, Clerk.'

E. A. Bedell and George Miller started at 8 p. m. to convey the above communication to Governor Ford. The night was so dark they lost their way twice and it was with much difficulty they reached Crooked Creek where they remained till break of day.

I conversed with Judge Ralston in relation to selling our property to the Catholics. He advised us to sell to them and said he would use his influence with them in Quincy to come and settle here.

Major Warren said this morning that no man would be permitted to go into Carthage [to attend trial of the Prophet's murderers] with any kind of arms. He swore he should search every man. It was thought best that about one hundred of the brethren should go and about twenty advance into town without arms, and the balance remain behind until they could ascertain Warren's movements; and if he declared martial law, all return, as in that case there can be no court held.

Plans for Attending Trial at Carthage.

Monday, 27.—Bedell and Miller reached Macedonia early, breakfasted with Wm. G. Perkins, changed horses and pursued their journey.

Elder A. W. Babbitt returned from Carthage and

reported that Backenstos had obtained a change of venue to Peoria to have his trial in five weeks. He is in the hands of the coroner who has permission either to take bail or select his own guard, at the expense of the state. The court adjourned until next May. The grand jury found bills of indictment against several of our brethren, none of the witnesses who had been burned out by the mob were admitted into the jury room, or allowed any opportunity to testify of their sufferings and so the farce ended with adding insult to injury. All Governor Ford, General John J. Hardin, Major Warren and Mr. Brayman's promise of administering justice and punishing the house-burners simply ends in compelling the sufferers to leave their destitute and helpless families and bear the loss of time and expense of spending several days at court to be told: 'You d—— Mormons shall not be admitted into the jury room to testify against the old citizens who have burned your houses, barns and grain, and turned your sick and helpless families out of doors to perish without food or shelter on the eve of winter.'*

Brigham Young's Reflections on the Procedure of State Officials.

Babbitt states that Dr. Abiather Williams has been before one of the judges of Iowa and sworn that the Twelve made bogus at his house in Iowa.

Charge that the Twelve Made Bogus.

They have taken out a United States writ and made a demand on the governor of this state for them, and the deputy marshal of Iowa (Silas Haight) is at Carthage with writs for all the Twelve. Warren is coming with the troops tomorrow, to aid the marshal in making the arrests. They had these writs with them on Saturday evening and this deputy was also with them, but when Elder Taylor made his speech it bluffed them off and they were afraid to serve them; since then Warren has sent to some of the eastern counties for volunteers to join his ranks.

*This cannot be supposed to be an actual speech from the grand jury, but it is implied as what their action inferred. Otherwise it would be a bald confession of what the old settlers had done.

The brethren in council expressed their feelings and all felt satisfied that the Lord would overrule this matter also for our good. The brethren of the Twelve all concluded to leave their homes tonight, so that if the *posse* come in during the night there will be no danger.

Defense by Prayer.

Tuesday, 28.—Ten a. m., President John Smith, Elders Newell K. Whitney, Joseph Young, Wm. W. Phelps, Orson Spencer, Joseph C. Kingsbury, and Lucien Woodworth met at Elder Taylor's and prayed.

The Twelve being apprehensive of treachery hid themselves until towards evening, when I received word from Major Warren that he wished to have an interview with us.

In the afternoon the Twelve held a consultation with Major Warren: I copy from Elder Clayton's Journal:

INTERVIEW WITH MAJOR WARREN

'Warren stated that when he came in with his troops on Saturday he had writs against the Twelve for 'treason' but he considered it unjust to serve them, he considered that if the Twelve were to be harassed with writs this people could not get away in the spring, that from Elder Taylor's remarks he understood we meant that no writs of any kind should be served in Nauvoo but intended to resist. This was explained by President Young who told Warren that we did not intend to resist. He also drew out of Warren that he was going to Springfield tomorrow and one part of his errand was to get his friends and relatives to come here and purchase some of our farms, for he was delighted with them. It appears that the Lord has softened his heart in answer to our prayers, for which we felt thankful.'

The following is extracted from George Miller's Journal:

REPORT OF BISHOP MILLER'S INTERVIEW WITH GOVERNOR FORD

'We (Miller and Bedell) traveled during last night, it was very dark, but by the light of the burning prairie we were enabled to proceed, we stopped fourteen miles from Springfield the latter part of the night and had a short nap while our breakfast was preparing, at the house of Mr. Bell all that we had conversed with during the past day disapproved of the course of the anti-Mormons in Hancock county.

We arrived at Springfield soon after breakfast and delivered the letter and affidavits to Governor Ford, whereupon he read several letters from individuals in Hancock county and others from different parts of the state insisting on the necessity of quartering a force in the county all winter sufficient to maintain law and order.

Mr. Bedell and I urged with the most earnest solicitude the disbanding of the forces stationed in our county, as we believed them to be a greater curse upon us than the real mob, as they have the effect to embolden rather than deter them [the mob] from committing acts of violence.   Governor Ford seemed to be friendly, he deplored deeply the situation of the country and said, if he were to exert the executive influence in our behalf as ought to be done in justice to us, it would result in his overthrow and ours also.   He also said, his private opinion was that the whole state were a mob and that he could not trust them to act in any emergency where we as a community were a party: Our interview lasted about three hours.

His final conclusion was to go to Hancock, and take a conciliatory course so as to prevent a collision until we should get away next spring: and when we should be gone bring them to justice and hang every devil of them [house-burners and murderers].

We conversed with several citizens who approved of the course of Backenstos in allaying the disturbances in Hancock, and reprobated with much severity the conduct of the house-burners, and expressed sorrow that Sheriff Backenstos did not kill five hundred of them.'

I copy from the *Nauvoo Neighbor*:

ADDENDUM

'Hancock Circuit Court:

This court commenced its session on Monday the 20th inst. at Carthage.   Present:—the Hon. Norman H. Purple, Judge; M. Brayman, states attorney *protem;* J. B. Backenstos, sheriff; Henry W. Miller, coroner; and E. D. Head, clerk.

After the grand jury were called an affidavit was presented to the court sworn to by a man named Michael Barnes, Jr., one of the known murderers of Joseph and Hyrum Smith, and also one of the grain and house-burners, which affidavit set forth that the county commissioners were prejudiced against him, and selected the grand jury with a view of having him indicted, whereupon the court set aside the array of grand jurors.   When Sheriff Backenstos addressed the court among other things he stated that he had been recognized by his Honor to appear and answer whatever indictment the grand jury might find against him, and hoped that the court would excuse him or any and all of his deputies in the selection of grand jurors. The sheriff and his deputies were then excused from performing that duty, whereupon the court appointed Thomas H. Owen and William D. Abernethy, elisors: objections being made to Wm. D. Abernethy the court set him aside and appointed Captain Morgan of Adams county in his place.

The grand jury, as selected by the elisors, were called and sworn on Thursday, and retired to investigate the crimes which have been committed in Hancock county unanswered and true presentments made. Little if anything was done on Thursday.

On Friday a rush was made by the mob party. Witnesses were brought in and examined before the grand jury and on Saturday about 11 o'clock the grand jury came into court and presented a bill against Sheriff Backenstos for the murder of Worrell, also several bills were found against the Latter-day Saints. In the meantime on Friday afternoon about forty witnesses appeared in Carthage to enter their complaints against the house-burners for arson, larceny and other crimes, knocking at the door of the grand jury room to be heard, and applying individually to some of the grand jurors with their complaints; but nothing could be done. There being a determination on the part of the grand jury that no evidence should be heard nor bills found against any of the anti-Mormons, whether for murder, burning houses or other outrages perpetrated against the saints; when the grand jury presented the bills the sheriff was placed in the hands of the coroner. The prosecuting attorney entered a *nolle prosequi* as to the bills found against the saints.

The court adjourned until Monday the 27th instant when Sheriff Backenstos was to be tried: the sheriff appeared ready with his counsel and desired an immediate trial, but by some judicial legerdemain the cause was sent to Peoria county to be tried at a special term of a circuit court, which is to come off in about five weeks. On motion of council, it was ordered that Sheriff Backenstos be admitted to bail in the sum of $3000, for his appearance at Peoria circuit court, which bail price has been executed and the sheriff is going about his business. The sheriff is in good health and spirits, and bears persecution with all commendable forbearance. His Honor Judge Purple visited Nauvoo on Saturday afternoon in company with M. Brayman, states attorney, Major Warren, and several gentlemen of the bar, and heard the Latter-day Saints tell their own story.'

Wednesday, 29.—I remained incognito at Brother A. P. Rockwood's, Brothers George A. Smith and Amasa M. Lyman came to see me; also

Brigham
Young
Incognito.

Brothers Henry G. Sherwood and John S. Fullmer who had just returned from their mission westward; Bishop Whitney and Brother Wm. Clayton also came to see me. Elder Sherwood made a report of their late mission, which was very satisfactory and gave us some very interesting information concerning our best route to the west.

I extract the following from John S. Fullmer's account of his mission to Vermilion:

FULLMER'S MISSION TO JAMES EMMETT'S ENCAMPMENT

'August 13, 1845: In company with Elder Henry G. Sherwood and James Emmett, I started from Nauvoo on a mission to James Emmett's company, encamped on the Vermillion, a tributary of the upper Missouri river.

We had one horse each, which carried us and all our provisions and bedding for the journey. Our course lay about west-north-west as far as Raccoon Barracks on the Desmoines river, seventy-five miles from Nauvoo.

Finding that we were suspected of being Indian traders we took a northwest course for four days and then turned towards Council Bluffs. While here Emmett's conduct became almost insupportable, and he appeared unwilling to pilot us to his camp, but finding Elder Sherwood and myself determined to push on at all hazards, he concluded to accompany us. Much of the country over which we traveled was very dry and water scarce so that we suffered considerably.

Finding there was some disturbance between the Pottawattomie and Sioux Indians we took our course up the river several miles from it keeping a sharp lookout for war parties and Indian campfires.

September 13.—We arrived at Emmett's camp (625 miles from Raccoon Barracks) and met our brethren. On our way we encountered many deep streams, with miry bottoms, and steep banks, also some severe storms which caused some of the streams to overflow their banks.

Emmett's camp contained about one hundred souls and were in a better condition than we expected to find them, they were tolerably well provided with provisions but somewhat destitute of clothing.

They feasted us on samp and milk and urged us to eat heartily of dried buffalo meat saying it would hurt no one, but we found to the contrary to our inconvenience and sorrow, its tendency is to swell to its natural dimensions as soon as eaten and this caused us to feel something like a beer barrel in a state of fermentation which no hoops can control.

Notwithstanding our caution and prudence, Elder Sherwood and myself were taken with violent ague and fever and for a week or more were unable to attend to business during which time Emmett sought to get the advantage of us, by intimating to the company that something was wrong with us, that the Lord was displeased with us, etc. John S. Butler and a few others had spirit enough to understand the spirit of these charges. Upon Elder Sherwood's recovery he rebaptized John S. Butler and reordained him. I was then carried to the river and rebaptized for my health by Elder J. S. Butler and walked back and was so far recovered in a few days as to be able to attend council.

We explained our mission to the people, and gave what instruction we could, as to their temporal welfare. We learned that many of them had been led away by Emmett's misrepresentations and such were glad to receive our counsel. Emmett opposed us and finally claimed equal authority with us. This drew forth our papers which gave us the presidency, while Emmett was only our conductor to the camp. The saints went forth and were all rebaptized by Elder John S. Butler.

To obviate any trouble with Emmett after we should be gone, we appointed him the president of the camp, with instructions. They were to remain where they were, build cabins for the winter, procure what buffalo meat they could, by sending out organized parties; to conciliate the friendship of the Indians, and prepare themselves for any instructions they might receive from Nauvoo in the spring, anticipating a removal to some place then unknown. After we had finished our business we appointed John S. Butler to attend us on our return, as we were yet too feeble to risk such a trip alone, and also to be the bearer of such instructions to the camp as might be given at headquarters. Emmett desired this appointment; but his recent behavior as a guide disqualified him.

A few days before we left a circumstance happened which came near proving fatal to the whole camp. Owing to our feeble health, we decided that it was impracticable to return on horseback: Accordingly we solicited Emmett to buy our horses for the use of the camp; but he gave us no satisfaction. We next applied to Brewyer, a French trader who gave us forty-five dollars for our horses: Emmett refused to deliver up the horses from his corral, although they had been paid for, stating that he wanted them for buffalo horses. This so enraged Brewyer that he immediately declared hostilities against the whole camp. There had been above a thousand Indians camped close by during our stay, but they had just started to the north. Brewyer who had married two of Eagle's (the chief's) daughters sent for him to return with all his warriors, which summons they promptly obeyed. He now stimulated them by giving them whiskey and sold them guns and ammunition on credit, in case they would wipe out the entire camp. Eagle promised to do so.

Fortunately there lived there a halfbreed named Ongee, an educated and influential man to whom Eagle communicated his intentions. Ongee opposed them with all the art he was master of, One device was this: Ongee said they would select the least baby they could find and kill it and he would give each of them a petticoat and make squaws of all them: to Eagle he said he should walk over his dead body first: but if they would desist Brewyer should have the horses he had bought, which we also determined he should have if that should settle up the affair.

Just before the difficulty was settled, an Indian brave appeared followed by a number of others on horseback, before Butler's tent, where Emmett was sitting and leveled his rifle at him: but was instantly prevented from firing by Ongee who was consulting with him on the subject at the time.

Ongee's wife also used what influence, tears and entreaties she had with the several chiefs, and with Eagle also, who was the head chief.

In ordinary circumstances these efforts would have proven unavailing but the Lord had compassion on his people and turned the wrath of the Indians aside.

Ongee had contracted a friendship towards our people which he so manfully displayed in the deliverance of the camp. And wishing to show his respect to the two strangers who visited the camp with authority, he made a feast, the best his table could furnish; and there was no mean variety of vegetables, fowls and meat served up in tolerably good style, and in great profusion. Among the latter variety was to them the choicest of all dishes, especially when they wish to do honor to their guests: that was a fine fat dog of small size. Being a dish of honor it became indispensable that we should partake of it, which of course we did, but I will not say, 'with a will', but with apparent good grace. It was also a rule with them that each guest must clear his plate or dish, however much it might contain, or of whatever kind or variety, or pay a horse in default; but from some cause or other, perhaps through respect for our feeble health, this rule was waived, in our behalf, to our no small gratification, for we had been served enough to do us half a week.

As we had concluded to return by the river we made a canoe of a large cottonwood tree and fell in company with a couple of traders who were going down the river with some furs.

We left camp on the third of October, taking provisions as we supposed to last us to Council Bluffs, but being unacquainted with the channel, and the river being low, we found ourselves out of provisions before we had got half the distance. About this time as we were camping (for we had to lay to by nights) we saw a large flock of turkeys going to roost near by. One of the trappers, Elders Butler and Sherwood started out for a hunt by moonlight, one shot nine, one eleven, and the other thirteen times without so much as ruffling a feather. The Frenchman cursed his luck and swore his gun had a spell on it.

In the morning Butler went out and at the first shot brought down his turkey, this served us one day, and now we had eaten our last bite and no prospects of anything but salt and Missouri river water. We continued our route watching for game, hours passed and we saw none. After camping for the night, the Frenchman who had cursed his luck, shot a fine buck deer, which lasted us to Council Bluffs, eight days.

Twenty miles above St. Joseph, Missouri, John S. Butler left us and struck across the country for Nauvoo, not wishing to go through Missouri.

At St. Joseph we took a steamer for St. Louis. The rest of our journey to Nauvoo was pleasant as we performed it by steamboat. It is reported that the apostates are trying to get up an influence with the president of the United States to prevent the saints emigrating westward, and that they have written to the president informing him of the resolutions of the General Council [Council of Fifty] to move westward, and representing that Council guilty of treason, etc.' "

CHAPTER XXXV

IMPORTANT LETTERS, FRIENDLY AND OTHERWISE—
SUMMARY OF RECENT PROCEDURE IN AND ABOUT
NAUVOO WITH COMMENT OF AN EDITORIAL FROM THE
TIMES AND SEASONS

*"Wednesday, October 29, 1845. — Evening, the
Twelve met at Elder Taylor's. The following letter
was read:*

WILD SCHEMES PROPOSED BY 'BACKWOODSMAN' OF PALMYRA, MIS-
SOURI, FOR THE CONJOINT OCCUPANCY OF 'CALIFORNIA' BY
THE LATTER-DAY SAINTS AND MIGRATING CITIZENS FROM
THE UNITED STATES, BUT TO LIVE IN SEPARATE
COMMUNITIES—FOUNDING OF INDEPENDENT
GOVERNMENT—'THE UNITED STATES
OF THE WEST'

'Palmyra, Mo., Oct. 22, 1845.

Sir: Owing to particular circumstances, I make free to address you,
though a stranger, and I do it with plainness and candor because I
think candor is always best, and may prevent difficulty hereafter. I
see from the papers that you Mormons as a body intend to remove
next spring to California, I myself am one of a very large number who
have for some time been making arrangements for a settlement there
with a view to the ultimate and not very remote establishment of an
independent government not with a view to annexation to this government at all, but for that and Oregon to form the 'United States of
the West'.

General Leslie Combs of Kentucky and several sons of Mr. Clay,
are of the number, and the design will be carried out, and it is folly
in you to think of settling there, unless it be on terms of compromise,
that will insure the peaceable enjoyment of your peculiar organization.
Experience ought to have taught you by this time, that it is impossible
for you to exist as a community collected together in a city in the
midst of another community, governed by other laws, than those you
esteem paramount to all laws. You cannot be tolerated long, in that
manner of living, anywhere; it is contrary to human nature and to
the nature of things. The very principles you inculcate, that as the
Lord's chosen people you have a right to everything you need, are
incompatible with civil government, and the rights of others, and will
not be tolerated, I again say, in any place long. If therefore you
locate in California when it has already commenced settling, you

interfere with the settlers already there, and you will create a prejudice against you, and so soon as enough others join them, which will soon be the case, you will again be expelled, this is inevitable.

I freely acknowledge, that although I have never taken any part against you, yet, I have felt a strong prejudice against your community because I believe that the natural tendency of your institutions is to make a part of your community bad citizens. No people have a right to interfere with your religious views, but if your religious views tend to disturb or resist the laws, or trespass on the rights or property of others, then the community have the right to interfere, and such is the case, too well established to be doubted by any person of intelligence, after making all proper allowance for false reports against you, of which I doubt not there are many. I think I understand you about as well as you do yourselves. There are three classes among you, the leaders, the fanatics and the dishonest part. The whole design of the leaders is to obtain power and wealth, the fanatics are conscientious and honest in their belief that they are doing God's service, but a large proportion have joined you, just to get the license and impunity which your numbers and strength give them, to pilfer and steal. This is the real state of the case, and it is useless to deny it. I do not charge all your denomination with the faults of a part, but I charge that the nature of your organization inclines the body to protect those committing depredations. I know there are good and bad in all communities, but the fear of the law with us, checks the vicious, with you they are emboldened, because they think your numbers will shield them from punishment, hence they indulge to a greater degree in bad practices, not because they are worse than others, but because of the nature of your social system. Whenever men have the strength, they tyrannize and even well disposed persons may be induced to connive at such practices by such arguments as these: 'The earth is the Lord's and the fulness thereof, and he giveth it to his chosen people, we are his chosen people, therefore we have a right to everything we need'.

The country around and on the Bay of San Francisco and in the valley of the Sacramento has already commenced settling, and in that part our party will settle and if you settle there you cannot stay there for the two communities cannot and will not live together, but if you are wise and will consent to the arrangement we propose, you will neither infringe upon, nor be infringed upon.

Mr. Hastings describes California as being naturally divided into two sections which he denominates the western and eastern sections. (I suppose you have read his book). In the eastern section there are no settlements, that section is watered by the great river, the Colorado of the west, which puts into the Gulf of California, or rather into the Bay of Colorado which is connected with the gulf; Hastings says that the harbor at the estuary of the river is very capacious and good, this affords a very elegible situation for an extensive settlement, and large city of commercial business; here, as there are no settlements, you can safely locate without infringing upon anybody and by a prudent arrangement being made beforehand the settlement may be permanent. I hope you may see the necessity of such arrangements, and avoid all occasion for such continual agitation and commotion as have been heretofore in connection with your community. I was often deeply pained on seeing your women and children, moving from Missouri through the snow and inclement weather, but notwithstanding these were my feelings, my acquaintances with the world and with human nature is such, that I know you cannot live in your organized embodied state in the midst of another community. We are willing to come to an understanding with you and reduce it to something like the form of a treaty that you shall settle at the mouth of the Colorado of the west and have assigned you a certain district of country, sufficiently large on that river, and in the eastern section exclusively and that we will not intrude on you within those bounds, provided you do not intrude on us, or on others without those bounds, and on the further condition that you join us and the original settlers to revolutionize the country from the dominion of Mexico and erect it into an independent government in connection with Oregon under the denomination of the United States of the West, Oregon and California including lower California will form sufficient territory to form twenty states.

Lower California would be forced into the confederation because it would be cut off from communication with any part of Mexico. It would evidently be your interest to join in the revolution because the Catholic religion being the established religion of the Mexican government, you could not be tolerated in the enjoyment of your views, but establish an independent government with full toleration of all religions, and then by a division of territorial limits as I propose, all difference will be prevented, for as we would have nothing to do with each other's religious views, and if each party were confined within its own limits we would know each other only as citizens. equally bound to protect each other and the country against all foreign invasion, and consequently to protect each other in the enjoyment of our respective peculiar views, then there need be no interruption of friendship and we could forget the past, as prejudice would die away. We could have an arrangement by which a due proportion of governmental patronage would be bestowed upon and enjoyed by each party, according to their relative strength as citizens, and to be wielded for the good of the whole republic and not for the exclusive benefit of either party so that as citizens of the republic we would all be precisely on the same footing and know no distinction any more, than if you had no separate social organization at all.

I submit this for your serious consideration and I request an early understanding and a positive statement in writing whether you abide by the proposed agreement or not, to be stated so definitely that it will admit of no misunderstanding.

You can write to this place addressed to 'Backwoodsman', distinctly defining your position in relation to this matter. We must know soon as measures have already been taken to send a messenger round by sea to put the settlers and the authorities on their guard so as to prevent your settling there, if you do not close with and come into this arrangement.

If you accede to this offer, I wish you to keep this letter and take it with you as evidence for it is written in good faith.

[Signed]   BACKWOODSMAN.'

BRIGHAM YOUNG'S COMMENT ON THE ABOVE PROPOSITION

The above letter contains the lucubrations of some of Senator Benton's mobocratic associations who, no doubt, desire to make us a barrier between them and the Mexican government. His falsehoods in relation to our social system, and interference with the rights and property of others, are too absurd to be noticed, but I copy the letter as a specimen of numerous others which I am constantly receiving and which show the vanity, folly and corruption to which the human heart has been prostituted.

We had prayers as usual.

I received a letter from Elder Willard Snow, dated at Boston, October 12th.

Thursday, 30.—Bishop George Miller and E. A. Bedell returned from Springfield at 10 a. m. and reported their interview with Governor Ford and informed us that the governor would be at Carthage today, and intends to see to matters himself and try to preserve peace until we can get away.

ORSON SPENCER'S LETTER TO GOVERNOR FORD (BUT WITH SANCTION OF PRESIDENT YOUNG AND HIS COUNCIL): OVERZEALOUS AND UNNECESSARILY HARSH TOWARD GOVERNOR FORD

'Nauvoo, City of Joseph,
October 23d, 1845.

To His Excellency Thomas Ford.

Sir: The familiar interview I have had the honor to share with you, and the portentious state of affairs in Hancock county induce me to write you. Not however without the impulse of President Young and his council. After our interview in June last, in presence of ex-Governor Reynolds and Samuel Brannan, Esq., I ventured unequivocally to assure the authorities in this place that you, Sir, would never, no never, lend your official influence to oppress or exterminate this people.

This was the prominent and emphatic object of my mission to Springfield, and made uppermost in our whole discourse, as you well recollect. The result of that interview was perfectly satisfactory to me and in the strength of your generous, noble avowal never to walk in the steps of Governor Boggs of Missouri, and never to jeopardize the lives of our leaders under writs and arrests as the Smiths had been, I made the most sanguine assurances to the council of your high-minded and patriotic bearing towards this people. You also will recollect that I labored to apprise you that by misrepresentation, and falsehood they might endeavor to array the state executive against us, before a full disclosure of facts could come to your knowledge. And, Sir, contrary to all these assurances and pleasing ground of joyful hope, that the high authority of the state would never be wielded against law and order, and consequently against a long persecuted and unoffending people, we find your troops, yes, *your troops*, clothed with the power of your own signature, and all the potency your official name can impart, right in our midst! And for what purpose have they been here the last six weeks? Let the facts speak, and what have they done?

Have they stayed the progress of crime? and spliced up the fragments of law and order? Have they looked with paternal charity after the fugitives that have been compelled to run for their lives, before the lurid flames of the incendiary? Have they administered to the sick, or afforded them shelter, when precipitated on the cold ground of autumn to die, under the excitement of threats, conflagration, and disease? Have they ever shielded those that humanely volunteered to go twenty miles and under to gather up scattered fragments of property and crops and dispersed cattle, hogs, and fowls that the wretched survivors might be protected? Have they come valiantly forward to help the high sheriff of the county in his perilous and arduous struggle, to stop the marauders in their hellish deeds of robbery, midnight arson, and murder? To all these inquiries I answer before all men, and before the Judge of quick and dead solemnly—no! But, Sir, the doings of *your* troops have been not only the negative, but the very ingenious and hypocritical counterpart of all this. In proof of this, if proof were necessary (when scores of journals and visiting spectators to these awful scenes have testified through the land), I ask you Sir, where now is the head and right arm of the law in Hancock county. Sheriff Backenstos severed; yes, completely amputated and severed. And for what and by whom, has this noble-hearted patriot, dared to break the midnight arson and the infuriated cupidity of fiends, and roll back the crimson current of onward desolation, and pick up the routed sick, and quench the rolling conflagration? In God's name and with retributive solemnity I ask where is this noble right arm of the law? Severed indeed but not by the mob: no—would to God it had been for the honor of our state and nation, and for the blushing glory of humanity. But it was not so, this 'valiant arm of the law', with the firmness and patriotism of Jackson, Samuel Adams and Patrick Henry had won a victory that will ever laurel his brow, or the circle of such worthies as Washington, Marion, and Howard for all time to come, he had rescued the sick from the tusks of the wild boar, and boldly struck down the midnight arson, with the torch in his hand, and routed the whole host of inhuman fiends when your troops arrived. Horrible to say, *your* troops Sir, forthwith arrested the benefactor and released 'Barrabas'. The sick and robbed hung aside their harps and mournfully exclaimed: Has Governor Ford become another Boggs? *Your* troops Sir, were immediately a safe-guard and shield to robbers and murderers, who speedily returned to their houses in quiet, while the veteran of law and order, with the whole *posse* of government were exposed to warrants and recognized for manslaughter. In no instance has an anti-Mormon malefactor been arrested. *Posses* of state troops continually throng our city and the vicinity with attempts at all hours of the night and day to make arrests. The consequence is, that peaceable, unoffending citizens, and those who have yielded prompt obedience to the order of the sheriff in authority, are filled with fearful apprehension of being ferreted out to undergo the like fate of the assassinated Smiths, and of being tried under the impanelment of the most notorious mobocrat as elisor. *Your* troops Sir, in the estimation of the public (soon after they were disbanded) murdered the defenseless Smiths in prison and the state force is now a perfectly legalized mob-sweetened arsenic—honeyed poison. The mob arsenic and poison when unadulterated we are not afraid of. But when they are administered to us by your potent arm, with all the authority of government our condition is appalling, and desperatives must be used. The only difference between *your* troops and the mob is like the difference between a keg of arsenic and a keg of choice flour fatally flavored with arsenic. The mob we dare to resist where they are purely mob: but the state force, though equally fatal we are obliged to submit to because of legal authority.

And now will you in the eyes of a nation and world that is canvassing your acts by their domestic firesides and in the reading room, continue to legalize the doings of an armed soldiery, that are more obnoxious to law than the mob. Then, Sir, for humanity's sake, speedily withdraw these troops, and allow us peace long enough to attend to our sick and prepare for a general departure in the spring.

Do not force us to blood shedding or a fatal dispersion in the inclement winter, when multitudes of the poor must inevitably perish, and your own exalted name, sink beneath that of Nero, Boggs and Williams. Withdraw then these troops and lend not a listening ear to aspiring politicians, or the cupidity of the cruel, but, let the oppressed bless your name, for permission to breathe the air of liberty long enough to escape in a warm season to the caves of the mountains, or to some distant island of the Pacific.

With high hopes of your bold philanthropic determination, in behalf of the council,

Your friend and obedient servant,

[Signed]   ORSON SPENCER.'

GOVERNOR FORD'S REPUDIATION OF SPENCER'S LETTER

'Springfield, Ill.,
October 30, 1845.

Sir: I return your letter of the 23d instant as not being respectful: as containing undeserved censure and as being in many particulars false and libellous: When were the Mormon people exterminated by my order?

It is acknowledged on all hands that there are some thieves in your city as in all other cities. These your people say, you have no power to restrain and punish for want of a city government and court. If you cannot restrain them I can and will. This is not extermination, or following in the footsteps of Governor Boggs.

I am very respectfully

Your obedient servant,

[Signed]   THOMAS FORD.

Orson Spencer, Esq.
Nauvoo, Illinois.'

GOVERNOR FORD'S LETTER TO GENERAL (BISHOP) GEORGE MILLER: FURTHER REPUDIATION OF SPENCER'S LETTER

'Springfield, October 30th, 1845.

General George Miller,

Sir: The two letters mentioned by you as having been mailed at Quincy by yourself and Mr. Spencer, were received the next morning after you left. Mr. Spencer is a man for whom I have felt a warm personal esteem but really his letter is a most uncalled for philippic containing the most extraordinary charge, that I have exterminated your people. It is true that I have sent troops to Hancock to quell disturbance. They were few in number and not sufficient for the work of extermination if they had been ever so willing. They were successful in everything except in arresting the rioters. This the sheriff's *posse* could not do, because they had run away. It is true also that the sheriff had apparently restored order before the arrival of General Hardin, but that order was not likely to continue. The anti-Mormons had fled from the county and were successfully enlisting forces in the neighboring counties. You may not believe it, but I assure you they would have raised four or five thousand men. Nothing has saved an attack on your city, by that number, but the march of General Hardin by my order. You may have beaten the assailants and a great number of good honest citizens, the dupes of anti-Mormon falsehoods, would have lost their lives, this was not to be permitted, it would have disgraced any government which would have permitted it.

Although neither your people nor the anti-Mormons were in a temper to appreciate the favor, it was no less my duty and that of General Hardin to stop you on both sides, both parties were so enraged that they were, as they said, anxious to be permitted to fight, though they were much like the two men whose disposition to fight increased as they were forced asunder by their neighbors; and their ardor sensibly abated when the obstacle to a fight should be removed.

It is supposed by your people that if the sheriff had not been interfered with by the state militia he could have kept the peace and preserved order. There are many reasons why this is not so. First, the anti-Mormons would have removed out of the county. The people of the surrounding counties were afraid in that event, that your people would get the whole of Hancock, and would be as troublesome to them as you had been to the anties of Hancock. For which reason they were determined to drive you off before you got stronger. They reasoned thus: these people, the Mormons, have for some cause or other been in difficulty with all the people they ever lived amongst. They were obliged to leave Ohio and Missouri and they have not agreed better with their neighbors of Hancock. If these neighbors move away their places will be occupied by Mormons, and we, the surrounding counties, will be their nearest neighbors and may expect with certainty to have the like difficulties with them. They said therefore we will take time by the forelock and drive them away before they get stronger and more capable of resistance.

Secondly, although the sheriff had put down the house-burners, he had not suppressed stealing and murder on the other side. One man had certainly been murdered between Carthage and Appanoose, another was missing in Nauvoo under circumstances which leave no doubt but that he was murdered in your city and most probably by order of some of your principal men. At least such is and was the popular belief. Stolen property has been traced to your city during the ascendency of the sheriff, and the owners who came to search were ordered away and fled for fear of their lives. None of the stolen property could be found and in fact the owners did not dare to go to look for it without the aid and protection of the state troops. You may say this is the work of only a few and that your people are not responsible for the few in your city any more than in any other city; this may be true, but its truth does not do away with the necessity for a military force. I have long believed that there are those in Nauvoo who carry on a pretty large business in stealing. Some have alleged that this gang are patronized by the church authorities. This charge, however, I never believed and would not believe it unless proved by the most satisfactory evidence. Be this as it may, the thieves are there and they do steal as is the case in all other cities of ten or twelve thousand inhabitants.

I think it likely that some of your people who were burnt out by the mob, have persuaded themselves that they have a right to indemnify themselves for their losses by taking the property of their enemies. It is also probable that many persons unconnected with the Mormons go to Hancock to steal on their credit. Be this as it may, stealing as well as burning has been done and the stolen property has been traced to your city. Other thieves have been captured whilst taking it there: all these things took place during the ascendency of the sheriff and was kept secret from him, or if he knew of it he had no power to prevent it. Under these circumstances it was considered advisable by General Hardin, Judge Douglas, Major Warren and Mr. McDougall the attorney-general to leave one hundred men as a permanent guard. General Hardin informs me by letter that your high council expressed a wish that this force might be left. It was also requested, as he says, by all the well disposed persons in the county and particularly by the Reverend Mr. Owen who has never been a mobocrat. I cannot hear that this force has annoyed your people in any other way than once in a while to be marched into your city in quest of stolen property. This must be what Mr. Spencer calls extermination, for I have never heard that the troops have annoyed you in any other way. Mr. Spencer complains that the presence of these troops prevents the Mormons from going on peaceably and quietly in making their arrangements to remove in the spring. I am at a loss to perceive how, unless it be really true that a part of those arrangements are intended to consist in making reprisals upon the property of your enemies to pay you for your losses. This must not be attempted and will not be permitted. A demonstration of your intention to this effect will cause an attempt by the anti-Mormon party to drive you out before spring. If there are more of you in Nauvoo than can live this winter, good sense would say scatter until spring and be making something by labor to live upon. At all events until I am better informed I will hold it to be my duty to continue a military force in Hancock, both to protect you from the attacks of your enemies, as well as to prevent stealing whether by the anti-Mormons on your credit; by the Mormons themselves; by interlopers who come to your city as a place of refuge or by those who have been burnt out and who may be tempted to take this method of indemnifying themselves for their losses; and if the civil law is not strong enough martial law must be resorted to. Because if these things are not put an end to, the surrounding counties will take up the guard and you may be driven in despite of the state, in the dead of winter.

In the course of my official duties I have had a great deal of trouble with both parties in Hancock. I have been called to do both of you some good and some harm. The harm is always remembered: the good is either not understood or is forgotten. I do not expect any gratitude or applause from either party; and you may be sure that the last things that I will think possible to be accomplished will be to please either you or the anti-Mormons, by any moderate conduct which, by taking the law for guide, repudiates the wildness and infatuation of both parties.

My health is bad or I should have started for Hancock on Wednesday morning last to see for myself what the state of things really are.

I am most respectfully your

obedient servant,

[Signed]   THOMAS FORD.'

Friday, 31.—At the Tithing Office, writing a letter to Brother V. Shurtliff to receive tithing in the east, and donations to help away the poor.

P. M., council met at Elder Taylor's.   We wrote the following to Bishop John B. Purcell of Cincinnati:—

LETTER TO REV. BISHOP PURCELL, ET AL, CINCINNATI

'City of Nauvoo, October 31, 1845.

To Reverend Bishop Purcell, and all Other Authorities of the Catholic Church—Greeting:

The Church of Jesus Christ of Latter-day Saints hereby take opportunity to inform you by letter and by our confidential messenger, Almon W. Babbit, Esq., that it is our fixed purpose to remove hence early next spring.

The hand of oppression and the lacerations of the tongue of calumny have compelled us to the determination to dispose of numerous lots, tenements, etc., in this city together with our public buildings, for instance our Temple, the Nauvoo House, the Academy, Seventies' Hall, Concert Hall, and other buildings, also our farms and other possessions in Hancock county, even all our effects and temporal interests.   The individual members of our community have also determined *en masse* to do the same with their effects and have empowered agents to sell.   The bearer, Mr. Babbitt, is empowered to represent as our authorized agent all our said property and interest in this city and county.   Through the suggestion of Judge Ralston of Quincy and other friends to your faith we are disposed to invite the authorities of your church, either personally or by authorized agents, to visit our city that we may negotiate with them, at as early a period as possible, the sale of our property.   We shall forbear any extensive sales to other communities until we learn your answer to this our epistle. The bearer may be relied upon as our confidential and highly esteemed brother who will furnish you any information preparatory to the proposed negotiation and sale.

With sentiments of high consideration, I have the honor to subscribe myself in behalf of the Council of the Church, your friend and obedient servant,

[Signed]   W. RICHARDS, Clerk.'

I received a long epistle from Elder Woodruff dated Liverpool, October 1st, relative to the course pursued by Elder Reuben Hedlock and Thomas Ward. I also received the following:

LETTER OF ORSON PRATT TO BRIGHAM YOUNG ON THE MATTER OF PURCHASING ARMS AND SELLING NAUVOO PROPERTY

'New York, October 31, 1845.

President Brigham Young and Council.
Dear Brethren:

I received a communication relative to obtaining six-barreled pistols for self-defense, (while journeying in western wilds). I immediately took active measures to obtain them and the present prospect is good. I think I shall obtain several hundred dollars for that purpose. The six-inch pistols can be obtained at retail for twelve dollars. The wholesale price is ten dollars but by agreeing to take some thirty or forty they can be obtained at nine and one-half dollars. As soon as I have raised the most of the funds that can be raised I shall make the purchase. I now have between one and two hundred dollars tithing subject to your order: tithing comes in very slowly since the exertions that were made for the canvass. The recent troubles in the west have put new life and zeal into the saints in the east, they are very anxious to assist all they can, and to gather westward.

The celebrated Robert Owen* has been to visit me several times. I have been endeavoring to persuade him to rent our houses and lands in Illinois, and he has quite a notion of so doing. He will let me know more about it in a few days: he thinks of locating the Owenites at Nauvoo.

Brother Brannan thinks it will be difficult to take his printing establishment and go to California unless he goes away dishonorably without paying debts. If we could sell he could pay his debts.

He is very anxious to go, and is willing to do anything he is counseled. He says that the church perhaps would consider it wisdom to buy his establishment and still keep up the paper.

I have not had an opportunity of visiting Philadelphia as yet, perhaps you may consider it wisdom to send two faithful elders to preside: one in Philadelphia, another in Boston.

Brother Willard Snow's pleadings to go home are almost irresistible, I believe that I will give him permission. I hope that it will meet with your approbation for I wish to do right. Since I heard of your

*This was the celebrated English communist seeking to establish his system in the United States.

persecutions and resolutions to leave Nauvoo in the spring I can hardly contain myself. I want to fly upon the wings of the wind and be with you, where you go, I want to go, where you stop, I want to stop. Brethren, give me counsel on this matter. Can I go with you in the spring? If so is it my privilege to return this fall? Count me worthy to receive counsel on these important items. Should my feelings get the upper hand of me and I start forthwith for Nauvoo I hope you will forgive me. I am willing to abide your counsel in all things.

I remain, dear brethren, your everlasting friend and fellow laborer,

[Signed]   ORSON PRATT.'

I received a letter from Charles A. Lovell, Mass., October 20th recommending us as a community to remove to California. Another from Thomas J. Farn-haus, New York, October 20th, on the same subject. Also one from Edward Warren, Boston, October 22nd portraying the Bay of San Francisco and country round as one well adapted for our location in the west.

Saturday, November 1, 1845.—I paid William Clayton one hundred and fifty dollars to purchase instruments for the brass band.

I met in council with the Twelve and Presiding Bishop, at 10 a. m.

The following editorial appeared in the *Times and Seasons:*

GREAT PERSECUTION OF THE CHURCH OF JESUS CHRIST OF LATTER-DAY SAINTS IN ILLINOIS

'After we had begun to realize the abundance of one of the most fruitful seasons known for a long time, and while many hundreds of saints were laboring with excessive, and unwearied diligence to finish the Temple and rear the Nauvoo House, suddenly in the forepart of September, the mob commenced burning the houses and grain of the saints in the south part of Hancock county. Though efforts were made by the sheriff to stay the torch of the incendiary and parry off the deluge of arson, still a 'fire and sword' party continued the work of destruction for about a week, laying in ashes nearly two hundred buildings and much grain.

Nor is this all: as it was in the sickly season, many feeble persons, thrown out into the scorching rays of the sun, or wet with the dampening dews of the evening, died, being persecuted to death in a Christian land of law and order; and while they are fleeing and dying, the mob, embracing doctors, lawyers, statesmen, Christians of various denominations, with the military from colonels down, were busily engaged in filching or plundering, taking furniture, cattle and grain. In the midst of this horrid revelry, having failed to procure aid among the 'old citizens', the sheriff summoned a sufficient *posse* to stay the 'fire shower of ruin', but not until some of the offenders had paid for the aggression with their lives.

This, however, was not the end of the matter. Satan sits in the hearts of the people to rule for evil, and the surrounding counties began to fear that law, religion, and equal rights, in the hands of the Latter-day Saints, would feel after iniquity or terrify their neighbors to larger acts of 'reserved rights', and so they began to open a larger field of woe. To cut this matter short they urged the necessity (to stop the effusion of blood), to expel the church, or as they call them, the Mormons, from the United States, 'peaceably if they could, and forcibly if they must', unless they would transport themselves by next spring. Taking into consideration the great value of life, and the blessings of peace, a proposition upon certain specified conditions was made to a committee of Quincy, and which it was supposed from the actions of conventions was accepted. But we are sorry to say, that the continued depredations of the mob and the acts of a few individuals, have greatly lessened the confidence of every friend of law, honor and humanity, in everything promised by the committees and conventions, though we have already made great advances towards outfitting for a move next spring.

A few troops stationed in the county, have not entirely kept the mob at bay: several buildings have been burned in the month of October.

We shall, however, make every exertion on our part, as we have always done, to preserve the law and our engagements sacred, and leave the event with God, for he is sure.

It may not be amiss to say, that the continued abuses, persecutions, murders, and robberies practiced upon us by a horde of land pirates with impunity in a Christian republic, and land of liberty, (while the institutions of justice, have either been too weak to afford us protection or redress, or else they too have been a little remiss) have brought us to the solemn conclusion that our exit from the United States is the only alternative by which we can enjoy our share of the elements which our heavenly Father created free for all.

We can then shake the dust from our garments, suffering wrong rather than do wrong, leaving this nation alone in her glory, while the residue of the world, points the finger of scorn, till the indignation and consumption decreed, make a full end.

In our patience we wil possess our souls and work out a more exceeding and eternal weight of glory, preparing, by withdrawing the

power and priesthood from the Gentiles, for the great consolation of
Israel, when the wilderness shall blossom as the rose, and Babylon
fall like a millstone cast into the sea.   The just shall live by faith;
but the folly of fools will perish with their bodies of corruption: then
shall the righteous shine: Amen.' "

CHAPTER XXXVI

MURDERS BY MOBS CONTINUED—CONFESSION OF DR.
ROBERT D. FOSTER—FAREWELL OF ORSON PRATT TO
EASTERN SAINTS — WESTWARD BY SHIPPING — THE
DURFEE MURDER CASE

"*Sunday, November 2, 1845.*—The first Emigration Company [for the west] organized by appointing captains of tens.

The second quorum of seventies held a festival at the Seventies Hall.

Monday, 3.—Brother Heber C. Kimball and I visited Dr. Willard Richards who was sick.

Evening, council met at Elder John Taylor's, Brothers Sherwood, Fullmer and Butler made a further report of the country west.

Abraham C. Hodge stated that he had some conversation with Robert D. Foster, who told him his feelings on the subject of Mormonism.　　He said, 'Hodge, you are going to the west—I wish I was going among you, but it can't be so, I am the most miserable wretch that the sun shines upon.　If I could recall eighteen months of my life I would be willing to sacrifice everything I have upon earth, my wife and child not excepted.　I did love Joseph Smith more than any　man　that　ever lived, if I had been present I would have stood between him and death.'　Hodge inquired, 'Why did you do as you have done?　You were accessory to his murder.' He replied: 'I know that, and I have not seen one moment's peace since that time.　I know that Mormonism is true, and the thought of meeting (Joseph and Hyrum) at the bar of God is more awful to me than anything else.'

Self-report of Dr. Robert D. Foster.

Organization
of Westbound
Company
No. 1.
Tuesday, 4.—Emigrating Company No. 1 met in the Temple, eighteen companies of ten families each were filled up and Parley P. Pratt and Amasa Lyman appointed captains over the first and second hundreds.

At 5 p. m., council met for prayers at the Historian's Office, (Dr. Richards').

Joshua Smith died. He was born in Nobleborough, Kennebeck (now Lincoln) county, Maine, February 13th, 1788. He was the son of Stephen and Miriam, and the eldest of four pair of twins, who lived to be men except one. Joshua was baptized at Kirtland, by John Smith in June, 1836. He was poison-

Joshua Smith
Died—
Poisoned by
Carthage
Militia.
ed by the militia while at Carthage where he was summoned to attend court; the militia searched for him and found a knife under his arm and arrested him, and while under arrest they gave him dinner, where no doubt he received the poison, he soon became very thirsty, and vomiting followed until death. He said, he had been poisoned by the militia and at a post mortem examination by Drs. John M. Bernhisel, Lucius P. Sanger and Jesse Brailey the suspicion was confirmed; he was a good man and his name will be registered among those who wear a martyr's crown.

He was second counselor to Samuel Williams, president of the elders' quorum, at the time of his death.

Miscellaneous
Items.
Wednesday, 5.—Attended council with the Twelve to direct the arrangement of the seats in the Temple.

Afternoon, in council at the Historian's Office.

Thursday, 6.—4 p. m., attended council and prayer meeting with the Twelve.

Friday, 7. — 4 p. m., attended council with the Twelve.

Saturday, 8.—Revising history in company with Brothers Heber C. Kimball, Willard Richards and George A. Smith till 4 p. m. Afterwards the Twelve and others met for council and prayer.

FAREWELL MESSAGE OF ORSON PRATT

'To the Saints of the Eastern and Middle States, Greeting:

Dear Brethren: The time is at hand for me to take a long and lasting farewell to these eastern countries, being included with my family, among the tens of thousands of American citizens who have the choice of death or banishment beyond the Rocky Mountains. I have preferred the latter. It is with the greatest of joy that I forsake this republic; and all the saints have abundant reasons to rejoice that they are counted worthy to be cast out as exiles from this wicked nation; for we have received nothing but one continual scene of the most horrid and unrelenting persecutions at their hands for the last sixteen years. If our heavenly Father will preserve us, and deliver us out of the hands of the bloodthirsty Christians of these United States and not suffer any more of us to be martyred to gratify their holy piety, I for one shall be very thankful. Perhaps we may have to suffer much in the land of our exile, but our sufferings will be from another cause—there will be no Christian bandit to afflict us all the day long—no holy pious priests to murder us by scores—no editors to urge on house-burning, devastation and death. If we die in the dens and caves of the Rocky Mountains, we shall die where freedom reigns triumphantly. Liberty in a solitary place, and in a desert, is far more preferable than martyrdom in these pious states.

Perhaps the rich may ask, how they are to dispose of their farms and houses so as to get to Nauvoo this winter and be ready to start early in the spring with the great company?—In reply to this inquiry, we observe that they can do it if they only have a disposition. Many of them might have disposed of their property years ago, but have been holding on to the same, for the purpose of getting a greater price, or for fear of losing their property by the ravages of mobs, if they gathered with the saints; thus they have not been willing to readily comply with the great commandment of God, concerning the gathering, and thus they are deprived of the privilege of sacrificing their property by being driven from the same: but still they can reprieve themselves in some measure, by selling immediately at all hazards, although they should not get one third of its real value.

The Lord requires a sacrifice, and he that is not willing, will fail of the blessing. Brethren now is the time for you to be up and doing, for unless you can get to Nauvoo this winter, it will be entirely needless for you to go in the spring, for you could not arrive in time to leave with the saints.

We would say to the poor in the east, that it will be of no use for them to go to Nauvoo, unless they have means sufficient to purchase horses, wagons, tents, etc., for it will be in vain for them to think of starting for the Rocky Mountains without these things; and the church at Nauvoo will have as much as they can possibly do to provide these things for the poor of that place. If they should have any

Mutual Help-
fulness of
Rich and Poor.
means left after having provided for their own poor, they would of course be willing to help the poor abroad; the rich in the branches abroad should help the poor to horses, wagons, etc.; and those who cannot possibly obtain these things, must raise means to pay their passage by sea around Cape Horn to the western coast of North America. Indeed our expenses by sea from here to the place of our destination would be but a trifle more, than our expenses from here to Nauvoo. Hence all the poor that can raise funds sufficient to go to Nauvoo, can with a little exertion, obtain sufficient to go by Cape Horn.

Company via
Sea Provided.
Those who go by sea, can carry with them many articles which it would be impossible to carry over the mountains. Elder Samuel Brannan has been counseled to go by sea. He will sail about the middle of January. Those who wish to accompany him are requested to give him their names as early as possible. If one hundred and fifty or two hundred passengers can be obtained, he can venture to charter a vessel for them, and thus their fare will be scarcely nothing. The voyage can be performed in four or five months.

Brethren awake!—be determined to get out from this evil nation next spring. We do not want the saints to be left in the United States after that time. Let every branch in the east, west, north, and south, be determined to flee out of Babylon, either by land or by sea, as soon as then. Judgment is at the door; and it will be easier to go now, than to wait until it comes.

Those who go by sea, should go as soon as possible, as it will be almost impossible to double Cape Horn in our summer months; as the seasons there are directly the opposite of ours. Their coldest months are in July, and August, their warmest months in January and February. There is too much ice in our summer months to admit a safe passage round the Cape.

Elder Samuel
Brannan Ap-
pointed to
Head
Sea-bound
Company.
Elder Samuel Brannan is hereby appointed to preside over, and take charge of the company that go by sea; and all who go with him will be required to give strict heed to his instruction and counsel. He will point out to you the necessary articles to be taken, whether for food or for raiment, together with farming utensils, mechanical instruments, and all kinds of garden seeds, seeds of various kinds of fruits, etc., etc. Several have already given their names to go with him, and I think he will soon raise a company as large as can conveniently go in one vessel.

Brethren, if you all want to go, charter half a dozen or a dozen vessels, and fill each with passengers, and the fare among so many will be but a trifle. The most of those, however, who can get teams this winter, had better go by land.

Do not be fainthearted nor slothful, but be courageous and diligent, prayerful and faithful, and you can accomplish almost anything that you undertake. What great and good work cannot the saints do, if they take hold of it with energy and ambition?

We can do almost anything, for our Father in heaven will strengthen us, if we strengthen ourselves. He will work according to our faith. If we say we cannot go, God will not help us; but if we say, in the name of the Lord we will go! and set ourselves about it, he will help us. The saints must do greater things than these, before many years pass away, and now is the time to try your faith and ambition, and thus by experience be prepared for greater achievements.

Brother Snow and myself are called upon to leave you, to visit our families and friends in the west. After our departure apostates will prowl around the branches here in the east, seeking to devour. They will present

themselves before you as very pious and holy beings, mourning over the corruptions of the church while the Twelve Apostles of the Lamb will be represented as devils incarnate. But dear brethren, our works you have seen, and our diligence and anxiety for your salvation, you are not ignorant of. We have labored with all patience and diligence with you. We have prayed with you, and taught and instructed, and counseled you according as the Lord has given us wisdom—And I hereby testify unto you in the name of the Lord God of Joseph, that, if after all the instruction you have received, you suffer yourselves to be influenced and led away by apostates, such as [Sidney] Rigdon, [George J.] Adams, William Smith, and others who have been legally cut off from the church—your sins shall be upon your own heads—our garments are clean. Remember these words, and let nothing move you. Let no apostates be in the least welcome under your roof. Be ashamed and blush at the very idea of attending one of their wicked meetings. Despise their principles, and all their apostate doings, as you would the very gates of hell. Touch not—taste not, and handle not any of their accursed doctrines; for they shall utterly perish, and all that follow them. The day shall come when they shall weep and howl for vexation of spirit, for their miseries shall come upon them; and all shall know and discern between the righteous and the wicked—between saints and apostates.

When the saints get this message, I shall probably be on my way to the west. Should they wish to forward me letters or assistance, they can direct the same to Nauvoo. I hereby tender my thanks to the saints for such assistance as they have rendered me. I have received in the neighborhood of twenty dollars in fulfillment of my dream. Those who have responded to the same, have the warmest gratitude of my heart. I have just returned from a tour of about eight hundred miles, all at my own expense. And I assure you dear brethren, that it is a difficult matter for the servants of God to spend all their time in the ministry unless the saints uphold their hands. I should have probably visited more branches of the church in the east if I had been in the possession of sufficient funds to have paid my traveling expenses. I have no fault to find. The saints in the east have done well in the main; for they have responded to the call of our brethren in the west, in relation to tithing, tabernacle, etc.; and they shall in no wise lose their reward. We love the saints, both in the east and in the west, and it grieves our hearts that circumstances should force any of you to tarry in the states after next spring. If it were in our power, our hearts would leap for joy at the prospect of taking you all with us: and thus would the fulness of the gospel be fully brought from among the Gentiles.

Brethren and sisters, remember the *Book of Mormon*, the *Book of Covenants*, and the instructions, teachings, and counsels, which the faithful servants have given you from time to time. Be strictly virtuous, pure, upright, and honest in all things; and comply faithfully with the instructions upon these points, as pointed out in my message. You can now see the consequences attending those who have violated those virtuous principles. They have apostatized, and become the bitterest enemies of the servants of God: thus fulfilling the words of Jesus—'He that looketh on a woman to lust after her, or if anyone commit adultery in their hearts, they shall not have the spirit, but shall deny the faith.'*

It is a fearful thing to violate the commandments of God, and depart from the strict laws which he has given concerning these matters. There is a right way, and there are many wrong ways; and blessed is that person who findeth the right way, and walketh therein even unto the end, for they shall be crowned with great glory, and of the increase of their kingdom, there shall be no end. Such shall be honored among the sons and daughters of God, while the corrupt, the whoremongers, and the vile seducer, shall be abased, where there is wailing, and wretchedness indescribable.

Who then, for a moment's gratification, will sacrifice an eternal kingdom, where pure virtue, and love, and affection shall beam forth like the rays of the morning from every joyful countenance?

O Virtue! How amiable thou art! Strength and beauty, and ex-

Apostrophy
to Virtue. cellency, and dignity, and honor, and immortality, are thine offspring—Gentle peace, pure affection, unbounded love, and omnipotent power, shall reign triumphantly in thy habitations forevermore!

And now I must say to the saints in the eastern countries farewell. Farewell till we meet on distant lands. May our kind Father hasten

Commends the
Saints to the
Lord. that time. Yea, O Lord God, remember these my brethren and sisters, and save them. Behold O Lord, they have received thy servants, and the message thou

Book of Covenants, p. 204, 5th paragraph, stereotyped [Nauvoo] edition; current—1921—edition. sec. xlii:23

gavest them to declare.   They have fed us and clothed us; they have
given their tithes for the building of thy Temple, and now, O Father,
reject not their offerings, neither cast away thy people who are called
by thy name.   Forgive their sins, and pity them even as a Father
pitieth his own children.   Behold O Lord, the desire of this thy
people to go forth from among the Gentiles, who have sorely persecuted them all the day long.   But thy people are poor.   Wilt thou
not help them?   Wilt thou not deliver them out of the hands of all
their enemies who hate them?   And when thou shalt visit this nation
in sore judgment, according to that which thou hast spoken, destroy
not thy people who are poor, with the wicked; but hide them with
thine own hand, and shield them from judgment.

Hear the prayer of thy servant kind Father, in behalf of his brethren,
over whom he has presided, and whom he is now about to leave.
For I ask thee for all these things, in the name of thy Son. Amen.

And again, with my heart full of blessings I say farewell.

[Signed]   ORSON PRATT.

City of New York, Nov. 8, 1845.'

Sunday, 9.—No public meeting; the floor of the first
story in the Temple having been taken up to put in
new timbers, the sleepers which were put in at the
commencement of the Temple having become rotten.

The brethren belonging to the different Emigrating
Companies assembled in and around the Temple, and
received instruction concerning emigration.

Eleven a. m., I addressed the saints.

Noon, I met with the captains of companies.

Two p. m., I met with Emigrating Company No.
1.

Monday, 10.—I spent the day with Elders Heber
C. Kimball, Willard Richards and George A. Smith
revising Church History; several of the   Suggested
Twelve and others called in the afternoon;   Purchase of
we consulted on the subject of purchasing   "Mother
the copyright of Mother Smith's *History;*   Smith's
and concluded to settle with Brother Howard Coray*
for his labor in compiling the same.

*The work of compilation for Mother Lucy Smith was really done by his wife,
Sister M. J. Coray, who was also her amanuensis throughout.   The work was finally
published und.r the direction of President Joseph F. Smith in Salt Lake City, Utah,
October, 1901.   It was revised by Elders George A. Smith and Elias Smith, close
relatives of the author.   See title page, etc.

Tuesday, 11.—Forenoon, Elders Willard Richards and George A. Smith revising history.

Afternoon, Elder Kimball and I joined them, and assisted in revising history.

Four p. m., the Twelve met, Elder Parley P. Pratt read an epistle to the churches which he had been instructed to write.

After council, accompanied by Brothers Heber C. Kimball and Levi Richards, I visited and administered to the sick.

Wednesday, 12.—Council met in the afternoon for prayer. A conference was held at New York City:

New York Conference

'The Church of Jesus Christ of Latter-day Saints met pursuant to appointment on the evening of the 12th of November at the American Hall. Many of the brethren were present from Long Island, Connecticut, and New Jersey.

On motion, Elder Orson Pratt was called to the chair, and G. T. Newell, secretary.

After prayer and a dedication of the assembly to God by the president, and a song of Zion by the whole assembly, the president arose and laid before the conference the present condition of the saints, and the necessity of all removing to the west. He exhorted them to a union of action for the benefit of the poor, that they might not be left behind. That as long as the church remained among the Gentiles, the fulness of the gospel could not be [said to have been] taken from them, and the *Book of Mormon* be fulfilled.

Elder Brannan then arose and presented the following Preamble and Resolutions, which were unanimously adopted by the whole assembly without a dissenting voice.

ELDER BRANNAN'S RESOLUTIONS

'*Whereas,* we as a people have sought to obey the great commandment of the dispensation of the fulness of times, by gathering ourselves together; and as often as we have done so, we have been sorely persecuted by the Protestant Christian Churches, our houses burned, and we disinherited of our possessions, and driven forth upon the charity of a cold-hearted world, to seek protection and sustenance for ourselves and families.

And *Whereas:*—Inasmuch as the people and authorities of the United States have sanctioned such proceedings, without manifesting any disposition to sustain us in our constitutional rights, but have rejected our many petitions to judges, governors, and presidents for the last twelve years, having hardened their hearts like Pharaoh of old, against the cries of the fatherless and the widow—That we now cease our cries, wipe away our tears, and prepare ourselves to 'enter into our chambers and shut our doors about us for a little season until the indignation be overpast.' Therefore,

'Resolved, That we hail with joy the Proclamation of our brethren from the City of Joseph [i. e. Nauvoo] to make preparations for our immediate departure, and give thanks and praise to our heavenly Father that the day of our deliverance is so near at hand.

'Resolved, That we look upon the Proclamation sent forth and published in the Warsaw Signal by our former brother, William Smith, as being actuated by purely selfish motives alone, for his own personal emolument and aggrandizement, at the sacrifice of the lives of his best friends, and the defamation of the character of the whole church; unchristianlike, even if true, because it brings persecution and affliction upon the innocent.

'Resolved, That we most heartily sanction the proceedings of the council and church at Nauvoo, in his excommunication; and that suffering innocence in this city by his hands, has demanded it long since. And in it we believe that prayers of the fatherless and widow have been answered. And further

'Resolved, That we caution all the honest in heart among the saints, where he has not visited in the east and elsewhere, that have not had an opportunity of proving his Apostleship as we have, to beware how they receive him into their houses, or bid him Godspeed, lest they bring condemnation upon themselves ignorantly.

'Resolved, That during the mission and ministry of our brethren, the Twelve, among us, since the absence of William Smith, their conduct has been of the most exemplary character, both in practice and precept; which we are sorry we are not able to say of our former Brother William Smith. And

'Resolved, That we advise him if he wishes to keep himself from trouble, shame, and disgrace—that if he has any feeling for the character of his family, and his martyred brethren, that he stay where he is, or go where he is not known. For we, the church in New York, have no desire to see him, unless he repent speedily, and go about making restitution for lifting his hand against the church and kingdom of God to destroy it.

'Resolved, That the church in this city move, one and all, west of the Rocky Mountains between this and next season, either by land or water; and that we most earnestly pray all our brethren in the eastern country to join with us in this determination, and carry it out effectually, to the delivery of the people of God from the daughters of Babylon, and not one left behind.

'Resolved, That there are no apologies required of those who do not go, but old age, sickness, infirmities, and poverty; 'For he that will not forsake father and mother, houses and lands, wives and children for me, and my name's sake, is not worthy of me'.'

Elder Brannan laid before the congregation his instructions from the authorities of the church directing him to go by water, and called upon all who wanted to accompany him, to come forward at the close of the meeting and put down their names. The conference was then dismissed by a benediction from the president.

[Signed]   ORSON PRATT, President.

G. T. Newell, Secretary.'

Wednesday 12 (continued).—Brother Rice's farm-
Action in Illinois. house on Camp Creek was burned by about thirty men of the mob who swore they were Governor Ford's troops, which was probably false, John M. Finch and Rollison were with them.

Thursday, 13.—Forenoon, I rode out to the prairie with Dr. Richards, my brothers John and Joseph, E. T. Benson and G. D. Grant, and dined at Brother Chamberlain's.

4 p. m., attended council with the Twelve. It was decided that Mother Lucy Smith should be furnished with food, clothing, and wood for the winter.

We prayed as usual.

Dr. Richards and I visited Stephen Markham who was cutting and sawing wagon spokes, at his place in
Brigham Young's Marksmanship. the woods. We helped him to cut and saw a while, and then took his rifle and shot at a mark, with my second shot I cut the pin that fastened the two-inch paper mark to a tree.

I wrote a lengthy communication to Noah Rogers giving him the general items of church news since he left on his mission to the Pacific Islands.

Friday, 14.—Evening, the Twelve met at Dr. Richards'. James H. Flanigan reports:

A MISSIONARY'S REPORT

'Nauvoo, Illinois, Nov. 14, 1845.

Having just returned from a mission eastward, appointed by the spring conference of 1843; according to order established by the Church of Christ, that elders should report their stewardship; I thought, although I was among the least, yet I would not be among the last in confessing my ignorance, and stating unequivocally, that I am but an unprofitable servant.

During my mission, which was in the fall and spring of '43 and '44, in the states of New Jersey and Maryland, in company with my fellow laborer, S. H. Rogers, we endeavored, according to our ability, and the trust reposed in us, to help rear up the standard of Latter-day glory, and to facilitate the great and momentous work of God in these last days.

I will also say, that although we were weak, yet we were made strong by the hand of the mighty God of Jacob! And although we were little, yet we confounded the great; and although our wisdom consisted in the simplicity of Christ's gospel, yet the wisdom of man was confounded before our eyes.

Many honorable men were enamoured of the truth, and many honorable men instructed in the plan of salvation. We baptized thirty-five or forty for the remission of their sins, and organized one branch of twenty-five or thirty members in Maryland; and thus the words of God were fulfilled, that 'the weak should confound the wisdom of the mighty, and the poor among men rejoice, the meek increase their joy in the Lord, those who erred learn doctrine,' etc., etc. Thus was the mission, and thus it ended.

May God bless his people, redeem and save Israel, and hasten his work in its time.

JAMES H. FLANIGAN.'

Saturday, 15.—Elders Heber C. Kimball, Willard Richards, and I visited through the city.

Evening, the Twelve met for prayer.

DEATH OF EDMUND DURFEE—SHOT BY A MOB OF HOUSE-BURNERS

A considerable party of the mob set fire to a stack of straw near Solomon Hancock's barn and concealed themselves. Hancock and others went out to put out the fire which was the only way to save the building, when they were fired upon by the burners, and Elder Edmund Durfee killed on the spot, many balls flew around the rest of the brethren, but none of the rest were hurt.*

Elder Edmund Durfee was born in Rhode Island, October 3, 1788. He was baptized by Elder Simeon Carter in Ruggles township, Ashland county, Ohio, May, 1831. (He had been a Methodist). He was ordained an elder by Simeon Carter and Solomon Han-

*See footnote p. 145 this volume.

cock; and accompanied Elder Brackenbury on a mission to Chautauqua county, New York, in December, 1831.

Elder Joseph B. Brackenbury died at Pomfret from the effects of poison secretly administered to him by

Case of
Poison by
Mob.

opposers, who afterwards boasted that Mormon elders had not faith enough to stand poison. The night after his burial there was a heavy snowstorm, about half past eleven o'clock Joel H. Johnson dreamed that some persons were digging up Brother Brackenbury's body, and was so exercised about it that he called up some of the brethren and went to the spot, about one mile distant, and

Body-
Snatching.

found a party of doctors at work, who had nearly cleared the grave of earth; the men fled with utmost precipitation. David Johnson took after the largest one who was caught and bound over in one thousand dollar bonds for his appearance at court, but was never tried.

DURFEE'S BIOGRAPHICAL NOTE

In the spring of 1832, Elder Durfee with nine others went up to Jackson county to put in grain, and build houses, and returned the same season.

He took another mission to the state of New York in the fall. In May, 1833, he moved to Kirtland. He was one of the twenty-four elders who laid the corner stones of the Temple in Kirtland, and moved to Caldwell county, Missouri, in 1837, and settled on Log Creek. In 1838 he was expelled from the state of Missouri with the saints, and settled in Yelrome, Hancock county, Illinois. After his death the mob boasted that they fired at Durfee on a bet of a gallon of whiskey that they could kill him the first shot, and they won.

Sunday, 16.—Meeting in the grove at 10 a. m.

Elders Orson Hyde, Heber C. Kimball and I preached.

I received the following:

BACKENSTOS' NOTE TO THE TWELVE

'*To the Twelve*:

On last night Elder Edmund Durfee was basely murdered by the mob in the Green Plains precinct, what shall be done to avenge his blood? the troops afford us no protection.

Yours, etc.,

November 16th, 1845.   J. B. BACKENSTOS.'

Edmund Durfee's body was brought into the city to be buried.

I learned that Elder Theodore Turley has been arrested at Alton on a charge of bogus-making.

Afternoon, council of the Twelve assembled.

Orson Hyde in behalf of the council wrote the following letter:—

HYDE'S LETTER TO MAJOR WARREN REPORTING DURFEE'S MURDER

'Nauvoo, Nov. 17, 1845.

Major Warren,

Sir: Intelligence reached us last evening of the murder of Mr. Edmund Durfee in the south part of the county by the mob who fired a quantity of straw to decoy him out, and while he was engaged in raking the straw so that the fire might not communicate with the buildings, six shots were made at him, one of which took effect in his breast and he died immediately.

His remains are brought to this city for interment.

Mr. Durfee was one of the most quiet and inoffensive citizens in these United States and from our acquaintance with him, and from the nature of his business in securing his crops we are persuaded that his murder was wholly unprovoked.

The burning of the house of Mr. Rice has created little excitement in the city, but on this occasion, we look to you to take such steps and adopt such measures as you, in your wisdom, shall deem expedient, and that you will make your views public as early as consistent.

Shall we send a sufficient number of men into the south part of the county to protect themselves while gathering their crops? or will you send your men for that purpose, or at least, a sufficient number of them? Be so good as to inform us so soon as convenient.

Affidavits will probably soon reach you of the above transactions.

Very Respectfully, in behalf of the Council,

[Signed]   ORSON HYDE'.

AN EPISTLE TO THE SAINTS

'All those who have letters, or documents of any kind in their possession, which in any way relate to the History of the Church of Jesus Christ of Latter-day Saints, are requested to leave them with the historian before tomorrow evening.

On Collection of Historical Items.

All elders who have been out on special missions within two years, and have not reported themselves in writing, are requested to do so before tomorrow evening.

Every individual who may be in possession of any fact, circumstance, incident, event, or transaction which they wish recorded in the *General History of the Church* will report it in writing before tomorrow evening.

The historian wants all books, maps, charts, papers, documents of every kind, name, and nature, and all information that may relate to, or have a bearing in any wise upon the History of the Church, before him, in his office within twenty-four hours.

Important items of history have frequently been presented at too late an hour to gain an insertion. Therefore I would say, that the history is written up to the year 1843, and the documents now wanting, are for the years 43-4 and 5. But if any of the brethren have any items of valuable history of any date, they may hand them in, and they will be filed away for future use.

The injunction of the Apostle 'owe no man anything' is excellent, and ought to be remembered by every one, and practiced, so far as circumstances will admit; this is a part of the religion of the celestial kingdom; I have endeavored to live up to it, and I am determined to live to it more perfectly if possible, therefore, I request every individual who has any account for or against me, to call and settle the same before next Sabbath; if they owe me I will not kill them, and if I owe them I will try and pay them, for I hope soon to start on a mission towards some Island in the Pacific ocean, and if I should go away in debt to God or man I should expect to be shipwrecked before I got there. And now, brethren, if you want to save me from such a dreadful calamity, don't fail to call and settle with me, for I expect that I owe some little accounts which have escaped my recollection and my mind cannot rest so as to prosecute my business in peace until these things are settled. Remember the time before next Sabbath and set me free for after that I have much business that will require my attention.

Payment of Debts.

May the God of Israel bless all the saints, help them to do right, prosper them in their business, and save them in his kingdom is the prayer of your brother,

         [Signed] WILLARD RICHARDS.

City of Joseph [Nauvoo], Sunday Morning, November 16th, 1845.'

Monday, 17.—I met in council at 4 p. m. with Elders Heber C. Kimball, Orson Hyde, Parley P. Pratt, John Taylor, George A. Smith, Joseph Young and Bishop George Miller.

In obedience to the call of the historian many elders furnished reports of their missions: I insert the following:

JAMES C. SNOW'S MISSION TO THE EAST

'May 17th, 1844, I left Yelrome, Hancock county, Illinois, for Rush county, Indiana, on a special mission.

On the 27th I commenced to lay before the people the views and policy of President Joseph Smith relative to the government and laws of the United States, presenting him as a candidate for the ensuing presidential election; at first, I met with opposition until the people became better acquainted with his principles; prejudice then gave way, and hundreds in Rush and other counties were turned in favor of President Smith and the saints.

Twenty were baptized into the church. When the news arrived of his death the people were disappointed and the shock was universally felt. Some of the most influential men immediately predicted the downfall of the nation because they looked lamely on and sang lulla-by-baby.

JAMES C. SNOW.

City of Joseph [Nauvoo], November 17th, 1845.'

Tuesday, 18.—The Twelve met in council at Dr. Richards'.

Mr. Brayman, attorney for the state, wrote a letter to the council desiring witnesses against the murderers of Durfee to be sent to Carthage, also affidavits forwarded in relation to the burning of Rice's house, and advising us of the arrest of George Backman, Moss and Snyder, who were charged with the murder of Elder Edmund Durfee, Sen.

Another Judicial Farce—Durfee's—to be Enacted.

The council replied immediately and requested the witnesses to start in the morning for Carthage to perform their part in another judicial farce.

I received the following:

SOLOMON HANCOCK'S LETTER ON DURFEE'S MURDER

'Carthage, November 18th, 1845.

President Brigham Young:

I am convinced that Major Warren and Mr. Brayman are doing all they can to ferret out and convict the guilty who have recently been engaged in lawless transactions. They have stationed troops at my house to protect it from the incendiary and things generally appear to be working out right.

As there appears to be a disposition to act in support of law I think we ought to aid in getting witnesses so that the truth may be proven.

I have learned that Calvin Beebe, Lester Herrick and Nelson Herrick were in Lima on Saturday night, and know something of the intentions of the mob upon my property. I believe their evidence is necessary. They should come to Carthage in time for the examination.

Please send all who know anything about the recent lawless outrages.

Yours Respectfully, etc.

SOLOMON HANCOCK.'

JAMES ARLINGTON BENNETT'S REQUEST

Tuesday, 18 (continued).—I received a letter from James Arlington Bennett urging me to appoint him military commander-in-chief in the church, the spirit of the letter shows a thirst for personal aggrandizement unbecoming a servant of God.

NAUVOO NEIGHBOR — EXTRA

Nauvoo, November 19th, 1845

MURDER AND ARSON
EDMUND DURFEE SHOT—TWO HOUSES BURNED

'As may be seen by the affidavits below, it falls to our painful lot to chronicle two more outrages upon the lives and rights of the Latter-day Saints, since they have been using all diligence to secure their crops, build wagons, and leave next spring.

Mr. Durfee was one of the most industrious, inoffensive and good men that could be found, and having his house burnt in September last, moved to Nauvoo and went on Saturday last for a load of grain, was shot dead in cold blood, at midnight while striving with others to save property from the flames by an armed mob!

As to the destruction of the houses and property, and the treatment on that occasion—let the affidavit speak for itself.

We have nearly two thousand five hundred wagons commenced for our Pacific journey next spring, but such outrages certainly are not calculated to aid us in getting ready. We have borne the Missouri persecution; we have mourned the loss of the Prophet and Patriarch, Joseph and Hyrum Smith; we feel the destruction of one or two hundred houses the present season, and our hearts are pained at the murder of Edmund Durfee, because he was a good man; but, we, as in all cases of the saints, leave the disposition of these matters in the care of a wise God, and the perpetrators, to the mercy of (as they say), a country of laws, and be those laws honored or disgraced we cannot be charged with revenge; and we do beseech the people and the authorities not to impute crime to us, to raise excitement, when we see our accusers wiping the blood of innocent men, women, and children, from their garments, as though this was the realm of Nero.

If thieves and robbers escape to Nauvoo, our rule is to deliver them up to the law of the land, and that is all that we can do.

We believe there is virtue and humanity among high-minded men, that know what honor is, and we appeal to them to lend a helping hand, while we are outfitting for our intended removal in the spring. Give us peace, for you that hold the balances of power can! And when we have settled on the other side of America you will know of a truth that we were friends and not enemies to life, law, and liberty! That we were good men, engaged in a good cause, and will receive the meed of praise we deserve for universal benevolence, and everlasting friendship to goodness.

The jealousy of the present generation is so great against the saints, that we have deemed it our duty to give this and the accompanying affidavits, that the world may know the continued ravages, and bloody outrages of a midnight mob; and for another important reason, that as Major Warren has pledged himself to use every exertion in his power to allay excitement, prevent the destruction of property, and stop the shedding of blood, we cannot feel anything better than that he will exhibit his honor and clemency in our behalf, that we may prepare for our exodus in peace henceforth.'

AFFIDAVITS IN THE DURFEE MURDER CASE

'State of Illinois ⎱ ss.
Hancock County ⎰

Personally appeared before me, Aaron Johnson a justice of the peace within and foresaid county, James H. Woodland, and after being duly sworn, deposeth and saith, that on the night of the 15th of November, 1845, in the south part of said county, near Solomon Hancock's house, about midnight, a stack of straw was discovered on fire and that several persons turned out to suppress the flames; they raked away the straw to prevent it from catching and firing the barn; while thus engaged, a whistle was heard east and one west; and presently a gun was fired at them, and they continued to fire till six guns were discharged at them; the ball of the fourth one entered the body of Edmund Durfee, just above his heart and he died instantly, and further deponent saith not.

[Signed]   JAMES H. WOODLAND.

Sworn to and subscribed this 17th day of November, 1845.

[Signed]   AARON JOHNSON, J. P. (LS).'

State of Illinois)
Hancock County) ss.

Personally appeared before me, Isaac Higbee, a justice of the peace within said county, Joseph Swymler, who being duly sworn according to law, deposeth and saith, that on the night of the 13th day of November, 1845, at about half past twelve o'clock, a company of men about thirty in number, made their appearance at the residence of Samuel Hicks in said county, near the head of Camp Creek, and called for Samuel Hicks, who got up out of bed and went to the door and asked what was wanted, they said they were the governor's troops right from Carthage, and had a writ for William Rice, who they said was there, and was told that he was not there. They laid hold of Hicks and forced him away without anything on but his shirt, Hicks and his wife and child all being sick with the ague, part of the company remained; they then called deponent and his brother up who were there, and ordered them to carry out the goods of the said Hicks and while his brother was in the chamber, they set fire to the stairs, which prevented him from getting all their goods, and when the fire had got to burning through the roof, they came back with Hicks who had suffered much with cold and ague, and after giving many insults and threats they went away. Deponent recognized in the company Jospeh Agnew, John M. Finch, and a young man by the name of Moss, and further deponent saith not.

[Signed]   JOSEPH SWYMLER.

Sworn and subscribed to before me, this 17th day of November, 1845.

[Signed]   ISAAC HIGBEE, J. P.'

Thursday, 20.—Council of the Twelve met in the afternoon.

I wrote a letter to Elder Wilford Woodruff, Liverpool, England, in reply to his communications.

Friday, 21.—The Twelve met and prayed.

COURSE OF MAJOR WARREN REPORTED—BACKENSTOS

Sheriff Backenstos came into council about 7 p. m., and said that he had watched Major Warren very closely for the last four days, thought he had turned Jack-Mormon, that he had been very busy and energetic in arresting the murderers of Durfee and the burners of Rice's house, that he had several of them under guard at Carthage and was in pursuit of more and had chased one of them into Missouri and forced him back at the point of the pistol without any requisition from the governor. He admitted to Backenstos that Durfee would not have been murdered had the troops not been in the county; notwithstanding Governor Ford's late letter to the contrary.

Major Warren has made several very sharp speeches to the anti-Mormons and told them if they did not help to bring those murderers to justice he would withdraw his troops from the county, and leave them in the hands of Backenstos; he had also intimated that if he could not bring them to justice without, he would establish martial law for a little season, try them by court martial, and have them shot. Stephens of Green Plains issued his warrant for the apprehension of the murderers, and came to Carthage on the day of examination and claimed his privilege of trying his own writs. Warren knowing him to be a mobocrat, caused Mr. Bartlett to issue new writs and took the prisoners out of Stephens' hands.

The sheriff also stated, that the clerk of the commissioners' court had had an injunction served on him, and had refused to issue the orders granted by the last commissioners' court for the payment of the sheriff's *posse* in quieting the rioters and house-burners.

Dr. Richards sick.

Saturday, 22.—The Twelve met with thirty-eight of the brethren who were expelled from Jackson county, Missouri, in 1833. Several of them spoke, some of them saying they thought they were neglected and cast off poor.

Echo from Jackson Co. Expulsion.

I made a few remarks, and showed that many had been slothful and had not preached nor magnified their callings in the church.

The plasterers finished the attic story of the Temple.

Sunday, 23.—Eleven a. m., seventies met in the Concert Hall.

I met with the captains of Emigrating Companies and gave them appropriate counsel.

Families organized, 3285.

Wagons on hand, 1508.

Wagons commenced, 1892.

Afternoon, the Council of the Twelve met. Several letters were read. Many threats by our enemies were afloat.

Monday, 24.—Ten a. m., Brother Heber C. Kimball and I called at the Historian's Office and read history with Dr. Richards and George A. Smith.

The council wrote Elder Theodore Turley who is now in jail awaiting his examination.

We have learned that the persons who murdered Edmund Durfee as also those who burned Rice's and Hick's houses were discharged by the magistrate without examination. Our brethren went according to Major Warren and Mr. Brayman's request as witnesses thereby fulfilling their part towards magnifying and making the laws honorable, but returned unheard, and the farce closed sooner than he had anticipated, without even a grand jury on the case.

Afternoon, council met for prayers.

Wednesday, 26.—At the Historian's Office with Elder George A. Smith and revised fifty pages history.

Elder Heber C. Kimball accompanied me to the Temple and examined the rooms. We were also engaged borrowing means to aid the Trustees, that they may go on with the work.

The presidents of the different quorums of seventies met and made some arrangements to furnish two rooms in the Temple. Elder Jedediah M. Grant gave a brief narration of his faith and standing.

The painters finished painting the attic of the Temple.

Thursday, 27.—At the Trustees' Office, arranging business.

Afternoon, Erastus H. Derby called upon Dr. Richards and informed him that Silas Haight, a deputy United States marshal of Iowa and another suspicious fellow were loitering about the streets, and endeavoring to see some of the Twelve to serve writs on them.

Friday, 28.—I went to the Trustees' Office, attending to church business. Elders Willard Richards and George A. Smith read and revised history to the end of 1843.

Saturday, 29.—I met with the Twelve, Bishops Whitney and Miller and a few others in the Temple and laid the carpet on the main floor of the attic story, and also on several of the small rooms ready for the First Quorum [of the Seventy] to meet in."

CHAPTER XXXVII

DEDICATION OF PARTS OF THE TEMPLE — ENDOW-
MENTS GIVEN — ROMAN CATHOLIC EFFORTS TO
PURCHASE THE TEMPLE AND OTHER NAUVOO PROP-
ERTY—THE CHURCH IN ENGLAND—UNITED STATES
FEDERAL CHARGES OF COUNTERFEITING AGAINST
CHURCH AUTHORITIES—CHURCH PUBLICATIONS FOR
1845

"*Sunday, November* 30, 1845.—At ten a. m. I
went to the attic story of the Temple with Elders Heber
C. Kimball, Willard Richards, Parley P. Pratt, John
Taylor, Orson Hyde, George A. Smith, and Amasa
Lyman, of the Quorum of the Twelve; also
Newel K. Whitney and George Miller, Pre-
siding Bishops; John Smith, Patriarch and
President of the Stake, Joseph Young, Pres-
ident of the Seventies, Alpheus Cutler and R. Cahoon,
Temple Committee, Cornelius P. Lott, Levi Richards.
Joseph C. Kingsbury, Orson Spencer, Wm. W. Phelps,
Isaac Morley, Lucien Woodworth.   At about 12
o'clock, sang 'Come All Ye Sons of Zion'.

I requested Wm. Clayton to keep minutes. I then
offered up prayer and dedicated the attic story of the
Temple and ourselves to God, and prayed that God
would sustain and deliver us his servants from the
hands of our enemies, until we have accomplished his
will in this house. Elder Taylor then sang 'A Poor
Wayfaring Man of Grief', after which Elder Heber C.
Kimball prayed, that the Lord would hear and answer
the prayers of his servant Brigham, and break off the
yoke of our enemies and inasmuch as they lay traps
for the feet of his servants that they may fall into them
themselves and be destroyed—that God would bless his
servant Joseph Young, heal his wife, and bless his

family—that God would bless and heal his own [Elder Kimball's] family and asked for the same blessings on all our families which he had asked for Joseph Young and himself.

Hans C. Hanson, the doorkeeper reported that there were two officers waiting at the foot of the stairs for me. I told the brethren that I could bear to tarry here where it was warm as long as they could stay in the cold waiting for me. Elder Amasa Lyman requested hands to be laid on him that he might be healed; five of the brethren laid hands on him.

Officers at the Door of the Temple Waiting for Brigham Young.

Joseph Young prayed that our enemies might have no power over our leaders, he prayed for our brethren in England and on the Islands of the Sea; Brothers Babbitt, Turley and the Reddens—also that the Trustees might have means to liquidate all the debts.

The side rooms were occupied as follows:

The first, in the southeast corner as a private office.

Assignment of Rooms in the Temple Attic.

The second by Heber C. Kimball, W. Richards and myself. The third and fourth by others of the Twelve; Fifth, by Joseph Young and Presidency of the Seventies; Sixth, for washing and anointing the elders.

On the north side: first, bishops and lesser priesthood. Second, president of the stake and high council; third and fourth, high priests' quorum; fifth elders quorum; sixth, washing and anointing room occupied by the sisters.

Hans C. and Peter O. Hanson were appointed to see to the fires, keep watch and guard the doors.

Every hundred have established one or more wagon shops; wheelrights, carpenters and cabinetmakers are nearly all foremen wagon makers, and many not mechanics are at work in every part of the town preparing timber for making wagons. The timber is cut and brought into the city green; hub, spoke, and felloe timber boiled in salt and water, and

Wagon Makers.

other parts kiln dried; shops are established at the Nauvoo House, Masonic Hall, and Arsenal, nearly every shop in town is employed in making wagons.

Teams are sent to all parts of the county to purchase iron; blacksmiths are at work night and day and all hands are busily engaged getting ready for our departure westward as soon as possible.

Very few sales of property are being made, the citizens of the country around instead of aiding us to Conditions in sell our property, are using their influence to Nauvoo. discourage sales and the authorities constantly haunt us with vexatious writs, efforts are making to bring us into collision with the authorities of the United States by means of vexatious writs from the federal courts. The brethren are doing their utmost to prepare amidst all the discouragements that surround us for a general exodus in the spring; but from the manner that our neighbors have kept their faith, it is very apparent that as soon as the strength of Israel is gone, that the remainder will be in danger of violence, from our cruel persecutors, the promises of governors, generals, judges, conventions of citizens, and mob leaders, and their hounds to the contrary notwithstanding; but we trust in God, we praise him that we have been thus far able to prepare his Temple for the ordinances of the priesthood, and we feel full of confidence that he will hear our prayers and deliver his unoffending people from the power of their enemies, and lead us to a land where we can enjoy peace for a season.

FOREIGN AFFAIRS

Elder Wilford Woodruff attended the Glasgow conference (Scotland). The branches comprising the conference were represented and contained 1181 members, including one high priest, 44 elders, 31 priests, 40 teachers and 30 deacons; sixty-eight were baptized since last conference.

Elder James Houston left Nauvoo, November 1,

1842, on a mission to preach the gospel in company with Elder Samuel Mulliner. They labored in Niagara county, New York, until the following summer, when Elder Houston, according to counsel, proceeded to Scotland, where he labored for about two years, mostly in the Glasgow conference; raising up a branch in Lanark. While on his mission he baptized 95 persons. He left Liverpool in charge of the company of saints that sailed on the *Oregon* in September, 1845, and returned to Nauvoo, November 15th.

Monday, December 1, 1845.—I met with several of the Twelve, the Temple Committee, and Trustees in the council chamber over the store.

Letters were read from J. B. Purcell,* Catholic bishop of Cincinnati, the Catholic bishop at Detroit, and other gentlemen, inquiring after the property and lands for sale in Nauvoo and vicinity.

Roman Catholic Effort to Purchase the Public Buildings at Nauvoo.

Elder Almon W. Babbitt made a report of his mission to St. Louis, Cincinnati and Chicago, relative to the disposition of property in Hancock county; and said the Catholics were making considerable exertions to have the members of their church purchase our property. They were very anxious to lease the Temple, but were not able to buy it. Mr. Quarters, the bishop at Chicago, has sent an agent who may probably enter into some arrangements for our property, he is expected tomorrow.

Brother Albert P. Rockwood was instructed to rent the upper stream mill for four months.

Bishop Miller answered a letter from Thomas H. Owen,† giving him an estimate of lands for sale in the several settlements in Hancock county under cultivation.

Tuesday, 2.—I received a letter from Messrs. Dun-

---

*This was Arch-Bishop Purcell who held a notable public debate with Alexander Campbell at Cincinnati in 1837, it was known as "The Battle of the Giants"! "Authority of the Catholic Church" was the subject of the debate.

†This was Thomas H. Owen the English Communist, temporarily in the United States to establish his system.

can and Co. of Bloomington, stating that a heavy firm in Philadelphia wished to know the condition and situation of our property, terms, etc., as they wished to buy, and for their ability to do so, referred us to Sheriff Backenstos and others; they proposed to pay specie for the whole, if a bargain were concluded.

Offer to Sell Nauvoo Property at Fifty Per Cent Valuation.

The council returned answer by letter that if their agent or agents would come here and examine the property, that we would sell the whole or any part of the city of Nauvoo, owned by our people, or the farms in the county, for fifty per cent under the valuation of like property, similarly situated in this country.

I spent the day in the Temple making preparations for the endowments.

Evening, Elders Heber C. Kimball, Orson Hyde, Parley P. Pratt, George A. Smith and I ordained Albert P. Rockwood, Benjamin L. Clapp and Jedediah M. Grant Presidents over the First Quorum of Seventies, filling vacancies which had been occasioned by the death of Daniel S. Miles, the apostacy of Josiah Butterfield, and the neglect of Roger Orton.

Vacancies in the First Council of the Seventy Filled.

Spent an hour in prayer.

Thursday, 4.—I was engaged with several of the Twelve fitting up the Temple preparatory to administering the ordinances of endowment.

Evening, the council met for prayer in the Temple.

Friday, 5.—Eight a. m., Brother Heber C. Kimball and I called on Dr. Richards who was sick, we proceeded to the Temple and were engaged in fitting up the upper rooms.

Sunday, 7.—I met with the Twelve and others in the Temple. We partook of the sacrament, exhorted each other and prayed.

The Lord's Sacrament in the Temple.

Monday, 8.—I have been actively engaged in the Temple since the painters finished, fitting up the apartments and preparing the rooms for administering endowments.

Tuesday, 9.—Forenoon, in the Temple.

Four p. m., Elders Heber C. Kimball, Orson Hyde, Parley P. Pratt, Willard Richards, John Taylor, George A. Smith, Amasa Lyman, Joseph L. Haywood, and I met at the Historian's Office with Father Tucker from Quincy and Father Hamilton from Springfield.

Father Tucker stated that Father Hamilton and himself had come here by direction of the bishop of Chicago, to see and inquire into the situation of the land and property for sale in and around Nauvoo.

Further Roman Catholic Inquiry into Purchase of Nauvoo Property.

I informed them that we would so reduce the value of the property as to make it an object for a society or speculators; and we wish to hand it over to the Catholics and so keep out those who want to have our property for nothing.

Evening, we wrote out propositions for the sale of our lands for the benefit of the Catholic deputation.

Wednesday, 10.—Nine a. m., I went to the Temple, weather fine, but cold.

I fitted up the curtains on the east windows, Brother Heber C. Kimball and wife, Sisters Parley P. Pratt and N. K. Whitney assisted me.

Eleven a. m., Messrs. Tucker and Hamilton, Catholics, were admitted into the Temple to an audience with the Quorum of the Twelve and a few other brethren.

Catholic Inspection of the Temple.

The propositions for sale of our lands were handed, by Brother Orson Hyde, to Father Tucker, who perused them, and handed them to Father Hamilton, his colleague. I gave him an explanation of the design of the rooms in the Temple, with which they seemed well satisfied.

Father Tucker said he thought it would be wisdom to publish our propositions in all the Catholic papers and lay the matter plainly before their people.

He should also think it advisable for the Catholic bishop to send a competent committee to ascertain the value of our property,

Hopeful Prospect of Catholic Purchase.

etc., etc.   At the same time they will use all their influence to effect a sale as speedily as possible.

Father Tucker thought they had men in St. Louis, New York and other cities, who could soon raise the amount we want, but the time is so very short he does not know whether it can be done so soon.

He asked if we would be willing to have our propositions published in their papers.

I answered that we would have no objections, providing it was understood that we reserved the right to sell when we had an opportunity.

Father Hamilton wished to ascertain upon what conditions they could obtain two of our public buildings, one for a school and one for a church.   They intended to write to the bishop, and wished to be able to supply him with some information on this subject.

I said I was well aware that there were many men in the Catholic Church who could furnish all the money we wanted immediately, but I supposed it was with them as it was with a Mr. Butler, a wealty banker, who, when asked, why he did not sign off more bills, replied it was a good deal of trouble to sign off bills!

Brigham Young's Comment on Proposed Catholic Purchase.

Perhaps it is too much trouble to dig their money out of their vaults, but I wished it distinctly understood that while we make liberal propositions to dispose of our property, we must have the means to help ourselves away.

I said I would like to add a note to our proposals before they are presented for publication, to this effect, that if a party agree to them, we will lease them the Temple for a period of from five to thirty-five years, at a reasonable price, the rent to be paid in finishing the unfinished parts of the Temple, the wall around the Temple block and the block west of the Temple, and keeping the Temple in repair.

The council agreed to the amendment, which was accordingly added to the proposals, and handed to Father Tucker.

Father Tucker gave much encouragement that an arrangement would speedily be entered into to accomplish the sale of our property; both of the gentlemen seemed highly pleased with the Temple and city.

Three p. m., Sisters Mary Ann Young, Vilate Kimball and Elizabeth Ann Whitney commenced administering the ordinances in the Temple [Dec. 10, 1845].

We consecrated oil.

ACQUITTAL OF SHERIFF BACKENSTOS FOR THE KILLING OF FRANK A. WORRELL

News has arrived that Sheriff Backenstos, who went to Peoria in charge of Henry W. Miller, coroner of Hancock county, and was tried before Judge Purple on the charge of the 'murder' of Frank A. Worrell, was acquitted. The moral atmosphere around the judge was so different, than when at Carthage, that in all his charges and rulings, he appeared like another judge, and as though he had never been afflicted with mobocratic mania.

The jury said if there had been no witnesses only on the part of the state, it would not have required more than two minutes to have made up their verdict. There are two of the mob witnesses in jail for perjury and Backenstos is gone to Springfield to request the governor to withdraw his troops.

At 3:45 p. m., we completed the arrangements of the east room, preparatory to giving endowments.

Completion of the Temple East Room for Giving Endowments.

The following persons were present on this occasion, *viz.*:—

Myself and wife, Mary Ann;
Heber C. Kimball and wife, Vilate;
Orson Hyde and Nancy Marinda;
Parley P. Pratt and Mary Ann;
John Taylor and Leonora;
George A. Smith and Bathsheba W.;
Willard Richards;
Amasa Lyman and Mariah Louisa;
John E. Page and Mary;

John Smith and Clarissa;
Mother Lucy Smith;
Newel K. Whitney and Elizabeth Ann;
George Miller and Mary Catharine;
William W. Phelps and Sally;
John M. Bernhisel;
Alpheus Cutler and Lois;
Levi Richards;
Reynolds Cahoon and Thirza;
William Clayton;
Lucien Woodworth and Phebe;
Orson Spencer and Catharine C.;
Agnes M. Smith;
Mercy R. Thompson;
Mary Smith.

The main room of the attic story is eighty-eight feet two inches long and twenty-eight feet eight inches wide. It is arched over, and the arch is divided into six spaces by cross beams to support the roof. There are six small rooms on each side about fourteen feet square. The last one on the east end on each side is a little smaller.

Attic Rooms of the Temple.

The first room on the south side beginning on the east is occupied by myself, the second by Elder Kimball, the third by Elders Orson Hyde, Parley P. Pratt and Orson Pratt; the fourth by John Taylor, George A. Smith, Amasa Lyman and John E. Page; the fifth by Joseph Young and Presidents of Seventies; the sixth, a preparation room.

On the north side, the first east room is for Bishop Whitney and the lesser priesthood, the second is for the high council, the third and fourth for President George Miller and the high priests' quorum, the fifth the elders' room, and the sixth the female preparation room.

Commencement of General Administering Temple Ordinances.

Four-twenty-five p. m., Elder Heber C. Kimball and I commenced administering the ordinances of endowment [Dec. 10, 1845].

Five o'clock, Isaac Morley and his wife

Lucy, Joseph Fielding, Joseph C. Kingsbury and Cornelius P. Lott came in.

Nine-thirty p. m., we assembled for prayers, Amasa Lyman was mouth.

We continued officiating in the Temple during the night until three-thirty a. m. of the 11th.

The following were administered to:

Willard Richards;
Heber C. Kimball and his wife, Vilate;
George A. Smith and Bathsheba W.;
Orson Hyde and Nancy Marinda;
John Smith and Clarissa;
Newel K. Whitney and Elizabeth Ann;
Brigham Young and Mary Ann;
William W. Phelps and Sally;
Parley P. Pratt and Mary Ann;
Amasa Lyman and Mariah Louisa;
George Miller and Mary Catharine;
John Taylor and Leonora;
Lucien Woodworth and Phebe;
John E. Page and Mary;
Joseph C. Kingsbury;
Mary Smith, widow of Hyrum;
Agnes Smith, widow of Don Carlos.

Thursday, 11.—Elder Heber C. Kimball and I went to Joseph Kingsbury's and ate breakfast and returned to the Temple.

Elder Orson Pratt returned from his eastern mission, bringing four hundred dollars worth of Allen's revolving six-shooting pistols (alias pepperboxes).

I officiated in the Temple with the brethren of the Twelve.   We administered the ordinances of endowment to:

Isaac Morley and his wife, Lucy;
Orson Spencer and Catharine C.;
Joseph Young;
Alpheus Cutler and Lois;
Reynolds Cahoon and Thirza;

William Clayton and Ruth;

Cornelius P. Lott and Permelia;

Mother Lucy Smith and Mercy R. Thompson.

At eight a. m., we assembled for prayer, Elder John
E. Page was mouth.   After which I called the Twelve
and bishops together and informed them that I had
received a letter from Brother Samuel Brannan, stating
that he had been at Washington and had learned that
the secretary of war and other members of the cabinet
were laying plans and were determined to prevent our
moving west: alleging that it is against the law for
an armed body of men to go from the United States
to any other government.

Extermination   They say it will not do to let the Mor-
Proposed.   mons go to California nor Oregon, neither
will it do to let them tarry in the states, and they must
be obliterated from the face of the earth.

We prayed that the Lord would defeat and frustrate
all the plans of our enemies, and inasmuch as they lay
plans to exterminate this people and destroy the priesthood from off the earth, that the curse of God may
come upon them, and all the evil which they design to
bring upon us, may befall themselves; and that the
Lord would preserve the lives of his servants and lead
us out of this ungodly nation in peace.

I said we should go out from this place in spite of
them all, and the brethren all felt that God would
deliver us from the grasp of this ungodly and mobocratic nation.

Brother Amasa Lyman and I tarried in the Temple
all night.

Friday, 12.—In company with my brethren of the
Twelve I officiated in the Temple until midnight.

Orson Pratt and his wife, Sarah Marinda, the First
Presidency of the Seventy and their wives and others
numbering in all twenty-eight males and twenty-seven
females received the ordinances of endowment.

Several tarried in the Temple all night.

Saturday, 13.—We continued officiating in the Temple; twenty-five males and twenty females were administered unto.

I drafted rules for the preservation of order in the House of the Lord.

Rules Drafted for Order in the Temple.

News arrived from Springfield that Lucien B. Adams, son of the late Judge Adams, has effected a complete revolution in the minds of the inhabitants of Springfield, so much so, that Judge Pope is convinced that Elder Turley is imprisoned through persecution and says he shall discharge him when he arrives at Springfield.

Courts of Springfield Modified Toward the Saints.

Sunday, 14.—The Twelve and others with our wives met in the attic story of the Temple.

After prayer and singing, Elders Isaac Morley and Charles C. Rich administered, and we partook of the sacrament.

I introduced the subject of establishing rules for the preservation of order in the House of the Lord which were agreed to and ordered to be printed.

Rules for the Establishment of Order for the House of the Lord.

* * *　　　　* * *　　　　* * *

There is too much covetousness in the church, and too much disposition amongst the brethren to seek after power and has been from the beginning, but this feeling is diminishing and the brethren begin to know better. In consequence of such feelings Joseph [Smith] left the people in the dark on many subjects of importance and they still remain in the dark. We have got to rid such principles from our hearts.

The Prophet Left the People Uninformed on Some Matters.

I referred to the manner in which the corner stones of this Temple were laid as published in the *Times and Seasons,* and said that the perfect order would have been for the presidency of the stake to lay the first or southeast corner; the high council the second or southwest corner; the bishops the northeast corner; but the high priests laid the southwest corner, though they had no right to do it.

Proper Order of Laying Temple Corner Stones.

I spoke of the brethren making objections to persons being permitted to receive the ordinances, and added, that when objections were made I should feel bound to determine whether the person making the objections was a responsible person, and if he is not, I should do as I pleased about listening to the objections; but if he was a responsible person I should listen to them.

To constitute a man responsible he must have the power and ability not only to save himself but to save others; but there are those who are not capable of saving themselves and will have to be saved by others.

When a man objects to another receiving the ordinances he becomes responsible to answer to God for that man's salvation; and who can tell but if he received the ordinances he would be saved, but if we refuse to give him the means he cannot be saved and we are responsible for it.

There is no law to prevent any man from obtaining all the blessings of the priesthood if he will walk according to the commandments, pay his tithes and seek after salvation, but he may deprive himself of them.

After much profitable instruction we united in prayer, Orson Hyde being mouth.

Meeting adjourned for one week.

Two p. m., many of those who had received their ordinances the past week met and received instructions from Elders Parley P. Pratt and William W. Phelps.

The Twelve met and read some letters, also an account of Sheriff Backenstos' travel from the *Peoria Register*.

We went down to the lower room and counseled on the arrangement of the pulpits.

I remained in the Temple all night.

Meeting in England. Elder Wilford Woodruff attended a special conference of the churches in the British Isles in the Hall of Science, Manchester.

10,956 members were represented; including 8 high priests, 392 elders, 590 priests, 311 teachers, and 188 deacons; 1570 were baptized since April last.

Monday, 15.—The ordinances of endowment were administered to sixty-four brethren and sisters.

The Twelve and others officiated.

Tuesday, 16.—I have been busy in the Temple dictating the order of business, appointing brethren to officiate in the various departments, and giving much instruction at different intervals; Elder Kimball assisted me. Sixty-nine brethren and sisters received their ordinances.

Wednesday, 17.—We continued our labors in the Temple, administered the ordinances of endowment to sixty-nine brethren and sisters.

Ten twenty-five p. m., eighteen persons assembled in my room and joined with me in prayer.

My son, Joseph A., remained with me in the Temple all night.

Letters were written to Stephen A. Douglas, M. C., J. P. Hoge, M. C., Wm. S. Marcy, Secretary of War, John Wentworth, M. C., and John Chapman in relation to our movement to the west, in consequence of learning that attempts were made to induce government to prevent our removal.

Thursday, 18.—Sixty-six persons were administered to in the Temple. I retired to bed about midnight.

In consequence of the great pressure of business during the past week, it had been decided to devote Saturday to the purpose of washing robes and garments used, but there being a general desire in the minds of all those officiating in the ordinances that the work should not cease, it was determined that the clothes should be washed during the night.

Friday, 19.—I appointed the following elders to officiate and labor in the Temple today:

Heber C. Kimball,
George A. Smith,
Joseph Young,

George Miller,
Phineas H. Young,
Lucius N. Scovil,

Aaron Johnson,	John Smith,
Wm. W. Phelps,	Jedediah M. Grant,
Hosea Stout,	John Scott,
Wm. Crosby,	Charles C. Rich,
A. O. Smoot,	Daniel Garn,
Erastus Snow,	John L. Butler,
Jesse D. Harmon,	John Brown,
Orson Hyde,	Alexander McRae,
Amasa Lyman,	Benj. L. Clapp,
Orson Pratt,	Franklin D. Richards.

7 p. m., I met with the Twelve in Elder Kimball's room for prayer; after which we counseled on the propriety of sending certain brethren to England.

Ninety-eight persons received ordinances.

I remained in the Temple.

Reading of Col. John Fremont's Works. *Saturday, 20.*—Beautiful morning. I dictated the arrangements for the day. Afterwards, with a few of the Twelve and others heard F. D. Richards read *Fremont's Journal*, giving an account of his travels to California.

We considered it prudent to devote today to cleaning and washing, and suspend operations in the Temple; but on account of the anxiety of the saints to receive their ordinances, the brethren and sisters volunteered to wash clothes every night. Ninety-five persons received their ordinances.

Sunday, 21.—According to appointment on Sunday last, a meeting was held in the Temple today of some of those who had received their ordinances.

Seventy-five persons were present.

Elder Heber C. Kimball presiding.

Sacrament Administered in tne Temple. The sacrament was administered by Father John Smith and Bishop George Miller. Elders George A. Smith and Heber C. Kimball preached, others made a few remarks confirming what had been said.

Elder John Taylor was mouth in prayer.

Meeting dismissed at 2:10 p. m.

Three p. m., many others who had been invited met
according to appointment.

Elders Amasa Lyman and Heber C. Kimball
preached.

At ten a. m., the seventies met in the Provision
Made for the
Seventy in the
Temple.
Music Hall. The thirty-second quorum of
seventies was organized; and arrangements
made to finish an upper room in the Temple for the
benefit of the seventies.

Monday, 22.—I stayed in the Temple last night
and early this morning gave direction for the arrangements of the day, assisted by George Miller,* as the
day was set apart more especially for the high priests.

One hundred and six persons received ordinances.

Tuesday, 23.—Early this morning the drying house
of Captain Charles C. Rich's Emigrating Co. No. 13
was burned to the ground, consuming $300.00 worth
of wagon timber.

The high council met in the Temple for prayer.

One-five p. m., Almon W. Babbitt came into the
Temple and informed me that there were United States
Authorities to
Arrest Brig-
ham Young.
some federal officers from Springfield accom-
panied by several of the state troops in the
city for the purpose of arresting some of the Twelve,
especially Amasa Lyman and myself.

It was soon reported that they were at the door of
the Temple and were intending to search it. George
D. Grant, my coachman, went below and drove my
carriage up to the door as if he was waiting for me to
come down.

William Miller put on my cap and Brother Kimball's cloak and went downstairs meeting the marshal
and his assistants at the door, as he was The Bogus
Brigham
Incident.
about getting into my carriage the marshal
arrested him, on a writ from the United
States court, charging him with counterfeiting the coin
of the United States. Miller told him there must be
some mistake about it, as he was not guilty of anything
of the kind, but the marshal insisted it was right.

*Brother Miller was president of the high priests.

Miller desired the marshal to go down to the Mansion where he could get counsel and ascertain if the proceedings were legal. On reaching the Mansion they went into a private room where Esq. Edmonds examined the writ and pronounced it legal. Miller gave Edmonds the name of four witnesses for subpoena for him, and asked the marshal to remain until morning; he consented, but soon got uneasy and said he must go to Carthage. Miller then inquired if he would wait three quarters of an hour until he could get his witnesses, but in fifteen minutes he said he must go, and would wait no longer. Miller got into his carriage, Esq. Edmonds rode with the marshal's guard and they started for Carthage, Miller protesting there was some mistake about it, for he certainly was not guilty of any such things as were charged in the writ: on the way to Carthage the marshal was very social, and remarked that the people had got quite a joke upon him for letting Turley give him the dodge. As they approached Carthage the troops began to whoop and holloa and went into town in high glee, performing the journey which was eighteen miles in two hours.

The marshal put up at Hamilton's Tavern, and the rumor soon spread through the town that Brigham Young was in the custody of the marshal at Hamilton's. Among others, George W. Thatcher, county commissioner's clerk, who was well acquainted with Miller came into the tavern to see me. The marshal at his request took Miller into a private room. After a little conversation one of the guards came in and the marshal went out. The marshal soon returned and said to Mr. Miller, 'I am informed you are not Mr. Young;' 'Ah!' exclaimed Miller, 'then if I should prove not to be Mr. Young, it would be a worse joke on you than the Turley affair,' he replied, 'I'll be damned if it won't.'

The marshal asked Miller if his name was Young, he answered, 'I never told you my name was Young, did I?' 'No,' replied the marshal, 'but one of my men professed to be acquainted with Mr. Young, and pointed you out to me to be him.' William Backenstos was called in and he told them William Miller was not Brigham Young. Another man came, and said he could swear Miller was not Brigham Young. The marshal said he was sorry, and asked Miller his name, he replied, 'it is William Miller'.

The marshal left the room and soon returned accompanied by Edmonds who was laughing heartily at him. Edmonds inquired if he had anything more to do with 'Mr. Young'. The marshal replied that he did not know that he had anything further to do with Mr. Miller.

Eighty-seven persons received the ordinances.

Seven-thirty p. m., I met with the Twelve in prayer, and thanked the Lord for deliverance from the snares of our enemies. *Prayer and Retirement from Enemies.*

Eight-twenty, I left the Temple disguised and shortly after Brothers Heber C. Kimball, Parley P. Pratt, George A. Smith and Amasa Lyman left, to elude the vexatious writs of our persecutors.

Wednesday, 24.—All the Twelve have been absent from the Temple the greater part of this day except Orson Pratt. One hundred twenty-two persons received the ordinances.

At 11:20, Elder Heber C. Kimball and I returned to the Temple and remained all night.

William Miller remained last night at Carthage at Jacob B. Backenstos'. Miller said he could not sleep being interrupted by *Aftermath of the "Bogus Brigham" Incident.* Edmonds' continued roars of laughter at the marshal's discomfiture.

Miller saw two of the marshal's guards, one of whom threatened his life. Miller came in with the stage, the driver told him that the officers said it would be like searching for a needle in a hay mow now, to undertake to find Brigham Young in Nauvoo.

Thursday, 25.—12:15 p. m., George D. Grant brought word that the United States marshal is in the city again. Elder Kimball sent a message to him by Elder Grant, and at 1:15 Elder Kimball and I left the Temple.

Six p. m., the high council met for prayer in room No. 4; the high priests met in room No. 8.

At twenty minutes before six, Amasa Lyman, George A. Smith, Orson Hyde, and John Taylor went into the Temple, at 6:10 Parley P. Pratt and Orson Pratt, and at 6:18 Brother Heber C. Kimball and I went in.

The Twelve met in my room for counsel and prayer. After considerable conversation about the western country we united in prayer: George A. Smith was mouth.

One hundred seven persons received their ordinances. The business of the day closed at twenty minutes past ten o'clock, and notice was given that no more washings and anointings would be attended to at present. Brother Kimball and I, with some few others, remained in the Temple all night.

Friday, 26.—Elders Heber C. Kimball, Orson Pratt and I were present in the Temple this morning and a few of those who had been officiating: I called them together in the east room about 11:30 a. m., and told them there would be no business done today and that they were all dismissed except the two Brothers Hanson, and three brethren for officers.

Instructions of Brigham Young on Temple Procedure.

I said we shall have no more anointing at present, and if the brethren do not get anything more than they have already received, they have got all they have worked for in building this house; and if there is any more to be received it is because the Lord is merciful and gracious.

The high council and high priests will meet together once a day as usual for prayer.

Two hundred sixty-eight high priests were reported to have received their endowments.

I further remarked, that when we began again we should pay no respect to quorums. Every man that comes in, is washed and anointed by good men and it makes no difference. Every man that gets his endowments, whether he is a high priest or seventy may go into any part of the world and build up the kingdom if he has the keys. We have been ordained to the Melchizedek priesthood which is the highest order of the priesthood, and it has many branches or appendages.

I said, my feelings were to rest a few days and let the Temple rest, and when we commenced work again I would make a selection of hands who will remain and officiate daily. No persons will be allowed to come in unless they are invited, and I shall feel insulted if they remain here. I felt it impressed upon me to rest a few days and make these regulations, and as our oil is done we cannot do much anyway.

Six p. m., the Twelve, the high council, the high priests and the Presidents of Seventies met for prayer, each quorum in their own apartment.

Sheriff Backenstos informed me that the United States deputy marshal was in town with writs for the Twelve and Brother George Miller.

Eight p. m., Elder Kimball and I left the Temple.

Saturday, 27.—This morning was a very pleasant one, moderately cold, the sun shining clear and bright in the heavens.

Orson Pratt was the only one of the Twelve present in the Temple.

Ten-fifteen a. m., the United States Deputy Marshal Roberts, went to the Temple in company with Almon W. Babbitt and searched for the Twelve and others. He was freely admitted to every part of the Temple, to which he desired access; he went into the tower, on to the roof, into the attic story and while viewing the city from the tower he expressed his astonishment at its magnificence and extent and said considering the unfavorable circumstances with which the people had been surrounded it seemed almost impossible that so much

A U. S. Deputy Marshal *et al* Visit the Temple.

should have been accomplished. He passed through the various departments into the east room where he very intently examined the portraits, and made inquiries as to whose they were.

On entering the attic hall he was requested to take off his boots and uncover his head, to which he complied; after remaining about half an hour he departed.

About two p. m., the marshal returned accompanied by a gentleman whom he introduced as from New Orleans, and Sheriff Backenstos. They visited the middle room and the tower and departed after about half an hour.

Letter of Emma Smith to *New York Sun.* Dr. Bernhisel went to the Temple about one p. m. and borrowed the *New York Sun* of December 9, 1845, which contains a letter said to have been written by Emma Smith, to the editor.

Lewis Robbins is cleaning and putting in order the washing rooms and furniture, Peter Hanson is translating the *Book of Mormon* into the Danish language. Elisha Averett is doorkeeper, John L. Butler, fireman, David Candland and L. R. Foster, clerks. Orson

Orson Pratt makes Astronomical Observations from the Temple. Pratt has been engaged in making astronomical calculations. From several observations he makes the latitude of Nauvoo 40°35'48" north.

In the evening I went to the Temple and met with Brothers Heber C. Kimball, Parley P. Pratt, Orson Pratt, Amasa Lyman and George A. Smith.

We retired to my room for prayer at six-forty-five. Elder John Taylor came in and joined us. Elder Heber C. Kimball was mouth. Elder Hyde arrived after prayers, and informed us he could not come at the hour as the officers were watching his house.

Nauvoo High Council in Prayer. The high council met and prayed for me and all the Twelve, that we might be preserved from our enemies that the faithful saints may be permitted to receive all the ordinances of the Lord's House—that the Lord would bless the quorums, and for several sick persons.

The high priests met in rooms Nos. 6 and 8 and prayed that those persons who are seeking our hurt may find themselves hedged up—for deliverance from bondage—means to remove, that I and all the quorums in the church may be sustained—for the sick—Elders Woodruff, Grouard [in the Pacific Islands] and all the missionaries on the globe, etc. High Priests in Prayer.

The First Presidency of the Seventies met for prayer. The Presidency of the Seventy in Prayer.

After prayers a general conversation ensued, in which the Twelve and bishops, J. M. Grant, and several others took part. The visit of the marshal and the emigration to California were the prominent topics. Elder Parley P. Pratt read from Hastings' account of California.

Nine-thirty-five the Twelve met in council and selected the names of persons who would be called upon to labor in the Temple the ensuing week. The names of Other Temple Workers Given.

The list is as follows, *viz.*:

Joseph Young,
Abraham O. Smoot,
Wm. Crosby,
Henry Harriman,
J. M. Grant,
Erastus Snow,
Orson Spencer,
Willard Snow,

Lorenzo Snow,
Lewis Robbins,
Benj. L. Clapp,
Charles C. Rich,
William Snow,
Ezra T. Benson,
Franklin D. Richards,
Elisha Averett,

John L. Butler.

The above in addition to those of the Twelve who will be present are considered sufficient to perform the work.

Elders Heber C. Kimball, Amasa Lyman, George A. Smith, Newel K. Whitney, and a few others remained in the Temple all night.

Sunday, 28.—About two hundred of the brethren and sisters met at ten-thirty a. m. in the attic story of the Temple, some of the A Sacramental Meeting Held in the Temple.

side rooms were filled, and the curtains withdrawn.

After singing and prayer, I addressed the meeting.

The sacrament was administered. Elder Kimball made a few remarks. After prayer the meeting was dismissed by benediction from Elder Orson Hyde.

High Council and High Priests in Prayer.

Six p. m., the high council and the high priests met for prayer.

Elder Kimball and I remained in the Temple.

Monday, 29.—Elder Kimball and I assisted by our wives, and the laborers in the Temple, cleaned up and arranged the furniture in the rooms.

Dragoons from Carthage at Nauvoo.

Four dragoons came in from Carthage and searched Nauvoo for hogs, said to have been stolen from Mr. Hibbard.

Elders George A. Smith and Amasa Lyman revised history.

Elder Parley P. Pratt read *Fremont's Journal* to Brother Kimball and me.

Report of Mission in Society Islands.

Three-fifteen p. m., Elder Noah Rogers just arrived from his mission to the Society Islands, in the South Pacific Ocean; he was accompanied by Mr. Tower, a fellow passenger on board ship, whom he baptized. He brings a favorable report of the progress of the gospel on those Islands. He came on foot from Paducah on the Ohio river.

1000 Received Ordinances to this Date.

Three-forty, a company numbering twelve commenced receiving their ordinances; this makes 1000 who have received the ordinances.

Six p. m., the high council, the high priests and the seventies met for prayer.

The Twelve in Prayer.

The Twelve met for prayer. We prayed for deliverance from our enemies, and that we might be spared to give the faithful saints their endowments, Orson Hyde being mouth.

I spent an hour reading, and with Brothers Kimball and Lyman remained in the Temple all night.

Tuesday, 30.—At eight-ten a. m., commenced to

administer the ordinances. Elders Heber C. Kimball, Parley P. Pratt, George A. Smith, Amasa Lyman, Joseph Young and myself consecrated oil.

Eleven-thirty, Almon W. Babbitt reported that the marshal had left for Springfield, and there would probably be no more danger of writs for the present.

Departure of the Marshal from Nauvoo.

Eighty-eight persons received ordinances.

Elder Parley P. Pratt has been engaged part of the time in forming a schedule for a Pioneer Company of 1000 men to precede the body of emigrants, to find a proper location and put in seed early in the summer.

Pioneer Company of 1000 for the West.

The labors of the day having been brought to a close at so early an hour, *viz.*: eight-thirty, it was thought proper to have a little season of recreation, accordingly Brother Hanson was invited to produce his violin, which he did, and played several lively airs accompanied by Elisha Averett on his flute, among others some very good lively dancing tunes. This was too much for the gravity of Brother Joseph Young who indulged in dancing a hornpipe, and was soon joined by several others, and before the dance was over several French fours were indulged in. The first was opened by myself with Sister Whitney and Elder Heber C. Kimball and partner. The spirit of dancing increased until the whole floor was covered with dancers, and while we danced before the Lord, we shook the dust from off our feet as a testimony against this nation.

Recreation in the Temple.

After the dancing had continued about an hour, several excellent songs were sung, in which several of the brethren and sisters joined. The 'Upper California' was sung by Erastus Snow, after which I called upon Sister Whitney who stood up and invoking the gift of tongues, sang a beautiful song of Zion in tongues. The interpretation was given by her husband, Bishop Whitney, and me, it related to our efforts to build this house to the priv-

Other forms of Entertainment—Singing in Tongues.

ilege we now have of meeting in it, our departure shortly to the country of the Lamanites, their rejoicing when they hear the gospel and of the ingathering of Israel.

I spoke in a foreign tongue; likewise, Brother Kimball.

After a little conversation of a general nature I closed the exercises of the evening by prayer.

Six p. m., the high council, and two companies of high priests met for prayer.

Wednesday, December 31, 1845.—Elder Heber C. Kimball and I superintended the operations in the

Readings of
the "West"
and Selection
of Locations
for the Saints. Temple, examined maps with reference to selecting a location for the saints west of the Rocky Mountains, and reading various works written by travelers in those regions; also made selections of names of persons to be invited to receive their endowments.

Eighty-four persons were received into the Temple.

Six p. m., the high council, high priests, and seventies met in their respective rooms and prayed.

CHURCH PUBLICATIONS FOR THE PERIOD

During the year 1845 there was published the *Times and Seasons,* fortnightly, octavo, edited by John Taylor, Nauvoo, Illinois.

The *Nauvoo Neighbor,* weekly, folio, edited by John Taylor, Nauvoo, Illinois.

The *Millennial Star,* fortnightly, octavo, edited by Wilford Woodruff and Thomas Ward, Liverpool.

The *Prophet,* weekly, folio, edited by Samuel Brannan, New York, which ended May 24th and was succeeded by

The *New York Messenger,* July 25th, quarto, edited by Parley P. and Orson Pratt.

Proclamation of the Twelve to the Kings of the World, pamphlet, 8 vo. 16 pages, written by Parley P. Pratt, and published by Wilford Woodruff, Liverpool.

Speech of Elder Orson Hyde, delivered at Nauvoo upon the course and conduct of Sidney Rigdon.

The *Voice of Truth,* containing some of the public writings, and a synopsis of a sermon of President Joseph Smith, as reported by Thomas Bullock, Nauvoo.

Account of the Murder of Generals Joseph and Hyrum Smith, by William M. Daniels, Nauvoo.

A Dialogue Between Joseph Smith and the Devil, which first appeared in the *New York Herald,* by Elder Parley P. Pratt.

Prophetic Almanac, by Orson Pratt, New York."

CHAPTER XXXVIII

LARGE NUMBER OF PERSONS ENDOWED IN THE TEMPLE—JANUARY AND FEBRUARY, 1846—CATHOLIC CHURCH EFFORTS TO PURCHASE L. D. S. NAUVOO PROPERTY—FRIENDLY ATTITUDE OF JUDGE JOSIAH LAMBORN—REPEATED HOSTILE EFFORTS OF STATE OFFICIALS—DEPARTURE OF THE TWELVE HASTENED BY FALSE REPORTS CIRCULATED BY GOVERNOR FORD

"*Thursday, January* 1, 1846.—At an early hour, Elder Heber C. Kimball and I went to the Temple. The plasterers have commenced to plaster the arched ceiling of the lower hall, the floor is laid, the framework of the pulpits and seats for the choir and band are put up; and the work of finishing the room for dedication progresses rapidly.

6:30 p. m., the high priests met and prayed, eighty-nine persons received ordinances.

10:20 p. m., after finishing the labors of the day, the company assembled in the large room in the attic story and united in prayer with Elder Heber C. Kimball, thanking God for his great mercy and goodness to us in granting this opportunity of meeting together in the House of the Lord, asking him that he would continue to bless us, that he would bless President Brigham Young with health and wisdom, that he might be able to lead and direct this people; and that the same blessings might be extended to all his brethren of the Twelve and all the saints; and that God would bless our wives and give unto them strength of body that they might live and administer to the servants of God, that they might see three score years and ten, and behold the kingdom of God established in the earth; and that we might be enabled to continue in Nauvoo in peace, until all the faithful saints

Ordinance Work in the Temple—Prayer.

had received their endowments; and that when the time to leave here should arrive that we might be able to sell our possessions and obtain those things that we need to enable us to go away in comfort. Also, that God would bless our children, and all that pertains to us.

Friday, 2.—Sixty-four persons received ordinances.

At 6 p. m., the high council, high priests, and seventies met in their several apartments for prayer.

This morning Elder Heber C. Kimball related the following dream: Last evening, before retiring to bed he asked God to enlighten his mind with regard to the work of endowment; while sleeping he beheld a large field of corn that was fully ripe, he and a number of others were commanded to take baskets and pick off the corn with all possible speed, for there would soon be a storm that would hinder the gathering of the harvest. The hands engaged in gathering the harvest, were heedless and unconcerned and did not haste, as they were commanded; but he and the man he assisted had a much larger basket than the rest, and picked with all their might of the largest ears of the field, they once in a while would pick an ear that had a long tail on each end and but a few grains scattering over the center of the cob, which were very light.
<!-- margin note: Heber C. Kimball's Dream. -->

The interpretation of the dream is, that the field represented the church, the good corn represented good saints, the light corn represented the light and indifferent saints, the laborers are those appointed to officiate in the Temple, the storm is trouble that is near upon us, and requires an immediate united exertion of all engaged in giving the endowments to the saints, or else we will not get through before we will be obliged to flee for our lives.
<!-- margin note: Interpretation. -->

Elder Kimball having invited Brothers William Pitt, William Clayton, J. F. Hutchinson and James Smithies [musicians], they performed several very beautiful pieces of music.

After a short time spent in dancing, Elder Orson

Hyde delivered a short address and requested the company present to unite with him in prayer.

I addressed the brethren at length, alluding to the privileges we enjoy—of the order of administering endowments: that the way to grow and thrive was to serve the Lord in all we did, exhorted the brethren to remember their covenants and not to speak evil of each other, and related some of the efforts made to arrest me and persecute the saints. If Joseph Smith had been living, we should have already been in some other country, and we would go where we would be 'the old settlers', and build larger Temples than this.

The High Privileges of the Saints.

Saturday, 3.—One hundred and fourteen persons received their ordinances.

At 5 p. m., several companies of high priests met for prayer.

At 7, the seventies met for prayer.

I had a chill today, accompanied by fever, and felt unable to attend to business. I remained in the Temple all night.

Sunday, 4.—No public meeting was held in the Temple this day, on account of the floor being insufficient to support a large congregation.

I attended a council of the Twelve in the Temple. David Candland was appointed a mission to England.

A letter was received from Samuel Brannan, New York, also one from Pittsburg, signed Wm. W. Salt; both of which were answered.

The different quorums met in their respective rooms for prayer, at the usual hour.

Sheriff Backenstos received the following:

LETTER OF GOVERNOR FORD TO SHERIFF BACKENSTOS

'Springfield, December 29, 1845.

Dear Sir: In the matter of the late attempt to make arrests by the deputy marshal in Nauvoo, you will understand that that was entirely an affair of the U. S. government, in which this state took no official part. A demand was made on me by the marshal for troops which was promptly refused. I am not yet advised that the troops under the command of Major Warren took any part. If they did they had no orders from me, and I cannot think that they did take any part in assisting the deputy marshal for that would have been contrary to the settled and solemn understanding between Major Warren and myself. I had heard some rumor of the matter before I received your letter, from which I inferred that some of the men may have gone with the deputy marshal as a mere personal guard.

You know that the impression has become pretty general that no officer can go with safety unattended to Nauvoo to arrest any of their principal men. The idea is, that an officer thus exposed would be liable to be murdered. This may be all idle supposition, yet it is sufficient to account for the men going with the marshal without supposing they went to assist him.

This indictment in the U. S. court against the leading Mormons puts a new face on the matter. It will bring them and the United States for the first time into collision. It is impossible for me to guess, with any certainty, as to the course of Mr. Polk in the matter, but I would think it likely that he will order up a regiment or two of the regular army, and perhaps call on me for the militia, in which event I will be compelled to order them as you know.

I hope that the administration will not act in the matter this winter. If the Mormons remain in the state a strong force will be ordered to Nauvoo by the secretary of war, to remain there until arrests can be made. This you know is all guess work, as I have no such official relations with the government at Washington as would enable me to know it certainly. I also think that it is very likely that the government at Washington will interfere to prevent the Mormons from going west of the Rocky Mountains. Many intelligent persons sincerely believe that they will join the British if they go there, and be more trouble than ever, and I think that this consideration is likely to influence the government.

If it should be the case that government will order and station a large force at Nauvoo, and they can keep their soldiers there with as little expense as anywherelse, and shall interfere to prevent their emigration, it will put the Mormon leaders who are indicted in a worse box than they have yet been.*

They will have to separate from their people and become fugitives in the earth, or submit to a trial on their indictments. These are all

---

*The statement in this letter about the probability of the United States government being likely to intercept the departure of the church leaders from Nauvoo is a most diabolical and self-conceived trick on the part of Governor Ford. For in his *History of Illinois*, (p. 413), after confessing that he purposely tried to mislead the church authorities to a belief of this kind he says:

"With a view to hasten their removal they were made to believe that the president would order the regular army to Nauvoo as soon as the navigation opened in the spring. This had its intended effect; the Twelve with about two thousand of their followers, immediately crossed the Mississippi before the breaking up of the ice."

mere speculations of mine, but it will be for you and them to calculate whether the results guessed at, are not probable.

I am most respectfully

Your Obedient Servant,

[Signed]   THOMAS FORD.'

Should Governor Ford's speculations and suppositions in relation to U. S. troops prove correct, and
the government send a regular force to arrest us, we will
run no risk of being murdered by them as our leaders
have been; and as to fearing a trial before the courts
it is all gammon for our danger consists only in being
held still by the authorities while mobs massacre us as
Governor Ford held Joseph and Hyrum Smith while
they were butchered.

Monday, 5.—My health being better I was ready
for duty at an early hour.   Spent the morning in hearing letters and newspapers [read], and giving directions
as to the business of the day.

8:45 a. m., commenced washing and anointing [i. e.
in the Temple].

Seventeen bottles of oil were consecrated.

One hundred four persons received their endowments.

The high council, two companies of high priests, and
the seventies met in their respective rooms for prayer.

9 p. m., the labors of the day being over, Brothers
Hanson and E. Averett played on the violin and flute
Dancing in
the Temple. and enlivened the spirits of the saints present: some embraced the opportunity and
danced to the lively strains of music.

Elder Heber C. Kimball and I returned home about
midnight.

The county commissioners' court met at Carthage.
Messrs. Coulson and Perkins, being in attendance, and
Bills
Protested. while allowing some bills for provisions and
provender furnished to Backenstos' *posse*—
during the late difficulties—Mr. Thatcher, the clerk,
stated that an injunction had been served on him,
which had been issued by the clerk of the circuit court,

forbidding all proceedings in relation to bills presented for the support of said *posse,* and this injunction he was determined to obey, and would not, therefore, place the order just made on record. The commissioners refused to recognize the legality of the injunction, on the ground that there was no provision in the statutes of the state to authorize such an interference with the county commissioners' court.

Tuesday, 6.—Seventeen bottles of oil were consecrated.

Ninety persons received ordinances.

6 p. m., Elder H. C. Kimball and I with our wives attended a party at Elder John Taylor's.

Three companies of high priests, the high council, and the seventies met for prayer in their respective rooms in the Temple.

Several musicians were present in the evening, some of the brethren danced.

I returned to the Temple about 10 p. m. and took part in the exercises. Brothers Erastus Snow and Levi W. Hancock sang hymns.

Wednesday, 7.—This morning there was an immense crowd at the reception room waiting for admission. The brethren brought all kinds of provisions for the use of those who are attending on the ordinances of the Lord's House.

A letter was received this morning from Father Tucker, informing us that the Catholic bishop could not raise money enough to purchase our property, but would either purchase or rent one of our public buildings, but would not insure it against fire or mobs.

Catholic Proposal to Rent Public Buildings in Nauvoo.

One hundred twenty-one persons received ordinances.

The supply of provisions brought in today has been very abundant, and much has been sent away to those families that are destitute.

The high council and three companies of high priests met for prayer.

The Presidents of Seventies met in council, in relation to keeping order in the Temple. The Twelve delegated to them the government of the Temple, while the ordinances were being administered to their quorums.

Service of Seventies in the Temple.

This afternoon, the new altar was used for the first time, and four individuals and their wives were sealed. The altar is about two and one-half feet high and two and one-half feet long and about one foot wide, rising from a platform about 8 or 9 inches high and extending out on all sides about a foot, forming a convenient place to kneel upon. The top of the altar and the platform for kneeling upon are covered with cushions of scarlet damask cloth; the sides of the upright part or body of the altar are covered with white linen.

A Temple Sealing Altar Erected.

The Twelve and presiding bishops with their wives were present at the dedication of the altar this afternoon.

* * *

Thursday, 8.—* * * Eighty-one persons received ordinances.

* * *.

Friday, 9.—One hundred and five persons received ordinances in the Temple. I attended to ordinances at the altar. The several quorums met for prayer.

I observed to the brethren that it was my wish that all dancing and merriment should cease, lest the brethren and sisters be carried away by vanity; and that the name of the Deity should be held in reverence, with all the due deference that belongeth to an infinite being of his character.

Dancing in the Temple Discontinued.

I received a letter from Samuel J. Hastings, of Boston, proposing to ship passengers, merchandise and freight to the Pacific coast for the saints.

Saturday, 10.—* * * One hundred and eighteen

received ordinances.   I received a letter from Elder Wilford Woodruff, Liverpool, informing me that he had made arrangements to send his family home by New Orleans and return himself by Boston, calling in Maine and Connecticut, to bring his kindred to Nauvoo to start with the church westward in their exodus from the United States.

Announcement of Elder Woodruff's Return from England.

Sunday, 11.—The General Council met and arranged to make an early start west.

Monday, 12.—One hundred and forty-three persons received their endowments in the Temple.   I officiated at the altar. Such has been the anxiety manifested by the saints to receive the ordinances [of the Temple], and such the anxiety on our part to administer to them, that I have given myself up entirely to the work of the Lord in the Temple night and day, not taking more than four hours sleep, upon an average, per day, and going home but once a week.

Anxious to Receive Temple Ordinances.

Elder Heber C. Kimball and the others of the Twelve Apostles were in constant attendance but in consequence of close application some of them had to leave the Temple to rest and recruit their health.

Tuesday, 13.—A council was held in the Temple.

The captains of fifties and tens made reports of the number in their respective companies, who were prepared to start west immediately, should the persecutions of our enemies compel us to do so: one hundred and forty horses and seventy wagons were reported ready for immediate service.

* * *

Thursday, 15.—I received a letter from George B. Wallace containing information that Samuel Brannan had chartered a ship to take a company of saints to San Francisco at twelve hundred dollars per month.

Elder Wallace had proposed to the brethren to purchase a ship, by shares of fifty dollars each to emigrate the saints to the Pacific coast: he gave an account of the progress of the work in the east.

Friday, 16.—A company of about forty saints including a portion of Elder Woodruff's family, consisting of his wife, Phebe, and two children, left Liverpool, on board of the ship *Liverpool,* for New Orleans. Elder Woodruff forwarded his family, he having to go by way of New York to Maine and Connecticut for his parents and daughter.

* * *

Saturday, 17.—Thirty-six persons received ordinances in the Temple.

I received the following [from Attorney-General Josiah Lamborn]:

JOSIAH LAMBORN PROPOSES TO WRITE HISTORY OF THE "MORMONS"

'Springfield, Illinois.

(Confidential)   17th Jan., 1846.

Dear Sir: I have been thinking of preparing for publication of a brief History of the Mormons and their difficulties in the different states where they have resided. My object would be to present to the public, the political, religious, and sectional motives, which have led to the persecutions of the Mormons. A well arranged statement of all these matters in a popular style of literature would have a tendency to correct public opinion and do much good.

I have lived in this state for many years, and have been intimately acquainted with the policy of office holders and office seekers, and without any particular intimacy with the Mormons themselves, I have become familiar with their peculiar condition.

A history of this kind would come with a good grace from one who has never had any personal, political or religious connection with your people. I presume that you are aware of the fact, that my feelings are as liberal and friendly as the feelings of any public man in the state. At no time have I failed to correct misrepresentations against you; and in some instances I have done so at the peril of losing favor and influence with men in high official stations.

I could prepare a work of the kind proposed and sell the copyright in New York, for five thousand dollars.

My object in addressing myself to you is to ascertain whether the Mormons would afford me any facilities in getting correct information, etc. If I should engage in anything of the kind I would wish to visit Nauvoo and have personal intercourse with some of the intelligent and respectable citizens for four or five weeks. Nothing could be done without some aid from your citizens, and if they will lend me their aid I will endeavor to make manifest my gratitude in a becoming manner. You can consult in confidence, with your friends upon this proposition, and let me know at an early day your views, etc.

Respectfully yours,

[Signed] J. LAMBORN.'

I attended a concert in the Music Hall; while my coachman, Brother George D. Grant, was taking his last passenger home, my horses fell through a bridge on Parley Street; I was in bed when I heard of it, but immediately arose, put on my clothes and hastened to the rescue of my team; on arriving I found they had lain nearly an hour between the timbers of the bridge, totally unable to extricate themselves from their distressing situation, and notwithstanding they were dumb animals they were sensible of their condition. We soon tore the timbers away and let down the horses one at a time, and rolling them over placed them where they could help themselves. (The depth of the gully was about six feet.) I returned home and washed the horses all over with spirits, using about half a gallon of whiskey in bathing them, which prevented stiffness and colds, so that in a few days they were able for service again.

Sunday, 18.—A meeting of the captains of Emigrating Companies was held in the attic story of the Temple, to ascertain the number ready and willing to start should necessity compel our instant removal, being aware that evil is intended towards us, and that our safety alone will depend upon our departure from this place, before our enemies shall intercept and prevent our going.

A general interest in the movement was manifested by the whole council, every man felt willing to yield to the circumstances that surround us, and let their property be used for the purpose of accomplishing the removal and salvation of this people.

We selected Almon W. Babbitt, Joseph L. Heywood, John S. Fullmer, Henry W. Miller and John M. Bernhisel, a committee to dispose of our property and effects and aid such in emigrating as may have to go, it was agreed that they should have letters of attorney to authorize them to act for us legally.

They were instructed to enclose the Nauvoo House and complete the first story of the Temple.

Meetings for prayer in the several rooms.

Monday, 19.—I administered at the altar all day with the exception of thirty minutes in which I took some refreshments.

Evening, I attended a concert in the Music Hall.

Tuesday, 20.—One hundred and ninety-five persons received ordinances in the Temple.

Public prejudice being so strong against us, and the excitement becoming alarming we determined to continue the administration of the ordinances of endowment night and day.

The high council published the following:

A CIRCULAR OF THE HIGH COUNCIL TO THE CHURCH

'To the Members of the Church of Jesus Christ of Latter-day Saints, and to all Whom it May Concern—Greeting:

Beloved Brethren and Friends: We the members of the high council of the church by the voice of all her authorities, have unitedly and unanimously agreed, and embrace this opportunity to inform you; that we intend to send out into the western country from this place, sometime in March, a Company of Pioneers, consisting mostly of young, hardy men, with some families. These are destined to be furnished with an ample outfit; taking with them a printing press, farming utensils of all kinds, with mill irons and bolting cloths, seeds of all kinds, grain, etc.

The object of this early move is to put in a spring crop, to build houses, and to prepare for the reception of families who will start so soon as grass shall be sufficiently grown to sustain teams and stock.

Our Pioneers are instructed to proceed west until they find a good place to make a crop, in some good valley in the neighborhood of the Rocky Mountains, where they will infringe upon no one, and not be likely to be infringed upon. Here we will make a resting place, until we can determine a place for a permanent location. In the event of the president's [U. S.] recommendation to build block houses and stockade forts on the route to Oregon, becoming a law, we have encouragements of having that work to do; and under our peculiar circumstances, we can do it with less expense to the government than any other people.

We also further declare for the satisfaction of some who have concluded that our grievances have alienated us from our country, that our patriotism has not been overcome by fire—by sword—by daylight, nor by midnight assassinations, which we have endured; neither have they alienated us from the institutions of our country.

Should hostilities arise between the government of the United States and any other power, in relation to the right of possessing the territory of Oregon, we are on hand to sustain the claims of the United

States' government to that country. It is geographically ours; and of right, no foreign power should hold dominion there; and if our services are required to prevent it, those services will be cheerfully rendered according to our ability. We feel the injuries that we have sustained, and are not insensible of the wrongs we have suffered; still we are Americans, and should our country be invaded we hope to do, at least, as much as did the 'conscientious' Quaker who took his passage on board a merchant ship and was attacked by pirates. The pirates boarded the merchantman and one of the enemies' men fell into the water between the two vessels, but seized a rope that hung over and was pulling himself up on board the merchantman. The conscientious Quaker saw this, and though he did not like to fight, he took his jack-knife and quickly moved to the scene, saying to the pirate, 'If thee wants that piece of rope I will help thee to it.' He cut the rope asunder—the pirate fell—and a watery grave was his resting place.

Much of our property will be left in the hands of competent agents for sale at a low rate, for teams, for goods and for cash. The funds arising from the sale of property will be applied to the removal of families from time to time as fast as consistent, and it now remains to be proven whether those of our families and friends who are necessarily left behind for a season to obtain an outfit, through the sale of property shall be mobbed, burnt, and driven away by force. Does any American want the honor of doing it? or will Amercians suffer such acts to be done, and the disgrace of them to rest on their character under existing circumstances? If they will, let the world know it. But we do not believe they will.

We agreed to leave the country for the sake of peace, upon the condition that no more vexatious prosecutions be instituted against us. In good faith we have labored to fulfill this engagement. Governor Ford has also done his duty to further our wishes in this respect. But there are some who are unwilling that we should have an existence anywhere. But our destinies are in the hands of God, and so also is their's.

We venture to say that our brethren have made no counterfeit money: and if any miller has received fifteen hundred dollars base coin in a week, from us, let him testify. If any land agent of the general government has received wagonloads of base coin from us in payment for lands, let him say so. Or if he has received any at all from us, let him tell it. Those witnesses against us have spun a long yarn: but if our brethren had never used an influence against them to break them up, and to cause them to leave our city, after having satisfied themselves that they were engaged in the very business of which they accuse us, their revenge might never have been roused to father upon us their own illegitimate and bogus productions.

We have never tied a black strap around any person's neck, neither have we cut their bowels out, nor fed any to the 'catfish'. The systematic order of stealing of which these grave witnesses speak, must certainly be original with them. Such a plan could never originate with any person, except someone who wished to fan the flames of death and destruction around us. The very dregs of malice and revenge are mingled in the statements of those witnesses alluded to by the *Sangamon Journal*. We should think that every man of sense might see this. In fact, many editors do see it, and they have our thanks for speaking of it.

We have now stated our feelings, our wishes, and our intentions; and by them we are willing to abide; and such editors as are willing that we should live and not die; and have a being on the earth while heaven is pleased to lengthen out our days, are respectfully requested to publish this article. And men who wish to buy property very cheap, to benefit themselves and are willing to benefit us, are invited to call and look; and our prayer shall ever be that justice and judgment— mercy and truth may be exalted, not only in our own land, but throughout the world, and the will of God be done on earth as it is done in heaven.

Done in council [stake high council] at the city of Nauvoo, on the 20th day of January, 1846.

[Signed] SAMUEL BENT   JAMES ALLRED
          GEORGE W. HARRIS   WM. HUNTINGTON
          HENRY G. SHERWOOD   ALPHEUS CUTLER
          NEWEL KNIGHT   LEWIS D. WILSON
          EZRA T. BENSON   DAVID FULLMER
          THOMAS GROVER   AARON JOHNSON.'

Wednesday, 21.—Two hundred and eight persons received ordinances. I received a letter from Hon. J. H. Ralston, Quincy, concerning our removal, etc., he says:

> 'I have long known many of the Mormons, who I have always thought good citizens, let them
>
> Admonition to "Suffer and Forgive!"   now show that they can suffer and forgive, and that amidst oppression their patriotism grows the brighter.'

Thursday, 22.—One hundred and ninety-eight persons received ordinances in the Temple. Elder Heber C. Kimball received a letter from Dr. Alphonzo Young of the 21st inst. in which he says:

> 'I have learned that the mob have been making preparations in Iowa to harass the brethren. Yesterday they got up a war dance in
>
> Warning of Hostilities in Iowa.   Keokuk and those participating in it were dressed in Indian garb, and as the report is widely circulated that the Twelve will soon leave for the west, I have no doubt
>
> but that the meeting was got up to concoct schemes to take the Twelve, when they cross the Mississippi or soon after.'

Friday, 23.—One hundred and twenty-eight persons received ordinances in the Temple.   Elder Woodruff and Joseph A. Stratton sailed from Liverpool on board the packet ship *Ashburton* for New York.

Saturday, 24.—One hundred and fifty-one persons received ordinances in the Temple.   I attended a general meeting of the official members of the church held in the second story of the Temple, for the purpose of arranging the business affairs of the church prior to our exit from this place.

The meeting being organized previous to my arrival Elder Orson Pratt was appointed chairman.

I explained to the brethren the object of appointing trustees, and informed them that the trustees would act in concert with Bishops Whitney and Miller while they remained here; and that when the Twelve left the bishops would accompany them, and that the trustees now appointed would carry on the finishing of the Temple and the Nauvoo House, also dispose of our property, fit out the saints and send them westward.   It is wisdom to take this course that we may have efficient men to act for and in behalf of the church and people.   I want Bishops Whitney and Miller here while we are here, and when we go, they will go with us.

Trustees Appointed to Take Charge of Property at Nauvoo.

We intend to start a company of young men and some few families perhaps within a few weeks.   This company will travel until they can find a good location beyond the settlements, and there stop and put in a summer crop, that we may have something to subsist upon, and a portion of us remain there until we can make further discoveries.

We are forced to this policy by those who are in authority [i. e. in the state].   I find no fault with the Constitution or laws of our country, they are good enough.   It is the abuse of those laws which I despise, and which God, good men and angels abhor.

I hope we will find a place, where no self-righteous neighbors can say that we are obnoxious to them; I exhort you brethren not to be self-important. We have covenanted to remove the poor that are worthy, and this we intend to do, God being our helper.

Let us walk humbly before the Lord, be upright and sustain yourselves and realize that we are engaged in a great and important movement. If any want to go with us that are not members of the church bid them welcome; for I look upon every man that is a true republican as bone of my bone and flesh of my flesh; and if any wish to follow Sidney Rigdon or J. J. Strang I say let them go; we will cut them off from the church, and let them take their own course for salvation.

President Favors Liberty.

I know where the power of the priesthood lies and I know that the enemy of all righteousness seeks our downfall, but God is our preserver.

A set of bogus-makers who recently commenced operations in this city, who are determined to counterfeit coin here by wagonloads and make it pass upon the community as land office money; [they] are determined to be revenged upon us, because we would not permit them to pursue their wicked business in Nauvoo, they have scattered through the country circulating their bogus money and spreading lies and every species of falsehood, saying that we are engaged in bogus-making in order thereby to conceal their crimes, and screen themselves from observation and punishment, and at the same time be avenged upon us for not consenting to the establishment of their bogus mints at Nauvoo.

Of Bogus Makers.

Nevertheless, we may have to suffer repeated wrongs in consequence of those falsehoods that are and which will be circulated about us; but my faith is that God will rule the elements, and the Prince and power of the air will be stayed, and the Lord will fight our battles, as in the days of Moses; and we will see the deliverance brought to pass. Although, there may be bloodshed frequently, still this must needs be that the scriptures may be fulfilled.

It is but a small matter for us to lay down our lives if we are prepared for the change; when we take our exit from this world we go into the society of disembodied spirits, and there become one of those who await the resurrection of the body; if humility and faithfulness has characterized our lives, our condition will be much better than the present. This nation is fearful that we will turn the world upside down and accomplish wonderful things in the land; our elders have confounded the wise men if they have not converted them. The nation are afraid that we will convert the savages of the forest; we will teach them and all with whom we may have intercourse, and further we will yet bring salvation to this nation if they will cease their hostilities against us, and repent of their sins. The Lord has said he would fight our battles, and if this nation still continues to be actuated towards us with a persecuting spirit, vengeance shall come from the Lord upon them, until they shall be utterly wasted; but I intend to preach and do all the good that I can.

Unimportance of Death to the Saints.

When the time comes to start westward we will continue to gather, until Israel is gathered; let there be no feelings about who shall go first; those who go first will lay a foundation for those who shall come after, and none will be neglected in their time.

I have one request to make of all the saints that expect to emigrate with us, that they be subject to their leaders, with their property and means, and if this is done I can say there never will be a lack in the church. If any man can say that he has been wronged out of his money by the bishops, let him speak and it shall be restored to him again; but I am aware it is not so. Keep your money in circulation and it will enable you to do good and you will be blessed in so doing; retain your money when the poor around you are crying for bread and it will prove a curse to you. Be honorable in all your

Justice in Financial Affairs Assured.

dealings, prompt and punctual to pay all your debts and restore confidence, let promptness and punctuality be the standard with you and the God of peace will pour out blessings upon you that there shall not be room enough to receive them.

We intend to finish the Temple and the Nauvoo House, as far as putting on the roof and putting in the windows are concerned, and we shall drop all political operations and church government, and by so doing we may preserve our public buildings from the torch. I propose that all the saints lay down their property to be used in building the Temple, the Nauvoo House and helping the poor away, such as must go in the first company.

I nominated Almon W. Babbitt, Joseph L. Heywood, and John S. Fullmer, trustees for the building The Committee of the Temple and Henry W. Miller and of Trustees. John M. Bernhisel, trustees or committee for the building of the Nauvoo House, which nominations were seconded and carried without a dissenting voice.

Two p. m., on motion, the meeting adjourned, after which I ascended the stairs—called at the dining room and partook of some refreshment, then repaired to room No. 1 where I continued administering at the altar until midnight.

Sunday, 25.—I attended to ordinances in the Temple.

Monday, 26.—Nine a. m., I went to the Temple and commenced the ordinances in the different departments which were set apart for the purpose; the washing and anointing was suspended until tomorrow.

Tuesday, 27.—One hundred and twenty-six persons received ordinances.

Elders Heber C. Kimball, Orson Hyde, Parley P. The "Higher Pratt, Orson Pratt, Amasa Lyman, and I Ordinances" of officiated in the higher ordinances. Elders the Temple. George A. Smith and Willard Richards were absent, being sick.

Sheriff Backenstos has returned from Increasing Unfriendliness of Governor Ford. Springfield, and says, that Governor Ford has turned against us, and that Major Warren is making calculations to prevent our going away.

I received a letter from Josiah Lamborn, Esq., Springfield, stating that Governor Ford was decidedly in favor of General J. J. Hardin's policy, which is, that of suspending all civil offices, the collection of taxes, and placing the county under martial law.

I officiated at the altar until 10 p. m. and remained in the Temple all night.

Wednesday, 28.—One hundred and seventy-two persons received ordinances in the Temple.

Nine-thirty p. m., the labors of the day closed. I remained in the Temple.

Thursday, 29.—I continued giving endowments in the Temple in connection with my brethren of the Twelve and others. One hundred and thirty-three persons received ordinances.

Quite a number of the governor's troops are prowling around our city; I am informed that they are seeking to arrest some of the leading men of the church.

This evening I read a letter from S. Brannan in which he said he had ascertained from Amos Kendall, the late postmaster-general, that government More Rumors of "Interception". intended to intercept our movements by stationing strong forces in our way to take from us all firearms on the pretense that we were going to join another nation.

Brannan said this jealousy originated from Arlington Bennett's letters in relation to our movements. We ask God our heavenly Father to exert his power in our deliverance that we may be preserved to establish truth upon all the face of the earth.

Friday, 30.—One hundred and seventy-two persons received the ordinances of endowment.

Nine a. m., the [wind] vane was put upon the tower of the Temple.

The weather is stormy, yet not cold. At ten a. m., I entered the Temple where I labored until evening.

Saturday, 31.—Two hundred and thirty-three persons received ordinances.

About noon, Brother Amasa Lyman came into the Temple being quite feeble; Elder H. C. Kimball administered to him.

The labors in the Temple came to a close at 10:39 p. m. I called the house to order and Elder Charles C. Rich prayed and we retired to rest.

Sunday, February 1, 1846.—Public meeting in the Sunday Service second story of the Temple. Elder Orson in the Temple. Pratt and myself addressed the meeting.

After meeting, I returned to the attic and partook of some refreshments.

Elder Heber C. Kimball, Amasa Lyman, and I administered at the altar.

Monday, 2.—Two hundred and thirty-four persons received ordinances.

Ten a. m., the Twelve, Trustees and a few others met in council, to ascertain the feelings of the brethren that were expecting to start westward. We Early Depart- agreed that it was imperatively necessary to ure of the Twelve from start as soon as possible. I counseled the Nauvoo Imperative. brethren to procure boats and hold them in readiness to convey our wagons and teams over the river, and let everything for the journey be in readiness, that when a family is called to go, everything necessary may be put into the wagon within four hours, at least, for if we are here many days, our way will be hedged up. Our enemies have resolved to intercept us whenever we start. I should like to push on as far as possible before they are aware of our movements. In order to have this counsel circulated, I sent messengers to notify the captains of hundreds and fifties to meet at 4 p. m. at Father Cutlers'.

At four o'clock, I met with the captains of hundreds and fifties, and laid my counsel before them, to which they all consented, and dispersed to carry it into execution.

I received letters from England and the eastern states.

At sundown, I returned to the Temple and continued there until 9 p. m.   Before leaving I gave instructions to my clerks not to stop recording until the records of the endowments were finished.

Elder H. C. Kimball and I went to Willard Richards' office, where we remained in council with him.   In the course of our council we walked out into the garden, and examined his grove of chestnut trees, and his wife, Jennetta's grave, and after returning to the office made inquiries of the Lord as to our circumstances and the circumstances of the saints and received satisfactory answers.   Retired about 1 a. m.

At the Home of Willard Richards.

Tuesday, 3.—Notwithstanding that I had announced that we would not attend to the administration of the ordinances, the House of the Lord was thronged all day, the anxiety being so great to receive, as if the brethren would have us stay here and continue the endowments until our way would be hedged up, and our enemies would intercept us.   But I informed the brethren that this was not wise, and that we should build more Temples, and have further opportunities to receive the blessings of the Lord, as soon as the saints were prepared to receive them.   In this Temple we have been abundantly rewarded, if we receive no more.   I also informed the brethren that I was going to get my wagons started and be off.   I walked some distance from the Temple supposing the crowd would disperse, but on returning I found the house filled to overflowing.

Great Anxiety of the Saints to Receive Endowments.

Looking upon the multitude and knowing their anxiety, as they were thirsting and hungering for the word, we continued at work diligently in the House of the Lord.

Two hundred and ninety-five persons received ordinances.

Brother Player and two others altering Jennetta

Grave of Jennetta Richards Opened. Richards' grave. I stayed at home until 6 p. m. I went to the Temple and returned again in an hour, busy preparing for my journey to the west.

Jennetta's coffin was opened, and the whole family looked at the corpse, which was but little decayed.

Wednesday, 4.—I continued loading up my wagons, preparatory to starting west.

Elder G. D. Watt received his letter of recommendation to preach the gospel in England.

Brother Player and others completed Jennetta's grave placing the inscription stone across her breast, one stone below, and another above, for a covering of the whole. It was first covered with a plank. A line passing ten feet south of the house, in a range with the west side of the building, thence west at a right angle twenty feet, thence descend at a right angle about three feet, and it will reach about the center of the vault containing the coffin.

Friday, 6.—Five hundred and twelve persons received the first ordinances of endowment in the Temple.

Bishop George Miller and family crossed the Mississippi river. They had six wagons.

Saturday, 7.—According to G. A. Smith's Journal upwards of six hundred received the ordinances [i. e. of the Temple]: One hundred and twenty-six of which were reported in the Seventies Record.

Sunday, 8.—I met with the Council of the Twelve in the southeast corner room of the attic of the Temple.

Prayer for the Nauvoo. Temple. We knelt around the altar, and dedicated the building to the Most High. We asked his blessing upon our intended move to the west; also asked him to enable us some day to finish the Temple, and dedicate it to him, and we would leave it in his hands to do as he pleased; and to preserve the building as a monument to Joseph Smith. We asked the Lord to accept the labors of his servants in this land. We then left the Temple.

I addressed the saints in the grove and informed them that the company going to the west would start this week across the river.

John Smith, president of the stake, and family crossed the river, accompanied by his clerk, Albert Carrington, and family.

Monday, 9.—A detachment of the governor's troops came into the city and apprehended a man named Samuel Smith, who soon escaped.

Elder George A. Smith sent his family across the river.

Three-thirty p. m., the roof of the Temple was discovered to be on fire. An alarm was immediately given, when the brethren marched steadily to its rescue. I saw the flames from a distance, but it was out of my power to get there in time Roof of the Temple on Fire. to do any good towards putting out the fire, and I said if it is the will of the Lord that the Temple be burned, instead of being defiled by the Gentiles, Amen to it.

I went to the Temple as soon as I could, after the fire had been extinguished, the brethren gave a loud shout of Hosannah, while standing on the deck roof.

Willard Richards called on the brethren to bring out all their buckets, to fill them with water, and pass them on. Lines inside were formed, and the buckets passed in quick succession. The fire raged near half an hour. It was caused by the stovepipe being overheated, drying the clothing in the upper room. It burned from the west stovepipe from the ridge to the railing, about sixteen feet north and south, and about ten feet east and west on the north side. The shingles on the north were broken in several places.

By the advice of President H. C. Kimball the brethren dispersed.

Several of the troops went to the Temple and attempted to enter, but were prevented by the brethren at the door.

At the same time that the Temple was on fire a

number of brethren were crossing the river in a flatboat, when in their rear a man and two boys
were in a skiff in a sinking condition, on
account of being overloaded and the unskil-
fulness of the helmsman. They hailed to the flatboat,
which soon turned, and rendered them assistance. As
soon as they got the three on board the flatboat, a
filthy wicked man squirted some tobacco juice into the
eyes of one of the oxen attached to Thomas Grover's
wagon, which immediately plunged into the river,
dragging another ox with him, and as he was going
overboard he tore off one of the sideboards which
caused the water to flow into the flatboat, and as
they approached the shore the boat sank to the bottom,
before all the men could leap off. Several of the brethren were picked up in an exhausted condition. Two
oxen were drowned and a few things floated away and
were lost. The wagon was drawn out of the river with
its contents damaged.

A River
Disaster
Incident.

The crossing of the river was superintended by the
police, under the direction of Hosea Stout. They
gathered several flatboats, some old lighters, and a
number of skiffs, forming altogether quite a fleet, and
were at work night and day, crossing the saints.

The undersigned wrote as follows:

JOHN E. PAGE OF THE COUNCIL OF THE TWELVE DISFELLOWSHIPED

'Nauvoo, Feb. 9, 1846.

To the Saints of God.

Dear Brethren and Sisters: We take this opportunity to say to you
that we have no fellowship with Elder John E. Page, in consequence
of his murmuring disposition, and choosing to absent himself from
our councils, and then saying that he is made a servant and slave of by
his quorum, and has had no privileges in the Temple, when the plain
truth is, he has chosen to stand aside from us, and because we would
let him do so, he has murmured about it. He has been on the back-
ground and in the shade ever since he failed to fulfill his mission to
Jerusalem in company with Elder Hyde.

Now, beloved brethren, you are not bound to look to him as one
of the Twelve Apostles, for he has yielded himself up to temptation,
and he cannot resist the spirit of apostasy which inspired him to find
fault with the organization of the church.

We, therefore, your brethren in solemn council, being grieved at his murmurings and dissension, and also at his yielding himself up to temptation willingly and without cause, have withdrawn the hand of fellowship from him until he comes to us and gives satisfaction for his dissension; and the saints are released from all covenants and obligations to abide his counsel.

Done in council the day and date above written.

[Signed]   BRIGHAM YOUNG, President,
HEBER C. KIMBALL,
PARLEY P. PRATT,
GEORGE A. SMITH,
ORSON PRATT,
JOHN TAYLOR,
WILLARD RICHARDS.

Orson Hyde, Clerk.' "

CHAPTER XXXIX

DEPARTURE OF BRIGHAM YOUNG FROM NAUVOO—
PROPOSITION OF "A. G. BENSON & CO."—PROPOSED
CONTRACT—PUBLIC MEETING IN THE TEMPLE—
MISSISSIPPI BRIDGED BY ICE—LIMITED NUMBER WHO
CROSSED ON THE ICE WITH TEAMS AND FAMILIES—
PETITION TO THE GOVERNOR OF IOWA—REFLECTIONS
ON COMMENCEMENT OF EXODUS FROM NAUVOO

"*Tuesday, February* 10, 1846.—Dr. Richards had a
very comfortable chat with Elder Noah Rogers who
had just returned from the Society Islands. Elder
Rogers related an account of Wm. Law and others
attempting to take the life of the Prophet Joseph.

THE SENIOR PRESIDENT OF THE FIRST COUNCIL OF THE SEVENTY APPOINTED PRESIDENT OF THE CHURCH AT NAUVOO

Joseph Young was appointed to preside over the
church during the stay of the saints in Nauvoo and
received his letter of appointment from the Quorum of
the Twelve.

Wednesday, 11.—President Joseph Young met in
the Temple with a company of saints for prayer, and
organized companies for prayer to meet every night.

Thursday, 12.—The Twelve Apostles making preparations to start on their journey westward.

Twelve brethren met in the Temple and prayed in
two companies. Elders Ransom Shepherd and Joseph
Young were mouth in prayer.

Friday, 13.—Two companies met for prayer in the
House of the Lord this evening, and prayed for the
preservation of the Twelve, and that they might have
wisdom to guide the saints in the paths of peace and
safety; for the healing of the sick, etc.

Saturday, 14.—Eleven of the brethren met for prayer in two companies.

Sunday, 15.—I crossed the river with my family accompanied by W. Richards and family and George A. Smith. We traveled on four miles, when President Young Departs from Nauvoo. we came to the bluff. I would not go on until I saw all the teams up. I helped them up the hill with my own hands. At dusk started on, and reached Sugar Creek about 8 p. m., having traveled nine miles. The roads were very bad. * * *

Monday, 16.—I was very busy in organizing the camp on Sugar Creek, Ambrosia township, Lee county, Iowa territory, where there was plenty of timber and water.

Ten a. m., I walked up the valley with Amasa Lyman and Willard Richards where we united in prayer, and I read to them a communication received two days previously, then returned to camp and continued the organization, acting the part of a father to everybody.

The night was clear and cold. Two companies met this evening in the Temple and prayed.

Tuesday, 17.—Nine-fifty a. m., all the brethren of the camp assembled near the bridge, when I arose in a wagon and cried with a loud voice—'Attention! the whole Camp of Israel'. I proceeded to explain the cause of delay of the Explanation of Delay of Movements. camp, which was, in short, that Bishop Whitney and Elders H. C. Kimball and Wm. Clayton were not ready, or were waiting to secure and bring with them church property needed in the camp. Some of the brethren have been here nearly two weeks, and if all had come on according to counsel, I should have been here sooner, if I had come without a shirt to my back.

I wish the brethren to stop running to Nauvoo, hunting, fishing, roasting their shins, idling away their time, and fix nosebaskets for their horses, Instructions on Camp Deportment. and save their corn, and fix comfortable places for their wives and children to ride, and never borrow without asking leave, and be sure and return what was borrowed, lest your brother be vexed with you and in his anger curse you, and then you would be cursed according to the power of the priesthood that brother possesses, and evil will come upon you. That all dogs in the camp should be killed, if the owners would not tie them up; and any man who would keep a horse in camp, that had the horse distemper, ought to forfeit all his horses. [This because horse distemper was rife in the camp and contagious.]

We will have no laws we cannot keep, but we will have order in the camp. If any want to live in peace when we have left this, they must toe the mark.

I then called upon all who wanted to go with the camp, to raise their right hands, and all hands were up.

Camp
Commissary
Appointed. I said we must wait here until we get the artillery, canvas, and public property; that the brethren must build a pen for corn and hay. George W. Harris was appointed commissary. That all spare men were for pioneers, guards, watchmen, and that all men of families must be organized into companies of tens, fifties, and hundreds. Wm. Clayton would be general clerk of the camp.

I requested the brethren to report all matters of history which might arise, to Willard Richards, historian.

At eleven o'clock, I returned to my tent and commenced organizing my division of the camp, consisting of four companies of tens, including the historian, his family, and teams.

Elder Heber C. Kimball arrived in camp at the same hour, and at half past one he and I dined on bean porridge in George D. Grant's tent.

Two-thirty, accompanied by Elders Heber C. Kimball, Orson Hyde, Orson Pratt, John Taylor, George A. Smith, and Willard Richards. Villainous
Proposition of
Amos Kendall
"A. G. Benson
and Co." I went up the valley east of the camp about half a mile and counseled. A letter from

Samuel Brannan and a copy of an agreement between Brannan and Benson were read.

Amos Kendall, of Kentucky, who was postmaster-general from May, 1835, till May, 1840, A. G. Benson and others represented to Samuel Brannan that unless the leaders of the church would sign an agreement with them, to which the president of the United States was a silent party, the government would not permit the Latter-day Saints to proceed on their journey westward. This agreement requires the Latter-day Saints to transfer to 'A. G. Benson and Company' the odd number of all the land and town lots they may acquire in the country where they may settle, and in case they refuse to sign said agreement, the president would issue a proclamation that it was the intention of the Latter-day Saints to take sides with other nations against the United States, and order them to be disarmed and dispersed. Brannan becoming fully satisfied that this was the secret intention of the government, and that the president was a principal party, signed it.

LETTER OF SAMUEL BRANNAN ON "A. G. BENSON AND CO."

'New York, Jan. 12, 1846.

Brother Young: I have written you three letters of late from Boston, Washington and New York, and I fear they have been intercepted on the way and I have thought it prudent to direct this to some obscure individual that it may reach [you] in safety; I have received positive information that it is the intention of the government to disarm you after you have taken up your line of march in the spring, on the ground of the law of nations, or the treaty existing between the United States and Mexico, 'That an armed *posse* of men shall not be allowed to invade the territory of a foreign nation.'

Amos Kendall was in the city last week, and positively declared that that was the intention of the government, and I thought it my duty to let you know that you might be on your guard. I declare to all that you are not going to California but Oregon, and that my information is official. Kendall has also learned that we have chartered the ship *Brooklyn* and that Mormons are going out in her, and it is thought that she will be searched for arms, and if found taken from us, and if not, an order will be sent to Commodore Stockton on the Pacific to search our vessel before we land.

Kendall will be in the city next Thursday again, and then an effort will be made to bring about a reconciliation. I will make you acquainted with the result before I leave. My company now numbers about one hundred and seventy-five. I chartered the whole ship, put her in the market and have already obtained one thousand dollars worth of freight for the Sandwich Islands, and a good prospect for more. I now have it in my power to learn every movement of the government in relation to us, which I shall make you acquainted with from time to time. God is at work in the east and so is the devil, but Moses' rod will be too hard for him. I feel my weakness and inability and desire your blessing and prayers that I may be successful. My cares and labors weigh me down day and night, but I trust in God that I shall soon have a happy deliverance.

All the saints in the east are praying and crying for deliverance; but I must now close by subscribing myself, your brother in the everlasting covenant.

[Signed]   SAMUEL BRANNAN.'

FURTHER REPORT OF SAMUEL BRANNAN

'New York, Jan. 26, 1846.

Dear Brother Young: I haste to lay before your honorable body the result of my movements since I wrote you last, which was from this city, stating some of my discoveries in relation to the contemplated movements of the general government, in opposition to our removal.

I had an interview with Amos Kendall in company with Mr. Benson, which resulted in a compromise, the conditions of which you will learn by reading the contract, between them and us, which I shall forward by this mail. I shall also leave a copy of the same with Elder Appleby, who was present when it was signed. Kendall is now our friend and will use his influence in our behalf in connection with twenty-five of the most prominent demagogues of the country. You will be permitted to pass out of the states unmolested. Their counsel is to go well armed, but keep them well secreted from the rabble.

I shall select the most suitable spot on the Bay of San Francisco for the location of a commercial city.

When I sail, which will be next Saturday at 1 o'clock, I shall hoist a flag with Oregon on it. Immediately on the reception of this letter you must write to Messrs. A. G. Benson [and Co.] and let them know whether you are willing to coincide with the contract I have made for our deliverance. I am aware that it is a covenant with death, but we know that God is able to break it, and will do it, the children of Israel from Egypt had to make covenants for their safety and leave it for God to break them, and the Prophet has said 'as it was then so shall it be in the last days.' And I have been led by a remarkable train of circumstances to say, amen—and I feel and hope you will do the same. Mr. Benson thinks the Twelve should leave and get out of the country first and avoid being arrested if it is a possible thing, but if you are arrested you will find a staunch friend in him, and you will find friends, and that a host, to deliver you from their hands—if any of you are arrested, don't be tried west of the Allegheny Mountains. In the east you will find friends that you little think of. It is the prayer of the saints in the east night and day for your safety and it is mine first in the morning and the last in the evening. I must now bring my letter to a close. Mr. Benson's address is No. 39 South Street —and the sooner you can give him an answer the better it will be for us. He will spend one month in Washington to sustain you—and he will do it, no mistake. But everything must be kept as silent as death on our part—names of the parties in particular. I now commit this sheet to the post praying that Israel's God may prevent it from falling into the hands of wicked men. You will hear from me again on the day of sailing if it is the Lord's will. Amen.

Yours truly,

A friend and brother in God's Kingdom,

[Signed]　SAMUEL BRANNAN.'

'New York, Jan. 27th.

Brother Young: Your letter confirming the contract I have made, which I directed you to address to A. G. Benson, must be written to me, and on the outside addressed to A. G. Benson and all will go well.

Yours very respectfully in haste,

[Signed]　S. BRANNAN.'

The following is a copy of a contract entered into between A. G. Benson of New York for Amos Kendall and others of one part, and Samuel Brannan of the other, done at the city of New York, previous to the ship *Brooklyn* sailing for California.

"CONTRACT" BETWEEN "A. G. BENSON AND CO." AND SAMUEL BRANNAN

'*Whereas,* the Latter-day Saints generally known under the name of Mormons, though devotedly attached to the principles on which the government of the United States and of the several states are founded, have become satisfied that owing to the prejudices against them which designing men have created in the minds of the great mass of the community, who do not appreciate their character, nor understand their designs, they cannot, under the jurisdiction of any of the present states, enjoy the privileges and security which their constitutions and laws promise to all sects and creeds.

And whereas, they have resolved to seek for liberty and security beyond the jurisdiction of the states, and under the fostering care of the United States, within their territories, not doubting that in becoming a nucleus on the shores of the Pacific, around which a new state shall grow up, constituted of a people, who, from their more intimate knowledge of them will be free from those prejudices, which now drive them into exile, thereby affording them peace and security, the only boons they ask at the hands of man, and

Whereas, it is their earnest desire to depart in peace, and reach their future homes, without that molestation on their pilgrimage which the government of the United States might, under a misapprehension as to their designs, feel themselves called upon to offer; and *whereas,* A. G. Benson states that he has it in his power to correct any misrepresentations which may be made to the president of United States, and prevent any authorized interference with them on their journey, and also to extend to them facilities for emigration, especially by sea, and afford them great commercial facilities and advantages at their new homes; *wherefore,*

It is covenanted and agreed between A. G. Benson aforesaid, on behalf of himself and such as he may hereafter associate with him on the one part, and Samuel Brannan, for and in behalf of the Latter-day Saints, by their principal men, duly authorized on the other part, that the said _____ shall take the necessary steps to guard the said Latter-day Saints against the effects of misapprehension, and prevent interference with them, by the officers or agents of the United States, on their journey westward, and shall, as far as in his power, facilitate trade with them in their new settlement, and promote emigration, to strengthen them there; and on the part of the said _____ for and on behalf of the Latter-day Saints aforesaid, it is covenanted and agreed that, in case the said saints shall be enabled to reach their new homes without molestation from the government of the United States, and they or any of them shall acquire lands from the said United States or from any other source, then one-half of the said lands shall belong and be conveyed to the said Benson, and those whom by written contract, he may have associated with him, his and their heirs and assigns, said lands if not surveyed to be held in common until a survey shall be made when they shall be *ipso facto* divided by alternate sections, the odd numbers belonging to the said Latter-day Saints, and the even numbers belonging to the said Benson and his associates; but if surveyed they shall be divided by sections, half sections, quarter sections, or otherwise, so as to carry into effect this agreement in its true nature and intent; and if the said saints or any of them, or the said Brannan or any of his associates, assigns or heirs shall within ten years, lay off and establish any city or cities, town or towns on the lands acquired by them or any of them, each alternate lot in said cities and towns, shall belong and be conveyed to the said _____ and his associates and assigns as hereinbefore stipulated by the said Brannan, that the said saints shall exert all their lawful authority and influence to prevent the imposition of any tax on the vacant lands held by said _____, his associates and assigns, so long as they use due diligence to settle the same, or any higher tax upon vacant city and town lots held by him and them, than shall be imposed on vacant lots held by resident citizens.

And it is further stipulated and agreed by the said Brannan in behalf of said Latter-day Saints, that they shall not in any manner on their journey, or after their arrival in the west, violate the laws or Constitution of the United States, it being hereby solemnly declared by him, that their dearest object, and most earnest desire is to enjoy for themselves, their wives, children and neighbors, of whatever religion or political faith, the protection which that Constitution and those laws promise to all men of whatever creed.

Witness our hands and seals at the city of New York on the . . . . . . day of January, 1846.

[Signed] SAMUEL BRANNAN, A. G. BENSON.
Witness: W. I. APPLEBY.'

'This is only a copy of the original which I have filled out. It is no gammon but will be carried through if you say, amen—it was drawn up by Kendall's own hand—but no person must be known but Mr. Benson.'

Samuel Brannan urged upon the council the necessity of signing the document.

The council considered the subject, and concluded that as our trust was in God and that we looked to him for protection, we would not sign any such unjust and oppressive agreement.

This was a plan of political demagogues to rob the Latter-day Saints of millions and compel them to submit to it, by threats of federal bayonets.

This evening was severely cold.

Thirty elders met in the Temple for prayer in two companies.

Wednesday, 18.—I called the brethren together and instructed the captains of hundreds to raise money in their respective companies and send for cloth for tent ends and wagon covers; and informed the Pioneer Company that it would be their duty to prepare roads, look out camp grounds, dig wells, when necessary, and ascertain where hay and corn could be purchased for the camp; that if the brethren could not bring their minds to perfect order, they had better leave the camp and I would have no feelings against them; that after dark no man must leave the camp without the countersign, nor approach the guard abruptly; that every family must call on the Lord night and morning at every tent or wagon, and

Instructions to the "Pioneer Company."

we shall have no confidence in the man who does not; that the police would be night and day guard; that every captain of ten would keep one man on watch every night; that Benjamin F. Johnson be authorized to receive and preserve for the owners all the lost property found; and that when I wanted to see the brethren together, a white flag should be hoisted, and that when the captains are wanted together a blue or colored flag should be raised; the captains of hundreds were instructed to form their companies in circles, without the circle surrounding the stand; Captain Hosea Stout formed the police; Captain Stephen Markham the Pioneers.

Elder Parley P. Pratt called out the companies of the Twelve. Captain Wm. Pitt called out the musicians. Captains George Miller, Shadrach Roundy, Charles C. Rich, Charles Shumway, Peter Haws, Samuel Bent, and Daniel Spencer called out their respective companies.

Those not organized were instructed to join the Pioneers, and all to organize into companies of tens.

I told the brethren they were the best set of fellows in the world, still there was a great chance for improvement: I blessed them in the name of the Lord.

Twelve-twenty p. m., Lyman O. Littlefield called on me in company with Dr. Clayton Tiffin of St. Louis, who was baptized last evening at Nauvoo, and wanted counsel.

I counseled Dr. Tiffin to meet the camp on the Missouri in April, bringing groceries principally.

The artillery was brought into camp in charge of Colonel John Scott, two six-pounders, one three-pounder and one short twelve-pounder carronade [cannon].

Elder Kimball, myself and a few others returned to Nauvoo: the night was moderate.

Twenty-four elders met for prayer in the Temple.

Thursday, 19.—From Dr. Richards' *Camp Journal:*

'The wind blew steadily from the northwest accompanied by snow which fell to the depth of seven or eight inches, but much thawed as it fell, the storm was unceasing, and the evening was A Fierce very cold, which caused much suffering in the camp, for Storm. there were many who had no tents or any comfortable place to lodge: many tents were blown down, some of them were unfinished and had no ends.'

Twenty-five elders met for prayer in the Temple. Elders Phineas Richards and Curtis E. Bolton were mouth.

Friday, 20.—From the historian's *Camp Journal:*

'Extremely cold, considerable ice floating on the Mississippi river.

About fifteen hundred bushels of tithing corn which had previously been gathered up in Lee county, together with a large amount of potatoes, turnips, and other vegetables and grain had been mostly consumed by the camp.

Dr. Richards was sick in bed with a severe cough, and at one p. m. invited Elders Parley P. Pratt, Orson Pratt, George A. Smith, Amasa Lyman, and Bishop George Miller to his tent; the council voted to purchase three hundred bushels of corn of Wm. Leffingwell and one yoke of oxen of Wm. Hawkes. The cold increased through the day, the night was very severe, at many points ice fastened on the banks of the Mississippi river.'

Twenty-five elders met in the Temple and prayed. Elders Franklin D. and Samuel W. Richards were mouth.

Saturday, 21.—From the *Camp Journal:*

'Cold continues. Two-thirty p. m., Elders Orson Pratt, Amasa Lyman, George A. Smith, George Miller and Albert P. Rockwood in council in the historian's tent.

Elder Willard Richards proposed that Bishop Miller assisted by Elder Charles C. Rich purchase five hundred or more bushels of corn and procure hay and straw to any amount—that Cap- Camp tain Stephen Markham of the Pioneers cause all the Provisions tithing wheat and rye at Ambrosia tithing office, and one Secured. hundred bushels of corn, to be ground immediately, and report to the council; that one load of wheat in care of David Dixon be ground and reported, and that John Scott cause the wheat in care of Captain Davis to be carried to the Buonaparte mills, floured and stored until further orders; also that the brethren meet at ten a. m. and at 4 p. m. on each day until President Young returns, to all of these propositions the council agreed unanimously.

The day was pleasant but the cold severe; the saints in camp were patient, and endured all their privations without murmuring.'

Twelve elders met in the Temple for prayer, Wm. Felshaw was mouth.

Sunday, 22.—I attended meeting at the Temple, the room was crowded and a great weight caused the new truss floor to settle nearly to its proper position. While settling, an inch-board or some light timber underneath was caught and cracked, the sound of which created great alarm in the congregation and some jumped out of the windows, smashing the glass and all before them. Philo Farnsworth smashed the northeast window while others ran out of the doors and many of those who remained jumped up and down with all their might crying Oh! Oh!! Oh!!! as though they could not settle the floor fast enough, but at the same time so agitated that they knew not what they did.

The Settling Temple Floor —Confusion— Hysteria.

I attempted to call the assembly to order to explain the cause of the settling of the floor, but failing to get their attention I adjourned the meeting to the grove. I went below, examined the floor and found it had hardly settled to its designed position, passed on to the assembly in the grove where the snow was about a foot deep, and told the people they might jump up and down as much as they pleased.

One man who jumped out of the window broke his arm and mashed his face, another broke his leg; both were apostates.

Afternoon, Elders Heber C. Kimball, John Taylor and I started for the camp; the ice was running in the river so there was no possibility of crossing only with a skiff which we accomplished with difficulty and danger, the skiff being very heavily laden, and arrived at camp at 7 o'clock.

From the [*Camp*] *Journal*:

'Ten a. m., Elders Orson Pratt, George A. Smith, Amasa Lyman and Willard Richards, in council.

Bishop Miller reported that he had purchased two hundred and fifteen baskets of corn.

Voted that Elder George A. Smith have a milk cow, which he had obtained on tithing, that Brother Thomas Grover have ropes to tie his oxen, and that Brothers Rockwood and Lee examine a load of tin belonging to Pulaski Cahoon and purchase such, as quality and prices would warrant, and raise forty or fifty dollars to send for such articles of tinware as were needed by the camp.

General Charles C. Rich reported that he had procured three hundred and fifty bushels of corn mostly on tithing.

Lucien Woodworth stated to the council that he could probably obtain five hundred bushels of corn, besides potatoes and other provisions, among the brethren in the vicinity, by donation: the council delegated to him that mission.

Voted that the brethren be lectured on domestic economy that the guard be instructed to lay aside their heavy arms during the day, that the Pioneer Company burn charcoal and that the blacksmiths and wagon makers organize and prepare for their several duties in the camp.

One p. m., the brethren came together at the raising of the flag. Elders Orson Pratt and Amasa Lyman lectured on the Camp health, comfort, success, peace, prosperity and salvation Lecture. of the camp.

Four p. m., the council convened as in the morning with the addition of Elder Parley P. Pratt.

Resolved that the second hundred bushels of corn be prepared for mill on the return of the meal of the first—that Bishop George Miller authorize Captain John Scott, of the artillery to gather provisions on tithing; that Parley P. Pratt and Amasa Lyman have leave to go tomorrow to the Clark Settlement for oxen, corn and provisions, etc.'

Twenty-five elders met for prayer in the Temple. *Monday, 23.*—I met in council with the Twelve and captains of hundreds as to moving the camp.

We agreed to pass up the divide between the waters of the Des Moines and Missouri rivers.

Henry G. Sherwood was appointed Pioneer Commissary to obtain grain and provisions for the camp.

Captain Stephen Markham was instructed to send a company of Pioneers to find a camping ground between Sugar Creek Encampment and Bonaparte Mills.

Captain Samuel Bent was instructed to move his company, consisting of twenty-five wagons, in the morning.

Several guns were discharged in and about the camp.

During the council Benjamin Stewart came up to the tent fire of the guards, caught up a large pistol and discharged it across the fire; it contained three small rifle balls which entered the left thigh of Abner Blackburn, son of Anthony Blackburn, two balls passed out the opposite side and one hit the bone and passed down remaining in the leg.

Evening, the Pioneers returned and reported a good camping ground ten miles from this, and corn plenty at 18¾ cents; 12¾ cents being the market price at Sugar Creek and Montrose.

PROSPECTUS OF THE HANCOCK EAGLE—"THE NEW ORDER OF THINGS"

W. E. Matlock issued the prospectus of the *Hancock Eagle* [Nauvoo], from which I extract the following·

'Our object in commencing the publication at this juncture, is to anticipate *the new order of things* which will inevitably result from the changes now taking place in the civil, ecclesiastical, and domestic polity of this large city and the country adjacent.

Nauvoo and its immediate suburbs, until recently, contained over 15,000 inhabitants—the greater part of whom were known as 'Mormons'—of these, some two or three thousand have already left together with an equal number from the country. A majority of those remaining, will, in due season depart upon their pilgrimage towards the setting sun. The high council is dissolved, and the church organization has been entirely broken up to be reestablished, we opine, in some distant region whose waters flow into the Pacific Ocean. The Twelve with their thousands of followers have abandoned their Temple and their city; with them, goes all that the enemies of Mormonism regard as inimical to the genius of our institutions and the well being of the community at large.'

Twenty-eight elders met for prayer in the Temple.

Tuesday, 24.—A son was born to John Redding in camp.

The cold has been severe the past night, a snowstorm this morning which continued during the forenoon, blowing from the northwest, which prevented Captain Bent's Company from moving; the cold was severe through the day and increased as night approached.

I was busy in unloading, weighing and loading my wagons preparatory to a removal.

I handed out to many of the brethren cloth for tent ends and wagon covers.

Evening, I met with Elders Heber C. Kimball and Willard Richards at his [the latter's] tent, to investigate some disaffection which existed between Bishop Miller and the guards which proved to be a misunderstanding.

Seven p. m., thermometer 12 degrees below zero, Fah. Mississippi river frozen over above Montrose.

Twenty-five elders met for prayer in the Temple in two companies.

Wednesday, 25.—The morning was colder than any one since the encampment, but the sun rose clear, the whole camp appeared cheerful and happy.

Nine a. m., the blast of the bugle and the raising of the flag called the brethren together.

President Young stated to the assembly that he had been informed by Bishop Miller, that jobs of chopping cord wood and splitting rails could be obtained to advantage by the brethren on the Desmoines river, at, and above Farmington; Bishop Miller said, that he had received his information from Mr. Crook, a merchant of Farmington. President Young asked, shall we go where we can get work? when the brethren responded in the affirmative, then, said the President, we will browse our cattle till Bishop Whitney comes up. *Prospects of Camp Employment.*

President Young then spoke against thieving, cutting strings from wagon covers, and said the brethren had gone contrary to counsel in cutting rail timber, etc., on the camp ground and they must stop all such practices; that they had not made him their leader of the camp as yet, but if they should do it, when they get out of the settlements where his orders could be executed, they would have justice done them, and, said he, I should be perfectly willing to see thieves have their throats cut; some of you may say, if that is your feelings Brigham, we'll lay you aside sometime, well, do it if you can; I would rather die by the hands of the meanest of all men, false brethren, than to live among thieves. He then called upon the captains of companies to report those who were most destitute and he would divide among them the corn and oats he had brought for horse feed; there is no need of stealing, if one suffers we will all suffer, this great 'I' and little 'you', I cannot bear, if the guard consider the Twelve as privileged characters they must consider the high council also, and if the high council, the high priests, etc., and we *Irregularities in Camp Life.*

should all be privileged characters; and what is the use of any guard?
None at all. When I want to pass the guard I will go to the sergeant
and get the password, and I want all the brethren to do the same. Let
no man crowd upon the guard and let the guard know no man as a
privileged character.

President Young retired from the meeting and went to distributing
his grain among the needy.'

About eleven a. m., Captain Charles C. Rich arrived
from Nauvoo and reported that he had walked over the
Mississippi river on the ice at Montrose.

Seven a. m., thermometer at 6° Fah.; one p. m.,
thermometer 18° Fah. Latitude of the Camp of Israel
by a meridian observation of the sun taken by Professor Orson Pratt this day was 40° 31' 50", longitude
91° 16' 0".

Bishop George Miller with about sixteen wagons
and thirty or forty Pioneers started for the Des Moines.

At seven p. m., thermometer stood 10° Fah.

This afternoon, Captain Samuel J. Hastings arrived
from Boston and in the evening was in council with the
Twelve at the recorder's office, Dr. Richards'
tent; when Mr. Hastings answered our
queries in a previous letter by stating that he
would take emigrants from New York, Bos-
ton and the Atlantic cities to California and the western
coast generally for $150.00 including provisions; that
from New Orleans there would be an additional expense
of about $4000 for every two hundred passengers and
to enter the Columbia river there would be an additional expense of about five per cent. Mr. Hastings
received a letter of introduction from the council to the
Trustees at Nauvoo. He retired in my tent about 11
o'clock.

*Captain
Samuel J.
Hastings—
Pathfinder
of the West.*

Two companies of elders met and prayed in the
Temple, thirty present.

*Cold
Intensity.*   *Thursday, 26.*—Six-thirty a. m., ther-
mometer stood at 2° below zero, Fah.
The weather being so cold it was not considered

prudent to remove the tents of families as had been contemplated.

John Gool let Thomas Grover, whose oxen were drowned on the 9th, have a span of horses and wagon to help him forward to be returned from the journey's end. This morning John Gool's wife came into camp and demanded the team; I tried to persuade her that it would be loss to her to take away the team under existing circumstances; but she persisted in her demand and took the team and drove off: I told Brother Grover to trust in the Lord.

Dr. Levi and Samuel W. Richards arrived in camp about eleven a. m. on a visit.

The trustees, Babbitt, Heywood and Fullmer arrived about noon.

The historian has been mostly confined to his bed since his arrival in camp, with a severe cough, and unable to write, but has dictated the *Camp Journal* from his pillow for the pen of Wm. Coray, scribe, since the 17th inst.

About noon, someone presented Brother Grover with a team.

Mr. Prentice, U. S. marshal, and several of the governor's troops from Carthage, came into camp and inquired for a grey horse which they said was stolen from McDonough county two weeks previously; that they had traced the horse to within six miles of Nauvoo and had caught the thief in Nauvoo but he was not a Mormon.

In the evening I met in council with Elders Orson Pratt, John Taylor and Willard Richards in my tent and decided to write to the governor of Iowa An Appeal and ascertain his views about the saints stop- to be Made to the Governor of Iowa. ping on the public land in Iowa to raise a crop this season; read the prospectus of the *Hancock Eagle;* also the *New York Messenger Extra,* which gave an account of the sailing of the *Brooklyn* with Elder Samuel Brannan and company of two hundred and thirty souls, or one hundred and seventy-five passengers.

The sky was clear in the forenoon, in the afternoon cloudy, and the wind veering to the southeast. Six p. m., thermometer 10° above zero, Fah.

George A. Smith went to Nauvoo.

Twenty-three elders met for prayer in the Temple.

Friday, 27.—Six a. m., thermometer 5° above zero, Fah.

This morning Captain Albert P. Rockwood slaughtered a fine ox which had been sprained, and distributed it amongst the most needy of the camp.

James Wallace came into camp and thought he ought to have pay for the timber which the brethren had cut; he was willing to leave it to them what the timber was worth.

Over the Mississippi on the Ice.

William Clayton arrived at three thirty p. m.; having crossed the Mississippi with his teams on the ice.

The sky was clouded through the day, the wind in the southeast and very chilly, and towards night a little fine hail fell; the camp generally healthy and happy.

Six p. m., 21° above zero, Fah.

Brother McKee protested my order for corn to the amount of $15.00, which he promised to the camp yesterday; when the teams called for the corn this morning, McKee told them he had concluded to keep the corn to help off the poor with, which caused the teams in camp to be fed on five ears of corn each.

Eleven elders met for prayer in the Temple.

Saturday, 28.—Six a. m., thermometer 20° above zero, Fah. Wind variable, changing toward the north.

Some of the Pioneers, Daniel Spencer, Charles Shumway, and part of Captain Bent's Company moved on four miles.

I met in council with the Twelve in my tent. We read and approved the following to the governor of Iowa:—

COMMUNICATION TO THE GOVERNOR OF IOWA

'To His Excellency,
Governor of the Territory of Iowa,

Honored Sir: The time is at hand, in which several thousand free citizens of this great Republic, are to be driven from their peaceful homes and firesides, their property and farms, and their dearest constitutional rights—to wander in the barren plains, and sterile mountains of western wilds, and linger out their lives in wretched exile far beyond the pale of professed civilization; or else be exterminated upon their own lands by the people, and authorities of the state of Illinois. As life is sweet we have chosen *banishment* rather than death. But Sir, the terms of our banishment are so rigid that we have not sufficient time allotted us to make the necessary preparations to encounter the hardships and difficulties of those dreary and uninhabited regions. We have not time allowed us to dispose of our property, dwellings, and farms, consequently, many of us will have to leave them unsold, without the means of procuring the necessary provisions, clothing, teams, etc. to sustain us but a short distance beyond the settlements: hence our persecutors have placed us in very unpleasant circumstances.

To stay, is death by 'fire and sword', to go into banishment unprepared, is death by starvation. But yet under these heart-rending circumstances, several hundreds of us have started upon our dreary journey, and are now encamped in Lee county, Iowa, suffering much from the intensity of the cold. Some of us are already without food, and others barely sufficient to last a few weeks: hundreds of others must shortly follow us in the same unhappy condition.

Therefore, we, the Presiding Authorities of the Church of Jesus Christ of Latter-day Saints, as a committee in behalf of several thousand suffering exiles, humbly ask your Excellency to shield and protect us in our constitutional rights, while we are passing through the territory over which you have jurisdiction. And should any of the exiles be under the necessity of stopping in this territory for a time, either in the settled or unsettled parts, for the purpose of raising crops, by renting farms or upon the public lands, or to make the necessary preparations for their exile in any lawful way, we humbly petition your Excellency to use an influence and power in our behalf: and thus preserve thousands of American citizens, together with their wives and children from intense sufferings, starvation and death.

And your petitioners will ever pray.'

Three-thirty p. m., I rode out two or three miles in company with several of the council and the band, and met Bishop Whitney, saluted him and returned.

I was so afflicted with the rheumatism it was with difficulty I could walk.

Bishop Whitney arrived in camp about 4:30.

Some of the brethren were engaged this day in building a log house to pay James Wallace for his wood which the camp had burned on his claim.

Noon, thermometer 41° above zero Fah., six p. m., thermometer 21° above zero Fah.

The camp consisted of nearly four hundred wagons all very heavily loaded with not over one-half of the teams necessary to make a rapid journey. Shortage of Teams. Most of the families were provided with provisions for several months. A considerable number, regardless of counsel, had started in a destitute condition, and some others, with only provisions for a few days.

Colonel Stephen Markham had about one hundred Pioneers to prepare the road in advance of the main body.

Colonel Hosea Stout with about one hundred men acted as police for the encampment; they were generally armed with rifles.

Colonel John Scott with about one hundred men accompanied the artillery.

A considerable number of the teams were to be returned as soon as an encampment could be selected for putting in spring crops; others expected to return as soon as the loads of provisions and forage which they hauled were exhausted.

Our encampment on Sugar Creek has had a tendency to check the movements of the mob, as they were generally of opinion, that our fit out was so insufficient that in a short time we would break to pieces and scatter.

The great severity of the weather and not being able to sell any of our property, the difficulty of crossing the river during many days of running ice President Young's Reflections. all combined to delay our departure, though for several days the bridge of ice across the Mississippi greatly facilitated the crossing and compensated, in part, for the delay caused by the running ice.

The fact is worthy of remembrance that several thousand persons left their homes in midwinter and exposed themselves without shelter, except that afforded by a scanty supply of tents and wagon covers, to a cold which effectually made an ice bridge over the Mississippi river which at Nauvoo is more than a mile broad. We could have remained sheltered in our homes had it not been for the threats and hostile demonstrations of our enemies, who, notwithstanding their solemn agreements had thrown every obstacle in our way, not respecting either life, liberty or property, so much so, that our only means of avoiding a rupture was by starting in midwinter.

Our homes, gardens, orchards, farms, streets, bridges, mills, public halls, magnificent Temple, and other public improvements we leave as a monument of our patriotism, industry, economy, uprightness of purpose and integrity of heart; and as a living testimony of the falsehood and wickedness of those who charge us with disloyalty to the Constitution of our country, idleness and dishonesty."

CHAPTER XL

DISCONTINUANCE OF DAILY QUOTATIONS FROM THE
MANUSCRIPT HISTORY OF BRIGHAM YOUNG—SUNDRY
EVENTS IN THE MARCHING ENCAMPMENT FROM THE
CLOSE OF FEBRUARY TO MID-JUNE.

With the close of February, 1846, I shall discontinue following the daily Journal known as the *History of Brigham Young, Ms.*, because of the inadequacy of the space in this volume to continue daily entries from that Journal, to the close of the period designed—October 8, 1848. The last hundred pages or so from the daily entries of that Journal up to now have been added to this volume at the suggestion of a committee of the Twelve Apostles to whom the manuscript was submitted, because they felt the desire to have the narrative of President Young continued throughout the crucial period of the exodus from Nauvoo; the importance of the official documents connected with the last days of Nauvoo being considered by them of such historical value that they ought not to be omitted from this volume. But these daily entries may not now be further continued if volume vii of the *History* is to be kept somewhat uniform in size with the previous six volumes, and hence I cover the period from the close of February, 1846, to the arrival at Council Bluffs in elliptical narrative with occasional verbatim brief quotations from the Journal at crucial points.

The first of March witnessed the breaking up of the encampment at Sugar Creek where some of the saints had been stationed for several weeks. Thence this encampment and others which followed on from Nauvoo continued marching intermittently westward amid renewing storms of the early spring months which with the breaking up of the frost in the mellow soil of the territory of Iowa made the

Breaking up of the Camp on Sugar Creek.

roads well-nigh impassable and the discomfort of the westward moving wagons of the really one encampment extremely slow and wearisome.

The hastened departure from Nauvoo of these early companies had enforced upon them an incompleted preparation, all which was unnecessarily enforced upon them by the constantly outbreaking hostility of their enemies, and Governor Ford repeatedly harassing the leaders of the church with manufactured statements about the likely intentions of the general government to hinder the departure of the people westward, and the arrest of the leading authorities of the church. This also prevented the perfect organization of the camps that had been projected for the departure from Nauvoo, resulting in some confusion in the organization projected, which in reality was not perfected until about half the journey between Nauvoo and Council Bluffs was accomplished. After that the organization as designed in the first place was carried into effect. Of course with the weather improvements which came in the latter part of March, and of April and May, many of the discomforts and distresses of the month of February and early part of March disappeared; and the great encampment, swelled into thousands both of people and wagons with large herds of oxteams, loose cattle and horses and mules, as it approached the Missouri frontiers.

Incompleteness of Preparations for the Westward Trek.

With the first sections of the moving camps a company of Pioneers was organized to forge ahead of the oncoming companies selecting the route, bridging some sloughs and streams, including the Chariton river. As springtime advanced selections of lands were made at different places, the prairie broken up and sown to early crops, which were left to be harvested by later companies as they arrived at these sections.

Development of Methods of Travel en Marche.

Meantime in the march individuals and small companies were sent to the north and south of the route to exchange household goods, excess bedding, crockery ware, etc., for corn, oats and other provisions for men and animals. Occasionally contracts for plowing, rail-splitting, building houses, etc., were secured from the settlers in this new country, for which compensation was had in provisions, corn and hay for the struggling teams, more especially in the time when spring had not brought forth the prairie grass for grazing the stock.

Thus the line of encampments resembled in many respects an industrial column, that had to be largely self-sustaining *en marche*.

A brass band led by Captain William Pitt to enliven the march of the camp segments was sometimes invited to give concerts at villages near to the line of march, which did much to change the feelings of hostility which occasionally was manifested in such places. Thus this band proved a very great benefit to the marching column, besides cheering the spirits of the pilgrims.

"Camp of Israel" was the name given to sections of the moving caravans, but more especially to the part of

"Camp of Israel." the encampment graced by the presence of President Brigham Young and his associate Apostles; from which headquarters instructions and orders were issued to the encampments along the whole line of march.

Principal and somewhat permanent encampments were formed at Richardson's Point, about 55 miles west

Prominent Encampments. of Nauvoo. Here President Young remained from the 7th of March to the 19th of that month, as heavy rains made the roads and swollen streams impassable. A similar encampment was formed on the Chariton river where the leader established his headquarters on the 27th of March and remained until the first of April. Thence he moved to an encampment on Locust river, reached on the 6th of April. Garden Grove, named by the marching saints, was headquarters of the camp on the 25th of April—150 miles from Nauvoo. Here extensive crops were planted; and again at Mount Pisgah some distance westward. This somewhat permanent encampment was located and named by Elder Parley P. Pratt. His description of arriving at the place and naming it is given in his *Autobiography* as follows:

"Riding about three or four miles through beautiful prairies I came suddenly to some round and sloping hills, grassy, and crowned with beautiful groves of timber; while alternate open groves and forests seemed blended in all the beauty and harmony   Mount Pisgah of an English park. While beneath and beyond, on the west, rolled a main branch of Grand river, with its rich bottoms of alternate forest and prairie. As I approached this lovely scenery, several deer and wolves, being startled at the sight of me, abandoned the place and bounded away till lost from my sight amid the groves. Being pleased and excited at the varied beauty before me, I cried out, 'this is Mount Pisgah.' "

When he reported the place that evening in camp, the name was adopted by the council, and Mount Pisgah thereafter became a permanent encampment to the marching hosts of Israel. Also extensive crops were planted there that spring.

The march under constantly improving weather conditions was continued until Council Bluffs on the Missouri river was reached in mid-June from which point it was proposed to send out into   Arrival at Council the western wilderness, beyond the Rocky   Bluffs. Mountains, a company of one hundred Pioneers to search out a place where crops could be planted and a resting place, as an objective, be established for the saints until perhaps more permanent locations could be determined upon.

It could not be otherwise in such a mixed company of people drawn together by the proclamation of the   Irregularities   New Dispensation from so many sections   *en Marche.*   of the United States, Great Britain and Canada, then that there would crop out in the great encampments some irregularities that bespoke uncertain training in righteousness and the outcropping of defective human nature. However, for the most part, the great leader of the expedition from Nauvoo could justly speak in high praise of the general character of the people whom he was leading into a distant wilderness.

On Sunday, April 12, he (President Young) met with the saints attended by his usual associates of the Council of the Twelve together with Bishops Whitney and Miller, Elder Charles C. Rich and about thirty of the brethren at the encampment of Elder Heber C. Kimball. Following is the report of Brigham Young of the services held that day:

"I told them that I was satisfied that we were taking a course that would prove to be salvation, not only to this camp, but to the saints

President Young's High Praise of the Camps.

that were still behind. I did not think there had ever been a body of people since the days of Enoch placed under the same unpleasant circumstances that this people have been, where there was so little grumbling; and I was satisfied that the Lord was pleased with the majority of the 'Camp of Israel'. But there had been some things done which were wrong. There were among us those who were passing counterfeit money and had done it all the time since we left Nauvoo. There were men among us who would steal; some pleaded our suffering from persecution, and said they were justified in stealing from our enemies because they had robbed us; *but such a course tends to destroy the kingdom of God.*

I propose that we proceed to the purchase [of lands] on Grand river, Iowa, and fence in a field of two miles square, build about twenty log cabins, plow some land and put in spring crops and thus spend our time until the weather settles; select men and families to take care of our improvements and the rest proceed westward. We will also send men back from Grand river to look out a new and better road to pilot the next company so that they may avoid the creeks, bad roads and settlements through which we have passed. Then those who follow can tarry on Grand river or go on to the Missouri bottoms and other places, where there will be plenty of feed for their cattle and tarry through the winter, and come on another season as soon as they can make their way through. I also propose that we select a number of men out of each company and send them tomorrow to Judge [i. e. Bishop] Miller's in the neighborhood of Grand river to work and get corn and other provisions for the camp. Also that we select a company to start about Tuesday and go on the northern route to Grand river, find the best road and good location and let the camp follow at short stages. One hundred wagons will be sufficient to cross the mountains this season.

Heber C. Kimball moved and it was voted that my views be carried out. I moved and the council voted to proceed direct to Council Bluffs. Heber C. Kimball, Parley P. Pratt, John Taylor, Orson Pratt, George A. Smith, Joshua H. Holman, Henry G. Sherwood, William L. Cutler and myself were selected to proceed to Grand river."

In this brief account of that meeting on Sunday, April 12, 1846, is given a picture of the spirit and nature of the many events that make up the history of that strange march.*

The matter of counterfeit money spoken of in the above remarks, is again referred to in the *Manuscript History of Brigham Young*.† It appears that the man who had the counterfeit money **Bogus Again.** in his possession had let another brother have some of it on shares, which he was to exchange among the settlers north and south of the line of march in exchange for goods, etc. This man had not shared the profits with the man who gave him the bogus and hence a quarrel between them. President Young being brought to the scene of the quarrel reproved them for dealing in base coin and told the originator of the trouble that he could not govern himself, his family or a company; and unless he repented and forsook such dishonesty the hand of the Lord would be against him and all those who partook of such corruption.‡

In another case two brethren had a disagreement over some wrongs sustained, fancied or real, and a challenge was issued by James M. Hemmic **Challenge** to Wilbur J. Earl to fight a duel. The **to a Duel.** matter coming to the ears of President Young, a council was called and an immediate judgment pronounced in this language—"That James M. Hemmic be discharged from the service of this camp forthwith by order of the

---

*History of Brigham Young, Ms., 1846, pp. 141-3.

†P. 171, for 1846.

‡The words of President Young were fulfilled: "The chief actor in the business," wrote George Q. Cannon, years afterwards, "and his whole family became apostates and very disreputable people, and the hand of the Lord was visibly against him. The man also to whom he gave bogus money to pass eventually lost his standing in the church and went down" (History of the Church, Cannon, *Juvenile Instructor*, vol. xvii, p. 293).

council." This was signed by Willard Richards, clerk.

After entering the Pottawattomie Indian country a piece of bogus money was passed upon an Indian; making the discovery, the red man and his friends took an ox from the next passing company and killed it. When the matter was reported to President Young he declared "the Indian had done just right".

Many of the brethren in the first companies leaving Nauvoo had left their families behind until the advanced companies could be well under way, and President Young and the council were quite severely tried by a number of these brethren constantly bringing up the request that they be allowed to return to Nauvoo to bring back their families. A number indeed did so return without the consent of the leaders. However, by the time the companies had reached Richardson's Point, quite a list of these men in the Pioneer Companies and those in charge of the artillery with other special detachments were formally released by official action to go back for their families, and gradually the number who were desiring to return to Nauvoo fell off until the annoyance ceased to exist.

Desire to
Return to
Nauvoo for
Families.

Those returning to Nauvoo, however, were able to be of service by carrying letters from the camp segments back to their friends, and letters also were forwarded from Nauvoo to the headquarters of the Camp of Israel, and thus was maintained a sort of postal service, the tent of Willard Richards being known as the General Post Office, both for outgoing and incoming mail. Sometimes this service was kept up by the appointment of men to go back and forth along the line of movement.

Improvised
Mail Service.

Letters from Nauvoo brought the acceptable news that companies of brethren—high priests, seventies, and elders—met in groups, almost daily, in the Temple to engage in prayer in behalf of the Camp of Israel and also for the benefit of the saints everywhere in the church. Especial prayer

Prayers
Well-nigh
Constant.

service was also frequently celebrated in the camps by appointment. Indeed, if one notices the frequency of prayer both in the camps and in the Temple, he is led to exclaim—If prayer can really serve its high purpose, then there was never a time like this in the church where the service of prayer was so constantly used, or more fervent appeals made to God for the deliverance of the saints!

Meantime, during this march of the saints from Nauvoo to Council Bluffs, two important things happened which had an effect upon the intended movements of the exiles. The first was the activity of Jesse C. Little at Washington, D. C., who had been appointed to preside over the Eastern States Mission with instructions to visit Washington and if possible secure the assignment for the saints in assisting the general government to settle California in anticipation of a conquest of that country by the United States then entering upon a war with Mexico. Elder Little contacted the federal administration and upon his representing the condition of the Latter-day Saint community at Nauvoo, and their westward traveling encampments, obtained the promise of President James K. Polk that an opportunity would be given for a company of at least 500 men to march with the "Army of the West" to California. They would be employed for one year, receive the usual compensation allowed to soldiers of the army of the United States, and be allowed to keep their arms and all their army equipment at the end of that time. Elder Little had proposed to raise 1000 settlers for California in the eastern branches of the church and 1000 men from their encampments on the Missouri, but the administration decided to take into service only 500 men.

The second thing was the order sent to General Stephen W. Kearny at Ft. Leavenworth to take the necessary steps to raise this Battalion of 500 men. The carrier of the dispatches to General Kearny was Thomas L. Kane who had

J. C. Little at Washington.

Raising the Mormon Battalion.

cooperated with Elder Little in presenting the cause of the Church of the Latter-day Saints to the administration and other friends in Washington.

The first knowledge of this opportunity of service with the "Army of the West" reached the Camp of Israel at Mount Pisgah, where on the 26th of June Captain James Allen of the United States army arrived, accompanied by three dragoons. The camp at Mount Pisgah was momentarily thrown into great confusion and excitement by this event, since the rumors, first set on foot at Nauvoo, that the United States would intercept the removal of the saints from the United States, was remembered, and the cry was echoed from tent to tent —"The United States troops are upon us!" "The United States troops are upon us!!" But as Captain Allen soon presented the intention of his visit, the excitement subsided, and Elder Wilford Woodruff of the Twelve Apostles, who at the time was at the encampment, referred Captain Allen's request for the enlistment of volunteers to President Young, then at Council Bluffs, and Captain Allen proceeded on his journey westward to make known his mission to the leader. Upon the proposition being submitted to President Young to raise a company of 500 volunteers the subject was referred to the council and a favorable decision rendered. Whereupon for several weeks the different sections of the encampment were visited as far east as Mount Pisgah—and word was sent on by letter to Garden Grove—150 miles west of Nauvoo, it will be remembered. These sectors of the camp were canvassed and men gathered together at Council Bluffs to enlist in the service of the United States.

Unfortunately there were many misapprehensions concerning the enlistment of this company of volunteers. For a long time it was represented as current traditional history that the opportunity given for enlistment was a "demand" or "requisition" or "draft"–sometimes one, sometimes another–

Misapprehensions of the Motives of the U. S.

of the United States government, unjust and out of all proportion to the membership of the church, and made from sinister motives of encompassing the destruction of the moving caravans either by scattering or annihilating them. First, in that if they refused to enlist, an excuse for halting their departure from the United States and their utter destruction would be justified; and on the other hand, if they complied and furnished the 500 young men, necessarily it would deplete their fighting force that they would fall victims to the large tribes of war-like Indians upon the plains and through the mountains. Nothing of this kind, of course, could be implied in the action of the administration at Washington, still it was so reported and believed.* In the first place, a much larger offer than 500 men was tendered to the administration, and the service was almost piteously pleaded for by a representative of the church —the president of the Eastern States Mission. In addition to that it was utterly impossible for the administration at Washington to make a "demand" or a "draft" for this service from the Mormon people, for at the utmost the president could only call for "volunteers"; since the law authorizing the president to organize an army to make war upon Mexico empowered him only to call for volunteers, 50,000 of them apportioned among the states. The quota in most of the states was over-subscribed by three times the number asked for, and the United States did not really need the service of the Mormon Battalion of 500 men in the sense that there was a lack of volunteers. The war was a very popular one.

Misapprehension also arose as to the time in which the Battalion was enlisted. It was popularly supposed that three days only were occupied in raising the Battalion. It is true the Battalion was mustered upon the rolls and commanders of companies were chosen from among the volunteers, and the Battalion put in march-

---

*See Sergeant Daniel Tyler's *History of the Mormon Battalion*, pp. 348-55.

Time Element
in Raising
the Battalion. ing order under Captain James Allen to be marched to Ft. Leavenworth in three days.

But before these three days of mustering in the Battalion at Council Bluffs, more than three weeks had been used by the principal brethren of the Camp of Israel in going through the various segments of the marching column selecting and deciding upon those who should form the membership of this Battalion. The remarks accredited to Brigham Young that he said to Captain Allen:—"You shall have your Battalion, Sir; and if there are not young men enough we will take old men, and if they are not enough, we will take women!"—was undoubtedly intended for humor; for after several weeks of recruiting throughout the camps from Council Bluffs to Mount Pisgah, President Young must have been well advised that the 500 volunteers were on hand to be registered in the service of the United States.

For further and full details concerning the calling of the Mormon Battalion, its departure from Council Reference
to the
Comprehensive
History of
the Church. Bluffs and Ft. Leavenworth, its record march of two thousand miles through what is now the states of Kansas, New Mexico, Arizona, and California, to San Diego on the Pacific coast, and its record in California, see *Comprehensive History of the Church of Jesus Christ of Latter-day Saints,* Century I, vol. iii, chapters lxxiii, lxxiv, lxxv, lxxxvii. Also the final and cruel expulsion* of the remnant of the church members left in Nauvoo, in the latter part of September, 1846, and all their sufferings on the west bank of the Mississippi, their journey through Iowa, and their final union with their fellow exiles at Council Bluffs will be found and given in detail in the *Comprehensive History of the Church,* Century I, vol. iii, chapters lxx, lxxii and lxxvi.

The founding of Winter Quarters and the trek during the summer of 1847 of the Pioneer Companies to

---

*It was in this final expulsion of the remnants of the saints from Nauvoo in which Daniel H. Wells figured so prominently, and so bravely, which won for him the title of "Defender of Nauvoo". (See references above to *Comprehensive History*).

the valley of the Great Salt Lake, their arrival and settlement there—all this is also treated in sufficient detail in the *Comprehensive History of the Church of Jesus Christ of Latter-day Saints,* Century I, and it will not be necessary to repeat these things in greater detail by following further the *Manuscript History of Brigham Young.* But the return of the Pioneers to Winter Quarters, late in 1847, and the steps taken to organize again the First Presidency of Three in December of that year, together with acceptance of the action by the various great divisions of the church, as then existing, is of sufficient importance to have the official account of it given from *President Young's Manuscript History* and with that account as given, chiefly by himself, we will close this seventh volume.

CHAPTER XLI

THE RETURN TO WINTER QUARTERS—THE ORGANIZA-
TION OF AND UNIVERSAL ACCEPTANCE OF THE FIRST
PRESIDENCY OF THE CHURCH, BRIGHAM YOUNG,
HEBER C. KIMBALL, AND WILLARD RICHARDS—1847-
8—PRESIDENT YOUNG'S LAST JOURNEY OVER THE
PLAINS

After having settled the Pioneer Company and the
contingent Mormon Battalion, invalided sections, which
had wintered at Pueblo, and who arrived in Salt Lake
City five days after the Pioneer Company, President
Young, a number of the Twelve Apostles, (a majority), and some of the Pioneer Company returned to
Winter Quarters late in 1847 to further the migration
of the saints still encamped on the Missouri frontiers.

Under date of October 30, 1847, President Young
records in his *Manuscript History* the following:

"*Saturday, October 30, 1847.*—At sunset about 20
wagons arrived from Winter Quarters with Bishop N.
K. Whitney, John S. Fullmer, Wm. Kay and many
friends, bringing food and grain.

Sunday, 31.—When we were about one mile from
Winter Quarters the wagons of the Twelve came to
the front, when I remarked:

'Brethren, I will say to the Pioneers, I wish you to receive my
thanks for your kindness and willingness to obey orders; I am satisfied with you: you have done well. We have accomplished more than we expected. Out of one hundred
forty-three men who started, some of them sick, all of
them are well; not a man has died; we have not lost a
horse, mule, or ox, but through carelessness; the blessings of the Lord
have been with us. If the brethren are satisfied with me and the
Twelve, please signify it, (which was unanimously done). I feel to

The Thanks
of the Leader
—His Report
of the Pioneer
Journey.

bless you all in the name of the Lord God of Israel. You are dismissed to go to your own homes.'

We drove into the town in order, about an hour before sunset. The streets were crowded with people to shake hands as we passed through the lines; we were truly rejoiced to once more behold our wives, children and friends after an absence of over six months, having traveled over 2000 miles, sought out a location for the saints to dwell in [in] peace, and accomplished the most interesting mission in this last dispensation. Not a soul of our camp died, and no serious accident happened to any, for which we praise the Lord.

* * *.

Wednesday, November 3, 1847.—The Twelve met in council at my house. John S. Fullmer reported the proceedings of the trustees in Nauvoo; when it was voted that the trustees gather all the papers and books pertaining to church affairs in Nauvoo, and as many of the poor saints together with as much church property as they can, and remove hither [i. e. Winter Quarters]. It was also voted that the saints in Garden Grove be advised to remove to Winter Quarters next spring.

Friday, 5.—I met in council with the Twelve. I signed a letter addressed to Colonel J. C. Little instructing him to resume his presidency over the eastern churches, and one to Elder John Brown and the saints in the southern states; also one to the trustees at Nauvoo recommending them to leave the keys of the Temple in care of Judge Owens and the building itself in the hands of the Lord*. The minutes of the con-

*DESTRUCTION OF THE MORMON [NAUVOO] TEMPLE

"*November 19, 1848:* 'On Monday the 19th of November, our citizens were awakened by the alarm of fire, which, when first discovered, was bursting out through the spire of the Temple, near the small door that opened from the east side to the roof, on the main building. The fire was seen first about three o'clock in the morning, and not until it had taken such hold of the timbers and roof as to make useless any effort to extinguish it. The materials of the inside were so dry, and the fire spread so rapidly, that a few minutes were sufficient to wrap this famed edifice in a sheet of flame. It was a sight too full of mournful sublimity. The mass of material which had been gathered there by the labor of many years afforded a rare opportunity for this element to play off some of its wildest sports. Although

ference of September 24, 1846, of the Chain Island group in the Pacific ocean were read, comprising thirteen branches on nine islands, containing 804 members, four elders, seven priests, thirteen teachers and twenty deacons.

Saturday, 6.—Evening, I met with the council and School of the Seventy.

Sunday, 7.—Elder Orson Pratt preached in the Council House. He gave an account of the Pioneer journey and described some of the lakes and valleys of the mountains.

Monday, 8.—I met with the Twelve, when it was voted that the saints vacate Winter Quarters in the spring and go westward. Elder Hyde informed the council that fellowship was withdrawn from George Miller, also James Emmett and his company; which was approved.

Tuesday, 9.—The Apostles, high council, Bishop

the morning was tolerably dark, still, when the flames shot upwards, the spire, the streets, and the houses for nearly a mile distant were lighted up, so as to render even the smallest objects discernible. The glare of the vast torch, pointing skyward, indescribably contrasted with the universal gloom and darkness around it; and men looked on with faces sad as if the crumbling ruins below were consuming all their hopes.

It was evidently the work of an incendiary. There had been, on the evening previous, a meeting in the lower room; but no person was in the upper part where the fire was first discovered. Who it was, and what could have been his motives, we have now no idea. Some feeling infinitely more unenviable than that of the individual who put the torch to the beautiful Ephesian structure of old, must have possessed him. To destroy a work of art, at once the most elegant and the most renowned in its celebrity of any in the whole west, would, we should think, require a mind of more than ordinary depravity; and we feel assured that no one in this community could have been so lost to every sense of justice, and every consideration of interest as to become the author of the deed' (*Nauvoo Patriot*).

November 1, 1856: Lewis A. Bidamon, (who married Emma Smith, widow of the Prophet Joseph, on December 23, 1847), [L. D. S. Biographical Encyclopedia, Jenson, vol. i, p. 692], landlord of the Nauvoo Mansion, Illinois, stated to Elders George A. Smith and Erastus Snow, that the inhabitants of Warsaw, Carthage, Pontusic and surrounding settlements in consequence of jealousy that Nauvoo would still retain its superior importance as a town and might induce the Mormons to return contributed a purse of five hundred dollars which they gave to Joseph Agnew in consideration of his burning the Temple; and that said Agnew was the person who set the building on fire.

Bidamon further stated, that the burning of the Temple had the effect of diminishing the importance of Nauvoo; for his 'Mansion' or 'Hotel' had not since the conflagration one-fourth the custom it previously had" (*History of Brigham Young, Ms.*, 1848, pp. 79-81).

Whitney, Presidents of Seventy and others, met in the Council House on business.

Wednesday, 10.—I met with the Twelve, high council and Seventies on business.

Thursday, 11.—I met with Elders Orson Pratt, Willard Richards, George A. Smith and Joseph Young to see to the distribution of the Nauvoo library which had been forwarded by the trustees.

Sunday, 14.—I met with the saints in public meeting; referred to our healthy locality in the mountains; suggested that those who could not go west next spring should vacate Winter Quarters and return to the east side of the river. The saints voted to leave Winter Quarters next spring.

Monday, 15.—I met with the high priests. Evening, I met with the seventies and high priests who were addressed by Elder Kimball and myself on the necessity of a reformation. I remarked that the government officials were looking on us more eagerly than when we were in Jackson, Caldwell and Clay counties, Missouri.

Tuesday, 16.—The council convened at noon in the Council House. Bishop Whitney was directed to preside over the high priests for the time being.

Thursday, 18.—I visited the sick and attended a high priests' meeting. The official members of the First Emigrating Division met at 7 p. m., and decided to fill up the old organization by new members.

Friday, 19.—The council wrote to Major Miller requesting his views and opinions on the saints vacating their winter quarters on the Omaha lands.

Saturday, 20.—The Council of the Twelve met in the Council House and selected twenty-seven persons to go on missions to preach.

Sunday, 21.—I was sickly. Elders Orson Pratt and Wilford Woodruff preached at the stand.

Monday, 22.—The Council of the Twelve met in Dr. Richards' office and wrote a letter to Oliver Cowdery, exhorting him to be rebaptized.

Oliver Cowdery Exhorted to be Rebaptized.

Tuesday, 23.—The Twelve and Presidents of Seventy met and selected seventeen elders to go on missions.

Thursday, 25.—I met with the Twelve and officers of the Emigrating Companies and instructed them pertaining to their further organization. We wrote to Elder N. H. Felt, St. Louis, to forward the emigrating saints to Winter Quarters.

Friday, 26.—I wrote a letter to Elder Orson Spencer giving particulars of Pioneer journey, their labors in Salt Lake valley and other interesting items.

Sunday, 28.—I met with the Twelve and high council in the forenoon, Theodore Turley and Joseph Fielding were voted members of the high council. In the evening I preached to the seventies and high priests concerning gathering to the Bluffs, and from there to the mountains, and aiding each other until all are located in a healthy country.

* * *

Friday, December 3, 1847.—The Twelve traveled to the Block House branch and met the high council and others, when I preached, followed by Elders George A. Smith, Amasa Lyman and Wilford Woodruff. Afternoon, I introduced the subject of organizing a Carrying Company hence to the Salt Lake country, for the purpose of taking as many thither as possible. I recommended the brethren to build a house 50 by 100 feet in time to accommodate the conference next spring, and called for help to assist the bishops on the west side of the river, who have to support three hundred poor persons daily. Elder Kimball preached.

Council met at Brother Daley's. Elder Wm. I. Appleby presented the gold pens and pencils sent by Colonel T. L. Kane to the Twelve Apostles. He reported the condition of the churches east.

Saturday, 4.—I attended conference and proposed building a big log house in the hollow, for temporary use, telling the congregation not to be surprised if a city should be built there. The conference voted that

Henry W. Miller be a committee of one to superintend the building, under the dictation of the Twelve. I told the conference that we must recommend ourselves as a people by our good works, to the Lord God Almighty. The conference was adjourned till December 24th to meet in the new house to be built.

The Twelve selected the site to build the house on and proceeded to Father Ezra Chase's Settlement.

Sunday, 5.—We traveled to Elder Hyde's house where all of the Council [i. e. of the Twelve] assembled in the evening. After remarks by myself, Heber C. Kimball, Orson Hyde, Willard Richards, Wilford Woodruff, George A. Smith, Amasa Lyman, and Ezra T. Benson [8 of the Quorum of the Twelve], I was unanimously elected President of the Church of Jesus Christ of Latter-day Saints, with authority to nominate my two counselors, which I did by appointing Heber C. Kimball my first counselor and Willard Richards my second counselor, and the appointments were unanimously sustained.*

*En route from Salt Lake valley, President Young conversed with his brethren of the Apostles on the subject of reorganizing the First Presidency of the Church. His conversation with Elder Woodruff on the subject is thus related by the latter in his Journal:

"*October* 12, 1847.—I had a question put to me by President Young: What my opinion was concerning one of the Twelve Apostles being appointed as the President of the Church with his two counselors. I answered that a quorum like the Twelve who had been appointed by revelation, confirmed by revelation from time to time—I thought it would require a revelation to change the order of that quorum. [But] whatever the Lord inspires you to do in this matter. I am with you" (*Woodruff's Journal*, entry for October 12, 1847).

In some remarks made by President Young while in St. George in 1862, he said to Isaac Morley and Levi Jackman, who were present with him: "You are both Jackson county members and I want you to live to go back to Jackson county with me." He also said: "Here is Brother Woodruff [who was present], he was the first man that I felt by the spirit to speak to about the organization of the church [i. e. First Presidency of the Church] (*Wilford Woodruff's Journal*, August 23, 1862; also copied into *Brigham Young's History, Ms.*, same date, pp. 779-80).

Wilford Woodruff also records concerning this meeting at Orson Hyde's house, that before the choice of Brigham Young for President of the Church "many interesting remarks were made by the various individuals who spoke, [this included all the members of the Twelve present], and we were followed by President Young. After which Orson Hyde moved that Brigham Young be the President of the Church of Jesus Christ of Latter-day Saints and that he nominate his two counselors, and they three form the First Presidency. Seconded by Wilford Woodruff and carried unanimously. President Young nominated Heber C. Kimball as his first counselor; seconded, and carried unanimously. President Young nominated Willard Richards as his second counselor; seconded, and carried unanimously" (*Woodruff's Journal*, entry for December 5, 1847).

Monday, 6.—The council met in the afternoon in Brother Orson Hyde's house and attended to several items of business; conversed about building a Temple in Salt Lake City and voted that Uncle John Smith be the Patriarch to the whole church; that Orson Hyde go to the east to procure means to help us and that E. T. Benson go with him; that Luke Johnson be ordained an elder, [formerly one of the original Quorum of the Twelve]; that Orson Pratt go to England and take charge of the affairs of the church there; that Amasa Lyman go to the southern states to get help.

Tuesday, 7.—Returned to Winter Quarters having accomplished much important business during this visit.

Thursday, 9—During my absence the past summer the Omahas [Indians] have killed more than twenty of my cows and calves.

Colonel Thomas L. Kane wrote me and enclosed a printed circular of a 'Meeting for the Relief of the Mormons in Philadelphia', copies of which had been sent to the president and vice-president of the United States, and to the members of congress; showing the colonel's great anxiety in behalf of a persecuted and suffering people.

Friday, 10.—Accompanied by Dr. Richards I visited Elder Kimball. I met Dr. J. M. Bernhisel and heard his report concerning the Nauvoo House affairs; also visited General Johnson, and attended meeting of First Division of Emigration.

Saturday, 11.—Philemon C. Merrill with fifteen others of the Mormon Battalion arrived in Winter Quarters; they left Great Salt Lake City, October 8th.
* * *.

Thursday, 23.—I started for Council Point and attended a meeting there at the schoolhouse when Elders Wilford Woodruff and Joseph Young preached.

Friday, 24.—Proceeded to Miller's Hollow, [later called Kanesville], where the brethren had built a log house forty by sixty feet, capable of seating about one thousand persons. The house was dedicated by Elder Orson Pratt as a house of prayer and thanksgiving. The congregation was addressed by Elders Wilford Woodruff and Orson Pratt and in the afternoon by Elders Amasa Lyman, George A. Smith and myself. Elder Wm. I. Appleby preached during the evening service.

Saturday, 25.—The council went to the Log Tabernacle and attended meeting. The congregation voted that the high council on the east side of the river have all municipal power given to them by this people, and that the bishops' courts have authority as civil magistrates among the people, until the laws of Iowa are extended over us.

* * *.

Monday, 27.—Conference convened again when Elder Kimball spoke, followed by Elder Joseph Young, myself, Elders George A. Smith, Orson Pratt and Amasa Lyman, when I was unanimously elected [sustained] President of the Church of Jesus Christ of Latter-day Saints.* Heber C. Kimball and Willard Richards were in like manner elected [sustained] respectively my first and second counselors. Uncle John

---

*This was a General Conference of the whole church from Winter Quarters, Kanesville and Council Bluffs. "The spirit of the Lord at this time," said Brigham Young a month later, "rested upon the people in a powerful manner, insomuch that the saints' hearts were filled with joy unspeakable; every power of their mind and nerve of their bodies was awakened." A dead silence reigned in the congregation while the President spoke following the vote which had been taken (See Letter of President Young to Orson Spencer, then in England, *Millennial Star*, vol. x, p. 115).

Subsequently this action of the saints in the settlements on the Missouri river in conference assembled—being the largest number of church members in one body, with several high councils presiding in various divisions of the church in those settlements—was ratified by unanimous vote by the saints of Salt Lake valley and in the General Conference of the church held in that place on the 8th of October, 1848; there being about 5000 people in the valley by that time.

Elder Parley P. Pratt nominated Brigham Young at that conference as the First President of the Church and the motion was carried *without a dissenting vote.* (See *Comprehensive History of the Church,* Century I, vol. iii, p. 318, note).

The action was also ratified by the saints of the British Isles in General Conference assembled at Manchester, England, August 14, 1848, at which there were present delegates from 28 different conferences with a membership of 17,902. (See *Millennial Star.* vol. x. p. 252. where the names of the officers are given; also the

Smith was unanimously elected [sustained] Patriarch to the whole church.

I spoke again referring to what had been accomplished by the saints and other topics; bore testimony that the communion of the Holy Spirit was enjoyed by those present, when the conference was adjourned till the 6th of April at the Log Tabernacle.

After benediction by Elder George A. Smith the congregation shouted three times 'Hosannah, Hosannah, Hosannah to God and the Lamb, Amen, Amen and Amen!'*

Tuesday, 28.—Wrote a letter to Elder Orson Spencer, Liverpool, England, with instructions to send the British saints *via* New Orleans and St. Louis to Council Bluffs.

Wednesday, 29.—The First Presidency, the Twelve, high council, and several others met in the Council House in Winter Quarters and attended to business.
* * *.

GENERAL ANNUAL CONFERENCE OF THE CHURCH, 1848

"*Thursday, April* 6, 1848.—I attended a conference at the Log Tabernacle, Miller's Hollow (named at this conference Kanesville), held on the 6th, 7th and 8th. I nominated, and Elder Orson Hyde was chosen, president [i. e. of the conference meetings]. The constituted authorities of the church were sustained, also the high council and other authorities in Pottawattomie. Elders Orson Hyde, George A. Smith, Orson Pratt, Wilford Woodruff, Joseph Young, Heber C. Kimball, myself and others preached. William Draper, Sen., was called to the office of patriarch. The appointments

names of the conferences and the statistics in detail; see also *Manuscript History of Brigham Young* under date of August 14, 1848, pp. 48-49, where the statistics are also given in detail.)

*This shout of "Hosanna" is given only on very great occasions. It is usually given three times in immediate succession; and when voiced by thousands and sometimes tens of thousands in unison, and at their utmost strength, it is most impressive and inspiring. It is impossible to stand unmoved on such an occasion. It seems to fill the prairie or woodland, mountain wilderness or tabernacle, with mighty waves of sound; and the shout of men going into battle cannot be more stirring. It gives wonderful vent to religious emotions, and is followed by a feeling of reverential awe—a sense of oneness with God.

of Elders Orson Hyde and George A. Smith to labor in Pottawattomie, Elder Orson Pratt in Great Britain and Elder Wilford Woodruff to the eastern states, Nova Scotia and Canada were sustained. A vote of gratitude was accorded to the saints at St. Louis for their liberality to the presidency and the saints at Winter Quarters during the past year. Committees were appointed to select locations and settle the poor of Winter Quarters on the Pottawattomie lands: Luke Johnson was recommended as a physician.

Appointments to Missions.

* * *

Sunday, May 21.—During this month I attended meetings each Sunday which were held at the stand. On the 14th, I preached at length and blessed the land at Winter Quarters and on the Pottawattomie purchase, for the benefit of the saints who should occupy it.

Friday, 26.—On the 26th I started from Winter Quarters on my journey to the mountains, leaving my houses, mills and the temporary furniture I had acquired during our sojourn there. This was the fifth time I had left my home and property since I embraced the gospel of Jesus Christ. All of my company had left Winter Quarters and were mostly, on the last day of this month, on the west side of the Elkhorn river, the place of rendezvous for organization.

President Young's Departure for the West.

Wednesday, 31.—On the 31st the organization was commenced by appointing Zera Pulsipher captain of a hundred with John Benbow and Daniel Wood captains of fifties; also, Lorenzo Snow captain of a hundred, with Heman Hyde and John Stoker captains of fifties. I gave some general instructions as to the necessity of observing order in camp—taking care of the cattle and not allowing them to be abused; not to have yelling nor bawling in camp; but to attend prayers—put out the fires and go to bed by 9 p. m.

Organization of President Young's Company.

Elder James H. Flanigan received a license to preach the gospel in Great Britain, under the direction of the presidency there. I gave my brother, Phineas H. Young a recommend to travel and preach in the states, and gather means to help himself and the saints westward. I also signed a letter of recommendation in behalf of Brother Willard Richards authorizing him to travel and preach in the United States and Europe and gather means to fit him out for his journey to the mountains. At the same time, I counseled him to gather up what teams and wagons he could and come on after us, as soon as he was able, even if he had to leave a portion of his family another year.

Thursday, June 1.—On the 1st Brother Heber C. Kimball with a company of fifty-five wagons arrived on the east bank of the Elkhorn river.

Heber C. Kimball's Company.

I proceeded to a further organization of my company. William G. Perkins was chosen captain of a hundred with John D. Lee and Eleazer Miller captains of fifties; also Allen Taylor captain of a hundred with John Harvey and Daniel Garn captains of fifties. The company voted that I should act as General Superintendent of the Emigrating Companies and Daniel H. Wells was sustained as my aid-de-camp. Isaac Morley was sustained as president of the company, with Reynolds Cahoon and William W. Major as his counselors. Horace S. Eldredge was chosen marshal, and Hosea Stout captain of the night guard. Captain Lorenzo Snow's Company moved out to the Platte river, and Captain Pulsipher's Company started out a few miles.

Elders Orson Hyde, Wilford Woodruff and Ezra T. Benson visited the organized camps at the Horn [Elkhorn] and returned to Winter Quarters on the third. The remainder of my company started from the Horn on the fifth.

Brother H. C. Kimball's Company started from the Horn on the 7th, and on the 9th they elected the following officers, *viz.* Henry Harriman, captain of the first hundred, Titus Billings and John Pack, captains of fifties; subsequently, Isaac Higbee was appointed a captain of fifty.

Wednesday, 14.—On the 14th my company reached the Loupe Fork whence I sent Brothers Daniel H. Wells and Daniel Wood back to Brother Heber C. Kimball's Camp, by whom Brother Kimball sent me a letter detailing the particulars of an unfortunate occurrence between William H. Kimball, Howard Egan, Thomas E. Ricks and Noah W. Bartholomew and the Indians; in which Brother Ricks was shot with three buckshot and Brother Egan was shot in the wrist. Dr. Bernhisel had dressed their wounds and both were doing well.

Indian
Difficulties—
Wounding of
Thomas E.
Ricks.

Thursday, 15.—I crossed the Loupe Fork on the 15th. Brother Kimball's Company came up on the 16th, and next day with the assistance of some of the best teams in my company, his company crossed.

Thomas Bullock, clerk, reported the statistics of my company to be 1,229 souls, 397 wagons, 74 horses, 19 mules, 1,275 oxen, 699 cows, 184 loose cattle, 411 sheep, 141 pigs, 605 chickens [and a variety of smaller domestic animals].

Statistics
of President
Young's and
Kimball's
Companies.

Subsequently the statistics of Brother Kimball's Company were obtained and showed 662 souls, 226 wagons, 57 horses, 25 mules, 737 oxen, 284 cows, 150 loose cattle, 243 sheep, 96 pigs, 299 chickens [and a number of smaller domestic animals].

Sunday, 18.—Brother Kimball and I gathered the companies together on the 18th, and preached to them.

In consequence of depredations committed by the Indians the saints on the Pottawattomie side of the Missouri prepared to organize themselves as militia by electing Charles M. Johnson, colonel, Abraham C. Hodge, lieutenant-colonel, and Philemon C. Merrill, major.

Pottawattomie
Indian
Depredations.

Winter Quarters, after its vacation by Elder Kimball's Company and mine, presented a desolate aspect.

Desolation
of Winter
Quarters.

A terrific thunder storm passed over, accompanied by a hurricane which tore wagon covers to shreds and whistled fearfully through the empty dwellings. A few straggling Indians camped in the vacated premises and subsisted upon the cattle which had died by poverty and what [else] they [could] pick up.

Some Indians stole three oxen from John Scott, who, assisted by others, pursued them and recovered the beeves.

Wednesday, September 20.—My company arrived in Great Salt Lake valley on and after the 20th and Elder Kimball's a few days after.

* * *

Friday, October 6.—The Semi-Annual Conference [in Salt Lake valley] was opened on the 6th, but postponed till Sunday the 8th, in consequence of the Battalion brethren having set apart the 5th to celebrate their return home, which day was so unfavorable that the celebration was deferred and came off on the 6th, by partaking of a dinner, firing of cannon at intervals, and meeting, which dismissed at sundown.

THE FIRST PRESIDENCY SUSTAINED

Sunday, 8.—On the 8th, the [regular church] conference met, when I was sustained by unanimous vote as President of the Church, with Heber C. Kimball and Willard Richards as my counselors.

The following officers were also sustained by unanimous vote:

THE TWELVE APOSTLES

Orson Hyde, Parley P. Pratt, Orson Pratt, Lyman Wight, Wilford Woodruff, John Taylor, George A. Smith, Amasa Lyman, and Ezra T. Benson, members of the Quorum of the Twelve Apostles.

THE PATRIARCH TO THE CHURCH

John Smith, Patriarch to the church. [This was

"Uncle John" Smith, brother of the Prophet's father, who was the first Patriarch to the church].

FIRST SEVEN PRESIDENTS OF THE SEVENTY

Joseph Young, Levi W. Hancock, Zera Pulsipher, Albert P. Rockwood, Henry Harriman, Jedediah M. Grant, and Benjamin L. Clapp, First Presidents of the Seventies.

PRESIDING BISHOP

Newel K. Whitney, presiding bishop [i. e. of the whole church].

PRESIDENCY OF THE SALT LAKE STAKE

Charles C. Rich, president of the stake, with John Young and Erastus Snow, counselors.

HIGH COUNCIL OF SALT LAKE STAKE

Henry G. Sherwood, Levi Jackman, Daniel Spencer, Ira Eldredge, Shadrach Roundy, Willard Snow, John Murdock, Lewis Abbott, Edson Whipple, John Vance and Abraham O. Smoot, members of the high council.

Arrangements were entered into for the building of a Council House.

I preached on the holy priesthood, showing the necessity of a First Presidency over the Church; for God had told me we would fall, if we did not organize a First Presidency."*

This acceptance by sustaining the action of a majority of the Quorum of the Twelve at Winter Quarters on the 5th of December, 1847, sustained also by the Annual Conference of the Church at Miller's Hollow (Council Point, at that particular conference named Kanesville, and subsequently Council Bluffs); and by all the branches in that region; by the church in Salt Lake valley, with more than 5000 members; and by the saints in conference assembled in Great Britain

*History of Brigham Young, Ms., 1845-6-7-8.

(then numbering, as stated in the text, 17,902 members) ; and by the churches in the Pacific Islands; completed the installation of Brigham Young and his counselors as the second First Presidency of the Church, of three Presiding High Priests, and bridges over the period of time and historic ground between the passing of the First Presidency in the administration of Joseph Smith, the Prophet, and the establishment again of the First Presidency by the selection and inauguration of Brigham Young, official Prophet in the Church of Jesus Christ of Latter-day Saints.   And with this, Period II of the *Documentary History of the Church* may be considered closed.

END OF VOLUME VII.

INDEX TO VOLUME VII

A

Oct. 6, 1845, minutes of, 457-77; general authorities sustained at, 458-63; printed word to be discontinued at Nauvoo, 473; provisions made for publication of school books in the wilderness, 474; general settlement of accounts proposed at, 475; New York, Nov. 12, 1845, 520; resolutions passed at, 520-2; Kanesville, Brigham Young sustained as President of the Church, 623-4; Sacred Shout at, 624 (and note); all general authorities sustained at, 624; general, in Salt Lake valley, Oct. 8, 1848, Brigham Young sustained as President of the Church, 628; all other general authorities sustained, 628-9; First Presidency of Three sustained by, in Great Britain and Pacific Islands, 629.

Cowdery, Oliver,—tenders service to the church, 482.

Curtis, Enos,—affidavit on houseburning, at Morley Settlement, 488.

D

Daniels, Wm. M.,—a witness at the Carthage trial of the Prophet's murderers, 49-50 (and note); affidavit of, 162; note on, 163; goes to Gov. Ford with his "testimony", 168.

Deming, General Miner (Minor) R.,—left in command at Carthage by Gov. Ford, 22; proclamation of, 133; satisfied with Dr. Willard Richards' proceedings, at Carthage, 168; receives letter from Dr. W. Richards anent Dr. R. D. Foster, 169; shoots Sam Marshal, 428; wealthy Nauvoo brethren become bondsmen for, 432; death of, 439.

Dreams,—Heber C. Kimball's, of preaching in Joseph Smith's presence, 228; on endowments, 561.

Duncan, Joseph,—Governor of Illinois, anti-Mormon, 58.

Dunham, Major-General Jonathan.—orders to Nauvoo guard, 129; orders to Nauvoo Legion, 134; call for more militia to check mob at Warsaw, 159; death of confirmed, 437.

Dunn, Captain,—comes to Nauvoo for state arms, 83.

Durfee, Edmund,—killed by mob of house-burners, 523 (and note); biographical note of, 523-4; report of murder of to Major Warren by Orson Hyde, 525-6; case of, *Nauvoo Neighbor—Extra*, 528-30; the accused in the case discharged by magistrate, 532; witnesses in the case discharged without hearing, 532.

E

Election,—state and national, 1844, 44; relation of Mormons to, 44.

Equipment,—for family crossing the plains, 454-5.

Explanation,—Church Historians', Part I, 1; Part II, 34; Part III—Taylor's Memoirs, 54; Part IV, 128; Part V, *Manuscript History of Brigham Young*, 246; of discontinuance of daily quotations from *Manuscript History of Brigham Young*, 604-5.

Emmett, James and Company,—report on, 377; official visit to, 383; report of status of, 383-4; desires retention of fellowship for self and company, 434; disfellowshiped with his company, 618.

F

Fellows, Colonel Hart,—Ford's messenger to Nauvoo, 149; communication to Nauvoo City Council, 150.

Flanigan, James H.,—reports mission—New Jersey and Maryland, 522.

Ford, Governor Thomas, of Illinois,—statement of conditions in Hancock county, 2; misled by false reports of thefts, 4; his zeal for law in Hancock county, 5; address of, to troops in Carthage, 5; promise of protection to Mormons in case they surrender, 5; threatens to call full force of the state unless they submit, 6; proposal to march state militia into Nauvoo, 6; dissuaded from act by militia officers, 7; makes requisition for the state arms of the Nauvoo Legion, 9; the amount of arms surrendered, 10; defense for permitting commitment of the Prophet to prison, 13; charges that anti-Mormons stimulated followers to

369; laying capstone of—ceremonies, 417-18; article about in *New York Sun,* 434; first meeting in—Oct. 5, 1845, 456; special inscription in west end—"Holiness to the Lord", 457; General Conference in—minutes, 457-77; dedication of attic story of, 534; officers appointed for, 535; sacrament adminstered in, 538; completion of east room for giving endowments —those present at, 541; proper order of laying corner stones— Brigham Young, 545-6; workers in appointed—list of, 547; procedure in—President Young, 552-3; U. S. deputy marshal *et al,* visit, 553-4; additional names of workers in, 555; ordinance work in and prayer, 560; sealing altar erected, 566; discontinuance of dancing and other merriment to cease in, 566; saints anxiety to receive ordinances of, 567; roof of on fire, 581; destruction of by fire, 617-18 (and note); conversation on building a, in the west, 622.

Thomas, Judge,—advises hearing of City Council before Esq. D. H. Wells, 92.

Times and Seasons.—L. D. S. Church publication, reviews martyrdom at Carthage, 186; proposition to cease publishing, 453.

Toronto, Joseph,—consecration of gold ($2,500) to church, 433.

Tribune, New York,—comment of on Troubles at Nauvoo, 170.

Tucker, Father Hamilton,—of Roman Catholic Church, attempts purchase of Nauvoo property, 539-40; reports inability of Catholic Church to purchase Nauvoo property, 565.

V

Voorhees, W.,—with mob at Carthage, wounded, 162.

W

Wakefield, J. R.,—report on destruction of *Expositor,* 130.

Wallace, James,—house built for to compensate for wood used, 602.

Watt, George D.,—Professor of Phonography—r e p o r t s conference speeches, 394; report of Carthage trial, 421-3.

Warren, Calvin A.,—counsel for defense of murderers at Carthage, 423.

Warren, Major,—reported turned Jack-Mormon, 530.

Warsaw,—committee of, reported a party of Mormons had attempted to rescue the Smiths, 25; committee of demanded expulsion of the people, 28; departure of *posse* from, to Carthage, June 27th, 30; movements in Illinois reported from, 195.

Warsaw Signal,—anti-Mormon paper, inflamatory articles in, 64.

Wells, Daniel H.,—Joseph Smith examined before and acquitted, 92; "Defender of N a u v o o"—l a s t phase, 614; aid-de-camp to President Young, 626.

Wells, John Patrick,—with mob at Carthage, wounded, 162.

Western Movement, — preparation for, 535; reading on the explorations in the west, 558.

Wheelock, Cyrus,—a r r a n g e s to leave Nauvoo with John Taylor, 80; visits Prophet at Carthage prison, 100; leaves pistol with those in Carthage prison, 100.

"Wolf Hunt",—the nature of, 46; dispersed, 47.

Works, Asa, Sen.,—American Revolution soldier, dies, 374.

Wight, Lyman,—one of the Twelve Apostles, letter of to Joseph Smith, 136; at his best, (note) 139; second communication, 157; political address at Bunker Hill, 159.

Williams, (p e r s o n named Col. Levi),—calls for volunteers to murder Smiths, 21.

Winter Quarters,—founding of, 614; return of the Pioneers to, 615-6; meeting of the Council of the Twelve at, 617; desolation of after departure of President Young *et al.,* 627-8.

Woodruff, Wilford,—one of the Twelve Apostles, excerpts from Journal—in Boston, 149; presides at conference in Scarborough, Maine, 170; preached at Franklin Hall, Boston, 185; excerpt from Journal—President Young in tears, 195; President Young urges him to keep up Journal, 212; excerpt from Journal—the Twelve returning to Nauvoo, 228; Journal outline of Brigham Young's discourse, 254; discourse by, on the Prophet Joseph, 262; obtains copyright of *Book of Mormon* and *Doctrine and Covenants*—Stationers Hall, London, 426.

Y

Yates, Captain,—accompanies *posse* to Nauvoo, 82; returns to Carthage, Ford's account of, 82.

Yelrome,—house-burnings at, 439-42.

Young, Brigham,—President of the Twelve Apostles, meetings with fellow Apostles at Salem, Mass., 170; acts as oxteamster, 224; at Nauvoo—position—Twelve hold the keys, 230; on the claims of the Twelve to lead the church in the absence of the First Presidency, 231; note discussing his proposition, 234; transformation of to Joseph Smith's likeness, 236 (and note); second speech at Nauvoo on Presidency, 239; *Manuscript History of*, Part V, 245-630; appoints Trustees-in-Trust for the church, 247; noted discourse of, 254-60; increase in number of seventies by, 260 (and note); presents a patriarch, 300; discourse against wickedness, 350; on doctrine of revelation, 372; premonition of evil, 376; comment on report of Emmett's Company, *et al*, 385; conversation on settling on the headwaters of the

Colorado, 387; setting the last trumpet stone on the capitals of the Temple, 388; revising History of Joseph Smith, 389; in retirement with associate Apostles, 414; comment of on death of Miner R. Deming, 439-40; prophecy of at General Conference Oct., 1845, 465; pledges to Mother Smith, 472; Bogus-Brigham incident, 549-51; comment on Gov. Ford's speculations on arrest of church leaders by U. S. troops, 564; kindness of to dumb animals, 569; appoints trustees to church property at Nauvoo, 573; names of, 576; instructions on camp deportment, 585-6; his high praise of Camp of Israel, 608-9; returns to Winter Quarters, 616; reception of, 617; nominated for President of the Church, 621; departure from Winter Quarters to the Rocky Mountains, 625; statistics on composition of his company, 627; arrival of in Salt Lake valley, 628; sustained as President of the Church at General Conference in Kanesville, December 27, 1847, 623; in Salt Lake valley, Oct. 8, 1848, 628; in Great Britain and Pacific Islands, 629-30.

Young, Joseph,—President of the First Council of Seventy, second dedicatory prayer at Seventies' Hall, 342; speech at Seventies Conference—stand against wickedness, 372; appointed to preside at Nauvoo, 584.